Bible Commentary
by
E. M. Zerr

Volume II
1 Samuel—Job

© **Truth Publications, Inc. 2018.** All rights reserved. No part of this book may be reproduced in any form without written permission from the publisher. Printed in the United States of America.

ISBN 10: 1-58427-182-5

ISBN 13: 978-1-58427-182-6

Truth Publications, Inc.
CEI Bookstore
220 S. Marion St., Athens, AL 35611
855-492-6657
sales@truthpublications.com
www.truthbooks.com

Foreword: The E.M. Zerr Bible Commentaries

Cecil Willis
Reprinted From *Truth Magazine* XX:26 (June 24, 1976), pp. 3-5

The Cogdill Foundation, which publishes *Truth Magazine*, has obtained exclusive publication rights to the six volume *Bible Commentary* written by Brother E.M. Zerr. . . .

Information About E.M. Zerr

Brother Zerr was quite well-known among a group of very conservative brethren, but he may not have been known among brethren in general. Hence, a little information concerning him is here given. Edward Michael Zerr was born October 15, 1877 in Strassburg, Illinois, but his family soon thereafter moved to Missouri. He was the second of six children born to Lawrence and Mary (Manning) Zerr. Brother Zerr's father was reared as a Catholic, but after he married Mary Manning, he obeyed the gospel. At the age of seventeen, young Edward was immersed into Christ in Grand River, near Bosworth, Missouri.

In June, 1897 young Brother E.M. Zerr received a letter from A. L. Gepford asking him to go to Green Valley, Illinois, and to preach in his stead. His first sermon was entitled, "My Responsibility as a Preacher of the Gospel, and Your Responsibility as Hearers." In the years between delivery of this first sermon on July 3, 1897, and the delivery of his last sermon on October 25, 1959, Brother Zerr preached about 8,000 sermons, from California to Connecticut, and from Washington to Arizona. It is noteworthy that his last sermon was built around Matt. 13:44, and was entitled "Full Surrender." Brother Zerr preached the gospel for a little over 60 years.

Among the brethren with whom Brother Zerr was most frequently associated, it was then common to have protracted periods of concentrated Bible studies, commonly referred to as "Bible Readings." Young Brother Zerr attended a three month "Bible Reading" conducted by the well-known teacher, A.M. Morris, in 1899. During this study which was conducted at

Hillsboro, Henry County, Indiana, Brother Zerr stayed in the home of a farmer named John Hill. After leaving the John and Matilda Hill farm, "E.M." began correspondence with their daughter, Carrie. The following year, while attending a "Bible Reading" conducted by Daniel Sommer in Indianapolis, "E.M." and Carrie were married, on September 27, 1900. The newlyweds took up residence in New Castle, Indiana, where their four children were born, one of whom died in infancy.

In 1911, Brother A.W. Harvey arranged for Brother Zerr to conduct a "Bible Reading" which continued for several months at Palmyra, Indiana. These "Bible Readings" usually consisted of two two-hour sessions daily. Young Brother Zerr's special ability as a teacher was soon recognized, and he continued to conduct such studies among churches of Christ for 48 years. Edward M. Zerr died February 22, 1960, having been in a coma for four months following an automobile accident at Martinsville, Indiana. His body was laid to rest in the little country cemetery at Hillsboro, Indiana, near the church building in which he had attended his first "Bible Reading."

Brother Zerr's Writings

In addition to his oral teaching and preaching, Brother Zerr was a prolific writer. He was a regular contributor to several religious periodicals. Brother Zerr also composed the music and lyrics of several religious songs. Two of these, "The True Riches," and "I Come to Thee," may be found in the widely used song book, *Sacred Selections*.

One of the books written by Brother Zerr is entitled *Historical Quotations*, and consists of the gleanings from 40,000 pages of ancient history and other critical sources which he read over a period of twenty years. These quotations are intended to explain and to confirm the prophetic and other technical statements of the Bible. Another book, a 434 page hard-cover binding, consists of a study course containing 16,000 Bible questions. This book, *New Testament Questions*, has at least 50 questions on each chapter of the New Testament. A smaller book, *Bible Reading Notes,* consists of some of the copious notes which Brother Zerr made in connection with the "Bible Readings" which he conducted. But the crowning success of his efforts was the writing of his six volume commentary on the whole Bible.

These six volumes were published between 1947 and 1955. Brother Zerr has the unique distinction, so far as is known to this writer, of being the only member of the church to write a commentary on the entire Bible. Many other brethren have written excellent and valuable commentaries on various books of the Bible, but no other brother has written on the entire Bible.

Foreword

The writing of this commentary consumed more than seven years of full-time labor. In order that he might devote himself without interruption to this herculean effort, Brother Zerr was supported by the Newcastle church during this seven year period. It is unfortunate, in this writer's judgment, that other competent men have not been entirely freed of other duties that they might give themselves to such mammoth writing assignments. Through *Bible Commentary*, Brother E.M. Zerr, though dead since 1960, will continue to do what he liked best to do—conduct "Bible Readings" for many years to come. The current printing is the fifth printing of the Old Testament section (four volumes) of the commentary, and the sixth printing of the New Testament section (two volumes).

Many Christians spend but little money on available helps in Bible study. Some own perhaps only a *Cruden's Concordance*, a Bible dictionary of some kind, and then *Johnson's Notes*. It would be interesting to know how many copies of B.W. Johnson's *The People's New Testament Commentary With Notes* have been sold. If I were to hazard a guess, it would be that at least 1,000,000 copies of this superficial commentary have been sold. *Johnson's Notes* contains the printing of the entire New Testament text in both King James Version and the English Revised Version (the predecessor to the American Standard Version), and his comments, all contained in two volumes. In fact, a single volume edition also is available. Thus one is buying two copies of the New Testament, and B. W. Johnson's *Notes*, in one or two volumes. So necessarily, *Johnson's Notes* are very brief.

If brethren somehow could be made acquainted with Brother Zerr's *Bible Commentary*, it is possible that it could be as widely used as has been *Johnson's Notes*, first published in 1889. Brother Zerr printed very little of the Bible text in his commentary. He assumed you would have your own Bible nearby. To have printed in the commentary the entire Bible would have required at least three other volumes. While it would have been helpful to have the Bible text printed by the comments, this unnecessary luxury would have been very expensive, since we all have copies of the Scriptures already. Furthermore, Brother Zerr intended that one be compelled to use his Bible, in order that his commentary never supplant the Sacred text.

A Word of Caution
I am sure that Brother Zerr, were he yet living, would advise me to remind you that his *Bible Commentary* is only that of a man, though a studious man he was. In fact, in the "Preface" to this set of books, just such a word of warning is sounded by Brother Zerr. The only book which we recommend without reservation is the Bible! But Bible commentaries, when viewed merely as the results of many years of study by scholarly men, can be very helpful to one.

Brother Zerr spent his life-time working among those brethren who have stood opposed to "located preachers" and to "Bible Colleges." However, he has not "featured" these distinctive views in his *Bible Commentary*. If one did not know of these positions held by Brother Zerr, he might not even detect the references to them in the commentary. However, I want to call such references to your attention. Along with the opposition to "located preachers," Brother Zerr also held a position commonly referred to as "Evangelistic Oversight." This position declares that until a congregation has qualified elders appointed, each congregation should be under the oversight of some evangelist. With these positions, this writer cannot agree. References to these positions will be found in his comments on Acts 20:28; Eph. 3:10; 3:21; 4:11; 1 Tim. 5:21; 2 Tim. 4:5, and perhaps in a few other places that do not now come to memory. Brother Zerr also took the position that a woman should never cut or even trim her hair. His comments on this position will be found at 1 Cor. 11:1-16.

But aside from a very few such positions with which many of us would disagree, Brother Zerr's *Bible Commentary* can be very helpful. Some restoration period writers of widely used commentaries held some rather bizarre positions regarding the millennium. Brethren scruple not to use *Barnes' Notes*, in spite of his repeated injection of Calvinism, and *Clark's Commentary*, in spite of his Methodist teaching.

Brother Zerr's *Bible Commentary* is far superior to *Johnson's Notes*. Though there are some extraordinarily good volumes in the well-known Gospel Advocate commentaries, there also are some notoriously weak volumes in this widely used set. Viewed from the point of consistent quality, Brother Zerr's *Bible Commentary* is superior to the Gospel Advocate set. Some brethren whom I consider to be superior exegetes of the Word have highly recommended Zerr's *Bible Commentary* and have praised the splendid and incisive way in which he has handled even those "hard to be understood" sections of God's Word.

Our recommendation regarding E.M. Zerr's six volume commentary can be paraphrased from the words of a well-known television commercial: "Try it; you'll like it!"

Bible Commentary

1 SAMUEL 1

General remarks: This book may properly be considered as the beginning of the major history of the Jews as it is found in the Bible. It should be noted that two of the men listed as judges, Samuel and Eli, are reported on in this book instead of the one bearing the name of Judges. The service of these men overlapped two periods somewhat, and the student will do well not to become confused by statements that might seem to bear on either.

Verse 1. The term Mount Ephraim included more than just a mountain, it included a territory extending down as far as Bethel. Ramah is an abbreviation of Ramathaimzophim; the exact location of the place is uncertain. Elkanah was a citizen of Ephrath, the ancient name of Bethlehem.

Verse 2. Plurality of wives was suffered (not "permitted") in those days, and Jesus explained it by saying it was because of hardness of heart. (Matt. 19: 8.) That particular instance, however, pertained to the putting away of a wife for various causes, but the same principle applied to plurality of wives. This man Elkanah had two wives at the time of our story; one was barren, thus being unfortunate according to the feeling of mankind in ancient times.

Verse 3. By reference to Deut. 16: 16 we learn that all males of the children of Israel were required to go to the place of the ark three times each year. While only the males were required to make this journey, others were permitted to go and as a rule many did. At the time of our story, the tabernacle and its services were at Shiloh, which was a city in the possession of Ephraim. Eli was the high priest and hence his sons, Hophni and Phinehas, were the common priests and the ones charged with the manual work pertaining to the sacrifices.

Verse 4. *Portions.* This word means rations. In Deut. 12: 17, 18 we learn that while the males were engaged about their duties with the sacrifices, the others would be partaking of meals in recognition of the goodness of God. It is said that Elkanah gave provisions for this purpose to Peninnah and her children.

Verse 5. *Worthy.* The literal meaning of this word is "anger," but the R. V. renders it "double portion." This is in agreement with the circumstances; the man loved Hannah as a man is supposed to love his wife, and he showed her this partiality by doubling his gift to her. See a like exhibition of partiality by Joseph in Gen. 43: 34. This favoritism shown to Hannah provoked the other wife to anger, therefore the writer used this peculiar word in describing the ration Elkanah gave to Hannah. Since the Lord had closed the womb of Hannah, the sympathy of the husband would be all the more in evidence.

Verse 6. Reference to Ch. 2: 3, together with all the factual context, indicates the "adversary" was the other wife. It was a reproach in those days not to be able to bear children. Thus we can understand why the more fortunate woman in this case would have occasion for her unkind attitude toward the other wife. This circumstance is like that of Jacob and his two wives. (Gen. 30: 31.)

Verse 7. The antecedent of "he" is "Lord" in the previous verse. There it states that the Lord shut up the womb of Hannah; here it means that the Lord continued to keep her thus from year to year. This would be brought out each time they went up to the house of the Lord, since that was the time Elkanah's partiality for Hannah was shown by the double portion. Peninnah, observing this partiality, gave vent to her anger over it by reproaching Hannah with her barrenness. This was done so persistently that the unfortunate woman wept. She even refused to eat. We need not conclude this to have been in the spirit of sullenness. It is a known fact that any state of extreme grief or worry will affect the appetite, and Hannah certainly had cause for worry. Elkanah understood the cause of his beloved wife's conduct and tried to console her with the reference to his own love for her; while that was no little consideration, yet nothing could take the place of the natural desire for children.

Verse 9. Hannah and other unofficial persons had been engaged in a meal, as mentioned above, which was not in direct connection with the service of the temple (a name here applied to the tabernacle built by Moses). In order to go into the temple to pray she would come into the presence of Eli, the high priest, who would be sitting near the post of the building; from this position he could see her and observe her actions.

Verse 10. The earnestness of the woman was indicated by the fact that her praying was accompanied with sore weeping.

Verse 11. While vows were not generally commanded under the law, they were encouraged. When a person made a vow he was bound to keep it, and certain regulations were made for the observation of the same. One special kind of vow was the Nazarite, which was distinguished by the promise not to cut the hair during the term of the vow. The term of this vow might be for any length of time up to life. In her vow to God Hannah promised to devote her son to the lord all the days of his life as a Nazarite, if he would grant her the favor of a son.

Verse 12. Eli marked or observed her mouth and could see that she was speaking.

Verse 13. Since Hannah did not speak out loud, only her lips moving, Eli concluded that she was drunk.

Verse 14. The command to "put away thy wine from thee" agrees with the following idea: wine was a slow intoxicant and required much time and continuous drinking to produce the condition sought; with this thought in mind, Eli used the words quoted.

Verse 15. The people of old times had certain other beverages with intoxicating effect, and some of them had a greater degree of alcoholic content than ordinary wine, hence we have the expression "strong drink" in a few places. The word "strong" is not in the original, however it is supplied by the translators from the word SHEKAR, which is defined by Strong, "an intoxicant, i.e., intensely alcoholic liquor." Thus Hannah meant that she was not using either wine or any other form of intoxicating drink, and instead of pouring out such for her own indulgence she was pouring out her soul to God.

Verse 16. *Belial*. This word is improperly capitalized here. It is not a proper noun in the Old Testament, but it is a descriptive word meaning one who is base, worthless, lawless. In the New Testament it came to be used as one name for Satan, and thus is a proper noun there. Hannah considered drunkenness as an indication of such a character and was quick to deny the accusation.

Verses 17, 18. Eli, being also a priest and thus one of God's spokesmen, was able to pronounce a blessing that would be effective. He granted to the woman a promise that her request would be fulfilled. This encouraged her to resume normal habits of life.

Verse 19. *They* refers to the ones in general engaged in the services of this occasion. (verses 3, 4.) After completing the activities about the tabernacle, Hannah and her husband returned home and resumed their domestic life. In fulfillment of the promise made by Eli, when Elkanah knew his wife the Lord caused her to conceive.

Verse 20. *Time was come about*. See comments at Gen. 17: 21, 22. Strong defines the original word for Samuel, "Heard of God." Hannah reasoned that since it was her request that was heard, it would be appropriate to give the child this name.

Verse 21. *Yearly*. Ordinarily this would mean once a year, but it is here from the word YOWM and defined by Strong, "Figuratively (a space of time defined by an associated term)." Thus the word is here used to mean that a certain sacrifice was offered every year. This sacrifice was required by the law and, in addition to it, a Jew could perform a vow that had been voluntarily made. On each occasion, therefore, when Elkanah went to the tabernacle to attend to the required sacrifice, he also performed his vow.

Verse 22. Since only the males were commanded to go to the place of national sacrifices (Deut. 16: 16), Hannah was wholly within her rights in deciding that she would stay at home until the child was weaned. The actual deliverance of the child to the Lord would not be expected until he was ready to be separated from his mother, and then the fulfillment of the vow would be due.

Verse 23. Elkanah agreed with Hannah's decision; he added his wish for the blessing of the Lord on her condition.

Verses 24, 25. These major sacrifices were not specifically required by the law in connection with the birth of a child (Lev. 12), yet they were always permitted, and the great joy of this woman because of her blessings prompted such an offering at this time.

Verses 26, 27. The acknowledgement that God's favor was bestowed on her is made, and it was in the form of a child born to one who was without the natural ability to become a mother.

Verse 28. Devotion of Samuel to the Lord for life was the substance of her vow.

1 SAMUEL 2

Verse 1. When *horn* is used figuratively it means power. Since Hannah did not previously have the power to become a mother, she attributed her present ability to do so to the Lord. In acquiring this power, she considered that she had triumphed over her enemies, just as in any other case of hostility. In this instance, however, the hostility referred to was the reproaches which had been heaped upon her by Peninnah, who was able to bear children naturally. In Hannah's day, this type of hostility was looked upon with more bitterness than that of actual warfare.

Verses 2, 3. When a rock was referred to figuratively, it meant a base for great expectations. The hope of Hannah in the matter of childbirth was based clearly on the power and goodness of God, and it was great in that it enabled her to win in her contest with the enemy who had been talking so proudly. Reference to 1: 6 shows that Peninnah had been sneering at Hannah because of her inability to become a mother, and that had been a source of great sorrow.

Verse 4. Most of the language of Hannah in this prayer is figurative. She was comparing her experience in social and sentimental matters to that of others in temporal and physical ones; therefore, she used terms that would apply literally to such contestants.

Verse 5. Being full at one time, and having to serve others for bread at another time, would be conditions of opposite character. Hannah used this as an illustration of her past and present condition. Seven is often used figuratively as meaning completeness. The fact that she was able to bear a child at all after being barren was so complete a change in her condition that she used this term. The complete triumph it gave her over the arrogancy of her rival caused her to refer to Peninnah as "feeble."

Verses 6-10. All this has the same bearing as the preceding verses. The fact that Hannah could now bear a child and thus contend with the other woman for God's favor, was the occasion for the passage. The words, *king, horn,* and *anointed* all refer to the power or ability which God had given her.

Verse 11. Samuel was left at the place of national service in Shiloh according to the vow of his mother. The fact that Elkanah is mentioned so much in connection with Hannah's vow indicates that he endorsed it. This was provided for in Num. 30: 6-15.

Verse 12. *Sons of Belial.* This is explained at Ch. 1: 16.

Verses 13, 14. Ex. 29: 31 and Lev. 8: 31 teaches us that certain portions of the beasts offered in sacrifice were given to the priests for food. This was to be attended to in an orderly manner, and the particular portion was to be observed. These wicked sons of Eli, had become so rebellious against the Lord that selfishness prompted their actions. They caused their servants to approach the offerings and sieze whatever and as much as happened to cling to the instrument thrust into the vessel. In so doing they would secure more than was intended by the Lord. This caused the priests to come into possession of an excessive amount which made them "fat" as expressed in verse 29.

Verse 15. The various places that speak of the fat of these animals are too numerous to cite here, but it will be remembered that no one was permitted to make personal use of that part. The Lord's service pertaining to the burning of this fat was to be attended to in preference to the personal rights of even the priests, but the sin of these priests had become so great that no respect was being had for the dignity of the law. They persisted in obtaining what they wanted regardless of the proper observance of divine service.

Verse 16. Such violation of the law brought protests from those who beheld it. The protests were ignored and, furthermore, the servants threatened violence if anyone tried to restrain them from obtaining the object called for by the priest.

Verse 17. One deplorable effect of violating the ordinances of the Lord is that the reproach of the world is brought on the services. The New Testament recognizes such a fact. That is why the Lord admonishes his people to live in such a manner that his ordinances will be honored. See Titus 2: 10 and other places.

Verse 18. Samuel was said to be a child. This is from a word that means one "from the age of infancy to adolescence." Hence he was old enough to be of bodily service at the direction of Eli the priest. Just what he did is not recorded, but the nature of his service called for the wearing of some form of girdle called an ephod.

Verse 19. Mention has been made more than once that all persons were permitted to come to the place of national service, but only the males were required to come. Hannah, however, would have a special motive for coming each year with her husband; she had given her son to the Lord. There is not the slightest indication that she regretted her act. In loving gratitude to God for the great favor bestowed on her in giving her a son, she continued to "lend" him to the divine service; but her mother's heart prompted her to provide him a new coat each year to wear in addition to the girdle.

Verse 20. *Loan* and *lent* mean "a petition." God had blessed Hannah with a son and she in turn had "loaned" him to the Lord as she had promised. Because of her faithfulness, Eli promised Elkanah that he would have more seed by Hannah. With this promise, the man and his wife returned to their own home.

Verse 21. Several years are covered by this verse. In fulfillment of the promise made by Eli, Hannah gives birth to three sons and two daughters.

Verse 22. The age of Eli is not mentioned as justifying the wicked conduct of his sons, but it would be rightly considered as a special reason why he should have been concerned with the character of the men who would soon take his place. The inspired writer tells us that Eli knew of the conduct of his sons, and therefore was responsible for the same. Women were permitted to come to the national services and usually they did so. These wicked sons of Eli took advantage of the occasion to commit immorality with them.

Verses 23, 24. The sinful conduct of Eli's sons was a matter of public knowledge, and when the report came to his ears he plead with them to change their ways. The word *transgress* is explained in the margin as meaning to "cry out"; in other words, the sin of these men was so great that the public outcry resulted.

Verse 25. In this verse Eli makes a distinction between sins that are between men and men, and men and God. Sins between men and men would be treated appropriately by the judge appointed for the purpose. The sin which his sons were committing, however, was one against the Lord and was being done, not only by the Lord's official servants, but in the place of the Lord's assembly. For such a sin there was no excuse, and thus no one could entreat the Lord to have mercy on them. In spite of this complaint from their father these sons continued their sinful conduct. The last sentence in the verse might be a little confusing to the reader as it sounds as if God's determination to slay them was why they continued their sinful life. But the meaning is as if it said they rejected the word of their father "and for this cause the Lord would slay them."

Verse 26. Many times the conduct that will win the favor of God will not win favor with men, and then sometimes it is the other way. In the case of Samuel his conduct received the favor both of God and men as he grew up.

Verse 27. A man of God in those days could be any person whom the Lord called on for any special form of duty. Such a person would be inspired to say the right thing to the one hearing him. The one sent to Eli reminded him of the history of his people in Egypt. "Thy father" refers to Aaron, from whom the priests came and who was, therefore, the official ancestor of Eli.

Verse 28. The question form of this language should not be misconstrued. It is just one form of a positive statement of fact, but used here in a manner that would rivet the attention of Eli on the important facts being considered. Not only was the house of Aaron to have exclusive charge of the priesthood, but was to receive the special parts of the animals offered in sacrifice by the other Israelites.

Verse 29. To kick at the ordinances of God meant to rebel at the lawful regulation concerning them. Not only was such being done, but such disorderly deeds were for the purpose of financial gain to make the families of the priests "fat" or prosperous.

Verse 30. This is a general threat

of the wrath of God to be poured out upon the house of Eli. Since it had dishonored the Lord he will dishonor it, and thus will get honor for himself at the hands of the sinful men.

Verse 31. The word *arm* means force, and the thought is that the days would come when the force of the family of Eli would be reduced. This was to apply not only to the immediate physical strength of his sons and their descendants, but would also affect their vitality to such an extent that they would all die prematurely.

Verse 32. In spite of the wealth and resources of the house of God, there would be such affliction that Eli would be a witness of it, and one result would be the death of the members of his family before they reached old age.

Verse 33. The very persons who will be the occasion of Eli's grief will be those connected with the service of the altar. The threat is repeated that his people would die in the flower of age; just when they became mature men they would be cut off.

Verse 34. As a special signal that he was no impostor, the man of God stipulated that the two sons of Eli would die on the same day.

Verse 35. This man of God logically would be able to make inspired predictions. Thus in direct connection with the rejection of Eli's house in the priesthood, he makes a jump of many centuries to the time when the final priesthood was to be ordained. This same prophecy is made in a different connection in Zech. 6: 13. Here we have the comprehensive thought that as Eli, one prominent representative of the Mosaic priesthood, was to be set aside because of his personal wrongs, so the whole national priesthood was to be rejected. This new priesthood that was to supplant the one rejected, is the burden of the book of Hebrews. The introduction of the word *anointed* signifies that the priest in the final institution was to be a king as well as priest. This also is seen in the reference in Zechariah.

Verse 36. The literal significance of this verse would seem to predict an attempt to get into the priesthood for the temporal advantage therein. While doubtless there were actual instances of such action, yet the prediction signifies something far more important. This last priest would be an Israelite and would primarily serve his people. The unqualified members of the family are pictured as asking for the same advantage with regard to personal favors as those enjoyed by the officials. It is similar in thought to the request of the Gentile woman for crumbs. (Matt. 15: 27.)

1 SAMUEL 3

Verse 1. The service or ministration of Samuel was under the supervision of Eli. The word of the Lord was precious, which means it was rare. The reason given for it was that there was no open or frequent vision; that is, the services of inspired men were not had often at that time. That called for special intervention of the Lord when he had some special message he wished to convey to his people.

Verses 2, 3. Since Eli was very old even to the extent of losing his eyesight, the Lord concluded it was time to introduce the next inspired prophet. The particular time selected for the revelation was while Eli was resting in his bed, but near the end of the night. This is indicated by the words "ere the lamp of God went out." This will be better understood if Ex. 27: 20, 21; Lev. 24: 2, 3 is consulted. In those passages we read that the candlestick in the tabernacle was to burn through the night only, and to be trimmed in the morning, by which time it had burned out. The revelation which Samuel is about to receive, therefore, came while the lights were still burning but near the time for them to go out. Just why the Lord selected that particular hour is not known.

Verses 4, 5. The Lord called Samuel. Of necessity we conclude the Lord mentioned his name, else Samuel would not have made the personal response to the call of the voice. Thinking it was his master Eli who had called him, he went to do his bidding; being told that Eli had not called him he was further told to lie down again.

Verse 6. The voice called again. There was no mistaking the person wanted this time for Samuel was called by name. Again the child responded to the call by going to Eli to do his bidding, but was again told to lie down as the master had not called him.

Verse 7. The statement that Samuel did not *yet know* the Lord cannot be restricted to the idea that he did not know him in the sense of being his prophet. The thought in the additional statement in the last of the verse teaches us first, that Samuel did not know what it was to be a prophet of God and, second, that he had not yet learned the truth about the existence of the God of the tabernacle service. We do not know just how old he was, except that he was old enough to serve about the tabernacle and to do the kind of service that called for a girdle. But in spite of that fact he did not know the Lord. It is interesting to consider Heb. 8: 11 in this connection. That passage deals with one difference between the old covenant and the new: in the latter it will not be necessary for one brother to tell another the knowledge of God, for he will have learned about him before becoming a brother; but in the former, a babe eight days old became a full brother to others upon circumcision, then when he became old enough he would have to be told about God just as Eli was here telling Samuel.

Verse 8. Upon the third instance Eli realized what was happening.

Verse 9. Eli expressed two important ideas; it was the Lord who was speaking, and Samuel was his servant. We might add the thought that when the Lord speaks, it is the duty of the servant to hear.

Verse 10. Samuel's sweet obedience to the command of the aged prophet is impressive and is a fine example of devotion to the Supreme Being.

Verse 11. Since Eli was a prophet of God and had been given revelations of his will in other instances, it would have been in order to have told him directly of this coming event. He had already been warned of it (Ch. 2: 27) through the instrumentality of "a man of God" who was doubtless commissioned specially for the occasion. Now it is time to start Samuel out in his great life work of teaching God's people, and he is introduced to the work by the announcement that a great surprise is about to come to the ears of the nation.

Verse 12. This passage indicates that previously the warning had been given as a prelude; now the final phase is about to begin.

Verse 13. In Chapter 2 we read how Eli spoke to his sons about their evil conduct, but that was all he did about it. Inasmuch as he was judge as well as prophet, he had the power to remove them from office had he been so disposed; but, seeing he did nothing more than talk to them about it, he must be brought to feel the weight of the Lord's wrath against his neglect of duty. It is not enough to cry out against a condition of wrong—we must also oppose that wrong with all the power we have.

Verse 14. A condition of evil may become so serious that nothing can be done to avoid the punishment of God. The nation in later years became so corrupt that all of the reformative work of Hezekiah and Josiah could not head off the great captivity, as will be learned when we come to that part of the Bible.

Verse 15. Since the house of the Lord at that time was the tabernacle, which had curtains at the entrance, we might become confused by the reference to doors. The Septuagint in this verse gives us THURA, and one definition Donnegan gives of the word is "an opening in general," and one meaning of the word "open" is "to loosen"; therefore, we can understand that Samuel pushed back the curtains. He was going about the daily tasks and was hesitating to tell Eli the sad news, but the aged prophet knew that something had been said to the young prophet that was important. He also sensed the state of mind of the lad.

Verses 16, 17. If Samuel was hesitating to tell Eli his vision, it was because the prophecy was unfavorable to Eli. "God do so" is a peculiar expression used in various places in the Scriptures. The meaning is, "if you keep back the news of the evil to come, then may God do the same thing to you that he has threatened against me."

Verse 18. At this, the young prophet told the aged one all of the Lord's prediction; Eli respected it and submitted to the divine will.

Verse 19. God will never forsake his faithful servants. When a prophet or other inspired person is instructed to communicate anything to the people, God will see to it that all will be carried out as revealed. As Samuel grew in stature and mind, his service as a prophet grew and God confirmed his words properly. This same principle was shown in his dealings through the apostles. (Mk. 16: 20.)

Verse 20. The city of Dan was at the northern extremity of Palestine, while Beer-sheba was at the southern. The expression "Dan to Beer-sheba" came to be a figurative one, meaning the extent of the country. The fulfillment of Samuel's words from time to time convinced the people generally that he was destined to be an established prophet of God.

Verse 21. The Lord revealed himself to Samuel in Shiloh, which was the place of the tabernacle and the headquarters of the national worship. It is significant to read that God revealed himself to Samuel by his word. That means he did not merely cause Samuel to feel some sensation and depend on him to interpret it, but he made his will known to him by words. God has always dealt thus with his inspired men.

1 SAMUEL 4

Verse 1. *Came to all Israel*. The marginal reading here gives, "came to pass," and the connection agrees with it. Samuel had warned of the coming misfortune of Israel, so now his predictions to the people are going to come to pass before their eyes. They are about to launch upon their long career of warfare with their prominent enemy, the Philistines. Eben-ezer and Aphek were places not far from each other and not far from the headquarters of the children of Israel.

Verse 2. In the first battle the Israelites were defeated; thus was begun the downfall predicted by Samuel.

Verse 3. It was not the purpose of God that the ark should be removed from its proper place in the second room of the tabernacle. It never does any good to make the wrong use of even a good thing. The children of Israel mistook the use of this sacred vessel, which finally they learned to their sorrow, but since they had already forfeited the favor of God and started on their downfall, they were suffered to proceed.

Verse 4. The people removed the ark of the covenant from the tabernacle and took it into battle with them; it was never returned to its place in the tabernacle. It will be interesting to keep track of the holy article from now on. To assist the reader in that matter, the various places where it is mentioned will be cited from one to another, and the same may be marked in the Bible as a chain of references. In this place the reference should be made to Ch. 5: 1.

Verse 5. The sight of the ark cheered the Israelites and caused them to make a resounding shout.

Verse 6-8. The first effect of this demonstration on the Philistines was one of consternation. They concluded that defeat was sure to come to them; they acknowledged it to be a circumstance without parallel and considered it to mean their ruin.

Verse 9. The Philistines recovered from their panic and cheered each other. *Quit yourselves like men* means, "act like men." The battle cry was spurred on by the suggestion that if they gave up they would become servants of the Israelites or "Hebrews."

Verse 10. The rallying cry had the desired effect. The army of the Israelites was routed and fled; thirty thousand men were lost.

Verse 11. The most significant item of bad news was the loss of the ark, and the death of the priests who cared for the article. That was a fundamental blow since the very life of the nation spiritually was centered in it.

Verse 12. The demonstration here described was an ancient way of showing grief at some calamity. This man had come to tell the sad news to the aged priest, Eli, and to the inhabitants of the city, since all were awaiting news from the battle front.

Verses 13, 14. In justice to Eli it should be said that his chief concern was still the ark of God; he showed that concern by faithful vigil. Hearing the tumult among the people, he made inquiry and the man just back from the battle front came into his presence.

Verses 15-18. The messenger gave to Eli the details of the battle that had just been lost by the Israelites. No one doubted the accuracy of the report since the man had just come from the battle. It seems that Eli showed no emotion during the recital until the messenger came to the item of the ark. Even the death of his sons did not move him; he had been expecting something along that line, but his greatest concern was for the ark. This was very commendable in him, and gives us an example of preferring the things of God to even our flesh and blood. At the mention of the ark, Eli slumped and fell backward off the seat. The fall broke his neck which caused his death. Here is another place in the chronology of the judges; the period of forty years should be noted.

Verse 19. The daughter-in-law of Eli was very much affected by the sad news. She was grieved over the death of her husband, of course, but mention of the ark was also a shock to her.

The pains of childbirth, which doubtless were about due, came upon her.

Verses 20-22. She passed through the ordeal unconsciously, then recovered to the extent that she could speak. She was able to give a name for the child that was appropriate to the occasion. She, like Eli, considered the ark as being a symbol of the glory of God, and since the ark had fallen into the hands of the enemy, thus the glory was gone. At this circumstance she died of shock.

1 SAMUEL 5

Verse 1. This is another place to mark a link in reference to the ark. Make it to verse 10.

Verse 2. The people of ancient times were generally idolaters, and their idols were of three classes: the artificial, such as those made of stone or metal or wood; the natural, or those of the planets and animals and other things in nature; the imaginative, such as Baal and Ashtoreth and others. Dagon was one of the imaginative idols and one worshipped by the Philistines who had a temple erected in his honor. To this place they brought the ark which they had captured from their enemy, the Israelites, in battle. It was significant that representative objects of the rival religions were brought together in this manner.

Verse 3. The test was made the first night. Which god will prove to be greater? In the morning the image of Dagon was fallen, face downward. But that might have been an accident not connected at all with the ark, so they set the image up again.

Verse 4. On the morrow the image was fallen down again. This time it could not be from accident, for the head and hands were severed. That meant that his ruling ability was overcome and that his power was taken from him. The Philistines were convinced that the ark was the cause of the calamity.

Verse 5. Like all false religionists, these people were superstitious. Attributing their misfortune to the presence of the ark, they were fearful of the place where it had been and refrained from stepping on the threshold of the room thereafter.

Verse 6. God punished the people of that city because of their possession of the sacred instrument by afflicting them with emerods. This is from a word that means "tumor." The emerods were hemorrhoids or bleeding piles. *Destroyed.* This need not be interpreted to mean that people died because of the emerods. The word is from SHAMEM, and Strong defines it, "to stun (or intransitively, grow numb), i.e., devastate or (figuratively) stupify (both usually in a passive sense)." The emerods would cause them terrible suffering, yet leave them conscious of their condition and able to account for it.

Verse 7. Concluding that the ark was the cause of their afflictions, the Philistines determined to get rid of it.

Verse 8. They called upon their leading men and counseled with them on what disposition to make of the ark. Their decision was to take it to Gath, a city in the possession of Benjamin.

Verse 9. When the ark was brought into the city of Gath, God decided to show his disfavor of the treatment the sacred article was getting. He smote those people with the same ailment he had put on the people of Ashdod.

Verse 10. The ark was next taken to Ekron, another city of the Philistines. Here is the place of another link in the chain of references to the ark; make it to Ch. 6: 1. When the ark came into Ekron the people of that place feared its presence might bring them death. Doubtless the experience of the other cities was known to them and they were unwilling to have it in their midst.

Verse 11, 12. The statement that the men who did not die in the destruction brought by God were smitten with emerods, indicates that such affliction was not fatal.

1 SAMUEL 6

Verse 1. Make reference to verse 15 for the chain on the ark. There is a general statement here concerning the time the ark was in the Philistine country.

Verse 2. The Philistines called their priests and diviners together to determine what to do with the ark. The sad experiences suffered thus far had taught them that the God represented by the ark would not suffer the sacred vessel to be mistreated without showing his disfavor in some way. The people were advised to send the ark away.

Verse 3. It must never be forgotten that the Patariarchal Dispensation of religion had been in force since the days of Adam. While about all mankind had departed from its principles, it is reasonable to conclude that some remnants of the usages thereof were still in their memory. Besides, the history of the Israelites would doubtless shed some information abroad on the subject so that the nations would know that the God represented by the ark often received offerings as a tribute of regard, and therefore it might avail to offer such now. The suggestion was made, therefore, that they should not send the ark away empty, but place in it a trespass offering to appease God that he might remove their affliction from them.

Verse 4. The Philistines concluded that a fitting offering would be one that harmonized with the circumstances. They acknowledged that their afflictions were brought about on account of the insult to the God of the ark, so the return offering should be significant of that. The emerods represented the affliction put on their bodies, and the mice represented the ravaging of their fields. This little creature spoken of here was not any specific kind, but stood for any of the ones that destroyed their crops. By making images of these two things, they were admitting that the misfortunes brought on both land and person justly came to them because of their trespass.

Verses 4, 5. The final plan was to make five images of the emerods and five of the mice to represent both the lords and the people. They were exhorted to be diligent about it and not suffer the punishment for stubbornness as others had suffered. Again we have an insight into the general knowledge the nations had of the history of the Israelites.

Verse 6. The Philistines had detailed knowledge of the experiences of the Israelites in Egypt. We may gather another lesson here. If those heathen nations had such itemized information of the actions of the children of Israel, we should conclude that it was a settled custom, even in that far-off time, to make records of events for general information. If so, it should not be difficult to believe that records were faithfully kept of the actions of God's people.

Verse 7. The Philistines concluded to make a sort of test of their performance. Usually the ox was the beast used for the service of the vehicles, but milk cows were selected in this case. That was because the Philistines wished to use their calves in the test. While they did sometimes use the female of the cattle for bearing of burdens, in this case they selected those not having been used before, and to make the test certain, they separated their calves from them and brought them home.

Verses 8, 9. These cows were not to be driven or guided, but permitted to go according to their own choosing. If they went in the direction of the Israelite country, the conclusion would be that God had been responsible for their afflictions. These cows belonged to the Philistines and had no interest in the country of the Israelites. If they voluntarily went in that direction, it would be evidence that a higher power than nature was directing the affair.

Verses 10-12. The beasts did what the Philistines expected and feared, and the fact that they were lowing for their calves at the same time not veering to either side in the journey, proved that God was directing their course.

Verse 13. When the people of Beth-shemesh saw the ark they rejoiced, because they were Israelites and interested in the holy article of furniture.

Verse 14. Instead of using the image in worship to God, these Israelites performed the kind of service that had been revealed in the law; they used the wood of the cart to make fire and the kine for a sacrificial offering.

Verse 15. Here is another place for a link in the chain of the ark; make reference to verse 21. The images sent by the Philistines represented actual value to the Israelites instead of being gods to worship, and in thankfulness for the substantial offering and in gratitude for the return of the ark, the men of Beth-shemesh made a sacrifice to God again.

Verse 16. This action of religious service was performed in sight of the lords of the Philistines, after which they returned home.

Verses 17, 18. This paragraph gives us a more detailed view of the Philistines' plan to represent their people with the images. The emerods stood for the lords of five of their chief cities, and the mice for the villages of the country.

Verse 19. There is no indication that the people of Beth-shemesh had anything but respectful feeling for the ark since it represented their own religion; but their error was in allowing their curiosity to lead them to look into the ark. In punishment for that error over fifty thousand of them were smiten with death.

Verse 20. The community was filled with terror and they asked who would be able to stand before the ark. They, too, wished to get rid of the instrument.

Verse 21. Make reference to Ch. 7:2 for another link in the chain of the ark. Kirjath-jearim was another city of the Israelites and the men of Bethshemesh wished to put their trouble upon the shoulders of that community; they asked the men of Kirjath-jearim to take the ark to their city.

1 SAMUEL 7

Verse 1. The men of Kirjath-jearim responded to the request of the people of Beth-shemesh and brought the ark into their midst. Reference to 1 Chr. 13:6 indicates that Kirjath-jearim was in the land of the tribe of Judah, and hence that the ark was now in the care of a chief tribe of the children of Israel. Smith's Bible Dictionary says that Abinadab was a Levite and that would make his son a proper person to care for the ark.

Verse 2. Make another reference in the chain to Ch. 14:18. The ark is destined to remain in its present location for twenty years. *Lamented after the Lord.* This means that they assembled or gathered after him. The ark was the highest symbol of the presence of God, and the article was the only part of the tabernacle service in that part of the country.

Verse 3. Samuel was now recognized as a prophet of God and authorized to speak to the people. Image worship was still practiced by the children of Israel, and Samuel charged them to put the image away. He called them "strange gods." That meant they were gods outside the proper kind. They were thus not merely to serve the Lord, but to serve him *only.* God will not accept a mixed service.

Verse 4. Baalim was the male god of the heathen and Ashtaroth the female. Each of these deities, represented by images made out of metal, were used in idolatrous worship. Upon the exhortation of Samuel these images were put away from among the people.

Verses 5, 6. Samuel proposed a gathering at Mizpeh for the purpose of religious activities and for prayer. The prophet was to pray for the people but they were to participate and show their sincerity by fasting. As the giving up of food in fasting indicated a sacrifice of something serviceable to man, so the pouring out of water on the ground would also be the giving up of something valuable to them. Here it is stated that Samuel judged the children of Israel. He was the last man to be considered in that classification.

Verses 7, 8. The Philistines were persistent enemies of the Israelites. When they heard of the gathering at Mizpeh they advanced to that place to make war. Then the people appealed to Samuel to take their cause on him and pray for them.

Verse 9. In those times the offering of a yearling was acceptable to God. Some irregularity in the service will be discovered here. The national sacrifices were to take place on the altar of burnt offerings which at that time was at Shiloh, but inasmuch as the whole system had been interrupted anyway, the Lord was very lenient with the people. We are told that the prophet was heard and the specific fact that proved this is recorded in the next verse.

Verse 10. While the Israelites were gathered near Samuel and he was in the act of offering the sacrifice, the Philistines gathered to make war against them. But the Lord will protect his divine service. He caused the enemy to hear a great thunder which "discomfitted them"; this means they were thrown into confusion—as a result, they were smitten in great numbers by the Israelites.

Verse 11. The men of war among the Israelites then gave chase to the Philistines and smote them all the way to Bethcar, which was some distance from Mizpeh.

Verse 12. This historic circumstance gives us the occasion for the expression, "here I lay my Ebenezer," found in one of the old hymns. Songs are supposed to be based on Scripture truth, and when they are sung the sentiment should be used intelligently. But that cannot be unless we know the connection in which the thought was brought out.

Verse 13. The last half of this verse must be taken as explanation of the first. The Philistines were enemies of the Israelites for many years after this, but while Samuel was living they were kept subdued.

Verse 14. The immediate effect of the good work of Samuel was the restoration of the lands that had been taken by the Philistines. The Amorites are mentioned here as they have been in numerous places. They were a distinct people, yet were so wicked and influential that the name was frequently used for other wicked nations.

Verse 15. The era known as the reign of the judges continued about 450 years, according to Paul (Acts 13: 20), but two of the judges, Eli and Samuel, are recorded in the book we are studying.

Verses 16, 17. This paragraph gives the name of the resident city of Samuel, and the three other cities he visited each year in his work as judge.

1 SAMUEL 8

Verse 1. There was nothing official in the judgeship of Samuel's sons. They are not referred to as judges when that subject is under consideration by an inspired writer. Samuel left the burden of the task to his sons in a sort of delegated arrangement, and, as might have been expected, they took advantage of the situation.

Verse 2. They became like modern "politicians" in their governing of the people by taking bribes in return for favoritism in their ruling.

Verses 4, 5. There could not have been any criticism due the people had they only protested aaginst the evil conduct of the sons of Samuel and demanded some relief, but they used the occasion to express a desire which was independent of the corruptions of these sons. In their request to Samuel, their actual motive was revealed in the four words "like all the nations." There is no indication that other nations had changed their form of government on account of the wickedness of a former ruler. The truth of the matter was that the Israelites had become influenced by what they saw, and wished to imitate it. They wanted an excuse, so they siezed on the situation caused by the wickedness of the sons of Samuel; a condition that was plain to be seen, and hence not to be denied. The desire to keep up with the world has been the downfall of God's people in many instances.

Verse 6. It is gratifying to note Samuel's reaction; he did not base his displeasure alone on the fact that he had been rejected, but on the idea of their being dissatisfied with the Lord's arrangement, and wanting to be like other nations.

Verse 7. When the Lord's constituted leaders in any age are rejected by the people, it is the same as rejecting the Lord. It frequently occurs that the professed children of God rebel against the scriptural rulers or leaders without realizing that in so doing they sin against God. Samuel is consoled in this truth and is told to let the people have their wish in this matter. Sometimes men have to learn a lesson in the school of experience that will not be learned elsewhere. When the people rashly wished to die in the wilderness (Num. 14: 2), God suffered them to have their wish. Now that a rash wish for a king has been made, God will suffer them to have their way in the matter, but to their sorrow. Had they observed the teaching of their inspired law (Deut. 17: 14-20), they would surely have profited by the implications therein. They should have gathered the warning couched in that passage and then would have hesitated about calling for a king lest he disobey those directions.

Verse 8. The Lord further consoles Samuel by showing him that the present case of rebellion is not new. From the birth of their nation down to the present time the Israelites had been inclined to disobey God and have their own way.

Verse 9. With all the evil of the people of God, he still was the merciful Being he always had been. While their request was to be granted, he did not take advantage of their ignorance of the future. They were informed of what they might expect if they had kings appointed over them; they could not say they had not been warned.

Verses 10-17. These verses need no special comment. Let the reader ponder well the various items of oppression that the king was destined to wage against this people. The history, as we shall see, confirms all these sad predictions.

Verse 18. Samuel warns them that after they have rejected the Lord and have been given their request for a king, it will be too late to complain. He predicted here that such would take place, and that the Lord would not change it then until they had fully received the effects of their rebellion.

Verses 19, 20. These warnings did not cause the people to change their minds; instead, they repeated their demand for a king. It is noticeable that in the response they made no mention of the wickedness of the sons of Samuel. That was not their real motive in the first place; they wished to be like others and engage in military operations.

Verses 21, 22. Samuel was the spokesman between the people and God. The response made by the people to Samuel's warning concerning the predicted oppression, was repeated to the Lord, but it did not alter the divine decision to grant a king to the people. The thing must be attended to, however, in a systematic manner. The people were dismissed for the time and told to go to their respective cities. This indicates that a general assembly had been formed, and that an uprising had been threatened.

1 SAMUEL 9

Verse 1. The significance of this verse may not be apparent now, but it should be observed that the first king will be from the tribe of Benjamin; no other was ever taken from this tribe.

Verse 2. *Goodly* is from an original word that has a wide range of meaning. It is not restricted to the character of the person considered, but applies also to his physical appearance. It is so used in this instance. Saul was evidently an attractive man in his personal appearance, and one to draw upon the admiration of his subjects. Hence, in selecting him for the first king, no fault could be found with the Lord by saying he intended to make them dissatisfied with their request for a king because of his outward appearance.

Verse 3. We are not always informed as to why the Lord uses certain plans for carrying out his decisions. He could have told the eunuch directly what he wanted him to know (Acts 8), but chose to use an indirect method. In the present instance he could have sent Samuel directly to the house of Kish for a king, just as he did the next time for David. God's ways are not man's ways. Were we to attempt an explanation of this circumstance we might be led into speculation.

Verse 4. Mount Ephraim has been explained to refer to an area greater than a mountain. It was a general territory south and west of Jerusalem. The various districts mentioned here indicate that God had a hand in the present situation. The beasts were induced to go so far away that it took the young man a great distance from home, and this would eventually bring him into contact with the man needed to bring about the Lord's purpose.

Verse 5. According to Smith's Bible Dictionary, Zuph was a city not far from Jerusalem, so the men were near that city when they gave up finding the lost beasts. It is evident that they had come a considerable distance from home from the statement of Saul about his father's anxiety. Perhaps it would be more accurate not to refer to Zuph as a city, but rather as a community in which was located the city of Ramah, the residence of Samuel.

Verse 6. A man as prominent as Samuel would be known by almost every person, so it was not strange that Saul and his servant were aware of the existence of the place. Being at their wit's end, Saul's servant suggested that they consult the man of God for the purpose of obtaining information concerning the whereabouts of the beasts.

Verse 7. We should not get the idea that prophets had to be "paid" for their services. It has always been customary to remunerate the servants of the Lord for their work, as a matter of respect, as well as for the actual benefit of the gift. Not having left home with the present situation in mind, Saul was not prepared to give the man of God the consideration he thought deserving.

Verse 8. This small piece of money would not be very valuable from a material standpoint, but it would be an expression of appreciation, and that is what means more to God than actual temporal value.

Verse 9. The meaning of seer is, "one who sees." The inspired prophets could see into the future, hence they were sometimes called by this name in much the same way that one who does things is called a doer.

Verse 10. The suggestion of the servant was approved by Saul and they proceeded to enter the city to consult the seer.

Verse 11. The word *draw* here is from SHAAB, and defined by Strong, "to bale up water." In Gen. 24: 11 is an account of this work. Wells were depended on for drinking water, and the women often were the ones who attended to that service. In the case of Saul and his servant it seemed to happen that they came near the city just at the right time to meet their informants. Upon meeting the young women they asked about the seer, whether he were there. We will recall the statement in Ch. 7: 15-17. Since the prophet had such a wide territory of operations, it might be that he would not be at home at the present time, hence their question of the maidens.

Verse 12. In view of their knowledge of the program about to be carried out, they gave Saul an affirmative answer. The language of this verse will be understood when it is recalled that a sacrifice was not always something burned on the altar. Deut. 12: 21-25 gives us the information that solemn feasts to the Lord were provided for in the law. Some place of elevation was usually selected for these public feasts, very much on the principle that people would wish some convenient place for a public meal today.

Verse 13. This spot or high place was evidently near the city, yet not exactly in it. Since it was about time to go to the particular spot, the women urged Saul to go at once in order to intercept the seer before he moved on. The people were waiting for the prophet to come to bless the sacrifice or meal. This did not mean he would do anything to the food to change its nature; the word means to bless or thank God for the food as a blessing from him. It agrees with the thought expressed by Paul in 1 Thess. 5: 18 and 1 Tim. 4: 4, that thanks should always be given for the blessings received from God.

Verse 14. Sure enough, when they entered the city they met the prophet on his way to the place of the feast.

Verses 15, 16. The prophets of God were to be inspired for the special duties of the time. It appears as an accident that Saul and Samuel met on this occasion, but we understand it was not just a happening by chance; the Lord had prepared the prophet for the occasion and was now bringing the two men together.

Verse 17. The instructions given Samuel previously were general as to the person involved. Now he is given specific information concerning the individual and told that he is before him.

Verse 18. Saul was not personally acquainted with Samuel, hence the inquiry.

Verse 19. An unexpected invitation to take part in the feast was now given to Saul. He was told also that the desired information would be given him on the morrow.

Verse 20. They are proceeding toward the place of the feast as Samuel begins to give Saul some preliminary information. For one thing, he will be able to appreciate the feast better if his mind is relieved about the lost beasts; therefore, the prophet tells him they have been found, but proceeds to inform Saul that a much more important subject is at hand, and that concerns his coming position with the people. Saul is informed that he is to be the fulfillment of the desire of the people for a king.

Verse 21. It would have been good for Saul and the people had he always maintained the humility here expressed. He represented his family as an unimportant one, and from one of the smallest tribes. The dignity of being a favorite of the whole body of the Israelites would suggest that the man should belong to a great tribe, thus the matter was indeed a surprise to Saul.

Verse 22. The trio reached the place of the feast, and entered the parlour or room appointed for some specially invited guests, number about thirty. In this room Saul and his servant were given the choice of seats.

Verses 23, 24. The word *left* does not mean a scrap, but something reserved. Having known that these special guests would be present, Samuel had instructed the cook to set this choice serving aside for them. The feast was then observed and Saul was the guest of Samuel that day.

Verses 25-27. This language is somewhat indefinite as to the time, but it should be understood to refer to the day after the feast. There was some conversation on the house top, a place often used in those times since the roofs were flat, and as the conversation drew near the close they were proceeding toward the edge of the city. It was then the time for Samuel to give to Saul the important message for which this whole meeting had been arranged by the Lord. At this point the servant was told to pass on from them in order to give opportunity for privacy; the word of the Lord was to be made known to Saul.

1 SAMUEL 10

Verse 1. Olive oil was used by the people of Old Testament times, and it was the practice to pour it over the head of persons to be recognized in any special position. It was also poured over inanimate objects which were to be set apart for a special purpose. See Gen. 28: 18; Lev. 2: 1; 8: 12; 10: 7; 21: 10; 2 Ki. 9: 6. This practice gave rise to the figurative use of oil as being poured on one's head, as in the case of Heb. 1: 9. Saul was told that he was anointed to be captain over the Lord's possessions.

Verses 2, 3. Reference to Gen. 35: 19, 20 will help us locate the scene of these events. The minute details concerning coming events which were given to Saul could only have been known by an inspired prophet and their fulfillment would convince Saul of that fact. It is easy to make circumstantial predictions, but only after they are fulfilled do they become evidence. On this thought see Ex. 3: 12 and Luke 21: 13. The importance of the office that Saul is about to assume requires that no doubt be left as to the legality of the appointment.

Verses 4, 5. Here are some more details. In addition there is mention of some other persons of importance; a group of prophets and a garrison of the Philistines. Since these people were the enemies of the Israelites, against whom Saul was destined to be pitted in war most of his life, it was fitting to have this demonstration take place here. These musical instruments mentioned were used in connection with prophetic statements of the men of God.

Verse 6. Inspiration required the special impartation of the spirit of the Lord. To be turned into another man means that he was to be changed from an uninspired to an inspired man.

Verse 7. In a general way Saul was told to act as directed. No particular instructions were needed further than are about to be given him on the spot. The reason for his assurance of proper guidance was that God would be with him. This is similar to an assurance Jesus gave his apostles recorded in Mark 13: 11.

Verse 8. Since Samuel was an inspired prophet and the one empowered to act with reference to Saul, his commands at present are equivalent to those of God. With this in view, Samuel gave directions for his conduct in the near future. In order to get the full import of this verse it must be observed that the command of Samuel had two phases, and they may be seen by dividing the words as follows: first, seven days shalt thou tarry, and second, till I come to thee. This distinction is not always made by the reader, and evidently was not observed by Saul. Hence his great downfall to come later.

Verse 9. The meeting of Samuel and Saul was now ended. After they had separated, events began to happen just as Samuel had said they would, and Saul received another heart from the Lord.

Verse 10. The company of prophets met Saul just as Samuel had foretold, and the spirit of God came upon him so that he prophesied. There is proof here that when the people heard him they recognized him as a prophet. Since no time had yet passed for the fulfillment of a prediction, we must conclude that prophesying then, as now, did not always require foretelling future events. The word is from NABA and defined, "a primitive root; to prophesy, i.e. speak (or sing) by inspiration (in prediction or simple discourse)"—Strong. But the character of the discourse was such that it was recognized as coming from an inspired man, as will be seen in the following verse.

Verse 11. These people had known Saul previously but had never heard him speak in this manner. In a somewhat surprising gesture they formed the question that became a kind of familiar saying.

Verses 12, 13. The insignificance which Saul himself expressed in Ch. 9: 21 was in the minds of the people, and that was the occasion for their surprise. One from so humble a source would hardly be expected to manifest this talent, hence the established saying," "Is Saul also among the prophets?" It reminds us of the statement of Jesus in Matt. 13: 57.

Verse 14. The lost beasts belonged to the father of Saul. The uncle was aware of the absence of the young man, but did not know the cause for it and asked about it. Saul innocently explained that he had gone in search of the beasts, and not finding them had contacted Samuel.

Verse 15. Naturally, the uncle wanted to know about the conversation; he knew the importance of Samuel and desired to know what communication he had given the young man.

Verse 16. *He told us plainly that the asses were found.* These are the words of Saul spoken to his uncle. All the rest of the verse are the words of the writer, and given to the reader to explain the attitude of Saul. Saul is still humble on the subject of his appointment; he is not boasting about it.

Verse 17. Following the anointing of Saul, Samuel went to Mizpeh and called the people together in a special meeting before the Lord.

Verse 18. The Israelites were reminded of the great deliverance which God had brought for them. Attention is now called to the most significant statement that it was from the kingdoms "that oppressed you." The idea should always be borne in mind that when God endorsed the action of war on the part of his people, it was always a defensive one. An aggressive war was not favored in ancient times and would not be so today. If our country should embark on a war of aggression, then a citizen could consistently be a "conscientious objector"; if a defensive one, then he could not.

Verse 19. About the same thought is found here that is in the preceding verse. In using them as instruments of war, God saved them from their tribulations, which is the same as waging a war of defense. In spite of all this help from God, they had become dissatisfied with divine guidance and called for a king. Their wish had been granted, so now they are directed to present themselves and prepare for the appointment.

Verses 20, 21. In some manner not detailed to us here, the selection among the tribes and families was made, and the lot fell on Saul. Now Samuel had already known who the king was to be since he was the one who had anointed him for that very office, but the present ceremony, whatever it was, was to show the people publicly just who was to be the man of their choice. The purpose of the action which Samuel took was evident, for the young man had followed the same humility as had already been manifested in him and had hidden himself from the public.

Verses 22, 23. Inquiry was made of the Lord and the hiding place was revealed. When the candidate was brought before the people he was "head and shoulders" above all. His physical appearance was thus imposing, and if he does not "make good" as a king they cannot lay the disappointment on the claim that God put them off with an inferior individual as a retaliation for their sin in asking for a king.

Verse 24. The comments on the preceding verse are verified here by the description which Samuel makes of their king. The response was favorable and the established way of acceptance was used by the exclamation, "God save the king."

Verse 25. In Deut. 17: 15 it was stipulated that if a king was ever to be chosen, they were to receive the one whom the Lord designated. In the present verse we see that God also decided the style of kingdom they were to have. And, that no misunderstanding might occur, the description of it was written down.

Verse 26. The word *touched* is from NAGAH, and part of the definition of Strong is, "to lay the hand upon." The thought is that God had personally designated a group of men to be associated with Saul in this important work now starting. The attitude of these men was favorable, as will be seen by the contrary one in the next verse.

Verse 27. The first word of this verse shows that these men were just the opposite in their attitude to those of the preceding verse. The sons of Belial were men of a very low and wicked type. The word is a descriptive one and not a proper noun. The term as used in the O. T. could be applied to any very wicked person. *Brought him no presents.* The last word is from an original that means "tribute." When used in cases like this, it means a formal acknowledgement of greatness or authority. In old times we will read of frequent instances where the use of the term carried such meaning. If a writer says that certain persons refused to bring presents to another, it means that the person involved was not recognized as being important. On the other hand, if the present were offered, it was to indicate a favorable attitude as being pleased with the other, and wishing to have his good will. A few outstanding references will be given here for the reader's information. Gen. 32: 13; 43: 11; Judg. 3: 15; 1 Sam. 9: 7; 1 Ki. 4: 21; 10: 25; 15: 19; 2 Ki. 16: 8; 2 Chr. 17: 11. Saul was not disturbed by this sentiment of the wicked men. He knew that since the prophet of God had anointed him to the office, he had the sanction of God; therefore, it was not reasonable to be upset by the condition. Had he always been conscious of this great fact and acted accordingly, how much happier he would have been.

1 SAMUEL 11

Verse 1. The Ammonites were among the old enemies of Israel. It will be recalled that Jephthah had to fight them (Judg. 11), and now they are here to threaten the men of Jabesh-gilead. The people of the city seemed to be frightened and expressed willingness to make a league with them. This would have been contrary to God's will, for the command had been given before (Deut. 7: 1, 2) not to make any covenant with the nations around them.

Verse 2. The leader of the enemy agreed to a league on the condition that the men of Jabesh-gilead sacrifice their right eyes. Such a condition would not only be a physical misfortune, but also a reproach or disgrace. One of the prominent instruments of war then was the bow and arrow. The loss of their right eyes would disable them for war; therefore, if they submitted to this shameful proposition, it would be considered a great military disaster.

Verse 3. The children of Israel asked for a truce of seven days for the purpose of securing reinforcements. It was granted.

Verses 4-6. The king was rightfully appealed to in their distress, and he was moved with anger at the impudence of the enemy and prepared to make war.

Verse 7. Sometimes it is necessary to rouse people with some kind of visible demonstration. We can see an instance of this in Judges 19: 29, 30. The method Saul used brought the desired result.

Verse 8. The distinction between Israel and Judah seems premature since it was a long time afterward that an actual division came in this sense, but an inspired writer could see the distinction when others could not. No formal distinction was made in the activities connected with the war, hence we should not consider the expression otherwise than given here.

Verse 9. Having raised a good military force, they sent the encouraging news to the city that had been threatened, and it was gladly received.

Verse 10. With the favorable news to cheer them, the men of Jabesh-gilead answered the besiegers that on the morrow they would expose themselves to them to take whatever they were able to impose upon them. This apparent submission was a feint and intended as the particular method for joining battle with the enemy.

Verse 11. The attack was made "on the morrow." It was done also in the "morning watch" which had to be before six o'clock. Hence we incidentally learn that at least in some instances the day was not considered as beginning at sunrise. This thought is further confirmed by the statement that the slaughter continued until the heat of the day, which meant the time of day for the sunlight. The destruction of the enemy forces was so complete that no two could be found in one place.

Verse 12. Another phase of human weakness was now shown. After Saul had given them military success they were eager to "come to his defense" by slaying the objectors, which indicates that had he been unsuccessful in this battle they would have turned against him. It agrees with the conclusion that people are friends of the one who is a winner. This too often is the case whether right or wrong.

Verse 13. Samuel quelled the clamor of the people with the statement that while Saul was the divinely chosen leader, yet the victory was from the Lord, and no retaliatory measures were to be permitted in the case.

Verses 14, 15. No man could actually be made king the second time unless he had been excluded from his throne for some reason, therefore the language in this paragraph must mean that Saul was recognized again and acclaimed as king. This idea agrees with that of making Christ king a number of times. One of the grand songs of the religious world is "Coronation." Critics have objected to this on the ground that we cannot crown Christ as king since that was done centuries ago. The criticism is not well founded. Every time a man recognizes him as king he "crowns" him in the same sense that the people made Saul king at Gilgal.

1 SAMUEL 12

Verses 1, 2. This paragraph might be considered as a prelude to a farewell speech, although Samuel will not leave them for a time. He wishes the people to realize their own responsibility, now that their request for a king has been granted. In order that no pretext could afterward be made as justification of their unlawful demand, by reference to any deficiency in his leadership, he makes a challenge.

Verse 3. The challenge mentioned in the preceding verse follows. Samuel called upon them specifically to state if he had come short of doing what was right in his treatment of them and government over them.

Verses 4, 5. The people answered that no charge could be made against him. The expression, "Lord is witness against you" means that an oath was taken in their statement. And if afterward they should ever bring up any accusation along this line it would be admission of falsehood in their former declaration.

Verses 6, 7. At this point Samuel gave God the honor of all success. In the case of Moses and Aaron, the Lord was doer of all success; it will be the same in the present time with them. Therefore they should give heed to what Samuel wishes to say to them since he is the man of God now, even as Moses was in former days.

Verses 8-11. Their divine deliverance from the oppressor in former times was now mentioned to them because of its relation to their present situation.

Verse 12. An implied doubting of God's ability to care for them further was seen in their calling for a king at the approach of the Ammonites. If the Lord could lead them out from their enemies in the former time he certainly could do so again; hence their call for a king indicated a weakening of their faith.

Verses 13, 14. Since a king had been asked for and granted, they are to make the best of it. While God was displeased at their request for a king, after granting one for their use both they and the king will have the blessing of God on condition that they obey his voice and walk in his ways.

Verse 15. On the principle set forth in the preceding paragraph, the rebellion of the people will bring the curse of God upon them and their king as surely as will their obedience bring the blessing. History proves all of this to be true.

Verses 16-18. Their lack of faith will be further emphasized by a physical demonstration of divine power. Samuel called upon the Lord to show his power and goodness by sending rain for their crops. It was done and the statement is made that they feared the Lord and Samuel. The word "fear" is here used in the favorable sense. It means that they were made to have great regard. It is significant also that they feared the Lord *and* Samuel. It was on the principle that no one can either regard or disregard an authorized leader for God without doing so to him.

Verse 19. As a result of the demonstration and speech of Samuel the people were convicted of their great mistake and made acknowledgement of the same. No attempt was made to excuse themselves nor to lessen the extent of their guilt. They even admitted guilt of previous sins as well as the mistake of asking for a king.

Verse 20. Samuel agrees with them that they have been wicked but reminds them that it was a thing of the past. Now it is proper for them to serve the Lord, and the kind of service expected is the cooperation of the people with God in the new arrangement.

Verse 21. Their calling for a king implied a need for something in addition to the help of God. If they now turn from the king given to them and trust outside sources, they will be as unsuccessful with a king as they thought they were going to be without a king.

Verse 22. When a person espouses another as his choice for any reason, then the reputation of the former is somewhat connected with that of the latter; therefore it is desirable to uphold the chosen person as long as possible. God had taken the people of Israel from among the nations of the world as his own. As long as it can be done he will sustain them. This would not be for the sake of Israel only, but also for the good name of God thus joined with his chosen people. Samuel declared that God would not forsake Israel for the sake of his own name. See the following passages for this thought: Josh. 7: 9; Psa. 23: 3; 106: 8.

Verse 23. There was no resentment in the heart of Samuel. In asking for a king the people had rejected him as well as God, but he will not cease to be interested in their welfare and will continue to pray for them. But prayer alone will not suffice. The people must be taught the right way of life and this was what Samuel promised to do for them. No specific ordinances were to be added to the established law of God already given to them through Moses. There will come times, however, when the proper application of that law will require inspired guidance; the prophets of old were for that purpose.

Verse 24. To serve the Lord in truth meant to serve him according to truth and not just as their own imagination might suggest.

Verse 25. To be consumed did not mean to be annihilated physically, but to be destroyed as a nation. This great threat was fulfilled. See 2 Kings 24 and 25.

1 SAMUEL 13

Verse 1. The peculiar language of this verse means that nothing much of importance occurred in the first year of Saul's reign, but after the second year his activities are reported by the inspired writer.

Verse 2. Saul made a selection of three thousand chosen men of Israel to be used in battle with the Philistines, the constant enemies of the people of God. He divided these forces between himself and his son Jonathan, who is here mentioned for the first time. After this draft the other people were sent to their homes.

Verse 3. The Philistines had a military post at Geba, and Jonathan showed his talent in battle strategy by smiting this post. The report of the event came to the ears of the Philistines, and Saul also saw to it that the people of his own nation heard about it.

Verse 4. When a deed is accomplished by an inferior officer, the credit in theory goes to the superior. It might have been on this basis that it is stated the Israelites heard of Saul's success, although they knew that Jonathan was in immediate command at Geba. But judging from the conduct of Saul afterward, it seems that the proper credit for Jonathan was left out of the report. There is a similar situation recorded in secular history that illustrates this condition of jealousy. In the war of the United States against Spain, a great naval victory was accomplished by the valor of an inferior officer in immediate command. Due credit was at first allotted to this inferior officer; the superior officer did not happen to be present when the victory was achieved. His jealousy led him to cause such a disturbance in government circles that the officer who actually had accomplished the feat was robbed of his credit. This kind of action is condemned by the Scriptures where it is taught that honor should be given to those deserving it. (Rom. 13: 7.) And this saying of the inspired writer was used while considering secular governments. Another thing that suggests this unfavorable attitude in Saul's report is the fact that the people gathered together after him. The place of proposed action seemed to be Gilgal which was the place previously appointed by Samuel for their meeting.

Verse 5. The Philistines mustered a mighty force of chariots and horsemen. They pitched in Michmash which was not far from Gilgal, the place where the Israelite forces were assembled and hence would be seen by them.

Verse 6. The sight of the enemy with such great strength frightened the children of Israel, and they seemed to forget all their former resolutions of faith in God. In their fright they sought shelter by hiding in caves and other places. (Heb. 11: 38.)

Verse 7. Some of the Israelites escaped even across the Jordan. Saul was yet at Gilgal and the people crouched after him in terror for a while, then indicated signs of desertion.

Verse 8. The reader's attention is referred to comments at Ch. 10: 8 in order to understand this passage. Saul tarried until the seventh day, but not until Samuel came. The desertion of the people from him misled Saul into sin. The same mistake is often made by people today. Too often man's dependence upon man is greater than that upon God.

Verse 9. In his discouragement and lack of faith, Saul proceeded to take some kind of action. It has been a popular idea that he was condemned in this case on the ground that he was not a priest, therefore he did not have the right to offer sacrifice. That is a mistake. There are numerous instances where men who were not priests offered sacrifices and were not condemned. (Ch. 6: 14; 7: 9; 2 Sam. 6: 18, 19.) The sin which Saul committed was in not waiting until Samuel arrived.

Verse 10. The margin gives us "bless" instead of "salute" and the lexicon agrees. After having disobeyed the command of Samuel, Saul has the impudence to expect a blessing. Often today when men do something that they think is good they expect the commendation of God or God's people on the ground of having done something "good." But the teaching of the Scripture is that our great deeds will not be *accepted*, much less be *blessed*, unless they are done lawfully. (Matt. 7: 22, 23; 2 Tim. 2: 5.)

Verse 11. Saul offered three facts as excuses for his disobedience. They may be summarized as follows: people were scattered; Samuel had not yet come; Philistines had appeared. But none of these were logical in view of the full command of Samuel. God does not depend on the people, so let them be scattered; it was not yet time for Samuel to come since the day was not yet gone; enemies should not frighten them if they had faith in God. Hence the defense which Saul offered was insufficient.

Verse 12. The word *forced* is from APHAQ and Strong defines it, "a primitive root; to contain, i.e. (reflexively) abstain." Saul's meaning was that he just could not refrain or control himself and had to offer the sacrifice. The foolishness of such an excuse is proved by many instances of history and sacred teaching. In the first place, no one is actually forced to do wrong; he may be forced to accept some terrible alternative, but God will always be with the person who resists to the end. (Matt. 10: 28.)

Verse 13. It was Samuel who gave Saul the command to tarry at Gilgal, but it is here called the commandment of God. It is on the basis that all commands uttered by the constituted spokesman of God are the same as coming directly from him. The idea that upon obedience his (Saul's) kingdom would have been established forever meant that it would have continued throughout that age, among his family and lineal descendants.

Verse 14. *Thy kingdom*. This is said in the light of the preceding verse and its explanation. The particular family (and even tribe) of Saul will be deprived of a place as rulers in the kingdom. *Man after his own heart*. Much speculation has been done as to the meaning of this statement. Since it refers to David, who was guilty of the terrible sin about Bathsheba, it is asked how could such a man be after God's own heart. It is no answer to say that David had not yet been guilty of that sin when this was said. Such a reply is an insult to the wisdom and foresight of God. Certainly the Lord knew that such a sin would take place and therefore uttered this description of David in spite of that. When David was charged with his sin he did not deny it nor even try to excuse it; he promptly acknowledged his sin and was willing to make any amends that God required. That is the kind of man that is after God's own heart. Here is another thing that must not be overlooked in this case. The main sphere of action that is under consideration is that of ruling God's people faithfully against the enemies. In this sense we know that David was faithful; such is indicated in this very verse by the reference to David as being captain over God's people.

Verse 15. After this painful circumstance, Samuel departed from Gilgal and went to Gibeah, another city in the inheritance of Benjamin. After Samuel left, Saul took an inventory of the men he had with him and they were six hundred; the others had departed for fear of the enemy.

Verse 16. Saul and his son both had their camps at Geba, a city of Benjamin, while the Philistines were at Michmash.

Verses 17, 18. The condition of panic among the Israelites gave the Philistines opportunity for looting. They formed three groups for this purpose and took a territory for each group.

Verse 19. Commercialism would not have kept the Philistines from plying their trade in the land of the Israelites under peacetime conditions, but under the state of affairs then existing they had withdrawn in order to hinder the progress of their enemies' military activities.

Verse 20. The children of Israel had to run the risk attached to getting work done in the land of their enemies. As the particular handicraft mentioned here was one requiring special qualifications, the Philistines were engaged in that business more extensively than the Israelites.

Verse 21. This verse merely names the minor tools that the Israelites had at the time; they were much handicapped in their defense with such tools as these.

Verse 22. The people in general felt the lack of equipment most severely. Saul and Jonathan had been successful in obtaining their weapons in the manner described in verse 20.

Verse 23. Due to the shortages in the forces of Israel, the post of the Philistines extended as far as here described.

1 SAMUEL 14

Verse 1. Jonathan was assigned a commission to himself, as we have seen previously; he now proposed to go into action as a faithful defender of Israel.

Verse 2. Saul had his present headquarters in his tent which was pitched under a pomegranate tree. His present force consisted of six hundred men; as we read in Ch. 13: 15; the others had deserted him.

Verse 3. It might be thought that Saul had one advantage in that he had a man with him of the priestly family who was authorized to wear an ephod. This is to be considered in view of the combined nature of that system which was both religious and civil in government. Verse 1 said that Jonathan had slipped away unknown to his father, and it was not understood generally that he was gone.

Verses 4, 5. It was the desire of Jonathan to constitute himself a sort of detachment from the main forces of his father, and to fight against their common enemy. His only help was the young man who attended him to carry his armor. This young man was faithful to Jonathan and ready to cooperate with him in all ways possible. The space between where Jonathan and the Philistines were, was taken up with two craggy rocks which served as a kind of screen so that his approach would not be entirely visible except as he desired to make it so.

Verse 6. Jonathan proposed to his young man that they make an attack on the enemy. It was true there were only two of them, but his reasoning was that if the Lord were for them they would be just as successful as if they had a host.

Verse 7. Like a true patriot the young man agreed to obey whatever was commanded.

Verses 8-10. In various instances we have seen that men of God would place their proposed action on some special test that was to indicate the will of the Lord about their conduct. (Judg. 6: 36-40; 1 Sam. 6: 12.) In all of such instances we should think of Heb. 1: 1. In the case at hand, therefore, Jonathan proposed to learn his proper course by the method described. ...

Verse 11. The rocky crags mentioned before served as a camouflage for Jonathan and misled the Philistines into thinking that the Hebrews were in hiding. With that kind of view they would not have a clear idea of how many were there. The very fact they were hiding thus indicated to the Philistines that their courage was down and therefore it would not be difficult to cope with them.

Verses 12. The ruse had the desired effect. *Shew you a thing*. This was their boastful manner of challenging them to come on to the attack. But it was the signal to Jonathan that the Lord was approving their proposed attack and would help.

Verse 13. The strategy was further carried out by their method of advance. In creeping on their hands and feet it would not be discerned clearly how many there were of the Hebrews; also, they would not be seen at all until near the enemy. As a result they fell before the two with much slaughter, considering that only two did the work.

Verse 14. The word *acre* is from MAANAH and defined by Strong, "a furrow." It is the word for "furrow" in Psa. 129: 3. The R. V. renders this place "half a furrow's length in an acre of land." This wording is evidently correct. The thought is that Jonathan and his young man slew twenty Philistines in a row half as long as a furrow across a square acre of land. That should be considered as quite a feat.

Verse 15. This unexpected action upon the part of two lone Hebrews spread fear and consternation among the Philistines. Not only so, but the Lord also made good his promise indicated through the answer of the enemy when Jonathan and the young man showed themselves; he caused the earth to quake and tremble. This threw the Philistines into such confusion that they began attacking each other.

Verse 16. This demonstration was so great that the watchmen of Saul could see it.

Verse 17. The report of the conflict called the attention of Saul to the situation and he then realized that some of his forces had left his presence. He ordered search to be made to learn who was gone, and the fact was discovered about Jonathan and his man.

1 Samuel 14: 18-35

Verse 18. This is another link in the chain of the ark. The reference to be made is 2 Sam. 6: 2. Saul thought to be assisted in his battle by the presence of the sacred vessel and thus he called for it.

Verse 19. Saul directed the priest to withdraw his hand. The reason for the strange order was not stated, but it was stated that the tumult among the Philistines was on the increase. That could have indicated to Saul that the presence of the ark, under the jurisdiction of the priest, had had an immediate effect.

Verse 20. Approaching the scene of battle, Saul discovered that confusion and self-destruction was going on among the Philistines.

Verse 21. It is natural for men to wish to be on the winning side. Previous to the present time, some of the Hebrews had associated themselves with the Philistines; now that the tide of battle had turned in favor of the action of the Israelites they came over to them.

Verse 22. Others, who had been hiding in the country round about, now came out of their seclusion and joined the battle.

Verse 23. However, these men were not credited with success; it was given to the Lord instead.

Verse 24. The evil results of rashness are here seen. While it is true that it was not an uncommon thing for people of God to resort to seasons of fasting in times of great importance, and it would not have been wrong in principle for Saul to call for one at this time, but he should have safeguarded it with proper conditions, which he did not. Without seeking to get his instructions to all people affected, he declared under oath that any man who would partake of food before evening would be cursed. The people who were aware of the oath observed it.

Verses 25, 26. Coming to a wood the people saw honey so abundant that it was on the ground; they did not partake of it because of Saul's oath.

Verse 27. Jonathan did not know of the oath of his father. Under the conditions of making oaths or vows (Num. 30: 1-8) it was necessary that all parties hear the oath before being bound to it or affected by it. Since Jonathan was not present when this vow was made he was not morally bound by it. The word *enlightened* is from an original that means "to shine." In view of the condition of exhaustion to be mentioned soon, and of Jonathan's comments on the case, we may see the whole subject in its true light. There was nothing supernatural in the effect the honey had on him. He, like the others, was faint and drooping from the weariness of the battle. Honey is one of the purest of foods; when he partook of it, his vitality revived and his eyes reacted to the nourishment.

Verse 28. The people then informed Jonathan of the curse pronounced by his father. The statement is made that people, also, were faint or weary.

Verses 29,30. Jonathan then reasoned, and correctly so, that his father had made a troublesome oath. Referring to the great help that a little honey had been to him in giving him strength, and the success which followed, he concluded that they would have had much more success against the enemy had the people been permitted to eat freely. No man can be at his best when exhausted by lack of food. Thus it was a foolish vow that Saul made and there is no indication that it had the sanction of the Lord.

Verse 31. The people were faithfully serving Saul even though they were faint, and they were successful. But that was not because of the oath; it was in spite of it, for God wished the enemy to be subdued.

Verse 32. When people are at the point of starvation, they become uncontrollable and act involuntarily. The Children of Israel had been obedient to the rash oath of Saul until a point of desperation was reached. When the battle finally exposed them to great quantities of food, their appetite led them to indulge. They were even so ravenous that they disobeyed the law of Moses and ate the blood, the part that must always be considered as belonging to the Lord.

Verse 33. The actions of the starving people were reported to Saul and he realized that the law had been violated. He applied their acts of disobedience to himself, however, more than to the Lord, for the word *transgressed* means to act treacherously, and referred to their rebellion against him. He was aware, however, that the law of God had been violated, and he proposed to appease God with a sacrifice. For this purpose he ordered them to bring him a great stone.

Verses 34, 35. Now the command

was given to go out among the people and provide animals for sacrifice to atone for the sin of the people in eating with the blood. That was indeed a grievous sin since the very basis of many of the restrictions in the commandments of the Lord was in the fact that the blood is the life. Saul does deserve credit for the distinction he made between his own vow and the law of God. The latter could not be atoned for by execution, as he afterward thought to do for his vow.

Verse 36. Saul seemed to have concluded that he had appeased God by his action with the sacrifices and now can go on with the war with success. He made a proposition to that effect, but the priest thought it would be better first to consult the Lord. After Moses was gone the priest was the lawful spokesman for the people, hence the suggestion here was in order. (Mal. 2: 7; Lev. 10: 9-11; Deut. 17: 9.)

Verse 37. Acting on the advice of the priest, Saul made inquiry of the Lord but did not receive any answer at that time.

Verse 38. This indicated that something was wrong. It was somewhat like the case in Josh. 7, where the failure of the army was attributed to sin in the camp. Saul directed that an investigation should be made.

Verse 39. In another rash outburst, Saul named his son as being the possible guilty person and declared that even he would not escape. The people did not say a word, they knew that Jonathan was the "guilty" person, but had too much regard for him to expose him to the wrath of the king.

Verse 40. An indefinite classification was first made in which Saul placed himself and his son on one side, and all the people on the other. The arrangement was agreeable to the people.

Verses 41, 42. The lot was one means sometimes used by the Lord in old times to show decisions. See Prov. 16: 33. By this process the lot fell between Saul and his son, then finally upon the son, only it did not show just what had been done.

Verse 43. The confidence Saul had in the truthfulness of his son was shown in that he left it to him to state what he had done. In a very sincere manner Jonathan told Saul what he had done, and in a declaration of submission concluded that he must die.

Verse 44. *God do so* must again be explained to mean that God would do to Saul what should be done to Jonathan were he (Saul) to disregard the oath. The fact that he was the son of Saul should not have provided any protection for Jonathan had the oath been a righteous one, but it had not been duly established in the first place.

Verse 45. Unlawful or irregular vows are not morally binding on anyone; neither is it necessary to suffer such rashness to be carried out. All such restrictions are automatically void, hence the people were wholly within their rights in protecting Jonathan from the wrath of his father. There is no indication that Saul tried to press his contention.

Verse 46. There is a lull in the warfare of the Israelites against the Philistines.

Verses 47, 48. The general conduct of Saul was faithful to the children of Israel, for he fought their enemies and waged successful warfare.

Verse 49. The principal point of interest to us in this enumeration of the family of Saul is the mention of his daughter Michal, because of what we will hear of her later on in the history.

Verses 50, 51. Let us note the name of Abner, for we shall read much of him in the chapter to follow.

Verse 52. The Philistines had been, and were destined still to be, long and bitter enemies of the Israelites. Saul was always eager to fight them and took opportunity to strengthen his forces by drafting all men who appeared to be strong.

1 SAMUEL 15

Verse 1. As the priests have been shown to be the authorized executioners of the law, and the proper consultants in connection with the services, so the prophets were the ones through whom the Lord made known many of the specific commandments. At the present time the prophet Samuel addressed himself to Saul the king and instructed him. He told Saul that what he was about to hear would be the words of the Lord.

Verse 2. This reminder refers to the record found in Ex. 17. At that time God decreed that the very remembrance (visible memorial) of Amalek was all to be blotted out.

Verse 3. This command included everything that would have left a sign of the existence of the Amalekites, and would have fulfilled the decree mentioned above.

Verses 4, 5. With a force of over 200,000 Saul came to *a city* of Amalek. The term emphasized will be explained in the following verse.

Verse 6. Seeing certain ones among the people of the city, he warned them to leave in order not to suffer with the rest. They took his advice and left. This accounts for the seeming discrepancy regarding the complete destruction of all the people except the king of the Amalekites. It means all of the ones immediately encountered. These people who took his advice and fled the city would include some remnants of the people of Amalek and they will show up in the book of Esther. This is the reason for the words pointed out in the preceding paragraph.

Verse 7. Saul covered a great deal of territory in his war against the Amalekites. However, it was indicated by the specific reference to "a city" in verse 5 that he did not make a "clean sweep" of all the places. This is another fact to be considered in the same connection with the book of Esther mentioned in verse 6.

Verse 8. The remarks in the preceding verse are not disproved by the statement that Saul destroyed all the people. That would be true of the particular group with whom they found the king. The motive in taking Agag the king alive could have been a good one, for it was usually considered a great feat to capture a leading enemy alive. Good motives, however, do not justify disobedience, hence the action of Saul will be found to be sinful.

Verse 9. With the same kind of motive that saved the king, the best of the beasts escaped destruction also.

Verses 10, 11. Samuel being the present national prophet, the word of the Lord for Saul will soon be revealed through him. *It repenteth me.* This calls for a repetition of the definition of the word repent. The outstanding principle always present is expressed by the word "change." Whether God or man is spoken of as repenting, the idea of change must be retained. The difference between them is this: when man repents he *changes* his will; when God repents he wills a *change*. In both cases a change is required by the word "repent." In the present case it means that God will change Saul from being king.

Verse 12. The word *place* refers to some kind of mark that Saul set up at Carmel in honor of his supposed great work against the Amalekites. Having accomplished that action he passed on to Gilgal, the noted place of his first sin. (Ch. 13: 8.)

Verse 13. The writer does not tell us whether Saul knowingly made a false report to Samuel; his motive might have misled him to think that he had actually performed the will of the Lord.

Verse 14. The sound of the beasts was evidently heard. There is no indication that Saul had tried to prevent Samuel from knowing he had saved them, hence the conclusion that he probably thought his action would be praised instead of condemned.

Verse 15. The use that Saul proposed to make of the animals was a lawful one. It was established as a part of the service under the law to offer beasts in sacrifie to God. The best of all such only would be accepted, therefore it seemed to Saul that his actions would be pleasing to God.

Verse 16. As a general introduction to what he has to say, Samuel told Saul to stay; that meant to be still and listen.

Verse 17. *Little in thine own sight.* See Ch. 9: 21 for the explanation of these words. Although he was insignificant in his own sight, according to his admission, he had been exalted to the high position of king over the people.

Verse 18. In his position as king, Saul was assigned the important task of destroying an inveterate enemy of the kingdom. He was not only to go against him, but continue his fight until he had utterly destroyed him. He had destroyed much of the enemy, but not utterly done so to the end.

Verse 19. Samuel placed the question squarely up to Saul as to why he took possession of the spoil instead of destroying it.

Verse 20. Saul seemed still to be saturated with pride over his great work, for he repeated his declaration of obedience to God. His claim that he had utterly destroyed the Amalekites could have been true as far as he went, but he was so eager to manifest what he thought to be an extra service to God in bringing back the king alive, that he failed to obey the letter of the command that the destruction was to be thorough.

Verse 21. The expression *should have been utterly destroyed* means that the said beasts would have been utterly destroyed had he not decided to make a better use of them. His plan was to sacrifice them to God on the altar at Gilgal.

Verse 22. Here we have a very famous declaration of Holy Writ. While no one of the commandments of God is more necessary than the others, yet when man thinks to make discrimination he generally chooses the wrong one. From that standpoint it is here declared that animal sacrifices are not so acceptable that they may be permitted to interfere with the positive commandments of God. Sacrifices must never be offered when some duty of an authoritative nature has been overlooked. This idea was taught by Christ in Matt. 5: 24.

Verse 23. Witchcraft and idolatry were generally considered by the Jews as great evils, which they were, but Samuel declares that rebellion and stubbornness are as bad as they. And the charge is not an arbitrary one. If a man is rebellious against the commandments of the God of Heaven there would be no logical reason why he should not turn his attention to idols. And stubbornness is another indication of self-gratification, which is the same as idolatry or self-worship.

Verse 24. The confession of Saul recognized the authority of Samuel the prophet in that he said he had transgressed the commandment of the Lord, "and thy words." This principle often has been set forth before the reader and doubtless will be again. It is so vital and yet so much overlooked by professed servants of God that it needs to be kept before the mind. When anyone disobeys the authority of God's constituted rulers it is the same as disobeying Him. Another weakness of mankind was acknowledged here. Saul said he had sinned because he feared the people. Many men who claim to be teachers of the Word will pervert it and refrain from preaching all of it because of a desire for popularity.

Verses 25, 26. Saul was eager to be restored to his former status and not only asked for the pardon of his sin, but that he might continue in the same favor of Samuel he had enjoyed before. That request was refused. Personally, he could have been forgiven of that sin, but his public trust had been twice violated already so he had forfeited his right to it. Therefore his kingdom was to be taken from him.

Verses 27, 28. In a visible gesture Samuel tore Saul's mantle which signified that Saul's kingdom was to be torn away from him. But not in the same way as was indicated later when the garment of Jeroboam was torn into many pieces. (1 Ki. 11: 31.) Then it meant the kingdom was to be divided, here it meant the kingdom was to be torn from Saul and given to a neighbor or associate of his.

Verse 29. The word *strength* means victory but is here used figuratively in referring to God. That was because the continued success of God's plans was not to be set aside by the disobedience of one man. Instead, it was going to continue by placing the human side of the work in the hands of another and better servant. Then the last part of the verse is added as a reason for the first part. We have previously seen that the term *repentance* has one common idea whether pertaining to God or man. That idea is *change*. The Scripture says in many places that God repents, yet here it sounds as if he does not. But the proviso should not be overlooked, "not a man, that." It means that God does not repent as man does. That would not prevent him from repenting in his own way. And so, since God had declared that Saul must be dethroned because of his great sins, he was not going to will a change in that decree.

Verses 30, 31. While God will not change his decree about the kingdom, yet his mercy is great toward penitent sinners. The man of God honored Saul to the extent of letting him worship the Lord in his presence as an inspired prophet. Sometimes a man will sin so grievously and frequently that confidence is destroyed, but that need not prevent him from performing the service called for in order that he might be saved. However, his activities should be done under proper supervision.

Verse 32. *Delicately*. This is from MAADANNAH and defined, "a delicacy or (abstractly) pleasure (adverbially, cheerfully)" — Strong. Since many others had been slain in this eventful time and he had been allowed to live this long, Agag was foolish enough to conclude that all fear or bitterness of death was gone. Thus he came into the presence of Samuel in a cheerful mood, but his mistaken ease of mind was destined soon to be changed.

Verse 33. *Mother be childless.* This was virtually the same prediction that was made in Ex. 17: 18, and fulfilled in the book of Esther.

Verses 34, 35. The king and prophet each went to his own city after this awful event in the affairs of the kingdom. The hostility of the enemy continued, but a lull was to come in the activities while an important move was being made. Samuel is said to have mourned for Saul. Not necessarily that he was sentimentally grieving over him personally, but he lamented the deeds of the wicked king. At the same time the Lord was holding out in his determination to remove the kingdom from Saul.

1 SAMUEL 16

Verse 1. This verse follows in thought the one at the close of the preceding chapter. Samuel was bidden to drop the matter of his lamentation over Saul's rejection. The thought is as if it read, "How long will you mourn at seeing my rejection of Saul?" As much as to say that it is time to be about doing something to replace the rejected king. The horn was a kind of flask to contain oil. Its use was brought about in those days by the custom of pouring oil over a man at his appointment as king, or in recognition of any other excellence. (Ch. 10: 1.)

Verse 2. The command to go to Bethlehem brought fear to the mind of Samuel. Saul had gone to Gibeah which was not far from this city and he might learn of the presence of the prophet. Saul's disgrace over his sins had been punishment coming through the hand of this very man, Samuel, and he might try to obtain vengeance at his expense. That is, he might do so for fear that Samuel was in that community for further acts of humiliation against him. It really was the thing about to take place. The humiliation would not be direct, it is true, but the appointment of a successor to the wicked king would have such an effect. Samuel was directed to offset the threat of harm from Saul by performing a sacrifice; that is, one of those religious feasts already described. There would be nothing untrue or unlawful in this. Reference to Deut. 12: 21 will inform us this sacrifice was not a burnt one but was a religious feast. That was entirely proper, especially as it was to be in connection with important affairs of the kingdom.

Verse 3. Jesse was to be invited to this sacrifie and during the time the Lord would show Samuel further what he was to do.

Verses 4, 5. The state of unrest that was then in the country made people have a feeling of uncertainty at the appearance of one from outside their community, so these people were fearful until Samuel made the announcement that God had suggested. He ordered them to make the necessary preparation for attending a religious feast. This had special application to Jesse and his sons.

Verse 6. Eliab was the oldest son (Ch. 17: 13) and naturally Samuel concluded that he was to be the new king. That would have been the usual and logical procedure.

Verse 7. The remarks of the Lord here were to be applicable in general, and not to the first son only. Hence the fundamental direction not to judge one's desirability for service to God by outward appearance. In temporal kingdoms the physical appearance is an important item; however, it is not the only one, nor the most important. A man might be qualified from that standpoint yet be lacking in some other sense. And since God was directing this choice it will not be necessary to depend on the outward appearance.

Verse 8. Samuel did not again think of judging by the mere appearance. He was to be shown expressly by the Lord which was the choice. Having said nothing in favor of this son, Samuel stated that he had not been chosen.

Verses 9, 10. Jesse caused seven of his sons to pass in turn before Samuel, yet no one of them was selected.

Verse 11. There was no indication of doubt in Samuel's mind as to the instructions he had received that a king would be found among these sons. His inquiry was in the form of a call for other members of Jesse's family to be presented. Jesse had not been informed of the purpose of Samuel's visit that we know of, hence he had not called the youngest son from the necessary work of tending the sheep. So now he was told to call him.

Verse 12. This rosy faced young man came into the presence of the group. The description given of him was very favorable and the reader might be confused into thinking of it as a contradiction of verse 7. Not so if closer attention is given to the whole context. It was true that David was a man of good appearance. But it is not said here that God chose him on that account. The reason he was selected was that the Lord could see the heart (verse 7) and David had the kind of heart that was pleasing to Him. (Ch. 13:14.) So the command was for Samuel to anoint him *for this is he.*

Verse 13. The usual formality was observed. Oil was poured on the head of David, which made him the "king elect" to succeed Saul. He will not actually take office while Saul is living. Howbeit, the spirit of the Lord now came upon him. This qualification will be useful in more than one instance as we shall see in the history to follow. Having accomplished his mission Samuel departed.

Verse 14. The word *evil* is from BA and Strong defines it "bad or (as noun) evil (naturally or morally)." The word has been rendered by such as adversity, affliction, calamity, distress, grief, and many others. Hence it does not mean that God caused him to have a sinful disposition. He already had shown that. Rather, that a spirit of affliction was sent upon him to punish him for his sins. The fact that music would relieve him proved that his condition was not of a moral character. The particular form of this affliction was that of troubling and terrifying him. Most of us know from experience what a profound effect it has upon one to be terrified.

Verses 15, 16. The affliction of Saul was such that it affected his appearance through his nervous system. That made it apparent to the ones around him. The suggestion was made, therefore, that someone be procured who could play well on a harp. This was the national musical instrument of the Hebrews according to Smith's Bible Dictionary. It was usually made with ten strings and played with an attachment for the fingers. Others were made of eight strings and played directly with the hand. Such was the kind David used and thus the suggestion was made that hand playing be done. This kind of instrument when played with skill would produce the soft tones that would soothe the nerves of one who was all wrought up with terror.

Verses 17, 18. Saul called for a man to perform the desired service. One of his servants described a man whom he had observed. This man possessed many talents besides that of playing the harp; the description pleased Saul as we shall see.

Verse 19. Being a king, Saul could properly call for the services of this son of Jesse. In order that no mistake could be made, the specification was given that the son caring for the sheep was the one Saul wanted.

Verse 20. Making offering of gifts in those days was a way of showing recognition for another. Saul was the king and Jesse was a subject, and his son was now to appear in the presence of the king. A respectful attitude was shown which contrasted with that shown by some others. (Ch. 10:27.)

Verses 21: 22. The appearance of David was pleasing to Saul and he not only took him for a musician, but placed him near in military service. Upon this decision he sent word to the father that he wished to obtain the services of his son for continuous relationship.

Verse 23. The primary object in calling David was for his service upon the harp. It did the thing desired and the music of the strings soothed the nerves of the troubled king, for the time being. This affliction is not to be thought of as a permanent one; it came periodically, whenever the Lord saw fit to bring it upon him.

1 SAMUEL 17

Verses 1-3. The lull in hostilities was over and war activities started again. The opposing armies pitched in a possession of Judah with just a valley between them.

Verse 4. Goliath is nowhere directly called a giant although we know he was one in physical stature. The word sometimes signified more than mere physical or bodily size. In the present instance the bodily proportions were the phases that the writer is concerned about. Goliath was about ten feet in height.

Verse 5. This verse describes the metallic covering the champion wore, called "coat of mail." It was made of brass and weighed 5,000 shekels. The tables of weights and measures used in ancient times are so variously given by the authorities that no definite statement is sure of being correct, but from all sources it is certain that this covering weighed many pounds.

Verse 6. The greaves are defined by Strong, "a shin-piece." It was a special protection for the lower part of the legs. The R. V. gives us javelin in place of the target, and the lexicon agrees. However, the context indicates that it at least might have referred to some kind of shield that he wore between his shoulders to protect his heart and lungs.

Verse 7. The great size of the spear with its staff indicated the physical might of this champion. He was further protected by a bodyguard who preceded him with a shield.

Verses 8, 9. The challenge that Goliath made is what is known as a "challenge to single combat," and was recognized as a legitimate way of settling military disputes. It had a retaining influence in the duels practiced later on in defense of "honor." It was considered a fair way of deciding an issue. But such contests were conducted on a stricter basis than could have been possible here. Even in the game of prize fights, a man is not permitted to enter the contest unless he is known to possess at least some show of equality to his antagonist. But Goliath knew there was no such man among the Hebrews to be compared physically to him. Hence his challenge to such a contest, as belonged only to men of equal chance, was just a pretense.

Verses 10, 11. The appearance of this mighty creature and his arrogant defiance of Israel made a profound impression on the people and filled them with dismay. The challenger appeared from day to day without having his proposition accepted.

Verse 12. All Bible students understand that much of the inspired writings will not conform to the chronological order of events. This fact should be considered in the case at hand. Verses 19-23 of the previous chapter, and verse 2 of chapter 18, should be placed after the events of this chapter. The personal identity of David and the description of his talents and influence are there given.

Verses 13, 14. Following the practice of nations in warfare, the oldest sons of a family were sent into the field of battle, while the others would be retained at home for family duties. Thus these three sons of Jesse were in the field of battle.

Verse 15. A brief explanation will be in order here in view of the remarks in a preceding paragraph. The main body of this narrative belongs before the permanent drafting of David for personal service under Saul. In the meantime there is indication that David had been sent for at special times just for his service as musician, and then he would be permitted to return to his daily task as a shepherd. So this verse is a sort of interpolation into the regular trend of things.

Verse 16. The period of constant terror lasted forty days in which no one had the courage or ability to accept the challenge of Goliath.

Verses 17, 18. Jesse was interested in the war, and especially interested in the welfare of his sons as all natural fathers would be, and for their benefit he wished to send supplies to them and their superior in battle. *Take their pledge.* The last word means, "token of safety." It signified that Jesse wanted to have some assurance that his sons were safe.

Verse 19. This verse gives us the information that while no one had accepted the challenge of the champion, yet the war otherwise was going on.

Verse 20. David obeyed his father and took the stuff to the area of the battle. He came to the trench, which means the field headquarters, where the stuff would be kept. Just as he arrived the unit was leaving with shouts of war to make an attack.

Verses 21, 22. Upon hearing and seeing this, David placed his carriage (the things he carried) in the hands of the regular custodian of those things and went into the area of the battle.

Verse 23. As he came into the midst of the soldiers, the champion made one of his accustomed appearances with the challenge and David heard it.

Verse 24. The people shrank away from fear at this, but no sign of fear upon the part of David was shown.

Verse 25. So helpless did the children of Israel feel in the matter of Goliath that great inducements were offered to urge someone to accept the challenge. His reward was to consist of money, marriage, and permanent freedom from all servitude.

Verses 26, 27. David thought he overheard the announcement of proposed reward for the conqueror of Goliath, but perhaps he was mistaken. He made personal inquiry and was told after the same words that he had thought he overheard.

Verse 28. This speech of Eliab was

certainly inspired by jealousy. He spoke what was untrue about David's purpose for coming there as the record shows. David did not know anything of what he would find when he left home. But it often happens in this world that true greatness in one person is so evident that others who do not possess like qualities will envy him and try to weaken the situation by false accusations. The fact that none of the regular army had the courage to even maintain good order in the hearing of the champion, while this youth was not only unafraid but making personal inquiry, roused Eliab to the jealous speech.

Verse 29. David in effect denied the petty accusation. His question meant, "is there not a reason for my being here?" And the reader will answer that in the affirmative by referring to verse 17.

Verses 30, 31. David did not let the little conduct of his jealous brother cause him to drop his interest. He turned from him to another with the same inquiry and was given the same answer as before. This conversation finally came to the ears of Saul and he sent for him.

Verse 32. David evidently knew that legal battle action even in time of war must be taken under proper enlistment or commission, therefore he offered his services to the king and agreed to take up the challenge of the champion.

Verse 33. Considering the subject from human knowledge and appearance, Saul thought of the offer as being out of the question. The great difference between the physical qualifications of the two would make the contest one of mere sacrifice for David.

Verses 35-36. David was not discouraged, yet he was respectful and proposed to furnish concrete evidence of his ability to cope with the monster. He cited the case wherein he killed a lion and a bear. There was no speculative theory about such evidence. If he could thus overcome those vicious and strong creatures, he surely can this other enemy. And the greatest of motives was present in this case. The challenger had defied the armies of the living God. That expresses a principle that holds good today. Whoever defies God's work should be regarded as an enemy of God's people.

Verse 37. In this verse David gave the secret of his hopes for victory. It was the Lord who had given him the victory in the other contests and would do so again. With this argument Saul was convinced and told the young man to go with the Lord's help.

Verses 38, 39. The word *armor* here means clothing or wearing apparel. Saul put it on David and then also put the metal covering on him. Then David further equipped himself by attaching his sword to the outfit. The word *assayed* is from YAAL and its outstanding definition is, "to undertake as an action of volition." The word *proved* is from NACAH and is defined, "to test." The thought in the passage is that David had a willingness to go in this outfit, but it had been willingness only as to his attitude of mind and not a final conclusion actually to go. As soon as he realized that he had not tested the equipment he concluded it was no time to wear an outfit that had not been tested by him; he put them off from him.

Verse 40. The critic may ask why David took five stones if he had so much faith in God. Well, David knew that the Lord helps those who help themselves. He did not know how many attacks would be required before victory would be given to him; therefore, the logical thing to do was to be prepared to cooperate with God.

Verse 41. The challenger and his armor bearer came on to the attack, the latter going before his master as his protector.

Verse 42. Goliath disdained him which means that he had a belittling feeling toward him. He thought him to be an inferior antagonist because of his youthful appearance, being ruddy and fair in complexion.

Verse 43. Verse 40 stated that David took his staff in his hand. This was merely a walking stick and not intended as a weapon at all. But the Philistine thought (or pretended to think) that he was intending it as part of his equipment for battle and thus he felt insulted. A man might take a club if he were going after a brute beast, but surely not if against a dignified fighter like this challenger. With such a feeling he called for the curses of his god upon David.

Verse 44. This is the language of a braggart and bully and not that of a brave man.

Verse 45. In this verse David contrasts the equipments of the antagonists. His mention of a spear throws light on the comments at verse 6. The giant depended on the physical strength of his armor and weapons while David relied on the very God whose armies had been insulted and defied.

Verse 46. David prefaced his warning of destructive victory over the Philistine with his reliance on the Lord. With this assurance he announced that his combatant would be disarmed and his body given to the same beasts mentioned in the boast of the giant. And the glorious motive for all this is revealed in the last words of the verse.

Verse 47. If the challenger is killed he will not realize his defeat, but the assembly will, and will be forced to know that the Lord does not rely on human means for his victories although he uses them through man. That is because he wishes man to have a part in the divine work.

Verses 48, 49. The attack now went forward. David did not wait for the giant to make the entire move but ran toward the army since the contender was in that position. The word *smote* is from NAKAH and defined by Strong, "a primitive root; to strike (lightly or severely, literally or figuratively)." I have quoted this definition to assist in understanding the passage, as it is sometimes made to be confusing as to whether the stone actually killed him or that it was the sword that did it. But it is not necessary to be specific on the subject. The word strictly means only that the stone struck the Philistine in the forehead. But as the result finally was his death, it could be said that the stone killed him. And yet it is stated that he drew the sword and slew him. The proper view of the whole matter is that all of the items involved in the action should be given proper credit for the death of Goliath.

Verse 50. By falling the giant with the stone David prevailed over him. But the mere fact of bringing him to the ground might not alone have brought his death. There would remain the work of making sure by beheading him. That would require a sword, something David did not have since he had discarded all such weapons upon discovery that he could not use the outfit offered him by Saul.

Verse 51. The Philistine was down and helpless. David therefore ran and stood upon him. We have previously learned about a practice of placing the feet in the necks of the enemies. Here is a similar action. The severing of the head from the body would be conclusive evidence to the Philistines of the defeat of their champion even had the work of the stone not been fatal. At the sight of it they fled. But there is no indication they intended to comply with the terms of the challenger, for he had stipulated that if he were killed then his people would submit to the Israelites.

Verses 52, 53. Israel and Judah are named again as being distinguished. See comments on this at Ch. 11: 8. The defeat of the giant had thrown the Philistines into a rout with panic and the pursuing Israelites wounded many of them in the flight. This made the present action very decisive in the war between the two peoples.

Verse 54. Bringing the head of the fallen foe into the city of Jerusalem was very much on the principle of the "triumphs" often carried out in ancient times by victorious warriors, while the act of depositing the armor of the foe in his tent was in the nature of storing a trophy as a keepsake.

Verses 55-58. For explanation of this passage please see the comments at verse 12.

1 SAMUEL 18

Verse 1. This describes a personal attachment that sprang up between David and Jonathan which continued undiminished as long as they lived and will figure largely in the history to come.

Verse 2. Again let the reader read comments at verse 12 of previous chapter.

Verses 3, 4. This exchange of apparel and weapons was only a demonstration of the deep affection which Jonathan had for David.

Verse 5. Saul, having taken David into his permanent service, sent him out on various missions. The words *behaved* and *wisely* are from the same original word SAKAL and defined by Strong as follows: "to be (causatively, make or act) circumspect and hence intelligent." The margin here gives us the word prospered. This is a true conclusion as to the result of such behaviour, for verses 14, 15 and 30 indicates such a conclusion. But the idea should be retained that the inspired writer in this verse wishes to state the manner of David's actions. And as a result of this conduct he was acceptable in the sight of the people generally. This fact will be evident in more than one way later on in our story.

Verses 6-8. This passage signifies the beginning of the enmity between Saul and David. The terms of the number of slain are figurative since neither of the men had slain the number stated, but the comparison was what angered Saul and filled him with the feeling of envy and pride. It also indicated to him that perhaps the time might come when popular sentiment would call for David to be king.

Verse 9. The word *eyed* means, "to watch (with jealousy)" according to Strong.

Verses 10, 11. This evil spirit that came on Saul was the affliction described at Ch. 16: 14 which see. The word *prophesied* here means that Saul was singing while David was playing on the harp. But the playing of David this time was not sufficient to allay the feeling of terror so he attempted to kill him with a javelin, which was a small spear. He intended to pin him to the wall with the weapon and made two moves for that purpose. But David was too quick for him and escaped both times.

Verse 12. Saul was afraid of David. This was a kind of regard for his influence and a recognition of his superiority. And this feeling was important since it was based on the observation that God was with David and not with Saul.

Verse 13. In his fear of David, also his jealousy, Saul removed him from his personal service and demoted him from the rank credited him by the women and gave him a command over a thousand men.

Verse 14. This did not cause David to swerve from his proper conduct which continued to bring him prosperity in his endeavors.

Verse 15. See comments at verses 5 on *behaved* and *wisely*. When Saul saw that David was successful on account of his prudent conduct, it made him all the more afraid.

Verse 16. *Israel and Judah*. See Ch. 11: 8 on this expression. David was loved by the people because he was evidently doing them faithful service.

Verse 17. The enmity of Saul for David was never cured although at times he professed it to be. He was ever plotting his downfall although he declined to destroy him personally if it could be accomplished otherwise. As a preliminary for such an end, he made an offer of marriage with his elder daughter. It was the rule for the elder daughter to be given in marriage first and thus it might seem to be a sincere action to make this proposition of honor to the young soldier. The inspired writer is telling the reader what was in the mind of Saul as he was making the proposition. This is what is meant by the last sentence of the verse.

Verses 18, 19. David believed Saul to be in earnest about the offer of marriage, but declined the offer as being unworthy of the honor. That is, he felt that his social standing did not entitle him to the place in the family of the king. And as he thus declined the offer of marriage, the daughter was given to another man to be his wife. There was no indication that she was interested in the match with David anyway.

Verse 20. But in some manner it was known that another daughter, Michal, loved David. This fact was revealed to Saul, although no evidence was present that David knew anything about her sentiment in his favor. But it suggested to the hypocritical mind of Saul that a still better opportunity would be furnished through her than it would have been through the other daughter.

Verse 21. *And Saul said*. But he did not say this outwardly. See comments on the latter part of verse 17. So he again proposed marriage for David and at this time suggested that one of his other daughters become his wife.

Verses 22, 23. The match was to be effected through the servants. They made the offer to David on behalf of the king and he declined on the same basis that he did the first time, when it was made by Saul personally.

Verses 24, 25. The servants had not told David all of the propositions yet, but now they did so. It was customary in those days for a man to give a present to the proposed wife which was called a dowry. According to Smith's Bible Dictionary this was to confirm the betrothal, hence it furnished a seeming occasion for the proposition of Saul in this case. David had professed his poverty and hence unworthiness of being related to the king. Now he is told that no money will be expected. Instead, he could meet the usual custom by an act that would not satisfy the social demand only, but also fit in with what was supposed to be a matter in which they both were interested; the destruction of their common enemies, the Philistines. However, Saul will not trust to the mere report that a hundred Philistines have been slain. He might be deceived as to their actual death. So if he required the foreskins, that would be evidence that the men had been slain. His expectation, however, was that in attempting to take the Philistines David would himself be slain, and that was what Saul wished.

Verse 26. The outward appearance here is that David wished to be son-in-law to the king, while the inner motive was that he had the desire to attack the inveterate enemies of his God. *Days were not expired.* This means that the offer made in verse 21 still was standing.

Verse 27. Upon the proposal from Saul the next thing was to make the attack. David took his men with him and doubled the required number by slaying two hundred of the Philistines. He brought the mutilated parts to Saul. There was now no pretense for refusing his daughter, and the match was made and Saul was again defeated in his wicked designs against David.

Verses 28, 29. All this confirmed the fears of Saul that David not only was loved by his wife, but that the Lord was with him. This increased his enmity for him and he continued ever after to be his enemy.

Verse 30. Even the prince of the Philistines recognized the superiority of David's conduct and success. *Set by.* This is expressed in the margin as "precious." That is, the very mention of the name David brought forth respect even from his enemies.

1 SAMUEL 19

Verse 1. Saul knew that his son and others were nearer to David now than he, and would have more opportunities to do him bodily harm. In his wicked jealousy he asked them to kill him. Nothing but the lowest depths of evil rage could have caused this.

Verse 2. Jonathan had no intention of obeying his father's orders, but he knows the hatred Saul has for David and considers that he is in constant danger from him personally and should always be on the alert. He warns David accordingly.

Verse 3. However, Jonathan proposed to make a test of the case on the morrow to see if Saul's rage had abated any. This he would do by bringing up the subject directly while in the field where David would be hiding. If it should be that his father had seen his wrong and was willing to treat him as he should, it would be an easy matter to show it, since he would be near and could come from his hiding.

Verses 4-7. The experiment worked out as Jonathan planned. He spoke to his father about David and cited the fact that he had been true and faithful as a servant, and had always been friendly toward him. Also that he had even risked his life in his fight with the champion of the enemy people. Saul agreed with the plea and David was called from his hiding and permitted to be in the presence of the king again for a time.

Verse 8. Another action now came in the war, and, as before, David went out and slew so many of the Philistines that they fled from his face.

Verses 9, 10. But the spirit of envy was ever present with Saul. And the spirit of affliction that we have already learned about was sent upon him as his punishment. When that condition came upon him, his faithful servant, David, was called to allay his terror with the harp. While the playing of the harp might soothe his afflictions, it was not intended to change his moral conduct. Hence, even while David was administering to his physical or nervous suffering, he was mindful of the superiority in conflict shown by the player. This roused his envy again and he forgot all his good promises. With the javelin or spear which he held he attempted to kill David; the attempt failed and David escaped.

Verse 11. In the night David came to his own house and prepared to repose. But Saul sent his men to the place intending to capture him in the morning. His wife was aware of the danger and warned him to flee, even from his own house.

Verse 12. She showed the sincerity of her warning by assisting him to escape by a window so that he could flee.

Verse 13. Michal expected them to come finally to take him by force. Perhaps, if she could make them believe that he was sick, they would have the heart to leave. For this purpose she took an image. This is defined by Strong as "a family idol." It was an object in the form of a human being and she placed it on a pillow of goat's hair and made it appear as if it were David there in the bed.

Verse 14. Sure enough, the servants of Saul came to take David and upon her report that he was sick they left and returned to Saul with the report. All this gave David more time for getting away to a place of safety.

Verse 15. The wickedness of Saul would permit no sympathy; he commanded that the sick man be brought to him in his bed. How different this case from that of the palsied man brought in a bed to Jesus; that was for his recovery, this for destruction.

Verse 16. The servants attempted to obey the orders of their chief, but had to report to him their disappointment.

Verse 17. We know from the language of the preceding verse that Michal made a false statement here. On this kind of situation see comments at Joshua 2. Another thing to be considered here is that David was in war with the Philistines and his life and services were needed for the conflict. Thus on the basis of strategy it would be just for Michal to deceive her father.

Verse 18. David escaped and came to Samuel and related his experience. On such information they fled and went to Naioth.

Verses 19, 20. Saul learned of the whereabouts of David and sent messengers to take him there. But upon the approach to the place they found that he was in the company of Samuel and that other prophets were there also. At this point the spirit of God came upon them and they joined in the activities of Samuel and the other prophets. This is a similar circumstance to that of Balaam in Numbers 23.

Verse 21. The report came back to Saul, but he was not discouraged in his evil designs and sent other messengers. This was like the act of Balak in Numbers 22: 15. But these other messengers were taken over by the Lord also.

Verse 22. Saul still is not convinced of his folly. This time he thought to carry out his plans more successfully by going himself. Coming into the neighborhood, he asked for and received information as to the location of David and Samuel.

Verse 23. The spirit of God that came upon Saul was not the evil one of affliction already known to us. It was the one directly of the Lord that inspired him to prophesy. This is not the only instance where God forced a wicked man to speak the truth. See the case of Balaam in Numbers 23. At various times in the past, God has used characters who were not his true servants, and at times those who were not even professed servants, to carry out his plans. But it should be borne in mind that in no case did that forced service make any change in the moral status of that person either for good or bad. The Persian king Cyrus was already a good man before God used him and thus was not changed in character by the special use God made of him. Pharaoh was a wicked man before the evil deeds against the Israelites and therefore was not made to be an evil man by the service God brought from him. It was thus in the case of Saul. God used him here as an instrument to show his divine power, but it did not have any reforming effect upon him.

Verse 24. In olden times persons wore outer garments generally. The outer was for more complete comfort and protection, and the inner was worn alone in times of special activity. These inner garments also were worn alone in times of either distress or humility. (Ex. 32: 25). For information on this point a partial quotation will be made from Smith's Bible Dictionary, article Dress: "1. The inner garment was the most essential article of dress. It was a closely fitting garment, resembling in form and use our shirt, though unfortunately translated 'coat' in the A. V. The material of which it was made was either wool, cotton or linen. It was without sleeves, and reached only to the knees. Another kind reached to the wrists and ankles. It was in either case kept close to the body by a girdle, and the fold formed by the overlapping of the robe served as an inner pocket. A person wearing the inner garment alone was described as *naked*." This description would apply to Saul in this instance.

1 SAMUEL 20

Verse 1. David was weary of hiding out and decided to expose himself to any charge that could be made against him and take the consequences. For this purpose he came to Jonathan as his good friend and also the one to carry his case to Saul.

Verse 2. Jonathan's usual intimacy with the plans of his father prompted him to tell David that he was not in such immediate danger since nothing on the subject had been told him. On this basis he tried to comfort David.

Verse 3. David tells Jonathan that Saul certainly knows of their close attachment and for that reason he perhaps would not let Jonathan know his plans. Therefore, David still fears that death is only a "step" away.

Verse 4. Jonathan did not wish to resist the desires of his friend if he had any plans in mind for his own safety, thus he gave him permission to express himself.

Verse 5. The occasion for testing the plan David had in mind was the feast of the new moon. A reading of Num. 28: 11 will show that each new moon meant a time of religious activity among the Israelites. While the proper officials were performing their work at the altar, others would be engaged in feasts in their own homes in honor of the season. The significance of this period as to date will be noted more in later verses of this chapter. David knew that he would be expected to appear with the family at this feast, since he was at this time a part of the family circle of Saul, but he proposed to hide in a field nearby.

Verse 6. There would not be anything irregular as far as the law was concerned in the fact that David wished to be with his own family at this sacrifice or feast. (Deut. 12: 21.) However, since he was now in the personal service of the king it might be regarded as his duty to be at his feast, and if he should be missed and inquired for the answer proposed would be a test of the king's temper with reference to him.

Verse 7. The reply that Saul would make was to determine, for the time, what the prospects were of peace with David.

Verse 8. Even with the close personal friendship between David and Jonathan, it was not desired to lead Jonathan into any conspiracy against his father if there was any real charge against David. If that were the case he would submit his lot to Jonathan directly for execution.

Verses 9, 10. Jonathan affirmed his friendship for David again and promised to tell him everything pertaining to his interests. Then David asked for more specific information as to when and how the plan was to be worked.

Verse 11. As the field was to be the place where the transaction would be put into effect, it was appropriate to go there for their present pact of friendship.

Verse 12. To *sound* his father meant that he would try out the plan mentioned in verse 6. If the reaction was favorable then he bound himself to show it to David.

Verse 13. If it should be unfavorable, still Jonathan declared that he would make it known to David. *Lord do so* is an expression often used in the Scripture. It meant that what the Lord would do to Saul as punishment for his mistreatment of David, he should do the like to Jonathan if he failed of his duty to David in telling him.

Verses 14, 15. Jonathan evidently expected David to survive the present distress and live on, even after the immediate families of Jonathan and Saul were gone. On such account he wished to provide for the future good treatment of their descendants by enlisting the friendship of David, and to do this it was necessary to help save him from the present wrath of Saul. The time did come when this service was performed for the house of Jonathan by David. (2 Sam. 9: 3, 7.)

Verse 16. The agreement was made that David was to continue kindness to the descendants of Jonathan. It was stipulated that if David broke the covenant, then the Lord would *require it*, or bring punishment on David through the instrumentality of his enemies.

Verse 17. The severe terms stated in the preceding verse were agreed to by David, and the reason he was willing to agree to them was his very strong love for Jonathan. This love never did abate toward him or his surviving family.

Verses 18, 19. The time for the scheme was near. Jonathan seemed to consider it would require the third day of absence to attract the attention of his father, hence he told David to come after that period to the place selected for hiding.

Verses 20-22. The casual performance of the lad with Jonathan and the arrows was to be the code agreed upon by the two.

Verse 23. This was merely another way of expressing the fact that an oath for faithfulness was between them in the sight of the Lord.

Verse 24. The idea to be noted carefully in this verse is that it was the time of the new moon.

Verses 25, 26. All through the first day of the feast, David's seat was vacant. But Saul did not think very strange of it. The Israelites were not permitted to partake of the religious feasts if something had occurred to make them unclean, and the king just concluded that such was the case with David.

Verse 27. Saul did not wait until the third day, the day that was to terminate by waiting in the field, to express his feeling about David. Yet it would naturally require some time to make the further preparations with the lad for the plan, so the agreement was to wait until the third day for its completeness. In this verse is the thought promised in verse 5. We know from the connection that the events of this verse were the next day after the new moon. And yet it is called the second day of the month. This proves that the month was started with the appearance of the new moon. David was still missing. But now it could not be accounted for on the basis of uncleanness, for the provision was made in the law that a state of uncleanness need not continue longer than the evening of the same day. (Lev. 11: 24, 25, 27, 31, 32.) Therefore, Saul was induced to make inquiry of Jonathan since he knew of the intimate association between the two and Jonathan doubtless would know about David.

Verses 28, 29. The answer was given Saul which had been agreed upon by the two friends. Yes, it was a deceptive answer, to be sure, and no special blessing was ever pronounced upon David or Jonathan because of this kind of conduct. It was in spite of it. We must not forget that David is the anointed king to come next, and his preservation would come under the principles of war since Saul had been trying to destroy him. It was necessary to take some means for his safety. Another thing that should be kept in mind is this: in none of the cases where people were blessed, even though they had made false statements, did any good person suffer from the effects of the falsehood. In the eyes of secular law even, a perjury is not considered unless a falsehood resulted in the injury of someone. In this instance no good person was injured, instead, a good man was benefited and preserved for the service of God.

Verses 30, 31. The reaction was as David feared. The word *woman* is in italics and not in the original. Neither is it appropriate in this connection. The language at the close of verse 30 indicates that no blame is laid on his mother, but rather that she is also disgraced by the conduct of her son. The correct rendering would be to say that Jonathan is a son or creature of rebelliousness. He further made the rash declaration that the destruction of David would be necessary in the interests of his (Jonathan's) political welfare. So Saul demanded that David be brought and slain.

Verse 32. Before giving up in despair for David's welfare, Jonathan tried to placate his father by placing him "on the spot," in calling for specific charges of misconduct in David.

Verse 33. Knowing that no such citation could be made, Saul showed his bitter feeling and determination of harm for David by attempting the death of Jonathan. This convinced Jonathan that nothing favorable for David could be expected.

Verse 34. Jonathan lost his taste for the feast and he arose from the table in anger, but did nothing more that day with regard to David.

Verses 35, 36. The plan with the lad and arrows was now arranged for the next day, which was the third day of the month. As a mere action of diversion he told the lad to bring the arrows back to him. The lad started to run to the supposed place of the target and, as he ran, Jonathan shot an arrow with aim that carried it beyond him, or overran his speed. Naturally the lad would be looking for the arrow, and, as a casual remark, Jonathan told him to go on further to find the arrow.

Verses 37, 38. Jonathan spoke to the lad as if he were eager for the arrows to shoot again, and for him to come back speedily. He obeyed his master, not knowing what all of the action meant.

Verses 38-40. Since the lad was unaware of the significance of all this, he would not think strange when given the artillery or instruments and told to carry them into the city. A question born of curiosity is sometimes asked here. Why did they go through with all this formality when no one was concerned in the affair but the two friends? Why not just come together at the start and impart the information? We will not speculate very much on this for it is not important. When this plan was agreed upon between them it was not known who else might be present that would make it unsafe for David to show up, but he could get the warning by hearing the conversation between Jonathan and the lad. And when the time came, Jonathan would not know the exact spot where David was hiding, thus he could find him only by the plan used. Since this specific plan had been agreed upon, if Jonathan should alter it materially by leaving the lad and the arrows out of the case, David might be confused in his fright.

Verse 41. David had overheard all and came out of his hiding and met Jonathan. He performed the custom of the East by prostrating himself before him in recognition of his fidelity in carrying out the covenant. The emotions of David were more expressive than those of Jonathan.

Verse 42. It was agreed that David should leave that community, and Jonathan wished the blessing of the Lord upon him and reaffirmed the covenant that was between them concerning the future of their kindred.

1 SAMUEL 21

Verse 1. The city of Nob was in the possession of Benjamin and one of the places where the ark rested. There were many many priests there at our present time of the story, and for that reason it was called a sacerdotal city. (Ch. 22:19.) Since verse 4 mentions the presence of men, the statement that no man was with David would have some special meaning. There was no man in any official or orderly capacity with him; the men mentioned below were some comrades unofficially associated with him.

Verse 2. Another instance of false statement appears here. Well, let the reader again consider the thoughts suggested at Ch. 20:28, 29.

Verse 3. As David asked for a specified number of loaves we can justly conclude he had that many of these personal associates with him. They were hungry, and David requested the priest to give him of whatever he had.

Verse 4. This was the bread that had been on the table of shewbread. Consult Lev. 24:5-9. This bread was replaced each Sabbath, and that which had been on the table for a week then became the food for the priest who was in active service. This was the bread that was eaten in the present instance, and not the bread on the table. (Matt. 12:3, 4.) While this bread had already served its original purpose by being on the table for a week, still it would be considered as hallowed bread. This was because its temporal use was considered the right of the priests only, but an emergency existed which would make it lawful for others to eat of it. This principle was recognized by Christ in the reference cited above. But this bread must not be used by any who have lately been connected with physical activities that rendered them ceremonially unclean. Such a condition would result from intimate relation with the opposite sex.

Verse 5. This verse has been rendered in various ways, but the thought evidently is that the young men were worthy to eat of the bread because they had not become unclean in the manner stipulated by the priest. As a physical reason for making the claim, David said it had been three days since they had left their homes and the women. Also, since the bread had been already used in the holy service it now could be considered in a manner common.

Verse 6. Upon the plea and explanation of David the priest gave him of this bread, and the statement was made that is explained in Lev. 24:9.

Verse 7. It would appear just at this verse that nothing but an insignificant event was meant by the mention of this Edomite who was a servant of Saul. But its connection will come to our attention before long.

Verse 8. The statement of David as to his lack of military equipment agrees with remarks made at verse 1 of this chapter.

Verse 9. How Goliath's sword came to be in this place is not stated. After the duel with Goliath, David had taken Goliath's armor to his tent, but nothing was said then of this weapon or what was done with it. But when it was offered to him at this time he was pleased, and said it was unlike any other. Reflection on his victory over the champion was the motive for the remark.

Verse 10. Fear of Saul was still in the mind of David, and he fled to Achish, king of the Philistines, who was located at Gath. Gath was one of the royal cities of the Philistines, and the city of the giant.

Verses 11, 12. When he came to this city the citizens recognized him and reported him to their king. They also referred to the fame concerning his accomplishments in battle. He overheard the remarks and took them under consideration. Since Achish was a Philistine and thus a friend of the giant whom David had slain, he might be resentful over the affair. This thought made him fear the king.

Verse 13. As a means of diverting attention from his ability in combat, David began the pretense of being mad or insane. He scrabbled or marked on the gate posts; he also made as if he were frothing at the mouth.

Verses 14, 15. The king of Gath was convinced that David had lost his mind, and was glad to have him out of the community. This took place as we will soon learn.

1 SAMUEL 22

Verse 1. In speaking of the vicinity of Adullam, Smith's Bible Dictionary says, "The limestone cliffs of the whole of that locality are pierced with extensive excavations, some one of which is doubtless the 'cave of Adullam' the refuge of David." His father and brethren heard of his hiding place and went to him there.

Verse 2. The place became a resort for various classes of disgruntled persons. It is a common trait of man to become bitter against society over his own misfortunes, whether those be on account of his personal mistakes or otherwise. About four hundred of these folk fled to David and he assumed a place as captain over them.

Verses 3, 4. With such a mob of disquieted people with him he did not consider it a very satisfactory place for his father and mother, so he left the place long enough to make other arrangements for them. He went into the country of Moab to the city of Mizpeh and requested a place of safety for them until he could know the outcome of his present situation. The request was granted and his parents remained at Mizpeh all the while he was in the hold or the cave.

Verse 5. The prophet Gad came and advised David not to remain in this hold, but to depart and go into the land of Judah, which he did.

Verse 6. Saul seems to have been at a loss to know David's whereabouts, but now it has been revealed to him where David and his men are. All the meantime Saul has been in a state of defense.

Verse 7. This is a plaintive cry for sympathy and bid for support on the basis of temporal advantages. It implies that citizens should support the man who could give them the greatest amount of money or land regardless of principles involved.

Verse 8. With what we have learned in the account, we know that Saul spoke what was not true against Jonathan; David's actions had not been instigated by Jonathan. It was true, however, that Jonathan recognized the wrong in his father's actions and the righteousness of David's, but it was false to state that he was helping David in any unlawful attempt against the king.

Verses 9, 10. This paragraph takes us back to the events of the preceding chapter. There it did not seem of much significance to mention the presence of this man Doeg, but his eyes and ears were open, and now we behold him as a talebearer. What he here stated was the truth, but told at a time and under circumstances that made a bad impression on Saul. As here reported it gave the appearance that the priest had acted in the interest of the king's enemies, whereas we know that it was not the case. In fact, David had led the priest to believe that he was there on behalf of the king. With that in view, it would make the motive of the priest in assisting him the very best. The whole circumstance gives us a signal illustration of how even a truth, when related without proper connections, may make a false impression.

Verse 11. Upon the report of Doeg, Saul summoned Ahimelech and all the other priests that were in Nob and they came to him. This fact should have convinced Saul that they had not designed any insurrection against him. Had they been doing so they would not have come to his presence; instead, they would have gone elsewhere.

Verses 12, 13. Upon arriving in the presence of the king, Ahimelech was accused in the matter of David, and asked for an explanation.

Verse 14. Ahimelech was still unaware of the gravity of his position. In explaining his attentions to David he reminded the king that David was the most faithful of his servants, and that in assisting him he considered it as an act of regard for the king.

Verse 15. This verse means that he was so sure of the faithfulness of David to his master that he never once thought it necessary to make any investigation about it.

Verse 16. Following his form of action for the last few months, Saul became enraged and pronounced the sentence of death on the priest and all his associates.

Verse 17. The footmen here were the bodyguard of the king. The command from him to attack the priests was too awful for their approval, even though they were under the highest authority in the realm. They therefore refused to obey the cruel order.

Verse 18. This Edomite could have no logical objection to obeying the order of the king, since he had but lately shown such interest in him as to tattle about the affair at Nob. Therefore he obeyed and killed 85 men of the priestly family.

Verse 19. Saul was not satisfied with slaying these men of the priestly class who appeared before him in Gibeah; the city of the priests also was attacked and all of its inhabitants from adult to infant were murdered.

Verse 20. Frequently a statement of mass destruction will be made in the Scripture, and then an exception will be made. (Judg. 9: 5; 2 Ki. 11: 1, 2.) One man named Abiathar escaped in this general destruction.

Verse 21. Having escaped, Abiathar fled to David and told the awful news.

Verse 22. Now the memory of David goes back to the occasion of his coming to Nob. At that time he concluded that a report of the conversation would get back to Saul, although there was no reason for him to know what the full consequence would be. Now that it has borne fruit, David blames himself for the death of all the priests, and mentions it to Abiathar in a form of speech that could be interpreted as an apology.

Verse 23. David cannot bring back to life the priests who have been slain through an occasion of his, although he can partly atone for it by furnishing protection to the one remaining member of the sacerdotal class. With this idea in mind, he told Abiathar that their interests would be identical, and that with him there would be safety.

1 SAMUEL 23

Verse 1. David and his men had fled the cave of Adullam because of fear of the Philistines. Now word came to him that a certain city in Judah was being attacked, and the products of the field robbed.

Verse 2. He inquired of the Lord whether he should make the attempt to recover the city and was told to do so.

Verse 3. The language might mislead the reader into thinking that Keilah was not in Judah. The comparison the men made was not between *where* the attack was to take place. It was the thought, rather, of being *in Judah*, let alone becoming the aggressor against the Philistines.

Verse 4. This necessitated another inquiry of the Lord by David, and he was given assurance of victory over the enemy.

Verse 5. It turned out as the Lord had promised, for David defeated the enemy in the city of Keilah and saved it.

Verse 6. This verse belongs, chronologically, after the last verse of the preceding chapter. Abiathar had fled and was with David in Keilah. He arrived there about the time that the battle against the Philistines in the city took place. Being of the priestly group, he was entitled to have in his possession an ephod, which was part of the garments of their class.

Verses 7, 8. The news reached Saul that David was in the city of Keilah and he concluded that God had lured David into that place as a cage to give him opportunity to take him. Accordingly, Saul called for his people to compose a siege of it.

Verse 9. David was aware of the treacherous actions of Saul, and wished to have reliable information concerning his prospects. We have previously learned (Lev. 10: 11; Deut. 17: 9) that the priest was an authorized medium of communication with God; Abiathar was therefore brought into service for that purpose.

Verses 10, 11. David's first inquiry was merely whether Saul would come down to take him in Keilah, and he was told that Saul would come down.

Verse 12. The next point was whether the men of the city would turn him over to Saul, even though he had saved their city for them. He was told they would do so.

Verses 13-15. Having been warned

of the intentions of Saul, David fled from Keilah with his men and hid in dens in the mountains. Saul made daily search for him but the Lord shielded him. This was because David was righteous and Saul was unrighteous.

Verses 16-18. Jonathan heard of the whereabouts of David and went to him to give him encouragement. He assured him that his father would not find him and that he would be king; also that his father was aware of this fact. After this friendly visit with David he returned to his own house.

Verses 19, 20. The Ziphites were inhabitants of the town of Ziph, which was in the near vicinity where David was hiding. These people informed Saul of the presence of his enemy in their neighborhood. They promised also to assist him in capturing David.

Verses 21, 22. Saul was much built up over this show of sympathy for him, and asked the blessing of the Lord upon him. However, he requested more definite information be obtained as to his present location with the warning that David was reported to have acted very cunningly in his movements.

Verse 23. Saul did not want to lose any time or activities in chasing David. He wished these friends of his to run that risk, therefore he instructed them to make diligent search and take notice of all David's hiding places. Then, when they have actually found him, they should pass the information on to Saul and he would make a forward move.

Verse 24. While these conversations were going on, David and his men had gone into the wilderness of Maon, so that he eluded his pursuers.

Verse 25. David had feared that Saul and his bodyguard were pursuing and that was why he had fled to the wilderness of Maon.

Verse 26. The chase continued with Saul in pursuit of David, a mountain being between them.

Verse 27, 28. Saul was now diverted from his chase by report of an invasion into the land by the Philistines.

Verse 29. At this time David changed his hiding place, and came to the strongholds of Engedi, which will be noticed further in the next chapter.

1 SAMUEL 24

Verses 1, 2. Saul made a short chase after the Philistines, then resumed his hunt for David. In this wilderness of Engedi were hiding places among the rocks and other kinds of surface of the earth. Saul had a force of three thousand men with him.

Verse 3. There was a cave in the community where David was hiding, and he took refuge therein. It happened that Saul went in there to attend to the call of nature, and David was hidden in the side of the cave unseen by Saul.

Verse 4. The men with David thought the situation was one purposely brought about by the Lord to help get the victory over Saul. It influenced David to the extent that while Saul was occupied with caring for the needs of the body, he slipped up privately and cut off part of the skirt of Saul's garment.

Verse 5. Afterward, David regretted doing even that much against Saul as will be explained in the next verse.

Verse 6. The motive for David's regret was that Saul was the Lord's anointed. He recognized the principle that as long as a man was in the authority of God's institution, he should be respected. The same idea is in the speech of Christ in Matt. 23: 1.

Verse 7. With this explanation, David prevented his men from doing Saul any bodily harm. Having finished his sanitary office of body, Saul arose and left the place.

Verse 8. David decided to use the circumstance as evidence to Saul that he was not his personal enemy, and that he did not intend any harm against him. After the distance between them made it safe, he called to Saul and got his attention.

Verses 9, 10. David made a general statement of the falsity of the reports that had come to Saul to the effect that he meant to do him harm. He further told Saul that his own men had bidden him smite him, and that he had prevented them from harming Saul.

Verse 11. General statements are not enough when so important an issue is at stake, therefore, David called Saul's attention to the part of the garment now in his hand. That would be positive evidence that he had been near enough to have killed him had that been his purpose. Apparently Saul had not missed the severed part.

Verse 12. We are not to conclude from David's treatment of Saul that he was excusing him in any of his mistakes. That was not the case. But he still recognized Saul as being the Lord's constituted official, and therefore to be respected. Furthermore, he expected the Lord to bring the proper punishment on Saul when the time came. This same thought is taught in Rom. 12: 19.

Verse 13. David then quoted a proverb that had been said by ancient people. That proverb is not in the Bible and thus we have another instance where outside literature is cited in connection with the inspired sayings. For other like places see Josh. 10: 13; 2 Sam. 1: 18; Acts 17: 28. This gives us the authority of examples to refer to evidence not in the Bible when it confirms or explains some of its statements.

Verse 14. David's reference to a dead dog or a flea is merely his way of saying that Saul's notion of David's being his personal enemy is purely a creature of imagination.

Verse 15. In harmony with his previous statement, David said that he would rely on the Lord to bring him the justice due.

Verse 16. Saul recognized the voice of David, and necessarily had to know that he had escaped from him when he had it in his power to kill him. For the present he was made to feel ashamed, and he wept.

Verse 17. Saul admitted that David had returned him good for evil. This is in harmony with the teaching of Paul in Rom. 12: 21.

Verse 18. Saul accounted the situation as an act of the Lord, in bringing him into a position where David could have smitten him had he been so minded.

Verse 19. The question in the beginning of this verse is the same as a positive declaration. It is as if he said that a man will not let his enemy escape if he came upon him. David had come upon Saul and let him escape, therefore David did not count Saul as his personal enemy. Saul then called for the blessing of God on David.

Verses 20-22. Saul then declared his conviction that David was destined to be king, and be established as such. He requested assurance that when such was the case, David would not cut off his family descendants. David made the promise, and Saul then departed for his home for the present. But this circumstance did not cause David to relax his vigilance for safety. He and his men got up to the hold, which means their hiding place.

1 SAMUEL 25

Verse 1. The mere act of lamenting over any cause of grief would naturally take place at the death of a beloved prophet like Samuel. So the gathering together of all Israel on the occasion of his death indicated some formal rites were performed in connection with the burial. Paran was the name of a considerable extent of territory on the south of Jerusalem, and in this general territory it is said that David went for the time.

Verse 2. Carmel was a city situated within the mountainous region of Judah, and was the location of a man of wealth. His wealth consisted chiefly of cattle or small animals, including sheep. At the time of our story he was shearing his sheep.

Verse 3. This verse describes the characteristics of the man and his wife as a preparation for the account to follow. The name of the man was Nabal, and that of his wife was Abigail. *Countenance.* This is from TOAR and defined by Strong, "outline, i.e. figure or appearance." We are to conclude, therefore, that this woman had a beautiful form of body in her general appearance. The man was churlish. This is from QASHEH, and the simple definition Strong gives is "severe." The word has been rendered in the A. V. by cruel, hard, heavy, obstinate, rough, stiff, stubborn and others. So here is a mean and hardhearted and stubborn man, with a wife that is beautiful in form and judicious in understanding. These facts will prepare us to appreciate more fully what follows.

Verses 4, 5. David was in the vicinity where Nabal was shearing his sheep, and decided to make a proposition of friendship to him in the name of the Lord. If men of some standing with the Lord's people are dwelling in the same community, it is always desirable to have an understanding as to each other's intentions. Hence David made the first move in this direction.

Verses 6, 7. Nabal dwelt at Maon and would not be present with his flocks except at the shearing time. So it was appropriate for David to inform this man of his attitude of friendship toward him, and that it was proved by the treatment he had accorded his herdsmen in the days past. Moreover, he wished to express interest in his continued prosperity in all that he had.

Verses 8, 9. David was willing to stake the truthfulness of his claims on the testimony of Nabal's own young men. In verse 8 the expression *young men* is used twice in close succession, but refers, respectively to the young men of Nabal and of David. The commission of young men from David delivered their message as directed and paused.

Verse 10. Now the reader will please reread the comments at verse 3, and observe how this speech agrees with the description given above. When the servants of David delivered the friendly greeting to Nabal, he made this hard hearted answer. He pretended not to know about whom they were talking, although he betrayed his hypocrisy by referring to a servant breaking away from his master, which it was supposed that David had done.

Verse 11. With this pretended ignorance as to the worthiness of David and his men, Nabal refused even the acts of common hospitality toward them.

Verses 12, 13. The young men returned and reported their experience to David. Now the mere failure to receive food and other items of hospitality was comparatively minor to what else it signified. David understood the principles of peace and also those of hostility. To him this all meant that Nabal was in sympathy with Saul and would, sooner or later, make an attack upon him. Therefore he decided to make a move in his own defense. He ordered his men to arm themselves. Leaving two hundred men to guard the property at home, he led four hundred to the attack.

Verse 14. One of the young men told Abigail of the affair and how the men sent from David with friendly salutation for Nabal had been insulted by him.

Verses 15, 16. They gave her further report of treatment they previously had received from David's men all the time they were associated with them. Not only so, but David's men had actually been a shield for them from danger that might have come to them in the wilderness.

Verse 17. Now these men of Nabal had not heard any report from David after his men had returned to him. Judging from the circumstances, they concluded that something would be heard, so they advised Abigail to do something about it. These men, even, described their master as being a man of belial. For the meaning of this word see remarks at Deut. 13: 13.

Verses 18, 19. Abigail acted on the advice of her servants and made preparations to greet David respectfully, according to the custom of those times. That is, she would have a present to offer him which was the manner of expressing respect or acknowledgment of another's rank in life. (Gen. 32: 13; 43: 11; Judg. 3: 15; 1 Sam. 9: 7; 2 Ki. 16: 8.) As the gifts were to be a token of good will it was appropriate to have them borne in the front of the procession. She did not tell her husband about her plan; he was a wicked and foolish man and would likely have interfered with it.

Verse 20. David and his men met Abigail near a hill. But before that had taken place, David had formed a resolution. He had reflected on the ingratitude of Nabal; after they had favored him by caring for his shepherds in the wilderness, he had insulted David and his men.

Verses 21, 22. This is the resolution about to take place, and introduced by the idea set forth in the preceding verse. The expression *God do so* means that if the one making it does not perform the thing he is resolving to do against an unworthy person, then may God do so to him, the speaker. The thing in particular that David determined to do was to destroy all of the males before morning. The obsolete word used here to express the act of discharging the excretions of the kidneys is just the old Biblical way of referring to males. We know that to be true, because it is the natural method of a man thus easing himself, and because a female would not use that method. The reason why the males are so often the object of destruction is the fact that they are the ones used in war and other activities of defense for a nation or people.

Verses 23, 24. Upon sight of David, Abigail alighted from her beast and made the proper curtsy before him, and respectfully asked permission to speak. From the suggestions made to her by her servant, and considering the character of her husband, she had reason to believe that David would stop at nothing short of complete punishment upon Nabal and all his house. With this in view she wished

1 Samuel 25: 25-39

to convince him that only Nabal was responsible for the insult given.

Verse 25. Abigail requested David not to regard or take seriously the conduct of this man Nabal. She did not condone nor belittle his wickedness in the least, instead she charged him with being a man of belial, which we have already explained. Also, he had the right name. The name Nabal is from the Hebrew word NABAL, which the reader recognizes as being spelled the same in the two languages. It is the word rendered "fool" in Psa. 14: 1, except that in that place it is a common noun while in this case it is a proper noun. The definition Strong gives of it is, "stupid; wicked (especially impious), dolt." Since her husband was such a character, she did not want David to take him seriously, although she did not excuse the wrong done. She declared that she did not know at the time of the presence of the young men sent from David.

Verse 26. This verse is her way of predicting some unpleasant end to Nabal, and the same to come to the enemies of David. She applied her intervention further, against David shedding the blood intended, as the work of the Lord; that is, she believed that the Lord had used her in preventing David from shedding this blood.

Verse 27. She had learned of the arrogant refusal of her husband to grant the young men the necessities of life asked for, and which were certainly due them considering the services they had rendered to the young men of Nabal. She now made up for that with the presents she had brought along with her by the hands of her servants.

Verse 28. Abigail accepted part of the blame, theoretically, for the trespass done against David, since she was the wife of Nabal. Yet she asked forgiveness for it. She also predicted the blessing of the Lord upon him because he was fighting the battles of the Lord. The use of capitals does not always have a basis in the thought of the writer; however, in this verse they are properly used.

Verse 29. Abigail spoke further predictions in favor of David, because a man had risen to injure him; by this she meant her wicked husband. She believed that David would be safe because of being bound up with the Lord.

Verses 30, 31. If David will heed her request and not shed blood unnecessarily, then he will not have any regrets after the Lord has given him the dominion over all his enemies. And when that happy time comes, she wishes him to remember her whom she here represents as his handmaid. To shed blood in cruel reprisal against rebellion is lawful, however, when the wrong can be righted legally without the extreme measures, it is to be preferred. This she was endeavoring to bring about with David.

Verses 32, 33. David recognized the hand of the Lord in these actions of Abigail, and blessed both the Lord and her. He made the significant remark that he had been kept from avenging with *mine own hand*. This allowed for the justice of vengeance on Nabal, and yet that it should not be done personally.

Verse 34. David repeats what he had threatened. See comments at verse 22 on the meaning of the language pertaining to males.

Verse 35. Had David carried out his previous purpose, it would have included the death of all that were near and dear to this woman. Now her voice has prevailed because of its good counsel, and her presence has pleased him so that he has respected her individually. With this announcement he dismissed her.

Verse 36. When she returned home she found Nabal engaged in a drinking party and in no frame of mind to be told anything.

Verse 37. When she told him the close call he had escaped it produced such a shock of surprise that he was stunned.

Verse 38. This condition continued with him until the Lord brought it to an end after ten days and smote him with death. Thus the vengeance that was due him was put on him by the Lord, and not by the hand of David.

Verse 39. When David heard about it he praised the Lord, not only for having put on Nabal the punishment he deserved, but also had kept him back from taking personal vengeance. He also remembered that he had been thus influenced by the good counsel of Abigail. Such a woman would be a desirable wife. We should bear in mind that in those times the Lord suffered (not permitted) men to have more than one wife. So that feature of this case is nothing new in the practices of the times. In making selections of women it is certainly commendable for a man to have the motive of choosing those of good counsel. We do not know that David was so minded in all of his selections, but he was in this case. He communed with Abigail. That means he did not think of appropriating her to himself without her consent. At least that was the way he conducted this selection.

Verse 40. The communication mentioned in the previous verse was conducted through the servants of David. That was not altogether unusual in those days. Abraham sent his servant to obtain a wife for Isaac (Gen. 24), and Samson asked his parents to obtain a certain woman for his wife. (Judg. 14: 2.)

Verse 41. Abigail was "flattered" by the proposal. Her expression of inferiority was unusual. It was thus: David will be king; he will have servants under him; those servants will need the assistance of still lower servants to perform the office of feetwashing; she wished to be one those lower servants. And evidently she was sincere. The most menial service, when performed for one who is loved and respected as Abigail surely loved and respected David, becomes a pleasure.

Verse 42. Without hestitation she made ready and journeyed to the place where David lived and became his wife.

Verse 43. What was said at verse 39 (see those comments again) on plurality of wives was to prepare the reader to understand this verse, and also, to help avoid confusion on remembering that David had been married previously.

Verse 44. This will not surprise us much when we recall that Michal had joined with her husband against her father as recorded in Ch. 19: 17. However, this is not the last we will hear about this woman. (2 Sam. 3: 13-16.)

1 SAMUEL 26

Verses 1, 2. Saul generally had spies who informed him about David. Now they told him of David's hiding place, and took three thousand men and went in search of him.

Verses 3, 4. Saul encamped at a certain place while being engaged in seeking for his prey. Word came to David that Saul was in search of him, but to make certain of the fact he sent out spies and learned that, sure enough, Saul was there after him.

Verse 5. Having this information it will not be necessary for David to come unexpectedly upon Saul, unprepared for his own safety. Thus he came near enough to the place where he was located to see the spot. Saul had his captain with him. That was Abner, of whom we will hear much. They lay in a trench. That was not a place dug in the ground, as the word generally means; it was a barricade composed of their wagons and other equipment. Not only did Saul have his captain with him, but his people also Ahimelech and Abishai. The latter also were pitched round him.

Verse 6. With the information as to Saul's exact location gained, David proposed to go near the camp and asked for volunteers to go with him. He made the proposal to Ahimelech and Abishai. The latter offered to go.

Verse 7. They reached the spot and saw that Saul was sleeping within the barricade described above. For immediate defense he had his spear stuck in the ground by him, near his bolster or pillow. As further guard, he had Abner and the people also lying round about him.

Verse 8. Abishai had only the personal interests of David in mind, and now proposed to take the life of Saul while he lay sleeping. So eager was he to make the attack that he assured his master he would not require more than one stroke.

Verses 9, 10. The distinction between a private individual and an official one was still the motive of David. The "Lord's anointed" was the basis of his consideration. That is a principle taught throughout the Bible. As long as a man is in lawful authority he must be regarded with respect, regardless of his personal shortcomings. See this principle set forth in Matt. 23: 1. David was determined to let fortune take its course with his personal enemy. It may be that the Lord will smite him (as he did Nabal), or that "his day will come to die," meaning the ordinary course of life and death, or that he might perish in battle; which actually did happen.

Verses 11, 12. However, David decided to furnish himself with positive evidence that he could have destroyed Saul had he that desire. For such purpose he directed Abishai to take the spear and vessel of water that were near the pillow. These would be unmistakable proof, since no question could be raised as to their identity.

The part God had in this performance was to depress the whole group with such a sleep that they were not awakened by this movement of David and Abishai.

Verses 13, 14. Verse 3 states that Saul had pitched in a hill. Now David took these articles and went over the space between this hill and the other, so that a safe distance was between them. From this place he cried so as to arouse them. Abner heard the cry and asked who was crying to the king.

Verse 15. The form of language here is what is known as irony. Abner was the captain of Saul's host, and was supposed to guard the body of his master. Thus, in this language of irony David chided him for his carelessness.

Verse 16. Ordinarily the rule would have been that Abner should be put to death for coming short of his duty to the king. We know why he did not awaken. However, it was appropriate to chide him thus, considering the unjust way his master had been treating David. To confirm the charge of neglect, he is invited to take notice of the articles of his master that are now in the hands of David.

Verses 17, 18. By this time Saul was awake and recognized the voice of David and made inquiry if it were true that it was his voice. David again confronted him with the accusation that he was pursuing a man he imagined was his foe.

Verse 19. David put the issue squarely up to Saul as to why he was thus pursuing him with hostile intent. If he had a reason from the Lord, then he was ready to meet the divine demands and make it right, but if he were being caused to do this by the influence of men, then may the curse of God be upon them. He charged that Saul's activity had driven him from the association of the Lord's people, and he was forced to fall among idolatrous ones who would have him join with them in the worship of their gods. Not that David really had done so, but that was the kind of people (the Philistines) he was forced to be with most of the time.

Verse 20. David knew that if one were to be guilty of deserting God and worshipping idols, he was liable to be smitten of the Lord for his sin. If Saul continued to force David to be with the idolaters, it would have the tendency to lead him into the sin that would cause him to die before the Lord. He plead with him not to do that. He then likened his act in trying to capture him to a man pursuing a flea. The significance of the comparison is clear when we observe the definition of the word in the original. It is from PAROSH and Strong defines it, "a flea (as the isolated insect)." Everyone knows about the proverbial flea that is always "not there" when an attempt is made to capture it. It is also like hunting a partridge in the mountains. Such an isolated place for a small bird would make capture impossible. As David is really not the personal enemy Saul thinks him to be, the Lord will care for him and make the search for him as fruitless as that for a flea.

Verse 21. When Saul was soberminded and used his good judgment he was capable of wise conclusions. He realized that he had been foolish and that David was righteous. While in that frame of mine he invited David to return to him with the promise of protection.

Verse 22. However, David had been betrayed before, therefore he invited Saul to send a young man over to recover the spear.

Verse 23. Appealing to the Lord for justice, David declared that his reason for not attacking Saul that day, although providence had thrown him into his hands, was that Saul was the Lord's anointed.

Verse 24. *Life was much set by*. This is a Biblical way of saying that Saul's life had been regarded as of much worth. On that account David requested that his life be regarded by the Lord as having much value.

Verse 25. Saul was gracious enough to predict great things ahead for David; however, it was considered best to go each his own way, which they did.

1 SAMUEL 27

Verse 1. When confidence has been betrayed it is difficult if not impossible to have it restored. More than once Saul had declared his regret at mistreatment of David, then betrayed him when an opportunity seemed to favor him. Now David came to the conclusion that, sooner or later, Saul would destroy him unless he got entirely out of his reach. For this purpose he decided to flee into the land of the Philistines. They were the people who were in constant war with Saul, and naturally he would not venture to pursue him among his enemies.

Verses 2, 3. Acting on his decision, David took his group of men that had been with him since he left Keilah and went to the city of Gath and dwelt with Achish. He had with him also his two wives, Abigail and Ahinoam.

Verse 4. Word of David's flight to Gath was brought to Saul. Then it is stated that Saul ceased to pursue him. From now on to the death of Saul, his activities and those of David will be independent of each other.

Verse 5. Gath was a city of a king, and David did not want to make that his permanent residence. He then requested Achish to provide him some country town to be his regular dwelling place.

Verses 6, 7. Achish granted his request and Ziklag was given him for a possession, and was occupied as a residence by David for a year and four months.

Verses 8, 9. The military spirit of David would not rest. He must do something along that line. Thus, leaving his family in the city, he took his men of war and attacked the people of that land in the immediate vicinities of Geshur, the Gezirites and Amalekites. These were not pure Philistines, but were associated with them and thus would be considered friends of the Philistines. So after making complete destruction of these people, unknown to Achish, he returned to him.

Verse 10. As might be expected, Achish missed David and asked where he had made a road, or, on what road he had gone that day. David used military strategy and gave him an evasive answer. It would not do for Achish to know that he had been attacking the people who were his friends.

Verse 11. In order that no one would be left to bear news to Achish, David had made complete destruction of all the people who could have been witnesses. Should the information reach the ears of Achish he would conclude that as long as David was in that country he would be an enemy in fact, and thus would be objectionable. He wished to maintain a peaceable relation with Achish so that he could continue to live there away from Saul.

Verse 12. The story had the desired effect. Achish was led to believe that the Israelites had come to abhor David, and hence he would be one to depend on for an ally. He then concluded to consider David as his perpetual servant. We can see in all this that David was at heart true to the children of Israel, although being compelled to take these inconvenient means of protection against the personal enmity of Saul.

1 SAMUEL 28

Verses 1, 2. There had been a sort of lull in the hostilities between Israel and the Philistines, but now another campaign was planned. As David was then with the last named people, he was offered service in their army, and the offer was accepted. This is a part of the story on the side of the Philistines.

Verse 3. On the other side were other conditions and activities. Samuel had died, and his absence was sorely felt. Saul had had a kind of change of heart, and had attempted to clear the land of the ones having familiar spirits. He knew that God did not approve of such characters, and had made an edict that all of them should be banished or killed.

Verse 4. The Philistines encamped in Shunem while the Israelites pitched in Gilboa. These places were about five miles apart. Here the strength of the opposing armies gathered for the great battle.

Verse 5. The sight of the hosts of the Philistines frightened Saul.

Verse 6. He was like men often are today. When their personal interests or safety are concerned, they turn to the Lord, but at other times they are unmindful of Him. This man had disobeyed the Lord so often and grievously that He had deserted him. Now he made an attempt to revive his standing with God, and appealed to him for instruction. The three channels formerly available for communication with God were: through inspired dreams; or by Urim, which signified communication by the instrumentality of the priest; or by inspired prophets. All three were now silent toward Saul.

Verse 7. In desperation he thought of conferring with a woman with a familiar spirit, otherwise called a witch. There was one such woman still living at a town called Endor. This woman was in hiding because of the edict that Saul had made against her class. In some manner the servants of Saul knew about her and told him about it.

1 Samuel 28: 8-15

Verse 8. Knowing that all such women would be afraid of him and refuse to have any communication with him, he disguised himself. Also, he chose the night-time for his visit, which would be an advantage to his plan of deception. Under this form of approach he was admitted into her presence and allowed to make a request. He wanted to have contact with Samuel, who was dead. There is no evidence that Saul would care anything about what information the woman would give from her own source of knowledge, but if she can get him in touch with the prophet, then the information obtained would be the truth. The word *divine* is from QACAM, and Strong defines it, "properly to distribute, i.e. determine by lot or magical scroll." Those people engaged in this business used some mysterious process of various kind to mislead their patrons into thinking they had some supernatural power or wisdom. It is true that in the days of miracles, God suffered the devil to work through evil channels as a test, although such kind of agencies proved to be a mere trick. Saul was so desperate that he was ready to try any kind of means to be thought of for relief.

Verse 9. Naturally, the woman would be hesitant about trying her old tricks since she knew about the edict of Saul. She thought this man was playing a ruse for the purpose of detecting her as one of the condemned persons, and would turn her over to Saul.

Verse 10. There must have been a great deal of weight in those days placed on the value of an oath, because the woman was prevailed on by the force of one.

Verse 11. Being satisfied that she was safe again to practice her accustomed art, she asked whom he wanted to contact and was told to bring Samuel up (from the dead).

Verse 12. There is nothing said here about what the woman said or what she did. We are not familiar with the course of procedure generally taken by these characters. Whatever it was, she went through with the formality. Now let the reader take note that the inspired writer tells us that the woman "saw Samuel," not that she just claimed to see him. She actually saw him. Yet when she did, *she cried with a loud voice.* Now the appearance of a righteous man like Samuel never had caused anyone to be affected with fear or astonishment in this way, therefore we cannot conclude that she was frightened by the nature of his appearance. No, it was the very fact that she saw him at all that affected her. All of which proves that she had not really expected to see him. And that fact proves that it was not the common experience of witches to accomplish actually what they claimed. Therefore, the success of this instance was an exception to the rule. Thus, instead of this circumstance being a proof of the genuineness of spiritualism, the theory of communicating with the dead, it is just the opposite. What happened is this: God decided to use this woman to carry out his purpose just the same as he used other evil persons for the like purpose. Other cases are the magicians in Egypt, and Balaam. And while causing Samuel actually to appear, contrary to the woman's real expectation, God also revealed to her the true identity of Saul so that she was made to be afraid. I do not mean that the woman knew the identity of Samuel, for that was to some extent still covered, but she did know that some actual presence was there from the unseen world, and could describe his outward appearance.

Verse 13. Saul assured the woman of her safety and inquired of the appearance that she saw. Her remark that she saw gods merely meant that she saw unearthly beings coming up from beneath.

Verse 14. Saul made further inquiry as to the appearance, and from her description he recognized it to be Samuel.

Verse 15. We should keep in mind that it is the inspired writer who is declaring what is taking place, and not just the claim of Saul. The writer plainly says that Samuel said certain things, and also that Saul did so, etc. Therefore, it was not any make-believe that was going on. It was another instance where God used an uncommon means of communication. (Heb. 1: 1.) The prophet chastised Saul for having disturbed him. Incidentally, we learn that when a righteous man passes to the next place of existence from the earth, he is in peace and rest. It will not do to say the language referred to his body. This took place at Endor while his body was buried at Ramah. (Ch. 25: 1.) Thus we are given the comforting information of the satisfactory state of the departed righteous. This all agrees with the story of Lazarus recorded in Luke 16: 25. Saul explained that his purpose was to obtain instructions for his conduct, since God had refused to answer any of his inquiries.

Verse 16. The question of Samuel implied that he was a man of God. Otherwise, there would have been no inconsistency in turning from God to a prophet. And while Saul did not offer any explanation of this, that we are told of, yet we can form our own answer; it was the desperate action of a man at the end of his resources.

Verse 17. In the margin "to" is changed for "for" which makes it clearer. God had carried out his previous determination as had been expressed through Samuel, that was to take the kingdom from Saul and give it to David.

Verse 18. The reason for this revolution to come on Saul was his disobedience regarding the destruction of Amalek. (Ch. 15.)

Verse 19. Saul was a wicked man and Samuel a righteous. According to Luke 16, we know that the two kinds of characters do not dwell together after death in any direct sense. And yet in a general sense they are together since the name Hades is applied to the general state of the dead. Two men may be in the same province and not be in the same county. So, Samuel and Saul were to be in the same general state in that they both were to be in the intermediate place. In this way we may understand the statement of Samuel that "thou and thy sons shall be with me." The overthrow of the army of Israel was also predicted to come on the morrow.

Verse 20. This speech of Samuel so shocked Saul that he fainted and fell prostrate on the ground. He was already weak from lack of food, and now this news overcame him.

Verses 21, 22. The woman then behaved as a normal woman of humanity. Having risked her life in his hands and received no harm, she was disposed to administer to his physical wants, and offered him food.

Verse 23. At first he refused to eat. Then he was prevailed upon by his servants and the woman to submit. They *compelled* him in the sense of convincing him that he should accept food and accordingly he sat up on the bed.

Verses 24, 25. The woman already had a young animal which Strong defines as a male or steer. It was in order for food and she used it as the base for a meal which she served to Saul and his servants. After this they went their way that night. There is no indication that Saul made any threat to disturb this woman afterward, although he had issued an edict against all such persons. But he had sworn protection to this woman. Besides, she had favored him with the desired information.

1 SAMUEL 29

Verse 1. The opposing armies were making movements for getting nearer and nearer to the attack which will prove so fatal to Saul and his hosts.

Verse 2. *Lords*. This word is defined by Strong as "peers." They were the leading men of the Philistines in point of rank and importance and made up the body of the army. David was in the immediate company with Aschish and they were with the rereward, which means the rear division of the army.

Verse 3. The princes were men of still higher rank or authority than the lords. They saw David and his men in the midst of their army and were displeased. By reference to Ch. 28: 1, 2 we may learn that Achish had invited David to go with him and that he had gladly accepted the invitation. Moreover, the Philistine king then notified him that he would be a guardian for his personal safety for all of his life. Upon discovering David and his men with them, the princes of the Philistines made a complaining inquiry of Achish about the presence of *these Hebrews*. Achish explained that David had been with him for years and had been faultless all the time.

Verse 4. The princes made more vigorous protest against the presence of David. They knew that he was a fellow-citizen of Saul and that at the present time he was at variance with him. They also supposed that he was eager to be reconciled to his master, and that he would use any opportunity for effecting the reconciliation. Now then, if he were permitted to accompany the Philistines in battle against the Israelites, he might wait until the armies had come in sight of each other and at that point he would turn against the very men near him in the Philistine army. The sight of this would naturally please Saul and he would weaken in his variance against David.

Verse 5. This verse presents the further idea, that not only might David be disposed to win his master over to him in the way indicated, but that he would be fully able to do so. For evidence of his success along that line they referred to the celebration he had been accorded by the women in their songs. That reputation was to the effect that he had slain more men than Saul.

Verses 6, 7. Achish yielded to the objections of his men with apologies to David in the form of words of praise for his faithfulness in the past. There was some difference between the rank of the princes and that of the lords, yet it was slight for Achish used both names almost interchangeably. At any rate, they were of such importance that he did not wish to incur their opposition just as they were entering what might be a decisive battle. He therefore requested David to return to his own city.

Verse 8. It might be expected that David would feel hurt over this turn of affairs. It implied to him that he had been untrue to the king of the Philistines. This was not the only reason for his disappointment. He wished to be engaged in warfare. Nor was that all of his motive. He wished to fight the *enemies of my lord the king*. We have read of his theory that no personal attack should be made upon the Lord's anointed. He never did excuse Saul's wickedness, but did not believe it right to oppose him as a private individual. He had made the remark once that perhaps he would perish in battle (Ch. 26: 10) and in that lawful way receive the just punishment for his deeds. Now it may be the time has come for that to happen. If David is enlisted in the regular manner in a war against Saul, and if in such an action he should assist in bringing about the downfall of his enemy, then it would be legal.

Verse 9. Achish still acknowledged the virtue of David and his faithfulness. Yet the leading men of his army objected, and as the success of an army depends much on unity, he did not wish to cause any dissension by retaining an objectionable soldier.

Verse 10. The Philistine king knew that David had some of Saul's servants with him. He then requested him to take them with him and depart.

Verse 11. David obeyed the request or command of Achish and returned into the land of the Philistines. The army of Achish, meanwhile, drew nearer the place of battle.

1 SAMUEL 30

Verse 1. This chapter will be a diversion from the regular story we have been reading. David was required to depart from the Philistine army and return to his city Ziklag. Upon arriving there he learned that it had been attacked while he was absent. The attack had been made by the Amalekites who had also burned the city.

Verse 2. They not only burned the city but captured the people therein, including the two wives of David. However, they had gone and were away from the community.

Verses 3-5. It would be expected that much consternation and sorrow would be caused by what they found upon returning to the city. The wives and children of the men were taken. It caused them to weep until they were exhausted.

Verse 6. In their bitterness, which is the marginal version of grief, they became unreasonable and threatened to stone David as being responsible for their losses, but it did not intimidate him for he took courage in his God.

Verses 7, 8. The mention of the ephod suggests the use of the Urim and Thummim that were provided with the priestly garments. (Ex. 28: 30.) This was one of the means of communication between God and the people at that time. Now, David wishes to inquire of the Lord for information regarding his proposed pursuit of the Amalekites. He was told to pursue and that he would succeed in his objective.

Verses 9, 10. David had six hundred men who started with him on this chase, but by the time they had reached a place called the brook Besor two hundred of them had become so faint that they had to stop. Leaving these to guard the stuff he took the four hundred men and pursued the enemy.

Verses 11 12. This Egyptian had been left behind because of his exhausted condition having had no food for three days. David's men gave him nourishment so that he regained his strength and was able to converse.

Verse 13. After the man was able to talk he told them of his nationality and of his reason for being in the present situation. He was a servant to one of the Amalekites and had been deserted because of his condition of body.

Verse 14. Through the conversation with this Egyptian David learned who had burned Ziklag and captured the people. A general invasion had been made by his masters which ended in the overthrow of this city of David.

Verse 15. Having recovered his strength he was able to assist David in identifying the people after whom he was pursuing. Upon guarantee that he would not be turned over to his master nor otherwise come to any harm he promised to direct David to the men.

Verse 16. The Amalekites evidently had paused in their activities after leaving the city of Ziklag and other points in the land of Judah and the Philistine territory. They were eating and making merry rejoicing over their success against the places which they had invaded.

Verse 17. David's attack upon the hordes that were scattered carelessly over the earth was doubtless a surprise. He continued his action against them for a whole day beginning his slaughter while it was yet dark and continuing until the evening. The destruction was so complete that none escaped except four hundred young men who made their getaway by the use of camels.

Verses 18-20. David made complete recovery of the persons, the cattle, and all of the goods that had been taken by the Amalekites. He took all of the Amalekites' own flocks and herds also, and it was counted as his personal spoil from the battle.

Verse 21. When David came to the brook Besor the two hundred men who had been left there went forth to meet him. Inquiries were made about the welfare of these who had been left behind because of their disability.

Verse 22. The four hundred men who went with David to the battle wished to make discrimination against the two hundred who did not go with them. They were willing to give back to each man his family, but not any of the spoil taken. The class of men among them that made this proposition are called men of belial. The A. V. puts the capital at the beginning of this word. However, in the Old Testament it is not a proper noun. This information has been given previously but will be given again now. It is from BELIYALL, and the following is what Young says about it: "This should not be regarded as a proper name. It is generally associated with the words 'man,' 'son,' 'daughter,' or 'children.' Hence 'son' or 'man' of Belial, simply means 'a worthless person.'" In the New Testament the form of the word is Beliar (BELIAR not BELIAL as given in the common version). Strong defines the word, "Without profit, worthlessness; by extension destruction, wickedness." The word has been rendered in the A. V. by Belial 16 times, evil 1, naughty 1, ungodly men 2, wicked 5. This description of the men will account for their selfish proposal to David.

Verse 23. The main idea to be noted in this verse is that the Lord was the one who had made their success possible anyway, therefore these men had no reason for their personal exultation.

Verses 24, 25. David declared that men who tarry by the stuff are as worthy as the ones who go to the war. He made it a statute for the future. That was right. In all times of war those who "keep the home fires burning" should be given credit along with the ones in battle. This is fair for all parties concerned. Why should men face the foes with risk of life on behalf of the home land if those at home do not preserve the home for them upon their return? It is true these men were not at home, yet the principle expressed here holds good. Moreover, David manifested this principle with regard to the home people in that he even divided his spoils with many of his fellow countrymen as will be reported in the following paragraph.

Verses 26-31. This paragraph names the places referred to in the preceding paragraph. The last verse gives the special motive for the selection of the places mentioned to receive these presents. They were the ones where David and his men were in the habit of passing time.

1 SAMUEL 31

Verse 1. This chapter resumes the main topic of the narrative. The Philistines and Israelites came together in fierce battle and the latter were being defeated.

Verse 2. This verse names the three sons of Saul, all slain in the battle.

Verse 3. *Sore.* The main difference is in the intensity of the meaning. The latter signifies a more complete or fatal condition, while the former means simply, "heavy."

Verse 4. This coincides with the preceding verse. Saul realized that he was fatally wounded. However, he wished to make it appear that the enemy had not actually accomplished his death and asked his armorbearer to finish it. He would not do it because he was afraid. That did not mean that he was afraid of death as the next verse will show. But the whole situation was horrifying, and besides, he had the same feeling as David had, in that he hesitated to smite the Lord's anointed. Then Saul took a sword and fell upon it. This would be accomplished by standing the handle of the sword on the ground and then allowing the body of the man to slump down over it.

Verse 5. Let the reader take notice that the inspired writer tells us that the armorbearer *saw that Saul was dead.* No one can see something that does not exist. Yet the statement of inspiration is that the man saw that Saul was dead.

Verse 6. The statement of Saul's death is again repeated, and in connection with the death of the three sons of Saul, and his armorbearer. These facts will be useful in explaining some questions to come up in the next book.

Verse 7. The death of Saul and his sons caused such dismay among the Israelites that they fled from the cities of that section of the country. Then the Philistines came and occupied those cities.

Verse 8. After the day of battle the Philistines came to plunder the slain of their clothing and any other things of value to be found with them. In this action they found Saul and his three sons among the fallen ones.

Verse 9. The personal defeat of the king in battle would be a thing to cause great rejoicing among the victorious people. Therefore, the Philistines took the head of Saul and sent it and the armor of his body among their people. The victory was published in the house of their gods, which was a signal that they were mightier than the one whom Saul worshipped.

Verse 10. Ashtaroth was one of the female deities of those people and they had a temple erected for her worship. In this house they placed the armor of Saul as a trophy of war. Cities spoken of as fenced or walled meant the ones fortified. To fasten the body of the king of the Israelites to the wall of a city supposed to be prepared against the enemy would be a sort of "triumph," a gesture often resorted to in those days.

Verse 11. Jabesh-gilead was a city east of the Jordan and opposite of the site of the fatal battle between the Israelites and the Philistines. These inhabitants heard of the shameful treatment that had been accorded their fallen king and his sons.

Verses 12, 13. It was a night's journey from Jabesh-gilead to the place of the shameful treatment of Saul's body. The valiant or brave men of the city made this journey and recovered the bodies of Saul and his sons. They brought them back with them to Jabesh. The text here says that they burnt the bodies. The same event is recorded in 2 Chr. 16: 14, but there it says they made a great burning for them. Jer. 34: 5 speaks of burning odors for Zedekiah, and that is the meaning of the language in the verse here. This conclusion is justified by the language in the last verse which says that the bones were buried under a tree. The fast of seven days was one of the formalities used in ancient times in connection with periods of great grief.

2 SAMUEL 1

Verse 1. Chapter 30 of 1 Samuel gives the record of this slaughter, and it was going on while the Israelites were engaged with the Philistines in battle. This verse brings us two days later, and David has returned to his city, Ziklag.

Verse 2. On the third day after the battle came this man to David. The use of earth on the head and the rent clothes was a practice in the East, indicating great grief or anxiety. We shall learn that this man was pretending grief in this case. He also was feigning his respect for David when he fell to the earth.

Verses 3, 4. Upon inquiry, the young man related the fatal end of the battle between the Israelites and Philistines. He stated that Saul and Jonathan were dead. The inspired record says that Saul and all his sons were dead. So there was something questionable about the report to begin with.

Verses 5-7. Another inquiry brought from the man his story of Saul's calling on him as he "happened" to be passing. This word is in itself a strong indication that something was wrong in the whole story. The battle was in its decisive stage and very hot. It is not reasonable to believe that a casual passer-by could be thus engaged.

Verse 8. This verse contains one consistent link in the story. Saul did not want the uncircumcised Philistines to boast of his death (1 Sam. 31: 4), therefore he inquired the nationality of this young man coming up. There is a weak point, however, also in the story. He told Saul he was an Amalekite, and as such would be an uncircumcised man also; however, according to the narrative, Saul had no objection to this person.

Verse 9. It is possible this young man was near enough to hear the conversation of Saul with his armor-bearer, for the pretended one between him and this man was about the same as the inspired record given us as having actually taken place.

Verse 10. Critics of the Bible have charged that a contradiction exists here; that this verse does not agree with the record in 1 Samuel 31: 4, 5. Certainly, the two accounts disagree. But one of the reports was made by the inspired writer and the other by this unauthorized Amalekite. It is not the first time that the word of inspiration has been contradicted. When a person is charged with a serious deed of evil it is expected that some motive for such deed be indicated. There is plenty of motive in the case of this Amalekite. He knew that Saul was the personal enemy of David, and thought it would be a favor to him to receive the news of his death, first hand. And to show that his story was true he brought some trophies from his body. This is not a mere guess; Chapter 4: 10 sustains the conclusion. The thing the young man did not know was that David regarded Saul as the anointed king of God's people, and that no personal victory should be wished to be had over him.

Verses 11, 12. Although Saul was the personal enemy of David, still he was engaged in battle against the Lord's enemies and was killed therein. For this reason David and the men that were with him lamented greatly, and put on a fast for the rest of the day.

Verses 13, 14. This additional inquiry brought to David the nationality of the young man. Being an Amalekite he would not be in the regular enlistment of the army fighting against Saul, therefore, would have no right to attack the king as a soldier. The regard for Saul as the Lord's anointed caused David to be aroused against the man.

Verse 15. The natural question here might be, why did David have the right to order the slaying of this Amalekite? It should be remembered that while Saul was the anointed of the Lord, which means the one still in active service, yet David was the one anointed in prospect to take the place of Saul. (Chapter 16: 13.) This would make it right for him to execute this private for his unauthorized act.

Verse 16. *Blood be upon thy head.* This expression is used in very numerous places in the Bible. It is based on the idea of guilt. The mere fact of shedding blood was not illegal. If a man committed murder, then he must have his blood shed in punishment. (Gen. 9: 6.) But when one sheds blood illegally, then another must shed his blood in execution, and that is the same as putting his guilty blood on his own head, not on the head of an innocent person. Please observe, David did not admit that the young man actually had slain Saul. The act of slaying him was based on his own incriminating testimony and David did not have to reject it, especially when he took so much delight in reporting the said affair.

Verse 17. While Saul and his three sons were slain, this lamentation was over him and one of the sons. It was because Saul was the Lord's anointed and Jonathan was the personal friend of David. According to Strong, this kind of lamentation was a funeral dirge, accompanied by beating the breasts or instruments.

Verse 18. *The use of.* These words are not in the original. The R. V. has "the song of." Either expression could be correct. The inspired writer said that David bade them to teach the use of the bow to the children of Judah. Whether it was a song about the bow, in memory of what it had meant to David and Jonathan, or that they were to perpetuate the use of the bow in honor of their friendship; either would harmonize with the facts. Jonathan had been successful in his use of the bow against the enemy, also it had been used as the token of friendship in the escape from Saul. (1 Sam. 14: 45: 20; 35-40.) *Book of Jasher.* Smith's Bible Dictionary says this of the book: "It was probably written in verse; and it has been conjectured that it was a collection of ancient records of honored men or noble deeds. It is wholly lost." Occasionally the inspired writers have referred to works of literature in circulation at the time. These books were of no authority, but often explained and corroborated the inspired statements. Another instance of this was the statement of Paul in Acts 17: 28. And such use of "outside reading matter," gives us an approved example of using works of uninspired men today when they help to throw light on the statements of Holy Writ.

Verse 19. It was no ordinary person who was slain. The king—the glory of Israel—was the one who fell. He fell from the highest place in the nation because he was king and therefore a man in the highest place.

Verse 20. Gath and Askelon were permanent cities of the Philistines. The language is a poetic expression of regret, and a wish that the sad news would not be scattered in these cities of the enemy. David had slain the Amalekite for rejoicing in the downfall of Saul and his son; for the same reason he shuddered at the thought of the daughters of the uncircumcised getting joy at Saul's downfall.

Verse 21. Since this is a song and figurative picture of the awful situation, David used terms that were not expected to have literal fulfillment. The speech of this verse is a poetic drawing of the humiliating condition over the beloved field, just as if nature itself was hanging its head in shame and refusing to function.

Verse 22. Jonathan and Saul were successful in their attacks upon the enemy. Even the mighty men among the enemy were not able to deprive them of prey. Naturally, we are to make an exception of their last battle in this statement of their success.

Verse 23. The question arises as to how this could be said of them in view of the things of which we have been reading. Well, the military operations of a man were the most outstanding ones of his life, especially the life of an official like Saul. And those operations, prominent though they were, did not actually occupy the major portion of their lives. Therefore, in spite of the events of the closing years, it still leaves sufficient time and opportunity for them to have been very congenial in their private lives and during most of the years. It was literally true that in their death they were not divided. They had certainly been fighting as comrades down to the very last, for they died together on the field of battle.

Verse 24. *Daughters of Israel* would refer to the women of the nation in general. Scarlet clothing with ornaments of precious metal had been provided by the king. For that reason his death would mean a great personal loss to them and call for weeping.

Verse 25. The *high places* was a term with the same significance as verse 19.

Verse 26. When David was ready to express his deepest feeling, he restricted his speech to Jonathan. *Passing.* There is no word in the original for this. The word *wonderful*, however, is from an original, which is PALA, and defined, "a primitive root; properly, perhaps, to separate, i.e. distinguish (literally or figuratively); by implication, difficult, wonderful."—Strong. The sentence means, the love of Jonathan was *equal* to that of women. The love of women is tender, personal, confiding, self-sacrificing, and clings to the object of the love amidst the most trying circumstances, and in spite of all opposition from flesh and blood relations.

Verse 27. This song of lamentation began and ended with the thought uppermost in the mind of David, the fall of the glory in Israel.

2 SAMUEL 2

Verse 1. For some time David has been living in Ziklag, a city of the Philistines that had been given to him by Achish, king of the Philistines. That had been a sort of internment for him and his family and some personal friends, because of the fear the Philistines had of having him in their army. Now the conditions have changed. Saul is dead, and the danger of personal violence to David from that source is gone. Perhaps now he should re-enter the territory of the Israelites. But the general state of affairs has been unsettled, and it was a question in his mind whether the way was open for him to venture forth. That is why he asked the question written in this verse. In answer to his second question David was told to go unto Hebron. This was a noted place in Old Testament times. It was the place where Abram dwelt after separating from Lot. (Gen. 13: 18). It is destined to be the home of David for a number of years.

Verses 2, 3. He had his two wives with him, Ahinoam and Abigail, and his men. They were the six hundred that were with him in Ziklag. (1 Sam. 27: 2, 3).

Verse 4. We recall that David had been anointed to be the next king over the children of Isreal, after Saul's reign ended. In the meantime the disturbed conditions coming up over Saul's wrong conduct had somewhat blocked the way for him to ascend the throne completely. The tribe of Judah, however, recognized his right and anointed him to be king over them. Having performed this honor for him, they informed him of the kindness shown to Saul's body by the men of Jabesh-gilead.

Verses 5, 6. David sent a message of appreciation and blessing to the men who had showed respect to Saul by burying his body. Not only the blessing of God was assured them, but he promised to return favors to them himself.

Verse 7. It is now necessary for them to take courage, seeing their master is dead. Furthermore, the house of Judah had anointed him king, which would indicate his opportunity for giving them assistance in whatever righteous acts they attempted.

Verse 8. Ner and Kish were brothers. (1 Chr. 9: 36). Abner was the son of Ner and Saul was the son of Kish. (1 Sam. 9: 1, 2). Therefore, Saul and Abner were first cousins, and Saul made Abner his commander-in-chief. And even after Saul was killed in battle, and David was the next lawful heir to the throne, Abner was set to continue the kingdom in the line of his relation and former master. To do this he took Ish-bosheth, Saul's son, and brought him over to Mahanaim. This was a city just east of the Jordan.

Verse 9. From Mahanaim, Ish-bosheth ruled over the territory of Gilead, a large territory east of the Jordan. The other towns mentioned in this verse were west of the Jordan. But he ruled over larger sections of the country, for specific mention is made of the tribes of Ephraim and Benjamin, then of *all* Israel. This means that only the tribe of Judah recognized David at this time.

Verse 10. Ish-bosheth was the youngest son of Saul, but all of his brothers were dead, therefore, he would have been the rightful person to reign had not the Lord determined to take the kingdom away from his father's house and give it to David. Because of this plan of God, we must consider this reign of Ish-bosheth as one of usurpation. He was strengthened for his action by Abner, the captain of the host under Saul. As long as he thought he could, he "pulled" for the only remaining son of his master. We shall learn, however, that the two-years' reign of this usurper was filled with unrest and the final overthrow of his supporter.

Verse 11. Notwithstanding the changing scenes in the opposition, David continued to have Hebron as his official headquarters for seven years and six months. He did not move it to Jerusalem until the opposition had been removed and all of the tribes were ready to recognize him as king.

Verses 12, 13. Abner was the commander-in-chief of Saul's forces, and Joab came into the same rank of service under David. As might be expected, these two were rivals. With a group of men each, they came to Gibeon and sat down on opposite sides of the pool at that place.

Verse 14. A contest was proposed by Abner to be acted on by men from each group. The word *play* is from SACHAQ, and defined, "A primitive root; to laugh (in pleasure or detraction); by implication, to play."—Strong. The word has been rendered in the A. V. by deride, have in derision, laugh, make merry, mock, play, rejoice, laugh to scorn, be in sport. It is the word for "sport" in Judg. 16: 25, where Samson was called to make sport for the Philistines. The statement under consideration here means that the young men were to act or perform, in physical contest, before their respective masters. The implied purpose of the contest was to decide the issues between the house of Saul and the house of David. Joab agreed to the proposition.

Verses 15, 16. Twelve men on each side engaged in the contest, man against man; forming twelve duels. The result was the mutual destruction of the duelists. The 24 men all died.

Verse 17. It would appear from the report of the contest just ended that nothing decisive was accomplished. The moral effect however, was great, for it weakened the forces of Abner and they were beaten by the servants of David.

Verse 18. Among the men with Joab at this time were his two brothers, Abishai and Ashahel. The roe is another name for roebuck. It was a species of antelope, an animal that was very swift on foot.

Verse 19. These brothers took up the support of David against the house of Saul. Abner had fled after the affair of the twelve duels, and Asahel pursued him, not stopping nor turning out of the path of the pursuit one way or the other.

Verses 20, 21. Abner pretended to think Asahel only wished to procure his armor, and, in order to detract him from his real purpose, suggested that he turn aside and take the armor from one of the young men. But Asahel did not have the purpose in mind, therefore he continued his pursuit of Abner.

Verse 22. It is evident that Abner did not wish to slay Asahel, because of his respect for his brother Joab, notwithstanding the feud between them, but to stop his pursuit he threatened to slay him.

Verse 23. The two were very near finally in the chase, so that Abner made a sort of backward stroke with the spear in his hand and smote Asahel. *Fifth rib.* The second word has no original in the text. But the first one is from CHOMESH, and means "the abdomen." The spear was an offensive weapon and used for casting or throwing. It was the largest form of that class of weapons. Abner could thus so use it as here described as Asahel was in such close pursuit. It went through his body and came out at his back. His death was immediate and he was permitted to lie there for a time.

Verse 24. It would be natural for Joab and Abishai, brothers to Asahel, to go after Abner after he had slain Asahel. They did not overtake him personally, but reached a spot called "hill of Ammah" near Gibeon. It was evening when they arrived there.

Verse 25. Saul was of the tribe of Benjamin, therefore these Benjamites formed a troop of themselves under Abner and came to the top of this hill.

Verse 26. The two groups were in speaking distance of each other. Abner then called to Joab and intimated that unless he ordered his men to cease their pursuing of their brethren, the sword would bring them to a bitter end.

Verse 27. This must be understood in the light of v. 14. It is as if Joab said, "You are the one who started this, when you suggested that the young men arise and play before us. Had it not been for that, the young men with me would have returned from the chase in the morning." The words *as God liveth* mean, as surely as that God lives.

Verse 28. While Joab charges Abner with being the cause of the conflict, yet he was willing to discontinue it. Therefore, he blew a trumpet as a means of giving orders to his men, and they ceased their activities.

Verse 29. After the difficulty was over, Abner and his men walked all night and came to Mahanaim, the headquarters that had been established for Ish-bosheth.

Verse 30. Joab likewise returned (to Hebron) and gathered his people together. When this was done, it was discovered that 19 of his men were missing, besides Asahel.

Verse 31. The loss sustained by David in this skirmish was light considering the number of slain on the other side. There were 360 of the Benjamites cut down, which means that the supporters of Saul's house suffered that loss, Saul being of Benjamin.

Verse 32. Before returning to Hebron as mentioned in v. 30, Joab and his men gave the body of Asahel respectful burial, in the sepulchre of his father. It was then morning by the time they arrived at Hebron.

2 SAMUEL 3

Verse 1. David was the rightful king, but Abner's attachment to the house of Saul caused him to hold out for Ish-bosheth, son of Saul, as long as possible. The contest finally began to prove one-sided, and the house of David was gaining.

Verses 2-5. Plurality of wives was suffered in those days. That is why it is common to read such family records as this. When the sons of a prominent man are named, their respective mothers will be named also. The two outstanding sons mentioned in this group are Amnon and Absalom. They are mentioned in that way here because of their connection with the bitter feud that afterwards came between Absalom and his father. Some special interest may be had in Adonijah also on account of his attempt to obtain the kingdom after his father.

Verse 6. As long as there appeared any chance of winning, Abner made strong efforts in the war on behalf of the house of Saul and against David.

In spite of these efforts, however, his side of the conflict began to weaken as was stated in v. 1.

Verse 7. For some reason unknown to us, the name of *Ish-bosheth* is not in the original text here. But we know he is the one meant because the other sons of Saul were dead at this time. Also, in the following verse the name is in the original, in direct connection with the same conversation. Rizpah was concubine to Saul and mother of two sons, (chapter 21: 8.) Mention was made in chapter 2: 10 of Ish-bosheth being the youngest son of Saul. That must be understood as applying to the sons in line as heirs to the throne. A concubine was a legal wife as far as moral consideration went, but she was not entitled to the same property and other rights. Therefore, in mentioning the sons of Saul, as king, the sons of his line only would be considered. Now Saul was dead at the time of this verse. We do not know what were all the circumstances connected with this affair between Abner and the concubine. Abner did not directly deny the charge, but implied that there was no fault or sin committed. We do not know whether he meant to deny any act of intimacy, or that any sin was committed in the act. Whatever was the true state of the case, Abner was very angry. It is possible that he "saw the handwriting" as to the future success of his contention against the house of David, and was wanting a "face-saving" pretext for changing his position. Such a thought is suggested by the facts stated in v. 1.

Verse 8. A part of Strong's definition of *dog* is, "a male prostitute." Abner asked him if he had such a low estimate of him that he might be compared to a male prostitute, in that he was intimate with the concubine of his master. Most of the verse recounts the services he has been rendering to Ish-bosheth on behalf of his father's cause. He has been kind to this son of Saul and has been acting against Judah, the domain of David, when it has been in his power to deliver him into the hand of David. The substance of the verse is an accusation against Ish-bosheth of gross ingratitude.

Verse 9. *So do God to Abner* means that God may do to Abner what is due Ish-bosheth. Abner would have expected such a fate were it not for the fact that he is going to cooperate with God in carrying out the oath sworn to David. This is what he meant by the word *except*. That God would do this except, that is, were it not that I will do as God wants to have done, according to his oath to David.

Verse 10. In keeping with the oath mentioned in the preceding verse, Abner now threatened Ish-bosheth with the loss of his kingdom, by having it translated or transferred to David. *Dan to Beer-sheba*. These cities were at the northern and southern limits of the land of Palestine, and this use of the names came to be a figurative way of referring to the whole land.

Verse 11. Had the accusation that was made against Abner been untrue, it would have been an easy thing to have recalled it and apologized. On the other hand, had there been good evidence of its truth, Ishbosheth could easily have produced it; therefore, we are still left with some uncertainty on that point. But whether true or false, the threat made about the kingdom filled Ishbosheth with awe and rendered him speechless.

Verse 12. Abner now began to carry out his plan to translate the kingdom by offering to David a proposal of a league. He promised to bring all Israel to David as a condition of the league.

Verse 13. In 1 Sam. 25: 44 we learn that Saul had given his daughter Michal, who was David's wife, to Phaltiel. Saul's motive for it was evident, because she had previously shown her love for David. (1 Sam. 18: 28; 19: 12-17.) Upon the proposition of Abner, David saw an opportunity for recovering his stolen wife. He made that a condition for favoring the offer of Abner.

Verse 14. David accompanied his demand upon Abner with a like one upon Ishbosheth, the usurper of the throne left vacant by the death of Saul. In this demand David referred to the bargain by which he had procured Michal from her father.

Verses 15, 16. Ish-bosheth was in a position to do as David requested, and did so. At first thought we may feel sorry for the husband. Then, since the receiver of "stolen goods" is considered as guilty as the thief, our sympathy weakens.

Verses 17, 18. True to his agreement, Abner began contacting the leaders of Israel by reminding them of their former friendship for David, and of their desire for him to be their

2 Samuel 3: 19-39

king. The way is now open for them to have their wish if they will act.

Verse 19. The tribe of Benjamin did not adhere to David in the matter of Ishbosheth, for he was of that tribe. Yet, the term "Israel" as it is used here, and in many other places later in the Bible, means the tribes exclusive of Benjamin and Judah.

Verse 20. With a group of twenty men, Abner came to David at Hebron, evidently to close up the negotiations for the league proposed between them. They were received with some formality and David made a feast for them.

Verse 21. The agreement was now made orally, and Abner said he would go and gather together all Israel, to the end that a league between them and David could be made. With this understanding, David sent Abner away in *peace*, which means that they parted as friends in the same sense as people who have been at war will come together as friends.

Verses 22, 23. While these conversations were going on between David and Abner, Joab and the servants of David were away pursuing a troop. They returned with the spoils of their conquest, and learned about the transactions between David and Abner; that although the latter had been opposing David, now he is being treated as a friend.

Verses 24, 25. Joab complained to David because of what he had done. He represented Abner in the role of a spy, and intimated that David should have taken him in hand while he had the opportunity.

Verse 26. Unknown to David, Joab sent messengers who overtook Abner at a place called the well of Sirah, not far north of Hebron. They brought him back to Hebron.

Verse 27. *Quietly*. This is from a word that means privacy. Joab pretended that he had some private message to give him. *Fifth rib*. This means the abdomen. The reason he assigns for this murder is different from what he said to David. He there made it appear as if he thought Abner was a spy, now he says it was for the slaying of his brother. The fact is, he considered him as his personal rival for honor and took this means for removing him.

Verse 28. When David heard of the death of Abner he disclaimed all approval of the act, either on behalf of himself or the kingdom.

Verse 29. David placed the blame for Abner's death on Joab and called for the punishment to fall on him and his father's house. *Let there not fail* meant that there was never to be a time when the following misfortunes would not be present in his posterity. There was always to be some one with an issue (running sore), or leaning on a staff (meaning that he would be infirm), or fall by the sword, or lack bread.

Verse 30. We know from the account of the slaying of Abner that Abishai did not have any direct hand in the act; moreover, David mentions only Joab in his curse in v. 29. And yet it is the inspired writer who tells us that Joab and Abishai were guilty of the bloodshed. This must be understood on the principle that persons who are interested in, or approve of, an act are to be considered as partakers of it.

Verse 31. David directed Joab to participate in the funeral rites for Abner. The king personally followed the bier, or litter.

Verse 32. This mourning at the grave of Abner was a form of burial ceremony, and showed that some formalities were practiced in the disposal of the body in that day.

Verses 33, 34. This paragraph means that Abner was a brave man, but did not have a fair chance. He had not been handled as a man would be by dignified officers, who would put him in chains in a legal way; instead, he had been the victim of foul play.

Verse 35. So deep was David's grief for Abner that he fasted for the day, in spite of the fact his friends urged him to eat.

Verse 36. The people did not persist in their attempt to get David to eat. But when they realized his plan was to observe a fast of mourning they took a favorable attitude toward it, on the general basis that whatever the king did was proper.

Verse 37. There was evidence that David did not approve of the slaying of Abner, even though he was or had been his personal opponent. But it had been demonstrated all along that David wanted all things to be done in the regular and lawful manner.

Verse 38. This verse gives a favorite statement, often used today at the death of some very important man in the church or the state.

Verse 39. The word *hard* means severe. These men were too severe, and their actions caused David to feel depressed or downcast.

2 SAMUEL 4

Verses 1-3. Although Abner had reversed his support of Ish-bosheth, the news of his death came as a shock. Abner had been in the services of Saul for some time and his death, especially in such an unlawful manner, caused Ishbosheth to be grieved. The death of Abner, and the revolution coming in the house of Saul, caused much unrest among the Israelites.

Verse 4. The writer goes back several years to explain the present physical condition of Mephibosheth, the son of Jonathan. This disability will account for the comparative obscurity that surrounded this heir in the line of Saul, until the gratitude of David later brought him to view again. (chapter 9: 1, 13.)

Verses 5, 6. These two men are mentioned in v. 2. They thought it would be a praiseworthy deed if they destroyed as many as possible of the remaining seed of Saul, now that his cause has lost out in favor of David. And they made the mistake of thinking it would be acceptable to accomplish this deed by "fair means or foul." Ish-bosheth was already weakened and discouraged at the news of his father's death (v. 1), and now these murderers pretended they were coming to bring him some food. They came into his house while he was taking his noon rest in bed, and slew him by thrusting him through the abdomen.

Verse 7. These are further details of the murder and mutilation of this son of Saul. No man can be killed more than once, but the writer wishes us to have the full force of the vicious attitude of these former captains of Saul. The word for *smote* means to strike, without necessarily causing death. So these men smote Ish-bosheth, then thrust him through the abdomen, then severed his head from his body, then fled with the multilated part. Since their master's house has been defeated, they want to be on the "winning side" by pretending to sympathize with the winner.

Verse 8. The idea these men had was that David would take it as a personal favor to have the head of this remaining heir to Saul's throne. The point in their speech that sets out what they thought would win the approval of David is expressed by the words, *thine enemy*. But they seemed not to know the spirit of David. He had always respected the lawful principles involved in any controversy, and had not wanted even Saul to be treated in any unmanly way. He therefore would not approve of any cowardly mistreatment of his family, especially when those members were righteous and harmless.

Verse 9. *As the Lord liveth.* This was a mild form of vow or oath. It meant that, as surely as the Lord lives, the things that will be said soon will be the truth.

Verse 10. The original account of this incident is in Chapter 1. The language here ignores the entire claim of the Amalekite for the slaying of Saul. The thing that aroused David was his attitude of pleasure at the death of Saul. Had the story he told been true, it would still have left the guilt of unlawful action upon him; therefore, whether true or false, the fact that he found pleasure in an unlawful act rendered him guilty.

Verse 11. To take pleasure in the death of Saul, as manifested by the Amalekite, was wrong, regardless of the fact that Saul had become sinful in his conduct as king. Then how much more wrong it is to find such pleasure at the death of a righteous man! And still more especially, when this death was caused by wicked men who took advantage of their victim. For such a deed these men deserved to be taken away in their own bloodguiltiness.

Verse 12. David did not make the execution personally, but called upon the young men whom he had in his employ to do the work. The bodies of the two murderers were mutilated, but not in as disgraceful a manner as they had done to Ish-bosheth. The mutilated parts were put up in a public place, while the head of their victim was given honorable burial.

2 SAMUEL 5

Verses 1, 2. The sincerity of these people might well be questioned. Not that they did not state the truth concerning the record of past conditions, for they did; but the question that may be asked is, why had they not recognized the right of David to be king instead of following the son of Saul. However, it is so evident now that David will be the recognized ruler that about all of the forces will want to serve him.

Verse 3. These elders of Israel were the leading men of the tribes and were in a position to represent the people. They anointed David king over Israel. This did not mean that he had never been anointed before, for we know that Samuel had done that. The thought is, they took that means of formally recognizing him as their king.

Verse 4. This short verse is informative in that it gives us the entire age of David, and the portion of his life which he spent as king. It will be understood that it is a statement made by the inspired writer in advance of the actual years of his life. At the present time David is 37.

Verse 5. This tabulates the places and divisions of David's reign. The 7 years of his reign while in Hebron included only the tribe of Judah, because at that time the other tribes were following Abner in the attempt to preserve the kingdom of Saul.

Verse 6. Jerusalem is to be the capital city of the Israelite nation hereafter. Now that David is approaching it to take rightful possession as king, he finds a group of people occupying it called Jebusites. They have been there for centuries. It is to be expected that they will object to David's entrance into the city as it will mean their ejection. But they make a sort of offer of admitting him to the city, and place it on the condition that he was to remove such conditions among the people as blindness and other physical disability. The text says *thinking*, David could not come in. The margin renders it "saying," and the lexicon gives the same. Either would be correct. The inspired writer would know what they were thinking, even though they had not expressed themselves in words. The situation shows that they counted on the generosity of David to permit them to remain undisturbed, and yet that would constitute a bar against his entering into the city according to their arbitrary stipulation.

Verse 7. The chronological place for this verse is after v. 8, and is introduced here as a conclusion to the events of v. 6. Zion was a fortification in the southwest part of the city. David took it and it became his headquarters. It also came to be called the city of David and will figure often and with importance in the history.

Verse 8. After the Jebusites made the challenge-like stipulation mentioned in v. 6, David disdained attacking them personally. Instead, he called upon his service men to make the attack. *He shall be chief and captain.* These words are not in the original, and have been ignored in the R. V. The statement of David was really an instruction to his men as to how and where to make the attack. *Hated.* This means that David hated them in the sense of their being his enemies regarding his lawful authority there. The word *wherefore* is rendered in the margin as "because." The last part of the verse would properly be constructed to read, "Because they said, that on account of the blind and lame, David will not be able to enter the city." And we should understand them to have in mind the stipulation which these persons had made (without any authority) to David. The thing that was overlooked was the fact that David never accepted the condition, therefore, it would not constitute any barrier to his entrance.

Verse 9. Millo was a rampart surrounding this hill called Zion. It had existed before the time we have been studying about, but had fallen somewhat in decay. David now repaired it. As it surrounded the hill we can understand the words here, "from Millo and inward."

Verse 10. Most of the opposition that had come from the house of Saul was now removed, and David grew in influence and favor of God and man.

Verses 11, 12. Tyre was a small, but important kingdom bordering on the Mediterranean Sea. That is, Tyre was a principal city of the kingdom known as Phoenicia. This kingdom was on friendly terms with Israel at this time and the king, Hiram, showed his friendship by furnishing materials for a house to be occupied by the King of Israel. This act of friendship on the part of a neighboring power, together with other favorable conditions, assured David that his kingdom was destined to be a great power.

Verses 13-16. The chief interest we have in this paragraph is connected with two of the sons of David, Nathan and Solomon. They were full brothers, being sons of David by Bathsheba, according to 1 Chr. 3: 5. One of the important facts regarding these full brothers was that each was an ancestor of Christ. (Matt. 1: 6; Luke 3: 31).

Verse 17. The old enemies of the

Israelites, the Philistines, heard of the coming into power of David, the successor to Saul, and came up to *seek* him. That word is from an original that means to search out or spy on. Upon hearing of it, David went into his *hold*, which means his fort within Millo.

Verse 18. The valley of Rephaim was not far from Jerusalem, and the Philistines encamped in great numbers in this place, thus forming a menace to David.

Verse 19. David inquired for advice about attacking them. He was told to do so, and that he would be victorious over the enemy.

Verse 20. Baal-perazim was a spot within the valley mentioned above. At this place David joined the battle with the Philistines and defeated them. He gave the Lord the glory for this victory.

Verse 21. The heathen peoples of that age and country worshipped small gods that they carried with them. In this battle they had to leave these images, and David and his men disposed of them, that is, they took charge of them. The word *burned* is from NASA and defined in the margin "took them away." The lexicon agrees with it, for Strong defines the word, "to lift." It has been rendered in the A. V. by bear 156 times, carry 25, lift 137, and many others. They were taken as spoils of war, and valued on account of the precious metals and other useful materials of which they were made.

Verses 22-25. The Philistines were not willing yet to give up the conflict, and came up again and occupied a position similar to the previous one. David inquired if he should again make an attack directly as before. God told him not to do that, but to make a semicircle and come up behind them. There is some uncertainty with the dictionaries as to the meaning of the name for these trees. What is pretty certain is that the leaves of the trees were very sensitive to the slightest breeze, and God decided to use the method described to notify David when to make the attack. It is another instance that should remind us of Heb. 1: 1. The battle was again successful for the Israelites, and the slaughter of the Philistines extended from Geba to Gazer, which were towns in this area comprehended by the valley of Rephaim.

2 SAMUEL 6

Verse 1. The word *chosen* means the select rank from the standpoint of usefulness in general, not especially from the standpoint of war. The service at hand was not one that necessarily called for military operations; it had to do with the ark.

Verse 2. Baale is the same as Kirjath-jearim, the place where the ark has been for some time. (1 Sam. 7: 2). David was at Jerusalem, and the statement means that he took these chosen men with him and went to Baale, and *from* there went to bring up (to Jerusalem) the ark. This verse is another link in the chain of the ark, and the reference should be made to v. 11. The two cherubims were on the ark and the Lord's name was represented between these images at the service of the high priest.

Verse 3. Ex. 25: 14, 15, shows that the ark was to be carried by hand, and the staves were provided for that purpose; therefore it was unlawful to place it on a cart to be moved. In moving the sacred vessel in this way a great danger of experiencing the wrath of God was present.

Verse 4. The antecedent of *it* is the cart, last word in v. 3. It is stated that *it* accompanied ("with" in the margin) the ark. One of the men, Ahio, went before the ark. That indicates that the other man, Uzzah, walked beside it.

Verse 5. David is known to students of the Bible as the great musician. As the ark was being borne along to the resting place provided, he was celebrating the occasion with these instruments.

Verse 6. It is a common idea that Uzzah was punished for touching the ark, he not being a priest; it is an erroneous idea, for no one was permitted to touch it. (Num. 4: 15). The staves were to be used for moving it. Uzzah was cut down for the simple act of touching the sacred vessel. A good motive is frequently offered to justify something that is otherwise questionable. This affair about Uzzah shows such reasoning to be wrong. The oxen "stumbled" (marginal reading) and the ark seemed to be in danger of being damaged, which would have been a tragedy. Notwithstanding, it was a sin to touch it.

Verse 7. The word *anger* is a proper translation. One definition in the lexicon for the original is "ire." The margin gives "rashness" for *error*, and the lexicon supports the rendition. Uzzah was prompted by his interest in the ark, and failed to consider what it would mean to touch it. His death by it proves that the presence of a sacred object will not protect one in a sinful act.

Verse 8. The word *displeased* is from the same original as *grieved* in 1 Sam. 15: 11, and *breach* is defined "a break, literal or figurative."—Strong. David was grieved because God had broken his favor toward Uzzah.

Verses 9, 10. David was overawed by the death of Uzzah, and hesitated about bringing the ark to his own headquarters in Jerusalem. Instead, he took it to the house of Obed-edom. It is significant that it was *carried*, which was the lawful manner for moving it.

Verse 11. This is another link in the chain of the ark. The reference is to v. 12. Obed-edom was a Levite and a friend of the Lord's people. The ark was in his house three months and treated with respect; as a result, the blessing of God came to him.

Verse 12. At this place make a reference to v. 17 for the ark. After three months, during which time the ark was in the house of this Levite, David went to complete his original purpose to bring it to Jerusalem.

Verse 13. This procession was one accompanied with joyfulness, and the gratitude of David was expressed by sacrificing oxen and other animals.

Verse 14. Dancing was practiced by men and women in old times as an expression of joy and gladness. There is no evidence, however, that the sexes danced together. An ephod was a girdle, similar to an article worn by the priests. David was wearing the ordinary loose skirt common to the men of that age, and the only thing to hold it down and near the body was this ephod.

Verse 15. The procession with the ark continued, accompanied with shouts and other exhibitions of gladness.

Verse 16. The action of dancing in the kind of garment David wore caused some exposure. Michal saw this and *despised* him in her heart. The word means she held him in low esteem.

Verse 17. This is another link in the chain for the ark, and the reference is to 15: 24. The *tabernacle* was a tent which David had provided for the housing of the ark. It was pitched in that part of Jerusalem called Zion. (1 Chr. 16: 1; 1 Ki. 8: 1.) The tabernacle that Moses built had been captured by the Philistines (1 Sam. 4), and was now at Gibeon. (1 Chr. 21: 29.) The ark, however, had been rescued by the Israelites, but had no satisfactory place of shelter; David, therefore, had provided this tent.

Verses 18, 19. When the ceremonies for the ark were over, David pronounced a blessing on the people. It would come from God. Then he bestowed personal favors on them in the form of the necessities of life. After this they returned to their homes.

Verse 20. The kindly feeling of David for his household would have been shown next, but Michal gave him an unfavorable greeting. The form of speech which she used is called irony. We know not whether she was actually humiliated by his conduct before the maidens, or was jealous of his apparent happiness in their midst. We are certain, however, that her attitude was wrong with regard to David.

Verse 21. This means his dancing was *before the Lord*, and not with any regard for the maidens present. He put a "sting" in his speech by saying the Lord had chosen him *before her father*. The first word is not in the original, but the context justifies its use. It does not mean before in point of time, for that would not have been true. It means that David was regarded higher than Saul, and more worthy of being king over Israel. (1 Sam. 13: 14.) For that reason he would play (joyously perform) before the Lord.

Verse 22. *Vile* and *base* do not mean bad morally. Michal had accused him of abasing himself before the maidens. His meaning is, if playing before the Lord constituted baseness, then he would do more of it; and his actions would be so evidently justified that he would be approved by these very maidens whom she represented as being displeased. Such a result would prove them to be more deserving of his regard than his wife would be.

Verse 23. Because of this behaviour of Michal, David did not cohabit with her afterward. *Had no child* means that she had none after this. The statement has no bearing on the question as to whether she had borne children previously.

2 SAMUEL 7

Verse 1. This rest from his enemies means only a lull in war activities; David will have many battles to wage.

Verse 2. We should distinguish between Nathan the prophet and David's son with the same name. From Samuel onward there was almost always a national prophet (Acts 3: 24) who served as an inspired teacher or interpreter of the law. David was concerned about the disregard for the ark. He was living in a home made of cedar (5: 11), while the ark had nothing better than curtains (tent Ch. 6: 17).

Verse 3. This assurance was given because of the general idea that God favored David, not that Nathan had as yet inspired information on the subject at hand.

Verse 4. That night the Lord spoke to Nathan. Prophets and other special spokesmen of God were inspired only when there was something for them to speak or write. Now, the Lord had a message to give David by Nathan.

Verses 5, 6. This paragraph indicates that David was more concerned than God about a house for Him.

Verse 7. The same idea is continued. The Lord has not complained about not having a house, why should David be so concerned?

Verse 8. The humble background of David's life, followed by his exaltation to the throne of Israel, is the subject of this paragraph.

Verses 9, 10. God assured David of continued favor for himself and the people. Furthermore, he was given the promise that the people of his kingdom would some day have a place of relief, and not be afflicted by their enemies as before.

Verse 11. The pronoun *thee* is variously related as to antecedents. The first instance refers to Israel, the second to David personally, and the third to him and the people combined.

Verse 12. This promise of the perpetuity of his kingdom was to be fulfilled through his own son.

Verse 13. There was no wrong in the idea of a house, for David's son was to be permitted to build one, and his kingdom was to be established *for ever*, or age-lasting.

Verse 14. This punishment with *the rod of men* was fulfilled in 1 Ki. 11: 14, and in other similar instances.

Verse 15. Saul was finally rejected and ignored completely, and suffered to come to a violent death (1 Sam. 28: 6; 31: 6), while Solomon enjoyed the leniency of God, even after his many sins. (1 Ki. 11; 13, 39.)

Verses 16, 17. Saul was of the tribe of Benjamin. Because of his sins, the throne was not only taken out of his family, but from his tribe. David was of the tribe of Judah, and as long as the kingdom existed, its kings were from that tribe.

Verse 18. These promises deeply affected David, and he entered the tent containing the ark and spoke to the Lord about his feelings.

Verse 19. The thing that especially impressed him was God's assurance for his house in the distant future.

Verses 20, 21. A sense of his inability fully to express himself was admitted. He then relied on the Lord's power to read the mind, and to see the regard therein existing for the divine purposes.

Verse 22. Not only did David confess that God is great, but also that he is without an equal.

Verse 23. God is great as a divine individual, but his people also is great. The greatness of this people was due to the might of God as demonstrated in the redemption of it from another strong nation. This was done in spite of the heathen gods.

Verse 24. This recognizes the fulfillment of the promise made to Abraham in Gen. 12: 2.

Verse 25. This is not a doubt of God's faithfulness; it is a form of expression just the opposite. It means that David fully expected God to carry out his covenant.

Verse 26. In those days of rival gods, it was significant that Israel was ruled by the Lord of hosts. Before such a God, David wished his house to be established.

Verse 27. God's promise to build a house for David's people encouraged him to offer this prayer.

Verses 28, 29. It is interesting to note that David was not concerned about himself only. He was more thoughtful of the welfare of his people who composed the nation of the Lord.

2 SAMUEL 8

Verse 1. *Metheg-ammah*. This is from a word defined by Strong, "bit of the metropolis, an epithet of Gath."

Smith's Bible Dictionary defines it, "the bridle of the mother city—namely, of Gath, the chief town of the Philistines." The statement is a figure of speech. Taking of the chief city, thus getting control, is like getting control of a beast by taking his bridle.

Verse 2. *Measured* is from MADAD and defined, "a primitive root; properly to stretch; by implication to measure (as if by stretching a line); figuratively, to be extended."—Strong. *Line.* This is from CHEBEL and defined, "a rope (as twisted), especially a measuring line; by implication, a district or inheritance (as measured); or a noose (as of cords); figuratively, a company (as if tied together)."—Strong. David had so completely subjugated the Philistines that he could dispose of them as he saw fit. Using the line or rope as a guage, he divided them into two groups; the number counted off by two lengths of the line into one, and those of one length into another. Then he cast them down on the ground, or compelled them to lie down. This was a performance corresponding to that when an officer orders a man to "throw up your hands." When this had been completed he slew the larger group, and kept the other for servants.

Verses 3, 4. Gen. 15:18 gives the promise made to Abraham that his seed should possess the territory extending to the river Euphrates. This accounts for the words *his border.* In attacking the men named he was taking possession of land already his by divine right. It had been unlawfully occupied, however, by these heathen people, therefore he had to *recover* it. To hough the horses means to cut the tendon just under the hock joint, which would disable them for service.

Verse 5. It would be usual for the heathen kings to sympathize with each other. That is why the Syrians tried to help Hadadezer. Their effort, however, was defeated.

Verse 6. A garrison is a military post, or stationary headquarters for defense. The first success over the Syrians needed to be safeguarded against future uprising, and these garrisons were for that purpose. *Syria of Damascus* is so worded to distinguish it from the country beyond the Euphrates, which was also called Syria sometimes. *Brought gifts* means they formally recognized the authority of David.

Verses 7, 8. These metals were taken as spoils of war, and appropriated to the service of God.

Verses 9, 10. Toi, king of Hamath, had been at war with Hadadezer, and the enmity still existed between them. The victory of David over this foe was in his favor; therefore, Toi sent his son to congratulate David. Furthermore, he followed the custom of sending gifts as tokens of friendship, and in recognition of the dignity of David.

Verses 11, 12. These gifts were added to others that had been received from the various nations as formal "presents," likewise, those taken as spoils of war.

Verse 13. The Syrians were a powerful and dreaded people, and David's success over them got him a name among the people. *Valley of salt.* The works of reference are not definite as to the location of this valley. It seems to be not far south of the Dead Sea, perhaps a flat stretch of land somewhat lower than the immediate surroundings.

Verse 14. The establishment of garrisons (military posts) in a country is evidence of the subjugation of the country; and such was the condition in this place. Since the Edomites descended from Esau (Gen. 36:9), this is a fulfillment of Gen. 25:23; 27:29.

Verse 15. *Judgment.* This is from MISHPAT and defined, "properly a verdict (favorable or unfavorable) pronounced judicially, especially a sentence or formal decree." — Strong. *Justice.* This is from TSEDAQAH, and defined, "righteous (abstractly), subjectively (rectitude), objectively (justice), morally (virtue) or, figuratively (prosperity)." — Strong. The verse means that David rendered his decisions according to rightous principles.

Verses 16-18. This may well be called David's cabinet. Most of the terms are self-explanatory; the last one, however, does not denote any authority. The marginal rendering properly gives us "princes."

2 SAMUEL 9

Verses 1-4. David had made a league with Jonathan that pertained to the descendants of his father's house. (1 Sam. 20:14-16.) It was this league that prompted the inquiry described. The investigation brought a servant named Ziba to David for more direct information, who cited him to a son of Jonathan's, then living in the house of Machir. He was a ward of that place, due to an injury received when five years old. (Ch. 4: 4.) Not being able-bodied, it was a real favor to be cared for as David wished to do.

Verses 5, 6. The name of this son of Jonathan's was Mephibosheth, and David had him brought to him. Upon their meeting, Mephibosheth performed the usual courtesy of that age by complete prostration of the body toward the ground.

Verse 7. David did not merely promise kindness to Mephibosheth, but told him the motive; that it was for the sake of his father, Jonathan.

Verse 8. *Dead dog.* These come from the usual originals for such terms, and are not given any special definition for the present use. The conclusion is therefore, that it is just an emphatic expression of humility and unworthiness, but used figuratively.

Verse 9. Calling Ziba to him again, David told him of his disposition of Saul's property that had come down to Jonathan; that it all was to belong to Mephibosheth.

Verse 10. The next command was for Ziba and his family group to till the land for the son of Jonathan, and bring the products in for his credit. Notwithstanding all such provision, Mephibosheth was to be a special guest at the table of David.

Verse 11. Ziba promptly agreed to comply with the instructions of the king, and was again told that Mephibosheth would be treated as one of the king's sons.

Verses 12, 13. The son of Jonathan also had a family group of some extent, and had need of household support. That accounted for his need of the land products which were to be administered by the servants of Ziba, by his directions. All this time, however, Mephibosheth received his personal care as a royal guest at the table of David. In this whole transaction of David's we have a worthy example of gratitude.

2 SAMUEL 10

Verses 1, 2. Gratitude again prompted David to act. The objective was to show kindness to Hanun, king of the Ammonites and son of Nahash, former king. This kindness was in return for some favor he had received from his father. David sent by his servants to offer condolences to Hanun on the recent death of his father.

Verse 3. The good intentions of David were misjudged by the princes of Hanun. They caused him to believe that the men were spies.

Verse 4. Hanun did not do them any bodily injury, but greatly abased them by mutilating their beards and clothing.

Verse 5. It would have been the work of only a few hours to restore the clothing, while a much longer time would be required for the beards to grow. David, therefore, gave them permission to tarry at Jericho until their beards grew.

Verse 6. *Stank* is from a word that is defined, "became offensive." In times of national unrest, to regard a nation as an offense is about equal to expectation of war. On this basis, the Ammonites concluded to secure an ally against David. They *hired* the Syrians to help them.

Verse 7. When soldiers are hired to fight in an army of a foreign commander, they are called mercenaries. Such an action is equivalent to a declaration of war. David so interpreted it, and sent his commander-in-chief of the field, Joab, with the best of his fighting men.

Verse 8. The Ammonites and Syrians arranged themselves as distinct units in the field, but prepared to fight together against Joab.

Verses 9, 10. Seeing the formation of his enemy, Joab did a like maneuver. He chose a detachment of the best men to serve under him against the Syrians, and placed the rest under his brother Abishai to meet the Ammonites.

Verse 11. Joab instructed his brother that if either division were failing in the battle, the other should come to his rescue.

Verse 12. Joab encouraged Abishai to trust in the Lord for the proper outcome.

Verse 13. The Syrians did not put up any fight, but fled at the approach of Joab.

Verse 14. The desertion of the Syrians disheartened the forces under Abishai, and they likewise fled.

Verses 15, 16. The Syrians decided to attempt recovery of their lost "honor." They allied themselves with Hadarezer, the man who had been defeated by David. (Ch. 8: 3, 4.)

Verses 17, 18. This alliance did the Syrians no good for they were again beaten before David, who had taken active command.

Verse 19. The servants of Hadarezer now realized that Israel was too strong for them, and came to peace terms. This put an end to the attempts of the Syrians to help the Ammonites.

2 SAMUEL 11

Verse 1. *Expired* is from a word defined "a recurrence." The wording means "at the return of the year," and applies to the time of year when it was usual to begin another campaign of war. David sent Joab, his military leader, out to war against the Ammonites, while he remained at Jerusalem. The army laid siege against Rabbah, an important, walled city of the Ammonites.

Verse 2. While the siege of Rabbah was being conducted, a sad affair occurred in Jerusalem. David was on the roof of his house, a place so used in old times, as the houses had flat roofs. (Deut. 22: 8; Josh. 2: 6; Judg. 16: 27; 2 Sam. 18: 24; Matt. 24: 17.) From there he saw a woman washing herself. The context shows that she was taking a general bath, although the original word does not always require that meaning. She exposed her body for it says she was *very beautiful to look upon.* This indicates that the appeal to one's eyes was the thing considered. The mere sight of a woman bathing her hands or face would excite no passion. We must conclude, therefore, the statement means a general exposure. Since David was in a place where he had right to be, and where it was customary for men to be, we would have to conclude that Bath-sheba was careless in selecting a place to bathe. Two wrongs, however, do not make one right, and the sin of David was so great that no mention was made of her mistake.

Verse 3. Upon inquiry, David learned the identity of the woman. Her husband was one of the valiant soldiers, then in service in the war against the Ammonites, and her name was Bath-sheba. She was alone, therefore, and her husband was some distance from home. She had a form that made great sex appeal, and David had beheld it.

Verse 4. Using his power as king, he sent for the woman and committed adultery with her. *For she was purified.* The R. V. renders this the same as the A. V., while the marginal rendering is, "and when she had purified herself," etc. The word *uncleanness* is from TUMAH, and Strong defines it, "religious impurity." The law considered a woman ceremonially and religiously unclean after her periodical function. (Lev. 15: 19-24); also, after intimate relations with a man. (Lev. 15: 18.) In the case at hand either rendering could be correct. If the one in the common text be accepted, it means that David would be free to be intimate with her as far as Lev. 15: 24 was concerned. If the one in the margin be accepted, it means that Lev. 15: 18 was obeyed.

Verse 5. When Bath-sheba knew of her condition she informed David of it. This is one case of conception that would not have occurred had mankind always been unclothed. See comments on Gen. 3: 16.

Verse 6. David was in supreme authority, and his order for the recall of Uriah was obeyed.

Verse 7. Upon arrival of Uriah, David pretended to be concerned about the progress of the war. Some such motive was necessary, he thought, for recalling Uriah, else he would have suspected some improper one, and that would have defeated the real purpose for his presence. This inquiry as to the war, therefore, was insincere.

Verse 8. David wished to escape responsibility for the child expected by Bath-sheba; for this reason he gave Uriah "leave of absence," that he might enjoy the comforts of home and the pleasures of married life. *Mess of meat.* The last word is not in the original, and the word for *mess* is defined in part, "a present." David wanted to make a very friendly feeling in the mind of Uriah, and this was just a token of his good will. If he can induce him to dismiss the cares of war for a little while, and go into the company of his wife from whom he has been separated, the way will be clear to place the paternity of the child on him.

Verse 9. Uriah was not in the frame of mind to carry out David's plans. Instead, he passed the night in company with the king's servants, near the royal house.

Verse 10. David was told of Uriah's actions, and again pretended to be concerned about his comfort. He did so by reminding him that he had been on a journey.

Verse 11. Like a true soldier, Uriah was concerned more for the success of the Lord's cause, than for his personal pleasure. This was especially so when he remembered that Joab and the ark were out in the field of battle. Under such conditions he could not conscientiously relax to indulge in the pleasures of home life.

Verse 12. Seeing his first plan did not work, David thought of another. He will let a day and night go by, which will permit the military ardor to cool off, perhaps, and also his natural desire for his wife may assert itself.

Verse 13. It is known that when a man is under the influence of intoxication, his lower or animal desires are often more urgent; likewise, his finer qualities are dulled. Now then, if Uriah can be made drunk, he may take up the king's offer and go home. This plan, however, did not succeed.

Verse 14. One more plan remained for getting Uriah out of the way. It is remarkable to note the confidence David had in the faithfulness of Uriah. The very letter that was to be his death warrant was entrusted to him for transmission.

Verse 15. There is no evidence that Joab knew the purpose of David in all this. Perhaps Uriah has offended the king, but he did not have the heart to execute him directly. At any rate, he knew it was David's will that Uriah must die.

Verses 16, 17. In obedience to the commands of his superior, Joab put Uriah in a place of greatest danger. The result was according to plans; Uriah was killed.

Verses 18-21. This message of Joab could be more easily understood if we knew he was aware of David's plans. In any case, he wanted to prepare the messenger with the means of quieting the king. He was to finish the conversation with the good news (to David) of the death of Uriah.

Verses 22-24. There is no indication that the messenger had to do anything to calm David. The whole report went through without interruption.

Verse 25. This again shows the pretense that David has been carrying on throughout the affair. He knew that Joab did not need any consolation, but the messenger must not be "let in" on the scheme, hence this speech.

Verse 26. Like a true wife, Bathsheba mourned the death of her brave husband. There is no evidence that she knew of his visit to the king.

Verse 27. This verse as a whole covers several months but begins immediately after the way was open for David's scheme. In this affair he was guilty of four distinct sins; adultery (v. 4); hypocrisy (v. 7, 8); alcoholism (v. 13); and murder (v. 15).

2 SAMUEL 12

Verses 1-4. Nathan the prophet is meant; he was national prophet in place of Samuel. This indirect approach to David was to cause him to realize the magnitude of his sin by viewing it with an unprejudiced mind. The parable uses him as the rich man, Uriah the poor. The many flocks refers to David's numerous wives, the one ewe lamb to Bath-sheba, Uriah's only wife. With this setup in mind, the application of the parable to the facts is easy.

Verse 5. *As the Lord liveth* is a Biblical expression used frequently and means, "as surely as the Lord liveth." David has no doubt that the guilty man should die.

Verse 6. Not only should the man die, but his property should be siezed to repay, fourfold, the wrong done. Since the poor man's life was not taken, the death sentence for the rich man was because he *had no pity*, and the property assessment was for taking that of the poor man.

Verse 7. There was nothing indefinite in the accusation that Nathan made. *Thou art the man*. The most important favors that had been given him were first mentioned. They consisted of his being delivered from Saul, and his elevation to the throne.

Verse 8. *Thy master's wives*. There is no evidence that David was ever intimate with a wife of Saul's, nor was he ever accused of irregularity along that line, except in the case of Bath-sheba. But the house of Saul had been turned over to him. That would include the women subjects of the realm, among whom he had found his wives. Nathan told him that any further need with which he had not been supplied, would have been given him when such need became evident.

Verse 9. *Wherefore* means "why?" *Despised* means to belittle or treat with disrespect. *Commandment* is in the singular form, but David had disobeyed three of the ten; the one against coveting a neighbor's wife;

2 Samuel 12: 10-23

against adultery; and against murder. The means of getting Uriah killed was indirect, but the charge of murder was direct. That proves that one is responsible for the result of any plot he may form.

Verse 10. One item of punishment that was to come upon David was the presence of the sword in unfriendly use.

Verse 11. Another was to be a violation of his marriage rights, which occurred through his own son. (Ch. 16: 22.)

Verse 12. *Thou didst it secretly.* The last word is from an original that means "under cover." The idea is that, while various ones knew of some things being done, they did not know "what it was all about."

Verse 13. David's confession was clean cut. No attempt to explain or justify the act. No reference to some others who had "done as bad, or worse." *I have sinned against the Lord.* This did not ignore the rights of Uriah and his wife, but all sins, regardless of any man affected, are primarily against God. This spirit of penitence is doubtless the reason for saying David was a man after God's own heart. (1 Sam. 13: 14.) In return for his confession, Nathan told him that his life would be spared.

Verse 14. Although David received the mercy of God as to his life, he must suffer the loss of the child. The purpose for this was to hush the blasphemies of the enemies. Had he been permitted to escape all punishment, after committing such a grievous sin, they would have said it was because he was a "favorite," and was to be shielded in wrong.

Verse 15. After Nathan went home, the Lord brought a severe sickness on the child. This seems strange to us, but God's ways are not ours. While it appears as an unjust treatment of the babe, we may consider it a blessing in disguise. The bodily suffering will be comparatively brief, while a life of uncertain experiences would be long. He would frequently be confronted with the shameful story of his birth. Instead of such a regrettable situation, he will be permitted, after a short period of physical suffering, to pass into that state of happiness that awaits all who die in the Lord.

Verse 16. "While there is life there is hope" is a familiar saying, and it seems to have been the thought of David. Nathan had told him the child would die. However, he knew that God was merciful, and perhaps he would "repent him of the evil" he thought to do, as he had done on many occasions. Fasting and prostrating oneself on the ground was a form of devotion used in times of great distress or desire.

Verse 17. The word *elders* does not have any official meaning unless the context requires it. As used here it has the ordinary meaning of the older persons of his household. Not being affected personally by the state of things, they could realize that David was neglecting his own body to no benefit of the child. But their attempts to get him to eat with them failed.

Verse 18. After a period of seven days, the child died. During this time David had refused to eat. The servants, however, misunderstood the state of his mind. They thought he was giving way to morbid grief; that was a mistake as verse 22 shows.

Verse 19. It is sometimes difficult to account for the shortsightedness of people. The servants wished to keep knowledge of the child's death from David. Yet, the very thing that would surely arouse his suspicions was what they did. Had they gone about their duties in the regular manner, he would not have been prompted to make the inquiry. They would have been compelled, however, sooner or later to tell him. Therefore, their conduct can be explained only by considering the awe, common to humanity, when in the presence of death.

Verses 20, 21. David's conduct, upon learning of the child's death, puzzled the servants. In verse 17 he resisted all efforts to get him to eat. Now that his grief (in their view) was greater than ever, why does he relax and call for food? In their confusion they asked him for an explanation.

Verse 22. His answer was consistent with the faith and practice of a servant of God. For further comments see verses 16, 18.

Verse 23. If it is true that "while there is life, there is hope," it is likewise true that death will end that hope. The original decree of God stood, hence there is no occasion for continued fasting. Such devotions were in order as long as the mercy of God was pending, but that mercy was not expected to bring the child back from the dead. *I shall go to him.* This shows David believed there was something in a human being more than the body. He still had the child's body and did not expect it to leave the earth. Moreover, since he expressed hope of going to the child, it meant he believed in another life after the one on earth was over.

Verse 24. The abruptness in the change of subject from the preceding verse is apparent only. The fact that this one verse reaches to the birth of another son shows it to be a concise statement, and allows for respectful waiting after the period of mourning, before engaging in the relaxation and pleasure of home life. It was during that period that David was comforting his wife. All of this shows another fine quality of his character. He treated her with tender consideration, and did not rush her into the obligations of married life until she had been comforted, and in the frame of mind, therefore, to cooperate with her husband normally. After this another son was born and was named Solomon, which means *peace*. That was appropriate; he never had a war and thus was a "man of peace" with regard to his official life. *The Lord loved him*. In a sense the Lord loves everybody; therefore, something special is meant. This son was destined to succeed to his father's throne, and go through his reign without any war. This will make him a type of the only begotten Son of God, who will be the *Prince of Peace*. For these reasons he also will be permitted to build the temple, to be a type of the glorious church, the spiritual temple of God.

Verse 25. This is related to the preceding verse. Since God had special reasons for loving Solomon, he added a significant name to him, Jedidiah, which is defined by Strong, "beloved of Jah; Jedidiah, a name of Solomon." He (the Lord) sent word by Nathan the prophet, telling David of this additional name he had given the new son. However, he was never referred to again by that name. It seems to have been used on this occasion merely as an expression of good will, and to cheer David and his wife.

Verse 26. In 11: 1, 25 we read that David sent Joab to take this city, while he remained at Jerusalem. The initial siege and conquest took place.

Verse 27. But Joab took only that part of the city called *city of waters*. Smith's Bible Dictionary explains this as follows: "The lower town, so called from its containing the perennial stream which rises in and flows through it." The citadel of the place remained to be taken.

Verse 28. Joab was willing to let his king and superior have the honor of the conquest, and accordingly sent word to him.

Verse 29. David acted on the suggestion, and completed the subjection of Rabbah.

Verse 30. Since he was king as well as warrior, it was befitting that he place this costly crown on his own head.

Verse 31. The words *under* and *through* are not in the original. *Brickkiln* is from a word that means brickmould. The verse means David made them work with the implements, and at brickmaking.

2 SAMUEL 13

Verse 1. It is the ordinary thing for members of a family to love each other, so the statement has some special meaning as regards Amnon. The word is from AHAB which Strong defines, "A primitive root; to have affection for (sexually or otherwise):" The context shows it means sexually.

Verse 2. Amnon's passion for his (half) sister was so great that he was in distress; to the extent that it affected his bodily appearance. The word *hard* is from PALA and defined in part, "great, difficult, wonderful,"—Strong. The meaning is that she was a virgin, and beautiful. That roused his feeling all the more, and suggested the unusual pleasure it would be to be intimate with her. He did not see any way, however, to obtain his desire.

Verses 3, 4. This friend observed the emaciation of Amnon and thought it strange. Being the king's son, having the benefit of the royal fare, there should be no reason for the condition. Upon inquiry, Amnon told him he was lovesick for Tamar. Of course, Jonadab understood that he was despairing of finding an opportunity for getting possession of the damsel, long enough to obtain his desires.

Verse 5. This shows the power of suggestion. Jonadab knew that if he would present the idea to Amnon, his craving for his sister would lead him on with the plan.

Verse 6. Amnon pretended he was sick, physically. In that condition his appetite would be weak and need some special inducement to prompt him to

2 Samuel 13: 7-24

eat. It is always desirable that the sick members of a family be able to take nourishment. Therefore, Amnon took advantage of such a sentiment, and asked that his sister be permitted to prepare him some food, in his sight.

Verse 7. The request of Amnon seemed reasonable, so the king instructed Tamar to serve her brother.

Verses 8, 9. The damsel did as instructed. That is, she was in the house, others being there also. But her work in preparing the cakes was in plain view of Amnon, even though not in the immediate room where he was lying. When they were ready to be served he refused to receive them as yet. Instead, he gave orders that all the men leave.

Verse 10. Complete privacy was now had. He directed her to come to his bedside and feed the cakes to him with her hand. She started to serve him as ordered.

Verse 11. This action brought her within arm's reach of this passionate man. Taking hold of her, he asked her to have intimate relations with him.

Verses 12, 13. She did not express any personal objection to him, but tried to show him the wrong of such a thing as he requested, and that it would bring shame on them both. Furthermore, she suggested that he ask the king for the lawful possession of her; that he would not be denied. There was nothing irregular in this suggestion since they were half brother and sister only, and such relatives married without criticism.

Verse 14. Amnon's real motive now expressed itself through his superior strength.

Verse 15. Love that is based on the coarser passion, only, is fickle; it will vanish when that passion is gratified. The moral reaction of the affair is perfectly logical. If a man does not love a woman because of *all* her qualities, but on the sensual basis only, when that is satisfied there is nothing of interest left. The alternative is sure to be the opposite of love. He ordered Tamar to leave.

Verse 16. *There is no cause.* Her meaning was that he had no reason for expelling her. The only honorable thing for him to do was to retain her and give her all the moral protection possible. Had his passion been associated with other considerations than sensuality, he would gladly have shielded her, as Shechem offered to do for Dinah. (Gen. 34: 3, 4.) That is why Tamar complained that the last wrong was greater.

Verse 17. She evidently was hesitant about leaving; he therefore ordered her to be put out by force and the door fastened against her.

Verse 18. Up to this event Tamar wore a garment that was a badge of virginity.

Verse 19. That garment would now be inappropriate, because she was no longer a virgin, although not by her own fault. She cancelled that badge by tearing it. *Crying* is from ZEAQAH which Strong defines, "a shriek or outcry." It shows she was not merely weeping as the term generally signifies, but was making a sound that indicated some terrible thing had happened to her.

Verse 20. Absalom knew the use and significance of the peculiar garment Tamar had been wearing. He saw it rent, which meant her virginity had been violated, and at once suspected Amnon. The necessary inference is that his condition of body had finally caught his attention and that of others, and the explanation of it had become known. By "putting two and two together," Absalom was able to name the guilty man. For her sake, he tried to make the situation look not too bad, since it was her brother who had been with her. As additional comfort he took her into his own home.

Verses 21, 22. Both David and Absalom detested this deed, and it might have been possible that both could have worked together in punishing Amnon, and not to have become so estranged as they did. But when Absalom "took the law into his own hands," as we shall soon see, it started a bitter feud that was never quieted until David stood at the bier of his beloved, but wayward son.

Verses 23, 24. Two years passed by and all that time Absalom was plotting to have Amnon killed. (v. 32.) The opportunity came, but he must be cautious not to rouse the suspicion of his father. Some distance from Jerusalem he had some sheep and the season for shearing had arrived. Such an occasion was often made into a time of festivity. On that pretense he invited his father, with his servants, to go with him. The invitation was general in order to hide his true motive.

Verse 25. David objected to going because of the charge it would cause. Amnon even insisted on his father's going, but we are sure he was not sincere. The purpose he had in mind would have been hindered had his father been present. That kind of conversation, however, deceived him, and paved the way for the next suggestion.

Verses 26, 27. If the king declined to go, why not let his brother go? There seemed to be little reason for even that burden. But he was urgent and the king permitted all his sons to go.

Verse 28. Drinking wine was a common practice on special occasions. *Merry with wine* refers to a state of mild intoxication in which the victim feels good, and unsuspecting of any danger. Under that condition it would be easy to get advantage of him. The assassins were to use the occasion for killing Amnon on Absalom's order. They were incited to the awful deed by the implied taunt of being lacking in valor.

Verse 29. The murder of Amnon frightened the other sons of David, and they fled.

Verse 30. While they were en route, the report reached David that all his sons had been killed. We do not know who was responsible for the false report, but the absence of the brothers, from both the place of the shearing and the king's house, would lend plausibility to it.

Verse 31. The king rent his garments, which was a custom on occasions of grief.

Verses 32, 33. Jonadab was the man who made the suggestion to Amnon that led to the whole situation. (v. 5.) Naturally, he had been observant of the events that followed, and was able to inform the king as to who was dead, also the motive for the slaying. With this he offered consolation to David.

Verse 34. Absalom fled, and many of the people with him.

Verses 35, 36. The sons of the king naturally did not follow their brother Absalom; they were too much frightened. But they came back to Jerusalem. As they approached the city, Jonadab saw them and called attention of David, confirming the statement he made in v. 33. When they arrived in the presence of the king, all of them mourned together.

Verses 37, 38. This flight was an admission of guilt. He knew that his father would resent the deed, and therefore would likely punish him. So here is when the bitter feud began, mentioned earlier in the chapter. This absence from Jerusalem lasted 3 years.

Verse 39. David was *comforted* or reconciled to the death of Amnon. Now he became concerned about his absent son, Absalom. Notwithstanding his great crime, he longed to have him return.

2 SAMUEL 14

Verse 1. Sometimes a man's official dignity conflicts with his personal or sentimental inclinations. David realized that Absalom had killed his brother treacherously, and that the least that should be done to him was to keep him away from Jerusalem. At the same time, his love for his son was active, urging him in the direction of mercy. This accounts for the last verse of the preceding chapter, and the first in this.

Verse 2. Joab sensed the situation; that David's heart really would favor the return of Absalom, while the thought of justice caused him to withhold any offers of leniency. He concluded a plan to break down official "pride" and permit mercy to have some consideration. For this purpose he contacted a woman of Tekoah who seemed to be shrewd, and had her put on the disguise of a woman in mourning over some grief of long ago.

Verse 3. Joab made the story and the woman delivered it to David.

Verse 4. She followed the custom of respectful posture, and called for help.

Verse 5. Not only her posture, but her distressed appeal caused the king to ask what ailed her. The answer, that she was a widow, and that her husband was dead, was not merely for emphasis. She might have been separated from her husband. In that case she would have been a widow in effect. At the same time, were the husband living, it would have left the possibility of reconciliation and help.

Verse 6. The sons in the story refer to Absalom and Amnon.

Verse 7. There has been no statement to the effect that any general clamor had been made for the punishment of Absalom; but in the absence of some action of David encouraging him to return, it was represented that he was virtually a fugitive from his father's house.

Verse 8. David attempted to dismiss the woman by a general or indefinite promise.

Verse 9. She said this to impress the king with the seriousness of the situation. She also implied that the king had some doubts of the importance of the case. As a form of vow and to show her good faith in the matter, she was willing to stake the peace of her household on the truthfulness of her claim.

Verse 10. Seeing the woman was not satisfied with the promise stated in v. 8, he strengthened his assurance of personal protection for her, expecting this to satisfy her and cause her to go on to her own home.

Verse 11. This is more along the same line, only more specific and urgent. The king repeated his assurance of protection for her son.

Verse 12. The woman was now ready to introduce the real purpose of her story, which she intended to do gradually. Before going further, however, she tested out the king's patience by asking permission to speak another word.

Verse 13. This is a virtual accusation of inconsistency against the king. She blamed him with faulty speech in that he did not carry out the same in action. This was the first direct reference to his *banished* son.

Verse 14. Without doing as God would wish, there would be no hope of recovering from the situation of sadness caused by the absence of the son. It would be as hopeless as the natural recovery of water spilled on the ground. But the "impossible" can be accomplished, even, in the present sad affair, if David will use his power, under God, for recovering the son now banished through fear of his father.

Verses 15-17. She seems to have dropped the actual subject of the banished son of the king, and gone back to the story. But she did this so that the king would see what it was to which he had committed himself. She had so impressed him with the justice of her complaint that he bound himself to assist her. After getting him to commit himself to an imaginary case, then presenting the true one, which was the same in principle as the imaginary one—after all this, she hoped to persuade David to act on behalf of Absalom.

Verse 18. The king now saw the point. He committed her to answer a question before she knew what it was about.

Verse 19. David suspected Joab of being the author of the story which the woman had told. He made a direct question to her regarding it. *As thy soul liveth* means, "as sure as thou livest." *None can turn*, etc., means there is no way of evading the question. She answered, therefore, not only that Joab was with her, but also had put the words in her mouth.

Verse 20. This goes one step farther than the preceding verse, and states the motive for the whole scheme.

Verse 21. Some time between the preceding verse and this, David had called Joab into his presence. Up to the present, no mention of the name of Absalom had been done. But the application of the story was so obvious that no pretense could be used to hide it. The king, therefore, instructed Joab to bring Absalom home.

Verse 22. Gratitude, expressed both by word and action, forms the subject here.

Verse 23. The permission of David, expressed in v. 21, allowed only of *bringing Absalom again*. Accordingly, Joab brought him to Jerusalem only.

Verse 24. The leniency of the king seemed to have been "held up," and his sense of dignity again asserted itself, for he refused to see his son after permitting him to return to the city. That would appear as a compromise between his paternal affection and his royal dignity.

Verse 25. The beauty of Absalom is applied to his entire body, from head to foot. That would indicate the writer was speaking of the perfection of his form, rather than the show of his countenance.

Verse 26. *Polled* means to cut the hair. It was not customary for men to have their hair long. This is indicated by the regulations of the Nazarite vow. The chief item of that vow was that the one making it would not cut his hair for the term of the vow. (Num. 6: 5; Judg. 13: 5; 1 Sam. 1: 11.) We should conclude, therefore, that the case of Absalom was an exception. For some reason he chose to depart from the common practice of men, and to let his hair grow long, in keeping with his quality of *beauty*. However, since the growth was unusual in weight, he cut it once a year for comfort.

Verse 27. The record does not say, but it is reasonable to conclude that he called the daughter Tamar in affectionate memory of his sister, who had been the unhappy occasion of his troubles.

Verse 28. These two years was the period Absalom had spent in his own house, during which he did not see his father's face.

Verse 29. The enforced separation from his father's face was made to appear the real source of his dissatisfaction. His true motive, though, was to get in better position for carrying out his plan of rebellion against the kingdom of his father. This will appear evident in the next chapter. He planned to be admitted to the presence of the king, and for that purpose sent for Joab. But he did not respond.

Verses 30, 31. Absalom caused the grain of Joab's field to be fired in order to force his attention. He got it, and was asked his reason for having the grain fired.

Verse 32. Having secured the attention of Joab, he told him he might as well have remained at Geshur, if he could not see the king, after being brought to the royal city. He proposed being brought before his father, and agreed beforehand to "take his medicine," whatever the king had against him.

Verse 33. The message was relayed to David who called for Absalom. Coming to his father, he performed the usual eastern custom of respect and bowed before the king, who kissed his son. There seemed to be a reconciliation, but the events soon to follow will prove his actions to have been a preparation for attack on the kingdom.

2 SAMUEL 15

Verse 1. After having effected an apparent peace with his father, Absalom waited a while, then began to lay his plans for a conspiracy.

Verse 2. The important cities were walled as a fortification against unfriendly strangers. That made it necessary to enter them through the gate. And that fact made it possible, also, to contact any person expected to enter the city. Naturally, there would be an almost daily appearance of citizens, coming with some sort of grievance or dispute, to have it settled by the king. But it would not be supposed that he could personally conduct all the cases brought up; deputies were appointed to handle the less important ones. This was according to an arrangement in the time of Moses. (Ex. 18: 23-26; Deut. 1: 9-16.) Absalom took advantage of this to make personal approach to the people. He manifested much interest in them, asking even about what particular cities they represented.

Verse 3. He next pretended to agree with the complainants, but deplored the lack of proper ones to hear their cause. He did not directly accuse the king of any injustice; only deplored the shortage of proper men to act under him. That, of course, would open the way for a suggestion.

Verse 4. He did not pretend that he wanted to be king; he asked only that he might be judge. If that were the case he would decide all their personal disputes justly.

Verse 5. When a man did the act of obeisance (formal courtesy) toward Absalom, he did not merely "return the salute," but condescended to contact him with a hand clasp and a kiss.

Verse 6. By such unusual acts of friendliness it was natural that he would capture the affections of the people. That is the meaning of *stole the hearts* of the people.

Verses 7-9. *After forty years.* It would be unreasonable to apply this term as counted from the time Absalom fled, or to his return, for we know he would not have waited that long to act on his plot. Neither could it be dated from the actual taking of the throne by his father; it had not been that long since. Therefore, it must mean forty years from the anointing of David at Bethlehem. Whether Absalom made the vow as declared to his father we do not know. It seemed plausible, however, and furnished a pious motive for requesting the royal consent to his absence. Such a plan would prevent any suspicions over his journey out over the dominions of his father.

Verse 10. Under cover of this pretended religious action, Absalom sent spies with instructions to acclaim him king in Hebron. It will be recalled that his father began his royal career in this place. (Ch. 2: 11.) Should any questioning arise prior to his reaching the city where he was to be acclaimed, it could be explained by David's permission for Absalom to go there on account of the vow.

Verse 11. These men were invited

2 Samuel 15: 12-34

to go. *Simplicity* means innocence. The whole passage means the men did not know what was going on. They thought they were merely going along with Absalom on a friendly journey.

Verse 12. The general uprising was becoming more apparent; it now included even Ahithophel, David's advisor, and that while he was engaged in the sacrifices.

Verse 13. News of the conspiracy was brought to David. It was not a hired uprising; it was based on an affectionate attachment to Absalom.

Verse 14. David realized the seriousness of the situation. As long as Absalom only had to be reckoned with, he could stand his ground, but a general conspiracy, and one backed by love for the leading conspirator, could result in nothing short of the destruction of the present king. He advised his servants, therefore, that they should flee for their lives.

Verse 15. The servants declared they would support David in whatsoever he wished.

Verse 16. Concubines had about the same moral status as wives in ancient times; they differed chiefly as to property rights, but they were considered as partners of their master's bed in the same sense as wives.

Verse 17. *All the people.* This could not mean that the entire population left the city; but all of the people that fled were following David. They paused when they reached a place far enough away to be safe from attack.

Verse 18. These people formed a bodyguard for the king.

Verses 19, 20. David referred to Absalom as *king*. We know that he was a conspirator and not entitled to the name, but his father recognized that he was now great in the eyes of the people. He would not antagonize them unnecessarily. Besides, he was his beloved and spoiled son. Ittai was a slave, lately come into the service of David, and was offered release from the present adventure.

Verses 21, 22. As surely as that the Lord and David were living beings, so that sure was Ittai that he would not desert his master. Seeing his determination, David permitted him to continue with him.

Verse 23. This was a pitiable and disgraceful flight. They crossed a small stream that flowed near Jerusalem, and were started on their way toward the wilderness.

Verse 24. In the panic of fear they had started to take the ark for assistance. This is another link in the chain for the ark. The reference is to v. 29.

Verses 25, 26. David "came to himself" and ordered the ark taken back to its rightful place. He reasoned that if his lot was to be favored by the Lord, he would not need to rely on some special use of the sacred vessel; and if he should, it ought to be left in its proper place.

Verse 27. *Seer* was the same as prophet or teacher. The priests occupied that position after the death of Moses. (Lev. 10: 11; Deut. 17, 9; Mal. 2: 7.)

Verse 28. This was in keeping with the idea David expressed in the preceding verse. Since the priests were scriptural consultants, he was to pause at his present place of hiding until further word from them.

Verse 29. The priests obeyed and carried the ark back to Jerusalem. It remained there as long as we have any history of it. The link of the chain refers to 1 Ki. 6: 19.

Verse 30. *Head covered.* This referred to some form of vail or shield for the face, in token of the feeling of defeat and shame. Removing the sandals was for the same reason. The whole situation was shameful.

Verse 31. Counselors were men close to kings and other important leaders. They served as personal advisers. Ahithophel was one of such servants. He was joined to Absalom in the conspiracy, presumably to advise him in his actions. It was logical, therefore, that David would pray to have his counsel turned into foolishness. That would defeat the interests of Absalom.

Verse 32. The *mount* is Olivet. (v. 30.) Hushai was one of the counselors, and will figure prominently in the affair of Absalom and David. He was a friend of David and expressed sincere grief over the distressful condition.

Verse 33. This speech to Hushai would seem to be an ungracious attitude toward a friend. The verses to follow will explain.

Verse 34. He was to return to Jerusalem and pretend to be a friend to Absalom. He was to address him as *king*, and declare his faithfulness to him as he had been to his father. This plan was to counteract the influence of Ahithophel.

Verse 35. Hushai was to spy on the *king*, Absalom, then communicate with the priests.

Verses 36, 37. These priests each had a son. They were to act as messengers. When they had any instructions for David, these sons were to take them.

2 SAMUEL 16

Verse 1. David passed on beyond Olivet. This servant met him with equipment and provisions for the journey.

Verse 2. David was informed of the purpose of these things.

Verses 3, 4. Ziba had been the servant of Saul. (Ch. 9: 2.) *Master's son*, therefore, would be Mephibosheth. Upon David's question, Ziba told him that Mephibosheth was abiding in the city in the hope that the kingdom (that should have fallen to his father, Jonathan), would soon be restored. That would put Mephibosheth in the position of a conspirator against David. As to the truth of the report of Ziba's, see Ch. 19: 24-29. At present, however, David believed the story, and in recognition of his faithfulness, promised him all the property that should have come to Mephibosheth.

Verse 5. Bahurim was a place not far from Olivet. Shimei was sympathetic for the house of Saul, whose kingdom had been lost to David. It is understandable, therefore, why he *cursed* him. The word is from an original that means, "to make light."

Verse 6. Casting stones in this ineffective manner was on the same plane as his belittling language. But the strong bodyguard around David protected him.

Verse 7. *Come out, come out.* The R. V. renders this, "Begone, begone," and the lexicons agree. It was just more contemptible language, coupled with his slanderous epithet *belial*, which meant a very wicked person.

Verse 8. Shimei taunted David about his present condition of defeat. Although Absalom never had shown any sympathy for Saul, this wicked man was taking delight in the present rebellion against the king. He had the insolence to charge the Lord with helping Absalom, and that in revenge for his opposition against Saul. The history will show this entire speech of Shimei to be false.

Verse 9. *Dead dog* was an expression of utter contempt. In the fiery zeal of devotion, Abishai proposed to slay Shimei. It was somewhat like the spirit manifested by Peter. (John 18: 10.)

Verse 10. *What have I to do with you* means, "I hardly know what to do with you." Perhaps the discipline was necessary for David. At any rate, that was the view he seemed to take of it. Later, Shimei made full confession for his sin and was pardoned.

Verse 11. David expressed no surprise at the unfriendly disposition of Shimei, when his own flesh and blood relative sought his life.

Verse 12. He took about the same attitude toward Shimei as he did toward Saul, when he was persecuting him. (1 Sam. 26: 9-11.)

Verse 13. This was more of his contemptible conduct. *Cast dust* is rendered in the margin by, "dusted him with dust." It would remind one of the actions of children.

Verse 14. No definite spot has been designated, referred to by *there.* It means, that when David and his men became weary in their enforced travel, they refreshed themselves there. It was no great distance from Jerusalem.

Verse 15. About this time Absalom entered Jerusalem, accompanied with the people and Ahithophel. This man, it will be remembered, was one of the counselors employed in those days by kings and other dignitaries. He had been in that service to Saul; now he is serving Absalom in that capacity.

Verse 16. Hushai carried out the request of his friend, David to go to Jerusalem and offer his services to Absalom; pretending to be converted over to his side of the controversy. *God save the king.* The proper noun is not in the original, and the second word is from an original that means "live." The expression could properly be rendered, "Long live the king."

Verse 17. Absalom chided him for his desertion. If he was his friend, why did he not accompany him before?

Verse 18. The explanation was very plausible. He would wish to be peaceable, and not be against the public opinion; especially when that is in harmony with the Lord's choice. Now that the choice has been made, he was ready to line up.

Verse 19. The speech of the preceding verse was not supposed to disagree with his conduct. If he had been with David for the reasons named, by the same token he would serve Absalom, since he was a son. For the present, the explanation seemed to satisfy Absalom. The whole story sums up to the idea that he formerly believed David to have been the Lord's choice; now it is evident that a change has been decreed. The son of the former choice has taken his place, and is now in the capital city, and the people are standing by him. Therefore, Hushai, like a faithful citizen, is there, ready to serve the new king. The reader will recognize all this as a piece of shrewd strategy, conceived by David. Absalom was satisfied with the explanation and accepted the services of Hushai as personal adviser, the same as Ahithophel.

Verses 20-22. Ahithophel was asked to give advice against David. The purpose was to make it evident to the people that a breach had come between Absalom and his father. The reason for wanting such an impression was that, since Absalom was then in actual possession of the capital, and no prospect of serving both him and his father, it would be wise to stick with the victor. The first piece of advice was to be an act of disrespect for David, in being intimate with his concubines. The tent was set up on the roof of the house. Such places were commonly used, but not for the purposes of housing. This tent, therefore, would attract attention and provoke inquiry. The answer would be given, and the people all would see the tent and know for what it was used. That is the meaning of the words, "in the sight of this sun," (Ch. 12: 11), and *in the sight of all Israel* here.

Verse 23. The counsel of Ahithophel was regarded as reliable by all the people of those days, including David and Absalom. *Oracle of God* means, Word of God. Since God frequently used these counselors, their opinion was not far from the truth.

2 SAMUEL 17

Verse 1. We should keep in mind that two recognized counselors, Hushai and Ahithophel, were in the service of Absalom. Each was regarded as trustworthy. Consequently, each will be consulted. The first to advise was Ahithophel, and he asked for an army of twelve thousand chosen men.

Verse 2. With this force he would attack David while weak and unprepared for resistance, and smite the king only.

Verse 3. *Bring back* all the people did not mean he would have the people in a body with him. But it would bring all the people over to Absalom's side when they saw their former king, David, had been killed. The defeat of David would be equivalent to the personal capture of all the people.

Verses 4, 5. The proposal was agreeable to Absalom and the leading men of the people. However, as there were two personal counselors, the suggestion was taken under advisement, and consultation to be had with the other.

Verse 6, 7. Hushai was very respectful toward Ahithophel. He did not belittle his advice as not having any merit; only that it was not good *at this time*. We recall that the specific purpose David had in sending him into the service of Absalom was to counteract the counsel of Ahithophel. (Ch. 15: 34.) That service was to be accomplished soon. If this counsel of Ahithophel be adopted it would leave Absalom out of the battle. He would still be safe in his fortified city, while his men would be taking all the risks of the encounter. That would be unfortunate since he, personally, was chiefly responsible for the whole conspiracy.

Verses 8-10. All that Hushai said in this paragraph was true in theory. But some of the facts were beside the issue. Regardless of all consideration of David's shrewdness in evading an army, and of his spirit of desperation, the speech was intended as a foundation for his main objective which follows.

Verse 11. This comprises the vital difference between the counsel of Hushai and Ahithophel. The latter would have left Absalom, the "public enemy number 1," in a safe place, and endangered David only, the rightful ruler. The former would expose this conspirator to the dangers of war, while the king would be in some safe place, according to the last clause of verse 8.

Verse 12. This action of the great crowd was to be in the nature of a dragnet. Although David would be in hiding, this would find him. *As the dew falleth on the ground*. This referred to the general but unheralded manner of the approach of the army.

Verse 13. The same dragnet could find him if he were hiding in some city. Without taking the time and effort to search out all the lurking places possible in the city, such a vast army could make a wholesale destruction which would be sure to include him.

Verse 14. There was a general approval of the counsel of Hushai. *Good counsel of Ahithophel* means it would have been good for Absalom. That is why God took a hand in the matter and had it counteracted by the advice of Hushai.

Verse 15. The priests were the proper ones to contact for information for the lawful ruler. This also was according to instructions of David to Hushai. (Ch. 15: 35, 36.)

Verse 16. Having advised Absalom to go out with a throng of people, he sent word of warning to David to move on out of the endangered territory.

Verse 17. Jonathan and Ahimaaz, sons of the priests, were to be the messengers for the priests, and were given the duty of taking the warning of Hushai to David. But they had been hiding by En-rogel, a spring not far from Jerusalem. It was necessary, therefore, that some neutral person take the message to them, and they to David. The person who did that was called a *wench*. That is from SHIPHCHAH and defined by Strong, "a female slave (as a member of the household)"

Verse 18. Before they reached David, the messengers were seen by a lad, who told Absalom. That made it necessary for them to seek hiding, as Absalom went out after them. They came to Bahurim, a village near Jerusalem. There they found a friendly family who took them in. This *well* is from a word that means pit. The *court* was a yard round the house, forming part of the premises.

Verse 19. *The thing was not known* means the camouflage had the desired effect.

Verse 20. This is another instance of falsehood that is recorded without criticism by the writer. Again, we should remember the condition was a military one; and in such cases it is the common practice to deceive the enemy. After all, what is called strategy is usually the same as camouflage; and that is falsehood acted out.

Verse 21. As soon as the danger was past, the messengers came out of the pit and resumed their journey. Coming to David, they delivered the warning sent by the priests. *Water*, of course, meant the Jordan River.

Verse 22. The "promised land," as we have seen, (Gen. 15: 18), included all the territory east as far as the Euphrates. But the Jordan was the eastern border of Canaan, which was the principal portion of the whole territory as pertained to the descendants of Abraham. By passing over Jordan, therefore, David practically fled from his dominions. In royal language, such an act is regarded as abandoning, for the present, one's territory to the invader.

Verse 23. *Order* is from TSAVAH, and one word in Strong's definition is, "enjoin." That agrees with the rendering in the margin which says, "Gave charge concerning his house." *Hanged* is from CHANAQ and defined in part, "to choke oneself to death."—Strong. It is the word for *strangled* in Nahum 2: 12. Ahithophel could not have expected any material gain had his counsel been followed. We must conclude, therefore, that his act was prompted by disappointed pride; and it verifies Proverbs 16: 18.

Verse 24. Absalom and all the men of war crossed over Jordan in pursuit of David, who had taken refuge in Mahanaim.

Verse 25. *Instead of Joab* does not mean that Absalom set him aside in favor of Amasa. Chapter 18: 2 shows that David had Joab with him. So the phrase means that Amasa was made captain, since Joab was not with the forces of Absalom.

Verse 26. Gilead was a term that included a considerable territory east of the Jordan and reaching to the Arabian desert; from Bashan on the north to the land of Moab on the south. It is referred to also by the terms "Mount Gilead," (Gen. 31: 25), and "the land of Gilead," (Num. 32: 1). In this territory both David and Absalom were stationed at the time of our story.

Verses 27-29. This paragraph describes the reception given David when he fled to Mahanaim. It proved the loyalty of those inhabitants to the throne of the rightful ruler.

2 SAMUEL 18

Verse 1. David was a systematic warrior; he now organized his forces for the conflict he knew was on hands.

Verse 2. Like a good organizer, David put his forces into three groups,

2 Samuel 18: 3-16

with a commander over each. They were to be superior to the *captains* mentioned in verse 1. He proposed, also, to go in person into the field of battle. That showed his personal valor, but it would have been contrary to the plan counseled by Hushai. (Ch. 17: 15, 16.)

Verse 3. The people thought that prudence was better than valor, and protested his proposal. *Worth ten thousand* of us meant from a military standpoint. *Succor us out of the city* means that he could help them better by sending reinforcements from the city, while they were fighting for him on the outside.

Verse 4. David agreed to the advice of his people; we are sure the Lord had a hand in it. Mahanaim was a walled city, which means one fortified, or else he would not have sought refuge there. He stood at the gate and personally oversaw the filing out of the forces to enter the field of battle.

Verse 5. The charge that David gave concerning Absalom was overheard by the people. It could not have added any special incentive for action to hear such a speech from their king, for whose sake mainly they were to fight. All people know that the leader of a conspiracy is justly chargeable with the situation, and should not be shown any favor. The fact, therefore, that they fought faithfully, in spite of the "setback," proved the sturdy character of the soldiers. Such an injunction can be understood only on the basis of paternal love for a child, though one who is personally unworthy.

Verse 6. *Wood of Ephraim.* We know that the general territory of Ephraim was all west of the Jordan, while this battle was fought east of it. Young explains it thus: "Perhaps it was so named from the tribe of Ephraim's being the chief sufferers in this battle. See also Judges 12: 4."

Verses 7, 8. *Wood* is from YAAR and part of Strong's definition is, "a copse of bushes; hence a forest." Moffatt renders the word, "jungle." *Devoured* is from AKAL and defined, "A primitive root; to eat (literally or figuratively)" —Strong. The meaning is clear. It was such a dense forest, with undergrowth like a jungle, that it contributed to the defeat of the forces, by hindering their movements.

Verse 9. Absalom now came into the immediate presence of David's forces.

It was natural that the action became more heated. In the encounter the mule on which Absalom was riding plunged into the bushy growth of a great oak tree. The beast was in a forward movement; and when Absalom's head became entangled in the thick growth of the tree it held him fast, while the beast went out from under him.

Verse 10. *Hanged.* This term usually is thought to mean that one has been killed; but Strong uses the word "suspend" in his definition of the original. That agrees with the following verses that show he was not dead.

Verse 11. Joab's attitude was more consistent with all the situation than was David's. This was being conducted by authority of the king, and Absalom was the ringleader of the conspiracy. It was foolish and inconsistent, therefore, to show any military leniency to him.

Verse 12. The speech of this man might be taken to mean that he was as solely influenced by sentiment for David. The next verse, however, will show that he was not.

Verse 13. *Falsehood* is from an original word that means, being untrue; and as used in this case it meant he would not be true to his own interests had he slain Absalom. David had given charge that Absalom was to be spared. Hence, if the man had taken advantage of Absalom's predicament, he would have endangered his own life. This shows his real motive in sparing him. He imagined that Joab also would have criticized him. That idea, however, was a mistake.

Verse 14. *I may not tarry thus with thee.* This means Joab did not have any time to waste on this man. He seemed provoked because a good opportunity had been let pass. He then thrust three darts into the body of Absalom while it was suspended in the tree.

Verse 15. The darts used by Joab did not produce instant death. Then ten attendants gathered round the wounded man, still alive, and hanging in the tree. *Smote* is from a word that means to strike, and the effects were to complete the attack made by Joab. That is why the verse concludes with the words *slew him.*

Verse 16. The death of the leader put an end to the conspiracy. Joab, therefore, signalled to his men to return from the chase.

Verse 17. David never saw the face of Absalom after he left Jerusalem with the pretended purpose of paying his vow. (Ch. 15: 7-9.) The men with Joab buried Absalom in the jungle where he died. They piled stones over his grave. The same was done in the case of Achan. (Josh. 7: 26.) It was a custom of those days, expressive of contempt.

Verse 18. Ch. 14: 27 shows that Absalom had sons. This statement, therefore, means either that the pillar was erected before the birth of any of them, or, he was doubtful of their being interested enough to attend to it.

Verse 19. Ahimaaz was one of the men who had been sent by the priests to warn David of danger. It was natural for him to think the death of Absalom, the arch enemy, would be good news.

Verse 20. Joab wished to observe a "period of mourning" over the death of a prominent man; prominent because of being the king's son. He knew the spirit of David, and suspected what would be his reaction at the news. For that reason he would defer the report a day. But some of his purpose is hard to understand. He told Ahimaaz not to go, and immediately told another to go. Doubtless he saw the eagerness with which Ahimaaz proposed telling David of the death of his son, and thought it well to slow him down.

Verse 21. Cushi was an Ethiopian in attendance on Joab. He was told to go and report what he had seen.

Verse 22. Ahimaaz repeated his request, only that he might run *after* Cushi. The first reason Joab gave against his going could not be used again, seeing he had just let the Cushite go; so another must be given. This time he said he did not have any tidings *ready*. If the Cushite reaches David first, which would occur if he made the same speed as made by Ahimaaz, he would tell the news. That would leave no news for him.

Verse 23. Notwithstanding, Ahimaaz insisted on being permitted to go. As the Cushite had the "start," Joab gave permission for him to go. He took another route and outran the Cushite.

Verses 24, 25. David was sitting between the gates, awaiting any report that might be brought. For a better view, the watchman went to the top of the wall. He informed the king that a man was running, and alone. That indicated he was a messenger.

Verse 26. Seeing another man running alone, the watchman shouted word to the porter, which was the gatekeeper, and he relayed it to David. His comment was that this man also was a messenger, as he was alone and running.

Verse 27. Ahimaaz was a good man, as David commented. It was true, also, that he was bringing good tidings. However, David wished to have the news good from the military standpoint, yet leave his beloved son unharmed.

Verses 28, 29. Ahimaaz evidently "saw the point" in the actions of Joab, and decided he would not break the news too suddenly. *All is well* was true, considering the main objective of the battle; the enemies had been overthrown. Upon specific inquiry about Absalom, Ahimaaz gave an evasive answer. The things he said were true, but not all of the truth.

Verses 30, 31. David wished more definite information. Perhaps the next messenger will have it, so Ahimaaz was dismissed. Cushi gave about the same general report as that of Ahimaaz. Both these messengers manifested much tenderness for David, in that they were hesitant about telling him what they felt sure would shock him.

Verse 32. The natural love of a father for even a wayward son, explains the attitude of David in this affair; otherwise we would be severe in our criticisms. A whole kingdom had been troubled with rebellion, and that, too, the kingdom of God's people. The leader of the rebellion had to be stopped or it would go on. In spite of these truths, David was concerned over the personal safety of this very conspirator. Cushi was still modest in his manner of answering the question which the king had asked for the second time. Now the truth must all be given him, only it was couched in as mild a speech as possible, to give him the facts. He had just been told (v. 28) that his enemies were slain; now he was told that his son was in the same condition.

Verse 33. This pathetic verse is a true picture of a doting father, stricken with grief over the death of a favored son. Had he let the subject remain in that status, no criticisms would be offered. He did not do that, as will be seen in the next chapter.

2 SAMUEL 19

Verses 1, 2. The grief of David was so excessive that it spread a pall of gloom over the people. The overthrow of the conspiracy, which ought to have brought a spirit of serious rejoicing, was turned into a season of general mourning by the conduct of David.

Verse 3. This undue grief of the king so intimidated the people they were made to act as if they were cowards, running from battle.

Verse 4. Joab was a mighty man, in ability and judgment. He knew the temperament of David; also, he had always wielded a strong influence over him. He, therefore, saw in his conduct, an instance of miserable, inconsistent grief.

Verses 5, 6. This rebuke was just; it exposed the shameful behaviour of David. Logically, it meant that he would not have mourned over the death of all his servants, if only his unworthy son had escaped.

Verse 7. *Speak comfortably* means to have a heart-to-heart talk; show a cheery spirit instead of so much gloom. The main objective of the battle had been attained; he should rejoice with the people, therefore, notwithstanding his personal grief. Joab asserted that if he did not do as suggested, all of the people would forsake him immediately, and leave him to pass the night alone.

Verse 8. The gate of the city was the most public place. A person seeking privacy would not go to that spot. Hence, this action was a reversal of what he had been doing, and showed he was accepting the advice of Joab, as he generally did. (Ch. 14: 19-21.) This movement recalled the people, who had fled in their fear and dismay.

Verses 9, 10. *The people* refers to those in Jerusalem and the nation in general. They were the ones who had accepted Absalom, not those now with David in the flight from the capital. Those folks now realized their mistake, and wished for the return of their rightful ruler. However, as it frequently occurs, each man looked to another for action in a matter that was a mutual duty. Such is the significance of the last sentence of this paragraph.

Verses 11, 12. This clamor came to the ears of David, which prompted him to take some action. But, although he was entitled to the throne, he was not disposed to attempt returning until the way was opened by those stationed near the capital. The priests had remained in the city as sentinels, ready to furnish information for David as occasion permitted. Now it was proper that they contact the elders, those of age and influence, and chide them for not being the most forward in bringing the king home.

Verse 13. Amasa was related to David by blood. (Ch. 17: 25; 1 Chr. 2: 15, 16.) He had served Absalom in the rebellion. Now that the rebellion had been put down, David was ready to "forgive and forget," and make him the captain of the army in place of Joab. He had two motives for this; one was in reprisal against Joab for personally smiting Absalom; the other, to induce him to use his influence in bringing the lawful king home.

Verse 14. Amasa *bowed the heart*, which means he inclined the minds of the men of Judah in favor of the request of David. They sent word, therefore, for the king and all his servants to return.

Verse 15. Leaving Mahanaim, where he had been taking refuge since fleeing his throne (Ch. 17: 24), David began his return and came to the Jordan, opposite Gilgal. To this place the representatives of Judah came in order to conduct him respectfully over.

Verse 16. Shimei was the man who cursed David (Ch. 16: 5, etc.) when he was fleeing. The fortunes have turned and he was eager to restore himself to the favor of the king. He hasted, therefore, to go forth to meet him.

Verse 17. To make a show of good faith, Shimei influenced Ziba, a former servant of Saul, with a thousand men, to come with him on this journey of recognition for the returning monarch.

Verse 18. *Ferry boat* is from ABARAH and defined, "a crossing-place." — Strong. There was no boat, according to the original, but a ford, that permitted a crossing on foot. The men mentioned in the preceding verse went over Jordan at this place to escort David and his group. As the king reached the western bank of Jordan, Shimei prostrated himself before him.

Verses 19, 20. There was no attempt at excuse for his past conduct; he frankly admitted his sin. As a token of the fervor of his repentance he was foremost in going to meet the king. *House of Joseph.* Chapter 16: 5 shows he was of the tribe of Benjamin. The phrase, therefore, was used figuratively of the people of Israel, and in respect for the cherished memory of Joseph. See Ex. 1: 8; Ps. 80 1; Amos 6: 6; Zech. 10: 6.

Verse 21. Abishai recalled the conduct of Shimei and doubtless was suspicious as to the sincerity of his confession. His suggestion was to slay him *for this*, which meant his previous action of contempt.

Verse 22. *What have I to do with you* means, "I hardly know what to do with you." David, however, did not offer any logical reason for his rebuke of Abishai; he only mentioned that he was again *king over Israel*. That is, he was so joyful over his return to favor of the people that he felt gracious unto all, regardless of their merit.

Verse 23. This verse is in agreement with the sentiment of the preceding one. However, in the time to come, when David's sense of justice moved him, he took the same view of Shimei's guilt as expressed by Abishai. (1 Ki. 2: 8, 9.)

Verses 24-28. In connection with this paragraph, the reader is requested to see Ch. 16: 1-4, and comments. The story of Mephibosheth given in this paragraph at hand seems plausible; and David did not wholly disbelieve it. However, he was just at the moment more interested in the good turn of affairs in his kingdom, than in some personal grievance. He decided on what could be termed a compromise, named in the following verse.

Verse 29. David was tired of the controversy between Mephibosheth and Ziba; besides, he was in a conciliatory frame of mind over his return to favor, and disposed to favor everybody. He therefore told the two men to divide the inheritance that was at first allotted to Ziba.

Verse 30. Mephibosheth was not interested in the land. To be restored to the favor of the king, and to know that the peace also had come to the kingdom, was enough to make him happy.

Verses 31, 32. When David and his men took refuge in Mahanaim, they had need of material support; Barzillai furnished it. Now that David was able to leave the place in peace, he came down to "see him off" in good will.

Verse 33. David was grateful for his former support, and offered to "return the favor" by taking him to Jerusalem to be a royal guest.

Verses 34-37. Barzillai had not come for the purpose of being repaid. Besides, he was so old and infirm that he could not enjoy such luxuries were he to go. Not only so, but he would be a burden on David without being of any benefit; for all these reasons he respectfully declined the offer. He did not want to appear unappreciative of his offered kindness, so made the suggestion that Chimham go. This was probably a son of Barzillai (1 Ki. 2: 7), and one who took the contributions of necessities to David.

Verse 38. David accepted the offer and agreed to give kindness to Chimham, according to whatever Barzillai would request.

Verse 39. After this friendly conversation, which took place at the western shore of the Jordan, David kissed Barzillai good-by and he returned to his home.

Verse 40. Judah and Israel are mentioned as separate groups in this and some following verses. See 1 Samuel 11: 8 for comments.

Verse 41. Envy is bitter sentiment. Now that David was returning in triumph from exile, the group that had a direct hand in escorting him was envied by the other.

Verse 42. The capital was Jerusalem and in possession of Judah. The king, also, was of the tribe of Judah. It was a matter of course, that these people would furnish the escort. They intimated that the other group suspected them of "graft" as a motive for their activity, which they specifically denied.

Verse 43. *Ten parts*. In addition to the comments at 1 Sam. 11: 8, the reader may see 1 Ki. 11: 31 which reveals the number of tribes that was grouped as Israel. The point of the argument in the present instance is at the fact of having the majority. That has always been a popular argument; but it is a misleading one. The majority was wrong in the days of the flood (Gen. 6: 8); and in Sodom (Gen. 18: 32); and will be wrong at the day of judgment. (Matt. 7: 13, 14.) *Despise* means to belittle or slight. It should be noted, also, that it was advice these people wished to give, not action. Frequently, those who are the most eager to give advice are the least willing to do anything. *Fiercer* is from QASHAH, and defined by Strong,

"A primitive root; properly to be dense, i. e. tough or severe." Young defines it "sharper," and Moffatt gives "heated." The thought is, that the men of Judah being in the right, logically their words had more point.

2 SAMUEL 20

Verses 1, 2. There *happened* or chanced to be, etc. Belial is a descriptive word in the Old Testament, meaning very base and wicked. The term *Israel* was not used in this place as it was in Ch. 19: 40. It referred to the nation as a whole as opposed to David's family personally. But since he was of the tribe of Judah, all the other tribes followed in the revolt, headed by this wicked man. His movement, though extensive at the first, was soon put down. (v. 22.)

Verse 3. Chapter 16: 22 shows the unfaithfulness of these concubines. That circumstance was a fulfillment of a prediction (Ch. 12: 11), and was a punishment on David for his sin with Bath-sheba. If God uses an agency to carry out a penalty against an individual, he also will penalize that agency for any unrighteous motive it may manifest in the affair. *In ward* means they were put under guard, not necessarily in a guardhouse. *Went not in unto them* means he did not have intimate relations with them. They had been unfaithful to him and he punished them in this manner. *Living in widowhood* means they were denied the privileges of concubines (equivalant to those of wives, morally), and thus compelled to live as widows.

Verse 4. David gave orders to Amasa, looking to the putting down of the rebellion of Sheba. He was charged with the work, which was in harmony with the promise made him (Ch. 19: 13). The limit set for his commission was three days.

Verse 5. The time limit expired but Amasa did not return.

Verse 6. Since Amasa did not appear, David became concerned about the activity of Sheba. Abishai was then instructed to take forces, composed of the servants of the king, and go to intercept the conspirator.

Verse 7. It should be remembered that Joab had been replaced by Amasa. Abishai was Joab's brother, and when this order was given to him, the men of Joab overheard, and went out voluntarily to join in the chase.

Verse 8. They overtook Amasa at Gibeon. Joab had armed himself with a sword; it was concealed about his garments, with the intent to use it at a proper opportunity. The sword, however, accidentally fell out and was exposed to Amasa. That made it necessary to act at once, but some pretense was necessary for getting near him.

Verse 9. Joab addressed Amasa as *brother*, which was a term with wide meaning, including anyone supposed to be a friend. Taking Amasa by the beard was a gesture of friendliness, but done to bring his face near enough to kiss. The special motive Joab had was to prevent him from seeing the sword in his left hand.

Verse 10. *Fifth rib* means the abdomen. See Ch. 2: 23 for comments on this term. *Struck him not again means* he was so skilful with the sword that one stroke was fatal. Jealousy over being supplanted by Amasa doubtless was the motive for the deed. With the rival out of the way, the two brothers pursued after Sheba.

Verse 11. The murder of Amasa left Joab in his former position as leader over the soldiers; it also gave boldness to his friends, hence the call was made for men to "take their stand," which was the significance of coupling the names of David and Joab. Naturally, if they stand with them, they will follow after Joab in the present conflict.

Verses 12, 13. A man dying from a fatal wound would be a gruesome sight, but the curiosity of human beings is so great that such a scene was enough to halt a pursuit after a conspirator. Seeing this, the man removed Amasa out of sight, and the people resumed their trailing after Joab, to capture Sheba.

Verse 14. He was not received as generally as expected, for he had to go from place to place, while the citizens pursued him.

Verse 15. Sheba took refuge in Abel, a city in northern Palestine. Joab brought his forces and prepared to lay siege. The *bank* was a ridge of earth, and it *stood in the trench*, which means it was as high as the outer wall of the city, the word *trench* meaning wall. From this mound of earth, Joab and his men began battering the wall with the hope of undermining it.

Verses 16, 17. There was a prudent woman in the city who asked for the privilege of speaking to Joab; it was granted her.

Verse 18. The woman then referred to some popular practice of the people seeking advice in cases of dispute; they would come to this city now being besieged by Joab's forces. By this speech she implied that it would still be well for him to listen to counsel offered to him here.

Verse 19. The woman next complained that she, *a mother in Israel*, was about to be destroyed with the city, although she was peaceable. *Inheritance of the Lord* means that the city had been given to the people by the Lord, and it should not now be destroyed without cause.

Verses 20, 21. Joab denied any intention of a general destruction. He explained that he sought only the man now taking refuge in the city, who had rebelled against the king. Assurance was given her that if this man were delivered up, the siege would be lifted. The woman promised that the man's head would be thrown over the wall. She knew that some time would be necessary for obtaining action from the citizens, therefore she set the date for the deliverance of the man wanted to be on the morrow.

Verse 22. The simple statement that the woman went unto the people in her wisdom is explained by the thing that immediately happened. The head of Sheba was thrown over to Joab, and he, true to his promise, withdrew with his forces from the city and returned to Jerusalem.

Verses 23-26. This paragraph is a repetition of Ch. 8: 16-18, there designated in the comments, "David's cabinet." Such an arrangement is necessary for good government. The *host* means the military, and Joab had that charge. The Cherethites and Pelethites formed the bodyguard for the king. *Tribute* is from MIC and defined, "properly a burden (as causing to faint), i. e. a tax in the form of forced labor."—Strong. It referred to the matter of exacting manual labor from men taken in war, and others falling into servitude under the king. Adoram had charge of the bureau. The *recorder* and the *scribe* had work much alike. About all the difference was, the former was more like that of a secretary, handling the transient and personal items pertaining to the king, while the latter had to do with the more permanent records for the kingdom. Zadok and Abiathar were officers in the religious activities about the altar and tabernacle. *Chief ruler*. The second word is not in the original. The first is from KOHEN and defined, "literally one officiating, a priest; also (by courtesy) an acting priest (although a layman)."—Strong. The regular priests, Zadok and Abiathar, are already named in this paragraph. We therefore would understand this last named man to have been a sort of valet to the king. The mixed group named in this paragraph is to be understood from the nature of the Mosaic system; it was one that combined civil and religious government.

2 SAMUEL 21

Verse 1. This does not teach that an innocent son might be punished for the sins of his father. Ex. 20: 5 clearly states that the children who hate the Lord will be punished; that they will be punished with similar treatment to that having been imposed on their wicked father. Saul had murdered the Gibeonites, thus breaking the oath that Joshua had made with them. Saul was dead, but this verse describes his descendants as a *bloody house*. We do not have the particulars of their actions; it is enough to know the Lord said these descendants composed a *bloody house*. This connected them in guilt with their fathers, and made them the victims of just vengeance of God.

Verse 2. Joshua 9 gives account of the league formed with the Gibeonites. It was obtained by fraud, but, having been made, the children of Israel were bound by it. Saul disregarded it and thought to show his zeal for God's people by slaying the Gibeonites. Such an act was counted illegal by the Lord.

Verse 3. David offered to make amends for the wrong done, and asked the Gibeonites to state their demands.

Verses 4-6. They said they did not require the death of *any man in Israel*. Since the sons of Saul were Israelites, we would question the meaning of their expression. The comments on v. 1 will help to explain. Since innocent persons should not be punished for the sins of others, it would not be just to select victims from the general public of the Israelites; they should be taken from the descendants of Saul since they were a *bloody house*.

Verse 7. Oaths were regarded sacred, and for that reason David spared Mephibosheth from the punishment. He was a son of Jonathan and thus of the second generation from Saul; the decree in Ex. 20: 5 reached to the fourth. This man, therefore, was a part of the *bloody house* of Saul, but escaped the penalty about to be inflicted, through the oath made with Jonathan.

Verse 8. Proper nouns were sometimes used indefinitely in old times. In 1 Samuel 18: 17-19 we may see that Merab, not Michal, was the mother of these five sons. But she had been suggested as a substitute for Michal to become the wife of David; that doubtless accounts for the exchange of names in this verse. The fact that seems clear is, that all of the seven (completeness) selected as victims of the punishment were grandsons of Saul.

Verse 9. If these men were hanged, why say they *fell?* The word has a figurative as well as literal meaning. Deut. 21: 23 gives the law requiring that dead bodies be taken down from the tree of execution on the day of death. When that was done, these men were represented as having fallen to the ground. This execution took place in the beginning of barley harvest, which came in the spring.

Verse 10. The law stipulated that the burial of a man dying on a tree must take place the same day; but the decree was not concerned especially with the fact of the burial; the main thing was that his body must not remain on the tree over night. The bodies of these men when taken down from the trees were not buried; they were laid on the ground, exposed to view. The mother of two of them, prompted by parental love, watched over them. With only some sackcloth for bedding, and the rock for a bedstead, she kept night-and-day vigil, being alert to keep the birds and beasts from making food of them. The barley harvest came in the spring months. Rainfall was seasonal in Palestine, the "early rain" coming in the fall and the "latter rain" in the spring. Between these rainy seasons there were several months of dry weather. Rizpah kept up her watch for all of this period. It is difficult to describe fully such an exhibition of devotion to one's offspring, and this mother has been celebrated in history and song.

Verse 11. This verse merely states that David learned of the deed of Rizpah; it does not give us any date. Between it and the next verse there must have been a considerable space of time, for v. 10 declares that Rizpah continued her watch until the rain began to fall, which was in the end of the season.

Verses 12-14. Sometime in the autumn David got the bones of Saul and Jonathan, together with those of the men who had been hanged, and buried them in the family sepulchre. After this, God reversed the stricken condition of the land.

Verses 15-22. This paragraph covers some of David's military exploits at various times. *War again, after this,* and such like expressions, found strewn in the passage, shows the writer was concerned more with the outstanding nature of some of the deeds than with the particular dates. David was unafraid of the men of giant proportions when they were arrayed against the Lord's army. His own men plead with him (v. 17) not to risk his life; that his guidance for the soldiers was of more value than the death of a few individual ruffians. He had, before this, been appealed to along this line. (Ch. 18: 3.)

2 SAMUEL 22

Verse 1. This chapter is practically the same as Psalms 18. A brief comment will be made at that place, but the chapter will be considered in detail here since the occasions of its composition are so near in date to that now connected with the history. David's victories over Saul, his personal and official enemy, together with those over his enemies in general, gave the incentive for this *song* or psalm.

Verse 2. Most of the terms used in this chapter pertain to war and other conditions of danger. Some of them are figurative and others literal. A rock signifies a solid basis; a fortress is a protected hiding place; and a deliverer is one who helps another escape his enemy. David ascribes all these to the Lord.

Verse 3. With such a Being for a rock he would trust the keeping of his interests. A shield is part of the protective armor of a soldier. *Horn* in figurative language means power. *High tower* refers to the places used in warfare for protection, also for look-out purposes.

Verse 4. Salvation will come from God if he is called upon; faith in him is necessary to obtain his help.

Verse 5. David had not died, but the danger of death had beset him in waves. *Ungodly* is from the word elsewhere rendered Belial in the Old Testament.

Verse 6. *Sorrows* is from a word that means literally a rope or strong cord. *Prevented* means to precede. *Hell* is from SHEOL and is rendered grave, hell, pit. The verse means that wherever David turned his attention he faced threat of violent death.

Verse 7. When human help seems useless it is well to call on the Lord. David did so and God heard him *out of his temple*. The last word is from an original that means palace. The thought is that God's place of abode is not too high nor far away to be reached by the prayers of the righteous.

Verse 8. The mighty voice of Jehovah overcame the attacks of the wicked.

Verse 9. As fire is used in destroying objectionable things, so God's power over sinful forces is compared to that element.

Verse 10. All the parts of the universe are subject to the might of God. He is able to overcome all forces of darkness.

Verse 11. A *cherub* is an imaginary creature of exalted flight; the wind would ordinarily be an element outside the power of man. But God is able to surmount all obstacles and bring them under his control.

Verse 12. *Pavilions* means a housing place, and God is able to sujugate the works of darkness to his use; also, the waters of oppression are made subject to God.

Verse 13. *Coals* of fire would indicate more life than a mere flame or flash. The force of God's brightness is compared to coals.

Verse 14. The elements of mighty storms are used to illustrate the power of God's voice.

Verse 15. The pronoun *them* refers to the various evil beings and things already mentioned in this chapter. God's figurative arrows had scattered these evil forces.

Verse 16. God's superiority over all things else is the thought most prominent in this verse. The channels or bed of the sea, and the foundations or strength of the world's inhabitants, were tamed by the Lord's rebuke. *Nostrils* is rendered "anger" in the margin, and the lexicon agrees. It means the things referred to are brought into subjection by the Lord's (righteous) anger.

Verse 17. *Waters* in figurative language means the floods of tribulations. God delivered David from such waters.

Verse 18. Human strength cannot endure the hatred of wicked enemies; but the help from the Lord will deliver the righteous from all evil.

Verse 19. These evil forces prevented David in that they tried to interfere with his service to God. This was done at a time of calamity, just when he needed help the most; the Lord gave him that help.

Verse 20. *Large place* refers to the bountifulness of the Lord's provisions. This idea is given much attention in the New Testament. See 1 Pe. 1: 2; 4: 10; Jude 2.

Verses 21, 22. David does not mean to boast of his goodness. The thought is that God would not have favored him had he not been a righteous man.

Verse 23. *Judgments* and *statutes*. There is not much practical difference in the meaning of these words, but there is a technical distinction. The first is from MISHPAT and defined, "properly a verdict (favorable or unfavorable) pronounced judicially, especially a sentence or formal decree (human or divine law, individual or collective), including the act, the place, the suit, the crime, and the penalty."—Strong. The second is from CHOQ and defined, "An enactment; hence an appointment (of time, space, quantity, labor or usage)."—Strong. To sum up, the first means laws brought about by some emergency or specific circumstance, while the second means those laws that were decreed regardless of special conditions.

Verses 24, 25. See the comments at verses 21, 22.

Verse 26. It is literally true that God is merciful to only those who are merciful to others. See Matt. 5; 7. God is upright, however, at all times, whether man is or not. But a wicked man will regard him in an unfavorable light, because he is judging others by himself.

Verse 27. This verse is explained by the closing sentence of preceding paragraph.

Verse 28. *Save* and *upon* are used as opposites. The afflicted will be favored of God, but the haughty will receive the frown of his eyes.

Verse 29. In figurative language a lamp refers to enlightenment, and guidance through the darkness of human uncertainty.

Verse 30. David was a man of war and frequently encountered the troops of the enemy. He also had to attack the cities that were walled against him. Such experiences gave him the basis for figurative reference to God's help as a faithful ally.

Verse 31. The special thought here is the condition on which God will help man. It is that he put his trust in the Lord.

Verse 32. The heathen worshipped many gods, but with David there was but one and that was the *Lord*, a word which Strong defines, "self-Existent or Eternal." The gods of the heathen were artificial, or were demons, and neither existed by their own power.

Verse 33. The margin gives "riddeth" for *maketh*. It means that, by ridding the pathway of life of unsurmountable barriers, it makes it perfect.

Verse 34. The hind is an animal very swift of feet. David means he was able to outrun his enemies, and mount to places above them.

Verse 35. The success which David had in war was due to the help of God. The enemies of him were those of God, hence the divine assistance was given.

Verse 36. *Gentleness* is from a word meaning condescension. When God looked down in pity on David, it caused him to react favorably and reach upward toward the higher plane of life. Such a life constitutes true greatness.

Verse 37. *Enlarge* means to broaden, and *steps* means the place for walking. The verse means that God made plenty of room for David to walk, that he might not slip.

Verses 38-40. The outstanding strain running through this chapter, as well as through much of David's writing, is his success in battle. That included both his personal and official enemies. It is noteworthy that he always ascribed it to the Lord.

Verse 41. Most warfare in ancient times was with the sword; in the attacks it was desired to behead the antagonist. That accounts for the repeated mention of the neck.

Verse 42. God will not assist those who fight against his people; therefore, it would be in vain for them to look for help from the Lord.

Verse 43. This verse adds no new fact; it is a description of the completeness of victory over the foes.

Verse 44. In one verse David remembers his difficulties with both his own relatives (Absalom), and the heathen or people of foreign blood.

Verses 45, 46. This is the same as the closing part of preceding verse.

Verse 47. *The Lord liveth*. This is not merely an assertion that the Lord was not dead. It has the strength of continuous existence; He is self-existent. For that reason he is a suitable Being to rest on as firm and solid rock.

Verses 48, 49. Vengeance is right when *it is God that avengeth*. This is taught in Romans 12: 19.

Verse 50. *Heathen* is from GOI, and Strong defines it, "a foreign nation; hence a gentile; also (figuratively) a troop of animals, or a flight of locusts." In the A. V. it is translated by Gentile, heathen, nations, people. It thus has a wide scope of meanings, and expresses the great extent of David's power.

Verse 51. A tower was much used anciently as a shelter from an attacking army. The word, therefore, came to be used figuratively of the special help from God in times of danger. It was most evident when *his anointed* was in danger.

2 SAMUEL 23

Verse 1. Chronologically, this chapter should be the last one of the book. But we have noted other places where strict order was not observed by the inspired writers. The original for *last* does not require the strictest sense; it means the words of David that were written in the latter days of his life. *Raised up on high* refers to his place as king over God's people, and the exaltation brought to him through divine favor. *Sweet psalmist of Israel*. The second word does not mean David personally; it means psalms that were used by the children of Israel in praise of him. The thought is along the same line as the statements just preceding it. The word is from ZEMIR, and defined by "a song to be accompanied with musical instruments."—Strong. David was held in such favor by the people that they celebrated him in their sweet ("pleasant") musical exercises.

Verse 2. This verse means that David spoke by inspiration.

Verse 3. *Must be* should be understood to mean that David believed God to be the kind of ruler described. We note that God is also designated a rock. It means the government for Israel was on a firm foundation.

Verse 4. A cloudless day following a refreshing rain is used to compare the glory of God.

Verse 5. The meaning of this verse is a little dim on account of the indirect form of language. David considers his house is secure through the favor of God, although it would not have been so without divine help.

Verse 6. *Belial* means very wicked characters, and such had long been a threat to the peace of David. The Lord had enabled him to overcome all such persons, since human power could not have done so.

Verse 7. In the previous verse the evil characters were likened to thorns. To cast such things into the fire would require use of a staff or iron. The assistance given by the Lord constituted that implement.

Verse 8. David was a man of great talents and accomplished much in his lifetime. But he depended not only on God for assurance of success; he brought into his service the men of outstanding ability. For a reason not given, the men were grouped in threes, and several verses are devoted to naming these trios. Not all of the three will be named, but the principal man will be, and in some cases the unusual deed of the same will be stated. In the present one, the slaying of 800 men was the feat.

Verses 9, 10. *Hand clave unto the sword*. This was because he had been so constantly engaged with the use of it that a sort of cramp siezed it and resisted the attempt to open it to release the weapon. After he had slain the vast horde of Philistines, the people reaped the results by coming on and taking the spoil.

Verses 11, 12. *Lentiles* were a podded vegetable like the modern beans; they were very desirable food. The Philistines planned to get the product on the ground and thus deprive the Israelites of their rights, who fled on account of the great number of the foe. Shammah, by the help of the Lord, defeated the purpose of the Philistines.

Verses 13, 14. According to the marginal reading, three men were over thirty. These verses are another instance of the unchronological manner of some parts of the Bible. In 1 Sam. 22: 1 we may read of this cave as being a hiding place for David. It is here given along with a general account of his life. The *hold* evidently was near Bethlehem from the following verse.

Verses 15, 16. David called for water to drink from the well near Bethlehem. To get it, the Philistines would have to be encountered, since they had possession of the well. The three men mentioned in verse 13 undertook the feat, and secured the water. But instead of drinking it, David poured it on the ground.

Verse 17. It is difficult to understand David's actions here. The men had already taken the risk of their lives and were safe back in their headquarters. The water would be no benefit if spilled on the ground. However, the circumstance serves to show us the kindly feeling David had for others.

Verses 18, 19. Differences in rank were recognized in those times as well as in the present. As a reward for his valor, Abishai was exalted above the others of the trio. He had slain three hundred men.

Verse 20. *Lionlike* is defined, "heroic." It means they were unusually strong and active. *Time of snow* is incidental, explaining why the lion was taking refuge in the pit. But the fact of the lion's being in the pit makes the encounter appear as one of extraordinary hazard.

Verse 21. A staff was a lighter weapon than a spear. The greatness of this feat was in the fact of disarming the Egyptian and slaying him with his own weapon.

Verses 22, 23. Honor to whom it is due entitled Benaiah to the present report, but he must not be thought to equal, in rank, another trio in David's service.

Verses 24-39. All of these men attached to David in service for the kingdom were outstanding. Special mention, however, should be made of Asahel because of his relation to Joab, the commander-in-chief; and of Uriah because of the affair with Bathsheba.

2 SAMUEL 24

Verse 1. One rule for interpreting language is to explain the more difficult passages by the simpler ones. This verse has an indefinite use of the pronoun *he*. Apparently, the antecedent is *Lord*, but the context will not agree with such conclusion. If the same incident can be found elsewhere in the scriptures, perhaps it will state it in more direct form. We have just that thing in 1 Chr. 21: 1. In that place we have Satan mentioned as the one who moved David to number the people. Taking the two passages together we get the thought. The antecedent of *he* is Satan, implied. Just why the pronoun is given in the present verse instead of the noun, we do not know. It is not the only place in the Bible where a pronoun is used with the noun not named. See "his" for the Lord in John 7: 38, and "he" (first instance) for God or Christ in 1 John 5: 16. The word *moved* is from CUWTH and defined, "properly to prick, i. e. (figuratively) stimulate; by implication to seduce."—Strong. The word has been rendered in the A. V. by entice, move, persuade, provoke, set on, stir up, take away. A question arising might be, why would Satan wish to persuade David to do this. The answer is to be seen in his main characteristic. In 1 Tim. 3: 6 we learn that the devil was condemned for his pride. And the connection shows the motive of David in numbering Israel was pride. And his pride over numerical strength caused him to neglect an important item of the law. See comments at verse 15.

Verse 2. *That I may know the number.* This is what reveals the motive; not that the people might be encouraged by their strength, but for David's satisfaction in knowing the number. It was somewhat like a miser counting his gold; not to see if he is able to make a purchase (he seldom does that), but just for the pleasure of knowing how much he has.

Verse 3. Joab protested the order of the king, and his use of the word *delight* confirms the comments in the preceding verse as to pride.

Verse 4. While it was against Joab's judgment to number the people, he was an obedient subject of the king, and complied with the order.

Verses 5-8. This shows the thoroughness of the work; the important parts of the territory were covered. It was not done in undue haste, either, for almost ten months was used.

Verse 9. A difference occurs between the numbers here and the corresponding account in 1 Chr. 21: 5. In some instances, differences in numbers are accounted for by the method of expressing numerals in ancient times, which was by letters. When manuscripts got worn it was easy for a transcriber (who was not an inspired man) to misread one letter for another. No attention was paid to that subject by writers and speakers in the Bible, because mere numeral discrepancies are unimportant, usually. In the case at hand, however, there is another explanation. In 1 Chr. 21: 5 mention is made of the omission of the tribes of Benjamin and Levi. Although that fact is mentioned in this place, where the number given is the larger one, it should be considered in the account in 2 Samuel, where the smaller number is given. It seems that Joab obeyed the king's order in the main, but finally became provoked at the whole project, and left off two tribes in his return. The larger account includes all the tribes; but when he came to deliver the report to David, he gave the number, less those of the two tribes.

Verse 10. True to his characteristic temperament, David repented of his wrong and made free confession.

Verses 11, 12. There was generally a national prophet in service in the times of which we are studying, such as Samuel, Nathan, Gad, etc. God sent the prophet (called a seer), to tell David the divine message. The mercy of the Lord is seen in that he leaves it somewhat to him as to what punishment is to be inflicted.

Verse 13. The three things from which he must choose are famine (shortage in natural products), be chased by the enemy (human chastisement), and pestilence (miraculous afflictions).

Verse 14. David concluded that he would rather fall into the hands of God.

Verse 15. This pestilence was in accordance with Ex. 30: 12. It will help in this place to quote Josephus who certainly understood the law of his own people. "Now King David was desirous to know how many ten thousands there were of the people, but forgot the commands of Moses, who told them beforehand, that if the multitude were numbered, they should pay half a shekel to God for every head. Accordingly, the king commanded Joab, the captain of his host, to go and number the whole multitude." Antiquities, 7-13-1. Pride is always wrong; in this case it brought a distinctly evil result. In his eagerness to gratify his feeling, David neglected to observe the requirements of the law.

Verses 16, 17. The actions of these verses were done simultaneously. God repented him of the evil (determined to *change* the conditions) because of his great mercy. He told the angel to stay his hand because the people had been punished enough. At the same time, David was moved with compassion for his people, whom he called sheep. Taking all the blame on himself, he asked God to let the punishment fall on him and his house. There is no evidence that such a change was made.

Verse 18. The actual atonement was made by the physical affliction. David was not permitted to assume that, but was required to perform a ceremonial service to God, to clear his personal guilt. He was commanded to build an altar and offer sacrifices. The place was designed for the service. David was not a priest; not even of the priestly tribe. Confusion sometimes occurs on this subject; it is supposed that a priest only could lawfully offer a sacrifice. It is true that all sacrifices offered on the brazen altar as part of the regular Mosaic system, had to be handled by the priest. But the particular ceremony that a priest only could perform, at any time or place, was the burning of incense. (1 Chr. 23: 13; 2 Chr. 26: 16-18.)

Verses 19, 20. In obedience to the prophet, David went to see Araumah. Their meeting was agreeable and the king was paid the homage due him.

Verse 21. Araumah was told what was wanted of him, and the use to be made of it. He was told that it was to be sold to David.

Verses 22, 23. Araumah was friendly toward the proposition, even offering all for David's use free of charge.

Verses 24, 25. In refusing to accept the property free, David gave us an excellent lesson on the subject of sacrifices. To offer to the Lord something that cost the giver nothing would not be a sacrifice at all. That principle is taught throughout the whole Bible. Christians are commanded to give out of their property. (1 Cor. 16: 2.) If we do not give up something of value, and that could have been used ourselves, we have not made any sacrifice. Jesus gave his life for us, and his Father before him had given him up to the sinful world, as "his unspeakable gift." (2 Cor. 9: 15.)

1 KINGS 1

Verse 1. *Stricken in years*. The first word is from the Hebrew BO, and defined, "a primitive root; to go or come (in a wide variety of applications)."—Strong. It is renedered "to come in" 1200 times in the A. V. Thus it has no meaning pertaining to the condition of the thing or person spoken of. What may follow its use must determine the condition. The term means only that David had come into years. The same could be said of Moses who was 120 at death and in his full vigor. Likewise, Abraham was at least 137 when he begat six sons. The last part of the verse was needed to tell us of David's condition. We are not told in any place why he became so infirm and lived to be only 70. (2 Sam. 5: 4.)

Verse 2. *Stand before the king* means to be always "in waiting" for his service. *Cherish* is from CAKAN and defined, "a primitive root; to be familiar with; by implication to minister to, be serviceable to, to cherish, be customary."—Strong. With such a relationship established under the practice of those times, this virgin would be permitted to occupy the same bed with the king, in order to give him the warmth of her body.

Verses 3, 4. The damsel secured ministered to the king in his infirmity. *King knew her not* means that he did not have the intimacy pertaining to husband and wife.

Verse 5. The death of David was evidently near, and another king will take his place. Haggith was one of his wives and Adonijah was her son. (2 Sam. 3: 4.) He thought he could get his father's place and prepared to do so.

Verse 6. This explains the vanity of the young man. He was a "spoiled" child; had never been denied any request of his father. He was half brother to Absalom, another son indulged to his father's sorrow. Parents should consider the evil results of being over indulgent toward their children.

Verse 7. Almost every man, though unworthy, will have a following, and Adonijah was supported in his conspiracy. He won over Joab, David's commander-in-chief, and Abiathar, one of the priests.

Verse 8. Another priest, Zadok, Nathan the prophet, and most of the important other men, remained true to David. The condition of the king, however, would seem to give Adonijah opportunity for working up sentiment for his scheme.

Verse 9. Conspirators often like to

use general gatherings as occasions for putting over their work. They give opportunity for contact with interested parties. Adonijah arranged a grand feast for the purpose and invited his father's sons, and servants.

Verse 10. Nathan the prophet, Solomon, and the men of influence, were not invited to the feast, and the reason is easy to understand. While the feast was going on, and the plot of Adonijah was in the making, there were persons active on the other side of the controversy.

Verse 11. Bath-sheba was the mother of Solomon, and he had been designated by the Lord before he was born (1 Chr. 22: 9) to be the next king. David had given this information to her. (verses 13, 17, 30.) Nathan the prophet knew about the movements of Adonijah and that David, as well as Bath-sheba, was unaware of it. As a friend to both, he came to Bath-sheba to get something done about it.

Verses 12, 13. Nathan advised her to go into the presence of the king, and make a report to him of the actions of Adonijah. She was to remind him of his promise to her, that her son was to reign next.

Verse 14. When two witnesses state the same thing, independent of each other, it strengthens the word of each. That was the plan suggested by Nathan for their plea with the king.

Verses 15, 16. Since the young woman was waiting on the king, it was not necessary for anyone else to offer such service. The appearing of Bath-sheba could not have been for that reason, so it was proper to ask why she was there.

Verses 17, 18. David was first reminded of his promise to make Solomon king. He was next told of the activities of Adonijah.

Verse 19. The aforesaid activities included his feast, and the class of persons he had invited, as well as those he had slighted.

Verses 20, 21. The plea Bath-sheba made was for David to decide who should be king next. Her point was that the selection should be made public while he was living, so that no opportunity would be open for the usurper to rob her and her son of their right.

Verses 22-25. These verses contain the same matter as the speech just made by Bath-sheba.

Verses 26, 27. There is still nothing additional in these verses. But it is well to observe the point that the rightful heir to the throne had been slighted in the invitations to the feast. Being thus treated would have been cause for complaint had there been nothing at stake but social enjoyment. Under the circumstances, however, it was significant of the conspiracy forming, that certain ones were left out.

Verse 28. Bath-sheba had retired after making her complaint and plea to the king. This was done, evidently, to give the speech of Nathan a meaning independent of hers. She was then recalled by Nathan on command of David.

Verses 29, 30. When Bath-sheba came into the presence of the king he renewed his pledge. *As the Lord liveth* means an emphatic declaration. There is no doubt about the existence of the Lord, and the assurance of the thing about to be declared is as great. The promise was repeated that had been already made, and confirmed with an oath, that Solomon should be king. Moreover, the decree was to be made known that day.

Verse 31. *Let my lord king David live for ever.* This must be taken as merely an expression of gratitude; not a serious wish. She had just been greatly concerned lest her son might not get to be king, and had gone through the entire audience with her royal husband to insure the success of her wish. But if David should live for ever, all her plans would fail.

Verse 32. David now proceeded to put into effect his guarantee to Bath-sheba, which must be done through proper persons. The importance of Nathan and Zadok is obvious. Benaiah had charge of the king's guard (2 Sam. 20: 23), hence his services were needed.

Verse 33. Smith's Bible Dictionary says: "It would appear that only kings and great men rode on mules." This accounts for the order of David in this affair. Gihon was a city near Jerusalem and a suitable place for the ceremony. Being near the capital city, there would be many witnesses to the transaction.

Verse 34. Anointing one for office was frequently done beforehand as a sort of formal announcement. (Num. 3: 3; Judg. 9: 15; 1 Sam. 9: 16; 16: 6.) The ceremony would be made more impressive and fixed by the blast of the trumpet, accompanied with the audible proclamation of the servants standing with them.

Verse 35. We should understand that David was actual king as long as he lived. But it was a practice for the reigning monarch to share the throne with the oncoming one, if such had been designated. When Solomon came from Gihon to Jerusalem, these men were directed to march after him in recognition of his appointment.

Verses 36, 37. It was fitting that Benaiah should be the spokesman at this point; he had charge of the king's bodyguard. He fully approved of the provisions made by David.

Verses 38-40. This paragraph repeats the subject matter of verses 33-35. The people added the sound of pipes (flutes) to the trumpet of the priest. *Rent* means literally, to fall apart. As this did not actually happen, we understand it to be a strong expression of the effect produced by the instruments and voices.

Verse 41. The sound mentioned in preceding verse was heard by the group at the feast of Adonijah about the time it was ended. Joab was the one who observed it and inquired for its cause.

Verse 42. At the same time, the priest's son came in. Adonijah said to him, "thou bringest good tidings." This was more in the nature of wishful thinking, for certainly the noise that was made did not all escape his ears.

Verses 43-46. The "good tidings" that Jonathan had was the report of what had been done for Solomon. Since he made a true report, and we know already what it was, no more space will be used here for it.

Verse 47. The king's servants had been among the ones invited to the feast of Adonijah. But this verse indicates that at any rate, some of them had "seen through" the conspiracy, and joined those who acclaimed Solomon as king. They did so in the presence of David, which proved their sincerity. It so pleased the king that he *bowed* upon the bed. The word is from SHACHAH and defined, "a primitive root; to depress, i. e. prostrate (especially, reflexively, in homage to royalty or God)."—Strong. It means that David acted as a subject in honor of Solomon as a king.

Verse 48. David further expressed thanks to God for having given him a son to sit on his throne. Not only was he assured that a proper successor would be forthcoming after his death, but he had seen the formalities of his appointment with his own eyes.

Verse 49. Upon hearing the report given by Jonathan, the guests that had remained with Adonijah became frightened and deserted him.

Verse 50. Adonijah then saw that his scheme had failed. When a would-be usurper is detected, the usual treatment meted out is death. This one fled to the altar for protection. Ex. 2: 28 stipulated that a murderer should be taken, from the altar even, for execution. The thought is, that such a reference to the altar would imply that for lesser wrongs it would serve as protection. In such a hope, Adonijah fled to it.

Verses 51-53. Adonijah plead for his life. Solomon granted it to him, but on condition that he "shew himself a worthy man." That would mean, of course, that he would be obedient to whatever orders were made for him.

1 KINGS 2

Verse 1. David knew that he was soon to die, so he gave a charge to Solomon, who was the son appointed by him to reign in his stead.

Verse 2. *I go the way of all the earth.* Joshua made the same statement. (Josh. 23: 14.) It means that all people of the earth are destined to die and he was to be no exception. This was written by Paul also in Heb. 9: 27. The words *shew thyself* are not in the original. *Strong* and *man* are, the second one meaning a male with individuality. The whole statement means, "be as a strong person with individuality."

Verse 3. The charge of the preceding verse could best be carried out by keeping the *charge* ("duty") of the Lord; walk in his *ways* ("course of life"); keep his *statutes* ("appointments"); and his *commandments* ("the law"); and his *judgments* ("verdicts"); and his *testimonies* ("record of witnesses"). It is further stated that all these important items of divine regulation are *written in the law of Moses.* This is another rebuke of those who seek to belittle the authority of Moses. The reward for Solomon if he observed all these things was that he would prosper wherever he went.

Verse 4. David had been promised by the Lord that if his children did right, he would always have a man to occupy his throne.

Verse 5. *Blood of war in peace.* The distinction should not be overlooked. When a nation engages in defensive warfare, the blood shed therein is lawful. But it is unlawful to shed blood under pretense of military action when not regularly enlisted as a soldier. *And in his shoes* is figurative, and means that when blood is shed unlawfully, the guilty person is walking in a wicked and bloody way of life.

Verse 6. The general charge was not to let Joab die in peace; Solomon was to use his best judgment in carrying it out.

Verse 7. Barzillai offered kindness to David when he was fleeing from Absalom. (2 Sam. 19: 31-39.) He had previously sustained him with necessities of life. In consideration for the convenience of the king, however, he declined to be a personal burden on him in accompanying him further than the river. Gratitude for his kindness prompted David to provide for his sons.

Verse 8. The words *with the sword* are added to what David said to Shimei recorded in 2 Sam. 19: 23. It explains the apparent disagreement between his two actions. These words refer to death in war; and Shimei was not drafted into military service.

Verse 9. The guilt of disrespect, however, was still on Shimei, and he was to be given capital punishment; the particular method was to be decided by Solomon.

Verse 10. *David slept with his fathers.* The second word is perverted by various materialists to favor the idea of soul-sleeping. It is from SHAKAB, and Strong defines it, "a primitive root; to lie down (for rest, sexual connection, decease or any other purpose)." In the A. V. it has been rendered by lie 98 times, lie down 30, lie with 2, sleep 48, be ravished 2, and a few others of the same class. There is not one single instance where the word is used except in reference to the body. *Fathers* is from AB and is defined by Young, "father, ancestor, source, inventor." It is defined by Strong, "a primitive word; father in a literal and immediate, or figurative and remote application." The verse means that David lay down in death the same as all his ancestors had done. See the comments at verse 2. He was buried in the "city of David." That was the part of Jerusalem called Zion. Young says it was "the southwest hill of Jerusalem, the older and higher part of the city; it is often called the city of David.". Strong refers to it, "in the sennse of conspicuousness (as a permanent capital), a mountain of Jerusalem."

Verse 11. 2 Samuel 2 gives the account of this division against David. After Saul's sympathizers were defeated, the entire nation recognized David as king and conducted him to Jerusalem.

Verse 12. To be *established* means to be made prosperous. The people were united behind the new king, and the prestige of his father's reign descended upon him.

Verse 13. We recall the attempt of Adonijah to obtain the throne by usurpation, which failed. He now thought to try another basis. To do so he must contact the mother of Solomon. In those days the movements of all persons related to the royal family were observed. This would be made more necessary by the plurality of marriages and the mixture of blood among the heirs that resulted. When Adonijah, son of one widow of David, came into the presence of Bath-sheba, another widow, and mother of the man then on the throne, it was natural to inquire for his purpose. He affirmed that he was coming peaceably, which meant that no evil intentions were prompting him.

Verses 14, 15. Adonijah falsified by saying that *all Israel set their faces on me.* He pretended next to acknowledge that his brother had obtained the kingdom and that by right from the Lord. All of this speech was in hypocrisy, and a preparation for introducing his request, the real motive for his coming to her.

Verses 16, 17. Obtaining permission to make his request known, he asked that he be given Abishag to wife. The request might seem fair and innocent. She was a virgin as David was too infirm when she came to him to live with her in the relation of husband and wife. Howbeit, as she was the latest woman to share his bed, it would place her in a close relationship with him. Adonijah was rash enough to think that if she became his wife, it would open up a way for him to seek the throne.

Verse 18. The request appeared so

reasonable that she agreed to speak to Solomon about it.

Verse 19. When she appeared in the presence of the throne, the king honored her by arising from it and doing homage to her. A queenmother was held in high regard, and Solomon provided a seat for his mother on his right hand. It was the most exalted position a person could be given except the throne.

Verse 20. *For I will not say thee nay.* Critics will charge Solomon with a breach of covenant, since we know he did deny her the request. There are two things to be considered. Bathsheba said it was a *small request.* The word in the original is defined by Strong as "unimportant," and doubtless she believed it to be so. With that sort of request in mind, Solomon would be willing to promise beforehand to grant it. Another consideration is, when a promise is obtained in ignorance of all the true state of affairs, and one that is wrong in principle, such a promise is not morally binding.

Verses 21, 22. When Bath-sheba made her petition known, Solomon saw through the scheme. He had not forgotten the first attempt of Adonijah to obtain the throne, and that it would have been by force. Now he proposed to secure it by marriage. Therefore Solomon said: "Ask for him the kingdom also." Another factor that would have lent a plausible basis for the petition was that he was older than Solomon, although seeking this young virgin for a wife.

Verse 23. *God do so to me.* This and similar expressions occurs in many places in the Bible. It means that if the thing threatened against some person is not carried out, then let the thing threatened be brought upon the one making the threat.

Verse 24. The threat alluded to in the preceding verse was that Adonijah was to die immediately. The mere asking for this woman as a wife might have been either granted or denied, and the matter dropped, had it not been that Solomen knew it to be but a scheme to get possession of the throne.

Verse 25. Benaiah had charge of the bodyguard of the king. This unit of service was in the nature of "secret service" today. It was proper, therefore, that he should be the executioner of the conspirator.

Verses 26, 27. Chapter 1: 7 shows Abiathar to have been with Adonijah in his first conspiracy. He was worthy of death, but in respect for the sacred service he had been rendering previously, Solomon spared him, for the present at least. But he would not permit him to continue in that service. Instead, he was ordered to retire to Anathoth, a city allotted to the priests for residence. In taking the priesthood from Abiathar, the inspired writer tells us that it fulfilled the prediction in 1 Sam. 2: 31-35.

Verse 28. Word came to Joab of the "purge" that Solomon was making. He had sided with Adonijah in the attempted conspiracy, and concluded that his life was in danger. He may have known of the benefit Adonijah obtained by fleeing to the altar; he tried the same thing. He had been true to David as against Absalom, but deserted him and Solomon in favor of Adonijah. That was not all of which he was guilty as will be seen below. Among the things of which he was guilty was murder, and Ex. 21: 14 required that the altar should not provide protection for a murderer.

Verse 29. When Solomon learned what Joab had done he ordered the captain of his bodyguard, Benaiah, to execute him.

Verse 30. Joab still thought the altar would serve for protection, and with that idea, said he would die there. He evidently thought the sanctity of the article of divine service would not be violated by such a turbulent act as capital execution. His proposal baffled Benaiah, so he brought word to Solomon.

Verses 31-33. While the act of conspiracy was the immediate occasion of Joab's death, it was the climax of a list of crimes. Solomon enumerated them, and the reader may refresh his knowledge of the deeds by reading 2 Sam. 3: 23; 20: 10.

Verse 34. *Fell upon him* is an expression found often in the Bible. It does not refer especially to the posture of the body. The first word is defined, "to impinge," and that means, to contact. It is sometimes used in a friendly sense, as "fell on his neck and kissed him," or in unfriendly, such as the above. The verse means he contacted Joab with the sword with enough violence to kill him. Men had their private burial place in some instances; Joab had one and it was in the open country, where he was buried.

Verse 35. The *host* was the army, over which Joab had held charge;

Benaiah was put in his place. Abithar, who had been sent home, was replaced by Zadok.

Verses 36-38. Shimei was the man who cursed David. He had apologized, however, and was promised leniency. In respect for that, Solomon allowed him to live, on condition that he confine himself to his house in Jerusalem. He agreed to the stipulation and observed it for some time.

Verses 39, 40. Shimei violated his parole after three years. Some of his servants escaped and he went in person to recover them, which took him out of Jerusalem.

Verses 41-45. Solomon called Shimei to him. He reminded him of the restrictions placed over him, and that he had agreed to them. *Knowest all the wickedness which thine heart is privy to.* The words *knowest* and *privy* are identical in the original, but the point is that Shimei not only was aware of his evil conduct, but it came from his heart, and hence it was with malice.

Verse 46. At the commandment of Solomon, Shimei was slain. The question is raised whether the account in this chapter contradicts statements in 1 Chr. 22: 8, 9. It does not, for they refer to actions altogether different. David was a man of war; Solomon never had a war. The three men slain in this chapter were executed by the officer charged with execution of those convicted of capital crimes; they were not killed as soldiers.

1 KINGS 3

Verse 1. *Affinity* loosely means any close attachment between any two or more persons. Its primary meaning, however, is defined thus by Strong: "To give (a daughter) away in marriage." Solomon had a multitude of wives in the legal sense of practice suffered in those times. But the daughter of Pharaoh was the woman he loved as a man should love his wife. She was the one whom he called "my wife" in 2 Chr. 8: 11, and is the heroine of the book, Song of Solomon. (Song, Ch. 1: 5.) *City of David* is explained at Ch. 2: 10. *Own house* means the palace, the *house of the Lord* means the temple. (Ch. 7: 1; 9: 10.) He lodged his wife in the chief part of Jerusalem until he had time to build a house for her elsewhere.

Verse 2. *High places* is a term used frequently and has a literal meaning. The first word is from BAMAH and defined, "from an unused root (meaning to be high); an elevation."—Strong. The tabernacle had been stolen by the Philistines (1 Sam. 4: 10, 11; Smith's Bible Dictionary, article Tabernacle). The people often wished to do formal service to God. In the absence of the altar, which was with the tabernacle at Gibeon, they used elevated places since they would seem to be appropriate for service to the High One. The fact of doing these services in high places was not condemned in itself. But in doing so it could be questioned whether that was the best they could do; they probably could have gone to the tabernacle. God was very lenient and tolerated many things not strictly according to the law.

Verse 3. Solomon's life in general was good up to this time, but he added the practice of using the high places in the same manner described in the preceding verse. That is, he did so although going also at times to the proper place at Gibeon. He respected the statutes of David his father who also had regarded the law of God that had been given to him in the writings of Moses. When kings and other high persons needed special guidance, they were inspired only for that occasion and purpose.

Verse 4. We have no definite information as to when or how the tabernacle got in possession of the Israelites from the Philistines. At the time we are considering, however, the change had been made, and thither Solomon went to offer sacrifices. The priests would do the manual part of the service, but the king furnished the animals from the royal treasury. The offering of animal sacrifices was not always for sin (Leviticus 3rd chapter), so the vast number of beasts offered at this time was in keeping with the favorable relationship that Solomon was observing toward the Lord.

Verse 5. *Ask what I shall give thee.* This is popularly misquoted, and made to say God told Solomon he could have whatever he asked for. This is far from correct. We have no right to say that his wish would have been granted had it displeased the Lord.

Verse 6. Solomon had great respect for his father, and appreciated the many things the Lord had done for him. *Mercy* generally implies a treatment less severe than one's conduct deserves. That was not what Solomon meant, for he stated as condition on which the favor of God had been shown him, that his father had walked before him righteously. The original word for *mercy* is defined in the lexicon as "kindness," which is the proper word. Among the favors that the Lord had bestowed on David was the giving him a son to sit on his throne.

Verse 7. The modesty of Solomon is refreshing. He attributes his good fortune in obtaining the throne of his father to the gift of God. *A little child* is a comparative expression, meaning he was inexperienced in the great task of ruling the kingdom left him by his father.

Verse 8. His sense of littleness was emphasized by recalling to mind the greatness of the people in whose midst he was. That greatness was due to the fact that God had chosen it to be his exclusive possession.

Verse 9. *Understanding* is from SHAMA, and defined, "a primitive root; to hear intelligently (often with implication of attention, obedience, etc., causatively to tell, etc.)." — Strong. *Good* and *bad* would not mean necessarily the questions of right and wrong morally. Solomon had the law of Moses and kings were required to keep a copy of it always by them to direct them in the right way. (Deut. 17: 18-20). But there would come times when proper judgment would be needed for determining between issues and disputes arising unexpectedly.

Verses 10, 11. None of the things mentioned would have been wrong in themselves, for God promised to give Solomon practically all of them. But they would have been favors of a personal character, and a wish for them would have been selfish. It would have indicated a greater interest in the things of self, than the ones pertaining to God. If a man puts the cause of the Lord above even the best of temporal blessings, such a man would likely make proper use of such blessings. Hence, God promised them to Solomon. This principle was taught by Christ. (Matt. 6: 33.)

Verse 12. The wisdom of Solomon has been a subject of discussion among the friends of the Bible. Some have said that, while it was far above what any other person had, it was not in the form of inspiration; that it was mental talent such as all people have through nature, except that his exceeded others. That will not hold, for Solomon was already a mature man, with all natural endowments possessed and developed, when God gave to him the wisdom we are speaking about. Again, it is claimed that his wisdom pertained to his ability as king and judge of disputes, not to his writings; wrong again. In Ch. 4: 32, immediately after mentioning his wisdom, the writer tells us of the songs and proverbs he composed. The conclusion is, then, that Solomon was a divinely inspired man in all his writings. The fact of his unrighteous life does not affect his inspiration, any more than Peter's hypocrisy at Antioch (Gal. 2: 11-13) affected his inspiration at Jerusalem (Acts 15: 7-11) or his epistles.

Verses 13, 14. God promised Solomon three things he had not asked for; riches, honor, and long life. But these favors were on condition that he "walk in my ways."

Verse 15. Dreams constituted one of the means used by the Lord in ancient times to make known his will. (Heb. 1: 1.) There was no doubt in the mind of Solomon that God had actually spoken to him. He immediately went to Jerusalem to appear before the ark (2 Sam. 6: 17), and to complete the worship begun at Gibeon, by offering more sacrifices near the sacred article, which always symbolized the presence of God in a special manner. While the tabernacle arrangement was intact, the high priest alone was permitted to come into the presence of this holy piece of equipment for purposes of worship. Solomon recognized the solemnity and dignity of the place.

Verses 16-18. It will be more satisfactory to consider these verses together. As the women were plying the same trade it was reasonable they might as well occupy the same house. Birth control was not as much developed as it came to be, and the natural result of their conduct gave occasion for the births to occur as they did. Such women would also be living alone, hence when time came for the deliveries they would be expected to assist each other.

Verse 19. This was the one born last and the mother was exhausted. The babe also was still unnourished and easily suffocated in being crowded by the mother.

Verse 20. Motherly instinct finally aroused her, only to find her child dead. The story of the other woman would seem plausible.

Verse 21. Along toward morning the other woman, whose babe was three days old and thus had started the function of nursing, thought to give her child its nourishment. It was easy to perceive, even while not very light, that the babe was dead. And when full light came, she was able to see that it was not her child.

Verse 22. There was nothing said about any marks of identity by which either woman claimed to know her child. The alleged action of the one woman would be the key to the situation. There could be no question as to which was the older, and thus the one for whom the nourishment had arrived would belong to the woman claiming it. All of the above reasoning pertains only to the truthfulness or falsity of the women. It would not disclose to Solomon which actually was delivered first.

Verse 23. The closing remarks in preceding verse are explanatory of this verse. Acting from human testimony only, all Solomon could say was that the claims of the women were on equal ground.

Verses 24-27. There is no doubt that Solomon's inspiration could have told him specifically which was the mother of the living child. But God used the occasion to exhibit an unusual mode of reasoning. After the transaction was accomplished, it was understood by the people that Solomon's judgment was more than human. Had there been sincere doubt in the minds of the women as to which was which of the babes each knew that she had borne a child. Each would know also that if the only living one were slain, hers would be dead for certain. A woman who would be willing for another to have her child rather than have it slain would be the more worthy of mothering a babe regardless of its parentage. The decision of Solomon, therefore, was correct from every viewpoint.

Verse 28. *Judgment* in both places means a verdict. The wisdom displayed by Solomon thereby filled the people with respect for him, and they attributed it to God.

1 KINGS 4

Verses 1, 2. *Princes* comes from SAR and is defined, "a head person (of any rank or class)."—Strong. The word cannot be restricted to any one group; instead, a prince in any group would mean an outstanding man of such group. This definition would apply whether considering religious or military or clerical departments of a kingdom. The word has been rendered in the A. V. by captain 125 times, chief 33, general 1, governor 6, keeper 3, lord 1, master 1, prince 208, principal 2, ruler 33, steward 1. It was thought well to give this extended view of the word because of the various and frequent use made of it in the Sacred Writings. Being the son of Zadok, Azariah would be in the priestly line independent of any provision made by Solomon. The word *priest* is from KOHEN and defined, "literally, one officiating, a priest; also (by courtesy) an acting priest (although a layman)." —Strong. All of Aaron's lineal descendants were eligible for the priesthood, but not all were in active service; only as many as needed. That is the reason for the expression "priest that is anointed" occurring in some places. (Lev. 4: 3; 6: 22; Num. 3: 3.) Azariah was the acting priest.

Verses 3-6. This paragraph sets forth members of the cabinet. See 2 Sam. 20: 23-26.

Verse 7. *Officers* means men stationed in the several places. *Victuals* is from a word with general meaning of provisions. The connection, however, shows it means the providing of food. Each man was responsible for one month's supply out of each year. He would have the power to commandeer all sources of necessities in the district where he was stationed, if such power were needed. Having one month only out of each year to be responsible for, there would be no reason for shortage.

Verses 8-19. This paragraph names the 12 men charged with the duty described in the preceding verse. Usually the mention of the name with brief reference to his territory is all that is given. A slight personal notice is occasionally made. (Vs. 11, 15.)

Verse 20. *Judah and Israel.* See comments at 1 Sam. 11: 8 on this expression.

Verse 21. Solomon was the first man to realize the fulfillment of the promise of Gen. 15: 18. The reason the Israelites never before did so was their disobedience of God's commands. In proportion as the conditions were neglected, God cut short the fulfillment of his promises. *The river* refers to the Euphrates, and *border of Egypt* is equivalent to "river of Egypt." *Brought presents* signified the subjection of the kings to Solomon. See comments at 1 Sam. 10: 27.

Verses 22-24. Solomon personally would not use these provisions, but his vast number of dependents would. *The river* again means the Euphrates.

Verse 25. *Judah and Israel.* (See 1 Sam. 11: 8.) Solomon was at peace with all kingdoms and hence his people dwelt *safely*, which is defined by Strong to be not only safe in fact, but also have the feeling of safety. *Under his vine and fig tree.* In times of national danger a citizen would need to take the products of his ground in haste and hurry to a place of safety to consume them. But now he could eat at leisure right on the spot where they grew. Dan to Beer-sheba was a symbol of the entire country. Dan was at its extreme north, and Beer-sheba at its south boundary. This condition of peace continued through the reign of Solomon.

Verse 26. *Forty thousand stalls.* The corresponding passage in 2 Chr. 9: 25 gives *four thousand.* Both cannot be correct. *Forty* is from ARBAIYM, and Strong defines it, "multiple of ARBA ["four"]; forty." Thus by adding the three letters it produces a multiple of the word. In the passage in 2 Chr. 9: 25 the suffix has been omitted. The word for *thousand* is in the original in both places, so the question would be with the words four and forty. In both passages, also, we have twelve thousand horsemen, and these with the horses were distributed among the cities, which were many. Twelve thousand horsemen to have charge of four thousand horses would make three men for each horse. That would be unreasonable, while forty thousand horses would give three or four horses in charge of each horseman, and that would be practical. Numerals were written with letters, and a letter in a used manuscript could become blurred so that the transcriber would overlook it. The question arising is, how does this affect the authenticity of the Bible. When Jesus was here he condemned the scribes for many sins. But not one instance is recorded where he even intimated they were unfaithful in their work as scribes. Had they been, that would have been the greatest of wrongs, and Jesus would certainly have mentioned it. We therefore understand that such omissions as we are considering were incidental, and did not discount the truthfulness of the Inspired Book.

Verse 27. This is explained at verse 7. The statement is added that nothing was lacking of the things needed.

Verse 28. These men were to provide feed for the beasts of service as well as food for the people. *Dromedaries* were swift beasts of various kinds, used in the post-routes.

Verse 29. We have another proof that Solomon was inspired. *Wisdom* and *understanding* are practically the same. The second specially means knowledge and the first means the ability to use it aright. *Largeness of heart* means breadth of mind. *As the sand* means his measures of wisdom were thus compared.

Verse 30. *The east* refers to the country of the Arabians and Chaldeans, whose people were reputed to be unusually wise.

Verse 31. The men named were noted in old times as outstanding in wisdom, and the reference to them is merely for purpose of comparison. *Fame* means the honor of the nations was extended toward Solomon.

Verse 32. *Spake proverbs.* The first word is defined, "to arrange," and the second, "a pithy maxim." From this verse we would know that not all of Solomon's literary compositions were written in the Bible. This is indicated also by the words "song of songs." (Song, 1: 1.) But enough of them are given to show his superiority.

Verse 33. Frequently what is called poetry and song today is chiefly a display of words without any attention to subject matter. This verse offers us the thought that Solomon did not waste words for mere sound, but had important subjects.

Verse 34. These great persons did not come so much for the benefit of his wisdom, as for the testing of the reports. Such is the direct statement regarding the queen of Sheba. (Ch. 10: 1.)

1 KINGS 5

Verse 1. Tyre was the principal city of Phoenicia, a country bordering on the Mediterranean, with the mountain range of Lebanon on its eastern line. Hiram had shown his friendliness for the Israelites previously by building a house for David. (2 Sam. 5: 11.) Upon hearing of Solomon's succession to his father's throne, he *sent his servants*. Nothing is said directly of the purpose of this, but the connection shows it was what we would call a "good will" mission.

Verses 2, 3. Solomon returned the good will in a substantial way. *Thou knowest how.* Just how definite this is to be taken is not clear. In the place where David had been put under the restriction mentioned (1 Chr. 22: 8, 9), nothing is said about Hiram. But the information given him now would explain why he had not been invited by his father to contribute more than for just his personal house.

Verse 4. The kingdom was then in complete peace. There was no adversary actually posed against it, nor even any evil *occurrent,* which means remotely indicated.

Verse 5. The way being now cleared, Solomon will build the house that his father was forbidden to build. It would be in harmony, also, with the understanding God gave to David concerning his son.

Verse 6. It may not be clear to the reader about the ownership of Lebanon. Hiram was asked to get materials therefrom, as if he were the owner. Again, if Solomon called for such to use in his building, he must have been the owner. It will be well to quote from Smith's Bible Dictionary. "Lebanon was originally inhabited by the Hivites and Giblites. Josh. 13: 5, 6; Judges 3: 3. The whole mountain range was assigned to the Israelites, but was never conquered by them. Josh. 13: 2-6; Judges 13: 1-3. During the Jewish monarchy it appears to have been subject to the Phoenicians. 1 Kings 5: 2-6; Ezra 3: 7. From the Greek conquest until modern times Lebanon had no separate history."— Article, Lebanon. The ownership, therefore, was so indefinite that the right to its products would be shared by the two kingdoms. *Sidonians* were the people in and near Sidon (otherwise called Zidon), a city of Phoenicia. They were especially skilled in woodworking, and were employed in the work requested by Solomon. They appeared, also, to have been already in the service of Hiram.

Verses 7, 8. The proposition of Solomon was highly pleasing to Hiram, and he agreed to furnish the cedar and fir, very fine timbers, to be used in the Lord's house.

Verse 9. The distance from north to south over land, between Lebanon and Jerusalem, was much greater than the combined distances from Lebanon to the sea, and from there to Jerusalem. And the distance over water could be made so much easier than would have been possible over an entire land transportation, that the water route was decided upon.

Verses 10-12. The two kings exchanged their possessions in a friendly way. Some fanciful theories have been devised regarding types and antitypes. The temple is regarded by New Testament writers as a type of the church. This is especially evident in the book of Hebrews. But care should be exercised not to run the comparison too far. Like the parables, some items have to be mentioned to make the story intelligible that might not have any application in the comparison. It is sometimes asked why Solomon called on Hiram, an "outsider," for help in building the Lord's house. It should be always borne in mind that the Jewish kingdom was political as well as religious. It was perfectly regular for one political king to have business dealings with another. But if it should be required, it can be shown that a parallel exists from a religious view. The church gets its new recruits (members) from the world, and has to take them by the water route (baptism) to their place in the spiritual temple of the Lord.

Verse 13. *Levy* is from MIC and defined, "properly a burden (as causing to faint), i. e. a tax in the form of forced labor."—Strong. This shows that if a government has the right to compel its men to fight, it has the right to compel them to work.

Verse 14. The thirty thousand went to Lebanon in relays. One-third went at a time and worked one month, then were relieved for two months at home. There was an overseer for them named Adoniram.

Verse 15. *Bare burden* is defined by Strong as porters. Their duty was to wait on the masons mentioned in this verse.

Verse 16. These officers were superior to the foremen directly connected with the workmen, and to them would be allotted the charge of seeing that all other officers did their duty.

Verses 17, 18. These forces were engaged in the work with the stone materials, while other workmen were in the forests of Lebanon getting out the timber. *Stonesquarers* were inhabitants of Gebal and made hewing of timber their occupation. This fact is the reason for their employment in the work of the temple.

1 KINGS 6

Verse 1. There appears to be some difficulty in chronology. This verse allows only 480 years from the Exodus to the 4th year of Solomon. We know there was more than that by adding the various terms plainly given. It is not like some of the chronological instances where the difference is a round number, and explained by the blurring of a numeral letter. The difference in the present case involves several numbers of odd amounts, and they cannot all be accounted for by the above mentioned method. The problem, however, is clearly solved by a noted chronologer, who has worded it so well that his statement will be here quoted: "According to 1 Kings 6:-1 it was 480 years from the Exodus to the fourth year of Solomon. But a glance at the various periods elsewhere noted, namely the 40 years wandering, period of the judges which Paul, in Acts 13: 20 says was 450 years, and the reigns of Saul and David taken together, show the length of time to have been far in excess of 480 years. Hence the clearest explanation is that the statement in 1 Kings 6: 1 recognizes only the years in which God's rightful leaders were in power and rejects the years of the servitudes and the usurpation of Abimelech. The six servitudes are Cushan 8 years, Eglon 18, Jabin 20, Midian 7, Ammon 18, Philistines 40, and the usurpation of Abimelech 3. These added give 114, the years ignored in 1 Kings 6:1. These added to the 480 gives 594, the exact time from the Exodus to the fourth year of Solomon." — Philip Mauro, in *Chronology of the Bible*. The number 594 includes the 13 years between the conquest and the beginning of the oppressions which started with Cushan. Any solution of a question that accounts for all the essential phases is a legitimate one, and the above solution does that.

Verse 2. The temple corresponded with the tabernacle in its general structure and purpose. But it was much more complicated in detail and far superior in costliness and beauty. *House* in this verse is applied to the central part of the structure as a whole. It was twice the length of the tabernacle, twice its width, and three times its height. No reason is given us for this increase in the dimensions.

Verse 3. The length of this porch corresponded with the breadth of the house described in the preceding verse. *Porch* is from ULAM and Strong defines it, "a vestibule (as bound to the building)." One meaning of *temple* is "capacity," and the thought is, the porch took in the capacity indicated by the breadth of the house.

Verse 4. *House* means the main building as a whole, including its two departments to be described at the next verse. *Windows; narrow; lights.* The first is from CHALLOWN, which Strong defines, "a window (as perforated)." The second is from ATAM and defined, "a primitive root; to close (the lips or ears); by analogy to contract (a window by bevelled jambs)."—Strong. The third is from SHAQUPH and Strong defines it, "an embrasure or opening with bevelled jamb." Transparent glass was not used in those times, and light was admitted through some form of open work like perforations or lattice. From the above information we may come to this conclusion: The walls of the building, being made of stone, were thick, and a narrow opening through them would admit very little light. And yet, if they were wide, too much exposure to the weather would result. Hence, the openings were narrow on the outside, reducing exposure to weather to a minimum, then the jambs were bevelled back on each side toward the inner side of the wall. That would remove some of the obstruction to the light without increasing the outside exposure.

Verse 5. *Chambers* occurs twice but is from different originals. The idea is that rooms or "lean-to" apartments were built all round the main building. These rooms were then strengthened and beautified with thin extensions like flanges. *Temple* and *oracle* were the two parts of the building, otherwise called holy and most holy. (Vs. 16).

Verse 6. The chambers were three stories high, which harmonize with the extra height of the main building. (Vs. 2). These stories were of unequal width, the lowest one being the narrowest. Each had heavy planks to support it. In order that these chambers could be in the nature of lean-to additions, yet not be injected into the walls of the main house, there were *narrowed rests*, defined "a ledge or offset," made in the main wall, and these supporting planks rested on the offsets.

Verse 7. Attention to this verse will show us that the stone parts of the temple were all that were considered in the statement about tools. It has been a favorite notion that the entire work of the temple of Solomon was done silently. 2 Chr. 3:9 says that fifty shekels of gold nails were used in the temple. It is unreasonable to say these could be used without the use of hammers, and a hammer would make a noise. The verse in our paragraph has reference to the tools for shaping the stone. Certainly, those large stones would have to be carved and shaped at the quarries before being brought on the ground.

Verse 8. The three-storied set of chambers described in verse 6 were entered by stairways from one story to the other. The lower one had been entered from a side door.

Verse 9. This refers to the heavy lining of the house, especially the top part.

Verse 10. This is just a detail of the work already described, giving us the height of the chambers whose widths are given in V. 6.

Verses 11, 12. God promised to bless Solomon and the house built if he would observe the *statutes*, *judgments*, and *commands*. See Ch. 2:3 for explanation of the words.

Verse 13. God has always had some formal method of indicating his presence among his people. In the Patriarchial Dispensation it was the family altar. In the Jewish Dispensation it was the tabernacle that Moses made, and now it was to be this temple.

Verse 14. This should be understood as a general statement regarding the work of the temple, that Solomon made a complete job of it. Further details will be given.

Verse 15. The principal thing to notice is the kinds of wood used in the interior of the house of God. The cedar is described by Strong as having very tenacious roots. The fir was a strong wood and adapted to heavy uses.

Verse 16. This *oracle* was also called *most holy*, which was the most exclusive room in the temple, as it was in the tabernacle built by Moses.

Verse 17. In contrast with the part considered in the preceding verse, and which was called the *most holy* place, the second important room was called *temple*. Otherwise, the word applied to the building as a whole.

Verse 18. The inside of the building was lined with cedar, and it was ornamented with carvings. The *knops* were formed like semi-globes, and the *open flowers* were just what the term indicates; flowers with the blossoms developed.

Verse 19. This gives a link in the chain for the ark, and the reference is to 8:1. The *oracle* was the proper place for the ark, and Solomon was preparing the room for it. At present it is in the tent which David pitched for it. (2 Sam. 6:17.) The tabernacle was at Gibeon. (1 Chr. 16:39.)

Verse 20. This room was a cube of twenty cubits. The corresponding room in the tabernacle of Moses was also a cube, but of ten cubits. (Ex. 26.) *Pure* gold is defined by Young as "refined." The *altar* was not in this room, but mentioned here because the writer was concerned with the use of refined gold.

Verse 21. There was a partition between the two rooms of the house which was plated with gold. And just by the partition there were golden chains stretched across.

Verses 22, 23. In one verse the altar is said to be "by" the oracle (most holy place), while in the other the cherubims are "within" the oracle. "Within" is more specific than "by." The conclusion is, therefore, that the altar (of incense) was not in the most holy place. *Cherubims* is from KERUWB, which Strong defines, "of uncertain derivation; a cherub or imaginary figure." These figures were made of wood, gold-plated.

Verses 24-28. These cherubims were ten cubits (15 feet) high, and the wings (including the bodies) reached over a space of ten cubits. The two cherubims with their wings extended completely spread out twenty cubits (30 feet), or, from wall to wall, and were fifteen feet high! They must have been beautiful and awe-inspiring.

Verse 29. This carving was for ornamental purposes. The literal or material beauty of the temple was appropriate, because it was a type of the spiritual temple, the church, which was to be glorious. (Eph. 5:27.)

Verse 30. *Within* and *without*. The interior of the temple as well as the places for treading on the outside, was paved with gold.

Verses 31. These doors were in the partition between the holy and most holy places. Many of the words of the verse are not in the original. *Side* and *part* have been supplied, and also the words in italics. *Lintels* and *posts* mean practically the same. The first having special reference to the strength of the support. *Fifth* is defined in the margin as "fivesquare." The idea is that some sort of doorway through the partition was so formed as to resemble a five-sided vestibule.

Verse 32. There were two of the doors and ornamented with carvings, gold-plated.

Verses 33-35. The entrance to the *temple* or holy place was similar to that in the partition wall, except they were foursquare.

Verse 36. This *inner court* corresponded with the court round the tabernacle. It was called "inner" because it enclosed the house proper. This court was made of three walls of stone, running parallel, and one of hewed cedar beams.

Verses 37, 38. This verse is important in that it states briefly the period of years used in building the temple of Solomon. *Throughout all the parts thereof* means that not only the main structure, but all the details were completed in the time.

1 KINGS 7

Verse 1. *Own house* means the palace, and the verse is a general statement, including all the parts directly and indirectly connected; details will come in following verses. The question has been raised why Solomon devoted almost twice as much time to his own house as he did to the temple. Josephus, the Jewish historian, gives the clearest explanation, which will be quoted: "After the building of the temple, which, as we have before said, was finished in seven years, the king laid the foundation of his palace, which he did not finish under 13 years; for he was not equally zealous in the building of the palace as he had been about the temple."—Antiquities, Bk. 8, Ch. 5, Sec. 1.

Verse 2. This begins the details on the building referred to in the preceding verse. The word *also* conveys the idea of something additional; that Solomon built something besides that of the first verse. That is not the case. The word is not in the original and means nothing to the story. After telling us in the first verse, in general terms, that Solomon completed the work of his palace in 13 years, the writer proceeds to give the details. The word *forest* is from a word that means "wood" as often as "forest," and the writer means to show of what wood the palace was made; that it was of the wood from Lebanon. The first sentence of this verse should read, "He built the palace of the wood from Lebanon." The three dimensions are then given, with the supports. Four rows of cedar pillars with beams tying them on top, supported it.

Verse 3. *Covered* means it was lined. In some way there were beams in the form of ribs or flanges that supported the heavy cedar planks lining the top of the house.

Verses 4, 5. The three rows of windows were so placed that they were exactly opposite to each other in the two sides of the house.

Verse 6. *Porch* is from ULAM and Strong defines it, "a vestibule (as bound to the building)." The remarks about the pillars being *before*, means that they were sufficient in number and so placed as to take care of the weight of the porch.

Verse 7. The building about which we are studying was quite a composite structure. As a whole it was called the palace. But it included departments for large assemblies. Also a room specially considered the throne room. That is what is meant in this verse. *Covered* means it was lined with cedar, which reached from the floor on one side, up and over and down to the floor on the other side.

Verse 8. This verse includes two special departments. One was the palace proper, corresponding to what is called the "living room or quarters" in a house today. The other was a special apartment for the king's favorite wife, the daughter of Pharaoh. Men with plurality of wives would naturally not be living in the same quarters with them. That made an occasion for providing special places according to sentiment of favoritism.

Verses 9-11. These verses simply itemize the kind and importance of the stones used in the various departments of the house.

Verse 12. This is what is described at Chapter 6: 35.

Verses 13, 14. This man was of mixed race. His mother was a Jewess and his father a Tyrian. The father was dead, and the son learned the occupation of brass casting. Solomon employed him to do such kind of work about the temple and its furnishings.

1 Kings 7: 15-45

Verse 15. These columns of brass were 27 feet high and 18 feet around.

Verse 16. A chapiter is an ornamental cap or head piece. These were seven and a half feet high, and as large in diameter as the columns, at least.

Verse 17. These chapiters were carved with ornamental net-like work, resembling lace. There were seven rows of such work around each chapiter or cap.

Verses 18-22. These various items of carving involve a great deal of repetition and might lead one to be confused. There were just the two columns, and were carved and fashioned in artistic designs all over. Being 6 feet in diameter, and 34 feet in height (including the caps), they were imposing in appearance, and appropriately named. *Jachin* is from YAKIYN, and Strong defines it, "he (or it) will establish." *Boaz* is from a Hebrew word similar to the English, BOAZ, and Young defines it "strength."

Verse 23. This *molten sea* corresponded to the laver of the tabernacle. However, it was doubtless much larger, inasmuch as the temple and its parts were generally on a scale larger than the tabernacle.

Verse 24. A knop is like a globe opened, or, a figure of a semi-globe, with the open side showing. They were about an inch and a half in diameter, and two rows of them ornamented the great vessel. The mold for them was prepared before the metal was cast.

Verse 25. Jer. 52: 20 says these beasts were bulls and made of brass. Standing in groups of 3 and looking outward, the 12 brazen beasts served as a base for the sea.

Verse 26. The walls of this vessel were a *hand breadth thick*. Strong defines the word to mean the width of the palm of the hand, not the spread of the fingers. The brim or edge of the opening was worked with ornamental designs like flowers. *Contained two thousand* baths. The corresponding account in 2 Ch. 4: 5 says *three thousand*. The conrtadiction is apparent only. *Contained* is from KUWL and Strong defines it, "a primitive root; properly to keep in; hence to measure; figuratively to maintain (in various senses)." Since the word has such a wide range of meaning, the difference in the two accounts is easily explained. The vessel measured up to the larger amount, but it certainly would not be kept brimful, which would be impractical for use. It thus would usually have the smaller amount in it. Young says a bath was about 8 gallons, hence this vessel would have 16,000 gallons of water in it.

Verse 27. These bases were to serve as pedestals, to hold up the lavers. (verses 30, 40, 43). They were 6 feet square and over 4 feet high.

Verses 28, 29. The sides of these bases had panels worked, called *borders*. Around the edges of the panels were raised framework parts called *ledges*. Both these panels and their surrounding frames were worked with ornamental figures of beasts and cherubim. These were cast into the pieces. (verse 46.)

Verses 30-33. The bases rested on brass wheels, and the whole unit was ornamented with various designs for beauty and general attractiveness. Part of the arrangement was to give the appearance of progress, in that chariot wheels were displayed.

Verse 34. *Undersetters* were shoulders or projections, to give the assembly an appearance of security, the bases having an ample provision for their rest.

Verses 35-37. The 10 bases were alike. Near the top edge, and just at the edge, there was an ornamental band, worked with cherubims and trees and lions. All of this work was according to the richness and beauty that could be seen throughout the temple.

Verse 38. The lavers contained 40 baths (320 gallons), and rested on the bases described in verse 27. The purpose of these lavers and the sea is well described by Josephus: "Now he appointed the sea to be for washing the hands and the feet of the priests when they entered the temple, and were to ascend the altar; but the lavers to cleanse the entrails of the beasts that were to be burnt offerings, with their feet also." Book 8, Chapter 3, Section 6.

Verse 39. The temple faced the east, which would make the south side the right. Five of these lavers were set on each side of the temple. The sea was at the southeast corner of the house, and it was so arranged as to be approached from the south.

Verses 40-45. This paragraph sums up the foundry work that Hiram did for Solomon, including the details that began with verse 13.

Verse 46. The size and number of the castings required for the work would make it impossible to do it in a regular foundry building, were any such in existence. It was done, therefore, in the open field where the plastic nature of the clay furnished a means for casting.

Verse 47. No attempt was made to weigh the vessels that Solomon had Hiram to make, on account of the great number and the enormous amount of metal used.

Verses 48-50. The tabernacle of Moses and its articles of furniture (except the ark) were at Gibeon. (2 Chr. 16: 39; 21: 29.) Solomon made these articles to be used in the temple according to the law of Moses, and they replaced those other pieces in the service. This means except the ark; it was at Jerusalem and never was duplicated nor replaced by another.

Verse 51. David was not permitted to build a house of God because of his many wars. But he contributed much material and had it in readiness for Solomon, which he now brought in (2 Sam. 8: 9-11; 1 Chr. 29: 1-5).

1 KINGS 8

Verse 1. The temple having been completed, Solomon called the leading men to him in Jerusalem. He gave them first a charge about the ark. This is another link in the chain for the ark, and the reference is to verses 6-9. The ark was in the tent that David had pitched for it in Zion, a part of Jerusalem. (2 Sam. 6: 12, 17.)

Verses 2, 3. It seems appropriate that this dedication of the temple should come in the 7th month. That was the month when the day of atonement came, at which time the high priest entered the most holy place to offer the yearly service for the nation. (Lev. 23: 27.) The standing of the congregation as a whole was brought down to date, thus making a significant occasion for the new start with the temple service.

Verses 4, 5. The tabernacle that Moses built had been at Gibeon for some time. It now was brought to Jerusalem, along with the holy vessels, except the ark; it had been brought up in the days of David. The fate of the tabernacle is largely a subject for secular history since no trace of it can be found in the Bible after the account given in this paragraph. It will be well to quote from Smith's Bible Dictionary concerning this subject: "Here [at Shiloh] it [the tabernacle] remained during the time of the judges, till it was captured by the Philistines, who carried off the sacred ark of the covenant. 1 Sam. 4: 22. From this time forward the glory of the tabernacle was gone. When the ark was recovered, it was removed to Jerusalem, and placed in a new tabernacle, 2 Sam. 6: 17; 1 Chr. 15: 1; but the old structure still had its hold on the veneration of the community, and the old altar still received their offerings. 1 Chr. 16: 39; 21: 29. It was not till the temple was built, and a fitting house thus prepared for the Lord, that the ancient tabernacle was allowed to perish and be forgotten."

Verses 6-9. This gives the final link in the chain for the ark. Make the reference to 1 Sam. 4: 4. The holy piece was taken from the tent that David had pitched for it and placed in the oracle, or most holy place, in the temple. There is no definite historic account of it after this, hence the reader has been referred back to the beginning passage for the chain of references. *Drew out the staves.* This expression is unusual, and will call for some critical study. The first word is from ABAK and Strong defines it, "a primitive root; to be (causatively, make) long (literally or figuratively)." It has the idea that the staves were made to appear longer (not actually so), and the effect was produced by drawing them partially out of the rings, thus protruding out from under the wings of the cherubims. This position made them visible to anyone in the oracle, but not without. This position of the staves remained to the time of the writing of this book. We do not know when or how the manna and rod were removed.

Verses 10, 11. The immediate need for the priestly service was over, therefore they were made to leave the holy place by the splendor of the cloud from the Lord.

Verse 12. *Thick darkness* is from ARAPHEL which Young defines, "secret or high place." We usually think of "darkness" as an unfavorable expression. But it is used in a figurative sense about God, referring to his exclusiveness of being; that he is infinitely above all others. For that reason he cannot be contained in any structure made by man, except in a representative way.

Verse 13. Solomon had built a house

for the Lord to dwell in according to the idea expressed at the close of preceding verse, as was predicted. (2 Sam. 7: 13; 1 Ki. 5: 5.)

Verse 14. *Blessed* as a verb is from BARAK and defined by Strong, "a primitive root; to kneel; by implication to bless God (as an act of adoration), and (vice-versa) man (as a benefit)." The word has been rendered in the A. V. by kneel 1 time, kneel down 1, blessed 72, be blessed 3, bless 211, congratulate 1, praise 2, salute 5, thank 1, and others. From the foregoing information we will understand the word to have both a manward and a Godward bearing. When used according to the first, it means that God or man makes another person happy, or wishes it so. When used according to the second, it means to acknowledge God as the source of happiness. In the verse now at hand, Solomon was wishing for the happiness to come on the congregation that he, as an instrument of God, could bestow on them. It is significant of great respect that the people stood.

Verse 15. The word *blessed* is used in the second sense, and refers to the happiness bestowed on the nation as promised to and through David.

Verse 16. The peculiar favor shown to David is mentioned. God had not as yet selected any city as a site of a dwelling place. But he had made choice of David to be ruler over his people.

Verses 17, 18. The desire to build a house for the Lord was righteous; God commended David for it. The circumstance shows that a motive can be right in principle, but objectionable from some other standpoint.

Verse 19. The expression "father and son" was used very indefinitely in Biblical language. It sometimes meant grandfather and son (Dan. 5: 18). But the importance of the relationship was made definite by saying it was to be one coming out of his *loins*, which is from a word that is defined, "the seat of vigor." That would apply only to a son of a man's body begotten; the offspring of his physical strength.

Verse 20. The outstanding thought is that Solomon's exaltation to the throne of his father was according to the Lord's promise; which included the privilege of building a house for the Lord.

Verse 21. The ark was of superior importance because it contained the covenant that God made with the fathers of the nation.

Verse 22. Solomon *stood* as he began his prayer. The prayer was accepted (Ch. 9: 2) which shows that prayer was acceptable to God if offered by a person standing.

Verse 23. *Heaven* means the realm of the air and the region of the planets. There was no one or thing in the third heaven claiming even to be equal with God. But everything in the first two heavens, also in the earth, had been worshiped, and Solomon exalted the Lord above all. It should be noted that God shows mercy to his servants provided they walk uprightly before him.

Verse 24. God requires his servants to carry out their professions with actions. He has set the example by his dealings with David.

Verses 25, 26. *So that* is worded "only if" in the margin, and harmonizes with the general requirements God makes of his servants. Solomon did not expect the Lord to carry out his promises to David on to his son except on obedience to the terms.

Verse 27. See comments at verses 12, 13.

Verses 28, 29. Solomon would not ask God to come bodily into a house which he had built, when the universe could not contain him. He would pray, however, that he would look toward the house; especially since he had said that his name would be there. That was said of the tabernacle that Moses built (Deut. 12: 5, 11), and the same was true of the temple after it will have been consecrated to the divine service.

Verse 30. *Toward this place* is rendered in the margin, "in this place." That is correct, for a part of Strong's definition of the original word for *toward* is, "near, with or among." This agrees also with the law of Moses that the males come 3 times a year to the place of national worship. (Ex. 23: 14, 17; Deut. 16: 16.) This *heaven* is the third one; Gen. 1: 20 is the first. Solomon prayed that God would forgive them *when thou hearest*. It is taught that forgiveness would be granted in time, but not until the N. T. Dispensation. The request was for the forgiveness to be granted at the time of the prayer, and Ch. 9: 3 says that Solomon's petition was to be granted.

Verses 31, 32. In Old Testament times God's people were permitted to make oaths. If a charge of trespass was made against a man, the issue was to be brought to the place of public worship. The accused was required to support his testimony with his oath. The judge in the case was to decide according to the merits of the case, not on any personal motive.

Verses 33, 34. This paragraph is related to Lev. 26: 35-42. The people actually did lament their condition while in captivity. (See Psa. 137; Ezkl. 37: 11; Neh. 1: 9-11.) This prayer of Solomon was answered. The sin of the nation was forgiven and it was brought back into the native land.

Verses 35, 36. In 1 Ki. 17: 1 is an account of the stoppage of rain. The people had been wicked and they were to be punished by a drought. It was broken in Ch. 18: 41-45. There is no direct record of the repentance and prayer mentioned by Solomon, but it is necessarily implied since the Lord said (9: 3) that his prayer was heard.

Verse 37. The calamities named were liable to come at any time as a punishment for wrongs of the nation, but no specific instance can be pointed out. The *caterpillar* was a form of locust, and was a pest on the vegetation. *Cities* is rendered "jurisdiction" in the margin. It is from the same original as "gates" in Deut. 28: 52, and that word is frequently used in the general sense of the territory under control.

Verse 38. This includes both the national and individual prayers. In either case, the petition was to be toward, or with respect to, the house where the Lord had his name recorded. (Deut. 6: 10.)

Verse 39. *Heaven thy dwelling place.* The first word is from an original that is used for either of the three heavens spoken of in the Bible; the atmosphere, the region of the planets, and the place of God's throne. The context, therefore, must be considered in determining which is meant. The last two italicized words tell us the answer in the present case; it means the place beyond the material universe. While God is spoken of as being everywhere, it means in the sense of his spiritual existence. His personality, however, is represented as dwelling in the same place as the abode of the angels; the place to be the eternal home of the saved of earth. *Ways* is from DEREK and Strong defines it, "a course of life or mode of action." Solomon prayed God to treat people according to their conduct, and the state of their hearts, since he knows that.

Verse 40. To *fear* the Lord means to have respect or reverence for him. A special motive for this fear is the privilege of living in the land inherited from the fathers.

Verses 41-43. The Mosaic system was a combination of religion and civil government, and hence certain privileges would be granted to *strangers* (those of another nation), that would not have been allowed had it been religious only. It was much like a foreigner visiting the United States. He would be granted certain favors that were being enjoyed by the citizens of the country. There is another fact that should be remembered; all the world was in some religious connection with God. If a man were not an Israelite, he was under the Patriarchal Dispensation. That would make it appropriate for him to be interested in the institutions of God, even though not directly related thereto. Again, both the Mosaic and Patriarchal Dispensations were destined to give way to the Christian. When that time will have come, the temple will be referred to as a type of the Church. That would make it a subject of interest for Jew and Gentile; therefore, it was proper for all the world to be "let in" on the significance of the literal place that was "called by thy name," which would prepare them to understand and appreciate the spiritual temple, the Church of Christ.

Verses 44, 45. *Whithersoever thou shalt send them* tells us that God sometimes sent his people out to war. If war is always wrong, it is so from a moral standpoint. Moral principles never change; if war is wrong morally, it was wrong at the time God sent his people out into it. Notwithstanding, Solomon prayed for the success of the arms of the Israelites, and Ch. 9: 3 tells us his prayer was accepted.

Verse 46. *No man that sinneth not* is the general fact on which Solomon presupposes the sin of the nation. *If they sin . . . and thou be angry with them.* The second group of words indicates that not every instance of sin would cause the anger of God to come on the nation. The Lord is very long-suffering and suffers his people to hold to the divine favor even though unworthy at times. If it goes too far, however, they will receive the severe punishment on the nation, even to the extent of captivity.

Verses 47, 48. *Bethink themselves* means that they will come to think on the situation. When they do so they will recall the threats that had been made and the fallen condition that has come on them will be realized. They will be convinced that all of this punishment has come on them justly. The prediction of this state of mind is recorded in definite terms in the 137th Psalm; the historical fulfillment of it may be seen in Ezkl. 37: 11. When the Israelites shall have come to this state of mind they will pray for deliverance, and in their heart will return to their native land.

Verses 49, 50. The specific point of interest in their prayer will be that God will *maintain their cause.* This is explained in the next verse to mean that their sins as a people will be forgiven. As evidence of this forgiveness, their captors will be induced to show them compassion. The prophetic prayer was fulfilled, and the history of it is in the books of Ezra and Nehemiah.

Verse 51. *Inheritance* as used here means possession. Ex. 19: 5 promised that Israel would be a peculiar treasure unto the Lord; peculiar means a possession exclusively the Lord's. Solomon reminded God of this great fact, which was a basis of the prayer. Egypt is called a *furnace of iron.* This is a figurative reference to the terrible afflictions endured in that land, and which had been foreshadowed by the burning bush; the bush was made to burn but was not consumed. (Ex. 3: 2.)

Verse 52. *Supplication* means entreaty and is a stronger word than mere request. It is an earnest begging for the favor of God.

Verse 53. The children of Israel were in Egypt for four centuries; in that time they had become sufficiently numerous to be formed into a separate nation as a people. This made it necessary to bring them out from under bondage. Now then, if they are again engulfed by bondage in a foreign land, may the Lord remember his inheritance and give them deliverance.

Verse 54. This verse shows Solomon in a kneeling position in his prayer, while v. 22 shows him standing. We do not know at what point in his prayer he changed. The fact that he used both positions, and that in the same prayer, indicates that God was not particular about the posture of the body while a servant was praying to him.

Verse 55. To bless means to wish and promise benefits on the people, when the word is used in the sense of direction toward them.

Verse 56. To bless the Lord means to recognize him as the source of the benefits. The particular benefit referred to by Solomon was the rest from their enemies. *Not failed one word* must be understood in the light of conditions on which the promises were made. See Josh. 21: 43-45; Judg. 2: 1-5.

Verse 57. See comments in the preceding paragraph. God was with the fathers when they obeyed him.

Verse 58. To walk in the *ways* of God means to walk the way he has directed. *Commandments* is a general term for the requirements of God; *statutes* has special reference to the original enactments of the law; *judgments* means the inspired decisions that were made from time to time as occasion called for them.

Verse 59. Solomon believed that if his prayer was acceptable to God, he would keep it under consideration constantly and deal accordingly. This would include such times as needed the divine help, whether prayer was being verbally spoken at the time or not. That is a principle also of the New Testament system. If a Christian's life in general is right, he will be in constant touch with the blood of Christ in its saving effects. This will apply whether he should be engaged in any specific act of the service or not, at the time the need for the favor came up. (John 1: 7.)

Verse 60. If the God of Israel maintained the cause of his people, that would prove to the world that he is unlike all other gods. The ones that were being worshiped by them would not help them in their time of need or distress; they could not even defend themselves. (Judges 6: 31.)

Verse 61. In one part of the verse Solomon plead with the people to let their heart be perfect with the Lord. This statement is explained to mean that they walk in His Commandments.

Verses 62, 63. No one man could handle this vast number of animals, hence the statement means that the king furnished the beasts, and *all Israel,* by the hands of the proper persons, did the manual work. The specific purpose of this service was to dedicate the temple. Such a service was once performed to dedicate one article of furniture in the tabernacle. (Numbers 7.)

Verse 64. This court corresponded to the court of the tabernacle, in which was the altar of sacrifices. The use of this space was necessary; an emergency arose which made it lawful. The emergency consisted in the large number of sacrifices.

Verse 65. Hamath was a city in the northern part of the country, and the *river of Egypt* was at the southern boundary. The congregation present at the service for the temple had gathered from all this territory.

Verse 66. *Eighth day* means the day following the second period of seven days. To bless means either to wish favor on one, or to acknowledge him as a cause of favor. In the light of the latter, they regarded the king as the instrument in God's hands in bestowing all these favors on them.

1 KINGS 9

Verses 1, 2. *House of the Lord* means the temple, and *the king's house* means the palace. The comparison to the time the Lord appeared to Solomon at Gibeon is to indicate that his appearance now was for a favorable purpose.

Verse 3. *I have heard thy prayer* means the Lord accepted it and would grant the requests. To *hallow* means to consecrate and consider as clean and holy. God's name was to be in this house *for ever* which means to the end of the age. Had the Jews retained their national organization through faithfulness, their temple would have continued to be the headquarters for their religious and civil life to the end of the Jewish Dispensation. After the Christian Dispensation came, the temple would still have been their headquarters, but for civil purposes only. And in all of those periods, down to the end of the world, God would have recognized them as his special people. (Psa. 144: 15.)

Verses 4, 5. *Integrity* means a condition of completeness of devotion to God, with the heart in true service to Him. *Uprightness* means a life filled with right doing. *For ever* is explained in the preceding paragraph. God had promised David that he would always have a successor to occupy his throne. Not that the same man would live perpetually, which we know was not done. But the throne would always be occupied by a man who was a lineal descendant of David. This promise, however, was made on condition that the several descendants follow the kind of life set forth in this paragraph.

Verse 6. Two trends in the conduct of the people are warned against; one is away from God; the other is toward idols. *Serve* is from ABAD and Strong defines it, "a primitive root; to work (in any sense); by implication to serve, till, (causatively) enslave, etc." *Worship* is from SHACHAH and Strong defines it, "a primitive root; to depress, i. e. prostrate (especially reflexively in homage to royalty or God)." The latter word refers chiefly to the attitude toward the idol gods; the former to the activities of life in their name.

Verse 7. This is a direct prediction of the Babylonian captivity, and the history of its fulfillment is in 2 Kings 24 and 25. *Cast out of my sight.* The last word is used figuratively since nothing literally is out of God's sight. But he will not look favorably on the temple when the time comes that is threatened. The Jews have been the target of jokes, sneers, and remarks of contempt for centuries.

Verses 8, 9. The ruin of the temple and city was to be so evident that all people would observe it. The natural inquiry would be as to why such a condition came on the people so favored of God formerly. The answer would also be ready for the inquirers, because the warnings will have been so often repeated that they will become public knowledge; and the historians will write on the subject.

Verse 10. The two houses are the temple and the king's palace. The years spent in building them are specified in Ch. 6: 38 and 7: 1. See comments on second passage.

Verse 11. These cities were not an exchange in the sense of payment for the materials that Hiram furnished Solomon. He paid for them as will be seen below. But it would be considered a great concession to be permitted even to buy such sites in another country. This favor was granted Hiram in appreciation for what he had done for Solomon.

Verses 12, 13. Hiram was not pleased with the cities, although he accepted them. He called their territory the land of Cabul. Strong defines the word as, "limitations; sterile." Young defines it, "dry, sandy." While the places were not of much value commercially, perhaps, they were very desirable as posts in a foreign land.

Verse 14. This exchange of money for the cities was a business transaction, and made their possession legal for Hiram.

Verse 15. *Levy* is from a word that means a tax in the form of enforced labor. See comments on this at Ch. 5: 13. The reason for such a levy was the work required for the buildings mentioned; also the strengthening of the cities. Millo was a fortification within Jerusalem, in the part referred to as the "city of David."

Verses 16-18. The cities named had to be *built*, which means they needed repairs. The reason for special mention of Gezer is, Pharaoh had taken it from the Canaanites and given it to his daughter, wife of Solomon, as a dowry.

Verse 19. *Cities of store* were those used for keeping provisions. Those for houseing the chariots as well as the horsemen, and all other structures that Solomon desired to use, he built and equipped.

Verses 20, 21. The people mentioned were not the Israelite line. Making bondservants of them fulfilled Gen. 9: 25.

Verse 22. While Solomon did not make bondservants of the Israelites, he did use them in his service. Such terms as *men of war, princes*, etc., are grouped round that of *servants*, which indicates they were servants of a dignified class.

Verse 23. It is true that Solomon required many of his own people to work. (See comments at Ch. 5: 13.) They even had to work at hard labor. (Ch. 12: 4.) The number of these workers was so large that 550 men were needed to oversee them; but they were not put under bondage as were the alien peoples.

Verse 24. Ch. 7: 8 tells of a house Solomon built for his wife, the daughter of Pharaoh. Her stay in that place, however, was to be temporary, and only to be built for her personal occupancy. 2 Chr. 8: 11 tells why this change was made. Solomon realized that his favorite wife (Song 1: 5) was an alien to the Lord's nation, and that it would not be appropriate for her to remain in the city of David. In this he showed a preference for the things of God over his deep love of woman; a principle that should be an example for everyone. Millo was a fortification located in that part of Jerusalem called "city of David." That is where the wife of Solomon had been living in a temporary residence. It was appropriate, therefore, that he postpone the extensive work of this fortification until his wife had been removed.

Verse 25. The three times referred to correspond with the requirement of the law of Moses. (Ex. 23: 14, 17.) The last sentence of the verse is merely reflective and not intended as additional information.

Verse 26. The reader should not be confused by the mentioning together of Eziongeber and the Red Sea. The map shows two long, narrow arms of the main body extending upward, one in a northwestwardly direction, the other in a northeastwardly one. The main body of this water, also either of these arms, is referred to in the Bible as the Red Sea. The former arm is the one the Israelites crossed in their flight from Egypt; the latter is the one meant in this verse.

Verses 27, 28. Hiram cooperated with Solomon in this expedition by furnishing experienced seamen. The object was to procure gold from Ophir, which was known to be of unusual fineness. The location of Ophir is a subject of dispute among the various authorities. I have consulted Smith's Bible Dictionary, Schaff-Herzog Encyclopedia and Josephus, and they leave the question in doubt with me. The specific location, however, is unimportant, since the Scripture does not state any. It is enough to know that it was accessible to sea travel, which opened the opportunity to obtain valuables therefrom.

1 KINGS 10

Verse 1. Sheba was a locality of the Sabeans, situated in the south part of Arabia. *Fame* is not as strong a word as commonly understood. It means merely a report; the weight of the word must be gathered from the connection. The report the queen was so much interested in was in connection with the house Solomon had built for the name of God. *Prove* means to test, and *hard questions* is from CHIYDAH and means a trick. The sentence as a whole means she came to test Solomon with puzzling questions.

Verse 2. *Train* refers to the forces and general equipment with which the queen came to Jerusalem. She communed with Solomon which means she had conversation with him, in which she opened her heart to him.

Verse 3. *Told* is from NAGAD and one meaning is "to explain." *Questions* means "words." The verse means Solomon explained all the words the queen used in his hearing.

Verse 4. The queen had a full hearing that revealed to her the wisdom of Solomon; also his ability at planning as seen in the house he had built.

Verse 5. *Meat of his table* refers to the ample provisions of life. *Sitting of his servants* means the number and situation of that group. *Attendance of his ministers* denotes the position of those who contributed to the king's comfort. On the *ascent*, see comments at Ch. 6: 8. *No more spirit in her* means she was overwhelmed with amazement.

Verse 6. *Report* and *acts* are from the same word, and have general reference to the doings of Solomon, directed by his superior wisdom.

Verse 7. *The half was not told me.* These words are used erroneously as a basis for a popular church song, in which the subject is the Gospel story. But that story has been all told. See Rom. 10: 18; 1 Cor. 2: 10; Col. 1: 23. The queen said the report was true; notwithstanding, she said the half had not been told. This gives us a specific instance showing that the truth does not always give a fair estimate of a situation; it takes the whole truth to do the matter justice.

Verse 8. The happiness the queen attributed to the servants and other men, was due to their relationship with Solomon. And this happiness was made possible by wisdom.

Verse 9. The queen was a heathen ruler, and did not know the Lord previous to her visit with Solomon. The conclusion is, therefore, that he had spoken to her about the God of Israel, and had given the credit for all present favors to Him.

Verse 10. 1 Sam. 10: 27 with comments will explain the occasion of this verse. The mere exchange of presents was a formal way of recognizing dignity. Solomon was the richest of men, and there was no financial reason why the gifts to him should be unusually large. But the exceptional degree to which the queen expressed her appreciation.

Verse 11. The *almug trees* were of red color; they were heavy, hard and fine grained. The wood evidently was similar to ebony, except in color.

Verse 12. These pillars were a reinforcing, not part of the original structure; it had been already completed. The harp and psaltery were stringed instruments. The former was of more ancient invention; it was usually played with a plectrum, which was a small attachment for the finger, unless the instrument were of the smaller type. The psaltery was played on with the fingers. The almug wood was well adapted to the making of these instruments.

Verse 13. This does not indicate any undue intimacy between Solomon and the queen, as is sometimes slanderously affirmed. The language is not the direct kind the Bible uses when revealing such acts. Solomon committed bigamy once, and polygamy 998 times, and it is plainly revealed in the Scripture. Had he been guilty of wrongdoing in this case, the writer would have said so. Here is the explanation of the verse. Distinction is made between the possessions of Solomon as king, and those he had as a private citizen. For a like distinction, see 1 Chr. 29: 3. The queen wished to receive the customary "presents" from both sources. For information about these presents see comments at 1 Sam. 10: 27.

Verse 14. According to Moffatt's translation, the amount of gold was nearly 29 tons.

Verse 15. Besides this income of gold from his direct sources, Solomon received much in the form of commercial trade and tribute from the nations mentioned.

Verses 16, 17. These *targets* and *shields* were in the same class except for size. Also, the former was more impressive as a menace to an antagonist. It was in the form of a large tablet and covered with sharp pointed spears. *House of the forest of Lebanon* is explained in detail at Ch. 7: 2.

Verse 18. Since ivory is such a valuable substance, we do not know why Solomon would use it, then hide it with gold. Evidently its texture insured strength, flexibility and non-shrinking.

Verse 19. The throne was so large that it required six steps to reach the seat. *Round behind* means it was not merely a surface form, but was filled out in the nature of an immense character. The *stays* on the sides were hands, projecting from the seat. The place was made further impressive with the presence of a lion at each hand.

Verse 20. There were 12 of those "monarchs of the forest" placed in such a manner that the ends of the six steps, on each side of the throne, were guarded by them. No other king had anything like this, which was according to the promise made to Solomon at Gibeon. (Ch. 3: 13.)

Verse 21. *Pure gold* means gold unmixed with any other metal. The reason given for such choice of materials is that silver was not thought much of in the days of Solomon.

Verse 22. *Tharshish* is the same as Tarshish, and is located on the western shore of the Mediterranean Sea. This fleet of merchant vessels had been made by Solomon and was used in conjuction with that of Hiram, to bring him the things mentioned.

Verse 23. This was what had been promised Solomon in his dream.

Verse 24. This verse is another declaration of inspiration to the effect that Solomon received his wisdom direct from God. So outstanding was the wisdom that it attracted the peoples of the earth.

Verse 25. For comments on this "present" see 1 Sam. 10: 27. A significant fact in this case is that they brought these presents *year by year.* That means a continuation of their recognition of Solomon and his greatness.

Verse 26. The reader should consult the comments on Ch. 4: 26 in connection here.

Verse 27. The abundance of silver and cedar was such that Solomon could use them as freely as he would stones and cheap wood.

Verse 28. The bringing of these horses from Egypt violated Deut. 17: 16; but this was only one of the errors Solomon committed as we shall see. Receiving the yarn at a *price* means it was purchased as a commercial transaction, not taken as a tax, nor even in the form of a "present."

Verse 29. The preceding verse does not say what was the price paid for the yarn. If the present verse is any indication on that subject, it was not very high. A chariot could be bought for 75 pounds of silver, and a horse for 20 pounds. Israelites and heathen alike could do such bargaining.

1 KINGS 11

Verse 1. *Loved* is from AHAB and Strong defines it, "a primitive root; to have affection for (sexually or otherwise)." A man could not love hundreds of women in a purely sentimental way, therefore it means that Solomon loved them "sexually." *Strange* is from NOKRIY and usually means "foreign." The full definition Strong gives is "strange, in a variety of degrees and applications (foreign, non-relative, adulterous, different, wonderful." We have no direct evidence that Solomon married even one Jewish. The peoples named are outside the Jewish nation which is the reason they are said to be *strange* (outside or foreign) women. The daughter of Pharaoh was also a woman from the outside, but is specially mentioned because Solomon evidently loved her in a sentimental way. She is the heroine of the Song of Solomon.

Verse 2. In taking these wives Solomon disobeyed the command not to marry strange women; also the one against marrying a multitude of wives. (Deut. 17: 17.) Plurality of wives was tolerated (not "permitted") in ancient times. But the chief reason for the command against marrying foreigners was that they were idolaters, and would lead their companions into the worship of strange gods. Solomon clave to these women in *love*, which is the noun form of the word in verse 1.

Verse 3. *Wives* is from a Hebrew word that means women in general. The connection must be relied on at each instance to determine the social and moral status. That is why the writer adds *princesses*, which means a social rank. *Concubines* were on equal terms with "wives" morally. The chief difference was in regards to social and property rights. The second occurrence of *wives* has no limitations, hence we would conclude that all of his women had an evil effect on Solomon.

Verse 4. *When he was old.* Solomon was true to God, as regards idolatry, through the years of young manhood and in his prime. That was the period when his physical nature was interested in the kind of "love" we have seen he had for the women. His fleshly interest, even, did not seem to predominate over that for the true worship. It was after the moving impulses toward the women had subsided that he permitted their bad influence to affect him. It is even so today in many cases. Christians will marry the wrong kind of persons, claiming all the while that interest in them is secondary. For a time it may appear to be so; but when the fleshly urge has subsided, they will relax also in their devotion to God. How well it would be if all Christians would restrict their marriage to others of like faith and interests. Then their fleshly interests (which are natural and right) and those for Christ would continue together through the years of youth, prime vigor and old age, and they would journey on down to the narrow valley, with all their original principles of life united.

Verse 5. The heathen believed the gods to be both male and female; also that each clan or district could have its particular god. Ashtoreth was a female deity of the Zidonians; Milcom (Molech, v. 7) was that of the Ammonites. *Abominations* is the comment of the writer. The worship of this god was especially abominable and disgusting.

Verse 6. *In the sight of the Lord.* Many things man does may look very good in his own eyes; they may even seem to be beneficial in a temporal sense. But that does not prove them to be right in the sight of the Lord. (Luke 16: 15.)

Verses 7, 8. *Abomination of Moab.* For explanation of the first word, see v. 5. The high places were elevations of earth or stone, on which the likenesses of heathen gods could be posted, and where altars could be installed for the burning of incense and animal sacrifices.

Verse 9. The two times God appeared to Solomon are recorded in Ch. 3: 5 and 9: 2. With such marked evidence of the divine favor, there was no excuse for his acts of ingratitude and wavering. *Angry* is a strong word; it comes from ANAPH and Strong defines it, "a primitive root, i. e. be enraged." Considering the many and great benefits the Lord had bestowed on Solomon, this attitude of anger toward him seems just.

Verse 10. To render him still less excusable in his wrongdoing, Solomon had been specifically told what he should not do.

Verse 11. A *covenant* is a pact between two parties; such had been made between the Lord and Solomon. (Ch. 3: 14.) This covenant had been broken on the part of Solomon in that he failed to keep the divine statutes. If one party to a contract breaks it, the pact is made void and the other party is released. Hence, the Lord announced that he would take the kingdom from Solomon and give it to another.

Verse 12. Consideration for David (not Solomon) was to defer the transfer of the kingdom until the days of his grandson.

Verse 13. The transfer of the kingdom was not to be total. Still remembering David, God promised to retain one tribe for his grandson, the son of Solomon. Actually, two tribes were left to him, Judah and Benjamin. But the latter was a small tribe and not always mentioned with the other.

Verse 14. God began to carry out the prediction of the 11th verse. By stirring up a human adversary, another prediction was fulfilled. See 2 Sam. 7: 14. *King's seed* means Hadad was related to the king of Edom.

Verses 15-17. This paragraph explains the occasion for Hadad's enmity against the kingdom of Judah. In the days of David a great slaughter had been made in the land of Edom. Hadad was a little child then, and escaped the general destruction, together with some of his father's servants and came into Egypt.

Verse 18. This verse records a stop en route to Egypt, as the location named was on the way to that country. Upon having passed through Midian they came to Paran, another point still farther on toward the south. Here they associated other men with them, and together they came to Egypt. Pharaoh provided for Hadad's comfort by giving him some land and a house.

Verse 19. This verse merely means that Pharaoh came to like Hadad as he grew to manhood. He expressed his friendship for him by making him his brother-in-law. Tahpenes was the wife of Pharaoh and her sister became the wife of Hadad.

Verse 20. A son named Genubath was born to Hadad and his wife. The intimacy of the two families was such that Pharaoh's wife took over the care of her nephew.

Verse 21. *Slept with his fathers* is a Biblical way of reporting death of some prominent person. Hadad heard that David and Joab had died; that meant the chief men who had opposed his people were out of the way. He then asked Pharaoh's consent to leave Egypt and return to his native land.

Verse 22. Pharaoh thought something was wrong with his surroundings and asked what it was. The answer showed that his desire to leave Egypt was not on account of any complaints. That left the implied conclusion that some special motive was drawing him toward home. With the facts before us as we have seen them, we may assume that his enmity for the nation of Israel was the motive. When he returned home he opposed Solomon in some way, unrevealed to us, which was indicated in v. 14.

Verse 23. Zobah was a city in some part of Syria, and its chief ruler was Hadadezer. He had a servant named Rezon, who deserted his lord.

Verse 24. Damascus was the chief city of Syria, and not far from the land of the Israelites. Formerly, while David lived and slew many of the people of his city, which was Zobah, Rezon had made a flight as mentioned in the foregoing paragraph. In doing so he gathered some men about him, with whose support he took possession of Damascus.

Verse 25. Being thus located near Solomon's territory, he had opportunity to harass him. He did so all the days that he lived; this was through the plans of God, who had said (2 Sam. 7: 14) he would chastise a disobedient son with the "rod of men."

Verse 26. *Jeroboam the son of Nebat* is a phrase that will become very familiar to the student of history concerning the Jews. The verse makes general mention of the fact that he lifted up himself against the king.

Verse 27. *This was the cause* is the introduction to a series of events leading up to the time when Jeroboam will receive his encouragement against Solomon. Millo was a fortification in Jerusalem, and the king was having it repaired.

Verse 28. Solomon observed that Jeroboam was industrious, and made him foreman of the repair work. *House of Joseph* is a figurative reference to Israel. See Ex. 1: 8.

Verse 29. This engagement of Jeroboam brought him to Jerusalem, in the vicinity of which was the prophet Ahijah. At this time the prophet was wearing a new garment, and he met Jeroboam coming away from the city.

Verses 30, 31. Manual or other literal demonstrations were used by the prophets in ancient times; the purpose evidently was to give emphasis to the prediction made. Note the cases of the girdle (Jer. 13: 1-11), the tile (Ezk. 4: 1-6), and the stuff for removing (Ezk. 12: 3, 4). Ahijah did a performance with the garment he was wearing by tearing it into 12 pieces, symbolical of the tribes of Israel. It would require more strength to tear a new garment than an old one; hence the superior might of God was pictured by this kind of garment. Giving the exact number of 10 pieces to Jeroboam, the prophet Ahijah made the prediction that the same number of tribes would be given into his hand. This encouraged him to seek for the transfer of power, and it is the explanation of *this was the cause*, in verse 27.

Verse 32. This verse is a parenthetical thought, and put in to explain why not all of the tribes would be given to Jeroboam. The tribe of Benjamin is not named, although it is to be included when the division takes place. See comments at verse 13.

Verse 33. The sin of idolatry was to bring about the rending of the kingdom. See explanation at v. 5 for the mention of these deities. It is well also to observe that the neglect of true worship is associated with the service for idolatrous gods. To walk in God's ways means to walk the way he requires. The statutes were the fixed and original enactments of the Lord; the judgments were the inspired decisions pertaining to questions that came up, and which also became fixed laws afterward.

Verses 34, 35. Frequent mention is made of God's regard for David as being the reason for leniency toward others. It is the reason given for retaining part of the kingdom for the son of Solomon, the son of David.

Verse 36. The Lord gave a personal reason for his retaining of the one great tribe (Judah), which was that David would always have a light in Jerusalem, the place of the formal recording of His name.

Verse 37. This was spoken to Jeroboam, and might seem to have given him an unbridled scope of authority. The limitations will be seen in the next verse.

Verse 38. The conditions on which the promises of the preceding verse were made, required that Jeroboam should walk in the ways of God. If he will do that, his *house* was to be made sure. The word "house" is from an original with a wide variety of meanings. It is from BAYITH and has been rendered in the A. V. by court 1 time, door 1, family 5, hangings 1, home 25, house 1789, household 52, inside 1, inward 7, palace 1, place 16, temple 11, web 1. The right to a throne was supposed to follow in the family line; for that reason an assurance that one would have a sure *house* was equivalent to that of a throne.

Verse 39. A question might arise as to why God would promise to bless a situation that seemed to have arisen through sin. The answer is in the verse at hand; it was for the purpose of punishment on the seed of David. And the consolation was given that the punishment would not be for ever. Since it consisted in the division of the kingdom, the removal of that condition would be ending of the punishment. The reunion of the twelve tribes took place, and it was specifically predicted in Ezk. 37: 1-22. The fulfillment of it is recorded in the books of Ezra and Nehemiah, and in the profane histories extant, too numerous to cite here. The fact of their restoration is also recognized in the New Testament. (Acts 26: 7; James 1: 1.)

Verse 40. In some way, Solomon heard of the "tip" that had been given to Jeroboam, and sought to kill him. How foolish to think he could prevent a plan of God by removing one of his servants involved. Had he succeeded in slaying Jeroboam, God would have replaced him by another servant. But the Lord evidently was already working against Solomon's interference by opening a way of escape, so that Jeroboam fled to Egypt where he was given a home as long as Solomon lived.

Verse 41. The books of Proverbs, Ecclesiastes and Song of Solomon, contain writings of Solomon; but reference is made to outside writings, and they are named in 2 Chr. 9: 29. There were other writings extant at the times covered by the Biblical ones, besides those included in the Bible; inspired writers referred to them. (Josh. 10: 13; 2 Sam. 1: 18; Acts 17: 28.)

Verses 42, 43. This is a brief and unadorned statement of the reign and death of Solomon. *Slept with his fathers* was a common way of reporting the death of a prominent person. For extended comments on *slept*, see 1 Ki. 2: 10.

1 KINGS 12

Verse 1. The inauguration ceremonies for a king did not always take place in the capital city. (1 Sam. 10: 1; 11: 15; 2 Sam. 5: 3.) Shechem was a city whose situation was beautiful, between the mounts of Gerizim and Ebal. It was about 34 miles north of Jerusalem. To this sheltered city all Israel came, supposedly to anoint Rehoboam.

Verses 2, 3. Jeroboam had fled to Egypt for fear of Solomon. (Ch. 11: 40.) Learning of the death of Solomon, he responded to the call of his countrymen to return to his native land. Their purpose was to have him represent them in a petition, which follows.

Verse 4. The complaints made against Solomon were all true. He had consumed 20 years of time building the temple and palace. This work had to have the services of many men. (Ch. 5: 13-18.) As far as we know, there was no fault found with Solomon in the matter. Such vast projects (which the Lord approved) could not be carried out without drafts upon labor. But that•work was all done, and there was no longer any need for the burdensome tasks. The request made to Rehoboam, therefore, was just.

Verse 5. The king dismissed the people with a promise to hear them again in 3 days.

Verses 6, 7. The king consulted the old men who had been with his father. They advised him to serve the people, which would induce them to serve him. Such a use of these words proves that the same word does not always have the same meaning. A king and his subjects could not serve each other in the same sense. We must understand, therefore, that it means the king would serve the best interests of the people by ruling well; and the people would serve the king by grateful obedience to his authority. The specific ruling the old men advised was that the king relieve the tax burden formerly imposed by his father.

Verses 8, 9. "Old men for counsel, and young men for war" was not the policy followed by Rehoboam. His associates of like age would likely be more sympathetic for his ambitions, and their advice was of that kind.

Verses 10, 11. *Little finger.* The

second word is not in the original as a separate word. The two came from a Hebrew word, meaning something little or insignificant. It is as if Rehoboam had said: "Comparatively speaking, that which is little about me will be greater than what was great in my father." *Whips; scorpions.* Literally, the chief difference between these is that of severity. The ordinary whip was merely a lash; the scorpion was a knotted scourge. The severity of this instrument was compared to a scorpion, a small animal with a poisonous fluid in its tail that was deposited in the flesh of the victim, resulting in very keen pain.

Verses 12-14. This paragraph is a repetition of what is in the preceding one.

Verse 15. Solomon had offended the Lord, and a punishment was declared against his kingdom. It was not to come, however, until the days of his son. This delay was in respect for David, the father of Solomon. Now the time had come to bring about the punishment. The stern attitude Rehoboam took, resulting in the division of his kingdom, was a judicial misfortune; not any moral wrong. It was consistent, therefore, for the Lord to influence Rehoboam into making such announcement that would result in the division of the kingdom.

Verse 16. This verse marks a decisive period in the history of the nation; the revolt of the 10 tribes.

Verse 17. Through the remainder of this book, and most of the next, we will be reading the history of the divided kingdom. Two tribes remained with Rehoboam and his successors at Jerusalem, and will be known as the kingdom of Judah. Ten tribes under Jeroboam and his successors will be known as the Kingdom of Israel. The history of the two kingdoms will run somewhat parallel. That is, the writer intends to keep the record of each kingdom "up to date," so to speak. To do this, he will write a while about one, then about the other. Since the length of reigns will not be uniform, it follows that accounts of the respective kingdoms will often overlap somewhat. That will cause a repetition of some of the events. This condition will be caused, also, by the fact that the two peoples were often engaged in conflicts with each other, making it necessary to refer to both in the same account. For instance, in writing of a certain event in the kingdom of Judah, it will be necessary to tell of contact with Israel. Then when on the history of Israel, the writer will need to mention Judah again, and on a subject that had been already treated. Occasionally, the writer will be telling of the actions of some king, when perhaps we have just read of his death. All of this may be explained by the zig-zag sort of the narrative; trying to bring the history of both kingdoms along together, or as nearly so as possible.

Verse 18. *Tribute* means the labor forces; Ch. 4: 6 tells us that Odoram had charge of them. Rehoboam thought he could ignore the revolt of the 10 tribes and continue to supervise their working forces. Evidently, he went in person to give authority to Adoram's position, since he was frightened away by the stoning of his agent.

Verse 19. *Unto this day* means the date of that writing.

Verse 20. This begins the history of the kingdom of Israel. The reason for mentioning only the tribe of Judah is explained at Ch. 11: 13.

Verse 21. Rehoboam failed in his attempt to foist his own foreman onto the working men of the 10 tribes; but he was unattended by military forces. He now thought he could put down the revolt with his soldiers.

Verses 22, 23. Shemaiah was a prophet. (2 Chr. 12: 5.) God usually spoke through them (Heb. 1: 1) instead of speaking directly to the people. *Remnant of the people* would mean the stragglers not identified with any particular tribe.

Verse 24. *For this thing is from me.* On the human side, the motives that brought about the division of the kingdom were evil. But since those motives deserved divine punishment, and since that was to be in the form of this revolt, it explains why the Lord said it was from him.

Verse 25. Shechem became the temporary capital of the kingdom of Israel, but changes were made soon after. It is important to note that it was in Mt. Ephraim.

Verses 26, 27. Jeroboam understood the system that the children of Israel got from Moses, and that it required them to go to Jerusalem at stated times for the national activities. He feared the influence the temple might have on them as they beheld it from year to year. To counteract that he formulated a wicked plan.

Verse 28. *Took counsel* means he thought over the matter. The sacred bull was a leading god among idolaters. The selection of calves for this plan was indicative of the long reign of idolatry that was just in the beginning. Jeroboam told his people it was too much for them to go to Jerusalem. This was an appeal to the longing of mankind for convenience. Today it is the same as of old; too far or too inconvenient to go to the assembly or to do other tasks. Jeroboam made the same claim for these calves that Aaron had made for the golden calf at Sinai. (Ex. 32: 4.) The history of that ancient event with its fearful results seemed not to be remembered.

Verse 29. Dan was at the extreme border of Palestine, and Bethel was near Jerusalem; just about as near as possible to be still inside the territory taken over by the ten tribes. By using these places, he counted on detracting the attention of his people from Jerusalem. He succeeded so well that it became a common thing to refer to Jeroboam as the man "who taught Israel to sin."

Verses 30, 31. Up to here, nothing has been said about the tribe of Levi when discussing the division of the kingdom. It was purposely reserved for this place. 2 Chr. 11: 13-15 should be read now. The tribe of Levi followed Jeroboam, but they were rejected by him when he was ready to form his religious system. When that occurred, the Levites returned to Rehoboam. We cannot feel very good over the wavering conduct of the Levites. However, we are relieved to know that the actions of Jeroboam gave the kingdom of Judah a lawful priesthood.

Verse 32. The particular feast referred to is Tabernacles. (Lev. 23: 33.) Other important feasts took place in the 9th month at Jerusalem, but they required use of the temple, which Jeroboam could not approach for his idolatrous practices.

Verse 33. *Devised of his own heart* means he had no authority for setting such a date. Having set up idolatrous images for worship, Jeroboam also erected an altar for sacrifices and incense. The priests whom he used in these services were the ones he had placed to supplant the rightful tribe of Levi.

1 KINGS 13

Verse 1. *Man of God* is an expression used very many times in the Bible, and with some variation in meaning. As a rule, however, it refers to men with special qualifications, such as prophets. God communicated with his people through them. (Heb. 1: 1.) Jeroboam was standing by the altar he had erected, preparing to burn incense.

Verse 2. This prediction was made about 970 B. C., and Josiah began to reign 639 B. C. The prediction, therefore, was made at least 331 years before the fulfillment, which is recorded in 2 Kings 23: 15.

Verse 3. It is easy to make predictions; but they do not become valid proof until fulfilled, unless something occurs immediately to demonstrate the authority of the prophet. Therefore, it was stated that on that day the thing would happen to the altar.

Verse 4. There were attendants with Jeroboam at the altar; he signaled to one of them to lay hold upon the prophet. But the hand by which he gave the signal withered at once so that he could not relax it to his body on account of the stiffness.

Verse 5. The demonstration mentioned in verse 3 took place just as predicted.

Verse 6. This brought Jeroboam to his proper frame of mind. He besought the prophet to pray for his recovery. It was done and the hand was restored to soundness.

Verse 7. Jeroboam was evidently grateful to the prophet and offered to reward him.

Verse 8. The kind offer was declined; not that the thing offered would have been wrong in itself. The reason for rejecting it will be stated in the following verse.

Verses 9, 10. God had commanded the prophet to go on his mission, then return by a different route. Also, he was told not to eat or drink in that place. These orders he began to carry out, and started on his return journey.

Verse 11. There is nothing unusual in this verse. Evidently this was a "retired" prophet whose sons believed he would be interested in an account of what had taken place. The part of the report that especially interested him pertained to the bones, and the treatment they were to receive in the future.

Verses 12, 13. Inquiring about the direction taken by the other prophet, this old one told his sons to saddle an ass for him; he then went in the direction indicated.

Verse 14. The old prophet overtook the other, sitting under an oak. To make sure of the identity, he asked him for the information, and received it.

Verse 15. This is another verse that would seem to have no special significance. However, we will learn that this old prophet had a far-reaching plan in his mind.

Verses 16, 17. The man of God then repeated the instructions that would forbid him to accept the hospitality of the old prophet.

Verses 18, 19. We know that God sometimes changes his mind and reverses a command he has given. How, then, was this person to know that the old prophet was lying to him? Well, if God changes his orders he had given to an inspired prophet, he does not call another inspired prophet to tell it. The first prophet should have suspected something when he remembered that God had not spoken again to him.

Verses 20-22. While the two were eating, God gave the old prophet a message for the other, who had ignored his own position as prophet and listened to another. Now when the Lord had a special message for him, he also ignored him as a prophet, and communicated through the other prophet. The prediction was made that his body would not be buried in the family burial ground. The explanation will be seen in next verses.

Verses 23-25. The unnatural action of the lion was the Lord's doing. Standing guard over the mangled body of the prophet, the passers-by reported it in the city.

Verse 26. This city was the home of the old prophet, and he heard the report. Recalling the word that God had given him concerning the disobedient prophet, he connected the circumstances.

Verses 27, 28. Another unnatural, or unusual circumstance awaited the old prophet. A lion will not stand quietly by when flesh is available for him, nor let another beast remain near him unmolested. The only explanation is that God was taking a hand in a plan to fix a prophetic scheme, serving as one of his "sundry times and divers manners." (Heb. 1: 1.)

Verses 29, 30. The old prophet took charge of the body, and there is no indication that he had any trouble with the lion; a further proof that God was in the matter. The prophet of Bethel used his own personal grave for the body of the other prophet, and the usual ceremonies at burial of the dead were performed. That is what is meant by the expression *mourned over him.*

Verse 31. There is no apparent reason for this strange instruction. No benefit could possibly be derived by having one's bones near another's. However, there is a certain amount of veneration for the body, which is right, since it was made in the image of God. The old prophet was looking out for the future "repose" of his body, based on the prediction made by the prophet from Judah. The fulfillment of it is in 2 Ki. 23: 16.

Verse 32. This explains why the instruction were given to his sons, by the old prophet of Bethel, to bury him in the grave with the other prophet.

Verse 33. *High places* means the mounds of earth, either artificially built, or found and consecrated to the service of idolatry. *Lowest* does not necessarily have any moral significance, but rather a social one. It is from a word that means the people in general. Jeroboam did not stop any place in selecting his priests; but when he saw a man whom he wanted to serve as priest, he consecrated him.

Verse 34. The tendency of all this sin was to lead the kingly line into sin and finally to plunge it into ruin.

1 KINGS 14

Verses 1, 2. This disguising was not for the public. Verse 5 shows that the woman had intended to mislead the prophet. Jeroboam knew that he was not a righteous man and that he was not entitled to the mercy of God. If the prophet did not know who was asking for the favor, perhaps he would grant it. He should have realized that, if no one can hide from God, neither can one hide the truth from his prophet.

Verse 3. *Loaves* is a general term for food made of grain, and *cracknels* means that which had been formed into cakes or biscuits. These are not to be considered as bribes; they constituted a customary expression of good will. Jeroboam believed that whatever the prophet said would be true, because he was the one who had predicted his rise to the throne of Israel.

Verse 4. The prophet Ahijah was blind from age, and it would have been easy to deceive him as to the identity of the woman.

Verse 5. Had the Lord waited until the conversation started to enlighten Ahijah, it might have been claimed that he recognized the woman's voice. But he did not wait for that; he had him informed so that her intended deception would be exposed even before she came to the inside of the room.

Verse 6. Ahijah let the woman know he was aware of her identity. That alone might not have been so unusual, since it could have been possible for some visible sign to disclose it. But the thoughts of one are not visible; therefore, the ability of Ahijah to read them to her would prove his divine authority. *Heavy tidings.* The second word is not in the original as a separate word. The first one is from a Hebrew word that means something hard or severe. The context shows that the speech of the prophet is what is considered, so the common wording is correct.

Verse 7. To us, the chief point in this verse is the information that it was God who brought about the action of Jeroboam, in drawing off the tribes of Israel.

Verse 8. Ingratitude is a cardinal sin in the eyes of the Lord, and Jeroboam was guilty of it. He was given a large portion of the dominions of David, yet the righteous life of that king seemed not to impress him.

Verse 9. The guilt of Jeroboam was said to be greater than that of any of his predecessors. *Other gods* would refer to idolatry in general, and molten images would mean those cast out of gold and other metals.

Verse 10. For comments on this obsolete word about the excretions of the body, see 1 Sam. 25: 22. The thought of the writer is that all the males would be destroyed. The importance of that threat lies in the fact that none but males were used in warfare, the chief activity of most of the nations in that day. Reference to dung at the close of the verse was to show the low estimate the Lord placed on the descendants of Jeroboam.

Verse 11. So debased will the descendants of Jeroboam be in the minds of the people, that their bodies will not be given burial. That will expose them to the dogs in the city, and to the birds in the open fields.

Verse 12. After giving to the wife of Jeroboam these "heavy tidings," the prophet Ahijah told her to go back home. A further display of his qualifications as a prophet was a prediction of the exact instant at which the child would die.

Verse 13. The age of the child is not given, but we know he was not an infant. He was credited with some favorable attitude toward God, which would not have been true of a babe. For this good that was in him, his body was to be given honorable burial, and not suffer the shame described in verse 11. Respectful burial of a body was regarded with much attention then, as well as in the present time. And it was especially desired that no shameful treatment be given the bones of a friend or relative. Hence the instances where sums of money were paid for burial places.

Verse 14. *Cut off the house of Jeroboam.* Ch. 15: 25-28 tells us that the line of kings was changed from the house of Jeroboam, and given to another family. *But what? even now.* The condition to exist when this change is to be made will be bad. The condition, also, was bad enough at the time Ahijah made the prediction. The words, therefore, have the meaning as if he had said: "What; do you think it strange that I should predict such a bad condition later on? *Even now* it is bad enough.

Verse 15. A reed growing in water would be always moving back and forth as if it were not permanently set. Israel shall also be made to waver. *Beyond the river* means beyond the Euphrates. The *groves* is a reference to idolatry, which was the chief sin of the nation, and which caused them to neglect their duties under the law of Moses.

Verse 16. Jeroboam was a wicked man and practiced his wickedness in the form of idolatry. Not only so, but he led the nation into corrupt practices.

Verse 17. Thus far was the speech of Ahijah to the wife of Jeroboam. She arose at his commandment (V. 12) and went home. The prediction about the death of the child came true just as she was entering.

Verse 18. *All Israel mourned for him* is a statement with formal as well as sentimental meaning. The third word is very strong as a primitive root, and describes the physical demonstrations of tearing the hair and beating the breast. Such outward expressions were not shown except in times of great concern.

Verse 19. *Chronicles* refers primarily to the official records of the kings of the Israelites, and the books in the Bible so named are partly formed after those official documents. The Schaff-Herzog Encyclopaedia has this to say: "Chronicles contains a reliable history, being drawn from the official records of the Israelites." God did not wish to take up space in his Bible for all the details of the lives of these kings. For the information of those who might wish to know more of the details, the inspired writers referred to these official records as we would consider "outside reading matter."

Verse 20. *Slept with his fathers* is a Biblical way of recording or reporting the death of prominent persons.

Verse 21. The scene now moves from the kingdom of Israel to the kingdom of Judah. The reader should consult the comments at Ch. 12: 17. The importance of Jerusalem is seen in that it was the city the Lord chose for the formal place of his name on earth. The name of a king's mother is often given for identification. The reason is that men had more than one wife in those days, and the statement is to show the complete naming of one's parentage.

Verse 22. When *jealousy* is coupled with the practices of the Israelites it is usually, if not always because of idolatry. Ex. 20: 5 states that God is jealous and the verse was on the subject of images for worship. This sin of idolatry was growing among the members of the kingdom of Judah. They did not become totally idolatrous, as did their neighbor, the kingdom of Israel. But they had many advantages over the other, in that they had the use of the temple and were served by the lawful priesthood. This made their partial idolatry more condemnable than the apparently worse state of Israel.

Verse 23. *High places* were what the term literally means. The physical fact of their being elevated spots would have been considered innocent in itself. But they came to be looked upon as something to be admired because of their loftiness, a great deal like religious people today who take "pride" in their elegant church buildings. Moreover, the idolatrous worship in most instances came to be connected with these high places. It became so much the rule that the very sight of an elevated place often suggested an idol. For these reasons the Lord condemned them and forbade his people building such places at all. The same sort of veneration was paid groves and even single trees, where the idea of idolatrous worship might be suggested.

Verse 24. *Sodomites*. The original is set forth in the lexicon as denoting a class of males who pretended to be devoted to a separate kind of life. Their character was very corrupt, and they made their profession an opportunity for gratifying their unnatural lusts. Smith's Bible Dictionary has this to say of Sodomites: "This word does not denote the inhabitants of Sodom; but it is employed in the A. V. of the Old Testament for those who practice as a religious rite the abominable and unnatural vice from which the inhabitants of Sodom and Gomorrah have derived their lasting infamy." The connection indicates undoubtedly that these sodomites were Israelites, and their presence and practices were tolerated by the nation. This conclusion is based on the fact that they are referred to in connection with the heathen nations that God had rejected. That is, they were compared with them as being as bad, while they were supposed to be a better class, seeing they belonged to God's nation.

Verses 25, 26. The *treasures* were the moneys and other items of value that had been collected from the various sources, such as tribute, toll and voluntary offerings. *Shields*, where actually used, were for the purpose the name indicates. But they were not always so used. Smith's Bible Dictionary says these shields were suspended about public buildings for ornamental purposes. Their presence suggested the protection of God and a figurative reference is made to them in Psa. 3: 3 and 28: 7. In taking these articles away the king of Egypt was foolish enough to think he was depriving Rehoboam of the protection of his God. He had also the motive of their material value.

Verse 27. As far as literal use was concerned, the shields made of brass would be better than the ones made of gold. The protection, therefore, that had been furnished by the former ones was not lost after the invasion of the king of Egypt.

Verse 28. The natural use of the shields would suggest that the guard should bear them while escorting the king. When they had served their purpose at an appearance of the ruler, they were taken back to their place of keeping in the guard chamber.

Verse 29. For comments on *Chronicles* see verse 19.

Verse 30. The statement was true of the two kingdoms in general. They were almost, if not entirely at war while they existed in power.

Verse 31. *Slept with his fathers.* See comments at Ch. 12: 17 for this. *Mother's name* is explained at Ch. 14: 21.

1 KINGS 15

Verses 1, 2. The date of a king of Judah is based on the reign of a king of Israel. See the comments at Ch. 12: 17. For *mother's name* see Ch. 14: 21.

Verse 3. Abijam could not have been the son of Rehoboam and David in the same sense. It was a common thing in ancient times to speak of persons in an important family line as father and son, etc. In Dan. 5: 18 Nebuchadnezzar is said to be the father of Belshazzar, whereas he was his grandfather. David was the first righteous king of Judah; for that reason he was frequently referred to when the writer was commenting on the character of some of his descendants.

Verse 4. The exceptional righteousness of David caused God often to be lenient toward the failings of his descendants. *Lamp* is used figuratively, referring to the son who should follow him on the throne.

Verse 5. *Save only.* We do not believe the Bible contradicts itself. At first sight this expression seems to say that the sin about Uriah and Bath-sheba was the only sin of David. In 2 Sam. 24: 10, 17, however, he confessed that he had sinned and done wickedly in the case of numbering the people. All apparent contradictions are explainable when the various angles are considered. One word in Strong's definition of the original for *only* is "although." The idea in his view of the case is that the life of David as a whole was exemplary, although he did sin grievously in the matter of Uriah. The history of David's life is one of perfect integrity up to the incident mentioned. The verse as a whole means that David's life and reign had been perfect, and he never deviated from the right path *until* the affair with Bath-sheba. And we might add that even in that case, David did what he could to correct it, by unreserved confession of his sin, and by respectfully bowing to the punishment God imposed on him.

Verse 6. The antecedent of "his" is Rehoboam since he died before Jeroboam.

Verse 7. For *chronicles* see Ch. 14: 19 and comments thereon. Note the mention of war again; it was a condition constantly prevalent between the two kingdoms.

Verse 8. *Slept with his fathers* is explained at Ch. 2: 10. It is usual to say of the kings of Judah that they were buried in the city of David. That was the most important part of Jerusalem, and the location of the capitol. It was fitting, therefore, that the kings of that line should be buried there. The kings of Israel were buried in various other places.

Verse 9. Again we see the reign of one king dated from that of another, and of a different kingdom. See Ch. 12: 17 and comments.

Verse 10. Some of the kings of Judah were good men, while all of the kings of Israel were idolatrous. Asa was one of the good kings and had a long reign. No less than 7 kings of Israel will have appeared on the historical horizon in course of the good reign of Asa. *Mother's name* is explained at Ch. 14: 21.

Verse 11. *Right in the eyes of the Lord* is a statement occurring in numerous places; it is a very significant one. A thing may be right in the sight of men, but be evil in the sight of God. This was taught by Christ in Luke 16: 15.

Verse 12. For explanation of *sodomites*, see comments at Ch. 14: 24. Removal of the idols would be in line with, or include the removal of the sodomites.

Verse 13. The mother of a reigning monarch was called a queen as an honorary title, not one that denoted authority; the full name was queen-mother. The word *idol* is not the ordinary one used when the worship of false gods is meant. It is from an original used in no other connection than this act of Maachah, recorded here and in its corresponding passage. (2 Chr. 15: 16.) The word is MIPHLETSETH, and Young defines it, "Horror, a cause of trembling." Strong defines it, "From PALATS, a primitive root; properly perhaps to rend, i. e. (by implication) to quiver)." Moffatt renders it, "an obscene object." It was evidently some horrible object so formed as to combine suggestions of lust and power. The ancients associated lust with religious services (Ch. 14: 24) and this wicked woman was making such a contribution to the vicious institution. The action of Asa is to be highly commended, in that he did not let his blood relation blind him to the errors and corruptions of the thing the woman was doing.

Verse 14. Since these *high places* were not wrong in themselves, the Lord tolerated them with a man like Asa, whose life as a whole was so good.

Verse 15. The law of Moses required certain contributions from the personal wealth of the Israelites. In addition, they might make freewill offerings and dedicate them to the service of the Lord. This was done by Asa and his father before him. The *vessels* were articles made of precious metals, such as bowls or platters, also any kind of armaments or items that could be used in national defense.

Verses 16, 17. The continuous state of war between the two kingdoms is mentioned to account for the action of Baasha. Ramah was an important city not far from Jerusalem. The word *built* means it was repaired and fortified and thrown into a state of siege.

Verses 18, 19. The action of Baasha alarmed Asa and he decided to make a move to counteract it. Damascus was the capital of Syria, a kingdom just north of Israel; the two kingdoms were leagued together at this time. Asa planned to divert the attention of Baasha from the city of Ramah by forming a league between himself and the Syrian kingdom. The treasures mentioned as being offered to the latter king are not to be regarded in the sense of a bribe. It was the form of official recognition in the practices of that time, and used to attest the friendship of the king of Judah for Syria.

Verse 20. The strategy of Asa had the desired effect. Benhadad king of Syria sent his soldiers against some of the important towns in northern Israel and smote their citizens. This was according to the league formed with Asa king of Judah.

Verse 21. The military actions of Benhadad drew Baasha off from his siege of Ramah, and he retired to Tirzah, the capital of his kingdom at that period.

Verse 22. With the forces of Baasha gone, Asa was free to undo the works that had been built against Ramah. To get this done, he drafted all the able-bodied men in his realm. The stones and timber were taken to repair Geba and Mizpeh, other cities of his kingdom.

Verse 23. *Nevertheless* usually introduces some thought that would seem to be against what had been just expressed. In this instance the idea is that Asa accomplished the many works enumerated in spite of the affliction that came on him toward the end of his long and useful reign.

Verse 24. *Slept with his fathers.* See Ch. 2: 10 for explanation of this form of expression. For *buried in the city of David* see Ch. 15: 8 and comments.

Verses 25, 26. The history again switches to the kingdom of Israel. See the comments at Ch. 12: 17 for explanation of why Asa is mentioned, although his death has just been reported.

Verses 27, 28. We have already read about this king (verses 16-21). But those verses were inserted into the history of Asa, king of Judah, to relate an episode that took place in course of his long reign. In the present paragraph the writer takes up the record of Baasha proper. The account shows the beginning of his reign, and the means by which he obtained the throne, which was by assassination of the reigning king.

Verse 29. One wicked man was sometimes used by the Lord to punish another. This act of Baasha in slaying the members of Jeroboam's family had been predicted by the prophet Ahijah. (Ch. 14: 10-14.)

Verse 30. The sins of Jeroboam were great even as they pertained to himself. What magnifies them is the fact that Israel was influenced by them to rebel against God.

Verse 31. This verse belongs after V. 28. The history was interrupted to relate some things about Nadab's successor. For explanation of these *chronicles* see Ch. 14: 19.

Verse 32. This is the same as verse 16.

Verses 33, 34. This is a repetition of V. 28. The reader should frequently consult the comments at Ch. 12: 17, to prevent confusion over the zig-zag form of the history.

1 KINGS 16

Verse 1. Jehu was a prophet (V. 7) and God used him to give a message to Baasha.

Verse 2. *Exalted thee out of the dust* is figurative reference to the elevation of Baasha from a lowly place. He was not in line for the throne, but was suffered to make successful conspiracy against Nadab. That was in reprisal for the sin of Nadab in laying siege against the city of Gibbethan. It had been given to the Levites (Josh. 21: 20-23) and should have been respected.

Verse 3. Baasha did not show appreciation for the honors bestowed on him. For this he was to feel the weight of God's wrath, by having the members of his family humiliated after the manner suffered by Jeroboam.

Verse 4. To be deprived of decent burial has ever been regarded one of the greatest of dishonors; it was to come upon the descendants of Baasha. Instead of being buried in respectful disposal, their bodies were to be given to the dogs and birds.

Verses 5, 6. For this paragraph see comments at Ch. 2: 10; 14: 19. Baasha was buried at Tirzah because that was his capital city. (Ch. 15: 33.)

Verse 7. The death of Baasha has just been reported. The present verse is a retrospective glance into some of the life of Baasha that had not been fully described. *Because he killed him.* Baasha did not kill Jeroboam personally; he killed his descendants. (Ch. 15: 29.) That punishment on the house of Jeroboam was intended of the Lord, yet Baasha's personal motive while acting as God's instrument was evil, and for that he was to be punished.

Verses 8-10. Assassination was not an uncommon method for reaching a throne. Zimri was only a servant of the king, but his place in the household gave him some advantage for carrying out his conspiracy. Selecting a time when his master was debased by drink, Zimri assassinated him and took the throne.

Verse 11. Baasha had slain the descendants of Jeroboam; in return for that, Zimri slew the male members of his family. For comments on the obsolete word for males see 1 Sam. 25: 22.

Verse 12. A true prophet was one who was inspired of God. No other could see the future and predict its transactions. When the Lord directed Jehu to make the announcement to Baasha that his posterity would be destroyed, he was able afterward to bring it to pass, which we have just seen fulfilled.

Verse 13. These wicked men were not content to practice their iniquity as personal entertainment. They urged their evil doings onto the people. Anger is not necessarily wrong; but if it is provoked by the wrongs of others, they are to be condemned. All of this conduct of Baasha and the people provoked the Lord to anger and brought his wrath justly upon them. *Vanities* is from a word that means something empty; the practice of idolatry had nothing of good in it, therefore it was vain.

Verse 14. For explanation of *chronicles* see Ch. 14: 19.

Verse 15. The reign of Zimri was mentioned at V. 10. The next few verses, however, were to record some things he did in fulfillment of divine predictions, including the slaying of Elah and other descendants of Baasha. After that interruption, the reign of Zimri was resumed. Gibbethon had belonged to the Philistines, but had been taken from them and given to the Israelites. (Josh. 19: 44.) At the time of this verse there was a host encamped against this city.

Verse 16. While in the camp around Gibbethon, word got around that king Zimri had obtained the throne by assassination. This roused their anger and they appointed Omri to be their king, and prepared to oppose Zimri.

Verse 17. Leaving the siege of Gibbethon, the people with their appointee marched to the capital city, Tirzah, and laid siege to it.

Verse 18. Zimri realized that he was defeated, and rather than fall alive into the hands of the besiegers, committed suicide by fire. But his resistance to the last was emphasized by his act of burning the palace, depriving his successor of its use.

Verse 19. Some of the acts of Zimri were fulfillment of God's predictions. That fact, however, did not justify his personal wickedness and motives.

Verse 20. The *treason* was committed when he slew the reigning king. It was necessary that Elah be chastised; but that did not justify Zimri for murdering him.

Verses 21, 22. This was a short-lived conspiracy against Omri and in favor of Tibni. The latter was the loser and Omri reigned.

Verse 23. In this and the preceding chapter we have mention of several kings of Israel, dated on the basis of the reign of Asa, king of Judah. This unusual continuation in the line of one of the kingdoms, instead of alternating more frequently, is due to the long reign of Asa (41 years, Ch. 15: 10) as against the short reigns of these kings of Israel. The entire length of Omri's reign is stated; also the portion of it that passed at Tirzah. This is because Omri planned to change the capital city.

Verse 24. *Samaria* was the name generally borne by a hill; Omri obtained formal possession of it by purchase. On this hill he built a city to be the new capital. He honored the man from whom he purchased the hill, by giving the city a name formed from his name. Samaria thus became the capital city of the kingdom of Israel, and it remained so as long as the kingdom continued in power.

Verses 25, 26. Omri was so exceptionally effective with his wicked examples that he was given special mention by a prophet. (Micah 6: 16.) For *vanities* see comments at V. 13.

Verses 27, 28. Omri was accredited with being a man of might. How regrettable that his talent was not used in the right manner. His life was given further detailed description in the annals of the kings. For *chronicles* see Ch. 14: 19; and for *slept* see Ch. 2: 10. He was buried in Samaria because that had become the capital.

Verse 29. This introduces one of the most famous of the kings of Israel; famous because he was so imfamous. The length of his reign is stated in this verse, but we are destined to read of many of his acts, running through several chapters, ere we get to his death. He began to reign three years before the death of Asa, king of Judah.

Verse 30. A comparison is made between Ahab and all his predecessors, so as to rank him ahead of them all in wickedness. The verse, however, is only a general statement. Some of the specifications will be cited in verses to follow.

Verse 31. God's people were commanded not to marry strangers. Ahab not only violated this command, but married one of the worst kind of strangers. Jezebel was wicked personally; she was the daughter of a heathen king, and wielded a great influence for evil over her already wicked husband.

Verse 32. Ahab not only "leaned" toward idolatry, but built a house for Baal in Samaria and equipped it with an altar.

Verse 33. *Made a grove* in itself would seem to have been an innocent thing, but the connection shows it was planted to shelter idolatrous worship. The comparison is again made, that Ahab did more to provoke God than all his predecessors.

Verse 34. There should be no responsible connection between the wickedness of Ahab and the rashness of Hiel. The significance is that the general effect of Ahab's wicked reign was such that men would be encouraged to defy the will of the Lord. The reader may see the comments on this subject of rebuilding Jericho at Josh. 6: 26.

1 KINGS 17

Verse 1. Elijah was a national prophet, a man of God who was used for the purpose of delivering divine messages to the people. (Heb. 1: 1.) These servants of God were given much authority, and were tenderly cared for, even by miraculous provisions. *Tishbite* is defined by Strong, "inhabitant of Tishbeh (in Gilead)." We will hear a great deal about Elijah. God determined to afflict the land with a dearth on account of Ahab. The prophet Elijah told this wicked king of the impending drought. A point of special importance is that the conditions of the weather were to be *according to my word* as Elijah expressed it. This was to demonstrate him to be a prophet of God.

Verses 2-4. When God plans a general state of destruction or other adverse condition, he always makes special provision to protect the worthy ones. In the flood he had the ark to save Noah and family. In Sodom he sent the angels to warn Lot. So in the case of Elijah; he was to be miraculously nourished during the general dearth.

Verse 5. The brook was before Jordan. Why depend on the brook if he was near the Jordan River? The river of Jordan is a swift flowing stream and its water is muddy. The brook is described in the reference works as a seasonal stream, and thus its water would not be muddy or stagnant either.

Verse 6. The raven was a tireless bird on the wing (Gen. 8: 7) and was constantly soaring to and fro in search of food. It would therefore not be a "hardship" to use this bird for the service of Elijah. The word *flesh* is from one that denotes "fresh meat." As the raven craves only tainted meat, he would not care for fresh, and would not have to overcome his appetite to give it to Elijah. *Bread* is from an original that has a general meaning, including grain. It is easy to see how the raven could find such an article without any miraculous help from God. The miracle was in causing it to make regular trips to the prophet with the food.

Verse 7. The brook was a seasonal stream; the absence of rainfall, therefore, would cause it to go dry.

Verses 8, 9. Usually it would be unreasonable to expect a widow to help one in time of general want. This is an instance for observing that when God commands one to do a certain thing, he always qualifies him for doing it.

Verses 10, 11. Even during a drought there might be some drinking water available. The request of Elijah, therefore, was not unreasonable. But as the woman started to get the water he gave another request that seemed more difficult under the circumstance brought about by the long dearth that had afflicted the land.

Verse 12. The morsel of bread that Elijah called for would be food already prepared from grain. The *cake* means the same; but provisions had become so scarce that all articles were consumed as fast as they were prepared. That is the reason the woman spoke as she did about not having a cake. She still had a small amount of ground grain and enough olive oil with which to mix it and which she was going to prepare. *Two sticks* indicates the scarceness of the woman's supplies, for that amount of fuel would not produce much fire, nor last very long. There is no reason to think the woman said this in the spirit of complaint. But she stated the facts so that Elijah would not be expecting much.

Verse 13. The nature of this command would indicate that an unusual person was speaking. She had just told him that she had only a handful of meal to divide between herself and son. Now she is told she may yet have it for their use, but must first make a cake for her guest.

Verses 14, 15. The original for *days* has a wide range of meaning, including a period of indefinite length. Since the meal and oil never ran out, we cannot give the word a definite meaning as used here.

Verses 17, 18. *My sin.* The idea might be suggested, since this is in the singular, that the woman was acknowledging the illegitimacy of her son; that is not the case. She was a widow and we have no reason to question her right to be a mother. The original for *sin* is in no other place so translated, which shows it is an unusual word, with an indefinite meaning. It has been rendered in the A. V. by fault, iniquity, mischief, punishment of iniquity. All persons realize they are "erring creatures," and if some unusual misfortune befalls them, they just consider it is a "judgment sent on them" for something they have done. Such was the idea in the mind of this woman. *What have I to do with thee* means, "what do you want me to do for you?"

Verse 19. *Loft* is from the same word as *chamber* in V. 23, and means an upper room. This was where Elijah's sleeping quarters were and he took the child's body there for privacy while praying and restoring the life to him.

Verse 20. *Evil* does not necessarily mean anything morally bad. One part of the definition of the Hebrew word is "bad physically." Elijah did not find fault with the Lord; his mentioning of the fact that he was a guest was to show his motive in praying for the restoration of the child.

Verses 21, 22. In various instances of miraculous healing, some kind of action has been done that apparently had nothing to do with the case. (2 Ki. 4: 29; John 9: 6.) In this case it was part of the plan for Elijah to apply his body to that of the child in bringing about the desired effect. *Soul come into him again.* This refutes the doctrine of soul-sleeping and all other forms of materialism. The soul could not come into a dead body had it not left it at death. So it is important to note that the child revived after his soul came into him again.

Verse 23. The chamber was a part of the house where the woman lived, but it was a separate room for sleeping purposes. The verse has the same sense as if we would say a person came out of a bedroom into the living room.

Verse 24. This shows the main object God had in mind when he enabled Elijah to perform this miracle; to demonstrate his divine mission and authority. This idea has been outstanding throughout the Bible. (Ex. 12: 2, 7; Num. 17: 5; Mark 16: 20; John 20: 30, 31.) The bodily benefits bestowed in the miraculous cures were incidental; the main purpose was to prove the divine power.

1 KINGS 18

Verse 1. The *third year* of the drought had come and God was about ready to end it. As Elijah had declared at the beginning (Ch. 17: 1) that no rain would come until he said the word, so the Lord will operate through his word in ending the affliction. Ahab was the king of Israel; that is why Elijah was told to appear to him.

Verse 2. The dearth was general, but Samaria was mentioned in particular because it was the capital of the kingdom of Israel.

Verses 3, 4. Obadiah was not in authority; he served as chief caretaker of the house. Being in that position, he had access to much of the provisions in store. He was a righteous man and not in sympathy with the conduct of his master and mistress. But he had to do his work for the prophets in secret because of the wickedness of the king and his wife. *Hid them by fifty* means he divided the 100 into two groups as a precaution. If one group should be discovered the other could escape. Such a precaution was taken by Jacob. (Gen. 32: 7, 8.) Food was very scarce, so the simple fare of bread and water was no doubt relished by these men.

Verses 5, 6. This would seem to us to be a very natural circumstance, for Ahab and his chief servant to divide the territory and go in search of sustenance for the animals. It will prove to be the occasion, however, for communication with Elijah.

Verses 7, 8. *He knew him.* The first pronoun is Obadiah. He had some acquaintance with Elijah, but under the strain of conditions, wished to make sure; that is why he asked for identification. *Lord* was a term of respect and meant to recognize Elijah as a man of God, since he was an inspired prophet. But Elijah referred to Ahab as Obadiah's lord. That was true in a secular sense, for he was his king. Then he asked Obadiah to bring his lord (Ahab) into his (Elijah's) presence.

Verses 9, 10. Ahab had made numerous attempts to locate Elijah. When some rumor came to him of the whereabouts of the prophet, he would go thither in hopes of taking him. When the search failed, he questioned whether the rumor was false, or that the people withheld the truth from him. To make sure, the king put the people under oath.

Verses 11, 12. As long as God wished Elijah to evade Ahab he assisted him in escaping. Obadiah did not realize that the time had come for the prophet to contact Ahab; and, not knowing it, feared for his life. Should he notify his king that Elijah was in a certain place, and then in the mean time he should vanish while Ahab was coming, he would slay Obadiah as a falsifier, and because of his disappointment. Obadiah protested such a circumstance on his profession of being one who feared God.

Verses 13, 14. As concrete evidence of his friendliness toward the Lord, Obadiah cited his care for the prophets hidden in the cave. On the basis of this practical proof of his devotion, he thought he should be spared.

Verse 15. *As the Lord of hosts liveth* is a mild form of an oath. It means, as surely as God lives, so surely will I; etc.

Verse 16. On the assurance given him by Elijah, Obadiah gave the word to Ahab. The word of his chief servant was doubtless of much worth in the mind of Ahab, for he acted upon it and went forth to meet Elijah.

Verse 17. *Art thou he that troubleth Israel?* This is in the form of a question, but was intended for an accusation. It is an old story to hear accusation of causing trouble, when opposing those who are really the ones responsible for the trouble. And when a person is in the wrong, he is likely the one who will object to any investigation of the situation; that was true of the guilty Hebrew in Ex. 2: 13. Truth does not fear the light, neither does a righteous man object to being questioned. If a person is doing wrong, he is responsible for all "trouble" that results from investigation and opposition to that wrong.

Verse 18. Not only did Elijah deny being the troubler of Israel, but he pointed out wherein Ahab and his people were the guilty ones. There were two angles of the case; they had forsaken the commandments of God, and had gone after Baalim.

Verse 19. The prophets of Baal were the ones specifically devoted to that god. The groves were also used generally as open temples for idolatrous services, and these prophets of the groves were the ones not devoted exclusively to Baal. They were the special guests of Jezebel. Ahab was challenged to have the issue put to a test, and was told to gather a group, 850 altogether, of the prophets of idolatry.

Verse 20. This states that Ahab gathered the prophets into a meeting, but no distinction was made between the two groups mentioned in V. 19. This shows there was no difference between them as to their actual standing.

Verse 21. *Halt* means to hesitate; that is, try to act as if they were in favor of both *opinions*. The last word is from an original that is also translated "thoughts." One word in Strong's definition is "sentiments." The idea of Elijah is, why try to hold to the two sentiments. Jesus set forth the same subject when he said that no man can serve two masters. (Matt. 6: 24.) The people had no answer to the question of Elijah, and the reason is clear. There could be no sound basis for trying to serve two gods that were opposed to each other.

Verse 22. If numbers count for anything, these idolaters had the advantage. Elijah was alone, while the prophets of Baal were 450, to say nothing about the prophets of the grove who numbered 400.

Verses 23, 24. Elijah had insisted on their choosing one god to the exclusion of the other. It would be logical, therefore, that some decisive test be made so that the choice would not be a blind one. He proposed a test that would be in keeping with the service of a god; it was the offering of animal sacrifice. And it would be consistent for the god to demonstrate his favor for the service that he accepted. The proposition was agreed to by the worshipers of Baal.

Verse 25. Elijah was confident of success, and if he made his test first, that would stop the proceedings. He wished the whole transaction to be a complete test; not only to demonstrate the power of God, but the utter weakness of Baal. He suggested to them, therefore, that it was fair for them to go first, since they were a multitude.

Verse 26. Note the fact that no voice was heard. Had there been any kind of sound, they could have maintained that it was from Baal, even though he did not send fire. The complete silence, therefore, drove them mad with disappointment. One meaning of the word for *leap* is to "dance." The word *upon* is translated in the margin, also in a number of versions I have consulted, as "about." The idolaters were dancing in a hysterical manner around their altar, because Baal did not answer them.

Verse 27. The facts about the case would justify their being *mocked* in the usual sense of that word. However, Elijah was using language that his contestants professed to believe in regard to their gods. It was the belief of idolaters that the gods were like men in many respects. They had their own territory (2 Ki. 17: 26) and would sometimes take journeys into that of another god. Also, being like men in some respects, they would become weary and need rest and sleep. Elijah reminded them of what they already believed. Baal might be *talking* (holding conversation with another god), *pursuing* (perhaps hunting), *in a journey* (visiting in another territory), *sleeping*. By calling their attention to all these professed practices of the gods, they could not afterwards use them as excuses for the silence of Baal. So they used enough time for Baal to have been finally contacted had he been engaged as described.

Verse 28. *After their manner* means according to a custom which they had as part of their religious practice. The law of Moses forbade the Israelites to mutilate their bodies. (Lev. 19: 28; Deut. 14: 1.) God wished his people to be different from the heathen nations round them.

Verse 29. The idolaters *prophesied* to the very last that Baal would hear them. *Evening Sacrifice* did not mean anything to these worshipers of Baal; it is mentioned as the time when Elijah "called time" on them. His reason for doing so was first, they had had sufficient time for their test; second, the Israelites had an established practice of offering a daily sacrifice in the evening. (Ex. 29: 39.) It was thus appropriate for Elijah to bring his test at the time usually devoted to sacrifices.

Verse 30. Elijah was not willing to use the altar built by the idolaters although that of the Lord had been broken down. See Ch. 19: 10, 14.

Verses 31, 32. The Lord's altar was repaired or rebuilt with a stone for each of the tribes. The trench was to receive water soon to be poured. *Two measures* is defined by Moffatt to be 1800 square yards.

Verses 33-35. The barrel was a vessel of indefinite capacity. It is sometimes translated "pitcher" and may be carried on the shoulders. We should not think, therefore, that the 12 barrels of water would fill such a large trench. The last expression of the paragraph tells us that filling the trench was an act in addition to the pouring of water on the wood. One barrel or pitcher of water might not thoroughly saturate the wood, so they were told to pour on four of them. But that might be questioned being enough to penetrate the fuel, and to make doubly sure, they were told to repeat the act. For fear that lingering doubt might exist, the act was done the third time. By then no doubt could be raised, because the water ran round about the altar. But perhaps by the time Elijah's prayers were ended the ground would absorb the water that was then visible, therefore, Elijah had the large trench filled with water. There could then be no doubt of the thoroughly saturated condition.

Verses 36, 37. *Abraham, Isaac* and *Israel* (Jacob) were the men usually meant in reference to the "fathers." They were regarded with special veneration as the founders of the nation. The primary motive, for the demonstration which Elijah was expecting, was to prove the divinity of Israel's God; also, to show that Elijah was a true servant of that God, and was acting on his orders. *Turned their heart back* means that the exhibition of divine power would force the minds of the people to recognize God as the true object of worship. Verse 39 shows such was the result accomplished.

Verse 38. We can see the advantage of having the large trench filled with water. That element is a natural enemy of fire and usually is the winner in a contact. In this case it was the loser, although being much "in the majority."

Verse 39. This was referred to in V. 37. With us there might seem to be no difference between *Lord* and *God;* that they mean the same person, and that the acknowledgment of these people meant nothing. Here is the point; the word Lord is from YEHOVAH and Strong defines it, "(the) self-Existent or Eternal; Jehovah, Jewish national name of God." The word *God* is from ELOHIYM, and the first definition of Strong is, "gods in the ordinary sense." What these people meant was that the being whom the Israelites recognized for their national Lord, was the one to be acknowledged as the One to worship.

Verse 40. Let us not forget that "all Israel" was called unto this demonstration (V. 19) as well as the prophets of Baal. It was the people, therefore, who made the acknowledgment of the preceding verse. The prophets had forfeited their rights to live under the law of Moses. (Deut. 13: 2-5.) But the people, having had their heart "turned back again," were to be assistants to Elijah in executing the law on the prophets of Baal. The brook Kishon was a seasonal torrent and dry at times. Its bed would therefore be a fitting place to slay the false prophets. There is no available information of what disposition, if any, was made of their bodies.

Verse 41. *Get thee up* meant for Ahab to leave the scene of the slaying, which was in the dry bed of the brook Kishon. There were indications of a heavy rainfall, and that place would soon become a torrent, and no place for living beings. Besides, the grand test of the gods was over and it was time to relax and partake of food.

Verse 42. Ahab and Elijah separated, the former going to his own habitation, to partake of nourishment. Elijah had accomplished his work for the time being and retired to Carmel, a famous mountain ridge in the southern part of Palestine. Much of the history of Elijah, and his successor (Elisha) is connected with this place. To it Elijah (with his attendant) went after the work at the brook Kishon, to await the immediate developments of the Lord's plans.

Verse 43. While in a meditative mood, Elijah put his servant through a little test of faith. For six times he saw nothing when he looked toward the (Mediterranean) Sea. But he was not permitted to give up until he had gone the 7th time.

Verse 44. The bringing of the rain was not much different from the natural appearances, except that it was brought at this particular time by the divine will, and that Elijah was given ability to hear it coming before there were any visible signs of it. The appearance of a cloud the size of a man's hand was due to its distance from the scene. Ahab had already been told to get back to his own headquarters, but the speed of the coming storm made it necessary to urge him on, which the servant was to do.

Verse 45. A great storm of rain and wind beat down, and Ahab drove his chariot ahead of it to Jezreel, his residence.

Verse 46. Ahab was equipped with a horse-driven chariot, while Elijah had none. The Lord gave him miraculous help, however, so that he traveled on foot faster than Ahab in his chariot, and got to Jezreel first.

1 KINGS 19

Verse 1. Ahab was under the domination of his wife Jezebel. (Ch. 21: 25.) When the occurrences at the brook Kishon were over, he reported them to her.

Verse 2. As would be expected, Jezebel was enraged at the report of the death of her prophets. *Do to me and more also* is an expression found often in the Bible. It means that she was determined to do a certain thing against Elijah, and if she did not, let the gods do something still worse to her. The particular thing she threatened for Elijah was to have him killed, even as he had killed *them*, meaning her prophets.

Verse 3. Jezreel was the residence of Ahab and his wife Jezebel. Upon her threat to kill Elijah he fled for his life into a "neutral" territory. The statement that Beer-sheba belonged to Judah is based on the original allotment of the land for Judah. Josh. 19: 1-9 tells us that a redistribution was made of the land, so that at the time of our study Beer-sheba actually was a city of Simeon, which was a part of the kingdom of Israel. The flight of Elijah to this city was because it was really a part of Ahab's dominion, although at a safe distance from his residence, and he wished to leave his servant in the proper country.

Verse 4. Elijah was not afraid to die, but had fled rather than be slain by the wicked Jezebel. Now that he had eluded her, and also since his work was accomplished, which was what he meant by *it is enough*, he wished to leave this world. Many of his fathers or ancestors had been called upon to die for the sake of the Lord's cause, and he felt no more worthy to live than they.

Verses 5, 6. Although the dearth had been broken, there had not been time enough to replenish the shortage of provisions. Elijah fell into a sleep under the tree; doubtless a state of exhaustion. He was awakened by an angel who had just brought some food. This was an instance of the service of angels according to Heb. 1: 13, 14.

Verse 7. Elijah had not partaken very heavily of the food before lying down again. That caused the angel to return and urge him to eat more in view of the strain soon to be put on his strength. His present location was not suitable for him, and the journey planned for him will be one of many days.

Verse 8. It is about 200 miles from Beer-sheba to Horeb, and God wanted Elijah to go there. In order to do so, the food he had taken in the two meals was made to sustain him for the journey, which took him 40 days and nights.

Verse 9. After reaching the vicinity of Horeb, Elijah was still dejected and took hiding in a cave. God spoke to him and asked what he was doing.

Verse 10. Elijah then made a speech that is often referred to by speakers and writers when discussing apparently hopeless conditions. The prophet was *very jealous* for the same reason God was jealous in Ex. 20: 5. The evils complained of had been done, but the destruction was not total as he thought. Moreover, it was Jezebel who had sought his life, and she was not an Israelite.

Verse 11. God will make a demonstration to show Elijah that noise and wind and physical tremors do not always indicate danger; neither do such appearances necessarily mean the presence of God.

Verse 12. The word *still* is from an original that means "calm." *Small* means about what the word usually denotes. A voice could be of large volume and yet not be boisterous; also, it could be small in volume and yet be rough. So the phrase means that God spoke with a calm voice and one with little volume. This was because a large volume was not needed, such as was heard at Sinai. (Ex. 20: 18-22.)

Verse 13. When Elijah heard the voice of God, he covered his face with his garment. Leaving the mount, he went back to the entrance of the cave. The Lord repeated the question he asked in V. 9.

Verse 14. Elijah gave the same answer he did in V. 10. His sincerity could not be questioned, for he was isolated from the public so much that he could not see all the conditions. In due time God will enlighten him on the matter, after giving him some instructions for a special service to the kingdoms concerned.

Verse 15. Damascus was the capital of the kingdom of Syria, just north of Israel. God has always been concerned in the affairs of earthly kingdoms, and has taken a hand in the appointment of their rulers. (Dan. 2: 21; 4: 17.) This verse, then, should be no surprise to us.

Verse 16. This Jehu must be distinguished from the prophet with the same name. (Ch. 16: 1.) The anointing of Jehu is ordered here, but he will not become king until 2 Kings 9. *Prophet in thy room* was said because there was a line of national prophets in service after the Israelite nation was established, beginning with Samuel. See Acts 3: 24; 13: 20. They communicated between God and the people. (Heb. 1: 1.)

Verse 17. The motives prompting the actions of Hazael and Jehu may prove to be different, but in each case the will of God will be served, for it will bring punishment upon the idolaters.

Verse 18. Appearances are often misleading. Elijah thought that everyone had gone over to idolatry but him. It was true that most of them had, and doubtless there were but a few in any one place who remained loyal. When all were counted, however, the number was great. It will be well to compare the statement of Jesus as to the number that will be saved. (Matt. 7: 13, 14.) When considered in connection with the ones lost, the saved ones will be few. When considered to themselves the number will be great. (Rev. 7: 9.) *Kissed* is from a word that Strong defines, "to kiss, literally or figuratively." It is the word for "kiss" in Psa. 2: 12. The meaning in this verse is that they had not shown any affection for Baal.

Verse 19. Elisha was not a prophet in his early life, but followed the occupation of a farmer. *With the twelfth* merely means to tell the place he took as driver of the oxen; it was behind the rear pair. Elijah threw his mantle on Elisha as he passed. Smith's Bible Dictionary, basing its conclusions on historical data, says, "he throws over his shoulders the rough mantle—a token at once of investiture with the prophet's office and of adoption as a son."

Verse 20. Elisha seems to have understood the action. Elijah had passed on in his journey, and Elisha ran to get in hearing distance of him. He wished the privilege of a formal farewell greeting for his parents before proceeding with Elijah. *For what have I done to thee.* The second word is not always a question, but is used also as an exclamation, or as a word to rivet attention on some important subject. Elijah permitted Elisha to return for the farewell party, but cautioned him not to forget what had been done to him with the mantle.

Verse 21. *Instruments of the oxen* were the yoke and whatever was needed in the work. These would be of wood and could be used for fuel. After the feast, to which the people were invited with his father and mother, Elisha left home. From now on he will be an attendant upon Elijah until the latter is taken from the earth.

1 KINGS 20

Verse 1. In Ch. 19: 15 we read of the anointing of Hazael as king of Syria. The anointing of a man for a place did not mean that he would take it immediately. In the mean time, Ben-hadad will occupy the throne of Syria. He brought a siege against Samaria, the capital of the kingdom of Israel; his forces included 32 kings. These were inferior rulers over small territories, and were confederate with Ben-hadad.

Verses 2, 3. From the camp of the besiegers the king of Syria sent messengers to the inside of the city. The demand was for Ahab to turn over his personal effects, including his wives and servants, for the use of the Syrian power.

Verse 4. It is difficult to understand why Ahab agreed to so disgraceful a demand. The clearest suggestion would be on the popular saying, "of two evils, choose the less." By turning over the things and persons demanded, the siege might be lifted and thus a still greater humiliation would be averted.

Verses 5, 6. The insincerity of Ben-hadad was exposed in his next demand. In the first instance, Ahab was left free to make the selection of things and persons to be turned over. The next time he was told that Ben-hadad's servants would sieze, upon search, *whatsoever is pleasant in thine eyes,* which meant the things regarded as most desirable. This demand not only would deprive Ahab of his belongings, but would admit the enemy into the privacy of the city and homes.

Verses 7, 8. The connection shows that Ahab reported both demands to his elders, although this paragraph mentions only the first. The advice of the elders was that the second demand of Ben-hadad be denied.

Verse 9. *My lord the king* was said in view of Ahab's agreeing to the first demand of the king of Syria. That agreement acknowledged Ben-hadad as his lord, to the extent that he had consented to turn over the things and persons demanded.

Verse 10. This was a virtual declaration of war. It also was a boastful threat based on numbers. It meant that if each grain of dust in Samaria were turned into a soldier, Ahab would not have as many as would be with Ben-hadad.

Verse 11. Ahab understood the boast, as his reply indicates. Girding on the harness means the putting on of the armor; and that would be done before any fighting had been done. Ahab's significant remark was to the effect that a boast before the battle might prove to be in vain, for it would not be known then who was going to be the winner. But the man who would be taking his armor off would have been through the battle, and in a position to boast.

Verse 12. The reply was delivered to Ben-hadad while he was drinking in the tents. It aroused him and he ordered his men to prepare for action.

Verse 13. God spoke to Ahab by the prophet. (Heb. 1: 1.) Although he was a wicked man, he was the king of Israel and was being opposed by a foreign army. Moreover, the events soon to follow were to teach him a lesson, and impress him with a fact of which he seemed to have slight appreciation, namely, that it was the Lord doing things.

Verse 14. Upon inquiry, Ahab was told that the forces to lead the charge were the 232 princes. The battle was to be commanded by him.

Verse 15. The princes were leading men of the various provinces. After them were to come the masses of the people, 7,000 in number.

Verses 16, 17. Ben-hadad with his 32 subordinate kings was relaxing and feasting in the pavilions or tents. Something caught his attention, and he sent messengers to learn of the situation. They returned and told their master that some men had come out from Samaria. They were the 232 princes under Ahab, who had taken the lead under orders from their king.

Verse 18. Ben-hadad did not know the purpose of the men in coming out; he did not care to take any risk, and ordered his forces to capture them regardless.

Verses 19-21. This paragraph pertains to Ahab's 232 princes. They defeated the plans of Ben-hadad stated in the preceding paragraph. Instead of being "taken alive," each of them took hold of a Syrian and slew him; that frightened the others who fled. They were pursued, however, and great numbers of them were slain. Ben-hadad and some others with horses, escaped. Other horses and chariots (their drivers) were slain by the king of Israel. This fulfilled the prediction of V. 13.

Verse 22. The Mosaic system was both religious and secular. That was the reason God's people were permitted to engage in defensive warfare. The inspired prophets, therefore, would properly be used when their services were needed. (Heb. 1: 1.) The king of Syria was so weakened by the defeat inflicted on him that he was not able to renew the war at once. But the prophet told Ahab to reinforce his army, for the Syrians would renew the war at the return of the year, which meant the next year.

Verse 23. See the comments at Ch. 18: 27 as to the belief in the personal characteristics of heathen gods. The Syrians considered the Israelites as just another nation like themselves, with their own special gods. As a balm for their defeat, they thought of the explanation about the supposed advantage of the hills as a place for combat. The servants of Ben-hadad suggested this idea to him as a piece of advice.

Verse 24. They further advised him to replace the kings with captains. Smith's Bible Dictionary says of *king*, "In the Bible the word does not necessarily imply great power or great extent of country. Many persons are called kings whom we should rather call chiefs or leaders." The word *captain* is more of a military term; in the next attempt against the Israelites, therefore, it was thought that the captains would be more efficient than the kings.

Verse 25. The servants further advised Ben-hadad to replace the army in full for all that had been lost in the first battle. With all the equipment, and by staking the battle in the plains, they assured their master of success. He believed them and planned on carrying out their counsel.

Verse 26. As the prophet had warned, Ben-hadad returned the next year to fight against Israel. *Numbered* means he mustered his men in army units. The Aphek of this verse was a city on the road leading from Syria to Israel.

Verse 27. The Israelites met the Syrians in the vicinity of Aphek and pitched their camp. *Two little flocks of kids* is an expression of comparison with the hordes of the Syrians. Great numbers, however, do not always count for success.

Verse 28. *Man of God* is a term used in the sense of an inspired prophet; such was the one who promised success to Israel in V. 13. The Lord wished his people to win the battle mainly because of the disrespectful remarks about him. The Syrians spoke of him in the same way they did of their gods; that he was limited by such considerations as the hills. These idolaters were to be given such a defeat they would be convinced they were dealing with the self-Existent, universal Being, not one confined to the hills nor to any particular spot in the universe.

Verse 29. Both armies lay in sight of each other for seven days and nights before the action. On the seventh day they joined battle and the Syrians lost 100,000.

Verse 30. Seeing the pitched battle was lost, the Syrians fled towards the city of Aphek nearby. There a further disaster befell them; a wall fell, killing 27,000 more. The king was not hit by the wall, and he sought hiding in a chamber that was on the inside of another chamber.

Verse 31. The Syrians realized their utter defeat, and that they must take whatever treatment the victors saw fit to inflict. In their extremity they were concerned most for their king, and advised throwing themselves upon the mercy of the Israelites. Sackcloth was used in times of great sorrow or extremity in the same way that crepe has been worn in modern times. The ropes entwined about the head acknowledged they were trapped and in grief.

Verse 32. The suggestions of the servants were carried out and they appealed to Ahab for the life of their king. Their plea met with a favorable reception; the king of Israel was even surprised, pleasantly, that Ben-hadad was yet alive. *Brother* is from ACH and Strong defines it, "a primitive word; a brother (used in the widest sense of literal relationship and figurative affinity or resemblance)." Ahab meant to grant the king of Syria his freedom; not only that, but to place him on friendly terms as a neighboring ruler. This gracious consideration was granted Ben-hadad, notwithstanding the Syrians had twice jeopardized the Israelite nation, and had insulted their God by comparing him to their heathen deities.

Verse 33. The servants of Ben-hadad did not intend to miss the least favorable word that might come from Ahab. When he used the term *brother*, they quickly grasped it and repeated it in recognition of the goodwill. Upon this overture they were bidden to bring Ben-hadad into the presence of Ahab, who, when he came, was invited to come up into the chariot occupied by the king of Israel.

Verse 34. Ahab not only agreed to let Ben-hadad go free, in peace, but made a covenant with him. It involved exchanges between the two nations that implied an equality of worthiness between them. Since Syria was a heathen country, and had held the God of Israel in contempt, this arrangement made by Ahab was displeasing to the Lord.

Verse 35. At various times inspired men have been called upon to go through certain physical performances as a form of predictions. Some of such instances will be cited. The torn garment, 1 Ki. 11: 29-31; The wounding of the prophet, present case; the cohabiting with the wife, Isa. 8: 3; wearing a girdle, Jer. 13: 1-7; eating of filth, Ezk. 4: 12, 13; cutting the hair, Ezk. 5: 1-4; moving of household goods, Ezk. 12: 3-7; eating a book, Rev. 10: 8-11. We are not told specifically why all this was done; but it was in line with the statement of Paul in Heb. 1: 1. It might be suggested that visible exhibitions of divine predictions are sometimes impressive where the simple wording is not. All that we know of the present instance is, the prophet was preparing for a protest against what Ahab had done in releasing Ben-hadad. *Sons of the prophets* means the men who were pupils of the older ones. *In the word of the Lord* means he had orders from the Lord to have himself wounded. No explanation was given as to why the neighbor was told to smite the other. While it would be natural to shrink from the deed, the fact that it was a prophet who gave the command should have influenced him.

Verse 36. An impostor could make a prediction; only when it was fulfilled would his authority be proved. The prediction was not general; it specified the manner and the time when the neighbor would be slain. Another thing proved is, when an inspired man gives a command, it is the same as if the Lord gave it direct; and the disobedience is counted as disobedience against God.

Verse 37. The next man obeyed the request to smite the prophet; the stroke wounded him. The original word is defined, "to split." Evidently, the skin was opened but no serious injury was caused; however, it would be sufficient to attract attention.

Verse 38. There could have been two purposes for the disguise. Ashes would indicate a condition of distress and thus cause the passers-by to be attentive. Another was to hide his identity until he got his message across to the king while he was still unprejudiced. See 2 Sam. 12: 1-7 for a similar plan.

Verse 39. The ruse worked and the king's attention was gained. While still behind the disguise he told what proved to be a parable, based on a supposed case. There was nothing questionable about the idea of being charged with a prisoner, since he had gone *into the midst of the battle*, and was thereby made a combatant and liable for any kind of military duty.

Verse 40. Ahab still thought he was talking with a soldier who had neglected his duty. By his own confession he was liable for the punishment threatened by the superior. When the king expressed this conclusion his remark was in the same class as David's "shall surely die" 2 Sam. 12: 5.

Verse 41. The disguise was then removed and Ahab recognized the speaker as one of the prophets, and thus as an inspired man.

Verses 42, 43. The speech the prophet made corresponds with Samuel's "thou art the man" in 2 Sam. 12: 7. The force of the lesson was made plain to Ahab while his mind was unprejudiced. After seeing it, and also being made aware of the authority of the speaker, he could say nothing against it. All he could do was to go home with a heavy heart. The prediction was fulfilled in Ch. 22: 34, 35.

1 KINGS 21

Verse 1. A Jezreelite was a citizen of Jezreel regardless of race. This man had a *vineyard* or garden, as such places were known also by that name. It lay near the palace of Ahab and would naturally be desirable to him because of its nearness to him.

Verse 2. Ahab was not thinking of commercial value or profit in his request. He offered to trade Naboth a better one for it, which would exclude the idea of profit, or to give him its *worth* in cash.

Verse 3. Naboth made no objection from the standpoint of the commercial value. He had sentimental reasons for retaining the garden, and rejected Ahab's request in memory of his ancestors, from whom he had inherited the property.

Verse 4. Ahab was so disappointed that he went into his house and sulked on his bed.

Verses 5, 6. Jezebel asked her husband for an explanation of his strange actions, and he related his disappointment at the hand of Naboth.

Verse 7. *Dost thou now govern the kingdom of Israel?* This statement represents the sentiment prevailing in the minds of many persons in authority. Private property and rights mean nothing to them. To govern for the good of all concerned is not their aim; they assume the privilege of taking to themselves whatsoever they wish.

Verse 8. The abuse of power indicated in the preceding verse shows up in this. Jezebel forged the name of her husband, and the seal or stamp from his signet ring would be genuine, though used unlawfully. The effect, however, would be to mislead them into thinking the signature was genuine.

Verse 9. Regardless of what Jezebel would write in the letters, with the king's name and seal attached, it would be effective with the people. Formal fasts were not required by the law of Moses, but were recognized and encouraged; they were also regulated when voluntarily observed. *On high* means in the front rank or prominent place.

Verse 10. *Sons of Belial.* The last word is a descriptive one, not a proper name. It means an extremely wicked person. The first is from an original with wide extent of meaning, such as subject or associate. The whole term means persons associated with the most vile and wicked men who have no regard for the truth. *Set two men* means to place them near Naboth so as to be witnesses against him. Being the kind of men described, they would not hesitate to lie against the victim of Jezebel. The law required that one who blasphemed the Lord should be stoned. (Lev. 24: 16.) This wicked woman had this in mind when she gave these awful orders.

Verses 11-14. This paragraph reports the carrying out of Jezebel's orders, which have just been explained. The elders and nobles were "on the spot" since the strange orders were backed up by the name and seal of the king. Under such pressure they did as they were bidden, and Naboth was put to death.

Verses 15, 16. This whole proceeding was prompted more by the wickedness of Jezebel, than by her desire for the property. To have merely confiscated it directly would surely be as easy as to get it indirectly through murder. It is an instance where a wicked character not only plotted murder and robbery, but was low enough to do so under the guise of the Lord's name. Ahab, like a cowardly truckler, thought to enrich himself through the fiendishness of his wife. (2 Ki. 9: 25, 26.)

Verses 17, 18. Again the Lord used a prophet to communicate his word. (Heb. 1: 1.) Ahab had gone into the garden of Naboth and Elijah was told to meet him there.

Verse 19. The question Elijah asked Ahab was really an accusation of a two-fold crime; murder and seizure of another's property. It might be said that Ahab did not cause the death of Naboth. He did not directly cause it, but was responsible in the case. He should have been more careful of his official seals; especially when he must have known of the wickedness of his wife. Moreover, after he learned of the criminal tragedy, he should have refused to profit by it. It is as bad to take enjoyment out of another's sinful acts, as it is to commit them. See Rom. 1: 32. The prediction about the blood of Ahab was fulfilled in Ch. 22: 38.

Verse 20. *Hast thou found me* is worded by Moffatt's version, "So you have found me out, O my enemy?" I believe this rendering is correct. It was an admission, mixed with a rather defiant resignation, that Elijah had again "caught up" with him. The use of "enemy" harks back to the previous contact with him. (Ch. 18.) One definition for *sold* is "surrender." Ahab had surrendered himself to the will of his vicious wife, with the understanding that she would require him to work evil.

Verse 21. See comments at 1 Sam. 25: 22 for the explanation of the obsolete word on the bodily discharges. If some of Ahab's posterity should escape the sword in active battle and be left alive in the city, God would even destroy them.

Verse 22. Ahab's conduct was likened to two other wicked men. Because of such likeness, his fate was to be like theirs. A factor in the case of Ahab that was also in the life of Jeroboam, was the sin in leading the nation after them.

Verse 23. Honorable burial has always been something to be desired by people of all classes. To be deprived of it at all was a misfortune. To have the body mangled and devoured by vicious animals, and especially by the dogs, was the extremity of humiliation. This was predicted of Jezebel and fulfilled in 2 Ki. 9: 33-36.

Verse 24. Ahab's body was to be given royal burial in the capital city of his kingdom. But his posterity was to suffer the same fate as Jezebel.

Verse 25. Ahab was not excused in his wickedness because of his wife; the subject is mentioned to explain why his life was worse than it would have been had it not been for her evil influence over him.

Verse 26. The *Amorites* were a distinct people and very evil. The name, however, came to be used as a symbol of wicked nations in general.

Verse 27. See the comments at verse 25. The actions of Ahab described in this place justifies those comments. Jezebel was never shown to have a penitent moment, while Ahab was. *Went softly* means he went gently or submissively. His arrogance was gone and he gave outward indications of repentance.

Verses 28, 29. The penitence of Ahab could not affect the evils predicted to come on his posterity. As a consideration, however, for his humility, he was to be spared the pain of seeing the calamity come.

1 KINGS 22

Verse 1. Ahab had released Benhadad (Ch. 20: 34), but he had such a close call that no attempt was made to make war with Israel for three years.

Verse 2. For some unrevealed reason, Jehosphaphat, king of Judah called on Ahab.

Verse 3. The presence of Jehoshaphat seemed to encourage Ahab to make a military venture, to repossess the city of Ramoth, which was located in Gilead, a district east of the Jordan. He made a proposition to that effect to his servants.

Verse 4. Ahab wished to have Jehoshaphat as an ally in the proposed attack on Ramoth, and asked him if he would go. The last sentence of the verse was Jehoshaphat's way of saying that they would merge their forces and use them as the forces of one man.

Verse 5. Jehoshaphat is classed among the good kings of Judah, although the project he agreed to with Ahab was ill-advised. However, his respect for God made him unwilling to make the venture without some instructions, and the method of obtaining such in those days was through the prophets. (Heb. 1: 1.)

Verses 6, 7. Ahab doubtless understood that the prophets were the means of hearing from the Lord. When Jehoshaphat asked him to enquire at the word of the Lord, he called for them. Prophets, like other teachers, sometimes give instructions they think will be relished by their hearers, whether such instructions are correct or not. Knowing such a fact, Jehoshaphat felt some misgiving at the advice of these 400 prophets, who were likely student prophets. So he asked for another prophet besides these.

Verse 8. It is significant that 400 prophets were acceptable to Ahab, while the one was not. The explanation is in the thoughts expressed in the preceding paragraph. When people do not want to hear unpleasant truth, they dislike the man who might give them such. Ahab made a rash statement about Micaiah and Jehoshaphat gave him a mild rebuke for it. But he did not consent to discard the calling of the prophet.

Verse 9. On Jehoshaphat's insistence, Ahab sent an officer to bring Micaiah.

Verse 10. *Void* means an open, level place near the gate of the city. Two kings were to give a hearing as royal personages. As they could not each be on his own proper throne, they provided a temporary one for each, in a place accessible for the group to be present. The prophets referred to were the 400 we read about in V. 6.

Verses 11, 12. When God needs to have some unfavorable work done, he uses an agency qualified for that purpose. In the present instance it was decided that Ahab be deceived, and the instruments by which it was to be done were the lying prophets. They were specifically qualified for such a work as we will see later in the chapter. The 400 prophets had a chief spokesman, named Zedekiah. He was led to do some acting (see comments at Ch. 20: 35) to impress Ahab, and a bright prospect was held out for the subjection of Syria. All the rest of the 400 were "yes men" and also encouraged Ahab to go on with the expedition against Syria.

Verses 13, 14. The messenger sent after Micaiah tried to prejudice him to join in with the other prophets in encouraging the king to go on with his plans. He was told that what the Lord directed him to say was what they would hear.

Verse 15. We cannot hear the voice of Micaiah, and thus do not know the irony manifested in it. The circumstances, however, show that Ahab understood it as such.

Verse 16. *Adjure* means to swear, and Ahab meant to charge Micaiah to tell the truth, as if he were under oath.

Verse 17. The prophet abandoned his irony and spoke seriously. The illustration he used about the sheep without a shepherd was specific as to the fate of Ahab, for he was destined to be taken from his people. It will be fulfilled in this chapter.

Verse 18. This speech showed that Ahab understood the indirect prophecy of Micaiah to have reference to him; it also showed that he really anticipated such a prediction. It is a curious trait of the human mind to "put far the evil day" by trying to avoid hearing what is known to be the unpleasant news awaiting, just as if ignorance of its actual form of speech would prevent its coming.

Verse 19. Micaiah is the speaker, reporting the vision he saw in connection with the present situation. *Host of heaven* means the soldiers in the services of heaven; specifically the angels. They were "standing by" in readiness for the Lord's services.

Verse 20. *Persuade* is from a word that is also defined "delude." The hard question is, why would the Lord be a party to deception? He has used agencies at various times to accomplish the results necessary to his plans. Some of the cases included pleasant, others unpleasant, experiences for the victims or recipients. When such results were to be brought about, the Lord called and qualified the agencies to be used. A few instances of these special services will be cited. Pharaoh oppressed the Israelites. The Babylonians destroyed Jerusalem and took the people into captivity. Cyrus freed the Israelites and helped reconstruct their city and temple. Judas betrayed Christ and thus helped in his crucifixion. The Romans destroyed Jerusalem and dissolved the national unity of the Jews. It should be noted that in no one of these cases was the agency made better or worse. When God was through with that agency, he left it in exactly the same status it had when brought into that service. We should not be confused, therefore, by these strange performances of the Lord. Ahab is going to be misled by the Lord, but it will not affect his character. He has been a wicked man and will be left a wicked man. God called for volunteers among the host to go and delude Ahab.

Verse 21. *Came forth a spirit* does not mean the others who had spoken were not spirits. Heb. 1: 14 says that the angels are spirits and no distinction is made. But our verse means that after the indefinite *manner* in which the other angels had spoken, at last came one offering to make a definite proposition.

Verse 22. This spirit was told to reveal his plan. He proposed to go into the world and inspire the 400 prophets to give a misleading prediction. Let the reader again carefully consider the comments on V. 20. The plan was approved by the Lord.

Verse 23. Having related the vision he saw and hearing what was said, Micaiah connected it with the occasion then being staged. It was his explanation of the difference between the prediction of the 400, and the one made when Ahab placed him on oath.

Verse 24. Micaiah was absent when Zedekiah made the favorable, but false prediction for Ahab. He evidently knew of the program planned among the heavenly host, which was for a spirit to go from the Lord into the mind of the false prophet. Now when he heard Micaiah first make the same kind of false prediction that he had (though in irony on the part of Micaiah), then change it, after describing the scene in heaven—hearing all this speech, Zedekiah realized that the same (lying) spirit had spoken to each; first to him, then to Micaiah. That is what prompted the question he asked of Micaiah. *Which way* was about the same as if he sneeringly had asked, "How come the spirit of the Lord to go from me to thee?"

Verse 25. Zedekiah does not again appear in history, so we cannot cite the fulfillment of this humiliating prediction. Knowing, however, that the question was asked more from jesting curiosity than sincere interest, Micaiah predicted that the false prophet would some day try to hide from God. When that time comes, he will learn by humiliating experience, how the Spirit of God works when an evil man is sought.

Verses 26, 27. See the comments at V. 8, considering them in the light of this. *Bread* and *water of affliction* means the coarse fare served to prisoners. Ahab gave these orders in retaliation for the unfavorable prediction Micaiah had just made. *Until I come in peace* was a defiant way of saying, "You have predicted my defeat; but I will return in peace finally, and you will have to be a prisoner, and live on prisoner's rations until I do return."

Verse 28. Micaiah staked his reputation as a true prophet on the outcome of the venture that Ahab was about to make. He called attention of the people to it, so that when the affair was ended, they would remember the word spoken.

Verses 29, 30. The two allies prepared to go up to battle. Let it be borne in mind that the king of Syria did not know he was to meet the king of Judah. Ahab was thinking of that, and planned to elude the Syrian weapons by not appearing in the attire of a king. Jehoshaphat would be the only one in such robes and hence would be the target for the foe. If this scheme could be carried out, Ahab hoped to frustrate the prediction of Micaiah and so be able to return in peace, as he had boasted.

Verse 31. To take the king is about the same as taking the army. The Syrian king, thinking only of the king of Israel, gave the orders recorded in this verse.

Verse 32. The charioteers were not personally acquainted with the Israelite kings. Seeing one man in the royal robes, it was natural to conclude that he was the man they wanted, and were about to make their attack on Jehoshaphat, who made an outcry. Ordinarily that would not have availed to ward off the attack. 2 Chr. 18: 31 says "the Lord helped him," which accounts for his escape.

Verse 33. The Lord helped Jehoshaphat by revealing to the Syrian soldiers that he was not the man they wanted, which caused them to turn away.

Verse 34. *Venture* commonly means something uncertain; that the man just shot the arrow in a haphazard manner, that it was shot without any regard for its mark. The original will not allow that conclusion; it is defined "completeness." The statement means that the pulling of the bow and the aim of the arrow was a soldierly act and intended to find one of the men in the other army. What the "certain man" did not know was that he was actually directing his arrow toward the king of Israel. That is where the Lord again took a hand, by guiding the arrow so it would find the man destined to fall, and fulfill the prediction made by Micaiah. The *harness* means the armor that Ahab wore under his ordinary clothing. The arrow found an opening in this armor and entered into his body, making a fatal wound. The marginal rendering is "made sick." It means that Ahab realized he was mortally wounded, and wanted to be taken to the rear.

Verse 35. The request of Ahab was not granted. He was held up by assistants through the day while the battle raged. His wound was bleeding all the while and covered the bottom of the chariot. In the evening he died, fulfilling Ch. 20: 42.

Verse 36. The death of the king discouraged his army and they dispersed.

Verse 37. In respect for the dignity of his position, Ahab was buried in the capital city of his kingdom.

Verse 38. A servant washed the chariot *in the pool*. The first word is rendered "at" by Moffatt, and "by" in the Revised Version. That is a clearer form, and agrees with the idea of the blood's running out into a place where the dogs could reach it. When they licked up this blood they fulfilled Ch. 21: 19.

Verse 39. The mention of an ivory house would give a glimpse at the luxury indulged in by Ahab. For *chronicles* see comments at Ch. 14: 19.

Verse 40. *Slept* is explained at Ch. 2: 10. The successor to Ahab is named in connection with his death, but nothing further here. See comments at Ch. 12: 17.

Verse 41. Going back a number of years, to the 4th year of Ahab (whose death has just been reported), the writer takes up the reign of Jehoshaphat. We have already heard a considerable amount about him, but it was in connection with the reign of Ahab, king of Israel. Again, let the reader consult Ch. 12: 17. Now we will read about the conclusion of his own reign.

Verse 42. Jerusalem is generally named as the place where the kings of Judah reigned. That city was the capital of the two-tribe kingdom is the reason. *Mother's* name is explained at Ch. 14: 21.

Verse 43. Jehoshaphat was one of the good kings of Judah. The fairness of the Scriptures in reporting the conduct of God's people is seen in that the weaknesses of the best of them are pointed out. One of those weaknesses was the use of the *high places*. However, that was not the most grievous of the faults. See the comments at Ch. 3: 2 for explanation of these places of sacrifices.

Verse 44. Peace is desirable and required by the Lord when it can be obtained properly. Peace through improper association, however, was not sanctioned by Him. 2 Chr. 18: 1, 19: 1 indicates the Lord was not pleased with the friendship of Jehoshaphat for Ahab. That was not because the latter was the king of Israel, for God had placed his blessing on that kingdom as a whole. (Ch. 12: 24.) The objection to this affinity was because Ahab was a wicked man and not worthy the friendship of a good one.

Verse 45. See Ch. 14:19 for comments on *chronicles*.

Verse 46. The *sodomites* are described at Ch. 14:24.

Verses 47-49. This paragraph is parenthetical in thought, specifying some of the "acts" of Jehoshaphat. *No king in Edom* means no man there was ruling in his own right. 2 Sam. 8:14 shows the subjection of the land of Edom to the children of Israel. This *deputy* was appointed by Jehoshaphat, and served in the enterprise connected with the plan to go after the gold, which failed. A son of Ahab had offered to furnish servants to go on the expedition, but the offer was refused. We are not told whether that fact had anything to do with the failure of the venture, or not.

Verse 50. Chronologically, this verse belongs immediately after V. 46. *Slept* is explained at Ch. 2:10. The successor to Jehoshaphat is named in connection with his death, which is the usual form of report. The incidents of Jehoram's own reign, however, will not begin until several chapters in the next book have been reached.

Verse 51. The reign of Ahab's son is dated from a certain year of Jehoshaphat, king of Judah. See Ch. 12:17 for comments on this point.

Verses 52, 53. These verses are concise and sum up the accounting for the wicked reign of this son of Ahab. It was because he followed in the counsel of his parents, both of whom were wicked, and of Jeroboam the first king of Israel. Many of the personal acts of Ahaziah are recorded in the book of 2 Kings which will immediately follow.

2 KINGS 1

Verse 1. David had brought the Moabites under tribute to the children of Israel. (2 Sam. 8:2.) They continued in that relation until after the death of Ahab, at which time they rebelled and made war. This verse barely introduces the subject of the situation, then the writer drops it to insert certain other happenings among noted individuals. It will be taken up again at Ch. 3:4, 5.

Verse 2. The injury that Ahaziah received by his fall was very severe. It was not immediately fatal, however, and the outcome was uncertain. In other words, the condition was apparently such that superhuman information was thought necessary to determine it. Baal was the general name of an idolatrous deity, and zebub was a special one located at Ekron, a Philistine city. To this place the wounded man ordered his messengers to go for the information on his case.

Verse 3. Had there been no man of God available, it would still have been an insult to God for one of his professed servants to recognize an idol god. The prophet Elijah was told by the angel to intercept the messengers of Ahaziah. *Is it not because*, etc., is in the form of a question. The meaning of it is an accusation of ignoring the true God of Israel, which was a deep offense to Him.

Verse 4. We do not know whether Ahaziah's injury was necessarily fatal; it might have been. But in whatever case the victim was involved, the outcome was as yet hidden from his knowledge. The information was thus given him by the prophet that he would die.

Verses 5, 6. The early return of his messengers caused Ahaziah to ask why. They gave a true account of their meeting with *a man*.

Verses 7, 8. *An hairy man* does not mean merely that he had a thick growth of hair, but the lexicon describes it as meaning it was in a ruffled and unkempt condition. Being apart from society much of the time, Elijah took this habit. Ahaziah had evidently seen him and recognized the description.

Verse 9. The king had previously known of Elijah's authority, else he would not have sent to him for assistance in this predicament of his. But the whole procedure indicated he appealed to the true God as a last resort only. We are not told just what form of speech the captain had been instructed to use in his request. He used the wrong one, however, as we can see; one of arrogance instead of humility. The words *man of God* acknowledge Elijah to be a servant of the true God, hence there was no excuse for the disrespectful demand expressed. *Come down* was a dictatorial expression, which did not recognize their master as being the one in need of aid, but rather, that Elijah was the one to be benefited by the occasion. The information had already been given Ahaziah from Elijah that the injury was to end fatally. It means, therefore, that Ahaziah thought to influence the prophet to reverse the decision and cause his recovery.

Verse 10. Turning the abject acknowledgement of the captain into a taunt, Elijah called upon that very God over him to destroy the whole group with fire.

Verses 11, 12. The scene with the first captain and his 50 men was repeated in duplicate, except the word *quickly* was added, thereby making it still more arrogant.

Verses 13, 14. Nothing has been said about spectators at the first two transactions. We know there was some means by which it was known what took place, for the third captain mentioned the matter in his pleading address to Elijah. The only request that is recorded was on behalf of him and his men. We know, however, that Elijah was requested to go with the men, from what the angel said to him in the next verse.

Verse 15. The angel gave Elijah assurance of his life, and on that he went to the king of Israel.

Verse 16. We still do not know what might have been the natural outcome of Ahaziah's injury. The prophet of God could have healed him with divine help regardless of the severity of the case. But the edict that the king was to die was due to his attempt to consult an idolatrous god. This conclusion is based on the fact that, after referring to the matter of consultation with the idolatrous god, Elijah said *therefore*.

Verse 17. The same name was common to more than one person in ancient times, even as it is today. In the line of rulers over Judah was a man named Jehoram. In his second year, began the reign of another Jehoram over Israel. The last named Jehoram was a brother to Ahaziah, who died of his injury. The reason this Jehoram reigned over Israel is stated, *because he* (Ahaziah) *had no son*.

Verse 18. For *chronicles* see the comments at 1 Ki. 14: 19.

2 KINGS 2

Verse 1. Genesis 5: 22-24; Heb. 11: 5 gives account of Enoch's being taken from the earth without death; the Lord will do the same thing with Elijah. There is no statement in the Bible that shows why God did this to these men, when the edict had gone forth that all men must die. (Heb. 9: 27.) It is an accepted idea, however, that an exception to a rule will emphasize and establish the rule. Elijah and Elisha had been close to each other, and the latter had been already designated as the prophet to take the place of the former. (1 Ki. 19: 16.) Considered mechanically, a whirlwind would be the ideal kind of storm by which to draw a man upward. It would affect a comparatively small area, and leave the persons and things nearby undisturbed. That will explain how Elisha could be near enough to see and talk with Elijah at the time.

Verse 2. Elijah knew that he was soon to leave the earth. Just why he appeared eager to get away from Elisha, we are not told. He mentioned more than one point to which the Lord was sending him; one after the other. His suggestions for Elisha to tarry at one of the given places intimated that the distance they would have to travel was great, and it was not necessary for him to make that journey just because Elijah had to. The Biblical statement at the close of this verse is one that is common in the Scriptures. It is as if he said, "As surely as the Lord and I are living, that sure it is that," etc. There was no principle against their traveling together, hence they did so for the present.

Verse 3. *Sons of the prophets* means the men who were pupils under the older ones, being trained in the work of prophets. They had some communication directly with the Lord, and had received some information regarding the present program for Elijah. Their term *thy master* was in respect for the seniority of Elijah over Elisha in the line of national prophets. (1 Ki. 19: 16.) Elisha also had information that Elijah was to leave him. That was an unpleasant thought and he did not want to be reminded of it, hence his demand for these student prophets to hold their peace about it.

Verse 4. Elijah named another distant point, and suggested that Elisha not go any farther. He received the same kind of answer he did before, so they traveled on.

Verse 5. The *sons of the prophets* at Jericho had received the same information about Elijah that had been given to the ones at Bethel. In answer to their reminder for Elisha, they received the same order that the others had.

Verse 6. For the third time, Elijah suggested that Elisha halt in his journey, and received the same kind of an answer. One difference in the last instance was, the place to which Elijah was to go (Jordan) was more indefinite as to exact location.

Verse 7. The procedure of the great prophets was arousing the interest of the student prophets. Fifty of them followed at seeing distance as they arrived at the Jordan.

Verse 8. Moses and Aaron used a rod in connection with their miracles. (Ex. 7: 17.) Jesus used clay in healing the blind man. (John 9: 6, 7.) Elijah used the mantle in forcing a passage across the Jordan. There was an important point in such performances. Had something been used that might have a physical or logical relation to the result desired and obtained, it might have been claimed that such was the cause. But since these things could have nothing to do with the actual problem the conclusion is clear, that the result was obtained through divine power.

Verse 9. Elisha has persistently refused to separate from Elijah, and he was no longer asked to do so. Let us note that Elijah did not tell Elisha he could have anything he wanted. This kind of distinction was made in the case of Solomon at Gibeon. (1 Ki. 3: 5.) Mathematically speaking, it would be impossible for one to receive more than all of another's spirit. We are sure that Elisha received that since he was to take the place of Elijah. (1 Ki. 19: 16.) The thought, then, is figurative. It was a desire to receive abundantly of the same spirit that had been possessed by Elijah. The request was an exalted one, and not one that looked for personal gain.

Verse 10. A thing could be *hard* or difficult or unusual, yet not wrong or impossible. That which Elisha asked for was very rare, but was right, and was promised to him on condition. Previously, Elijah had designated certain places he expected to be and asked to be left alone. Now the attitude has been changed and Elisha was placed on his guard, to be always on the alert lest his master slip away from him. There is no explanation given for the change in Elijah's attitude.

Verse 11. *Parted them* means the fiery chariot separated the two prophets. *Went up into heaven.* The Old Testament uses the same original word for "heaven," whether the 1st, 2nd, or 3rd heaven is meant. The connection in each case must be relied on to determine which is meant. It was the first heaven, or domain of the atmosphere that received Elijah as far as Elisha could see. From other considerations, however, we understand that he was taken to the 3rd heaven, the abode of God. (Matt. 17: 3.) There is another important thought about this. Elijah had to leave the earth in order to get to heaven where God is. That disproves a doctrine among men that all the heaven there is to be is on the earth. The word translated *fire* is defined in the lexicon as having both a literal and figurative meaning. The case at hand means the chariot and horses were of a flaming or fiery appearance.

Verse 12. The word for father is so rendered in most places, but by "chief" in a few other places. It was evidently used in that sense by Elisha. As chief person among the children of Israel, he would mean to Elisha as much as all the other chariots and their drivers. With such a loss to him and his people, he expressed his grief by a well known custom of rending his garment.

Verse 13. A popular saying supposed to be based on this circumstance is, that the mantle of Elijah fell on Elisha, when people are moralizing on the subject of one person's committing his work to another. A careful reading will show that to be erroneous. The mantle had fallen to the ground, and Elisha picked it up voluntarily.

Verse 14. *Where is the Lord God of Elijah* was said in the sense of calling upon that God. As Elisha made that call he also used the same mantle and for the same purpose as did Elijah in V. 8. See the comments at that verse. After invoking, successfully, the mantle, Elisha recrossed the Jordan back into Canaan proper.

Verse 15. Jericho is near the Jordan, and that was the place from which the *sons of the prophets* had stood to *view afar off.* (V. 7). By this we learn of the place where the two great prophets had crossed the river Jordan. When these *sons of the prophets* saw the miracle that Elisha did with the mantle, they concluded it was done through the same spirit that Elijah had possessed. With due respect for the successor of the great prophet Elijah, these young prophets bowed before Elisha.

Verse 16. The sons of the prophets had twice told Elisha (Vs. 3, 5) that his master was to be taken from his *head that day.* That meant merely that he would be deprived of his master's personal association, but no evidence is apparent that they knew it was to be permanent; neither did they know that he was to leave the earth. All of this explains why they were so concerned about his bodily safety. They offered their services for a search of Elijah. But Elisha had a better knowledge of the affair, and objected to their proposal.

Verse 17. Elisha knew he was correct in his judgment, and therefore had nothing to be ashamed of as the word is commonly used. The original is defined by Strong, "to pale, i. e. by implication to be ashamed; also (by implication) to be disappointed, or delayed." It has been translated in the A. V. by delay, be long and others. The thought is that the men insisted so long that Elisha concluded he would not delay longer, but would let them learn a lesson by their own disappointment. Upon his consent the eager group went in search for Elijah; three days of fruitless search followed.

Verse 18. Elisha was so sure the men would return that he tarried at Jericho for them. Upon their coming back, he chastised them mildly by reminding them of his advice.

Verse 19. *Situation* means the site of the city, that the "view" was agreeable. *Naught* is from RAH and defined, "bad or (as noun) evil (naturally or morally)"—Strong. *Barren* is from SHAKOL and Strong defines it, "A primitive root; properly to miscarry, i. e. suffer abortion." This condition was practically admitted by Elisha, so that we need not doubt the statement by the citizens. Something must have come up to cause the condition, for Jericho was a popular city and no such complaint had been made of it. Some kind of germ had crept into the source of drinking water, causing abortion with expectants who needed to use it. The citizens would know of Elisha's miraculous power, for he had just performed the feat of forcing a passage across the Jordan nearby. They told him of the defect in their city, with the hope that he would do something about it.

Verses 20-22. *Spring of waters* means the source of their drinking water, thus showing that it was the water that was infected and not the ground. This observation is important in meeting the critic who would say that salt would kill the ground instead of causing it to yield fruit.

Verse 23. *Bald head.* The second word is not in the original. The first is from QUERACH and Strong defines it, "bald (on the back of the head)." It is the word for "bald" in Lev. 13: 40, where it is seen to contrast with "forehead bald" in V. 41. *Children* is from NAAR and Strong defines it, "A boy from the age of infancy to adolescence." *Go* is from ALAH and defined, "A primitive root; to ascend, intransitively (be high) actively (mount)."—Strong. The wording of the common text is correct. In derision with reference to the ascension of Elijah, the master of Elisha, these boys made fun of the prophet. For some reason the back of his head was bald, which could be seen by the boys as they followed him. As an impertinent remark, which they probably thought was smart, they taunted Elisha with the suggestion that, as he was a baldheaded old man, he was ready to leave this world, and should follow the other old man who had just gone up from the earth.

Verse 24. *Cursed.* Unfortunately, this word has acquired an exaggerated meaning in the popular mind. It is thought of as being some profane and harsh language, expressed against someone with the idea of inflicting a specially dire penalty. It is from QUALAL, and Strong defines it, "a primitive root; to be (causatively make) light, literally (swift, small, sharp, etc.) or figuratively (easy, trifling, vile, etc.)." The passage means that Elisha pronounced them as very insignificant and unworthy; also very rash and inconsiderate in what they said, and deserving of some punishment. As far as the text shows, however, Elisha left it for the Lord to decide on what it should be. He caused 42 of them to be destroyed by wild beasts. This was a severe punishment, but disrespect for their elders was also a serious offense, and children need to know how wrong it is; a severe punishment was the necessary penalty for that lesson.

Verse 25. After all these experiences, Elisha went on his way. Passing on to Mount Carmel, he went on to Samaria where he spent much of his time. It is in this place where we will see some of his most noted exploits. The city was the capital of the kingdom of Israel, and thus a fitting headquarters for this national prophet.

2 KINGS 3

Verse 1. It is important that the reader avoid confusion over the switching back and forth of the accounts concerning the kingdom of Judah and Israel. Read the comments at 1 Ki. 12: 17 frequently. Also remember that the Bible is not always chronological in its historical reports in other parts; much less would it be in this place, where two rival, but related kingdoms, are being reported simultaneously. Jehoram's reign was mentioned in Ch. 1: 17 and then dropped to give us accounts of the two great prophets, Elijah and Elisha, whose lives were so closely woven together for a time.

Verses 2, 3. The Bible gives credit where it is due. Jehoram was the son of Ahab and Jezebel, who were exceptionally wicked people. This son was not as bad as they, and had corrected a part of their evil work by removing the image of Baal. He was bad enough, however, and followed the example of Jeroboam, the first king of Israel.

Verses 4, 5. The revolt of Moab was barely mentioned at Ch. 1: 1 but is resumed here. The particular act that signified the break was the withholding of tribute. The king of Moab had been *rendering* or delivering to Israel 100,000 each of lambs and rams per year. That tribute was stopped which amounted to a declaration of war.

Verse 6. One word in the definition of the original for *numbered* is "muster." Jehoram was preparing for war with Moab, and went out to get his soldiers together.

Verse 7. It is highly probable that Jehoram knew of the alliance that was formed between Jehoshaphat and Ahab, father of Ahaziah and Jehoram, in the war with Syria. That encouraged him to ask for a similar alliance with him for the war with Moab. He was not disappointed, and the answer was the same as that given to Ahab. See 1 Ki. 22: 4.

Verse 8. After agreeing to the alliance, Jehoshaphat asked Jehoram his advice as to the proper route in the approach to Moab. The reply was that they go by the wilderness of Edom. That land was south of Moab, while these Israelite kings were north and west. That made it necessary for them to take a roundabout route. The object for the move is not stated, but from the facts of the next verse, Jehoram must have had reason to expect some favor from Edom.

Verse 9. Sure enough, the king of Edom joined as an ally of Jehoram and Jehoshaphat. *Compass of seven days* means the route they chose was out of the way to the extent that it took seven days longer. It also took them into a territory where there was no drinking water.

Verse 10. Jehoram became uneasy and feared that perhaps the situation was brought about by the Lord; if so, it was in order to entrap them with the Moabites.

Verse 11. After the law of Moses was completed and left with God's people, it was regarded as all the Lord wanted in the way of statute law, or formal enactment. That is why we have the words "and he added no more" in Deut. 5: 22. As time went on, it was necessary to have the services of inspired men in interpreting that law to show its proper application, also to give specific information in emergencies. For such purposes God used the priests (Lev. 10: 8-11; Deut. 17: 9, 10; Mal. 2: 7) and the prophets. See Heb. 1: 1. Jehoshaphat had good reason, therefore, to call for *a prophet of the Lord*. He was told of an available one by the name of Elisha. *Poured water on the hands of Elijah*. This fact is not mentioned in any other place, and is doubtless merely a reference to his ministrations to the head prophet over him. Moffatt's translation is, "who used to be servant to Elijah."

Verse 12. Jehoshaphat recognized Elisha as an inspired prophet, and the three kings went to confer with him.

Verse 13. *What have I to do with thee* is the same as saying, "What are you coming to me for?" *Prophets of thy father* means the prophets whom Ahab and Jezebel relied on when they wanted advice to their liking; they were the idolatrous ones. Jehoram still believed the Lord had brought about the alliance of these three kings for the purpose of some punishment. But it was Jehoshaphat who insisted on their advising with the prophet before venturing on their military enterprise.

Verse 14. Jehoshaphat was a good king, and his presence caused Elisha to respect the group of kings standing in his presence.

Verse 15. The *minstrel* was a musician. Just why Elisha wished the services of this person we do not know. It was in line, however, with the practice of the prophets and other miracle workers in the Biblical times. It gives a concrete exhibition of the fact mentioned by Paul in Heb. 1: 1 that, not only did God speak to the fathers by the prophets, but he did so "at sundry times and in divers manners."

Verses 16, 17. *Ditches* is from a word that means pools. God proposed to bring a flow of water into the valley, and the pools would store up and save the precious liquid after the general spread had served its purpose, and had flowed away. This was to be a miraculous supply of water, and not brought by ordinary weather conditions.

Verses 18, 19. *Light thing* means that it is unimportant compared with the other miracle they will receive. Managing an army of men would be a mightier feat than bringing forth a supply of water. *Fenced city* means a walled or fortified city. *Choice city* means a city very desirable from standpoints other than being walled. To *mar* the fields with stones means to strew it with them so they cannot be cultivated.

Verse 20. *Meat offering*. The first word is not in the original as a separate word. The expression as a whole refers to the regular time of morning sacrifice which was nine o'clock. The miraculous supply came from the direction of the land of Edom, until the country had the appearance of a lake.

Verse 21. About this time the Moabites awoke to their danger, and gathered all their fighting men for battle.

Verses 22, 23. This body of water was between the allies and the Moabites. From the angle where the latter looked in the direction of the water, it was made to look like blood. This could be aptly called a miraculous camouflage, for the Lord certainly caused it to occur to deceive the Moabites. They concluded the enemies were slain and that their blood was causing the red which they saw. With the enemy slain, nothing was to hinder them from taking the spoil, so they thought, and thus announced it.

Verse 24. The camp of the allies, which was in charge of the Israelites, was kept quiet. The soldiers were lying low, looking for the Moabites to come on with no expectation of meeting any resistance. All of this was an effective maneuver, doubtless inspired by the Lord as his means of causing fulfillment of the promise in verses 18, 19. The allies sprang to the attack and overcame the Moabites. They were put to flight and chased even to their own country with great slaughter.

Verse 25. *Only in Kir-hareseth*. The first word is not in the original. The R. V. words it, "until in Kir-hareseth," etc. The verse means they made exception of this city in their general destruction with the large stones. But it was not to escape entirely, for the men with the slings encompassed the city and smote the people.

Verse 26. This kind of maneuver is called a storm attack. It sometimes obtains an entrance through the enemy's lines when all other means fail. The attack was a failure in this case and the Moabites were forced to retire.

Verse 27. This human sacrifice was not with sincere devotion to the idolatrous god of the Moabites, for in that case it would have been done at some proper shrine of the gods. It was done *upon the wall*, in sight of the Israelites. That created such a sentimental protest among them that the leaders were forced to leave the scene.

2 KINGS 4

Verse 1. The *sons of the prophets* were sometimes married men, although only students of the older ones. The widow of one of them was the complainant before Elisha. It was a practice among certain ones to sieze upon human chattels as security for debts. In consideration of her devotion to the Lord, she thought the prophet should help her.

Verse 2. *What shall I do for thee* was asked in the sense of merely introducing the subject. It might be considered as a meditative form of speech, leading up to the more specific inquiry into her own resources.

Verse 3. There is no limit to divine power, whether in connection with human effort or not. But it has always been a rule of God to require man to do what he could. This woman had a supply of oil and it will be used as a starter. See a similar situation in the widow and the meal, in 1 Ki. 17: 12. Note that the woman in the present paragraph was admonished to borrow *not a few*.

Verse 4. Elisha left direct connection with the case after giving instructions.

Verse 5. In obedience to the order from Elisha, the woman closed the door and began filling the borrowed vessels, using the pot of oil that she had as a source.

Verse 6. The supply of oil was continuous as long as there was any provision to care for it. When that failed, the flow of oil stopped. This was what was signified when Elisha cautioned, "borrow not a few" in V. 3.

Verses 7. Olive oil, which was the only kind known in that day, was valuable in many ways. Now that the woman had a large store of it, she did not know what Elisha intended for her to do with it, until he authorized her to use it in meeting her debt, and as a source of future income.

Verse 8. *It fell on a day* is the same as if we would say, "one day Elisha came to Shunem." We are not told what business took him there this time or afterward. But a certain woman of some prominence saw him and offered him her hospitality. Having been treated thus kindly, he made it a regular thing to stop at this house.

Verses 9, 10. Houses were built with flat roofs. A chamber *on the wall* was an "addition" to the main building, and could be entered and left independent of the rest of the house. That would be very appropriate for Elisha, as he was coming and going frequently, and this arrangement would accommodate him without always joining in with the family life. So a little furniture was installed and the guest room turned over for the use of the *man of God*.

Verse 11. It fell on a day is an obsolete form of saying, "so one day," etc. Elisha had accepted the hospitality with appreciation.

Verse 12. The woman of the house was called by the servant, Gehazi, and stood in talking distance of him, so that he could act as a go-between for her and Elisha.

Verse 13. The message passed from Elisha to the woman was to bid her name a wish. It was suggested that a good word be spoken in her behalf to the king or general of the army. Perhaps they would provide a more suitable place of residence. But she declined the offer and preferred to remain with her relatives.

Verse 14. Elisha asked his servant to suggest something for the woman. He was told that she had no child. She evidently was much younger than her husband, for only he was mentioned as being old. Had she been old as well as he, it certainly would have been as logical to refer to her age, as to his; if any difference, more so to her.

Verse 15. The woman was recalled and stood in the door of his room.

Verse 16. *Time of life* refers to the natural period of carrying the unborn child. The promise of a son seemed incredible to the woman. Nothing was said about her age or condition otherwise in view of becoming a mother. All we have that would bear on the subject is the remark of Gehazi, that her husband was old. That fact, and the remark of doubt by the woman, leaves the conclusion that the husband was thought of as being too old to beget a child. The word *lie* sounds so harsh to us that we shrink from it. To "deceive" is the same principle but not so severe on the ear; the original has been so rendered in other places. The woman was so surprised and taken aback that she instinctively used the term. The whole statement might be worded, "You are a man of God; surely, then, you would not deceive me about this."

Verse 17. The promise was fulfilled and the child was born at *the time of life*, meaning the proper time after conception.

Verse 18. *Grown* is from an original with indefinite meaning. It does not necessarily mean *fully* grown; but only that the child had grown enough to perform the action of walking out into the field to his father.

Verse 19. *Lad* is from NAAR and is sometimes translated "servant" in the A. V. Some convulsive attack came upon the boy that caused his complaint. Since it was a time of harvest (reapers), it is possible that it was a sunstroke.

Verse 20. The child was old enough to walk to the field, but young enough to be carried by the servant, and nursed in his mother's arms until he died.

Verse 21. How natural it was for the mother to take the body of her child into the room of Elisha. He was the one who had promised the son to her, and through whose intercession the Lord had granted it. Besides, she must leave the body for a time, and she would desire it to have as much privacy as possible. Therefore she *went up* (the room was on the wall) and laid him on the bed of *the man of God*.

Verse 22. This verse would indicate that the regular dwelling places of Elisha and the woman were not far apart. Mount Carmel was a range 12 miles long. Shunem was in the same general territory of this range, hence the statement above. Furthermore, the distance could not have been too great, for it is evident that some of the actors in this drama traveled on foot.

Verse 23. It appears that the husband was not aware of the child's death. The usual occasion for calling on the prophet was for observance of some feast, such as that on the new moon or on a sabbath day. *It shall be well.* The last word only is in the original, but the thought of the group is authorized. The word is from SHALOM and Strong defines it, "safe. i. e. (figuratively) well, happy, friendly; also (abstractly) welfare, i. e. health, prosperity, peace." The expression indicates the woman's faith that it would finally be well with the child.

Verse 24. Some factors in this arrangement are not clear. Nothing is said about a second beast, yet the servant is urged not to slacken his riding. Neither is anything said about a vehicle for their common use; and that would have made the saddling of the beast unnecessary. The best solution in my mind is, they each rode a beast, and the servant was expected to stimulate the speed of hers by urging the one he was riding.

Verse 25, 26. The appearance of this woman under the circumstances made Elisha suspect that something was wrong. He bade his servant go to meet her, and to ask the questions about the welfare of the family. *It is well* is explained at V. 23.

Verse 27. Taking hold of Elisha's feet seemed to be an intrusion in the eyes of Gehazi. The prophet thought otherwise; that some great sorrow was upon her heart, and that Gehazi should not molest her.

Verses 28, 29. The entire conversation is not recorded. In the previous verse Elisha said the woman's grief had not been told him by the Lord, but in this paragraph he gives directions on account of the death, which shows that the woman told him about it. Laying the staff on the child was another instance of using a material, though not logical means, in connection with the miraculous results. See Ch. 2: 8.

Verse 30. "As sure as the Lord lives, just that sure will I not leave thee" is the meaning of the woman's statement. Upon this, Elisha went with her to her home.

Verse 31. Had there been any virtue in the staff, the child would have reacted when Gehazi laid it on him. Again, read the comments at Ch. 2: 8.

Verses 32, 33. We should understand that the *twain* were Elisha and the dead child. Why he wished no one else in the room we know not. Peter did a similar thing in the case of Dorcas. (Acts 9: 10.) It is one of those things that belong to the Lord and not to be revealed to us. See Deut. 29: 29.

Verse 34. When Paul restored the life of the young man at Troas (Acts 20: 10), he did so by embracing him, after which his life was in him. In the case of Elisha and the child, he made contact between their bodies, after which *the flesh of the child waxed warm.* The life was then returned to the body, although there was no activity as yet. The mere fact of contact by a living body with a dead one would not restore life, else it could still be done. But it was the Lord's way of doing the work this time. And once more, the reader is asked to see comments at Ch. 2: 8.

Verse 35. *Returned, and walked,* etc. This does not mean that he had left the house. The first word is defined in part by Strong, "to retreat." It means that Elisha retreated from the child so as to make his to-and-fro movement in the house. Moffatt's translation says, "rising up, he walked to and fro." After this, he contacted the child again, but not to restore his life. When warmth comes into a body that has been cold and dead, it is evidence of life. Just why it was desired to carry out the peculiar actions of this verse we are not told. We know it was not to restore life.

Verse 36. *Take up thy son* indicates that the child was not large, also that he might still be somewhat weak from the ordeal he had gone through. Elisha could have overcome even that, had it been the divine will. The Lord has always dealt on the principle of leaving it to man to do what he could. Jesus raised the daughter of Jairus from the dead, but commanded the people to feed her (Mark 5: 43), and he raised Lazarus to life, but told the sisters to remove the graveclothes. (John 11: 44.)

Verse 37. Gratitude prompted the mother to do this act of homage. *Bowed herself to the ground.* This room was on the wall and therefore had no literal ground in it. The key is in the word *to*, which has the meaning of *toward* the ground. The main thought is, the woman was so thankful and humble that she took a prostrate attitude of body before the prophet, bowing downward or toward the ground. A person could be said to do that if he were in the top story of a skyscraper.

Verse 38. In times of distress or emergency, the student prophets looked to their master prophet for relief. At this time the shortage of food was caused by the dearth, and the group of prophets expected something from Elisha. The large boiling vessel was ordered put on the fire to *seethe pottage*, which means to boil soup.

Verse 39. While one servant was making ready the pot for the soup, another was out foraging for something to use in the pottage. As there was a dearth, there would not be a great supply of vegetables. Strong defines these wild gourds as wild cucumbers. They resembled other vine products and hence the servants made the mistake of getting a poisonous plant.

Verse 40. By the time the soup was ready to eat its true character was discovered, and they appealed to Elisha to help them out of their predicament.

Verse 41. The *meal* was ground grain and an ordinary article of food. It had no power of removing poison from another food without miracle. The student should frequently refer to the comments at Ch. 2: 8.

Verse 42. *Full ears of corn.* The first word is not in the original. The others are from one word and defined in part by Strong, "garden produce." *Husks* is from TSIQLON and defined by Strong, "a sack (as tied at the mouth)." This part of the verse should be worded, "twenty loaves of barley, and garden produce, in a sack." The man who brought these provisions was told to feed the people with them.

Verses 43, 44. The word *servitor* means "contributor" and refers to the man who brought the bread and produce. He was puzzled at the thought of feeding so many people with such a small supply of food. His remark was similar in thought to that made by the disciples to Christ. (Matt. 15: 33.) In using this comparatively small amount of food for the multitude, Elisha followed a principle already mentioned a number of times. God will not do for man what he can do for himself. The widow's meal and oil contributed to the miraculous favor of God. The people before Elisha ate of the food set before them. They were abundantly satisfied, for they left some over.

2 KINGS 5

Verse 1. Naaman was commander in chief of the Syrian army. He was *honorable* which means he ranked high in the esteem of his king. The reason given for this high standing, is the fact that the Lord had given victory to his arms. This favor from God agrees with the declaration made to Nebuchadnezzar (Dan. 4: 17.) It also should be considered in connection with Rom. 13: 1-6. Since the existence of human governments is of divine origin, we should not wonder at God's interest and participation therein. He even has used them in chastising his own people. Naaman was afflicted with leprosy, an incurable disease by any natural remedy.

Verse 2. Syria was just north of Israel, and was frequently engaged in battle with that kingdom. In one of the raids into the territory of the Israelites, the Syrians had captured a little maid who became the attendant of Naaman's wife.

Verses 3, 4. The little maid remembered Elisha and his ability to cure disease. Her interest in the welfare of her master was sweet and unselfish. She had been taken out of her native land, and under the command of this very master. In spite of that, she was desirous of having him cured of the terrible disease. She spoke to her mistress about the matter, and another person revealed the message to the king, who was naturally eager that so valuable a soldier be healed.

Verse 5. *Go to, go.* This was an obsolete way of saying, "come, and I will send," etc. It was a mistake, doubtless due to some misunderstanding, that the king of Syria wrote to the king of Israel, instead of to the prophet Elisha. The articles mentioned to be taken along should not be considered as a bribe. It was customary to recognize kings and other dignitaries by making them presents. See 1 Ki. 4: 21; 2 Ki. 17: 3; 2 Chr. 17: 5; Psa. 68: 29.

Verse 6. If the king of Israel had been respectfully addressed, and then requested that the services of Elisha be tendered him, there might not have been any friction. The error was in asking the king to *recover him of his leprosy.*

Verse 7. Jehoram was the king of Israel at that time. He had never professed to have miraculous power, and this direct request, made by the king of a foreign nation, was equivalent to a declaration of war, or at least, a threat of one. Friendly nations are supposed to be willing to grant favors to each other, and the refusal is considered as an unfriendly act. By asking a favor on this established basis, and yet one that he knew would be impossible of fulfillment, it seemed that the king of Syria was laying plans for a pretext on which to make a complaint.

Verse 8. Word of the affair came to the ears of Elisha. The humbleness of the man of God, as well as his respect for the Lord, was indicated by the message he sent to the king. He brought out the significant motive he had for seeking the chance to cure Naaman; that he might know there was a (inspired) prophet in Israel.

Verse 9. The word was passed on to the unfortunate Naaman, and he arrived at the door of Elisha's house, eager to have him administer to his stricken condition.

Verse 10. The original word for *wash* applies to part or the whole of a body. The command was understood by Naaman, however, to mean to dip or plunge, for that is what he finally did, receiving the desired result. At the same time, much unnecessary speculation has been done on this case. Whether Naaman was afflicted in whole or in part of his body with the leprosy we do not know. The conclusion remains that what was done was a plunging into the water, not a mere application of water to the affected parts.

Verses 11, 12. Naaman belonged to a race of idolaters, and such people were more or less superstitious. They believed in the ceremonies of conjuration as a means of obtaining some superhuman result. Naaman was describing such a ceremony in this place. He reasoned on the theory that Elisha expected the leprosy to be healed through the virtue of the water. Had he been acquainted with the ideas offered to our readers at 2 Ki. 2: 8, he might have made a different speech. The rivers of Damascus were fed by clear and clean water, while the Jordan was a swift, muddy stream. The reasoning from a material standpoint, therefore, was sound. Naaman's disappointment caused him to turn away in a rage, and he was about to return home.

Verse 13. *Servant* and *father* are used as opposite terms in the present connection; the conclusion is that Naaman was regarded as their master. The line of thought the servants were following was that some *great thing* would have been done on the theory that it would have accomplished the desired end naturally, or as a logical consequence. The simpler instructions, however, should have commended themselves as coming from a person of authority. An uninspired man would need to use some great method, if the outcome sought were to be obtained. Therefore, this simpler and illogical plan should indicate to the interested party that it was no ordinary person who was directing him.

Verse 14. The inspired writer tells us that when Naaman *dipped* himself, it was according to the saying of the man of God. See comments on *wash* in V. 10. When "seven" is used figuratively it denotes completeness. One dipping would have ended in the cure of the leprosy, had the prophet seen fit to command only one. The desired result was obtained from the Lord, because Naaman went to the end of the commandment.

Verse 15. Gratitude is one of the greatest of virtues, and very unworthy is he who does not manifest it in return for favors. The benefit was already bestowed upon Naaman; his offer of the *blessing*, therefore, was from a pure and unselfish motive. The *blessing* is elsewhere translated "present" in the A. V. Naaman was a lord over others, but called himself a *servant* to Elisha, which was in humble respect for his benefactor.

Verse 16. There could not be anything morally wrong in offering or accepting the present. We are not told why Elisha refused it. He was so positive about it that he emphasized his determination by making it as sure as that the Lord lived.

Verse 17. We know there was earth available in the land of Syria. The use Naaman proposed to make of this was to build an altar on which to offer sacrifices. He had the erroneous idea that earth from the country where he had been converted to the God of Israel was more suitable for the purpose. Elisha made no objection to his taking the earth, nor to his proposal to offer sacrifices to God. The Patriarchal Dispensation was in force, and any man not an Israelite was eligible for proselyting to that form of religion, even if he were not in direct line. See Ex. 18: 12; Job 1: 5.

Verse 18. Naaman was a servant of the king, and he was an idolater. When they entered the house of Rimmon, an idolatrous temple, Naaman would still need to accompany his master to give him bodily support. By that sort of service he would have to move his body up or down in conjunction with his master's body. In this verse he is reserving the right to do that, and it was not to be regarded as a breaking of the promise just made to Elisha to worship God only.

Verse 19. The reservation was approved as indicated by the words, *go in peace*. *A little way* means he got only a short distance homeward until something happened, of which we will read in the next paragraph.

Verse 20. Gehazi, the servant of Elisha, had overheard the conversation between his master and Naaman. Being of covetous mind, he thought he saw an opportunity to get some valuables for his own possession, and Elisha would not know about it. *As the Lord liveth* means, "as sure as the Lord lives."

Verse 21. Naaman had not gone far, which is signified by the words *a little way* in V. 19. He saw Gehazi coming and stopped his travel to greet the approaching servant of his benefactor. *Is all well* was a courteous expression of good will.

Verse 22. The story that Gehazi told seemed reasonable. There was nothing morally wrong in the proposition to give something to Elisha; he merely was not disposed to accept it for his personal use. But this emergency of the arrival of the student prophets would change the situation; there would be nothing wrong in helping them.

Verse 23. Naaman would be glad for the opportunity to show his appreciation. In asking for only one talent of silver, Gehazi appeared very modest in the estimation of Naaman. That is why he *urged* him to take more. The amount of the gift called for some help in carrying it back to Elisha, and two servants were sent for that purpose.

Verse 24. Gehazi did not intend for Elisha to know anything about the ill gotten articles. As soon as they reached the tower, which would afford a hiding place for the goods, he took charge of them and dismissed the servants, who returned to resume the homeward journey with their master.

Verse 25. We may wonder that Gehazi ever imagined he could deceive Elisha. He had been his servant and in close touch with him. He knew of his inspiration and other superhuman ability; but covetousness is a strong sentiment. It is so dominating that Paul calls it idolatry; not merely as bad as idolatry. (Col. 3: 5.) With such an evil desire in his heart, it should be no surprise that he would lie to the prophet.

Verse 26. One definition of *heart* is "the mind." Through inspiration, Elisha's mind was present at the transaction between Naaman and Gehazi. *Is it a time*, etc. The mere fact of receiving some material gift would not be wrong. But when a serious circumstance had called for a test of the authority of God's prophet, it was not an appropriate time to be interested in money and clothing. That would be especially true when obtained by fraud, and by playing on the generosity of another.

Verse 27. According to Smith's Bible Dictionary, the leprosy of the Old Testament was the white variety. It was not fatal at once, and in some cases the leper might live to old age and die of some other disease. But it was a loathsome malady, and subjected the victim to great shame. *Leprosy of Naaman* does not mean that Gehazi "caught" the disease from Naaman. The expression is figurative, and means that as he was so eager for Naaman's valuables, he would receive his disease also.

2 KINGS 6

Verse 1. *Too strait* means too narrow or cramped for their needs.

Verse 2. A *beam* was the body of a tree, and the plan was for each man to cut down a tree, then use the log in building a dwelling.

Verse 3. Elisha had approved of the proposal of the prophets, and upon their request agreed to go with them to Jordan to get the timber.

Verses 4, 5. These men were cutting down the trees growing on the bank of the Jordan. The ax slipped off the handle and disappeared in the water. It showed a good principle to be concerned over the loss of the article because it was *borrowed*. It indicated unselfishness and a regard for the interests of another.

Verses 6, 7. This is another place to consider the comments at Ch. 2: 8.

Verse 8. Syria was the country lying immediately north of Israel, and Damascus was the capital. There was war frequently between the two kingdoms. *In such and such a place* meant that the location of the camp was named to the servants of the king of Syria, so that they would be informed about it. At the same time the expression denotes the fact that Elisha could locate the camp through his inspiration, in spite of the indefinite language used by the Syrian king.

Verse 9. With the knowledge mentioned in the preceding paragraph, Elisha gave the warning to the king of Israel, definitely pointing out *such a place* to him, though the king of Syria intended *such a place* to be so indefinite an expression that no stranger could find it.

Verse 10. The king of Israel acted on the warning of Elisha. When he would be thinking of making a journey near the danger zone, he would first send out a reconnaissance force to learn of the conditions. By doing this he saved himself *not once nor twice*, which means he saved himself one or two times.

Verse 11. The king of Syria kept looking for the king of Israel, and wondered why he never came into sight. He finally concluded there was a traitor in his camp who was keeping the Israelites informed. In his distress he called upon his people to inform him of the guilty person.

Verse 12. Some servant of the Syrian king thought about Elisha and his superhuman knowledge. He was correct in his idea that no secret could be hid from Elisha.

Verse 13. If the knowledge of an inspired man cannot be outdone, it should be realized that he cannot be defeated by mere human strategy. But the king of Syria was so desperate that he overlooked all such reflections, and made plans to capture the man of God laying siege to the town where he was at the time.

Verse 15. In the morning the besieging forces were seen around the town. The servant of Elisha was frightened at the sight and made a distress call to him.

Verse 16. The forces with Elisha were not visible to the natural eye, but the prophet was aware of their presence and help.

Verse 17. For the benefit of the young man, Elisha prayed God to give him a vision of the forces on their side. God answered the prayer and he saw the mountain covered with the hosts of Heaven, in the form of flaming chariots and their horses.

Verse 18. *They* in this place means the Syrians besieging the city. Elisha prayed again and in answer God smote the enemy with blindness.

Verse 19. Elisha misled the people, but such action was according to military practice, and this was a military action according to the words *captive* and *sword* in V. 22. While Elisha misled his enemy, he did not mistreat him. Instead, he chastised the king of Israel for wanting to do so, and commanded him to treat them with kindness.

Verses 20-23. Much of this paragraph was commented on above. Had the king of Israel been allowed to carry out his suggestion against these captives, he would have become a "war criminal." The treatment accorded them had the desired effect, by putting a stop to the inroads of the Syrians for the present.

Verse 24. The war spirit is a restless one. Some time after the events of the preceding paragraphs, the Syrians again came into the land of Israel. They laid siege to Samaria, the capital of that kingdom.

Verse 25. In all ages and in every country, a prolonged siege of a walled city results in a famine; and a famine results in the inflation of costs of necessities of life. Ordinarily, no one would care to eat the head of an ass. In this siege it was not only accepted as food, but was sold for the enormous sum of 80 pieces of silver, which Moffatt says is ten pounds. A cab was about a pint, and one fourth of a cab of dove's dung was sold for five pieces of silver, or about three dollars. The dung was used for fuel in that country, and as all kinds of fuel would be difficult to find in a siege, this article was obtainable from the fact of the birds' being winged creatures, and not affected by a siege.

Verse 26. The king of Israel was on the wall of the city, looking out to view the position of the enemy. This brought him into sight of one of his distressed subjects, who cried to him for help.

Verse 27. Threshing was done by piling the whole straw on a barnfloor, then beating out the grain by driving oxen round and round over it. When that was done, the loose chaff and grain was tossed up into the air with a winnowing shovel (called a fan in Matt. 3: 12), where the wind would blow the chaff away, letting the grain drop back on the floor. In times of famine there would be no grain to thresh. The winepress also would be empty as there would be no grapes to press. The first of this verse means that if a miracle is not performed to help them, it would be in vain to look to a man for relief from natural sources.

Verses 28, 29. There was some indication that a special situation prompted the woman to call on the king to intervene. Upon his inquiry she related her terrible story. Hunger had driven two mothers to the extreme plan of devouring their own flesh and blood. This very thing was predicted in Deut. 28: 53. After eating the flesh of one child the pangs of hunger were relieved and the mother was restored to a saner mind, and it was natural for her to back down from the agreement that hunger had impelled her to make. The other mother was thus expecting the king to take a hand in the case.

Verse 30. The king did nothing about the affair of these women, but the case made a profound impression on him. He rent his clothes and covered his nakedness with a coarse material, commonly used for making sacks. In this condition he walked by the people as he was still on the wall of the city.

Verse 31. *God do so* is a Biblical expression found frequently. It means that if the speaker does not carry out the thing he is threatening against some one, then may God do that thing to him, the speaker. In the case at hand, the king threatened to have Elisha beheaded. The prophet had performed miracles when it was God's will. The king of Israel was so rash as to think a miracle could be performed at will at the request of a wicked ruler. In his distress he threatened vengeance against Elisha.

Verse 32. Elisha was a national prophet of God, and was informed by inspiration of the king's plot. He prepared himself against attack by having the elders, men of outstanding rank, to bar the door against the entrance of the execution party.

Verse 33. While Elisha was talking with the elders, the messenger of the king of Israel came, the king immediately following. When they got to the door of Elisha's house they found it locked against them. By this time the king concluded that the whole difficulty of the siege and famine was from the Lord, and that it would be vain to oppose it farther. *What should I wait*, etc., means he was despairing of receiving any help from the Lord. However, Elisha assured him that the situation would soon be eased. This assurance is shown in the next chapter.

2 KINGS 7

Verse 1. In the preceding chapter, the king of Israel realized the Lord had brought about the condition of distress then upon the capital city, or at least that he had suffered it to be so. He concluded also that it would be of no avail to ask God for help. In the present paragraph he will be promised a change. The prices named for necessities of life are so small that only by great plenty could such a thing be.

Verse 2. The king made no comment on Elisha's prediction, that is recorded, but the personal attendant doubted it. He is called a lord, and Strong defines it as a general of the third rank. In response to the expression of doubt, Elisha made another prediction: that the great plenty would come and the lord would see it; but he would not get to eat of it. The fulfillment of this strange prediction will come soon.

Verses 3, 4. The apparently abrupt change of subjects is necessary to lead up to the great plenty just predicted by Elisha. Lev. 13: 46 shows the isolated kind of life imposed by the law on lepers. They were not prohibited entirely from going abroad, but they must observe certain restrictions for the protection of others. Within these regulations they could leave their individual dwellings and go abroad and about the country. In a state of helplessness, these lepers had sat down on the outside of the city near the gateway. Under the general situation confronting them, they concluded that nothing could come to them any worse than by remaining there until death. If they entered the city, they would perish from the famine. The proposal of falling in with the Syrians had the advantage of its being no risk of anything worse than would come to them by any other procedure.

Verse 5. Having decided to take their chance with the Syrians, the lepers rose up in the evening and started toward their camp. When they reached the outskirts of the camp they found it deserted.

Verse 6. The idea that the Lord would mislead the Syrians is to be understood in the light of military procedure. For more comments on this point see 1 Ki. 22:20. The Syrians did not feel able to cope with all these other forces which they were sure had been hired against them.

Verse 7. The flight of the panic-stricken people was timed to coincide with the approach of the lepers. Consequently, when they came to it they found everything belonging to a well-equipped camp intact.

Verse 8. They went from tent to tent, eating and drinking. They also carried much of the valuable property and assets to some place of hiding.

Verse 9. The lepers suddenly realized they were being selfish in not reporting their "find" to others so that they could share in the good things. Moreover, should they continue in their selfishness till morning, they might justly come to some punishment. It was then decided to let the king's family know about the conditions.

Verses 10, 11. A leper would not venture any farther than to a porter, which was the janitor or gate keeper. They gave the news to this person, describing the conditions as they found them. The one who was on duty at the time passed the word to other porters and they told it to the king's family.

Verse 12. The king did not doubt the scheme of the Syrians. He took it to be a trick to get the Israelites drawn out of their entrenchments. The hunger that famine would naturally bring, might impel them to rush into the trap set for them. All this was the scheme of the Syrians as the king of Israel feared.

Verse 13. A servant had a plan for testing the purpose of the Syrians. *They are as all the multitude.* This means that this small number could learn the true state of affairs just as well as the whole number in the city could if they went. If these five horsemen were sent out on this "suicide" sort of mission and were slain, they would not be any worse off than the ones who remained in the city. On the other hand, if they survived, their discovery would result in the preservation of the other citizens.

Verse 14. The suggestion pleased the king and he adopted the plan in principle. He selected just two, however, for they would answer the purpose as well as five. He commanded them to go and discover the real situation.

Verse 15. The camp of the Syrians was near the city of Samaria, since they had been conducting a siege of that place. But they had fled their camp, and the two horsemen would need to track them some distance to get the information desired by the king. They kept up the pursuit as far as Jordan. That was not the direction they naturally would have taken, for the country of the Syrians was north of Samaria. But they were panic-stricken and doubtless had taken the direction that first appeared to them. And the two men in pursuit were guided in their chase by the articles that the enemy had strewn along the way in their hasty flight.

Verse 16. To *spoil the tents* means to take the goods found in the tents, especially the articles of food. The great plenty of the provisions caused the low price at which they could be bought. In selling them at these low prices, one prediction of Elisha was fulfilled. The one pertaining to the doubting lord will be described next.

Verses 17-20. After a period of distress from hunger, people are apt to be disorderly and need to be put under restraint. The sudden discovery of so much food threatened a state of disorder and a rush to obtain the much wanted articles. Samaria was a walled city, and the passing in and out would have to be through the gate. For the purpose of order, the king made an appointment for the very lord who had been his personal attendant, that he should have charge of the gate. The people were mad with hunger and paid no attention to the gate keeper. In their stampede to get access to the food, they bore down upon the lord and trampled him to death. By this tragedy the prediction made by Elisha (V. 2) was fulfilled. The lord saw the great plenty of food but did not get to eat of it.

2 KINGS 8

Verse 1. The famine of the preceding chapter was local, confined to a city and caused by a military siege. The one predicted now will be a miraculous one and will affect the land in general. A natural famine would not likely continue for a definite number of years as this one is to continue. In two respects it will be like the famine in Egypt in the time of Joseph. It is to last just seven years, and the Lord was to call for it. (Psa. 105: 16). In kind appreciation for past favors from the woman, Elisha warned her of the coming distress so she could arrange some place to live.

Verse 2. Acting upon the advice of Elisha, the woman went into the land of the Philistines where she remained for the duration of the famine. This land seems to have been more fortunate in times of famine. Isaac went there (Gen. 26: 1) at such a time and prospered. Now this woman went there to escape the famine in her country.

Verse 3. In the absence of the owner during the famine, the woman's property had been unlawfully seized by some person. She was unable to dislodge the intruder and had to appeal to the king for relief.

Verse 4. Before the woman came to the king, however, he had entered into conversation with Gehazi, personal servant of Elisha. It would be expected that he would make mention of his master, the prophet, and of his greatness in general. But general reference to the accomplishments of the man of God did not satisfy the king.

Verse 5. Among the *great things* Gehazi told the king was the feat of restoring to life the son of a certain woman. Just as he was telling the king about it, that very woman came into their presence to make the petition mentioned in V. 3. That served as an excellent introduction, and Gehazi confirmed her plea by connecting her with the miracle then being reported.

Verse 6. The word *famine* is from RAAB and Strong's definition is, "hunger (more or less extensive)." From this definition we would conclude that even in a time of famine, there would be some products of the land available. In Gen. 43: 11 we read that in spite of the general famine, Jacob was able to send nuts and other products as a "present" into Egypt. Some things could be staples that had been stored for many years, but nuts and other such things would not likely be suitable for food after too many seasons. The conclusion is, therefore, that a state of general dearth would not entirely stop the production of such articles as would be brought forth from the deeper moisture of the earth. This all agrees with the "more or less extensive" part of the definition. There would not be sufficient for sustenance of the whole citizenry, but a scant subsistence might be maintained by a person here and there, through the use of these commodities. They could be exchanged at some market within reach for the more necessary items of food. Such use had been made of this woman's land in her absence. The king ordered her property to be given up by the usurper, and also to have her reimbursed for these things that had been produced while she was out of the country.

Verse 7. Damascus was the principal city of Syria, and was located just north of Israel. Elisha went to that place where an occasion came up for making a prediction. Ben-hadad was the king of Syria, and he was sick. He heard of the arrival of Elisha.

Verse 8. The Syrian king had knowledge of the talents of Elisha, and decided to appeal to him for information. Hazael was an attendant upon Ben-hadad and did service at the royal court. He was told to take the customary "present" and call upon Elisha. *Shall I recover of this disease?* All that Ben-hadad had in mind when he sent for answer to this question was whether his illness was necessarily fatal. He knew nothing of the other conditions that might arise.

Verse 9. The extent of the *present* which Hazael took to Elisha would tell the reader that such was not to meet any material need for just one man. See the comments at Gen. 32: 13 for further explanation. *Thy son* was a figurative term that denoted a feeling of respect. Hazael delivered the very question of his king to Elisha.

Verse 10. We do not believe that an inspired man would contradict himself. When a statement is made that seems to disagree with another, an explanation will be apparent if an attempt is made with fairness. As far as the illness was concerned, Ben-hadad need not die, and the message that Elisha intended for the Syrian king went that far only. The prediction of the last half of the verse was made to Hazael, and of course he did not tell that to his master.

Verse 11. *Ashamed* is from an original that means also "to be long." It here means that Elisha had set an expression on his face that continued for a long time, and he finally burst into tears. Inspired men can write or speak only what they see revealed, and such revelations often come to them as the occasion arises. When Elisha had delivered the prediction that Ben-hadad was to die, the Lord opened up another vision regarding the future of Syria. That had so much sorrow in it that it brought forth the weeping just mentioned.

Verse 12. Up to this point in the conversation, there is no indication that Hazael knew the significance of Elisha's prediction of the death of Ben-hadad. When he asked the prophet why he was weeping, the answer connected it with his own mistreatment of the people of Syria. Among the acts of violence he was going to commit, were the dashing of the children against the ground or other hard surfaces, and the murderous mutilation of expectant mothers.

Verse 13. The Old Testament has one word only for "dog." The literal meaning is the same as we understand by it today. The next definition is "a male prostitute." It next has a figurative meaning, being used to express the idea of unworthiness, and a general state of weakness. Hazael used the word in its figurative sense. "How could I, a private man, and one as insignificant as a dog, accomplish all these things thou hast predicted of me?" Hence the word as used in the present connection does not mean a dog in its moral sense, for that would be the very kind of character that would commit the horrible deeds described. The remark of Hazael brought forth the additional prediction that he was to become king of Syria. With such power, and with the disposition to misuse that power which so many kings show, he would be in a position to do the things predicted by Elisha.

Verse 14. The report that Hazael gave his master was a faithful one. He was not instructed to say anything on the subject of his death; that prediction was made to Hazael only. The words *shouldest surely* are not in the Hebrew text. The word *recover* is from a word that has been translated "live" 148 times. The answer, therefore, that Elisha sent back to Ben-hadad was that he would live, but nothing was said as to how long. The Lord had his own reason for withholding part of the truth from him.

Verse 15. We do not know how far Elisha's predictions influenced Hazael in his actions. In 1 Ki. 11: 27 we are told that Jeroboam's rebellion was caused by the prediction recorded in V. 31 of that chapter. Elisha told Hazael that his king would die, and that he would reign in his stead. If the Lord predicts some evil act of mankind, that prediction will be fulfilled. But that fact will not justify the evil motive of the one doing the evil. See Luke 17: 1; 1 Cor. 11: 19. Hazael committed the brutal murder of his helpless master by suffocating him with a damp cloth. By that act he brought about the fulfillment of a prediction, but we have no intimation that God was pleased with it. His motive for the deed was a selfish one.

Verse 16. Joram and Jehoram were forms of the same name. Ahab, king of Israel, and Jehoshaphat, king of Judah, each had a son with that name. The wording of this verse is somewhat unusual. The writer seems eager to give us plenty of details. The meaning is that the Jehoram who was the son of Jehoshaphat began to reign in the fifth year of the Jehoram who was the son of Ahab. The extra detail is put in, that Jehoshaphat was still reigning in Judah, down to the fifth year of Jehoram, king in Israel. The reader should again consult the comments at 1 Ki. 12: 17.

Verse 17. The item of where the kings reigned is given because there were two kingdoms of the children of Israel. Jerusalem was the capital of one, Samaria the other.

Verse 18. There was no law against marrying into another tribe. The fact of Jehoram's taking the daughter of Ahab to wife is stated, therefore, to help account for his evil reign. It is a strong argument against marriage with a family of doubtful principles, because of the evil influences. See 1 Cor. 15: 33.

Verse 19. In spite of the evil conduct of Jehoram, God suffered the kingdom of Judah to continue for the time, in respect for David. *A light* means a representative to sit on the throne in the royal line.

Verse 20. This verse shows the fulfillment of the prediction made by Jacob to Esau. (Gen. 27: 40). The Edomites were descendants of Esau.

Verse 21. Joram, king of Judah, attempted to force the Edomites back into subjection. He took some forces and attacked the people at Zair, an Edomite city, and defeated the people of that place, driving them into their tents.

Verse 22. The victory over the forces at Zair was local only, and the Edomites continued to be independent. Their success encouraged the people of Libnah, a Canaanitish community, also to declare their independence.

Verse 23. For *chronicles* see 1 Ki. 14: 19.

Verse 24. *Slept with his fathers* is explained at 1 Ki. 2: 10. *City of David* was the principal borough of Jerusalem, and the place of headquarters for the kings.

Verses 25, 26. The preceding verse had said merely that Ahaziah took the throne after the death of his father. This one gives us the date, based on the reign of the king then on the throne of Israel. He reigned one year only, and it was a turbulent time for him. The mother's name is given according to the thoughts at 1 Ki. 14: 21.

Verse 27. *Son-in-law of the house of Ahab* means he married into that line. The fact is mentioned as an explanation, in part at least, of his wicked reign.

Verse 28. Ramoth-gilead was an important city east of the Jordan, and had been in the control of the Syrians for several years. The kings of Israel and Judah joined in an expedition to wrest the city from Hazael, the king then on the throne of Syria. The action was successful although Joram was wounded.

Verse 29. Jezreel was a city that became noted in the days of Ahab. To this place Joram went for treatment of the wounds inflicted on him by the Syrians. Ramah was another name for Ramoth-gilead. The close of the verse is merely an incidental mention of the sick call of one king upon another.

2 KINGS 9

Verse 1. *Children of the prophets* is the same as sons of the prophets, referring to the students associated with the older, national prophets. *Gird up thy loins* meant to put a belt around the waist. That would equip the man for the journey, which would be from Damascus (Ch. 8: 7) to Ramoth-gilead. Olive oil was used in those days as one of the formalities connected with the appointment of kings.

Verses 2, 3. The Lord was going to change the dynasty, or family line of kings over Israel. In such a radical move it would not be any surprise that some formality would be used, such as this prophet was directed to do. And this act of the Lord agrees with what the Babylonian king was told regarding the placing of men on the thrones of the kingdoms of men. (Dan. 4: 17). The Jehoshaphat named was the son of Nimshi, who was not a member of the royal line. The application of oil to Jehu was preliminary to his actively taking the kingdom, and hence it was to be a private affair.

Verses 4, 5. When the young prophet reached Ramoth-gilead he found the military leaders in a war council. His announcement was that he had a message for a captain. All of the group were captains of the same rank, therefore he was asked to say which he meant, and he designated Jehu.

Verses 6, 7. The first verse records the fact of the selection of Jehu to be the next king. The other verse states why God was going to change the dynasty from the house of Ahab to another. Through the influence of his wicked wife Jezebel, Ahab had suffered the servants of the Lord to be slain.

Verse 8. The change of dynasty or family line was to be brought about by the avenging from God, causing the death of all the male heirs to the throne. See the comments at 1 Sam. 25: 22 for explanation of this obsolete word for the discharges of the male body. Also, for the reason why the males were specially marked for death.

Verse 9. The comparison was for the purpose of showing the complete overthrow of the family line.

Verse 10. This prediction about Jezebel had been made before. (1 Ki. 21: 23). Death may come to a person under circumstances of honor to the victim. But in the case of Ahab and his wicked wife, great dishonor was to be thrust upon their memory. He was to have no male descendant left, and she was to be denied respectful burial.

Verse 11. Curiosity is a strong sentiment. The other captains appeared to be concerned about their comrade. At least they made as if they were thoughtful for his welfare and pressed him for some information. Jehu tried to put them off with some indirect remark about what might be expected from such a man; one who gave the odd kind of speech that he did upon his arrival.

Verse 12. That did not satisfy them, for they felt sure that Jehu was keeping something back, either through fear or modesty. When they urged him to tell them what had been said, he told them the mission of the man sent from Elisha.

Verse 13. The other captains gave Jehu an ovation and gladly hailed him as king.

Verses 14, 15. *Jehu . . . conspired* against Joram, but it was with the consent of the Lord. At the battle of Ramoth-gilead, the Syrians lost the city to Joram. But he was wounded in the attack and had to go to Jezreel to be treated. While he was there the affair of Jehu's anointing took place, and Joram did not know anything about it. The comrades of Jehu had expressed themselves favorably for him. On the strength of that, he requested that no one go to Jezreel to inform Joram of the conspiracy. He wished to have first opportunity of contacting Joram, soon to be deposed, and that by the decree of God.

Verse 16. Jehu went to Jezreel and approached the city, at the time that Ahaziah, king of Judah, was visiting with Joram during his recovery.

Verse 17. Important men like Jehu did not travel alone. The watchman on the tower could see that a company of men was approaching. He told Joram about it and a man was directed to meet the company to learn the object of the mission.

Verse 18. *What hast thou to do with peace?* That was Jehu's way of telling the horseman that the mission he had was no concern of his, and for him to fall back to the rear of the company. This was done to prevent his returning to Jezreel with any information. The watchman told his master that the horseman had disappeared.

Verse 19. The second watchman was sent to meet the company, and he was commanded to do the same as the first.

Verse 20. The watchman reported the circumstance to Joram. By this time the company was nearer, and he thought he could identify the leader. There is no other information available to me on the matter of Jehu's driving. It is evident, however, from the remark of the watchman, that he had a reputation of being a reckless driver.

Verse 21. The report of the watchman roused Joram to action. He ordered his war chariot to be made ready for travel. He and his royal guest, Ahaziah king of Judah, then went to intercept Jehu. Each of the kings was in his own chariot. They met in the the field that belonged to Naboth, an interesting coincidence. In 1 Ki. 21 the account of the murder of Naboth on the orders of Jezebel. Now her son is about to meet his fate at that very spot.

Verse 22. Upon their meeting, Joram inquired if the mission of Jehu was a peaceful one. His question was entirely inconsistent with other conditions with which he certainly was acquainted. *Whoredom* means the idolatrous practices of the people, under the encouragement of the wicked Jezebel. While such things were being permitted by Joram, it was a hypocritical question he asked.

Verse 23. When Joram heard the statement of Jehu he knew he was in danger. *Turned his hands* means he caused the chariot to be turned round, intending to flee; at the same time he gave warning to Ahaziah. *Treachery* means deceit or fraud. The definition would not justify Joram's use of the word; there was no underhanded action going on. Jehu was in the open and frankly coming against a wicked man. But it is a common trait of guilty persons to accuse others of intrusion, when they propose to interfere with the evil doing. See Ch. 11: 14; 1 Ki. 18: 17; Acts 7: 27.

Verse 24. Joram (which is the same as Jehoram) had turned to flee, which would expose his back to danger, that part of the body not being as well protected as the front. Jehu used his full reach and shot an arrow at his fleeing victim. It struck him between the shoulderblades with such force that it went through his body. As it penetrated the heart it caused instant death, and he sank down in his chariot.

Verse 25. The captain attending Jehu was told to fling the body out of his chariot, onto the field that had been the possession of Naboth. The incident mentioned took place when Ahab was being pursued. At that time the Lord had put this *burden* (predicted punishment) on Joram. That was because he was "of Ahab" and thus came under the prediction of 1 Ki. 22: 24.

Verse 26. *Yesterday* is figurative and means "a short time ago." Naboth was murdered through a plot of Jezebel, and vengeance was to be had by casting the body of Joram, a son of Jezebel, on the same piece of ground that had been seized through unlawful bloodshed.

Verse 27. Ahaziah had been friendly with Joram, and had shown partizan interest in him by accompanying him in his attempt against Jehu. He not only must have felt guilty, but saw that his life was in danger. A garden house was a small building near a garden, built for the use of the keeper. It would not be a very conspicuous thing and seemed to offer a way for Ahaziah to escape. He succeeded in getting away from the immediate presence of Jehu; but he was seen, and the command was given to smite him in his chariot. They overtook him as he was trying to drive his chariot up an incline approaching Gur, a place near the city of Ibleam. At this place he was given a fatal stroke which did not result in instant death. He got away again and reached the city of Megiddo where he died from his wound.

Verse 28. Ahaziah was a king and died in office. His servants took his body in a chariot to Jerusalem, where he was buried in the family tomb.

Verse 29. This verse is parenthetical in thought, and is an item regarding the reign of Ahaziah, whose death was just recorded. By the aid of the marginal reading, and the reference to 2 Chr. 21: 18, 19, we learn he was acting ruler for his father who was seriously ill. After a year of such rule his father died, and he began to reign in his own rights. See Ch. 8: 24, 25.

Verse 30. According to the lexicons and various translations, the part of her face that Jezebel painted was her eyes; *tired* means "adorned." Thus we can see this wicked, idolatrous, murderous woman, with her head decorated and eyes gaudy with artificial coloring, impudently gazing from a window as Jehu approached the city.

Verse 31. The question Jezebel asked was a veiled threat against Jehu. She called him (figuratively) another Zimri because he had slain his master, the king, as Zimri had done. But she perverted the facts about Zimri. It is true that his reign was short, just 7 days, and ended with suicide. But the troubles imposed upon him were not for his slaying his master. That was according to the will of the Lord and in fulfillment of an inspired prophecy. Please read 1 Ki. 16: 8-19. But in making this insinuating remark, Jezebel let her true mind be known, that she was in sympathy with the wicked men just slain by Jehu, who had been selected by the Lord to be king.

Verse 32. Primarily, a eunuch is a male who has been deprived of his manhood. Such persons were employed in the service of bedchambers, which were used by women as well as men. In time, however, the word came to mean any special and personal attendant, regardless of his physical condition. In response to Jehu's question, two or three of these servants appeared to his view.

Verse 33. Actions speak louder than words or looks. The eunuchs were told to act by casting the wicked woman down from the window. It must have been from the second story or higher. The fall brought her in contact with the wall with such violence that she was mangled and her blood was shed. It was sprayed over the wall and the chariot horses, and Jehu drove them over her body in contempt.

Verse 34. In respect for the royal line to which Jezebel belonged, Jehu directed that she be buried.

Verse 35. Almost the entire body had been eaten by the dogs. That fulfilled a prediction made by Elijah in 1 Ki. 21: 23, and quoted here.

Verses 36, 37. *Be as dung upon the face of the field.* This was true figuratively and literally. The absence of honorable burial, and the shameful and violent death imposed upon her, covered her memory with shame and suggested the article. Also, as the dogs made food of her body, it would be cast out upon the face of the ground with the other discharges of the bodies of the dogs.

2 KINGS 10

Verse 1. *Samaria* is used to refer to the kingdom of the 10 tribes because the city of that name was the capital. However, Ahab had chosen Jezreel as his personal residence (1 Ki. 21: 1), hence the word of Jehu was sent to that particular city. It was addressed to the older men of influence, who had much to do with the rearing of Ahab's 70 sons. Normally, one of these sons should have inherited the throne.

Verses 2, 3. The Lord had decreed to change the royal line to the family of Jehu. The fleshly heirs to the throne might not have learned about it; or, if they had, they might wish to contest it. At any rate, Jehu did not intend to leave them any pretext for complaint. Should they have known about the situation and wish to defend their "rights," he was ready to fight the "best and meetest" of them.

Verse 4. I am sure their answer was about what Jehu expected. The *two kings* were Joram and Ahaziah. (Ch. 9: 24, 27).

Verse 5. The men to whom Jehu sent the letters were frightened by them. They humbly recognized him as their lord, and agreed to do whatsoever he would bid them.

Verse 6. *Be mine* is not in the original, and the King James' translators got the idea from the word for *hearken*. It is SHAMA, which is defined by Strong, "a primitive root; to hear intelligently (often with the implication of attention, obedience, etc.)." Jehu was taking them up on their profession of being his servants. Such persons are supposed to do what their masters command them. So therefore, make your word good and do as follows. Behead the 70 sons of Ahab and bring their heads to me at Jezreel by this time tomorrow. A man with no head could never become a rival, and Jehu was not taking any chances with the future.

Verse 7. The men receiving the severe orders had ample opportunity for destroying the sons of Ahab, because they had them in charge and had been controlling them from their youth. They slew the men and sent the 70 heads to Jezreel.

Verse 8. We are not told the purpose of Jehu in directing the heads to be piled in two heaps. But we know one thing that was made possible, whether that was his motive or not. By having 35 instead of 70 heads in a pile, the exact number could be counted by the spectators. And by the exact count of the heads, the public would know that all of the royal seed had been destroyed, and that nothing was left but to accept Jehu as the lawful king.

Verse 9. *Righteous* is defined in the lexicon as "just." It means that Jehu gave the people credit for being fair-minded, and able to form logical conclusions. He admitted having slain his master, the king reigning immediately before him. But here are the heads of that master's sons, and the question was, who had slain them? Jehu did not do it, neither had any of these people present done it. The conclusion ought to be easy for the people since they were fair-minded.

Verse 10. Without awaiting an expression from the people, Jehu attributed the circumstances to the Lord, and said it was the fulfillment of the prediction of Elijah.

Verse 11. Consistently with the foregoing conclusion, Jehu proceeded in his "purge" as predicted by the prophet. He killed the friends and relatives of Ahab that were in Jezreel, the former residence of the wicked king.

Verse 12. *Samaria* means the city of the name, as Jezreel was already in the territory of the kingdom whose capital was Samaria.

Verses 13, 14. Ahaziah was king of Judah and had been slain by Jehu. These relatives of Ahaziah made the mistake of sympathizing with the royal line of the former dynasty. The "purge" that Jehu had begun required that these persons also should be destroyed. The command was given for their slaying, which was carried out.

Verse 15. Jehu continued his journey toward Samaria, and on the way he met Jehonadab. *Is thine heart right, as my heart is with thy heart?* This was Jehu's way of saying, "Are you as willing to be my friend as I am to be yours?" Upon receiving a favorable answer, he took his hand and invited him into his chariot.

Verses 16, 17. *Made him ride* does not mean they forced him to ride. The first word is not in the original, but has been supplied by the translators. The thought of the whole passage is that Jehonadab was caused to ride in the chariot by the friendly attitude of Jehu. He was invited to witness the zeal that he was going to show for the Lord. They finally reached Samaria, the chief city of the kingdom. There were still some distant relatives of Ahab who might cause trouble for the new ruler. All of these were to be slain, fulfilling the prediction in 1 Ki. 21: 19, 21.

Verse 18. Jehu was taking this plan to get a complete roundup of the worshipers of Baal, including all who merely sympathized with the idolatrous practices.

Verse 19. By threatening all with death who failed to respond, Jehu expected to make a complete assembly of the wanted victims. The motive of the man Jehu could be known by the inspired writer, and he tells us that it was to destroy the worshipers of Baal, and that his scheme was done in *subtilty* which is defined in the lexicon as "trickery." The motive was good and no undue advantage was taken of the people.

Verse 20. *Solemn assembly.* Both words are from ATSERETH and Strong defines it, "an assembly, especially as a festival or holiday." To *proclaim* such an occasion meant not only to announce it to the public, but also to make preparation for it.

Verse 21. Upon pain of death, the worshipers of Baal responded to a man, and they were gathered in the house that had been used for the service to their false god.

Verse 22. The *vestments* were the garments worn by the worshipers of Baal. The act of receiving and wearing them was additional proof of their alliance with him.

Verse 23. This verse gives the climax to Jehu's plan to make a complete corralling of the idolaters. All who did not respond to the call at the start were to be put to death. On that principle, all of the halfhearted persons would be drawn over to take an evident stand for idolatry. The question might arise whether it was fair to use such measures. It was certainly fair, because in so doing no one would be drawn into the net except those who cared more for their temporal life than for righteousness. All such characters were no better than the active adherents of Baal. Jesus taught this idea in Matt. 12: 30.

Verse 24. The sacrifices for Baal were to take place in the house of Baal. While the services were going on, the place was guarded by 80 men. They were threatened with death if a man of the worshipers was allowed to escape.

Verse 25. The men with their officers who had been standing guard outside during the sacrifices, were next told to go and act as executioners. They were charged not to let one man escape. After they had been slain, their bodies were flung out of the building. *City* is from a word with very wide meaning, including "a mere encampment or post." In this verse it has special reference to that part of the *house of God* where they had the images of Baal.

Verse 26. After slaying the worshipers of Baal, they brought out his images and burned them.

Verse 27. *Draught house* means a public rest room. While such a service is necessary for health and convenience, it was intended as a perpetual condemnation and shaming of idolatry.

Verse 28. "Honor to whom honor is due" is an old saying that has much meaning. The Lord will have the truth told about the evils of Jehu's life, at the same time he was given credit for the services he rendered to the nation of Israel.

Verse 29. Jehu destroyed the avowed worshipers of Baal, which was an important work. But the golden calves that Jeroboam placed at Bethel and Dan were suffered to remain. The religious use that was supposed to be the motive of the first king of the ten-tribe kingdom might have misled Jehu.

Verse 30. It is natural to be concerned about things that will happen after one's death. This was true as to the inheritance of a throne. Jehu had done much service for God and, as a reward for it, he was promised that his family line would continue to hold the throne to the *fourth generation;* this prediction was fulfilled. The four descendants in the family line from Jehu were Jehoahaz, Joash, Jeroboam II, and Zachariah. Ch. 15: 10 says that Shallum, son of Jabesh, slew the fourth and reigned instead.

Verse 31. Nothing is said about the personal life of Jehu except his idolatry. And that evil was not total, for the accusation was that he did not walk in the law of the Lord *with all his heart;* he did walk to some extent, however.

Verses 32, 33. God often used foreign nations to chastise his own. At this time he suffered Hazael, the Syrian king, to make inroads against several cities of Israel, and to destroy many of the citizens.

Verse 34. For *chronicles* see 1 Ki. 14: 19.

Verses 35, 36. *Slept with his fathers* is explained at 1 Ki. 2: 10. The reason

Jehu was buried in Samaria was the fact that it was the capital of the 10 tribes, of which he had been king.

2 KINGS 11

Verse 1. Our study takes us to the kingdom of Judah again. See 1 Ki. 12:17. *Seed royal* means the regular heirs to the throne. Athaliah was a wicked and ambitious woman. She craved authority, and sought to obtain it by murdering all the male heirs to the throne left vacant by the death of Ahaziah. That is, she intended to destroy, and thought she had destroyed, all of the royal seed. The fact that she missed one child did not make her guilt any the less.

Verses 2, 3. The escape of one intended victim was similar to the case of Gideon's son. (Judges 9:5). Athaliah was a murderer and usurper, but is listed among the rulers of Judah. Her reign, however, will come to a violent end.

Verse 4. The priests under the Mosaic system were vested with much authority, and sometimes acted on behalf of others who were unable to act for themselves. Joash (also called Jehoash) was the one heir who escaped the murderous hand of Athaliah. He was hid for 6 years by Jehosheba, who was his aunt, also the wife of Jehoiada, the high priest. There is an interesting and informative article in the Schaff-Herzog Encyclopaedia on this subject which will be quoted: "Jehoiada, high priest, and husband of Jehosheba, the aunt of Joash, who alone of the family of Ahaziah escaped the murderous hand of Athaliah (2 Kings 11:1-12:2). Jehoiada was the guardian of the young king, put him upon the throne, killed Athaliah, and, so long as he lived, so wisely directed Joash that all things went well."—Article, Jehoiada. After the 6 years of hiding, the high priest brought the youthful king forth. He called together the officers of different ranks and presented to them their lawful ruler, and obtained from them an oath of allegiance.

Verse 5. Jehoiada assigned the men to separate duties. In addition to the services of the holy days, they were to serve as guards for the king.

Verse 6. Not only must the king's house be guarded, but also the gates to the place. Sur was one of the gates, and another one was near the position of the guard.

Verse 7. Another group of service men was to be nearer the king.

Verse 8. These precautions were being taken because Jehoiada expected opposition from Athaliah or her sympathizers. The *ranges* means the proper bounds for would-be intruders. The service men were to be armed, and must slay any one trying to cross the limits. All of these arrangements were lawful, because they were on behalf of the lawful ruler, and against a usurper who was a murderer.

Verse 9. The officers obeyed the orders of the high priest, and presented the men under them to him.

Verse 10. The weapons that David had used might not have been any better than others. The psychological effect, however, on the men appointed for guard duty, would not be insignificant. The memory of David as a warrior was great.

Verse 11. The place described was an important one in the temple, and the guard took position there with full equipment, all set for any emergency that might spring up at the appearance of the king.

Verse 12. *Gave him the testimony*. This was the law, and giving it to the king was in line with Deut. 17:18. This verse describes the ceremony of Joash's coronation, and its reception was indicated by the words, *God save the king*.

Verses 13, 14. The commotion attending the crowning of king Joash attracted the attention of Athaliah. She came to the temple to investigate. When she arrived she beheld the scene in all of its splendor and authority. *Treason, treason*. The act of only one person in opposing a government unlawfully would be treason. But the word here is from GESHER, and defined by Strong, "an (unlawful) alliance." It has been rendered in the A. V. by confederacy, conspiracy. It means that Athaliah not only accused the king, but others who were his allies. It is true that Joash and those with him were allied against Athaliah. But it was not true that it was treason, for that word requires that said alliance must be unlawful. Athaliah was a usurper and murderer, and it was not unlawful to overthrow her with force if necessary.

Verse 15. In respect for the temple, Jehoiada had directed that Athaliah not be slain there. She was to be taken outside, and if any person presumed to follow who was not of the guard, he was to be slain.

Verse 16. It was not a very sentimental spot chosen for the execution of this wicked woman. She was slain at the gate where horses entered toward the king's house.

Verse 17. First we read of a covenant involving the Lord, the king, and the people. Then we have a covenant involving the king and the people. This does not imply any difference. It is a form of expression to show the unity of the whole government, and its being one compact system, each unit of which was necessary to the others. The same idea was taught by Jesus in Matt. 10: 40; Luke 10: 16.

Verse 18. It usually happens that an unlawful ruler will violate the laws of the very nation he assumes control over. During the reign of Athaliah, the worship of idols was again allowed to flourish. When she was out of the way, the people destroyed the instruments of such corrupt practices. The priest also appointed the proper kind of men to take charge of the Lord's house.

Verse 19. With a great throng of officers and people, Jehoiada gave the king dignified escort from the temple to the palace. There he sat on the throne that had been occupied by his predecessors.

Verse 20. This verse is merely a resume of the day's proceedings, with a statement of the general condition of the public mind.

Verse 21. It must be understood that the reign was by the priest. The king was an infant when he was tucked away by his aunt in her private apartment. When he was 7 years old, the demonstration described above was put on, and he began to be recognized as the next king. His duties, of course, were performed by the priest until he became old enough to rule on his own responsibility.

2 KINGS 12

Verse 1. Going back to the reign of Jehu, king of Israel (see 1 Ki. 12: 17) for a date, the writer gives the entire length of Joash's reign over Judah. His *mother's* name is explained at 1 Ki. 14: 21. The 40 years reign includes the ones of his childhood, when Jehoiada managed the kingdom for him.

Verse 2. The righteousness of the reign is attributed to the influence of the priest. But it is commendable that he was willing to be guided by that righteous man.

Verse 3. The Lord never overestimates the good done by a man, any more than he does the evil. Joash gave the people a good administration, but he had a small defect in with the good. He did not remove the *high places*. However, that was a mild error, and further comments will be found on the subject at 1 Ki. 3: 2.

Verse 4. The verse as a whole means the money intended for the treasury, whether that specifically assessed upon the people *(that every man is set at)*, or the voluntary contributions *(cometh into any man's heart)*.

Verse 5. The priests were to collect this money from the men nearest in contact with them. The funds were to be used for repair of the house where such was needed.

Verse 6. Several years went by and the king discovered that the repairs which he had ordered had not been made. It appeared that the money had been taken from the people, but kept in the possession of the priests.

Verse 7. Joash called the priests into his presence and rebuked them for their neglect of duty, also for their retaining the money. He directed that no more money be delivered into their hands, but that arrangements be made to insure its proper use.

Verse 8. The priests agreed to the orders of the king. *Neither to repair*, etc. That means they were not to be considered as having direct responsibility for the repairs, since they had proved themselves untrustworthy. Instead, they were to take the money that was collected otherwise, and deliver it to the workmen, who were to appropriate it in their discretion about the repair work.

Verse 9. This chest was a kind of public receptacle for the money, to be used instead of the pockets of the priests. There is no intimation of actual fraud in the conduct of the priests. Their willing cooperation with the king in the plan ordered by him shows a good attitude. The situation was evidently one of carelessness.

Verse 10. When the chest was filled, the proper officers took charge of it and *told* or counted the money. It was put up in bags for safe handling and convenience.

Verses 11, 12. The money was delivered from the hands of the priests, and put directly into those of the men having charge of the repair work. Some of it was used to buy necessary materials for the work, and some was to pay the workmen.

Verses 13, 14. 2 Chr. 24: 14 states that some of this money was used to make such vessels as are mentioned in this verse. But the verse means that the money was first used for the repair work. When that was done, the balance was used for vessels.

Verse 15. The men who had been given the money were not reckoned with; that is, they were not "checked." They had given evidence of honesty and it was unnecessary to look into the accounts.

Verse 16. Money collected on account of trespass and sin was considered as the Lord's. See Lev. 4: 24; 5: 15. Such money could rightfully be used personally by the priests, as their support in the services about the temple worship.

Verse 17. Gath was a city in the Philistine territory; a place of much importance, west of Jerusalem. Hazael was the king of Syria, and he took possession of Gath. This success encouraged him to go on for more conquests, so he prepared to attack Jerusalem.

Verse 18. Hazael's motive was to obtain money or its equivalent rather than power or territory, for he left the community as soon as he received those chattels. It was a regrettable thing for Jehoash (Joash) to take all those valuable things that had been accumulated by former kings. However, that was better than suffering the house of the Lord (temple), and the king's house (palace), to be destroyed.

Verse 19. *Chronicles* is explained at 1 Ki. 14: 19.

Verses 20, 21. Murder, assassination, suicide, and other forms of violence, were not very uncommon in ancient times. No motive is given us for the conspiracy of the servants against Joash. Since the son was permitted to take the throne, who was the rightful heir, we know the motive was not desire for power. Sometimes a servant gets peeved from enforced labor and rises in violent rebellion. *Millo* was a fortified place in that part of Jerusalem called "the city of David." Silla is from CILLA, and Strong says it is from still another Hebrew word meaning "an embankment." Being the king, it would not be strange that Joash would be in that place. But the conspirators selected a time when their victim was in the open, on his way from the tower to this embankment. The city of David was the proper place for the burial. It was where his royal ancestors were buried, it was the headquarters of the kingdom, and where he died.

2 KINGS 13

Verse 1. Since Joash reigned 40 years, this verse takes us to about the middle of his reign. And, as Jehoahaz reigned only 17 years, the reign of Joash was still going at the death of Jehoahaz. See 1 Ki. 12: 17 in regard to this alternation.

Verse 2. This king was worse than some others of Israel. Like the others, he allowed himself to be influenced by the example of the first king, Jeroboam, who not only did wrong personally, but caused the people of Israel to sin.

Verse 3. Hazael and Ben-hadad, his son, each reigned in turn over Syria. Because of their many sins, God suffered his people to be punished by these Syrian kings.

Verse 4. The preceding verse is a general statement, covering a long period of punishment for his people, but not giving any details. Some of them will be given below, after the narrative is intercepted to relate the merciful answer of God to prayer.

Verse 5. In answer to the prayer of Jehoahaz, God gave his people a *savior*. The word is from one that is elsewhere rendered "deliverer," and refers to some military leader who led the Israelites to victory over their oppressors. *Tents* is from a word that means homes in general. After the oppression was lifted, Israel lived in their homes *as beforetime*. Not that they had been entirely driven from their homes, but life in them was not like it was after being delivered from the Syrians.

Verse 6. Ingratitude is a common weakness of mankind. Notwithstanding the favor of the Lord, the nation of Israel continued in its idolatry. *The grove* was the place used to shelter the idols, and for the activities of the idolatrous religion.

Verse 7. Having halted in the account to tell us of the goodness of God toward his disobedient people, the writer gives some details of the oppression. All of the army of Jehoahaz

2 Kings 13: 8-21

that was left him was what is listed in this verse. After a row of wheat has been threshed out by beating, nothing but light dust would be left. That is used to compare the depleted condition of the army after the Syrians got through with it.

Verse 8. Jehoahaz was no insignificant king, and reference is made to his *might*, which means his valor and success against his foes. See 1 Ki. 14: 19 on *chronicles*.

Verse 9. *Slept with his fathers* is treated at 1 Ki. 2: 10. He was buried in Samaria because that was the capital of his realm. *Joash*, his son, also called Jehoash, should not be confused with the man by the same name who was king of Judah. (Ch. 12: 1).

Verse 10. See comments in the preceding verse on two men named Joash; also 1 Ki. 12: 17.

Verse 11. It is bad enough to commit evil occasionally. But Jehoash (or Joash) *walked therein*. That indicated a general practice of life. A statement made here and at many other places, is that a man did evil *in the sight of the Lord*. The actions of a man may be good in the opinion of another, yet be evil in the Lord's sight. Jesus said something about that in Luke 16: 15.

Verse 12. The *might* of Joash is mentioned, as it was in the case of Jehoahaz; but in this a specification is given. His war with a king of Judah is merely mentioned, but will be described in the next chapter.

Verse 13. For purposes of distinction, this new king should be known as Jeroboam II. Joash *slept* according to 1 Ki. 2: 10, and was buried in Samaria, the capital.

Verse 14. We have more than once observed that the Bible is not as strictly chronological as we would think of writing a book. That does not affect its truthfulness, but it does make it necessary for us to use care in our study. The preceding two verses gave a summing up of the life of Joash. The present one goes back to some incidents in his life. He heard of the serious illness of the prophet Elisha, and called to see him. The kings and other men in public life depended on the national prophets for guidance. That is why Joash called him *my father*, meaning a term of respect. *The chariot of Israel*, etc. This means he considered Elisha to be worth as much to Israel as their whole military. See Ch. 2: 12 and comments on this thought.

Verses 15, 16. At 1 Ki. 20: 35 some thoughts are offered on the subject of prophets "acting." The same idea is present here, except that the prophet authorizes and enables the king to do the acting.

Verse 17. The window looking eastward was opened because the Syrian territory was in that direction. Aphek was a city where the war forces had met previously (1 Ki. 20: 26), and will again witness an encounter between Israel and Syria.

Verses 18, 19. This is some more acting. (Verses 15, 16). When a supernatural result is connected with an arbitrary and illogical means, the extent of the human contribution is considered. See the case of the vessels for oil, Ch. 4: 6. The success of Israel's arms will be limited by the number of times the king strikes the ground. Not that God is actually aided by the work of man, but to teach the lesson of man's responsibility in his cooperation with the Lord.

Verse 20. The burial of Elisha and the Moabite invasion have no connection with each other in this verse, but are mentioned preparatory to the following.

Verse 21. A funeral procession was going on when they spied a band *of men*. These words are not in the original, but the previous verse authorizes their use, and we could properly add, "of Moabites." The panic at sight of the invaders caused the pallbearers to seek a hiding place for the body. Sepulchres are described as follows in Smith's Bible Dictionary: "A natural cave enlarged and adapted by excavation, or an artificial imitation of one, was the standard type of sepulchre. Sepulchres, when the owner's means permitted it, were commonly prepared beforehand, and stood often in gardens, by roadsides, or even adjoining houses." —Article, Burial. From the nature of these sepulchres, we can understand how they could be entered, in much the same way that one can enter a modern mausoleum. The tomb of Jesus could be entered in this way. And it also explains how more than one person could be "buried" in the same place. (Gen. 49: 31). *Bones* does not mean that the flesh of Elisha had been literally decayed; the word means the body. There was nothing magical in the body of a prophet to restore life, else a general use could be made of such a body. The Lord willed this demonstration of his respect for the prophet.

Verses 22, 23. This history is a repetition of verses 3-5. But in this place is added a motive for the Lord's regard for the nation, the memory of the fathers.

Verse 24. This Hazael was a servant of a former Ben-hadad, whom he murdered and reigned in his stead. (Ch. 8: 15). He had a son whom he called by the same name his slain master had worn.

Verse 25. Again the writer ignores chronology and takes us back a few years. Jehoash had died in V. 13, but his father, Jehoahaz, had lost some cities to Ben-hadad, king of Syria. Hazael had been succeeded by his son Ben-hadad, and Jehoahaz was followed by his son Jehoash. The writer is telling us that Jehoash recovered these cities, carrying out three successful campaigns.

2 KINGS 14

Verse 1. The reader must never forget the zigzag character of this history, and should frequently refer to 1 Ki. 12: 17 and the comments. Because of this style of recording, the same man and events will be mentioned more than once. Furthermore, it should be remembered that different men had the same name. Thus, in the present verse, we have Joash as the name of two kings; one of the kingdom of Israel, and the other of the kingdom of Judah.

Verse 2. Jerusalem was the capital of Judah where Amaziah reigned. Mention of his mother is explained at 1 Ki. 14: 21.

Verse 3. Both David and Joash are called the father of Amaziah. The latter was his father by bodily offspring, and the former in the sense of an ancestor. Both were good men and served the Lord, but David served him better. Amaziah imitated the latter father rather than the former.

Verse 4. One defect in the reign of Amaziah was the retention of the *high places*. For notes on that term see 1 Ki. 3: 2.

Verse 5. The first official act of Amaziah was to execute the murderers of his father. That crime is recorded in Ch. 12: 20, 21.

Verse 6. Individual responsibility is taught in this law. Moses enacted the law and the king respected it.

Verse 7. *Slew of Edom* means he slew the Edomites, who were located near the south of the Dead Sea, which gave the name of *valley of salt* to the place. *Selah* was a city in that section that was based on rock formation. It was the most important city of the Edomites and had been fortified. Amaziah took possession of it and called it Joktheel, a word meaning the "good will of God." He doubtless attributed his success in that campaign to the goodness of God.

Verse 8. *Look one another in the face* was a form of challenge to battle. Amaziah was flushed by his victory over the Edomites, and let it lead him into rashness.

Verse 9. "Cedars of Lebanon" has long been a synonym for that which is lofty, elegant, and useful. A thistle would be an opposite of a cedar. Joash used the fable to illustrate the proposal of Amaziah. He likened himself to the cedar and Amaziah to the thistle. For a thistle to ask a cedar's daughter as a wife for his own son, would be about as appropriate as for Amaziah to challenge Jehoash to combat. The king of Israel continued his comparison by an implied prediction that if they came to battle, the challenger would be defeated and brought to shame.

Verse 10. Jehoash accused Amaziah of being puffed up because of his victory over Edom. *Glory of this and tarry at home* means that he ought to be contented with such glory, and remain at home.

Verse 11. Amaziah would not take the advice of Jehoash, so the two came together. *Looked one another in the face* means they came face to face on the field of battle.

Verse 12. When a man has been killed he cannot flee to his tent. The verse means that so many were killed that all the rest fled in fear.

Verse 13. Note the care that is taken to designate which kingdom and which Jehoash (Joash) is meant. It is because of the same thoughts treated at 1 Ki. 12: 17. Having taken the king alive, Jehoash took his captive to his capital, Jerusalem, and made great havoc of the city. The wall had a number of gates, each one bearing some particular name. The purpose for mentioning this one was to designate the part of the wall attacked, and also the extent of the damage. It was from this gate to the one at the corner of the wall, and the distance was about 600 feet.

Verse 14. The precious metals and the vessels were taken as spoils of war. *Hostages* is from two original words, and the meaning is "pledges." Some kind of surety was exacted from Amaziah, to the effect that he would not disturb Samaria again.

Verses 15, 16. This is the same as Ch. 13: 12, 13.

Verses 17-20. Verse 14 of this chapter left Amaziah in Jerusalem, his capital. This paragraph gives us the account of his death. Personal enemies conspired against him and threatened his life. He escaped temporarily and got to Lachish, but the conspirators followed him and killed him there. He was brought back on horses, and buried in Jerusalem. See 1 Ki. 14: 19 for *chronicles.*

Verse 21. We are not told the motive for killing Amaziah. We know, however, it was not to change the dynasty or family line, for they placed his son on the throne.

Verse 22. Having introduced the king Azariah (also called Uzziah), the writer mentions one item of his reign, the rebuilding of the city Elath. He then drops the history of his reign to take up the reign of a king on the other side of the divided kingdom, or, the kingdom of Israel. We will read of some incidents which took place there, after which the account will come back to Azariah in Jerusalem. See 1 Ki. 12: 17.

Verses 23, 24. Two men named Jeroboam are mentioned in this paragraph. Since they occupied the same throne at various times, the last named should be known as Jeroboam II. No man is justified for evil doing on account of the influence of another. But frequent mention is made of the kings who followed the example of the first king over the 10 tribes. The lesson to be had is in observing the far-reaching influence of a wicked character. Paul taught that fact in 1 Cor. 15: 33.

Verse 25. The word for *coast* in the original means "boundary," whether a writer is considering the territory of land or water. The line of the kingdom of Israel had been pushed back; Jeroboam restored it to its former survey. *Hamath* was a place in Syria near the territory of Israel, and the *sea of the plain* was the Salt or Dead Sea. A long boundary line had been infringed upon, and Jeroboam restored it. This prophecy of Jonah is not mentioned elsewhere in the Old Testament.

Verse 26. *Shut up* is a term meaning "maintained," and *any left* means about the same. The whole passage means that the foreign nations had so oppressed them that no helper seemed in sight until Jeroboam came to the rescue.

Verse 27. God often gave his people some bitter punishment through the instrumentality of the heathen nations. He never did threaten to blot out their name entirely. When the chastisement had been sufficient in his eyes, he would strengthen some man for the work of relief. That is what was done through the services of Jeroboam.

Verse 28. *Recovered Damascus.* That was a city of Syria, and never was considered as a part of the territory of Israel. But sometimes the neighboring nations were brought under a form of subjection to the children of Israel. That had been done in the case of Damascus, according to 2 Sam. 8: 5, 6. What Jeroboam did was to restore that subjection. *Chronicles* is explained at 1 Ki. 14: 19.

Verse 29. *Slept with his fathers* is explained at 1 Ki. 2: 10.

2 KINGS 15

Verses 1-3. Azariah (Uzziah) had a long reign (52 years), yet part of a chapter only is devoted to his history. Even in the book of Chronicles, one chapter (26th) only is used. The affairs of a reign may be important, but if they are not of a military nature, the historians do not pay so much attention to them. Some writer has coined the remark, "Happy is that nation whose annals are brief." Azariah is included among the good kings of Judah, although he made some mistakes for which he suffered.

Verse 4. Retaining the *high places* was one of the defects of Azariah's reign. See comments on these places at 1 Ki. 3: 2.

Verse 5. The occasion for this leprosy is recorded in 2 Chr. 26: 20-23. *Dwelt in a several* (separate) *house* was according to the law of Moses. (Lev. 13: 46). Because of this quarantine regulation, the king could not come in contact with the people, and his son acted in his stead.

Verse 6. The *chronicles* here mentioned should not be confused with the book of that name in our Bible, and referred to above. For this word see 1 Ki. 14: 19.

Verse 7. *Slept with his fathers.* (1 Ki. 2: 10). The city of David was the part of Jerusalem that David had selected for his headquarters, and was the center of attraction on various accounts. Jotham reigned in his own right after the death of his father. He had been acting king since the leprosy came upon his father.

Verses 8, 9. This chapter gives the names of all the remaining kings of Israel. None of them had a long reign, and some were short. Assassination was a common thing through those years, and the life of a king was uncertain. Since Azariah reigned over Judah so long, he will be referred to in dating the reigns of all the kings of Israel mentioned in this chapter except the last one. The death of Azariah (Uzziah) is recorded in V. 7, and the writer then goes back into the years of his reign to take up the line of the kings of Israel. See again 1 Ki. 12: 17.

Verse 10. The family line was broken off by violence more than once in the period covered by this chapter. Some of the conspiracies were open and brazen, such as the present case. *Smote* and *slew* are used as if they were different in meaning; they differ in degree only. To smite could mean only to wound, while to slay would be fatal.

Verse 11. This *chronicles* is the document explained at 1 Ki. 14: 19.

Verse 12. This verse fulfills a promise made to Jehu. See Ch. 10: 30 and comments.

Verse 13. *Full month.* The first word seems an emphatic term, yet the reign of this king was by far the shortest of all. The word is from YOM and translated "day" 1167 times in the A. V. Since the reign of this king was a matter of days only, it was proper to state the exact number of them. The marginal reading, "a month of days" is a correct rendering.

Verse 14. The family line was again broken, and the throne fell into that of Gadi. This man lived at Tirzah, which is significant with the assassination since that city was once the capital of Israel. See 1 Ki. 15: 33; 16: 8.

Verse 15. The acts of Shallum in general are mentioned, while his conspiracy is given special notice. They were all recorded in the greater fullness in the *chronicles* we have spoken about so frequently.

Verse 16. These actions were in the line of conquest, but in the form of violence. The *coasts* or regions about Tiphsah and Tirzah were attacked thus to overcome their resistance to the new king. His brutal treatment of expectant mothers could not be condoned by any kind of motive. However, it was not purely for the sake of brutality that he did it. His main object was to prevent the increase of children who might grow up to oppose him. But even if that were his expectation, he did not reign long enough to realize it, for it continued for ten years only.

Verses 17, 18. This reign was longer than those of his two predecessors, but was not long enough to accomplish all of his plans. Like most of the kings of Israel, he followed in the steps of the first king.

Verse 19. Assyria was a kingdom in the territory of the Euphrates River, and should not be confused with Syria that was just north of Israel. Pul, king of Assyria, came up to attack the king of Israel and dethrone him. He might have attempted it had he not been bought off. Money is a mighty power, and Pul agreed with Menahem for that sort of consideration.

Verse 20. The money was raised by a heavy levy of taxes against the wealthy Israelites. With that inducement, Pul returned to Assyria.

Verses 21, 22. There was not much to say about the reign of Menahem. A fuller account could have been seen by those interested in those days, by reading the *chronicles* as explained at 1 Ki. 14: 19.

Verses 23, 24. The long reign of Azariah (Uzziah) was about ended in Judah, when Pekahiah began to reign over Israel. He repeated the usual practices of kings in that period, and followed the example of Jeroboam, the first king of the 10 tribes.

Verse 25. The throne was again diverted from the family line by assassination, a common occurrence then. The murderer had been in an important relation with the king, that of captain in the army. He took advantage of his rank and slew his master. *Palace* means a fortress of defense for the king's house. Being engaged as defender of the king and the nation, Pekah had an easy access to the monarch. The two men named were accomplices of Pekah and, with the backing of 50 men of the Gileadites, dethroned the king.

Verse 26. So unimportant was the reign of Pekahiah that no act of his was recorded in the inspired record.

The only way of reading about him was by the *chronicles* explained at 1 Ki. 14: 19.

Verses 27, 28. As king Azariah was ending his long reign over Judah, Pekah began his reign over Israel. His reign, like that of his predecessor, ended with murder.

Verse 29. The cities named were depopulated by the king of Assyria, and the inhabitants taken to his country, which was beyond the Euphrates River. This is not to be regarded as a national captivity; that tragedy will take place in the reign of the next king of Israel. But the Lord was so displeased at the general corruption of the kingdom that he suffered this foretaste of their trials to come upon them.

Verse 30. See comments at V. 10 on the difference between *smote* and *slew*. Hoshea was the last king of Israel, or the kingdom of the 10 tribes, and is merely introduced in this verse. His history will be dropped for the present, then resumed after relating that of some kings of Judah.

Verse 31. Nothing further of importance is recorded here of the reign of Pekah. But a brief mention is made of him in 1 Chr. 5: 26, and in the national *chronicles*, explained at 1 Ki. 14: 19.

Verses 32-34. The narrative switches back to the kingdom of Judah. (1 Ki. 12: 17). The long reign of Uzziah (Azariah) had ended, and his son Jotham was on the throne. He was considered one of the good kings, as was his father before him. *His mother's* name is given for reasons explained at 1 Ki. 14: 21.

Verse 35. For comments on *high places* see 1 Ki. 3: 2. Among the good things Uzziah did was to build an elevated entrance to the house of God.

Verse 36. Some account is given of Jotham in 2 Chr. 27: 7 of our Bible, and further information was given in the *chronicles* of the nation, already explained often in this volume and at 1 Ki. 14: 19.

Verse 37. A partial punishment was suffered to come upon Judah from the king of Syria. That was the kingdom just north of the land of Israel.

Verse 38. *Slept with his fathers* is explained at 1 Ki. 2: 10. *City of David* is also called Zion. It was the most important division of Jerusalem, and the site of the temple and other official structures.

2 KINGS 16

Verses 1, 2. The reign of Ahaz in Judah is dated from that of a king in Israel. See the remarks at 1 Ki. 12: 17. His conduct was not right *in the sight of God*, whether man approved of it or not. David was called his father in the sense of an ancestor.

Verse 3. The horrible practice of human sacrifice was done by the heathen, but it should have been far beneath men who had been instructed of the Lord. However, it was a liability and actually was committed by them, otherwise there would not have been the occasion for the warning against it. Read Lev. 3: 21; Deut. 12: 31; 18: 10; 2 Ki. 17: 17; 21: 6; 2 Chr. 33: 6; Jer. 7: 31; 19: 5.

Verse 4. See 1 Ki. 3: 2 for comments on *high places*.

Verse 5. Sometimes one of the divisions of the nation of Israelites would ally itself with a heathen nation, and they would attack the other division. Here the king of Israel and the king of Syria came against Jerusalem, whose king was Ahaz; their attempt failed because that city was so well fortified.

Verse 6. Failing in the action at Jerusalem, the king of Syria turned his attention to Elath, a city that had become the possession of Judah under Azariah. (Ch. 14: 22). It was recovered from the king of Judah, and the Jewish inhabitants were driven out, and their places taken by Syrians.

Verse 7. Israel and Syria had formed an alliance against Judah. Now the latter proposed an alliance with Assyria, against the other Jewish kingdom. *I am thy servant and thy son* just meant that he was willing to grant him great favor if he would help him out of his difficulty with Israel and Syria.

Verse 8. Ahaz proved his proposition was sincere, by taking the valuables from the Lord's house, and sending them as a "present" (Gen. 32: 13) to the king of Assyria.

Verse 9. The king of Assyria responded to the money inducement, and came against Damascus. That city was the capital of Syria, and by reducing it, the king of Judah would be relieved.

Verse 10. The king of Assyria had done Ahaz a favor at Damascus, and he went to that city to greet his ally. While at that place he saw an altar.

It must have been erected for idolatry, for the Syrians were not worshipers of God. Ahaz was interested in the style of the altar and wished one like it for his own use. Accordingly, he sent a description of it to the priest at Jerusalem.

Verse 11. Ahaz must have sent instructions for the priest to make a like altar, for he had it done by the time the king returned.

Verse 12. The inspired writer is giving an account of the actions of Ahaz from the standpoint of history, not that he approved of them. We were told in Vs. 2, 3 that he was an unrighteous king, and the movements being described in these few verses are in keeping with the general description of him. Like many professed servants of God today, Ahaz mixed his own devices with the divine arrangements.

Verse 13. The offerings named were all commanded in the law of Moses. The *burnt offering* in Lev. 1: 3; the *drink offering* in Ex. 29: 40; and *peace offering* in Lev. 3: 1. While the offerings were of divine origin, the proper place for their devotion was also divinely stipulated. But Ahaz had already departed from God, so this corruption of the divine services is not surprising.

Verse 14. The word *altar* occurs three times in this verse. The first and third refer to the brazen altar that Solomon had made; the second is the one Urijah had just made. Ahaz had put the new altar in front of the brazen altar, so that the brazen one was between the house of the Lord and the new altar. Now, Ahaz moved the brazen altar from where it was, and placed it north of the new altar.

Verses 15, 16. The *great altar* was the new one that had been made at the king's commandment. He changed the ordinances of God and substituted his own inventions. All the offerings mentioned were prescribed by the law. The *morning burnt offering* was known elsewhere as the "daily sacrifice." The *meat offering* was the one composed of grain, and described in Lev. 2. The brazen altar, the one that Solomon made under the blessing of God, was to be used only *to enquire by*. That meant Ahaz thought he could use it as a sort of supernatural means of communication with God. There was no authority for such a notion, and no evidence that it was ever recognized by the Lord. It was just another item in the long list of departures from the divine system.

Verse 17. Ahaz had launched out on an adventure of innovations and went to great lengths for the purpose of being different. Read 1 Ki. 7 for a description of the pieces named in this verse. This mutilation of the sacred articles was to get the materials for the king of Assyria. The *sea* was the large tank that Solomon made to contain water. It was supported by 12 brazen oxen. (1 Ki. 7: 25). Ahaz discarded all these valuable pieces of metal and let the sea rest on a foundation of stones.

Verse 18. *Covert* is from MEYCAK and Strong defines it, "a portico (as covered)." Young defines it, "a covered walk." This was an addition to the house of the Lord that *they had built*, meaning some people of more recent times. There is nothing said about this place in the works of Solomon. It could well be likened to the covered entrance seen today, conducting guests from the street to the entrance door of public buildings. This one was built for the special use on the holy days. The materials used in it were turned over to the king of Assyria.

Verses 19, 20. *Chronicles* is the same as explained at 1 Ki. 14: 19, and *slept with his fathers* has notes at 1 Ki. 2: 10.

2 KINGS 17

Verse 1. In the margin of many of our Bibles we have a note, stating that Hoshea began to reign after an interregnum, meaning an interval. Ch. 15: 30 states that he slew the king in the 20th year of Jotham. The present verse says he began to reign in the 12th year of Ahaz. A look at the chronology will show a space of 10 years. This fact also recalls the comments in this volume at Ch. 15: 30. The history of Judah will be dropped for a few verses, to take up that of Hoshea in the kingdom of Israel.

Verse 2. God always recognizes any merit in his people; Hoshea was one of the bad kings of Israel, but not as bad as his predecessors. We should have in mind the idea that, as far as spiritual outcome is concerned, the Bible makes no distinction between big and little sins. But the Mosaic system was both spiritual and temporal. It made some difference, therefore, that a ruler was not as bad as another; the people under him would fare better in their national life.

Verse 3. This was Shalmaneser IV, according to George Rawlinson, who says that the Assyrian king began his reign in 727 B. C., and that he led several expeditions into Palestine. It was on one of them that he forced Hoshea to become a tributary to Assyria; which is meant by the words *gave him presents*. It constituted a form of political subjection to Assyria, with an agreement to continue the payments of the "presents."

Verse 4. Hoshea broke his covenant with Shalmaneser, which was indicated by his discontinuance of the tribute or "presents." As a reinforcement in his revolt from Assyria, Hoshea appealed to Egypt, but there is no evidence that it did him any good. The king of Assyria took him into custody and put him into prison.

Verse 5. Personal imprisonment of Hoshea was not enough to satisfy the king of Assyria. The reduction of the capital and citizens of the nation was planned. For that purpose a siege was begun about Samaria, which continued three years. Smith's Bible Dictionary states that Shalmaneser lost his crown to Sargon about this time. It is not clear in history whether the former or the latter king of Assyria was in power at the close of the siege. In the 3rd verse the inspired writer states that Shalmaneser was the one who started the siege, and all history agrees with it. In the 6th verse the same writer merely states that the *king of Assyria* came up, leaving it an open question which king is meant. But since it is pretty definite that not more than a year's margin is probable, it will be reasonable to attribute the following performances to Sargon, who had usurped the throne from Shalmaneser.

Verse 6. The events of the whole chapter have to do with the great tragedy of the Assyrian capitivity, and the details will be discussed as we pass from verse to verse. But a suggestion will be made to those who are marking their Bibles. This verse may properly be marked, "Assyrian Captivity of the 10 Tribes." Gozan is defined by Strong, "a province of Assyria." The river of Gozan would mean a river flowing in that province, and is a tributary of the Euphrates, and the cities of Halah and Habor were on that stream. Media was a small power located in that general territory, and some of the Israelites were placed in cities there after being taken captive.

Verses 7, 8. Reference is made to the deliverance from Egypt to call attention to their ingratitude. It also exposes the folly of turning from a God who can do such things, to those who have no power. *Which they had made* means the things the heathen had practiced for religion.

Verse 9. Nothing can be hid from God. When men think to hide from him, however, it is accounted as bad as if they actually did so. *From the tower of the watchman to the fenced city.* Small towns depended on watchtowers for protection, while the fenced (walled) cities had the more extensive kind of protection. The phrase means they made these provisions for idolatry at all of such localities.

Verse 10. We usually think of a grove as a group of trees. But the word *grove* here means an image of some goddess, which they erected under the trees.

Verses 11, 12. *High places* is explained at 1 Ki. 3: 2. Idolatry was wrong, even when instigated by the professed servants of God. What made it still more grievous to the Lord was the borrowing it from the heathen about them.

Verse 13. The Israelites could not plead ignorance as an excuse, for the Lord had repeatedly warned them. There was not much difference between a *prophet* and a *seer*, and the words are used interchangeably in the Bible. The slight distinction is, the latter may mean an inspired man merely, while the former includes some authority.

Verse 14. *Hardened their necks* means they became stubborn.

Verse 15. *Statutes* means the specific enactments of God, and *covenant* means an agreement or promise that was made, on condition of their obedience. *Testimonies* means the same law referred to by other terms. The special idea is that the law had been confirmed by the oath and proof of the Lord. It may be expressed by saying it had been divinely notarized. *Vanity* means that which is useless, and following it makes persons vain or useless in the sight of God.

Verse 16. These calves were not the first metallic images the Israelites made, but they were the beginning of their practice as the kingdom of Israel. (1 Ki. 12: 28). Care must be had when considering *grove* in connection with idolatry. The word is from ASHERAH and Strong defines it, Asherah (or Astarte) a Phoenician goddess; also an image of the same." Young defines it, "a shrine." Smith's Bible Dictionary says of grove, "It is also probable that there was a connection between this symbol or image, and the sacred symbolic tree, the representation of which occurs so frequently on Assyrian sculptures." The Schaff-Herzog Encyclopaedia says in part, under *Groves and Trees, Sacred:* "In the Hebrew Old Testament there is no mention of sacred groves, for the word so translated in the A. V. means properly an image to Asherah; but sacred trees are repeatedly mentioned. . . . Worship under trees was commonly idolatrous." Because of the facts named above, groves, trees, and oaks are used in the Bible generally to refer to idolatry, when used figuratively. This is true whether natural or artificial trees is meant. *Host of heaven* means the sun and other heavenly bodies.

Verse 17. *Pass through the fire* is explained at 2 Ki. 16: 3. *Divination* was the same as witchcraft, or some form of trickery. *Enchantments* was similar to divination, and meant the practice of magic. *Sold themselves* means they surrendered themselves to a life of evil. *To provoke him* does not necessarily mean they did it for that purpose, but that was the effect their evil conduct had on Him.

Verse 18. Judah was mentioned as being the only tribe left. That is a comparative term, and used because it was by far a stronger tribe than Benjamin.

Verses 19, 20. Judah had some good kings which caused God to delay their captivity. But they were guilty, and walked in the statutes which the 10 tribes had made. Altogether, the children became so corrupt that God suffered them to be oppressed by the foreign nations, and finally cast *out of his sight*, which means out of the land of Canaan, since that land represented the presence of God on earth.

Verse 21. *Israel* means the 10 tribes as a separate kingdom. They were torn from the other two, because the king in Judah was rash. After being separated from Judah, or the house of David, the 10 tribes appointed a wicked man, Jeroboam, to be their king. And this wicked king *made them sin*, which means he caused them to sin.

Verses 22, 23. This is a summing up of the subject matter pertaining to the Assyrian captivity and the causes. We are told that such a calamity had been predicted by the prophets. *Unto this day* means up to the date of this writing, which was about 600 B. C. according to the Schaff-Herzog Encyclopaedia.

Verse 24. The reader should consider verses 24-33 as one paragraph, in a general setting, its subject to be named later. But we shall study the verses separately first. The land had been depopulated by the captivity, and taken over by the Assyrian king. He wished the country to be occupied by other people of his own choosing. The places named were cities or provinces mostly in the Assyrian kingdom, or other localities under its domination.

Verse 25. *Feared not the Lord.* In its full sense, to fear the Lord means to love and respect and obey him. In a restricted sense, it means to respect to the extent of standing in awe of the Lord. These newcomers did not fear the Lord even to that extent. In punishment, God sent wild beasts to destroy some of them. It was not to be expected that these heathen would become a group of fully devoted servants under the Mosaic system. But it was right to expect them to respect the God of the land.

Verse 26. *Manner* is from MISPHAT which has a wide variety of meaning. In the present connection it has the force of law or requirement. It was one of the notions of idolaters that different countries and provinces had their own peculiar gods. These gods might differ from each other in their wishes and requirements. In order to get along with any of these deities it was necessary to comply with their personal demands. It would be impossible to do that, unless one knew those tastes and demands. Of course these immigrants were not acquainted with the god of their newly found country, hence had failed to please him, which brought the misfortune of the wild beasts.

Verses 27, 28. It was logical to think of the priests for the purpose suggested to the Assyrian king. They were the men supposed not only to understand, but to preside over the services given to a god. Accordingly, one of the priests whom they had taken from Samaria, which was the capital, was returned to the land. Bethel was a prominent place, it being where one of the golden calves had been erected by Jeroboam. Here the priest informed them as to the God of that country (which means, of course, the God of the Hebrews). They were told to fear or regard him.

Verse 29. *Every nation* has reference to the various places from which the king of Assyria had taken people to occupy the cities of Israel. The newcomers used these places for their services, but each particular group erected its own kind of idol.

Verses 30, 31. According to the statements at V. 29, the several localities named here made images according to their own personal choice. The words listed are names of various deities, each of which had some peculiar form of worship. One group had adopted that of human sacrifices. See 2 Ki. 16: 3 for comments on that subject.

Verses 32, 33. *Feared the Lord* in the limited sense as explained at V. 25. In connection with that, they continued their services to idols. It was a combination of idolatry and the acknowledgement of the God of the Hebrews. This is how the Samaritan religion got started. In course of time some Jewish blood got mixed with the foreign type, so that the national complexion was affected thereby. This is the place to give the name of the paragraph of verses 24-33, promised above. Those who are marking their Bibles may title this paragraph, "Origin of the Samaritan Nation and Religion." It is proper to state, before considering the rest of the chapter, that the Samaritans did not always remain idolaters. We shall quote from Prideaux's Connexion, for the year 676. "But they (the nations sent to replace the tribes of Israel) only took him (the God of Israel) hereon into the number of their former deities and worshiped him jointly with the gods of the nation from whence they came; and in this corruption of joining the worship of their false gods with that of the true they continued, till the building of the Samaritan temple on Mount Gerizim by Sanballat; but, on that occasion, abundance of Jews falling off to them, they reduced them from this idolatry to the worship of the true God only, as shall hereafter be related; and they have continued in the same worship ever since even to this day." We shall return from this digression to the affairs of the Samaritans as treated in this chapter.

Verse 34. *Unto this day* means the date of the writing. *Feared not the Lord* in the true sense of faithful service as described at V. 25. *Statutes, ordinances, law and commandments*, means the requirements of the law of Moses.

Verse 35. The former citizens of this territory had been deported because they violated the covenant God made with them. Now the new citizens were not profiting by their experience, but doing the same as they did.

Verse 36. This was not said directly to the Samaritans. It is cited for the reader, explanatory of the statement in the preceding verse.

Verses 37, 38. The warnings given the Israelites very specifically pointed out the practices of the nations of the places through which they must travel.

Verses 39, 40. The very nations whose idolatry they were warned against, could have no power over the people of God, unless they proved unfaithful. In that case, the Lord would use those heathen nations as scourges to punish his own people.

Verse 41. *These nations* means the idolaters brought in to take the place of the former citizens. They had been removed because of the very practices now being done by the new occupants. It is remarkable how little effect a stern lesson sometimes has.

2 KINGS 18

Verse 1. We have just read of the captivity of Israel, with their last king, Hoshea. Now we are reading of events that happened in the *third year of Hoshea*. This makes us recall the note at 1 Ki. 12: 17. From here on to the end of the book we will not be reading about the kingdom of Israel, except as an incidental reference from the main subject, the history of Judah.

Verse 2. The name of this king's mother is given for the reason explained at 1 Ki. 14: 21.

Verse 3. Hezekiah was one of the good kings of Judah. He made many reforms, of which we will read as we go on through his history. David was his father in the sense of being an important ancestor.

Verse 4. For comments on *groves* see 2 Ki. 17: 16. The brazen serpent had been made for one purpose only, to look at in case of the serpent's bite. It was never intended as an object of veneration, much less to be worshiped with the burning of incense. That made an idol out of an object that had a divine origin, and the king destroyed it. People are doing a like thing with the cross. It was only the mechanical means to an end, and when that was accomplished it was not to be used as an object of veneration. Thus, when a cross is erected on a church building or grave stone, or is worn as a charm about one's person, it becomes an idol. The references to *the cross* of Christ in the N. T. mean the scenes of the cross, not the literal object of wood. *Nehustan* is from a word that Strong defines, "something made of copper." The idea is, the serpent had no inherent qualities to cure disease. Only when God was using it for the purpose could any benefit come from it. After that it was still the metal it was while in the earth, and not something that was entitled to be worshiped.

Verse 5. *None like him* is not the same as saying there was none as good or as great or as useful. Josiah was a great and good king and did wonders in the way of reform. But even at that, he was not *like* Hezekiah. It means he had individual characteristics in his service to God unlike those of any others.

Verses 6-8. A part of this is prospective, for we have not as yet read about his opposition to Assyria. *From the tower of the watchmen to the fenced city* is explained at Ch. 17: 9.

Verses 9-12. This passage is the same as Ch. 17: 3-7. Its use in this place is to account for the actions of the Assyrians soon to be related. Their success against the 10 tribes encouraged them to try their fortunes against the 2 tribes.

Verse 13. Urged on by the success against the kingdom of Israel, the Assyrian king Sennacherib conducted an expedition against the kingdom of Judah. He took the fenced (walled) cities, among which was Lachish, where he pitched his camp.

Verse 14. *I have offended* could not mean an acknowledgement of any wrongdoing, for Hezekiah had not committed any. That is, he had not done wrong morally, nor gone beyond his rights as a king, although the original word could mean that sometimes. It is CHATA and Strong defines it, "a primitive root; properly to miss; hence (figuratively and generally) to sin; by influence to forfeit, lack, expiate, repent, (causatively) lead astray, condemn." From the connection, and with the definition for our authority, the meaning is that Hezekiah admitted he was the loser. He had made a military miscalculation, and was ready to pay whatever the king of Assyria demanded. The amount set was 124,000 pounds of silver, and 174 pounds of gold, according to Moffatt.

Verses 15, 16. Part of this precious metal had been added to the building by Hezekiah, and now is used by him in remitting the fine imposed by the Assyrian king. It was a diplomatic move, and obtained a brief lull in disturbances from Sennacherib.

Verse 17. Some little time had elapsed since the events of the previous verse. The Assyrian king had maintained a post at Lachish, and from that place sent his officers to Jerusalem to demand the surrender of the city. In the meantime Hezekiah had formed an alliance with Egypt, according to the Schaff-Herzog Encyclopaedia, which will be quoted: "But Sennacherib demanded more than this [the fine of silver and gold] from the Judean king. He had taken up his position at Lachish with the expectation of a battle against a most formidable enemy, Egypt, which had joined the league against Assyria, and whose army, although too late to protect most of its allies, was on the way to meet Sennacherib." — Article, *Sennacherib*. The *conduit* was a watercourse to bring water from a pool that Hezekiah had built for the service of the city; it is mentioned in Ch. 20: 20. The fuller's field was a place used to do various kinds of washing, which would be supplied by this conduit. This spot was chosen by Sennacherib's men because it was in speaking distance from the wall to Jerusalem.

Verse 18. Eliakim was a good man, and had charge of the king's household affairs. The two other men were part of the "office force" of the king. This trio came out to represent their master in the conversations.

Verses 19-21. Rabshakeh was the chief butler to the king, and was speaker for the group representing him in the conversation. *Staff of this bruised reed* was a figure, intended to describe the uselessness of the alliance with Egypt. This alliance was recorded and explained at V. 17. The substance of the speech was to the effect that Hezekiah was foolish to think he was strong enough to resist the great king of Assyria.

Verse 22. Rabshakeh make a false accusation against Hezekiah. The *high places* and *altars* which he destroyed were not of God, but institutions opposed to God. History repeats itself, and today if a man opposes the religious institutions of men, he will be accused of opposing the work of God.

Verse 23. As an insulting statement, Rabshakeh offered to furnish Hezekiah some help if he cared to risk his fortunes in a battle. He offered to furnish 2000 horses, and then impudently intimated that he could not muster that many riders. And he also showed his contempt for Hezekiah by requiring pledges that due treatment would be given the horses while in the possession of the Jews.

Verse 24. Rabshakeh took it for granted that Hezekiah could not furnish that many riders. In that case, how could he hope to *turn away* or repulse even the weakest of Sennacherib's men, by trusting in Egypt?

Verse 25. It was known that the Lord sometimes used foreign nations to chastise his own people. He had recently done so against the 10 tribes. But the claim was false in this instance, for the expedition failed, and the Lord's plans do not fail.

Verse 26. Eliakim did not wish his Jewish brethren who were listening, to be discouraged by the theratening words of Rabshakeh. They knew that God did occasionally help foreigners against them, and perhaps this was one of those occasions. Eliakim believed he and his associates could endure the insults of Rabshakeh, but the others might not. For that reason he requested him to use his native tongue, since it could be understood by the three representing Hezekiah.

Verse 27. The language of Rabshakeh was vile in view of a more modern translation. But the meaning that he had was significant of a siege. It was a threat that if they did not surrender to Assyria, the siege would be prolonged until all rations would be cut off. In that state of want, they would be forced to eat and drink the discharges from their own bodies.

Verses 28, 29. In a spirit of spite, Rabshakeh took particular pains to have the men on the wall hear him. He used a *loud voice* and spoke in the Jews' language. He tried to instigate a rebellious attitude against their king. They were warned that Hezekiah would not be able to deliver them from the Assyrian king.

Verse 30. Rabshakeh knew the Jews relied on the Lord for help, and he was rash enough to declare to these listening to him that their Lord would not deliver them.

Verses 31, 32. The next move of Rabshakeh was an offer of a bribe. If the people would desert to the king of Assyria, and come outside to him, they would immediately be supplied with the good things of life. That would continue throughout the siege, then they would be conducted kindly to the land of Assyria. That land would be as good as the one they were leaving, with an abundance of provisions.

Verses 33-35. As proof that no god can rescue a people from the hand of Assyria, Rabshakeh cited the captivity of the 10 tribes, that the gods whom they had served, and because of which the Assyrians had been brought against them, could not deliver them. He either did not know, or did not care to admit, that the God of the Hebrews was behind that action of the Assyrians, while he was not behind the present one.

Verse 36. Nothing the people could have said would have satisfied a vile character like Rabshakeh. Another thing, the king already had men deputized to speak for him, hence he had before instructed the unofficial people to attempt no speech.

Verse 37. Eliakim and his associates were much overcome by the tirade of Rabshakeh, and indicated it by rending their clothes, which was a custom in olden times when one was in grief or confusion. They reported their interview to their chief.

2 KINGS 19

Verse 1, 2. Hezekiah was much distressed by the report of his men. It was natural for him to go into the temple at such a time, for that was where the Lord's presence seemed to be the most vividly portrayed. He then decided to appeal to Isaiah the prophet for instruction and comfort. This is the first mention of this prophet, who was one of those who wrote as well as spoke prophecy. The prophets and priests were the public men employed by the Lord to communicate any special message to his people. (Heb. 1: 1). These representatives of Hezekiah arranged their appearance properly to indicate anxiety and distress, and went to the man of God.

Verse 3. This language is figurative, of course. A woman's time comes for the birth of her child. Her labor pains are calling for relief, but she does not have the strength to expel the child without help. So the kingdom of the Lord's inheritance is in pain from trouble, but will have to have help to overcome it.

Verses 4, 5. Eliakim and his associates explained their figure of speech, and asked Isaiah to make his prayer to God on their behalf.

Verse 6. Isaiah did not claim any personal wisdom, but reported what God said. He also comforted them by assuring that they need not be afraid of the king of Assyria.

Verse 7. Isaiah specified his promise by saying the Lord would help them. The Assyrian king would be kept from attacking Jerusalem by a miraculous impression from God. Something will "rumor" to him that he would better look after his interests at home. In the meantime, however, he will be engaged in war with other forces. That will not keep him from his bitterness against Hezekiah, and even while busy with his affairs of war, will make more efforts to irritate him, which will be discussed below.

Verses 8. This meant that Rabshakeh returned to Sennacherib at Libnah, having learned that he had left Lachish.

Verse 9. There are four pronouns in this verse that might confuse the reader; *he, he, thee,* and *he.* The second refers to Tirhakah, the others to Sennacherib. When the Assyrian king heard that the Ethiopian king, Tirhakah, was coming against him, he was goaded into some more agitation against Hezekiah.

Verse 10. Sennacherib sent his messengers to Hezekiah to intimidate him into submission, with a possible alliance against the common foe. He warned him not to trust his God to protect the city of Jerusalem from capture.

Verses 11-13. Sennacherib tried the same boasting that his servant Rabshakeh had. He referred to the success of the Assyrian arms against the 10 tribes and other kingdoms, and that in spite of all the gods. He also made the mistake of likening a case where God was the real force, to one where the motive was against God. The messengers sent by Sennacherib were vested with a written communication, which they delivered to Hezekiah.

Verse 14. When the king of Judah received the letter sent from Sennacherib, he did the same as when Rabshakeh made his defiant speech. He went into the house of God and spread the letter before the Lord.

Verses 15-19. *Dwellest between the cherubims.* This is a reference to the creatures Moses made for the mercy-seat over the ark. (Ex. 25: 18-22). It was in the most holy place, and the high priest went there on one day of each year to converse with the Lord. *Open, Lord, thine eyes.* Strictly speaking, the Lord never closes his eyes. The word is from PAQACH and one definition is, "be observant." Hezekiah is reverently asking the Lord to take notice of them in their distress over the Assyrian king. The finest motive Hezekiah expressed for his prayer is, that all kingdoms may know that God is the only one. Such despots as Sennacherib had destroyed the gods of the nations they attacked. If he, in turn, is overcome by the God of Israel, then his supremacy over all other gods will be demonstrated.

Verse 20. Isaiah was an inspired man. God informed him of the prayer of Hezekiah and told him how to answer. He directed him to give answer in a message, for it says he *sent to Hezekiah,* which reminds us again of Heb. 1: 1.

Verse 21. This is the beginning of the message Isaiah *sent to Hezekiah,* which will include a goodly number of verses. *Virgin* is from BETHUWLAH and Strong defines it, "feminine past part. of an unused root meaning to separate; a virgin (from her privacy); sometimes (by continuation) a bride; also (figuratively) a city or state." Daughter is from a word meaning any relation, either by blood or other tie. Jerusalem was separated to God, and the capital of the state composed of his people. *Him* and *thee* means Sennacherib, the king of Assyria, and the man who has caused the condition of distress and threatening. *Despised* means to belittle the actual power of the enemy; *shaken her head* has the same significance. The past tense in *hath* is characteristic of inspired prophecy. With God, everything is an absolute "now," and he can speak of the future events as if they were already taking place, or even had done so. God knew what Sennacherib was planning on doing, and inspired Isaiah with information.

Verse 22. The prophet is represented as speaking to Sennacherib, and charging him with offense against God. Not speaking directly to him; but since God can read all minds, he is reading that of this boastful king. The making known of this state of Sennacherib's mind, and God's attitude toward it, is for the encouragement of Hezekiah and his people. The point is, that in using this attitude against Hezekiah and Jerusalem, it is accounted as against *the Holy One of Israel*.

Verse 23. The verse starts with the same thoughts described in the preceding one. The rest of the verse regards the boastful claims of the Assyrian king, how he proposed to occupy the choice places of the land within his siege.

Verse 24. *Strange* means "outside," and Sennacherib boasted (to himself) that he would use the waters of another land. Furthermore, he would stop the use of such waters that were not desired for his own use.

Verse 25. At this point God acts as if he would interrupt the boastings in the mind of Sennacherib, to remind him of certain facts. He asks the Assyrian king if he had not long known that "I have done it," meaning that the very things he threatened to destroy were the work of God. The last part of the verse means that God would be the one to consider when he thought about doing such havoc.

Verse 26. *Therefore* and the rest of the verse means that if Sennacherib carries out his boasts, to subdue the inhabitants in the way figuratively described, it will be in spite of the same God mentioned in the preceding verse.

Verse 27. From here on to the end of V. 34, (which by the way is the end of the message to Hezekiah), God is represented as speaking to Sennacherib about his boasting. We do not know that the king of Assyria ever actually saw this message; it was so worded for the encouragement of Hezekiah. God asserts that he knows all about the king and his raging against the people of the Lord's kingdom.

Verse 28. The original for *hook* is defined in the lexicon, "a ring for the nose (or lips)." *Bridle* is from a word that means to curb with a bit. The passage is a figurative description of the humiliating degree to which the proud Assyrian monarch would be brought, in his retreat to his own country.

Verse 29. Some specific proof of divine foresight is often given for the benefit of God's people. While the passage is still represented as a warning to Sennacherib, its purpose is to encourage Israel. They are in siege and distress, and not free to go about their usual pursuits. Not that a material siege had been thrown around the city as yet. Sennacherib was away, engaged in war with other combatants. But the state of fear and uncertainty, caused by the overawing war clouds in the not too distant fields, had the effect of making the people hesitant and suspicious. They are assured that they may find subsistence from the voluntary fruits of the land for two years, after that they will feel free to engage in the cultivation of their land.

Verses 30, 31. It is so near, comparatively, to the captivity of the kingdom of Judah, that the prophet goes even beyond it to give a few words of encouragement to the people now in distress.

Verse 32. Returning to the subject immediately at hand, Isaiah declares that Sennacherib will not approach Jerusalem, not even near enough to shoot an arrow.

Verse 33. *By the way*, etc. If an army travels on a new highway, it might not be known whether the leader was still moving in his original plan. If he is on the same road on which he arrived at the given camp, but going in the opposite direction, it would be evidence of a retreat, which means defeat.

Verse 34. A double motive prompted God to defend Jerusalem. His own honor was involved, also that of the great king David.

Verse 35. Irreverent or frivolous critics think there is something to laugh at in this verse. If they were *all* dead, they ask, how could they arise? For one thing, the pronoun *they* occurs twice; once for the ones smitten, the other for the ones living. The word for *smote* is NAKAH, and Strong defines it, "a primitive root; to strike (lightly or severely, literally or figuratively." So a person could be smitten and not killed, and it would be proper information to add the ones smitten were dead. Another criticism is that the word *dead* is unnecessary, since the word *corpse* tells that. The critic again exposes his lack of information. At the time the A. V. was composed the word meant "a human or animal body, whether living or dead," according to Webster. Hence, a corpse does not always mean one dead. Moffatt's translation gives us, "they were all found to be dead corpses in the morning." The R. V. words it, "and when men arose early in the morning, behold, they were all dead bodies."

Verse 36. The foregoing event was the *blast* predicted in V. 7. With such a stroke of misfortune to his army, Sennacherib was induced to give up all his malicious designs against Jerusalem, and return to Nineveh, the capital of his kingdom. He never again attempted anything against Palestine, but history gives accounts of many important campaigns elsewhere.

Verse 37. About 20 years after his return from the attempt against Jerusalem, Sennacherib met a violent death, and that by assassination at the hands of his sons. This fulfilled another prediction made by Isaiah in V. 7. Secular history does not give us any information on this affair, as to the motive of the murder. But we know it was not thirst for power, for the murderers escaped to Armenia, otherwise called Ararat, and another brother took the throne.

2 KINGS 20

Verse 1. *Sick unto death* means he was sick enough to die, and would do so unless some miraculous intervention occurred. *Set thine house in order* means for him to arrange his household affairs as he wants them to be conducted after his death.

Verse 2. *Turned his face to the wall.* Hezekiah was seriously ill, and not able to leave his bed for a season of prayer. He wished to have the privacy of secret prayer, and could have it only by turning his face toward the wall.

Verse 3. *Walk in truth* means to walk according to the truth of God. *With a perfect heart* means with all the heart. The word *perfect* always takes the definition "complete." To do something with all the heart is the same as doing it with a perfect heart. Hezekiah offered a scriptural reason for expecting the favor of God. It was not that he was wiser or more necessary to God than other servants, but he had served God truly. That is the teaching of the whole Bible. God does not depend on human assistance in carrying out his plans, for he is the All-powerful One. But he is pleased to have the faithful cooperation of his children.

Verse 4. *Court* is from a word that means "city." Isaiah had scarcely reached the center of the city when the Lord stopped him.

Verse 5. God sometimes spoke directly to his servants, but more often he did so through the prophets. (Heb. 1: 1). Hezekiah was called the *captain of my people* because he was the king of Judah. The specific promise was made that the recovery would come to a climax on the third day.

Verse 6. From this verse it seems that Hezekiah's sickness occurred in course of the disturbances from Assyria; the exact date is not clear. At any rate, God assured him of 15 years more of life, and of the full relief from the threatening of Assyria.

Verse 7. Strong defines the *boil* as an inflammatory ulcer. There are some medical qualities in figs, yet they alone would not cure a malignant infection. This is another instance where the Lord combined human and superhuman means in effecting a result. See comments at 2 Ki. 2: 8.

Verse 8. The preceding verse covers the three-day period, from the application of the figs to the recovery. That style of writing is common to the various instances in the Bible. This verse goes back to the first of the conversation to relate some details. Hezekiah was not the first person who desired and received some miraculous evidence that a prophecy would be fulfilled. One instance only will be cited, that of Gideon in Judges 6: 36-40.

Verse 9. The shadow was on an instrument made by king Ahaz, and used to indicate the time of day. It is rendered "dial" in the A. V., but the marginal reading is "degrees," which is correct. It is from MAALAH, and Strong defines it, "elevation, i. e. the act (literally a journey to a higher place, figuratively a superior station); specifically a climactic progress." It has been translated in the A. V. by stair, step, story and other words. The definition is simplified in Smith's Bible Dictionary which I quote: "Dial. An instrument for showing the time of day from the shadow of a style or gnomon on a graduated arc or surface;" rendered "steps" in A. V., Ex. 20: 26; 1 Ki. 10: 19, and "degrees" in 2 Ki. 20: 9, 10, 11; Isa. 38: 8, where, to give a consistent rendering we should read with the margin the "degrees" rather than the "dial" of Ahaz. It is probable that the dial of Ahaz was really a series of steps or stairs, and that the shadow (perhaps of some column or obelisk on the top) fell on a greater or smaller number of them according as the sun was low or high. The terrace of a palace might easily be thus ornamented." Article, *Dial*. The reason the King James translators used "dial" was the use of the modern instrument which is actually a dial, and used for the same purpose as the steps of Ahaz. Hezekiah asked for a sign and Isaiah suggested one with the dial. For the shadow to go suddenly in either direction would require a miracle, yet the king was told to suggest which direction.

Verse 10. *Light thing* means "easy." Hezekiah used the word in a comparative sense, not that it would not be a miracle either way. For the shadow to go down would indicate the hastening onward of time. The going backward would be the retracing of time, which Hezekiah thought would be the greater miracle, and chose that evidence.

Verse 11. In answer to the prayer of Isaiah, the shadow went back 10 steps or degrees. There was no logical relation between the 10 degrees and the 15 years to be added to the life of Hezekiah. He had been promised that much more of life, and this movement of the shadow was miraculous assurance of its fulfillment.

Verse 12. The events of this verse occurred after the recovery of Hezekiah. 2 Chr. 32: 31 gives us the additional information that the king of Babylon sent to Hezekiah to inquire about the miracle of the shadow, of which he had heard. He also professed to congratulate him on his recovery. The *present* was a bid for diplomatic alliance. See comments at Gen. 32: 13 on the word. Consistent with the principle of the alliance, a request was made to see the building of God, with the treasures therein.

Verse 13. *Hearkened* means he granted the request of the ambassadors of the king of Babylon. He *shewed them all the house* means he shewed them all through the house. In other words, he held a sort of "open house" for them, so that they obtained information of the desirability of the place. Doubtless, Hezekiah had the best of intentions, but the king of Babylon turned the courtesy unto his own favor.

Verses 14, 15. Again the prophet Isaiah enters the scene, and is told of the visit of the men from Babylon. He is not hesitant nor evasive in his statement, for he is not conscious of having done anything wrong. At that time Babylon had not risen to the power it was destined to reach, and no intimation of the danger that might come from such a source could have been apparent to an uninspired man.

Verse 16. *Word of the Lord* shows the significance of the work of a prophet. As a man, Isaiah might not have been any wiser than others, but when speaking for God, it was the same as if spoken directly by the Lord. See Heb. 1: 1.

Verse 17. *The days come* is a prophecy, meaning the days will come. The immediate calamity of predicted things was the taking of the valuables that had been just shown to the men from Babylon.

Verse 18. However, a graver fate was coming to Hezekiah than the loss of his collected articles. His descendants were to be taken to the country from which these men had come, who just saw the precious things. They not only were to be taken away from their native land, but would be forced to serve as *eunuchs* in the palace. The word means primarily one not possessed of manhood, and thus a desirable person to be a servant about the bed-chambers. It came to be used with reference to the personal attendants of kings and queens and other dignitaries.

Verse 19. It is difficult to understand the frame of mind which Hezekiah exhibited. The cold idea that his sons, and not he, were to see the predicted misfortune, gave him comfort. The most reasonable commendation one can offer is that his flesh and blood was not as important in his estimation as the quietude of the kingdom.

Verse 20. The pool is mentioned in Ch. 18: 17 and Neh. 2: 14. See the comments at the former place. *Chronicles* is explained at 1 Ki. 14: 19.

Verse 21. *Slept with his fathers* is explained at 1 Ki. 2: 10.

2 KINGS 21

Verses 1, 2. See 1 Ki. 14: 21 on reason for mention of *mother*. Manasseh began to reign at the age of 12 years. We would hardly think of a lad at that age doing very many things on his own responsibility. It was the rule for young kings to reign through the priest. (Ch. 12: 2). Manasseh's reign was 55 years long, and the account of his activities given here does not tell us at what year he began the evil works described.

Verse 3. The *high places* are described at 1 Ki. 3: 2. They were not as bad as some other institutions of those times, yet they were objectionable. King Hezekiah had destroyed them, but now his son rebuilt them. Baal was the supreme male false god of the people of Canaan, and altars raised for him were used for burnt sacrifices. It was the most prominent form of idolatrous worship, to offer sacrifices to Baal. For information concerning the *groves* see at 2 Ki. 17: 16. *Host of heaven* means the sun and other heavenly bodies, that were worshipped by idolaters.

Verse 4. The house of the Lord was in Jerusalem. So the objection was not that Manasseh built altars *in the house of the Lord*, for that would have been the proper place for them, had it been right to have them. The point is that he built altars in the place where the Lord said he would put *his name*. It was the substituting the altars for the name of God that was condemned.

Verse 5. These altars were for sacrifices to the sun and other heavenly bodies. The *two courts* were the *inner court* (1 Ki. 6: 36) and the *great court* (1 Ki. 7: 12) that Solomon had made.

Verse 6. *Pass through the fire* is explained at 2 Ki. 16: 3. *Observed times*. The second one is not in the original. The first is from ANAN, and Strong defines it, "to cloud over; figuratively to act covertly, i. e. practice magic." *Use enchantments* is similar to the preceding practice, but has special reference to pretended ability to make predictions. *Familiar spirits*. The first does not appear in the original as a separate word. The second is from a Hebrew word of somewhat indefinite meaning, but generally refers to persons claiming some superhuman knowledge. *Wizard* has practically the same meaning as *spirits* above. The practices of Manasseh provoked the Lord to anger, so that he threatened to bring shame upon him and his people.

Verse 7. The words *my name* form the central thought of this verse. See comments at V. 4. *A graven image* is one carved out by hand, in the form of the idolatrous *groves* already explained at Ch. 17: 16.

Verse 8. This is a statement of the Lord, which was begun in the preceding verse, beginning with the words, *said to David*. The Lord is repeating his promise to maintain his people in the land, but on condition they keep his commandments.

Verse 9. This is the writer of this history, making comments on the conduct of Manasseh and the people under him.

Verses 10, 11. Isaiah and other prophets of his day were inspired to give the warnings from God, over the corrupt practices of the people of Judah. The Amorites are referred to because they represented the most corrupt type of idolaters.

Verse 12. The form of language is present tense, but it is prophecy, for the things threatened did not come to pass for some years. *Tingle* means to "redden with shame" at the humiliating punishment that would be put upon them.

Verse 13. *Upside down* is merely an indifferent incident if one were only considering the manual act of drying a dish and then putting it on a table with the face downward. But in using it as an illustration, it means that as a dish turned upside down would be empty, so the Lord will empty Jerusalem of its people.

Verse 14. The inheritance means the people whom the Lord inherited from the fathers, and whom he had made into a nation. Because of their wickedness, they were threatened with desertion.

Verse 15. The sinfulness of the people dated from the time they left Egypt. The *fathers* is a term used variously; in the present connection it applies to the heads of the families in all of the tribes.

Verse 16. *Innocent blood* means the blood of persons who were righteous as far as bloodshed was concerned. If a man commits a crime that deserves capital punishment, the shedding of his blood is not innocent blood. (Gen. 9: 6). *Beside his sin* has reference to his leading the people into idolatry.

Verse 17. *Chronicles*. See 1 Ki. 14: 19. In addition to the chronicles mentioned above, see the account in the Bible in 2 Chr. 33: 11-19.

Verse 18. *Slept with his fathers* is commented upon at 1 Ki. 2: 10. Manasseh was not buried in the sepulchre of the other kings. The garden of Uzza was a somewhat private burial place near the palace of the king.

Verse 20. Again it is stated the king did evil *in the sight of the Lord*. Regardless of how a thing may seem to man, the thing that counts is what the Lord thinks.

Verses 21, 22. Amon not only forsook the Lord, but took up the worship of idols. It is bad enough to become inactive as to the service one owes to the Master. Mere neglect will condemn in the end. (Heb. 2: 3). But to add the sin of false religion is still more grievous. Amon served the idols his father served. It was no more sin to serve those idols than any others. The point is the thought of his father's responsibility. By setting the example of heathen worship, he left a trail on which his descendants and others were encouraged to travel.

Verses 23, 24. This passage furnishes a concrete case, showing both kinds of bloodshed, guilty and innocent. Amon was an unrighteous man, yet he was the lawful king and the act of slaying him was murder, or the shedding of innocent blood. When the people slew the murderers of Amon it was lawful, for they were not shedding innocent blood. It was an act of lawful execution, and in harmony with Gen. 9: 6.

Verses 25, 26. *Chronicles* again calls for the comments at 1 Ki. 14: 19. The sepulchre where Amon was buried was called *his* because it had been that of his father, and he inherited it.

2 KINGS 22

Verse 1. The reign of Josiah is said to have begun when he was eight years old. This is to be understood in the same light as the reigns of Jehoash (Ch. 12: 2) and Manasseh (Ch. 21: 1, 2). The reign of Josiah was one of the good ones, and would include the years he was guided by the priest.

Verse 2. The kingdom of Judah had a few good kings, and some were better than others. Josiah was one of the best, and emphasis is put on his case by the wording of this verse. He did what was right *in the sight of the Lord* which was the prime motive of his life. Walked *in the way of David*, which means he imitated the ways of an outstanding man of God. *Turned not* is significant, because it is not enough to do the right thing part of the time only. It is desired that a servant of God continue doing the right thing, which will not leave him any time or energy for "side trips" from the strait path of duty and righteousness.

Verse 3. Comparing 2 Chr. 34: 8, we learn the 18th year means that of his reign, and when he was 26 years old. Josiah was acting on his own responsibility, giving instructions to the priest, instead of taking them from him. *Scribe* is from CAPHAR and defined by Strong, "A primitive root; properly to score with a mark as a tally or record, i. e. (by implication) to inscribe, and also to enumerate; intensively to recount, i. e. celebrate." The primary meaning of the word is given in the lexicon's definition. It acquired various shades of meaning at different ages, depending on the particular time, and the class of service employed. In the case at hand it had the meaning of a king's personal secretary. He was sent to the house of God on a mission of inquiry on behalf of the king.

Verse 4. Money was taken in from the people by the priest. Some of it was voluntary as a gift to the treasury (Lk. 21: 1-4), and other amounts came in through the tithing system of the law. Josiah directed that an inventory be taken of the silver.

Verse 5. After the amount of silver had been noted, it was to be put into the hands of the overseers of the work. They were then to give it to the men doing the work being planned. *Breaches* is from BEDEQ and defined, "a gap or leak (in a building or a ship)." Any kind of a structure will need repairs from time to time, the temple of God not excepted. The money in the treasury of the Lord would very properly be used to repair the house of the Lord.

Verse 6. Different classes of workmen are named, which shows a systematic plan of work. Each man to be assigned to the particular task for which he is fitted, is in keeping not only with good human judgment, but with the principle of God's dealings with man.

Verse 7. *No reckoning* means they were not checked. Their record of honesty had been made and the reckoning was not necessary. However, we observe that the money had been in the hands of two classes of men, the priest and the foremen, before it was in those of the workmen. That would be sufficient safeguard against unintentional error. It would be also a protection for each party in case some discrepancy should be suggested. The whole arrangement points to Rom. 12: 17 and 2 Cor. 8: 18-21.

Verse 8. See the comments at Deut. 31: 24-26 regarding the location of this book. Had it been on the inside of the ark, which the sabbatarians claim was a more important place, it is doubtful whether the priest would have found it. Had he not found it, the great reformatory work of Josiah might not have been done. Hence, if any valid argument is to be based on the particular place where this "ceremonial" book was kept, it was more important than the decalogue, for it led to a great reformation. An imaginary difficulty may appear to the reader. The high priest was to enter the most holy place, where the ark and the book were originally placed, on one day only of each year; what business did he have in there at this time? But the text should be read more carefully, which says the book was found *in the house of the Lord.* That would not necessarily be in the most holy place. Many changes had taken place since Moses put this book in the side of the ark. The Philistines had the sacred piece for a while, then it was in various other hands before it was taken by David and housed in a tent pitched specially for it. After his death, and Solomon had built the temple, with its many rooms and other details, the ark was finally put into the most holy place. It would be unreasonable to suppose that the book was kept in that particular spot all that time, especially when the statement of our own verse states only it was found *in the house of the Lord.* Another point to be considered is, they found the book while looking after the money, and we know the treasury was not in the most holy place, for it was approached at various times in the year and by different persons.

Verse 9. The scribe did his duty as secretary, and made the report about the money. For *gathered* the marginal reading has "melted." Lest the reader be confused it will be explained. The original word is NATHAK and Strong defines it, "a primitive root; to flow forth (literally or figuratively); by implication to liquefy." The word hence could mean actually to melt, but it does not necessarily mean that. The idea here is, the money was made to flow freely into the hands of the proper persons.

Verses 10, 11. In modern times it might seem strange that a copy of the law of the Lord would cause so much surprise, or that the finding of it was noted as such an event. But all copies of such documents were made by hand and were very scarce. Among the other items of neglect chargeable against the kings of those years was their failure to observe Deut. 17: 18-20. Had that been done, they would have been spared the surprise that shocked Josiah.

Verse 12. The persons named were the religious and personal "cabinet" of the king. The revelation brought to him by the reading of the book made him fear that the Lord's wrath might be soon poured out on them.

Verse 13. The law of Moses was complete and needed no general interpretation. But all along the line of their experiences as a nation, the Israelites needed the services of prophets and other inspired persons, to give immediate instructions and warnings. (Heb. 1: 1). Josiah knew the law had been disobeyed, and now he wished to learn just what was about to happen and what to do about it.

Verse 14. In about all of God's systems for the use and benefit of humanity, the leaders and authoritative teachers have been men. The exceptions have been inspired women, which would qualify them to speak conclusively regardless of their sex. Huldah was a prophetess and was inspired. That was why the men of Josiah went to her when he told them to *enquire of the Lord.* Her husband had charge of the clothes worn by persons of prominence about the capital city. She dwelt in Jerusalem, in the *college*, which means "second" or subordinate. Being a wife, she did not occupy the first place in the capital city, but since she was a prophetess she occupied a place next. To her the men appealed, who had been sent by Josiah.

Verse 15. *Saith the Lord* proves that Huldah did not speak on her own knowledge or responsibility. What she was about to say would be the word of the Lord.

Verse 16. *Words of the book* means the things threatened in the book against the people if they committed idolatry.

Verse 17. The nation had been guilty of idolatry and the evils connected with it for centuries. God had endured it from time to time, and more than once had allowed his wrath to be turned away by the pleas of the prophets. But his patience was exhausted at last, and now he determined to carry out the extreme penalty that had been threatened, which is the meaning of the words *shall not be quenched.* In connection with these words, which might seem to disagree with other places in the Bible, the reader is requested to read carefully the following comments: Some apparent contradictions may be understood by an acquaintance with all the facts and truths concerned. The nation was told, in very decided terms, that it must go into captivity. Such reformers as Josiah endeavored to correct the corruptions of the nation and made sufficient progress as to receive the commendations of God. Yet he and other reformers were told that nothing could be done now to prevent the captivity, since the nation had become so corrupt as a whole that nothing but captivity could cure it of its leading iniquity which was idolatry. Yet there are always individuals in any community who are not in harmony with the corruptions of the community as a whole and who try to avoid those corruptions. With reference to these individuals there are various exhortations to repentance or to continuing in righteousness as the case might be, with the promise that those who were righteous or who would become so would receive the personal blessing of God, even though they, as members of a community, must share in the national calamity. Such men as Daniel and his three companions; Ezra, Nehemiah and others were among those who were already righteous. Doubtless others heeded the exhortations to repentance and thus brought themselves under the blessing of God. Because of this they were saved the humiliation of serving idols in the land of their captors, while the nation as a whole was required to worship these idols, so that the apparent contradiction between the definite threat of captivity and the exhortation to repentance is to be understood by considering the difference between the nation as a whole, and certain individuals therein. The above comments should be considered in connection with the following passages: 2 Ki. 22: 17; 23; 26, 27; 2 Chr. 34: 25; Isa. 1: 6, 18; 55: 6, 7; Jer. 3: 1, 7: 16, 27; 8: 20; 11: 14; 13: 23; 14: 11, 12; 17: 1, 24-27; 18: 8; 22: 1-6; 35: 15, and others of similar character. Apply these comments in all places where an apparent discrepancy occurs as to divine favor to some and disfavor to others.

Verses 18-20. Josiah furnishes a concrete instance of the comments on the preceding verse, even as he is mentioned in those remarks. It is probable that his earnest exhortations and practical reforms saved many individuals from personal loss of divine favor. If that was done, and they were living when the captivity came, they were protected from the corruption of idolatry in the land of Babylon. For Josiah to end his days in *peace* did not mean that he would not be slain in battle (for he was), but that he would be at peace with his God, in spite of the error in judgment.

2 KINGS 23

Verses 1, 2. The discovery of the book, and the revelation of conditions, caused a complete change in Josiah's work. The plans for repairing the material building of the Lord were dropped, and full attention was turned toward repairing the spiritual house. The king called for a gathering of all the people of Judah, with special mention of the elders (older and experienced, but unofficial men), and the priests and prophets. The priests were the immediate custodians of the worship of the sanctuary, the prophets were the men inspired for special interpretation of the law in emergencies. (Heb. 1: 1). Josiah read to this great assemblage the words in the book just found, that had caused such consternation and alarm.

Verse 3. *Made a covenant* does not mean that Josiah enacted a new law to take the place of the law of Moses. It was more in the nature of a personal promise or assurance that he would do what he could to enforce that law. The promise was made in the hearing of the people, and *all the people stood to the covenant,* which means they agreed to it, which made it their obligation also.

Verse 4. Priests of the *second order* means the common priests. All buildings of importance have doorkeepers to guard against the entrance of improper persons. Very logically, then, they would be included in this order of Josiah. *Vessels* means any apparatus, such as a utensil or implement, hence it here refers to anything that was used in connection with the worship of Baal. See comments at 2 Ki. 17: 16 on *grove.* Utensils made to use in connection with those images were included in this destruction. *Ashes* is from APHAR and Strong defines it, "dust, (as powdered or gray); hence clay, earth, mud." When metal is burned it corrodes and can turn to dust, here called ashes. We may recall what Moses did to the golden calf recorded in Ex. 32: 20. It was ironically proper for Josiah to carry this dust to Bethel, for that was one of the places where the national practice of idolatry was first set up. (1 Ki. 12: 29).

Verse 5. *Put down* means he stopped the practices of the idolatrous priests. The mere burning of incense in *high places* might not have been so bad in itself (1 Ki. 3: 2), but when it was done by the idolatrous priests it was done for the wrong purpose. Baal was an imaginary intelligent god, the sun and other heavenly bodies were inanimate deities. The people of Judah had turned to the worship of all those false gods, and Josiah sought to overthrow the corruption.

Verse 6. The *grove* was an object made of metal, as explained at Ch. 17: 16. By burning it the corrosion would make it possible to grind it to powder. The dust was put on the graves, and the companion passage in 2 Chr. 34: 4 shows it was the graves of the idolaters. That was a sort of contempt for fake gods, showing them to be as dead as the persons who had worshiped them.

Verse 7. *Sodomites* is explained at 1 Ki. 14: 24. They were people who practiced the vile sin as a religious ceremony. *Hangings* means tents the women fabricated to shelter the *grove*, or idolatrous image.

Verse 8. *Defiled the high places* denotes that he desecrated them so they could not be used again. Joshua was a governor of a city in Judah, and he gave his name to a gate of Jerusalem, just as noted people will give something to a particular building and have a room named for them. At one side of this gate there were provisions made for idolatrous worship, and Josiah demolished them.

Verse 9. This verse shows the charactertistics of many professed servants of God. They will spend most of their time in the things that interest them personally, but neglect the service to their Lord. Then if trouble comes, they want to claim the benefits of the church. These idolatrous priests would not go to the lawful altar in Jerusalem, yet they were impudent enough to partake of their share of the bread that had been contributed by others to the service.

Verse 10. There was a noted valley near Jerusalem called after the children of one Hinnom. In that valley was a place called Topheth, and at that spot the most horrifying acts were committed in the name of religion. Parents took their infants there and offered them in burnt sacrifices to Molech, one of the imaginary gods. Josiah desecrated this place so that it could not be used thereafter for that purpose.

Verse 11. In those days of prevailing idolatry, various places and persons were singled out for some object of the wicked cult. In the suburbs, which was a borough of Jerusalem, a chamberlain or eunuch had a room for his personal occupancy. In this place the different kings of Judah had made artificial horses and placed them there in honor of the sun as a god. The mention of chariots in direct connection with the horses, which were burnt, indicates the horses were of metal.

Verse 12. *Upper chamber* is from one word, meaning some elevated room of some kind and belonging to Ahaz, one of the idolatrous kings. Being devoted to idolatry himself, he permitted the others to build altars for idol worship on the roof of this chamber. The *two courts* were the *inner court* (1 Ki. 6: 36) and the *great court* (1 Ki. 7: 12) that Solomon made. King Manasseh had made altars in these courts for the service of idols; Josiah burnt them and cast their dust into the brook. That manifested not only a contempt for the false worship, but consigned the material to a place from which it could not be recovered.

Verse 13. It should not be forgotten that the *high places* were comparatively indifferent as to being wrong (1 Ki. 3: 2), for they occasionally were used for service to God. Although not in strict regulation, the Lord gave them some tolerance when used for Him. But they came to be used most generally for idolatrous worship and had to be condemned. *Mount of corruption* was the Mount of Olives, and 1 Ki. 11: 7 tells us the corruption was placed there by Solomon. Various tribes of heathen had their own gods. Many of them were the imaginary or invisible type, and their particular deities had places erected for their worship. Since such practices were an abomination to God, they were called the *abomination of the Zidonians*, etc.

Josiah *defiled* or desecrated all these places and rendered them unfit for idol worship.

Verse 14. *Image* and *groves* were about the same in principle. The first were statues of the invisible gods, the second were metallic likenesses of their sacred trees. By filling their places with the bones of men, two objectives were attained. It indicated a condition of death, also it served as a standoff in view of the feeling men had toward human bones.

Verse 15. *High places* is mentioned three times in this verse, and it is said that Josiah burned them and crushed them to powder. That indicates they were made of metal, whereas we often think of them as being places of eminence, either by natural elevation or architectural work. The idea is that on these high places there were altars erected for idolatrous worship, and the altars were burned, likewise the *grove* which was the metal image of their sacred tree.

Verses 16-18. Before reading this passage, the student should read 1 Ki. 13: 31, 32. It is the place where these things were first referred to, in part. The respect that men had for human bones, and especially those of a prophet, was great, almost to the extent of superstition. The old lying prophet of Bethel knew this, and prepared to have his bones respected when the time predicted came, by ordering his body to be buried in the same sepulchre with that of the disobedient prophet. By that time the bones would be sufficiently decayed that it would not be realized there was more than one person's remains in the tomb. The inspired writer knew that the bones of both prophets were there and preserved together. Josiah knew only from the title, and the information the men of the city gave him, that there were any certain bones there at all. The motive for burning the bones in these sepulchres was because they were those of idol worshipers. By desecration of their bones, the great disapproval of Josiah was shown.

Verse 19. Every form of religion in every age had temples erected for its headquarters. In such buildings the devotees of the *high places* would assemble at times for some of their heathen practices. These were the houses Josiah destroyed.

Verse 20. Josiah found the idolatrous priests engaged in their services at the altars and slew them. He further showed his abhorrence for the system by burning the bones of those who had been dead for some time.

Verse 21. Among the things which had been dropped from their observance was this great national feast. The Israelites had been so much interested in the worship of false gods, they had forgotten that of the true; such a state of affairs might be expected. It is the principle Jesus taught in Matt. 6: 24. If the illogical thing should be imagined, that idolatry is as good as the true worship, still no man can do justice to both. Either would take up all of his time and energy. That is why their idolatry caused the Israelites to neglect the passover; also the seventh year rest for the land, and many other ordinances.

Verses 22, 23. The specific items of the passover were set down by the law, so that no radical difference should have been possible between any of the observations. The comparison is not to the items observed, but to the interest manifested. In 2 Chr. 35: 18 the same instance is recorded, and it mentions the thought of who and how many of the nation attended. A similar expression is often used today when we speak of some particular meeting that had been largely attended, and where unusual interest was manifested. It might be heard said at such a time that "we had a great meeting today."

Verse 24. *Familiar spirits* and *wizards* were persons who used magic to take the attention of the people from the worship of the true God. Josiah put all of such evil workers away. He destroyed also the visible objects of false worship such as those made in honor of the imaginary gods, and the *images* supposed to be like celestial beings.

Verse 25. There had been some very good kings before Josiah who opposed the corruptions existing among these people, but none of them carried their reforms as far as he. There was nothing that was left undone through inattention, that was possible for him to do to purify the situation of the nation.

Verses 26, 27. The thing that was impossible for Josiah to accomplish was to prevent the captivity. The case had gone too far to be altered. This zealous king did what he could to remove the corruptions, and doubtless succeeded in bringing many individuals to repentance. In spite of all this, however, the nation had to go. The reader should again read the long comments at Ch. 22: 17.

Verse 28. Once more a reference is made to notes on *Chronicles* at 1 Ki. 14: 19.

Verse 29. This is the sad part of Josiah's record. It is given in more detail in 2 Chr. 35: 20-23. The king of Egypt was not intending to attack Josiah, but had been instructed by the Lord to go against the Assyrians. We have previously known that God sometimes used one heathen nation to punish another. That was being done in this case, and Josiah seemed to doubt the words of the Egyptian king. His zeal took him too far and he lost his life.

Verse 30. Josiah was treated with great honor and taken back to his capital city for burial. The regular succession to the throne should have been taken by Eliakim, since he was the elder brother. For a reason not stated *the people* put the younger son on the throne. But he did not keep it long as we shall see.

Verses 31, 32. Jehoahaz should be regarded as a usurper since he had an elder brother who had not been disqualified. The reign was only 3 months long and he was taken from the throne.

Verse 33. Pharaoh-nechoh was the name of an Egyptian king. The line of rulers in that country for many centuries was called Pharaoh. Each had his personal name and this one was Nechoh. He it was who slew Josiah when he interfered with the expedition against the Assyrians. Since Jehoahaz obtained the throne in an unlawful manner, it was not surprising that the Lord accepted this act of the Pharaoh in dethroning him and placing on the throne the lawful ruler. At the same time Pharaoh put a fine of 100 talents of silver and a talent of gold on the land.

Verse 34. Eliakim was the elder brother of Jehoahaz, and the rightful ruler. He was put into his proper place but had his name changed to Jehoiakim. We have no information as to why the change was made. After Jehoahaz was dethroned he was taken into custody at Riblah. He was afterward taken to Egypt where he died. He had received the additional name of Shallum in the meantime. This information, and the prediction of his death in the land of his exile, may be seen in Jer. 22: 10-12.

Verse 35. Jehoiakim paid the fine mentioned in V. 33 to Pharaoh, and he obtained the money by taxing the people. *Exacted* is from NAGAS and Strong defines it, "a primitive root; to drive (an animal, a workman, a doctor, an army); by implication to tax, harass, tyrannize." *Taxation* is from EREK and defined, "a pile, equipment, estimate."—Strong. Jehoiakim forced the people to give to the utmost that was possible, although he had to use severe measures to accomplish it.

Verses 36, 37. This passage is a general statement of the length and character of Jehoiakim's reign. The most noted event of his reign was the rebellion against the king of Babylon, which brought on the great 70-year captivity of the Jews. That will begin in the next chapter.

2 KINGS 24

Verse 1. *His days* means the days of Jehoiakim, who had been placed on the throne of Judah by Pharaoh-nechoh of Egypt. After having done that, Pharaoh disappeared from the scene, because the king of Babylon had taken most of the territory, and the Egyptian king was shut up in his own country. (V. 7). About the time Jehoiakim began to reign, Nebuchadnezzar, king of Babylon came up and *Jehoiakim became his servant three years.* That means that the king of Judah acknowledged the king of Babylon as his superior and agreed to a national alliance. Jehoiakim continued in that state of dependency to Babylon for three years, *then . . . rebelled.* That set the stage for the beginning of the noted Babylonian captivity of 70 years; it was in the year 606 B. C. While this great captivity began then and continued till 536 B. C., it was carried out in three stages, recognized in the scriptures and in secular history as the 1st, 2nd, and 3rd captivities. Unless these divisions of the historical epoch are recognized, some statements in other parts of the Bible will be confusing. For instance, in Ezk. 1: 2 we read the words, *Jehoiachin's captivity.* In Ch. 40: 1 of the same book we have the words, *our captivity.* We know there was only one captivity as a whole, so the various references to some specific captivity must be understood in the light of these divisions. The dates of the 2nd and 3rd will be stated at the proper places in this and the following chapter. Ch. 23: 36 states Jehoiakim reigned 11 years. Since the captivity started at the end of his 3rd year, he continued to reign for 8 years. But while he occupied the throne of Judah in Jerusalem, he was subject to the Babylonian king through those years, and the great captivity is to be dated, therefore, from his 4th year.

Verse 2. Jehoiakim was permitted to sit on his throne in Jerusalem, but the several tribes of heathen people mentioned were suffered by the Lord to make inroads against the country, which began to weaken the kingdom.

Verse 3. Most of the kings of Judah were evil men, but Manasseh was an outstanding one for wickedness, which is the reason he is mentioned in connection with the national distress. *At the commandment of the Lord.* It might be somewhat confusing to think of these idolaters doing anything in order to obey the commandments of the Lord. While God did sometimes give direct instructions to the heathen to perform certain services (Ezra 1: 2), there is nothing to indicate these people were acting with the motive or knowledge that they were obeying the Lord. The word *commandment* is from PEH, and a part of the definition is "according to." The thought of the passage is, the action of the people mentioned was according to the will of the Lord. Men and even beasts can fulfill the will of the Lord without knowing it. (Isa. 43: 20).

Verse 4. Manasseh committed many sins not specified, but the shedding of innocent blood was one of the most horrible sins. So while the captivity did not come until the days of Jehoiakim, the wickedness of one of his predecessors was known to him, and he did not profit by it, therefore was the one on whom the blow came.

Verses 5, 6. *Chronicles* is explained by my comments at 1 Ki. 14: 19. *Slept with his fathers* is explained at 1 Ki. 2: 10.

Verse 7. The facts of this verse were commented upon at V. 1.

Verses 8, 9. The reign of Jehoiachin was only three months in duration. It was so short and so little was accomplished that it is ignored in the statements that pertained to dates of the captivities. Any date based on "Jehoiachin's captivity" would coincide with any that was reckoned from Jehoiakim's death. See my notes on *mother's name* at 1 Ki. 14: 21.

Verse 10. What is to be known as the 2nd captivity is recorded in verses 10-16, and readers who are marking their Bibles should make the notation accordingly. But the several verses will be considered somewhat separately. The verse of this paragraph begins the 2nd of the three captivities explained at V. 1, and the date is 598 B. C. Nebuchadnezzar was the king of Babylon, and it was he who had subjugated Jehoiakim for 8 years. Now that Jehoiachin, the son of Jehoiakim, was on the throne and was a very weak ruler, the king of Babylon decided to increase the servitude of the kingdom of Judah. He came with his servants to Jerusalem for the purpose of subduing it still more than it had been in the days of Jehoiakim.

Verse 11. Kings and other great men are said to have done things when it may mean only that their servants did them. But according to secular history and other evidences, Nebuchadnezzar was present in person at the siege of Jerusalem, although he operated by the aid of his servants.

Verse 12. This verse means that Jehoiachin surrendered to Nebuchadnezzar without a struggle, and that he delivered into his hand his chief men. *Eighth year of his reign* means the 8th year of the reign of the king of Babylon. *Officers* is correctly rendered "eunuchs" in the margin of the Bible, for it is so defined in the lexicon. Eunuchs were employed much by kings and other men of prominence. They served as valets, also in other specific positions about the residence.

Verse 13. These precious articles that Nebuchadnezzar took are the ones mentioned in Dan. 1: 2; 5: 2, 3. *Vessels* is not confined to containers as we think of the word, but includes any article used in the service of a place. It takes in the ornaments of the holy building as well as the instruments for serving food and drink. That explains how the king could *cut in pieces* the vessels, yet Belshazzar could use them for his wine the night of the great feast. This circumstance fulfilled the prediction Isaiah made to Hezekiah in Ch. 20: 17.

Verse 14. *All Jerusalem* means the inhabitants of the city in general. The inspired writer then specifies some of the classes of persons taken. A *craftsman* is a fabricator and a *smith* is a "fastener." In other words, the craftsman fabricates things and a smith puts them together. *Valour* means "strength" of any kind. As used in this place it means the men with great force and influence. The *poorest sort* would not mean only those of limited means, but included all classes with little or no important talents, and thus of limited usefulness.

Verses 15, 16. There is not much new information in this passage except what pertains to Jehoiachin in person. He and his attendants and his mother were taken to Babylon. He was kept in prison in Babylon for 37 years, then released and treated with royal courtesy by the king of Babylon then reigning. (Jer. 52: 31-34).

Verse 17. Jehoiachin had sons (1 Chr. 3: 17), but Nebuchadnezzar did not permit any one of them to occupy his father's throne in Jerusalem. Instead, he took one of his uncles, Mattaniah, and put him on the throne. At the same time he changed his name to Zedekiah, for no reason that is stated to us, and he will be known from now on by that name. He will be the last king that the Jews as a political nation will ever have. Having reached the last king of the Israelite nation, I will suggest a chart the reader can make which will be helpful in the study of the history. We have already had our attention called to the zigzag way the account has been given since the tribes divided into what were called the kingdoms of Judah and Israel. Take the kings of Judah for a basis of the chart, starting at 975 B. C. Draw the chart on a schedule that will allot the proper space for each reign, according to the years stated in the books of Kings. Then under the line thus made for this kingdom, place the names of the kings of Israel in their proper position under the line of the kings of Judah. This will form a chart for reference while reading the history of the divided kingdom, and may be considered in connection with the comments I made at 1 Ki. 12: 17.

Verses 18, 19. It is stated that Zedekiah reigned in Jerusalem, and yet we know that the Babylonian captivity was going on at the same time. We must understand the last three kings to sit on the throne in Jerusalem were doing so as tributaries to Babylon, and were regarded as being subject to that country, just as surely as were the citizens who had been taken into it. Their permission to occupy the throne was a kind of courtesy, and was to be enjoyed on condition of loyalty to Babylon. They were so restless and wavering, however, that the king of Babylon finally lost patience with them and completely demolished the government, taking entire charge of the country. This part of the history will be given in the next chapter.

Verse 20. This verse means that God's anger was held back until he finally turned his people over completely to Babylon. The captivity of the nation as a whole had been going on since the 3rd year of Jehoiakim. But Zedekiah could have prolonged the time when he personally must go, had he done right in the sight of the Lord, and respected the authority of the king of Babylon. His rebellion displeased God, and he suffered the king of Babylon to lay siege and finally complete the whole captivity, which will be learned in the next chapter.

2 KINGS 25

Verse 1. *Ninth year of his reign* means the reign of Zedekiah. Nebuchadnezzar became tired of the rebellious conduct of Zedekiah and determined to complete the subjugation of Judah by taking its king off his throne, and destroying the city. To do this he saw the need for an effective siege, and prepared to attack the walls. As a means to that end he built forts around it, which is defined in the lexicon, "a battering-tower." — Strong. That consisted in a series of the towers, practically comprising a wall all round about, from which the besiegers could apply their battering rams against the wall of the city to overthrow it.

Verse 2. The siege lasted 2 years, coming to a close the 11th year of Zedekiah, which will prove to be his last.

Verse 3. *Fourth* is not in the original in this passage, but is at Jer. 39: 2, where the same event is recorded. The famine *prevailed* on the above date, which means it had grown so bad that it reached a climax. The result was that the people in the city ceased to resist or try to hold the city against the besiegers.

Verse 4. See the author's comments on the *garden* wall as a means of escape at Ch. 9: 27. The inhabitants having relaxed their vigilance, the wall was attacked with greater fury and a breach was made through it. The soldiers escaped through the breach, the king with them, and they chose the night for their flight; this had been predicted in Ezk. 12: 12. *Chaldees* or Chaldeans is another name for the Babylonians at the time of our present study. In ancient periods there was a distinct group that had the name Chaldees, and the term was not applied to any others. They finally settled in the city of Babylon and grew in power until they dominated, not only the city but most of the surrounding country of Babylonia. For this reason the name Chaldeans and Babylonians came to be used commonly for the same people.

Verse 5. King Zedekiah made the mistake that multitudes of others have made. It had been predicted that the city would be taken and that by the will of God. Moreover, it was plainly taught that resistance to the enemy would be in vain. Had Zedekiah heeded all these warnings and surrendered to the king of Babylon he would have fared better. Trying to run from him was the same as running from God, since the actions of the Babylonians was the carrying out of the plans ordained of God.

Verses 6, 7. While Nebuchadnezzar doubtless spent some time near Jerusalem in person, most of it was at Riblah, a temporary headquarters used by him and other monarchs of the East. Smith's Bible Dictionary has this to say of the place: "Riblah in the land of Hamath, a place on the great road between Palestine and Babylonia, at which the kings of Babylonia were accustomed to remain while directing the operations of their armies in Palestine and Phoenicia. Here Nebuchadnezzar waited while the sieges of Jerusalem and Tyre were being conducted by his lieutenants." This explains why Zedekiah was taken to Riblah after his capture. He was brought before Nebuchadnezzar, whose throne of judgment during the war operations was at Riblah, and there tried and condemned, which is the meaning of the words *gave judgment upon him.* His sons were then slain in his sight, after which his eyes were put out, and he was bound and taken, blinded, to Babylon where he died. This simple and consistent narrative explains what some enemies of the Bible claim to be contradictions, because not all of the facts are stated in each place. When studying this subject, the reader should always read the following passages. Jer. 32: 4; 34: 3; Ezk. 12: 13.

Verse 8. About a month after the events of the foregoing paragraph, Nebuchadnezzar sent his chief military leader, Nebuzaradan, from Riblah to complete the overthrow of Jerusalem and bring the Jewish nation completely under his power.

Verse 9, 10. Most of this chapter has to do with the 3rd captivity, otherwise known as the 3rd division of the great captivity. Since it is well to have clearly defined limits for certain important dates, those marking their Bibles should title this paragraph, the 3rd captivity, B. C. 587. As a brief résumé, I will state some of the outstanding things that took place at each of the three captivities. At the 1st, Jehoiakim was weakened by having several tribes of heathen attack his country. At the 2nd, the best of the citizens were taken to Babylon, including the prophet Ezekiel. At the 3rd, the buildings were demolished and the walls of the city broken down. This was when "the city was smitten" in the words of Ezk. 40: 1. The last king of Judah having been taken to Babylon, and now the city being completely destroyed, the great Babylonian Captivity was complete, although its beginning should be dated at 606 B. C., when Jehoiakim was put under forced tribute by Nebuchadnezzar.

Verse 11. When an enemy attacks a community, there are often some who will betray their people and go over to the invaders. That happened in Jerusalem when the king of Babylon came against it. But it did not do them any good, for they were taken out of their native land to the land of their captor. At the same time, about all of the citizens that had been left in the city were taken off to the foreign land.

Verse 12. These *poor* of the land is explained at Ch. 24: 14.

Verses 13, 14. In Ch. 24: 13, mention is made of the more valuable vessels and ornaments that the king of Babylon took away. The things named in this paragraph were those of brass. They were very necessary to the temple service, but not as desirable from a commercial standpoint. In the 2nd captivity the king of Babylon did not bother with these materials, but since he was making a "clean sweep" of things in the final attack, he took possession of about all that could be turned to his account.

Verse 15. In the general ransacking of the place, Nebuchadnezzar's men found that some gold and silver had been left from the previous raid, and all of it was taken merely as precious metal, not because of the form in which it was found. That is what is meant by the words, *such things as were gold, in gold,* etc.

Verse 16. The *two pillars* are mentioned in 1 Ki. 7: 15, also in V. 13 in this chapter. But the subject is again brought up to tell us something of the great amount of "loot" the king of Babylon obtained. The *sea* was a great tank containing water for the various services about the temple. *Without weight* does not mean they were light, but they were so large and many and heavy that they had never been weighed. (1 Ki. 7: 47).

Verse 17. A chapiter was a sort of ornamental cap or head piece on the pillars. *Wreathen work and pomegranates* refers to the ornamental formations in the metal.

Verse 18. *Chief priest* means the high priest, and *second priest* means the common priest who was acting at the time. All of the lineal descendants of Aaron were eligible for the priesthood, but their services were not always needed. Therefore, when a specified man is mentioned as being a priest, it means he was the one in active service.

Verse 19. When a revolution takes place in a government, men of prominence are often destroyed as a protective measure against possible future revolt. If such men were influential in the former government, they might some day exert enough control over the emotions of the people to rebel against the new government. So we read that Nebuchadnezzar's leading military man took charge of a great number of such persons who had been in the service of Zedekiah.

Verse 20. Nebuchadnezzar was still at Riblah, therefore these "key" prisoners were taken to him there for judgment.

Verse 21. *Smote . . . slew.* The first word means merely to strike, but not necessarily hard enough to kill. The second is added to tell us the result of the stroke. This verse is the concluding statement that the captivity had become a reality in full.

Verse 22. There could have been various reasons why Nebuchadnezzar wished to leave a small group of people in the land. We learned in V. 12 one of them was that they might care for certain crops. But since the country had been taken over by a foreign power, the people left needed some supervision, and for that service Nebuchadnezzar appointed Gedaliah with headquarters at Mizpah. He also left some of his own Chaldeans as a guard, and the whole setup was to care for the land subject to the king of Babylon. This arrangement pleased the Jews who were scattered in various places in fear, and they came out from their hiding to Mizpah to enjoy the privileges permitted them under Gedaliah.

Verses 23-25. Jealousy is a terrible sentiment, and will lead men to commit great crimes. It appears here that the people who came to Mizpah were favorable to Gedaliah and that they appreciated his suggestions. But we have additional information in Jer. 4: 7-16; 41: 1-3. Gedaliah was warned of the treachery of Ishmael by Johanan but would not believe the accusation. He and several others were murdered, including the Chaldeans whom the king of Babylon had left to guard the place.

Verse 26. This verse is very brief, and omits many details that would shed information on the reason they fled to Egypt for fear of the Chaldees. It appears that Johanan became panicky after the affair of Ishmael, fearing even for the lives of all the rest, lest the sympathizers of Bablyon attack them. He advised their flight to Egypt in spite of the instructions of Jeremiah the prophet, and even took some of the people by force (including Jeremiah) and fled to Egypt. The student is urged to read Jer. 42 and 43 to complete the information on this tragic episode.

Verses 27-30. This paragraph passes over about 26 years to pick up a few incidents concerning Jehoiachin. He had been taken from his throne in Jerusalem after reigning only 3 months, and taken to Babylon. After 37 years in prison he was released by the king then on the throne in Babylon, and treated with royal attention. *Set his throne* does not mean that Jehoiachin was permitted to act as a king. It means that he was treated with more courtesy and distinction than any of the other kings in captivity. In Jer. 22: 26 it was predicted that Jehoiachin (there called Coniah) would die in Babylon; our present paragraph fulfills that prediction. If he was treated in Babylon in the manner described *all the days of his life*, he necessarily died there.

1 CHRONICLES 1

General remarks: A few comments were made on the subject of *Chronicles* at 1 Ki. 14: 19. Having come to this part of the Bible, I believe it will be helpful to quote from two authentic secular sources some further information before entering upon the chapter-and-verse study of the books just before us. The first will be from the Schaff-Herzog Encyclopaedia, Vol. 1, P. 468. "Chronicles, The First and Second Books of. The name, since Jerome, for the Hebrew 'Book of the Events of the days,' called in the Septuagint PARALEIPOMENA ("things omitted"). Originally our present First and Second Chronicles, Ezra and Nehemiah, formed one book. The proof of this is the similarity of style, language, point of view, and the identity of the last two verses, of Second Chronicles XXXVI. 22, 23) with the first two of Ezra. These books, therefore, were once one book, a history of the Israelites from the beginning; although the first part is exclusively genealogical tables to the post-exilian period. [Period after the exile or captivity]. Our present division of this book into four parts is very ancient, originating with the Seventy. [Translators of the Septuagint Version]. Chronicles contains a reliable history, being drawn from the official records of the Israelites, which explains the numerous instances in which it coincides even verbally with *Kings*, and where it differs in names, etc., and the discrepancy can be explained by textual corruptions, either in Chronicles, Kings, or their common source. But the point of view is priestly, and therefore the author dwells at greater length upon those features of the history which are ecclesiastical. Accordingly we find his narrative very full about David's religious reforms and arrangements, Solomon's erection of the temple, its consecration, and his care for religion (he passes over his defection). In regard to the other kings he emphasizes those like Asa, Jehoshaphat, Joash, Hezekiah, and Josiah, who were zealous for the Jewish religion."

The next is from Smith's Dictionary; article, *Chronicles*. "Chronicles, First and Second Books of, the name originally given to the record made by the appointed historiographers in the kingdoms of Israel and Judah. In the LXX [the Septuagint version] these books are called PARALIPOMENA (i. e. things omitted), which is understood as meaning that they are supplementary to the books of Kings. The constant tradition of the Jews is that these books were for the most part compiled by Ezra. One of the greatest difficulties connected with the captivity and return must have been the maintenance of that genealogical distribution of the lands which yet was a vital point of the Jewish economy. To supply this want and that each tribe might secure the inheritance of its fathers on its return was one object of the author of these books."

There are some special advantages in having these books of Chronicles; one is similar to that of having more than one record of the Gospel in the New Testament. Frequently a subject that is treated in one of the books will be given additional information in another. So with the books of Chronicles in the Old Testament. Subjects that appear in the books of Samuels and Kings will have more light shed on them in one of these books. The prevalence of so many proper names may seem unnecessary to us on first thought. In the first place, we should bear in mind that the Lord has a good purpose for everything he does, whether we can see the reason or not. But in this case we can see at least one reason for the circumstance. As stated in the quotation last made above, after the return from the captivity, every family was eager to show the proper claim to the inheritance coming from the ancestors. To do this it was necessary to prove the relationship, and that called for the registration records. Hence we have the necessary though tedious long list of names. Let us place ourselves in the place of these Jews, with a personal interest in the religious and temporal rights inherited from our forefathers. If we will do so, I believe we will study this book with interest. Due to the very nature of the subject matter, many of the verses will be grouped in a paragraph and comments made on the group as a whole. Where the names are of historical interest to us, special attention will be called to them; either for the purpose of citing the reader to other places in the Bible where they occur, or in order to explain some other spelling of the name for identification.

Verses 1-4. The 10 names represent the "blood line" through that many generations. After Cain killed Abel he was rejected although the older son of Adam. Then Seth (here called Sheth) was born and took his place in the line, and became the ancestor of the "sons of God" mentioned in Gen. 6: 2. This is indicated by the marginal reading, "call themselves by the name of the Lord" at Gen. 4: 26. See my comments at that place, also at Gen. 6: 2. By the blood line is meant the lineal descendants from Adam to Christ, passing through many generations, and often including men of prominence from various standpoints. The name or person of Christ was not made known to mankind until the time of Abraham, (Gal. 3: 16), but God had it in mind all down through the ages, and guarded it to help keep it a pure strain. We shall observe this line running through patriarch, prophets, kings and preachers. Sometimes the members of the line will be good men and at other times wicked men. Occasionally a woman was allowed to get into the line from the outside, after the strain had been pretty well established, but the masculine side of the line was kept strictly with the lineal descendants of Adam. The general rule was for it to pass through the oldest son, but there are some exceptions, although we will not be able always to discover the basis for the change. This line of descendants has commonly been called the "blood line" from the fact that Christ was to have human blood in his body, received from the first man, and through a carefully guarded line of generations. In most cases the particular group of these men is determined by the mention of some man who was of special importance besides being in the line. The group of this paragraph stops with Noah, made famous by the flood. His three sons are named, and later we shall see one of them placed in the blood line as the story goes on.

Verses 5-7. Much of this chapter corresponds with the 10th chapter of Genesis. After running the blood line to Noah, the author gives us information on the three sons of that great man, naming their respective descendants for a few generations. It will be interesting to identify some of the later groups of people with these members of Noah's family tree. This paragraph deals with the descendants of Japheth. Although mentioned last, he was the oldest son of Noah. (Gen. 10: 21). He was the ancestor of the great mass of the earth's population who came to be referred to as the Gentiles. The Gaulic Celts came from Gomer; the Slavs from Magog; the Medes from Madai; the Greeks from Javan; the Germans from Tiras. This information is from Origin of Nations, by George Rawlinson.

Verses 8-16. The inferior nations came from Ham, and some of the most noted ones will be identified in this paragraph. Cush originated the Ethiopians, the Canaanites and Philistines. *Nimrod began to be mighty.* A more specific reference to his power is given in Gen. 10: 10 where he is connected with the kingdom of Babylon. The several "ites" of the Bible history are shown to have originated with Canaan, son of Ham.

Verses 17-23. Shem was in the blood line, and from him came the great Israelite nation. There were other noted people who came from him. This is explained by the fact that the line always continued through only one of his sons, until the time of David, when two sons were admitted into it, carrying the blood stream down to the time of Christ and terminating on the two sides of his house namely, his mother and foster father. If one of the fathers of the line had more than one son, he might become the founder of a somewhat noted people, and they would be considered as indirectly related to the regular line. Thus we have the Assyrians springing from Asshur, one of the sons of Shem. Other branches of Shem's family are mentioned in this paragraph, including a number who were directly in the line. However, they will be named distinctly from those on the outside in another paragraph.

Verses 24-27. This is another group of 10 in the direct blood line. It terminates with Abram (called also Abraham) for the reason that he was another outstanding man in the Biblical history. With this paragraph we have the blood line brought down to the 20th generation from Adam.

Verses 28-31. Isaac was 14 years younger than Ishmael, but is named first because he was the son chosen to be in the line. The members of Ishmael's family will be given more notice sometime later, but are only casually named in this paragraph.

Verses 32, 33. The woman who is here called Abraham's concubine is called his wife in Gen. 25: 1. That is because there was no moral difference between the two words in ancient times. The difference was in regard to property rights. That is why Gen. 25: 5, 6 states that Abraham gave *all that he had to Isaac,* and gave only *gifts* to the sons of the concubine. Abraham married Keturah after the death of Sarah. There were 6 sons born of the last marriage, and the name to note is Midian, because he was the founder of the famous Midianite nation.

Verse 34. In a verse above, two of Abraham's sons are named. Now the author is concerned about the one who is in the direct blood line, but who also had his family tree divided into two branches, Esau and Israel or Jacob.

Verses 35, 36. The readers marking their Bibles should underscore *Esau, Eliphaz* and *Amalek*. That will assist the eye in selecting the names of special importance. The Amalekites were a famous people, and this passage shows at a glance the origin of, and hence the relation to, the regular blood line.

Verses 37-42. This paragraph is a list of the members of Esau's family down to the 2nd or 3rd generation. There is nothing in their history of special interest to us.

Verse 43. There were two noted groups of people that came from Esau. The Amalekites are named in V. 36, and now we have *Edom* introduced, which gave the name of Edomites to another group. *Edom* was another name for Esau, and was given to him from the fact of his being red, also because of his fondness for red pottage. (Gen. 25: 25, 30). But the name *Edomites*, while being related to the meaning of the word, came to refer specifically to that portion of Esau's descendants who were located near Mount Seir. The references to Seir or Edom, therefore, have in mind this portion of Esau's descendants, and these people were by far the most important of his family tree. Some favor was shown to the Edomites in that they had kings before Israel. We recall that Jacob had cheated his brother about the birthright and blessing, but Esau was never entirely forgotten by the Lord.

Verses 44-50. The main point of interest to us in these verses is the fact that Edom had quite a succession of kings, not just one who perhaps sprang up "over night" and soon died out.

Verses 51-54. The Edomites had not only a line of kings, but a group of dukes, which means leaders or chieftains.

1 CHRONICLES 2

Verses 1, 2. Israel was another name for Jacob, which he received from the angel after his wrestling with him. (Gen. 32: 28). These 12 sons of Israel were born in Mesopotamia, except Benjamin who was born near Bethel. (Gen. 35: 16-20). The family history of Esau is given in the preceding chapter. There is nothing said as to why it is given before Israel or Jacob. We do know, however, that Esau was the older of the brothers and that would make it regular to enumerate his family first.

Verse 3. A number of chapters will be devoted to the families of the sons of Jacob. They will not be considered in the order of their birth. The first one named is Judah, although he was fourth in age. But he was first in point of importance, because he was the one through whom the blood line passed, making him a lineal ancestor of Christ. In Gen. 38: 3-5 is the account of these sons, showing the circumstances under which they were born. A few verses onward is the record of the death of Er. Neither there nor here are we told what particular thing it was of which he was guilty. We are told merely that he was evil in the sight of the Lord, which brought death to him.

Verse 4. The brevity of this book has a significant example in this verse. The mention of Judah's begetting a son by his daughter-in-law, *Tamar*, would arouse our curiosity at least, and some who are critical against the Bible might make more of it than the facts would justify. The Lord is not giving us this short statement of the case from the principle of evasion. The whole 38th chapter of Genesis is given to the case, and the reader is urged to consult it with care.

Verses 5, 6. Since *Pharez* and *Hezron*, son and grandson of Tamar, are in the blood line, their names are set down in the record.

Verses 7, 8. Not all of the sons of Judah are named above, neither does this verse tell us that Carmi was one of them. But Ch. 4: 1 says he was, so in the present verse we should read the statements with him in mind. The special item of interest to us is the relation of *Carmi* to *Achor*, another form of Achan, famous for his sin at Jericho.

Verse 9. We are particularly interested in the names of the men who are in the blood line. *Hezron* had three sons, but *Ram* is the one to mark, because he was in line.

Verse 10. Three of the men descended

through Judah, and forming part of the line, are named in this passage. *Nashon* is specified as a *prince;* it has no necessary official meaning. It comes from NASI and Strong defines it, "properly an exalted one, i. e. a king or sheik." It could include the idea of an official as far as the definition is concerned, but the connection would have to show such a meaning before it could be thus understood.

Verses 11, 12. These verses correspond with the closing 3 verses of the book of Ruth. See the comments made at Ch. 4: 18-22 in that book.

Verses 13-15. Not only was David in the blood line of Christ, but the inspired historian gives enough of the names preceding and following him, that we can get a view of his family connection. He is said to be the 7th son of his father, but in 1 Sam. 16: 10 it is shown that he had 7 sons besides David. All this is on the basis that some one of the sons was of such little importance that he was left out of the royal list, and the document compiled by Ezra for the Bible followed that list.

Verses 16, 17. As a rule, there was not much attention paid to the birth of daughters. But a special point of interest called for the notation of David's sisters. Their sons became prominent in the affairs of the nation. Read 2 Sam. 2. Joab became especially noted on account of his connection with the military service of David.

Verse 18. This *Caleb* must not be confused with the man associated with Joshua as a spy. His father was Jephunneh; the father of this one was Hezron.

Verses 19, 20. Similarity of names should not be allowed to confuse us. This *Hur* was a son of Caleb who was a son of Hezron. The one in the days of Moses was from another family.

Verse 21. *Went in to* is one Biblical way of mentioning the intimate relation of the sexes. *Whom he married.* The last word is defined in the margin by "took," and the lexicon gives the same. There were no formal marriage ceremonies in those days. A man took a woman from her family association, went in unto her, which means he became intimate with her, and that made them one flesh, the only Biblical basis of marriage.

Verse 22. *Had* the cities means he held them or controlled them, and it means the cities that had belonged to the land of Gilead.

Verse 23. *From them* means Jair took these towns from the communities of Gilead. *Of Jair* means that at the time of this writing, the towns mentioned were considered as belonging to Jair, having been taken from the people of Gilead.

Verse 24. The construction of this verse is a little vague. The thing that happened was this. After Hezron was dead, Caleb had relations with Ephratah, and they had a son named Ashur.

Verses 25-33. This paragraph is a list of the family tree of Jerahmeel, one of the sons of Hezron. There is no special connection with other parts of the history.

Verses 34-41. Because it was unusual to record the birth of a daughter, or at any rate to attach much importance to it, the writer tells us that Sheshan had no sons, which is the reason for mentioning his daughters. He gave his daughter to his servant in order to have a son by "proxy." *She* bare *him* means, his daughter bare a son for her father, but who had been begotten by the servant. We will not have much occasion to consider this family elsewhere, so the paragraph may close here.

Verses 42-55. I have grouped all of these verses into one paragraph because they pertain to the family names of Caleb. The exact identity of this man is uncertain. Young does not attempt to clarify it, and Moffatt's translation throws little or no light on the subject. It is sufficient for us to know that no other historical matter is dependent on the identity of this particular man or any of his family. Such passages doubtless were useful in determining the settlement of an inheritance; but further than that we need not be concerned.

1 CHRONICLES 3

Verses 1-3. Because of friction in the nation, David did not reign over all the tribes at the beginning. Also for that reason he did not at first reign in Jerusalem, but in Hebron. While there he had 6 sons from as many wives. Three of these sons became more or less prominent afterward; *Amnon, Absalom* and *Adonijah.*

Verse 4. In detailing the years of David's separate divisions of his reign, the extra 6 months is mentioned. When the reign as a whole is referred to it is stated to be 40 years.

Verses 5-9. The chief item of interest in this paragraph is the fact that Nathan and Solomon were full brothers, sons of Bath-sheba, here called Bath-shua. The significant thing about that is that the blood line of Christ divides with these brothers. Solomon retains the genealogy that ends on the foster father's side, and Nathan becomes an ancestor of Mary, the mother of Christ. See the genealogies in Matt. 1 and Luke 3. A reference only is made to the sons of the concubines. That is because a concubine was inferior to a wife in the matter of property rights. There was no moral difference recognized, hence these persons are called sons of David with the same kind of expression as used for the others.

Verses 10-16. I have made one group of these verses because of the interesting facts that they contain the complete blood line from Solomon to the end of the kingly descendants of Judah. It is a coincidence of interest that the same men who were in the pedigree through that period were also the kings of Judah, Zedekiah being the last man of the line ever to occupy a temporal throne. Verse 15 shows a break in the line as regards proper succession. Instead of the line running successively from father to son, etc., three of the sons of Josiah occupied the throne. The transactions of this irregular arrangement are shown in the last chapter of 2 Kings.

Verses 17-24. The account of activities of the people had to be made by the inspired men during the period covered by this paragraph, because they were in captivity in Babylon. Only a part of the line is shown here; for fuller information see Matt. 1: 11-16 and Luke 3: 24-27. Jeconiah is called also Coniah and Jehoiachin.

1 CHRONICLES 4

Verses 1-4. Plurality of wives was tolerated in ancient times, and that gave occasion to think of a man's posterity in different groups. Hence we have an account of Judah's sons in this paragraph, although we had one in Ch. 2: 3. And again, we should keep in mind the special reason for the importance of family registration in view of property inheritances, and also the interest in the promises to be fulfilled through the descendants of Abraham and David.

Verses 5-8. Evidently the point in this paragraph is signified by Ashur's having two wives, and their respective sons were named.

Verse 9. It was decreed from the beginning that childbirth should be attended with pain; and after the sin of Eve that pain was to be increased. See my comments at Gen. 3: 16 regarding this subject. While this increase of pain was to be general, there would be exceptions where still greater suffering would have to be endured. The last word of this verse means pain, and the word *Jabez* in the Hebrew means sorrow. The birth of this son was attended with unusual pain and sorrow, so he was given a name that signified the experience.

Verse 10. While it was through no fault of his that Jabez was so named, he seemed to fear it might act as a "bad luck" omen in his life. In view of this, he earnestly prayed to God for help, that he would bless and prosper him in the ways of life. It is pleasant to read that the prayer was granted.

Verses 11, 12. *Chelub* is mentioned to begin this paragraph. The only reason I can find for his mention is the fact that he was a part of the family tree of Judah. All that Smith's Bible Dictionary says of him is, "A man among the descendants of Judah."

Verse 13. *Othniel* is the name to have our attention here. He was the man who fought a battle to obtain a wife. (Josh. 15: 16, 17).

Verse 14. *Craftsmen* is from CHARASH and Strong defines it, "a fabricator of any material." These people were engaged in the special trade of preparing materials to become parts of some larger unit. They happened to live in this certain valley which gave it the name *Charashim*, which means "craftsmen."

Verse 15. *Caleb* is a familiar name to us because he was one of the 12 spies who went to search out the land of Canaan. He was one of the faithful ones, who, with Joshua, was permitted to enter the promised land.

Verses 16-20. All of the persons named in this paragraph were members of Judah's family stock. Some of them are identical with others of note, such as Ezra, Miriam, Heber, Pharaoh, Amnon; but the similarity to the ones of note is purely a coincidence.

Verse 21. *Er* was the grandson of Judah, not his son who was slain by the Lord for his evil conduct. Sometimes the thing that won a place of honorable mention was some special trade. As an instance of it, we read of the fabricators in V. 14, and now the workers in linen in this verse.

Verse 22. The verse means that these men were dominant persons in the land of Moab. *Ancient things* means that it had been a matter of established note, from ancient times, that the men referred to did occupy that sort of dominion in the land of Moab.

Verse 23. This verse is a kind of detail of the preceding one. The statement is there made that the men were prominent. This verse explains that they had a special trade, that of working in pottery, and that they were employed by the king. So important was this work that it made them something like the "indispensable man." They not only worked in pottery, but had care of the shrubbery so important in the palace grounds.

Verses 24-31. Simeon was the 2nd son of Jacob. He was put out of the direct blood line on account of murder (Gen. 49: 5-7), so that his posterity was not recorded for the purpose of showing his right to that position. It was still important in connection with the settling of inheritances. They retained their hold on the cities named until the time of David. We are not told why it was changed then.

Verses 32-38. After giving this group of names, the last verse states the occasion for their being recorded. *Mentioned* is from BOW and Strong defines it, "to go or come." *Names* is from SHEM and we have the definition, "an appellation, as a mark or memorial of individuality; by implication, honor, authority, character."—Strong. *Princes* is from NASI, which Strong defines, "properly an exalted one, i. e. a king or sheik." With this critical information as a basis, the conclusion is that the persons presented were entitled to special notice due to their important character or personality; that as a result of their influence, they added to the prestige of the house of their fathers.

Verse 39. According to Young, *Gedor* was a place in the extreme south of Judah. It was not far from the vicinity of the Edomites. These people were industrious and willing to bestir themselves to make their condition better. They dealt in cattle and went in search of pasture for their flocks.

Verse 40. Their activities were rewarded, and they found fat or rich pasture with plenty of room. Some of the descendants of Ham had occupied the territory several years before, and had left the country quiet.

Verse 41. This verse is a detail of the preceding one, and states the time when their activities for territory took place. *These written* means the ones named in Vs. 34-38. *Tents . . . habitations.* The first word means the same as the word denotes today; the next means the places of residence in general. The idea of conquest by might seems to be outstanding in the account, and we might be inclined to shrink from their conduct. However, we should remember that these people were of the seed of Abraham and had been promised this land, even though they had to fight to obtain it.

Verse 42. This is another specification of the activities referred to in V. 39. *Mount Seir* was the territory in general, of which the mount of that name was a part. This was a rather wide stretch of country, and sometimes was occupied by the various portions of Esau's seed.

Verse 43. In 1 Sam. 15 is the account of Saul's attack on the Amalekites. He was told to smite all of them, and the record says he did so, except the king. But that was to be understood as applying to the ones engaged in combat. I mean, the claim that Saul had killed all but the king was his own declaration. He had actually been commanded to destroy all the people, including the women and children. We know, however, that he restricted his movements to the combatants, letting others escape. Those whom he allowed to escape are the ones meant in our present verse, where it says *Amalekites that were escaped.*

1 CHRONICLES 5

Verse 1. In several preceding chapters and some to follow, the family registers receive attention from the inspired writer. But it has not been done according to the order of birth. The present verse takes up the register of Reuben the firstborn of Jacob. After stating that he was the firstborn, an explanation is injected into the account of why he did not retain his place in the blood line genealogy; that it was because of his sin about his father's bed. (Gen. 35: 22). That sin not only deprived him of this honor, but also of his property rights, which was a part of the advantage of being the firstborn. This inheritance was given to the descendants of Joseph, and by that a prophecy of Jacob was fulfilled. See Gen. 48: 22; Deut. 21: 17; Josh. 17: 14.

Verse 2. *Chief ruler* refers to Christ, who was from the tribe of Judah. Hence Reuben lost his property rights to Joseph, and the genealogy to Judah.

Verses 3-6. Tilgath-pilneser is the same as Tiglath-pileser who was of Assyria. Beerah was a prince among the descendants of Reuben, and this Assyrian king carried him off into the Assyrian captivity. (2 Ki. 15: 29; 16: 7).

Verses 7, 8. Beerah had some brethren who were chief men, and they are named in this paragraph.

Verse 9. This particular man, Bela, took possession of some pasture land as far as the Euphrates River. The reader may ask whether this was justified by the promise to Abraham; Gen. 15: 18 shows that it was.

Verse 10. The *Hagarites* were a people named after Hagar, the handmaid of Sarah. They occupied a territory east of Palestine that is otherwise called Gilead. While Hagar's son was begotten by Abraham, the inheritance was to come through the son of his wife Sarah. (Gen. 25: 5). It was proper, therefore, for these sons of Reuben to take this land, since they were descended from Isaac, the son of Sarah.

Verse 11. Gad was another of the tribes, and had some territory in the same place as that of the descendants of Reuben. The specific spot where they settled may be recognized by the mentioning of Bashan, the place where Og was king at the invasion of the Israelites under Moses.

Verses 12-16. This paragraph specifies some of the men of God who occupied this space formerly held by the king of Bashan.

Verses 17. The names given in the preceding paragraph had been enrolled in the time of Jotham and Jeroboam, kings of the two bodies of Israelites. Their right to some of the inherited land could therefore not be disputed.

Verse 18. The two and a half tribes named here are the same whose request is recorded in Numbers 32. This request was granted, but they were expected to fight for the territory. Their military strength for doing so is described in this paragraph.

Verses 19-22. Some of this territory had been taken by Moses as the children of Israel were coming from Egypt. (Num. 21: 35; 32: 33). While it was given to them, there was some resistance from part of the natives and they had to be fought. But God was with his people and caused the battle to be a success. They obtained the territory and kept it until the Assyrian captivity.

Verses 23, 24. The two and one half tribes are usually mentioned as one unit. But in the matter of settling the inheritance, the half tribe maintained its tribal distinction and occupied the land in its proper place.

Verses 25, 26. The inspired writer goes onward many generations to the overthrow of these tribes of Israel. The reason for their downfall is given to be the sin of idolatry. The very thing for which God enabled his people to drive out those nations, became the popular sin of them, so that he saw fit to punish them by a national downfall. This has already been mentioned in this chapter (V. 6), and the original history of it is recorded in 2 Kings 15.

1 CHRONICLES 6

Verse 1. Levi was the 3rd son of Jacob. He was eliminated from the blood line for the same reason as was his brother Simeon, which was murder. (Gen. 49: 6). This applied to him personally, however, and did not affect the standing of his descendants in their work for the Lord. The tribe that sprang from him was honored by being chosen as the one to have entire charge of the religious services of the tabernacle. And the three sons of Levi were assigned their respective parts of the service. That is the reason the three are named in this one verse.

Verse 2. Special importance was attached to one of the sons of Levi, named Kohath. And his son Amram became peculiarly important in that he was the father of the two brothers who will be named next, and who became the outstanding men in connection with the religious activities of the nation.

Verse 3. Amram had two sons and a daughter. The two sons became famous in the history of Israel, each for a special cause. Aaron was the first high priest, and father of the entire priestly line throughout the life of the nation. Moses was the lawgiver, and the man who was inspired to write the first five books of the Bible. Since Aaron was exclusively the founder of the priestly group of God's people, his four sons are named in this verse.

Verses 4-15. All of the sons of Aaron were eligible for the priesthood and served whenever needed. But the high priesthood normally descended through the oldest son, unless some circumstance made a switch to another necessary. This paragraph cites the line of high priests to the Babylonian captivity. The account starts with Eleazer, although he was not the firstborn son of Aaron. The reason is that the two brothers older than he were slain for their sin about the strange fire. (Lev. 10: 1, 2.) The priesthood was then passed to the next oldest brother because neither of them had left any children. (Num. 3: 4.)

Verse 16. This chapter starts with the names of Levi's three sons. That is for the purpose of introducing the priestly and legal lines of Aaron and Moses. Now the same three sons are mentioned to introduce some of the other special work.

Verses 17-30. The three sons, Gershom (also spelled Gershon), Kohath and Merari, had families, and the work of these groups was assigned to them. A list of these registrations is hereby given, which was put into the records in order to settle any misunderstanding that might arise concerning the work in the future.

Verse 31. Since the preceding paragraph extends to the captivity, it would include the period of David's work. *After the ark had rest* refers to the time when David had brought the ark to Jerusalem and placed it in the tent pitched for it. (2 Sam. 6: 1-17.)

Verse 32. The *tabernacle* was the building that Moses erected at Sinai, and *the house of the Lord* was the temple that Solomon built to be used instead of the tabernacle. Not being descended from Kohath, these people had no work in the priesthood. They were therefore employed in this service according to David's appointment. *According to their order* means according to the directions that David gave them. Each of the men served as he was bidden, so that order was maintained in the service.

Verses 33-38. The group of the Kohathites was eligible for the priestly service. However, since their service in that capacity was not always needed, they could be employed otherwise. In the present instance we see they were engaged in the song service. Furthermore, the descendants of Kohath were in the priestly group, yet some of them might be disqualified for that service because lacking in some personal requirements. (Lev. 21: 1-8.) But while disqualified for that service, they could be useful in other forms of service about the Lord's institution.

Verses 39-47. *Stood . . . left hand.* This was arranged for the purpose of maintaining good order in the service. God has always manifested a desire for order and not confusion. Paul taught this principle in 1 Cor. 14: 33.

Verse 48. There were many services pertaining to the tabernacle in general, that did not require the special qualifications of a priest, and yet which should be done by the specially chosen tribe. Also, by the ones who did have the priestly qualifications previously, but had lived past the age limit. There was plenty of useful work to be done and they were to have the privilege of doing so. (Deut. 18: 6-8.)

Verse 49. The teaching of this verse cannot be considered with too much care. It is not generally understood that the priesthood was the exclusive right and office of Aaron and his lineal descendants. Hence it should be remembered that while all priests were Levites, not all Levites were priests.

Verses 50-53. This paragraph has to do with the line of high priests only, and they descended from Aaron through Eleazer, who was next oldest after the two who were dead.

Verse 54. *These* refers to places yet to be named in the following verses. *Castles* refers to walled towns or cities. The tribe of Levi was not to have a general allotment of land as did the others, but was to be given cities throughout the whole land. Read carefully Num. 35: 1-15 for particulars concerning this subject of the Levitical possessions. Among the cities to be given the Levites were 6 used as refuge for the slayer, and 3 of them will be named in this chapter. *Coasts* means borders or territories regardless of whether land or water is under consideration.

Verse 55. *Hebron* was one of the cities of refuge given to the Levites. See my comments at Num. 35: 4, 5 on the meaning of "suburbs."

Verse 56. Caleb had made a special request for this territory, and Moses gave it to him in recognition of his faithfulness in wholly following the Lord. (Josh. 14: 6-14.)

Verses 57-81. It will be just as well to comment on this group of verses as a whole. On the west side of the Jordan River there were cities selected from the various families of the tribe of Levi, three of which were cities of refuge. They were *Hebron* (V. 57), *Gezer* (V. 67) and *Golan* (V. 71). These several cities were scattered throughout the land in general, hence were taken from the different tribes. This long paragraph is a list of the various cities given to the Levites, showing from whose possessions they had been appropriated.

1 CHRONICLES 7

Verses 1, 2. *Generation* means family history as the word is used here. The statement means the history of that family was one of valor. Their number had been taken by David, and it was 22,600.

Verse 3. *Obadiah* and *Joel* are mentioned in this verse, but it is a mere coincidence that their names are the same as those of two of the minor prophets.

Verses 4, 5. In the family register of these men of Issachar were 36,000 military men. The simple explanation of the large number of that kind of men is that there were many wives and sons. The conclusion is that a general military training was given the sons of the rising generations.

Verses 6, 7. Another tribe is introduced, that of Benjamin. *Reckoned by their genealogies* means they were not counted unless they had been born in line with the family record of births. These were men of valor which means strength or power.

Verses 8, 9. The main reason for noting these verses is to show the close distinction between the words *genealogy* and *generations*. The first means the pedigree of the stock, and the second is the history of that pedigree. To illustrate, an animal might possess the pure blood of a certain strain, yet not get credit for it because no record had been kept of it. Therefore, a prospective purchaser would demand that the pedigree be "registered" to show the purity of the stock. Likewise in our case of the sons of Becher, the number of men counted for the military came from those not only of the pure stock (genealogy), but it was a matter of history or registration.

Verse 10. *Benjamin* is another familiar name, but its presence here is a coincidence.

Verses 11, 12. *Heads of their fathers.* The last word is plural because the group being considered descended through the various posterity of Jediael. The number 17,200 was the military strength of this group.

Verse 13. This short verse is all that is given to the tribe of Naphtali. If any landed interest was due the members of this tribe, it could be established through this brief but direct pedigree.

Verses 14-19. This paragraph includes all of the names that the present record gives of the tribe of Manasseh who was a son of Joseph. An interesting item of this account is concerning the status of Zelophehad, a near descendant of Manasseh. This man had no sons, and that fact brought an embarrassing situation to the daughters about their property rights. They made an appeal to Moses which resulted in an interpretation of the law in their favor. This account is in Num. 27: 1-11.

Verses 20, 21. This book is a list of the families of Jacob's sons. Not much attention is paid to consecutive chronology, nor to the relative dates of the events written about. The transactions of this paragraph and the following verses took place in the land of Canaan before they went down to Egypt. We know this is true, for none of the original heads of the tribes would be living after they came out of Egypt. These sons of Ephraim were killed by the natives of Gath on the ground that they were going to get their livestock.

Verses 22-27. It was natural for Ephraim to mourn over the violent death of his sons, regardless of what they may have done to provoke the attack. The lexicon definition of *Beriah* is, "in trouble." There are many instances recorded in the Bible where children were given names with a significant meaning. Hence there is nothing unusual in the present case. Aside from explaining why this son was so named, there is no significance in the mention of Ephraim's loss in close connection with the fact of his relations with his wife. That particular fact was the introduction to the list of his descendants connecting the line down to a familiar name. It has a different form from what we have known; *Non* is the same as Nun, and *Jehoshua* is the same as Joshua.

Verse 28. We think of *Bethel* and the other places named in this verse as cities or towns, yet the text gives, them and also their *towns*. The word is from a Hebrew term with a very wide range of meaning. Its primary definition is "daughter," but it has figurative applications also, and when so used it means something closely related, such as a daughter who would be related to an older person. Moffatt's translation gives it "Bethel and its townships," etc.

Verse 29. Ephraim and Manasseh were full brothers and it seems appropriate to write of the two in this way of close association. We were told that the descendants of Ephraim had certain places "with their towns" (townships), now it is fitting to say something of the kind about the descendants of Manasseh.

Verses 30-40. This paragraph recounts the prominent descendants of Asher, another of the tribes of Israel. Most of the comments made in the preceding paragraph will apply here. The familiar name, *Jephunneh*, is another coincidence only.

1 CHRONICLES 8

Verses 1-27. This concerns Benjamin although we have already seen some account of him in the preceding chapter; however, a slight variation will be noted in the names. It is explained by the fact that property rights had to be considered when giving the names of a man's descendants. Furthermore, that was a military age, and sometimes the writer was enumerating the members of a family in view of their general qualifications for military service. That is why we so often see the expression "able to go forth to war."

Verse 28. *Heads of the fathers* means they were leading men, whose descendants included fathers of important generations, and who lived in Jerusalem.

Verse 29. *Father of Gibeon* means the founder of the city, and that he lived in the city he founded. His name was Jehiel according to Ch. 9: 35.

Verses 30-32. The preceding paragraph showed us that Jehiel was the man last referred to; and the one meant by the pronoun "his." He had a son named Kish, but he was not the father of Saul.

Verse 33. The importance of this verse is evident. According to 1 Sam. 14: 51, Ner was the father of Abner, the captain under Saul. This verse shows him to have been also the father of Kish. Since Abner and Kish were brothers we see that Saul had his uncle as his chief military head. The three brothers of Jonathan are named, but only Jonathan became noted in the later activities of the family.

Verse 34. Dissimilarity of names of the same man may be as confusing as similar names for different men. Here is Merib-baal which refers to Mephibosheth, who is connected with the movements of David. (1 Sam. 4: 4.)

Verses 35-39. These are descendants of Jonathan, and among them are a few names familiar in form but it is just another coincidence.

Verse 40. *Archers* means men who were able with the bow, which was one form of weapons used in those days. The men named were descended from Jonathan who was an expert in that form of action. See 2 Sam. 1: 18, 22. The last sentence uses *these* to mean the chapter as a whole, since Saul was of that tribe being considered.

1 CHRONICLES 9

Verse 1. *Genealogies* is from YACHAS, and Strong defines it, "to enroll by pedigrees." *Written in the book* is explained by my comments on 1 Ki. 14: 19.

Verse 2. The preceding verse closed with a reference to the Babylonian captivity. Up to that point in this book, the writer was giving a list of the different families of Israel, showing the proper place and rank of the people. Between the 1st verse of this chapter and the one we are studying, the 70 years of the captivity took place and the people were released to return to Jerusalem. This verse, as well as the rest of the chapter, will give us a brief list of those who returned, and their places of residence, as well as the particular rank and service accepted. It will be instructive for us to note the list, to compare it with that contained in the preceding chapters of this book. *First* is from a word that Strong defines, "first, in time, place or rank." The connection indicates the last word of the definition is the one that applies here. This conclusion is justified by the special naming of *priests, Levites* and *Nethinims.* The last word was never used until after the captivity, although the special temple service, which distinguished them as a class, had been used previously.

Verses 3-8. This paragraph begins stating the various persons who located in Palestine after returning from Babylon. Men from four tribes, Judah, Benjamin, Ephraim and Manasseh, dwelt in Jerusalem.

Verse 9. There were 956 of these, said to be *chief* men, which agrees with the definition of *rank* as the meaning of *first* in V. 2.

Verses 10-12. The priests would logically dwell in Jerusalem since their work was there. *Ruler of the house of God* means he was a leader through prestige.

Verse 13. The reason for naming this group as a unit is expressed in V. 13; they were *very able men.*

Verses 14-16. The Levites as a tribe were mentioned in V. 2. Now certain men *of the Levites* are singled out for honorable mention. The *Netophathites* were the inhabitants of Netophath. These people spread out and occupied the villages in the surrounding territory, and Levites already named resided in some of these villages. Not all Levites would need to be in active service at the same time, so they could reside in places other than Jerusalem.

Verses 17, 18. The *porters* were janitors or doorkeepers. These men attended the gate at the east side of the city.

Verse 19. *Gates of the tbaernacle.* We know the tabernacle proper had vanished long before this time, which was after the return from captivity. In describing the work assigned to these men it is based on their former work. Moffatt's translation throws light on this passage which I will quote: "Were in charge of the service as keepers of the sacred thresholds, as their fathers had been keepers in the sacred camp of the Eternal."

Verse 20. Phinehas was doorkeeper in early times; now that the people get their liberty to return from the captivity, some others will need to take up the work; that prepares us for the next verse.

Verse 21. Zechariah performed the service that was referred to in preceding verse.

Verse 22. These 212 were admitted to this service after the return because their names were found in the register. This was an official record, having been made under the supervision of David and Samuel the seer, or prophet.

Verse 23. The *tabernacle* is mentioned again because that had been the institution that originated this kind of service. After the return from Babylonian captivity the same kind of service was rendered for the temple.

Verse 24. This means the four points of the compass. The original word for *quarters* is literally defined as "winds." When used to denote directions it is as when we say "the four winds under heaven."

Verse 25. This means the brethren changed shifts on this service every seven days.

Verse 26. The Levites that were the chief porters or doorkeepers for these four gates had their position as a *set office,* which means "trust," and they had also the charge of the treasury. However, they would need some help, so their brethren relieved them by turns at intervals of seven days.

Verse 27. While they were relieved at times of some of the weight of the office, they remained near the temple to supervise the opening of the gates in the morning.

Verse 28. *Vessels* means any implement or utensil. These men had a general charge to care for the utensils needed about the temple. *By tale* denotes a counting of the utensils when they were taken out of their storing place for service, then counted again when ready to be put back. This was in the nature of a "check."

Verse 29. Every man had his own task. Some had that of supervising the utensils, also the materials used in the service.

Verse 30. In Ex. 30: 23-25 the formula was given for the anointing oil. There were restrictions about the making and using of this ointment, therefore it was appropriate that the sons of the priests have charge of its mixing as indicated here.

Verse 31. According to Lev. 2: 5 some of the materials used in the service were prepared in pans. Mattithiah had charge of this part of the work.

Verse 32. *Kohathites* were the descendants of Aaron through his son Kohath. Their special charge was to see after the bread for the table in the holy place. To *prepare* it meant to see that the 12 loaves were put on the table each sabbath, to replace those that had been there since the previous sabbath. This was according to the law in Lev. 24: 5-9.

Verses 33, 34. The singers were *free* from other duties because their services kept them in the temple day and night.

Verses 35-44. This paragraph is practically the same as Ch. 8: 29-38.

1 CHRONICLES 10

General remarks: There seems to be an abrupt change of subjects. Up to this point the author was concerned with the pedigrees of the families of the Jews, to establish their proper repossession of the land. The next thing he wishes to do is to restore the respect for and interest in the institution of the national life. Its true greatness really dated from the reign of David, and hence the main history from now on will be on that basis. However, since David was not actually the first king, the author realizes the moral necessity of paying at least a little attention to Saul, the first king. In that way it could be said that the writer of the books of Chronicles gave a history of the kingdom at Jerusalem from its beginning. But only enough of the history of Saul was given to show there was such a king, then state briefly the account of his shameful death. We therefore have the explanation of the sudden change of subjects, plunging into the very midst of Saul's last battle. As to its historical setting, this chapter corresponds to 1 Sam. 31.

Verse 1. The Philistines were long the enemies of the Israelites. Their country lay along the western border of Palestine, and the people were from a very old stock. They fought with the Israelites in a fierce battle. The action was in the vicinity of Mt. Gilboa, which was a range of mountains in the northeast part of Palestine.

Verse 2. It is a piece of good strategy to get the generals in an enemy army. The Philistines concentrated their actions against Saul and his sons. This verse says they were slain, but the details of Saul's death will be given in some verses to follow.

Verse 3. The Philistines succeeded in hitting Saul with their arrows, and the wounds would have proved fatal had he not interfered by his own action.

Verse 4. This verse shows why I said the wounds of Saul might have proved fatal. At least Saul believed them to be that serious, else he would not have wanted to "cheat the gallows" by taking his own life. *Sword . . . fell upon it*. The kind of sword used in battle was so long that it would have been difficult, if not impossible, to use it upon one's self in the ordinary way. That is why a man who committed suicide with a sword did it by standing it with the handle on the ground, then, leaning over and down upon it, the weight of his body would force the weapon through it.

Verse 5. It does not say the armorbearer just thought Saul was dead; it says he *saw that Saul was dead*. Now we know a man cannot see that which does not exist. The inspired writer is the one who says the armorbearer saw that Saul was dead, which proves that he was dead after falling upon the sword. These comments should be considered when thinking of the story of the Amalekite in 2 Sam. 1: 1-12. That young man thought he would win the favor of David by his falsehood.

Verse 6. Saul had been told the kingdom was to be taken from him, and that did not mean merely from him personally; it included an entire change of family for the throne. The death of *all his house* prepared the fulfillment of that prediction.

Verse 7. The result was doubtless as the Philistines expected. If the leader in battle is killed, especially when it is the king of the nation, the depression would be great. After fleeing in their fright, their cities were left to the mercy of the enemy.

Verse 8. *Strip* is from a word that means "to plunder." It did not mean to remove the clothing, but to take the valuables that might be upon them. In their general search for dead bodies they came upon those of Saul and his sons.

Verse 9. *Carry* is from LASAB which Strong defines, "to be fresh, i. e. full (rosy, figuratively cheerful)." The announcement that the king of their enemy was dead would be good news. The sight of his head and armor would be proof that the news was true.

Verse 10. Dagon was the national god of the Philistines. The image itself was a combination of man and fish. Of course an image like that was intended to represent some invisible deity who would guard their human interests. By including the likeness of a fish, it would suggest something encouraging for the men who spent their time on the sea. Since the Philistine country was near the sea, the people would naturally be interested in a god who was interested in them. To fasten the head of their enemy in the house of Dagon signified the superiority of their god over all others.

Verses 11, 12. The general meaning of *valiant* is *"to be strong,"* whether applied to an individual or an army of men. The people of Jabesh-gilead were strong and brave. *All the valiant men* came to rescue the bodies of Saul and his sons; that would be for two reasons. It might be the Philistines would resist their taking the bodies, and force would have to be used. Another thing, it was a demonstration of the respect they had for the leading men to come in a body, as it were, to perform these rites to a fallen monarch. The fast of 7 days was a formal ceremony, done on the same principle that funeral ceremonies, the use of flowers, etc., are practiced today.

Verses 13, 14. These sins are only mentioned here. The detailed account of them is in 1 Sam. 13: 8-14; 15: 6-29 and 28; 5-20.

1 CHRONICLES 11

Verse 1. This verse goes past the 7 years that David reigned in Hebron. During those years he was recognized by the tribe of Judah only. Abner, the captain over the military in Saul's reign, put his son Ish-bosheth over the other tribes, and they kept David from his rightful place until after the affair of Abner and Saul's concubine. Then Abner revolted the party of Saul and went over to David, which brought about the actions referred to in the present paragraph. The history of the change described above is in 2 Sam. 3: 7-21. Seeing that the house of Saul had gone down in its plot for power, these people came to David and professed to be devoted to him.

Verse 2. There might be some doubt as to the sincerity of "all Israel" in these flattering remarks, considering their attitude for 7 years just past. But now they see the "handwriting" and want to be on the winning side. However, all the good things they said to David were true, only they should have recognized it before.

Verse 3. With their "change of heart" toward David, the elders and leaders of the Israelites came to Hebron, where he had been reigning for 7 years over Judah, and anointed him as their personal recognition of his true rank, spoken of by Samuel.

Verse 4. Up to this time it seems that no attempt had been made to occupy Jerusalem. Ish-boseth the usurper had his throne at Mahanaim. (2 Sam. 2: 8.) Now that the nation has come together in the matter of a king, it was proper that Jerusalem be used as the capital for the king. When they did so, they found the city in possession of an ancient tribe called Jebusites.

Verses 5, 6. These ancient citizens of Jerusalem were unwilling to be disturbed. This verse makes only a statement of the fact, but 2 Sam. 5: 6 gives the conditions on which David had to obtain possession of the city. The noted man Joab made his reputation good by leading in the attack on the opposition and gaining control of the city.

Verses 7, 8. There are some terms that might confuse the reader, that refer practically to the same thing. In the city of Jerusalem there was a section or borough that was more important than others. In this place was a fortified castle, and it is sometimes called Millo. David settled in that part of the city and for that reason it was called the city of David. The same place was also what was meant by Mount Zion, or by the one word, Zion. And because so much of the Lord's institutions took place in that locality, the term "zion" or "Mount Zion" came to have a spiritual or figurative meaning in later years.

Verse 9. It is significant that David's growth is accounted for by the fact that the Lord was with him. In all ages of the world, true greatness has consisted in doing and being what is pleasing to God.

Verses 10, 11. All men were not counted great for the same reason. Later on Solomon will be given an important commission from God because of his success against his military foes. There is no contradiction in the situation. The times of David required the activities recorded of him, for there were many mighty forces that had to be subdued to make ready for the peaceful reign of Solomon. The success of David in his many conflicts was due largely to his wisdom in selecting the proper men for his service. In this and several verses to follow, the statements of greatness of his men will be verified by specific citation of their deeds. In the present paragraph the man slew 300 with a heavy weapon called a spear. It was an instrument composed of a long shaft with a head of hard metal, and was hurled by hand against the foe.

Verse 12. No explanation is given in the Bible why David's great men were grouped in threes. It is easy to see some advantages in the arrangement, however. These men were expected to meet the foes of the kingdom as well as David's personal enemies. A trio of good men would be more successful because of mutual encouragement. It would be also an advantage in case of casualties, so that the survivor could care for the fallen comrade. Of course, David would not put three of the best in one group and then form some other group all of the inferior kind. He associated one of the best with others in forming the groups. But if some special occasion required only one man's services, he would select one from some of these trios.

Verses 13, 14. Barley was a valued food and the Philistines planned to take this field. They had frightened the Israelites from it when David, aided by one of his mighty men, beat off the Philistines and saved the food.

Verse 15. *Three of the thirty.* This is rendered "three captains over the thirty" in the margin, and Moffatt's translation gives practically the same wording. Adullam was a city in Judah that is referred to in a number of places in the Bible. According to Smith's Bible Dictionary, there were limestone cliffs in that locality which were pierced with extensive excavations, one of which was the "cave of Adullam" in the time of David. The valley of Rephaim was in the same general vicinity as the cave, and the Philistines brought their army there to oppose David.

Verse 16. The Philistines had a general mass of soldiers in the valley, but their garrison, which means a fortified post, was at Bethlehem which also was in the vicinity of the valley. David, in the meantime, was hiding in the *hold*, which means the cave of Adullam which was of such a character that it provided a stronghold for safety.

Verse 17. This event about the water is a sidelight on the main subject, the bravery and might of David's chief men. Whether he really intended to drink the water we are not told. The point is to give an instance of the achievements of the great men in his service. But in order to give an intelligent view of the occasion it was necessary to relate the request of David and his activities afterward. The well was in the very shadow of the garrison of the Philistines, and it would be necessary to face them in obtaining the water. We may reasonably conclude, therefore, that David's expressed wish was to test the courage of his men.

Verse 18. Drawing water from a well in those days was not as simple a matter as might be the case today. It was done chiefly by the use of an earthen pitcher and rope and would be a very visible performance. This would make it a dangerous occasion.

Verse 19. *Drink the blood* is figurative, and refers to the risk of being slain, that the men took when they got the water. *These things did these three mightiest.* This expression gives the main object the writer had in telling about the water.

Verses 20, 21. Differences in rank were recognized in those times as well as in the present. As a reward for his valor, Abishai was exalted above the others of his trio. He had slain three hundred.

Verse 22. *Lionlike* is defined, "heroic." It means they were unusually strong and active. *Time of snow* is incidental, explaining why the lion was taking refuge in the pit. But the fact of the lion's being in the pit indicates a very great hazard.

Verse 23. A staff was a lighter weapon than a spear. The greatness of this feat was in the fact of disarming the Egyptian and slaying him with his own weapon.

Verses 24, 25. Honor to whom it is due entitled Benaiah to the present report, but he must not be thought to be equal, in rank, with another trio in David's service.

Verses 26-47. All of these men attached to David in service for the kingdom were outstanding. Special mention, however, should be made of Asahel because of his relation to Joab, the commander-in-chief; and of Uriah because of the affair about Bath-sheba.

1 CHRONICLES 12

Verse 1. David had fled to the land of the Philistines as a final escape from Saul, and had been given Ziklag as his own residence (1 Sam. 27: 1-7). It was natural that many of his associates would come to him, to render whatever service they could.

Verse 2. It is noteworthy that some of these men were relatives of Saul, the very man from whom David had fled. This shows the sentiment that was held for him in his flight from Saul.

Verse 3. These men were of the tribe of Benjamin, but the "ite" appellative is added to designate the town or other location of each one's residence.

Verse 4. Ismaiah is named as a special man in that he outranked the 30 of whom he was one.

Verses 5-7. No particulars are given as to the deeds or rank of these men, but their being included by the inspired writer is proof of their importance.

Verse 8. The tribe of Gad was situated east of the Jordan, yet these came over to David in a goodly number. The character of the tribe as described here, is borne out by Smith's Bible Dictionary as follows: "The character of the tribe is throughout strongly marked—fierce and warlike." A shield was a defensive piece, held at the left side to ward off the darts of the enemy. A buckler was a similar piece, but used more as a shield for the front of the body. The reference to lions is for comparison only, indicating the boldness of the men. The roe was a kind of deer that was very swift on foot, hence the comparison.

Verses 9-13. Having given a description of the Gadites in general in the preceding verse, this paragraph names some of the men who came.

Verse 14. The men named above were so able in war they were given a position over others. Their qualifications were indicated by the fact that the least of them could manage 100 men.

Verse 15. At harvest time the Jordan overflowed all its banks (Josh. 3: 15). The fact is mentioned in this place to indicate the rugged character of the Gadites. Being on the east of the river, they had to get across the torrent in some way in order to get to David.

Verse 16. Judah and Benjamin were adjoining tribes, and men from their territories went over to the land of the Philistines to offer their services to David.

Verse 17. Since Saul was of the tribe of Benjamin, it is understandable why David would question these men as to their purpose in coming.

Verse 18. Amasai was spokesman for the group. He assured David that they wished him peace, and indicated they were ready to fight for him. He then received them and enlisted them in his service.

Verse 19. When David was preparing to fight in the Philistine army against Israel (1 Sam. 28: 1, 2; 29: 1-10) these men offered to fight by his side. However, since David was rejected from the Philistine army, we have no further information as to the activities of these Manassehites.

Verse 20. Ziklag was the city that had been given to David by the Philistine king of Gath. (1 Sam. 1-7.) *Fell to him* means they became friendly to him. These men of the tribe of Manasseh were not ordinary persons, but were captains. This shows the standing that David had in those troublous times.

Verses 21, 22. *Rovers* is not in the original, but *band is*, and is defined in the lexicon, "a crowd (especially of soldiers)." Moffatt's translation gives us "the raiders." These men who came to David from the tribe of Manasseh were themselves men of experience as soldiers, and were able to help him against the hostile bands. Encouraged no doubt by the favorable appearances, the number of men coming over to David's side increased daily, until it became a *great host*, which means it became an army.

Verse 23. The reader is taken back to the time David was king in Hebron. At that time he reigned only over the tribe of Judah as a whole. But there were individuals who had friendly feeling for him and came to his aid. They believed that David was the rightful ruler, and that the attempts to hold the kingdom for Saul's family were unlawful.

Verse 24. It would be expected that men of Judah would be in sympathy with David in the controversy. Yet it sometimes occurs that professed sympathy is all the assistance one gets, while these men of the home tribe where David was reigning showed their sincerity by being *ready armed to the war*.

Verses 25, 26. Here we see that some men of the tribes who were supposed to be under Saul's son came over to David's side. They were not just those who might have been considered the weaklings seeking some recognition. They were *mighty men of valor*, which means they were strong men.

Verse 27. The previous verse had mentioned the children of Levi. That would mean the tribe as a whole which consisted of three important groups from the three sons of Levi. The present verse considers one family of Levi only, *the Aaronites*. They were the priests since only the family of Aaron was eligible for the priesthood.

Verse 28. There were several men named Zadok, some of them in the priesthood. The one in this verse is different from all of them, and is known simply as a young man of much strength. He led 22 captains, or military leaders, in the service for David.

Verse 29. Saul was from the tribe of Benjamin. It is significant, therefore, that 3,000 men of that tribe adhered to David, for the most of the tribe still clung to the house of Saul.

Verse 30. Almost if not quite all of the tribes furnished men who were faithful to David, even while the tribes as a whole held with the conspiracy for Saul's house for some years. But special reasons for mentioning the particular ones are often given. The men of Ephraim are said to have been *famous*. Strong defines the original word, "an appellation [or name] as mark or memorial of individuality; by implication honor, authority, character."

Verse 31. Mention of the *half tribe of Manasseh* does not mean that part of the tribe was opposed to David. Half of that tribe had settled on the east side of the Jordan River, which would explain why they had not taken active part in the movements. Verse 20 had already mentioned 7 men of this tribe who came to David's side, and they were captains. Our present paragraph refers to 18,000 of that tribe who, though not as prominent as the ones in verse 20, were men of sufficient importance that when they came to David they were all named out to him.

Verse 32. *Understanding of the times* means they were men of good judgment, to know what to do in all emergencies; the less efficient men cooperated with these.

Verse 33. These men are mentioned because of their expert ability in battle. They could make formations for the actions that were helpful towards victory. *Not of double heart* means they were not wavering in their purposes.

Verse 34. The men of this tribe are mentioned because of their expertness in handling the *shield and spear*. The spear was a long rod or pole with a sharp, heavy head, and used by hurling with the hand at the enemy. This was done with the right hand, and the shield was a plate of metal held in the left hand to ward off the spears thrown by the enemy.

Verse 35. The simple statement that these men were *expert in war* is the motive for taking note of this group of the Danites.

Verse 36. In this and two other verses above the word *expert* is used to describe the quality of the men referred to. The particular meaning of the original word is defined by Strong thus: "A primitive root; to set in a row, i. e. arrange, put in order (in a very wide variety of applications)." The practical meaning of the word is ability to keep in order under the excitement of battle.

Verse 37. *Other side of Jordan* means the east side, because the author is writing from the main part of the Jewish territory which is Palestine proper, west of Jordan.

Verse 38. The writer extends the date of his narrative to the time when David was to be accepted as king of the whole nation. Many of the men cited above had shown their sympathy for him before; now they are taking an active part in the developments. The qualification *could keep rank* is the same as being "expert" which was defined at verse 36. *Came with a perfect heart* means they were wholehearted in their friendship for David. The various tribes were sincere in their offer to recognize him, although some of the individuals had been slow in seeing the injustice of the usurpation of the house of Saul after his death.

Verse 39. The people had come to Hebron because that was the place where David had been located during his restricted reign. They had been expected, and preparations were made for a feast that lasted 3 days.

Verse 40. This verse describes a gathering of many people of Israel. It was a joyous time because the opposition to David had subsided, and the outward expressions of support for him caused all to have a sense of relief. The general feeling of joy prompted these men of the tribes mentioned to contribute the food for the entertainment, so that the three-day feast was an occasion of great joy.

1 CHRONICLES 13

Verse 1. David was the absolute king of the Israelite nation. But he was a man of systematic principles and knew the value of cooperation. He therefore took his great men into his confidence and consulted them about the important proposition at hand.

Verse 2. The proviso that David made in connection with his proposal was that it be *of the Lord our God*. With such a condition understood, all of his suggestions would be righteous. Among the brethren generally scattered, special mention is made of *priests* and *Levites*. The distinction between these two is in the fact that all priests were of the tribe of Levi, yet not all Levites were eligible for the office of priests; only the family of Aaron had that right.

Verse 3. In 1 Sam. 7: 2 it is stated that the ark was in Kirjath-jearim 20 years; that was before Saul was made king. He reigned 40 years (Acts 13: 21) and David had been reigning at least 7 years at the time of the present paragraph, making fully 47 years since the ark was taken to Kirjath-jearim. The clearest explanation is the statement in 1 Sam. 7: 2 is based on some special conditions connected with the ark, and not on the period as a whole. The ark had not been consulted in the days of Saul because he was not much interested, and also because it was not in its proper place in the tabernacle where the high priest could have access to it.

Verse 4. It is not necessary for a thing to be right in the eyes of the people, to be right before God. It is gratifying, though, when the people approve of that which is right. That was the case in the matter of bringing the ark home.

Verse 5. *Shihor of Egypt* is the same as "river of Egypt" in Gen. 15: 18. It was the southern boundary of the land of Canaan while Hemath was at the north. The statement means that David made a general call for the people all over the country to back him in bringing the ark home.

Verse 6. Baalah was another name for Kirjath-jearim, the place where the ark had been so long. *Belonged to Judah* means it was located in the territory possessed by the tribe of Judah. The cherubims were on the cover of the ark and God had said he would meet the high priest there on behalf of the people. (Ex. 25: 10-22.)

Verse 7. *Carried* is from BAKAB and Strong defines it, "to ride (on an animal or in a vehicle); causatively, to place upon (for riding or generally), to dispatch)." A cart was used to move the ark which was contrary to the law which required that it be borne by the staves in the sides. (Ex. 25: 14, 15.)

Verse 8. *David and all Israel played* means they were merry and expressed their feelings by using instruments of music. The corresponding passage in 2 Sam. 6: 14 says that David danced also. Individual dancing was a common practice in those days. It was not like the mixed dancing of the sexes with each other in our times. It was perfectly logical that a feeling of joy would be caused by seeing the sacred vessel arriving toward the city from which it had unlawfully been taken almost half a century before.

Verse 9. It was common for more than one name to be given to the same person or place. *Chidon* here is the same as "Nachon" in 2 Sam. 6: 6. *Stumbled* is from an original word with a stronger meaning than this. It is defined, "to fling down; incipiently [indicating] to jostle."—Strong. It means that the movements of the oxen actually caused the ark to be shaken so that it was in danger of being thrown from the cart. That would have been a tragedy, for it would doubtless have been burst open and its sacred contents exposed. With all that in view, Uzza had the best of motive in putting his hand on the ark.

Verse 10. Good motives will not excuse a man in wrongdoing. The ark was to be borne by the hand with the staves, and no reason existed for carrying it on a cart. The Lord was angry or displeased with Uzza for his violation of the law and punished him with immediate death. The circumstance should be a lesson on the importance of obeying God regardless of how matters look to us.

Verse 11. *David was displeased* does not mean he found fault with the Lord. He was worried over the whole thing because it was necessary for God to break off (breach) his favor from Uzza, which threw the situation into confusion.

Verse 12. *Afraid of God* means he was overawed by the event and intimidated against doing anything further with the moving of the ark as far as Jerusalem.

Verse 13. For the time being David had the ark deposited in the house of Obed-edom the Gittite.

Verse 14. The Lord blessed the family of Obed-edom for the respectful care given the ark during the three months it was there. According to Young and other authorities, Obed-edom was a Levite, which made it appropriate for the ark to be in his house, although there is no indication that he attempted any priestly use of it. *Gittite* was a locality term and not related to his nationality.

1 CHRONICLES 14

Verses 1, 2. From a strictly religious standpoint, there should have been no fellowship between Hiram and David. The former was of the heathen nations while the latter was of the nation of God. But the Mosaic system was a combination of civil and religious government. From the civil standpoint it was in order for the two to be on friendly terms. The fact that Hiram contributed valuable materials toward the building of a house for his kingdom, indicated to David that Providence was in his favor and that his acquiring the entire kingdom of Israel was to be permanent. These verses, however, are introductory only, and nothing will be done for some time about the building.

Verse 3-7. In a book of this kind we may expect to find a repetition of some details and see them scattered. The list of David's sons is given in Ch. 3: 3-9. In that place it is shown that Nathan and Solomon were his sons by the same woman, who was Bath-sheba. This is interesting from the fact that the full brothers were ancestors of Christ. Nathan headed the line ending with Mary the mother of Jesus, and Solomon headed the line ending with Joseph, the foster father.

Verse 8. News of David's rise to power over the whole nation of Israel was displeasing to the Philistines, the old enemies of God's people. They came up to oppose him, but he went out against them.

Verse 9. The valley of Rephaim was a field south of Jerusalem. It was the scene of some of David's greatest conquests. The Philistines spread in this locality in a position threatening to David.

Verse 10. David was a man with great faith in God. He depended on his counsel and help in the duel with Goliath, now he asked for divine guidance in the matter of meeting the Philistines. Upon inquiry the Lord told him to attack the enemy with the promise that he would win.

Verse 11. Baal-perazim was a place within the valley of Rephaim. At that spot David won a great victory over the enemy and gave the credit to God.

Verse 12. In their flight the Philistines left their gods behind; David commanded that they should be burned.

Verse 13. The enemy was persistent in the conflict and returned to the valley.

Verse 14. The Lord directed David to make a different mode of attack. The reason for it is not stated.

Verse 15. According to Smith's Bible Dictionary the mulberry trees referred to are not the same as our trees of that name, but something like the aspen tree. The original word is defined by Strong, "The weeping tree (some gum-distilling tree, perhaps the balsam)." As the leaves of the aspen tree are very sensitive to the slightest disturbance it is significant that God used the *sound of the going in the tops of the mulberry trees* as the signal for attack. See my comments at 2 Ki. 2: 8 as to unusual and arbitrary means used in connection with a miracle.

Verse 16. *From Gibeon even unto Gazer* means David defeated the Philistines who were pitched against him in the territory between those two cities.

Verse 17. The nations feared David in the sense of respecting him. They regarded him as a man of such dignity and power that it would be unwise to ignore him.

1 CHRONICLES 15

Verse 1. *City of David* was the borough in Jerusalem otherwise called Mount Zion. These houses were not official buildings, except that they were for the housing of the king's household. *Prepared a place* means he arranged a suitable site to pitch a tent for the ark. We have learned of David's plan to bring the ark to its proper city, and that the plan was temporarily halted over the affair of Uzza; now he will try again.

Verse 2. David profited by the experience of Uzza. The language of this verse implies that Uzza was not a Levite. However, that does not account for his death, for no one was authorized to touch the ark since it was provided with the staves.

Verse 3. We are not to take this to mean each individual of the whole country came to Jerusalem, but the call was for certain representatives *out of* all Israel. This is indicated by the specifications of some verses to follow soon.

Verse 4. *Aaron and the Levites* are mentioned as separate groups. That is because Aaron's family only of the Levites had right to the priesthood.

Verse 5. Kohath was the son of Levi and he was the father of Aaron the priest. At this time that family had increased to 120.

Verses 6, 7. Levi had two other sons besides Kohath. They could not act in the priesthood but had other important activities. Their combined number was 350.

Verse 8. According to Num. 3: 30 Elizaphan was a Kohathite. While not all Kohathites were eligible for the priesthood, their near relation to Aaron made it appropriate that they have a special charge of the articles of service. Among the groups there were certain ones who were considered as chief or outstanding which is the point in this verse.

Verse 9. Ch. 6: 18 shows Hebron was a son of Kohath. He had 80 descendants of whom Eliel was a chief.

Verse 10. Uzziel was another son of Kohath, and the group springing from him numbered 112. Since these men have been singled out in the work of moving the ark, it should be considered in connection with the statement in V. 3 about *all Israel.*

Verses 11, 12. A still more specific appointment was made of the priests and others related, to prepare themselves for the duty of bringing the ark to its place.

Verse 13. David's comment on the tragedy about Uzza is that God had not been sought *after the due order.* That refers to their moving the ark on a cart instead of carrying it with the staves.

Verse 14. *Sanctified themselves* means they got themselves in readiness for the service by whatever might be necessary for their cleansing if they were unclean. Also, the word "sanctify" means to consecrate or devote oneself. Not all men eligible for the priesthood were acting at the same time. Some of these might be engaged in other activities that were lawful, yet which would prevent their taking part in the emergency of moving the ark. David meant for them to dismiss all other engagements and be ready for the special work at hand.

Verse 15. The mistake made in the affair of Uzza was not to be repeated. The Levites bore the ark by placing the staves on their shoulders. This was according to the law of Moses. (Ex. 25: 14.)

Verse 16. These instruments were not originally provided for in the law, but David was a man of God and his works were blessed, all of which indicates that God was favorable towards the instruments.

Verse 17. The various men were to perform their own proper items of the ceremonies. Nothing was left to chance or haphazard action. An old and true saying is, "that which is everybody's business is nobody's business." David avoided such a failure by ordering a set task for the men appointed. In obedience to his directions, the Levites appointed a group of singers under the charge of Heman, son of Joel.

Verse 18. The word *degree* has nothing in the original. The word *second* is from a Hebrew word with a variety of meanings, one of which is "second in order." It therefore does not mean that the men under Zechariah were inferior to those under Heman. All that is meant is that the Levites appointed two groups of singers, each group to be under a leader. The group of V. 17 was mentioned first, and the group of this verse was mentioned second, without any distinction of merit.

Verses 19-21. The various musical instruments named in this passage, together with some words in connection, constitutes an orderly arrangement for the proper musical effect. Some of the words refer to the instrument, and others have in mind the part of music to be played. I have examined the lexicon of Strong, also Smith's Bible Dictionary, and find that Moffatt's rendering of these three verses is correct. I shall therefore quote them for the information of the reader. "Of the singers, Heman, Asaph, and Etham had to beat time with bronze cymbals; Zechariah, Jaaziel, Shemiramoth, Jehiel, Unni, Eliab, Maaseiah, and Benaiah had to lead the praises with lutes set for soprano voices, while Mattithiah, Eliphlehu,

Mikneiah, Obed-edom, Jehiel, and Azariah had to use harps set for bass voices."

Verse 22. *Song* is translated "lifting up" in the margin of some Bibles, and Strong's lexicon agrees with it. Moffatt renders the word "transport" which also agrees with the lexicon. The idea corresponds with our "crescendo" performance in song. From the four verses just considered it is clear that some attention was paid to "parts" in those days. It gives us the example of Old Testament usage, at least, for having the four voices in our church songs.

Verses 23, 24. The ark was to be kept in the tent which David pitched for it. The sacredness of the article made it necessary to have it carefully guarded. The men named in these verses were to serve as guards at the entrance of the tent.

Verse 25. Having arranged his groups of helpers out of the elders and captains, David went to the house of Obed-edom to get the ark. *Ark of the covenant* refers to the tables of the covenant that Moses had put there at Sinai. (Ex. 25: 16.)

Verse 26. Gratitude for favors is one of the finest of principles; especially when it is backed up by some action. The Levites knew it was a very momentous occasion, for it was a sort of correction of the terrible mistake made in the case of Uzza. Now the procedure was going according to the law, and there was evidence that God was blessing the work. In their joy over the goodness of God, they paused to offer these sacrifices. This account does not tell us just when this was done. We again see the advantage of two books covering the same period. 2 Sam. 6: 13 says they made these offerings when they had gone six *paces.* The lexicons are indefinite as to the meaning of this word, defining it as "a step." The thought is that as soon as they had gone a few steps, far enough to see that their mission had the blessing of God, they paused long enough to perform the service of the offerings. They did not wait until the next day, or the next week, or until some "more convenient" time, but did it at once. They gave us an excellent example of devotion to God.

Verse 27. The physical actions of transporting the ark did not require any particular form of dress, but David and the others were attired as described out of respect for the ark of God. While it is not strictly true that "clothes make the man," yet there are times when one's attitude of mind may be indicated by the attention given to outward appearances. When Joseph was called to appear before the king, "he shaved and changed his raiment." (Gen. 41: 14.) It sometimes happens that professed Christians will attend the services of God with much less concern about their dress than they would if going to some social function. They justify their actions on the ground of "comfort," as if it were more necessary to be comfortable in a religious meeting than at a wedding.

Verse 28. *All Israel* brought up the ark. As a quartet of men only would be necessary to carry the ark, it is clear that the term is accommodative. It gives us another light on the expression, "all the congregation," in Ch. 13: 2, 4. *Making a noise.* The first two words are not in the original as separate words. The last is from SHAMA, and Strong defines it, "to hear intelligently." Hence it was not a mere sound they were making, but a service of such a nature as to be understood.

Verse 29. The procession successfully reached its destination. See my comments at 2 Sam. 6: 20-23 on this circumstance.

1 CHRONICLES 16

Verse 1. All of the articles of furniture for the regular services were at Gibeon except the ark. That would constitute an emergency which justified David in making the sacrifices in another manner in Jerusalem. Many items of the law were somewhat neglected under the various difficulties forced upon the nation. Wanton disregard for the ordinances was not passed over, but circumstances for which a leader was not responsible often tempered the justice of God.

Verses 2, 3. A blessing pronounced by a man of authority, such as David, was more than a mere expression of good will. It carried with it the favor of God. These people had just completed a march of some distance, hence the dealing out of food was in order and would be considered one of the blessings.

Verse 4. David again showed his interest in a systematic method by making specific appointments among his men. *Record* does not mean to put something in writing. It is from

ZAKAR and Strong's definition is, "to mark (so as to be recognized), i. e. to remember; by implication to mention." The thought of the verse is concerning gratitude due God for his many favors. These men were to serve continually near the ark, to be praising the Lord, to keep before the minds of the people the wonderful works of God. The principle is similar to that of Peter who would "stir up" the minds by way of "remembrance." (2 Pe. 3: 1.)

Verse 5. These men are mentioned in the preceding chapter, among those who went to bring the ark to Jerusalem. The cymbals were not musical instruments in the strict sense of the word. They were used for about the same purpose as the drums of modern times, and intended to give emphasis to the other instruments, and to indicate the beats.

Verse 6. The trumpets differed from other musical instruments in that they were wind instruments. However, they were not made with valves as are cornets today. They were made of the horns of rams, or of metal in the shape of horns, and the tone was the result of the lip movement in blowing into the cavity of the instrument.

Verse 7. Smith's Bible Dictionary says this of Asaph: "A Levite, son of Berechiah, one of the leaders of David's choir." According to 2 Chr. 29: 30 Asaph was a composer also. David gave him and his brethren the assignment to express the words of verses 8-36. *Psalm* is not in the original because the passage to follow is too general to be covered by the definition of the Hebrew word for Psalm. That word is MIZMOUR, and Strong's definition is, "from ZAMAR; properly, instrumental music; by implication a poem set to notes." While on the subject I shall give the reader Strong's definition of ZAMAR, referred to in the preceding definition. "A primitive root; properly to touch the strings or parts of a musical instrument, i. e. play upon it; to make music, accompanied by the voice; hence to celebrate in song and music." We can see why the writer of 1 Chronicles did not call the passage a psalm. It contains so much "doctrine" and historical information that he made an indefinite introduction and allowed the subject matter to speak for itself.

Verse 8. They should not only have a thankful heart, but should let the people know of the deeds that prompted it.

Verse 9. See comments at V. 7 for meaning of "psalm."

Verse 10. The glory of the Lord means very little to those who do not seek him; rejoicing is in store for the ones who do.

Verse 11. The important thought is in the word *continually*. Some people seek the Lord when convenient or when in special trouble. True servants are those who are constant in their devotion.

Verse 12. The things God does are great and many persons will extol them. But the same people often reject the teaching of God, while the truth is that the divine judgments are as wonderful as are the works of his hands.

Verse 13. Israel is one of the names for Jacob, and his people were the chosen of God. Such a favor should bring forth the best of service.

Verse 14. Even where the written Word of God is not known, there is great evidence of his wisdom in the arrangement of the universe, of which the earth is a small part.

Verse 15. God is always true to his covenants, although the generations for whom they were made often forget.

Verses 16, 17. This passage specifies the covenant David had in mind in the preceding verse. We should not forget that he was inspired and the teaching in this outstanding passage is that of God. The three fathers, Abraham and Isaac and Jacob, are named as a group, yet an important distinction is made between the first two as against the third. The covenant is said to have been *made* with Abraham and considered as an *oath* with Isaac. But it was not *confirmed* until the day of Jacob. This should always be considered when studying the length of Israel's sojourn in Egypt, in connection with Gal. 3: 17. That passage says the law was 430 years after the covenant was *confirmed*. The verse of the present paragraph shows that the covenant was confirmed in the time of Jacob. We know that it was in the days of Jacob that the children of Israel entered Egypt, corresponding with the time the covenant was *confirmed*. Then, since the law came 430 years after the covenant was confirmed, and also since the law came just after their coming out of Egypt, the conclusion is that the sojourn in Egypt was 430 years. See also my comments at length at Gen. 15: 13-15.

Verse 18. The three fathers named in the preceding paragraph never lived to see the promised land possessed. The exhortation here is addressed to the *seed of Israel*, (V. 13), because they were the ones who lived to see the promise carried out. *Lot of your inheritance* means that the Israel of David's day were the heirs of the country promised to the fathers.

Verse 19. As late as the time the covenant was *confirmed* in Jacob, the number of the group was only 70. (Gen. 46: 27.)

Verses 20, 21. As far back as the days of Abraham this declaration of God's care was true. See Gen. 12: 17 for an instance of it.

Verse 22. In Gen. 20: 7 Abraham is called a prophet, and the king of Gerar was reproved for his treatment of the patriarch. That proves the statement of this verse.

Verse 23. *All the earth* means all the people of the earth, not the material planet as in Psa. 19: 1. This *earth* is to *shew forth* salvation, which indicates the intelligent creatures on the earth are meant.

Verse 24. *Heathen* and *nations* may often be used interchangeably. In this verse the first refers specifically to individuals of foreign blood, the second to groups of persons formed into units of government. Both kinds of humanity were to be informed of the glory of the Lord.

Verse 25. The word *fear* has two meanings; one is to respect, the other to dread. The connection must determine in each case which is meant. This verse directs us to *praise* and *fear* the same Being, so we know the fear required is "respect." Idolatry was almost universally practiced, hence the contrast between the Lord and all false gods.

Verse 26. *The heavens* means the material world, and everything in it was worshiped as idols. The point of the writer is that the very things that were adored by the heathen as gods, were themselves the work of the true God.

Verse 27. The greatest *glory* and *honor* one can have is to be in the presence of his Lord. It is true also that the *strength* that comes from *gladness*, and the *gladness* that comes from *strength*, can be had only in the *place* or locality occupied by the Lord. We may be in that place, spiritually now, and personally in the future, if we serve him faithfully while here.

Verse 28. It is impossible for people actually to give strength to the Lord. It means to give him the glory for all true strength or greatness possessed by anyone.

Verse 29. The name *Lord* is from the Hebrew YEHOVAH, sometimes spelled YAHWEH. It is defined by Strong, "The self-Existent or Eternal; Jehovah, Jewish national name of God." Young defines it, "He (who) is." The word occurs several hundred times in the Hebrew Old Testament. In view of the meaning and extensive use of the term, we should not be surprised at the statement of the writer of glory due to the Holy Name.

Verse 30. The security of the earth is dependent on the Lord, therefore the *fear* called for means "respect."

Verse 31. The *heaven* and *earth* are material things and cannot rejoice; but the creatures in them can, and are called upon to do so. They also are bidden to acknowledge the Lord as the one who is reigning.

Verse 32. *Fields . . . all that is therein.* Dumb creatures do not know how to express joy in its true sense. However, the pleasure that is enjoyed by them is due to the might and goodness of God, and that is the meaning of the writer.

Verse 33. To the eye of the true worshiper of the Lord, even the trees furnish subjects for song. (1 Ki. 5: 32, 33.) To sing at thought of God's judgments implies that they are just.

Verse 34. *Endureth* has no word in the original. The strength of the sentence is in the word *ever*, and means there is no time when God's mercy does not exist. Man is merciful at times, but God always has mercy for those entitled to it.

Verse 35. Contrary to a common notion, the word *heathen* does not necessarily mean uncivilized people. It refers to the peoples of the world in general who are not of the chosen race belonging to God.

Verse 36. *For ever and ever.* The simple word *ever* means "always," and is unlimited. The repetition, therefore, is for emphasis.

Verse 37. This repeats the announcement made in verses 4, 5, which see. The task was daily but might be varied according to the performances of the worshipers.

Verse 38. The special charge of Obed-edom was to guard the tent containing the ark, that David had pitched in Zion for it.

Verses 39, 40. After the ark was captured by the Philistines, the tabernacle became reduced in its importance. It was not entirely abandoned, for Solomon went there to make his great sacrificial offerings. But it was located at Gibeon by some circumstance not revealed to us. The brazen altar was there, hence David made the appointment stated, for the priests to preside over the animal sacrifices offered at that place. The priests were normally the ones to have charge of that work.

Verses 41, 42. The performance of animal sacrifices combined the activities of the priests and the ones making the offering. At the same time, David arranged for the other exercises to accompany the offerings. See the comments on this subject at Ch. 15: 19-22. *Musical instruments of God* is an inspired expression. David was never condemned, nor even criticized for making and using them. But it was a part of the procedure under the Old Testament regulations and has no bearing on the religious activities of the New Testament. The *porters* were gatekeepers or janitors.

Verse 43. The great service on occasion of installing the ark in its tent was ended. The assembly departed for their private homes, and David also returned to his home in Mount Zion. With the authority of a king and the effectiveness of an inspired man, he bestowed on his household his blessing.

1 CHRONICLES 17

Verse 1. David had built himself a house, for which Hiram, King of Tyre, had furnished men and materials. (Ch. 14: 1, 2.) But the ark was kept in a tent which seemed inappropriate. He felt unworthy to have a better dwelling-house than was provided for the ark of God. The mere statement of this fact was all he said to Nathan the prophet. This was a different man from Nathan the son of David.

Verse 2. Prophets were inspired to write or speak when God wished to give some communication through them. (Heb. 1: 1.) At other times they were as other men, and might express an opinion that would prove to be in error. David had been so well favored of the Lord that Nathan supposed he would approve of the plan to build a house.

Verse 3. This verse gives a clear instance of how God worked with his prophets. When he had some communication he wished to give, he would contact the man for the service. It was done in the case of Samuel (1 Sam. 3: 4), and once with Isaiah. (2 Ki. 19: 20, 21.)

Verses 4, 5. There was but one tabernacle built by Moses which was used all through the wandering. But it was moved from place to place, which is the meaning of *from tent to tent*, etc. The same tent (tabernacle) was used for many generations after the children of Israel got settled in Canaan.

Verse 6. The point in this verse is that no reason existed for David's feeling of neglect, for God had not made any complaint at not having a house for his name.

Verses 7-9. It is best to group these verses into one paragraph because of the one thought running through them. David feared that he would be charged with indifference toward the matters of the Lord, and that the nation might be in danger of some penalty for the neglect. Against such an idea the Lord recalled the promotion that had been made for him, elevating him from the humble calling of tending sheep to the great honor of being king of God's people. And no fear needed to have been felt as to the security of the people, for the cutting off of the enemy nations was evidence that God would not neglect his inheritance. Therefore, the absence of a building for the Lord was not endangering the welfare of the nation.

Verse 10. The watch-care of God had continued through the long period of the judges, and it was destined still to continue. All of these things were said to David to set his mind at ease as to the immediate necessity for a permanent building. However, lest he might get the impression that God opposed his desire because it was wrong to build a house, he was told that such a structure would yet be built. He will be told later why he was not permitted to build it.

Verse 11. Many of the predictions made in olden times, both favorable and unfavorable, were to be fulfilled on the generations after the ones to whom the predictions were made. (Gen. 12: 3; 48: 22, 2 Ki. 20: 17-19.) It was good news to David to be told that his son was to continue in the kingdom after him.

Verse 12. Had it been wrong in principle to have a permanent structure, God would not permit anyone to build it. The reason why David was not permitted to build the house is stated in Ch. 22: 8, 9, which will be commented upon in the proper place. *For ever* means "throughout the age." Had all things gone well, the house and throne built and enjoyed by Solomon would have continued to the end of the (Jewish) age. The Babylonian Captivity was brought on because of the disobedience of the nation, and it made an interruption into the existence of the temple and reign of the nation over which Solomon had been king.

Verse 13. *Father* and *son* are named in this way to express the closeness that was to exist between God and the king. *Him that was before thee* refers to Saul, who became so unworthy that God withdrew all favors from him and permitted him to die in disgrace. Solomon was chastened of the Lord, but did not end his days as did Saul.

Verses 14, 15. *Forever* and *evermore* are explained by my comments in V. 12. The communication was delivered to Nathan the prophet and he gave it to David. (Heb. 1: 1.)

Verses 16-19. Gratitude is again expressed by David for the great attention God gave to him. He was humble and felt unworthy of such favors. He was unselfish also in that he appreciated the promises that were to be fulfilled after his death.

Verse 20. In those days of prevailing idolatry it was especially appropriate to contrast the God of Israel with all the heathen gods.

Verse 21. Two great events in the history of the children of Israel are referred to; deliverance from Egypt and settling in Canaan. Both required a powerful hand, for Egypt was a strong nation and Canaan was being usurped by strong idolatrous nations. God took his chosen race and gave them success over all foes. A *name . . . terribleness.* The second word is from the same Hebrew word as "reverend" in Psa. 111: 9. One meaning of it is, "to revere." The expression means to respect the name of God. It is true also that the name of God means something terrible in the common sense of the word, to those who will not respect it. The heathen nations learned to their sorrow how terrible it was to show disrespect for the holy name of God.

Verse 22. In the general sense of the word *ever*, God designed Israel to be his people to the end of that age. In an extended and moral sense, he offered to make them his beloved possession endlessly on condition of their faithfulness to him.

Verse 23. David gladly submitted to the plans of the Lord, and connected himself with the house that was to be built. That is, he regarded his own honor as being bound up with that of the house.

Verse 24. The worthy motive of David's wish was that God's name might be magnified. His own glory was not important, but it was more desirable to have the glory of God's name become manifest to the idolatrous nations.

Verses 25-27. The promises of God gave David the heart to offer this prayer. That principle is true today with the true servants of God. By the same token we may justly conclude that when a professed follower of the Lord does not have the heart to pray, it is because he does not believe the promises made by the Lord.

1 CHRONICLES 18

Verse 1. This book is a general collection of the outstanding facts concerning the nation of God. It does not claim to give all the details, neither does it profess to be always connected chronologically. We have just read a psalm and prayer of David for the promise made to him concerning the house to be built by his son. Now the sacred writer or historian goes into some of the military operations of the great man of God. We shall finally learn that David was not permitted to build the house of God because of his warlike activities. It was consistent, therefore, for the writer to break away from the happy subject of the temple to be built in the future, and to take up the narrative of David's military movements.

Verse 2. *Brought gifts.* See my comments at Gen. 32: 13 on the meaning of this.

Verses 3, 4. Gen. 15: 18 shows that Abraham's descendants were to possess the territory reaching as far as the River Euphrates. It was never fully realized until the days of Solomon, (1 Ki. 4: 21), but was partially taken by David. It was necessary, though, for him to be on the alert to hold the points taken. At this time he went on one of such missions, and on the way encountered this man Hadarezer and took over his holdings as far as Hamath. *Houghed the horses* means he cut the tendons of the horses that is a part of the leg near the hoof. That would disable the animal for use yet leave him in possession of his strength otherwise, thus making him a care or burden.

Verse 5. The Syrians were north of Canaan and often showed their sympathy for the foes of Israel. They thought of helping Hadarezer against David, but were met with great defeat and loss of their own forces.

Verse 6. A garrison is a fortified post in the territory of an enemy, or at least a territory in doubt. Syriadamascus means that part of Syria in which was located Damascus, the capital. The garrisons placed there would be for preventing another attempt like the one just made on behalf of Hadarezer. It brought the Syrians into subjection to David to the extent that they gave him "gifts." See comments at Gen. 32: 13 on the meaning of such gifts.

Verse 7. These shields of gold were valuable as precious metal, not as implements of war, as far as David was concerned.

Verse 8. Among the cities which David took from Hadarezer there was much brass or bronze. This proved to be useful in the future, when Solomon son of David, came to the work of the temple and its vessels of service.

Verses 9, 10. Tou, also spelled Toi, had previously been oppressed by Hadarezer. He was therefore thankful for the relief resulting from David's work, and expressed his appreciation in a practical way. He not only sent his son to congratulate him on his success, but sent useful materials to him in the nature of these "gifts."

Verse 11. Whenever David subdued the enemy he took from them their valuables, which he reserved to be used in the service of the Lord.

Verse 12. Abishai was one of David's mighty men. This verse is put in at this place because it is another item in the long list of the exploits against the numerous foes of the Israelites. The *valley of salt* was a broad open plain just south of the Dead Sea. This Sea was otherwise called Salt Sea, which accounts for the name of this valley. The territory of the Edomites was not far from the Dead Sea.

Verse 13. See V. 6 for explanation of the garrisons and their use. The ability to plant them was evidence of success against an enemy, hence the words *thus the Lord preserved David*.

Verse 14. *All Israel* is significant because at first he reigned only over one tribe. *Judgment and justice* means his decisions were wise and fair to all.

Verses 15-17. See the remarks at 2 Sam. 8: 16-18 on the cabinet of David.

1 CHRONICLES 19

Verses 1, 2. Gratitude is one of the finest principles, and David always manifested a great degree of it. His kingdom was secular as well as religious, hence he would have more or less to do with the kingdoms around him. Such dealings might be agreeable or otherwise, depending on the conduct of those kingdoms. The Ammonites had been generally against the Israelites, but one particular king of that people had shown some kind of favor to David. We are not told what that was, but David sought to show his gratitude by expressing his sympathy to his son.

Verse 3. Gratitude is indeed an excellent trait, and therefore to reject it is an indication of an opposite one. Without any investigation that we know of, the son of the former king of the Ammonites listened to the suggestions of his princes, who imputed to David a bad motive in sending his servants to console him.

Verse 4. Hanun did not wish to do any bodily harm to the servants of David; he planned only to humiliate them. Most men wore their beards at the natural length in those days. They were cherished because of the masculine significance. To rob a man of the natural ornament meant to deprive him of one sign of manhood. And men usually wore outer garments consisting of long robes, reaching nearly to the ground. To cut away the lower half of these garments not only exposed their bodies to shame, but would force them to become an offense to others. Hanun imposed both these indignities on the servants of David.

Verse 5. Being under orders from their king, the men were faithfully journeying on their return although very much humiliated. Some persons informed David of the circumstance and his humane spirit again showed itself. The replacement of the clothing could have been done at once, but it would take some time to grow another beard. Jericho was not a very conspicuous city, so the king permitted his servants to remain there until their beards were grown.

Verses 6-8. *Odious* means they realized they had offended David. They could have avoided serious trouble with him by proper acknowledgements, but their pride prevented them from doing so. They concluded that David would make war on them, for their insults to his men meant insults to him. They prepared for the conflict by hiring men out of Mesopotamia and other places, to come and help them in their conflict with David. Such allies today are called mercenaries, meaning men who fight for money and not because of sympathy for the cause for which they pretend to be fighting. Mesopotamia was the country east of the Euphrates, and Syria-maachah was a small district in the territory of Syria, which lay nearer Palestine. Military forces from these communities were induced to come to the aid of Hanun, and they pitched their camp before Medeba, a town just east of the Jordan. The Ammonites brought their forces and joined themselves to their hired allies to fight against David.

Verse 9. While the Ammonites were allies in this battle, they arrayed themselves as units distinct from the forces hired to help them. They operated near the gate of the city, and their hired allies were out in the field. That was a piece of good strategy, because it presented two fronts to the other side.

Verses 10, 11. Joab was an expert in war, however, and planned at once to meet the challenge. He formed a special detachment from the Israelites, composed of the *choice* men. The original for this means a young man. With this special group he proposed to contact the hired forces, and gave the rest of the Israelite soldiers into the hands of his brother Abishai to contact the Ammonites, the ones starting the war.

Verse 12. This verse shows more good judgment. No one could tell in advance which unit of an enemy would be the stronger, and to make special plans of attack with that question in doubt would be a risk; the method David proposed would avoid that uncertainty. Another lesson we may obtain from the circumstance is that of cooperation and the strong helping the weak. The New Testament puts much stress on that idea as may be seen in Rom. 15: 1 and 1 Cor. 12.

Verse 13. David showed a fine spirit of resignation to the will of God in his statement to his brother. He proposed that they do their best in the battle, then leave the result with the Lord. That should be the motive of all who profess to serve God. We are not responsible for the results of doing right. If we do what God directs us to do, he will take all the care about what comes from it. On the other hand, if we act upon our own wisdom and desires, we must be held responsible for all.

Verse 14. The very sight of Joab with his forces caused the hired soldiers to flee. Having no interest at stake but the money they were to receive, they would not stand their ground against danger.

Verse 15. Fear is contagious. Seeing their allies were running from the contest, the Ammonites fled also. They entered the city which was Medeba. As the enemy had all deserted the field of action, David returned to Jerusalem which was his capital.

Verse 16. The Syrians had very little interest in the cause when they entered the alliance with the Ammonites, except the money they were to receive. But the "pride of life" is another strong sentiment, and they were goaded by it into trying once more to "save their face" by calling on their own people for help. The *river* means the Euphrates, which was one boundary of Mesopotamia. The terms *Syria* and *Assyria* are sometimes used interchangeably because of some points of relation common to both. But when the subject under consideration is strictly geographical and political, Syria was directly north of Palestine and Damascus was the capital. Assyria was east of the Euphrates and Nineveh was the capital.

Verse 17. When David heard of the new plans of the enemy he did not wait for their advances. Crossing over Jordan, (since that territory was a part of the promised land according to Gen. 15: 18), he moved on the enemy.

Verse 18. The chariots mentioned in the Bible usually are vehicles used in war. To state that a number of chariots was slain means the men of those chariots were slain. Some men in the war forces were on foot, and 40,000 of such soldiers were slain by

David in the encounter. The captain of all the forces also was slain.

Verse 19. The servants had offered to fight with the Syrian leaders against David. When they saw that it was a losing battle they came to terms with him. The Syrians realized also that it was foolish to think of overcoming the children of Israel, so they refused any further alliance with the Ammonites.

1 CHRONICLES 20

Verses 1, 2. This corresponds with the account in 2 Sam. 11: 1, but nothing is said here about the affair with Bath-sheba and her husband, although it is the same period. *After the year was expired* means the time of year had come when the kings waged a campaign of war. David was the king and hence was commander-in-chief of all the forces. He directed Joab, his general of highest rank, to lead the army out in the war with the Ammonites, while he, the king, tarried at home. It was at this time that David had his affair with Bath-sheba. At that time Joab attacked the royal city of Rabbah and captured the king. As a loyal subordinate, Joab turned the conquest over to his chief, who took the crown from the head of the captured king. This crown weighed 100 pounds, made of gold. *It was set upon David's head* means the jewel of precious stones was placed on his head, not the heavy crown. There was much other valuable material in the royal city of the Ammonites, and David took possession of that.

Verse 3. *Them* is not in the original and should not have been in the translation for it conveys a false impression. The verse means that David made these people work for him by using cutting tools and other implements of iron.

Verse 4. While on the subject of the Israelite successes, the historian tells of the fight that Sibbechai, one of David's guard, had with the Philistines at Gezer. He slew a member of one of the group of giants, which brought the enemy under there.

Verse 5. This verse singles out another personal encounter with the giant forces. A brother of the noted Goliath was the personal contestant this time. The mentioning of the weight of his spear handle was to give some idea of the strength and size of the Philistine; that he was no ordinary antagonist.

Verses 6-8. These men of the Philistines were abnormally large and strong. The description of them was given that we might have an idea that no force amounts to much when arrayed against the servants of the Lord.

1 CHRONICLES 21

Verses 1, 2. This verse should be read as an explanation of 2 Sam. 24: 1, where it sounds as if the Lord induced David to number Israel. It is an established rule of literature that where two different accounts are given of the same event, the easier one should be used to explain the other. We know that God would not cause a man to do a certain thing, then punish him for doing so. Therefore, the whole story is that God was angry with David because he allowed Satan to mislead him.

Verse 3. The speech of Joab indicates the motive of David in ordering this enumeration of the people. He was especially interested in numerical strength, which would rather be a questioning of the power of God, which can operate independently of the great numbers of man. When a man decides to do a thing with the wrong motive, even if that thing would be right in itself, he is liable to neglect some duty connected with it. David was guilty of such neglect as we shall see. Joab was a wise man and saw through the purposes of his king, and tried to get him to change his mind.

Verse 4. We again see the loyalty of Joab. Although he felt sure a mistake was about to be made, he prepared to carry out the word of his chief.

Verses 5, 6. There is a difference of numbers between the two accounts of this transaction. I have explained it at the other place in 2 Sam. 24: 9.

Verse 7. *Smote Israel.* This was according to the threat God made in connection with this subject. (Ex. 30: 12.)

Verse 8. The penitence of David again showed itself and the reason he was said to be a man after God's own heart. (1 Sam. 13: 14.) It was not because he never made any mistakes, for all men do that, but because he always was fair and honest about it afterward. He did not try to justify himself in his wrong but confessed that he had "sinned greatly."

Verses 9, 10. The national prophet was Gad, who was directed to give a message from God to David. (Heb. 1: 1). The threat of a plague was already made in the passage in Exodus referred to above. So there must be some form of punishment brought, but God was lenient in that he allowed David to have something to say about it.

Verse 11, 12. Gad told David to select one of the three punishments named. *Famine* would affect the nourishment of his people; the *sword* would affect their lives violently; *pestilence* would affect them through some kind of disease. These three things, "famine, pestilence and the sword," seem to have been a familiar combination of calamities in the history and prophecies of old times. (Jer. 14: 12, Ezk. 5: 12.)

Verse 13. Of the three misfortunes threatened, David regarded the last as offering the greatest opportunity for the Lord's mercy. He had much confidence in the divine compassion, therefore he chose that proposal.

Verse 14. The first effect of the pestilence was the death of 70,000 men.

Verse 15. Chronologically speaking, this verse should come after the next two. God sent the destroying angel to attack Jerusalem and the work was begun. But the plea of David (soon to be considered) caused the mercy of God to "repent," which means he was to *change* his decree against Jerusalem.

Verse 16. The sight of such a misfortune upon his capital city caused David to feel sorrowful. He and his "elders" or leading men put sackcloth over their bodies and got down to the ground, having their faces downward. That was a practice of those times when one wished to express great anxiety and penitence.

Verse 17. The fine character of David was manifested on so many occasions. Many persons in royal position feel so important that consideration for others is absent from their minds. The thing that grieved David was the fact that others were having to suffer for his misdeeds. *These sheep* was said to indicate his sense of responsibility. As king over the people, he regarded himself as one who should have protected them as a shepherd would his sheep. Instead of doing that, he had brought harm to his flock by his own acts. In such a frame of mind he begged the Lord to lift the affliction from the innocent and place it on the guilty.

Verse 18. The Lord heard the plea of David and decided to grant it. He was commanded through the prophet Gad, the national prophet at that time, to build an altar. It was to be built *to the Lord*, which means that the Lord was to be given some service by it. A threshing floor was an open space that was used on which to pile the harvested grain, to beat it in the process of separating the chaff from the grain. There could have been other places just as suitable for the erection of an altar, but the Lord had a special purpose in mind when he directed that David use this place.

Verses 19, 20. *Turned back* comes from one original and means that Ornan looked up from his threshing and beheld the angel, (in the form of a man), and he and his sons were so shocked at the sight that they hid themselves. Wheat threshing was a very important work, and Ornan would not have paused in it had the circumstances not been unusually impressive.

Verse 21. Ornan must have recognized David on sight, and followed the prevailing custom of bowing in a gesture of profound respect.

Verse 22. God's instructions for David to build the altar at this particular place brought him in contact with the owner, since it was the threshing time and he would be on the ground then. That gave him opportunity for proposing the purchasing of the property. *Full price* meant he wanted to pay the actual value of the real estate, not merely a "token" payment. David not only told Ornan the use he wished to make of the ground, but also the result he hoped to accomplish; to turn away the plague from the people.

Verse 23. Ornan was a Jebusite which means he was of the ancient inhabitants of Jerusalem. He doubtless was familiar with the practices of the worshipers under the Mosaic system of altar service. He wished to contribute the articles for the service by donating the ground as a site for the altar. Besides that, he knew that the law called for animals for the blood sacrifices, and offered the oxen for the purpose. These animals were being used at that moment in the threshing. The work was done by heaping the reaped straw on the ground, then driving the oxen round and round to trample out the grain from the husk so that the wind could separate the wheat from the chaff. (Deut. 25: 4.) *Threshing instruments*. The second word does not appear in the original as a separate word. The two are from a Hebrew word that means "a sledge." It was used to haul the crop from the field to the threshing floor. It was made of wood and Ornan was willing for it to be used for fire in the sacrifice. The law provided for meat (meal or grain) offering, and the material for such an offering was naturally available since the work of threshing was going on then. We can thus see that "all things were ready" for an important religious performance. Ornan offered to contribute the entire list free of charge for David's use.

Verse 24. In this verse David gives us a view of what constitutes a genuine sacrifice. Unless we give up something of value, or give that which costs us some real value, we have not made any sacrifice. Many professed servants of God shrink from a service that would interfere with their personal interests. When they have looked after all of their personal matters, if there is any time or money left, they want to offer it to God. Such conduct puts God second in the line and there is no evidence that service offered on such terms will be accepted.

Verse 25. *By weight* means that no guessing was done as to the price to be paid for the property. After the full price of it had been determined, the amount was exchanged on a legal basis according to the established table of weights and measures.

Verse 26. *Called upon the Lord* is said in connection with the offerings David made on the altar. That indicates that calling upon the Lord consists in more than merely speaking his name. There must be some practical evidence of devotion if one expects the Lord to recognize the "call." It is the same today, and we have a specific instance of the subject in Acts 2: 16. These *burnt offerings* and *peace offerings* are described in Lev. 1 and 3.

Verse 27. The Lord was entreated by the offerings of David, and commanded the destroying angel to cease the use of his sword.

Verse 28. David made some sacrifices with his plea to God for mercy. The plea was granted, and he then made additional offerings in gratitude for the divine favor. That was another fine example and one that is worthy of following today. Many people will pray or do other religious services when they are in trouble. When the trouble is removed they will forget God and give themselves over to their own personal interests.

Verses 29, 30. In spite of the fact that God caused the angel to withdraw the sword from the slaughtering, David was so overawed by the whole procedure that he hesitated about going to the institution that was at Gibeon. He therefore was content to perform the service on the altar he built on the ground purchased from Ornan.

1 CHRONICLES 22

Verse 1. David was told that he could not build the house of the Lord. He was permitted, however, to do some preparatory work for it, and this verse is an introduction to that subject. *This is the house* means, "this is what I propose to do in preparation for the house of the Lord."

Verse 2. *Strangers* is from a word that means foreigners or aliens. The work of hewing stone was purely secular, so it was appropriate to employ such men in that work. The church should not call upon any but its members to participate in the congregational worship. But it would be altogether lawful to employ a man of the world to do any secular work needed.

Verse 3. The *joinings* were some kind of clamps to be used where nails alone would not be sufficient. *Brass without weight* means that he did not take the trouble to weigh it; he just got a great amount of it ready.

Verse 4. Tyre and Zidon (sometimes spelled Sidon) were prominent cities of Phoenicia, a country just north and west of Palestine. It included a part of the land where the famous "cedars of Lebanon" grew, and the inhabitants of these cities delivered much of this timber to David as a gift from a neighbor country.

Verse 5. Having been told that his son would be permitted to build the house of the Lord, David did what he could to help by having some things in readiness. *Young and tender* means he was inexperienced, being young, and David was desirous of having the building made properly. *Magnifical* means large and conspicuous. It was to be of such proportions as would impress the people of the surrounding countries. The closing sentence indicates the general scope of the verse and the others of the chapter preceding this one. That is, David did what he was permitted to do by way of preparation for the building that his son was to construct. All of this was going on before Solomon knew of the conversation the Lord had with his father relative to the temple.

Verse 6. After making the preparations referred to above, David informed his son of the same, and explained why the work was to be left for him to do.

Verses 7, 8. David did not want him to think that his father was putting some task upon his shoulders in order to be relieved of the responsibility. He told him it had been his desire to do the great work but was not permitted to do so. And now we have the statement as to why David was not permitted to build the house. It was not because of any personal defects, for he certainly would have compared favorably with Solomon in that. The reason is given in the statement, *thou hast shed blood abundantly*. This shedding of blood had reference to war.

Verse 9. The reason that Solomon was to build the house is given in the statement, "who shall be a man of rest." A question might come to the mind of the reader, if this would not constitute a charge against David personally. It would not, because the Lord even commanded the destruction of the heathen nations through war. The key to the proposition is the fact that the material temple was to be a type of the immaterial church. Christ was to be the builder of the church, and he is represented in the scriptures as the "prince of peace." (Isa. 9: 6.) It was therefore appropriate that the type of the church be erected by a man who was free from wars. It is true that Solomon caused the death of three men. (1 Ki. 3.) But they were slain under the criminal section of the civil law and not by the sword of *war*, which was the item under consideration with Solomon. It is true that in all of the activities of the "wise monarch," and his contact with so many foreign nations, he never had to resort to war to accomplish the desired results. In harmony with that truth he alone reached the full enjoyment of the promise as to subjugation of the entire promised land. (Gen. 15: 18, 1 Ki. 4: 21.)

Verse 10. The terms *father* and *son* are used as figures of speech, to give the idea of nearness and affectionate cooperation.

Verse 11. The absence of bitterness in David's attitude is gratifying. He must have been disappointed at being denied the honor of building the house of the Lord. But it did not cause him to show the least resentment toward another who was given the work. Instead, he manifested a spirit of absolute unselfishness, both in his speech and actions, by wishing Solomon good fortune in the work, and by furnishing some of the material. A common trait would have caused him to fling the proposition from him with the attitude of, "Well, if some one else is to have the honor of the job, he can just have all the burden also, and I will not have a thing to do with it."

Verses 12, 13. *Wisdom* and *understanding*. There is very little difference between these words. If a technical distinction is made, the first means the natural intelligence, the second the information a person has acquired by the proper use of the natural intellect. The three words, *law, statutes* and *judgments* are used in this paragraph. There are some more words with slight difference, yet with some minor distinction. The first pertains to the government as a whole; the second means the formal enactments of the governments; the third has special reference to the decisions of God, made necessary by some issue arising from the indefiniteness of the statutes. This paragraph closes with an encouraging word of cheer, and inviting his son to take courage for the great work before him.

Verse 14. *In my trouble*. The last word is from ONI and is defined by Strong, "depression, i. e. misery." He further says it is from another Hebrew word that means, to depress, literally or figuratively," and has been rendered in the A. V. by, "abase self, deal hardly with, submit self." The statement in Ch. 29: 3 should also be considered in this connection, where David is speaking on the same subject, and where he distinguishes between his personal assets and those of his royal income. The central thought in the passage of this paragraph is, David was disappointed in not being permitted to build the house of God. But he would not let that slow him down any in doing what he could to prepare stuff for Solomon's use. In the midst of his concern, and at great sacrifice from his private possessions, he had "earmarked" the amounts named to be used by his son in the work of the temple. *Without weight* means he did not take the time to weigh the brass; just got together a vast amount of it regardless of its weight, since it was so plentiful. David did not expect what he had collected to be all that might be needed, he therefore suggested that Solomon might add to it.

Verse 15. The workmen of Tyre and Zidon had offered their services to David in some other building projects, now they may be available for Solomon when needed.

Verse 16. *No number* is a figurative expression, meaning there was no end to the resources for all these materials. With such an opportunity, Solomon was urged by his father to set himself about the task before him.

Verses 17-19. David was near the end of his life and therefore he was making these immediate arrangements for his son, who was soon to take actual charge of the kingdom. As an aid to him, the leading men of Israel were commanded to work with him. Their services had been needed previously in the defense of the country. That need was past, and the Lord had given them rest from their enemies. They were free, therefore, to turn their attention to peacetime activities. The special reason for the building program being prepared was to provide a permanent place for the ark. It was then in the tent that David had pitched for it in Jerusalem.

1 CHRONICLES 23

Verse 1. *Made Solomon king*. This means he made him acting king, not that he occupied the throne. That kind of action was never done lawfully while the rightful ruler was living. But David had become infirm near the end of his life, and some unrest had been created by persons who wanted the throne. To settle the dispute while he lived, David made it clear to his people that Solomon was to be king after him. See the account of the controversy about the rulership in 1 Kings 1.

Verse 2. *Princes* is a very commonly used word in the Old Testament. It comes from various Hebrew words, but the general meaning is, one who has prestige or influence, not necessarily one in official standing. The definition given by Strong for the word is, "a head person (of any rank or class)." So the word could sometimes include men in official position, but the term would be applied to them on account of their personal influence, not because of their official standing. This accounts for the mention of the *princes*, and *with* the priests and Levites.

Verse 3. The numbering of the people was done at different times, and the rules or limits to regulate the list were also different at times. On the occasion of this verse the beginning age for the Levites was 30 years. *Polls* means heads, and there were 38,000 of them at that time.

Verse 4. *Set forward* means to oversee or engage actively in the work. 24,000 of the numbered Levites were given such a charge. 6,000 were officers and judges, which means they were the technical authorities over the work.

Verse 5. The porters were doorkeepers or janitors. The other 4,000 made up the choir.

Verse 6. *Courses* means divisions or sections or groups. The three sons of Levi had been dead for centuries, but the lines of their descendants were in existence. David formulated the three lines into groups in such a way that each man could know from which of the three sons of their common father he had come.

Verses 7-11. The descendants of each of the three sons of Levi were next divided and designated into their individual groups. This paragraph concerns the men who descended from Gershon.

Verse 12. Kohath was another son of Levi. He had four sons, but Amram was the only one who had any special significance. That was due to his relation to the priesthood as will be seen and explained in the following verse.

Verse 13. We have been told a number of times that the priesthood belonged exclusively to Aaron and his sons, and to their lineal descendants. This verse contains that information, but goes further with the information about the priesthood. It gives us the very item that was the exclusive right of the priests, which was the burning of incense. The supervision of the sacrifices was in their hands, and they were the ones who generally took the active part at the altar, but the restrictions were not as close on that. Others than priests were permitted to officiate in offering sacrifices. As instances, we will cite the cases of Samuel (1 Sam. 16: 2) and David (2 Sam. 6: 17). But no one who was not of the sons of Aaron could participate in the burning of incense. There is an outstanding case of error regarding this in 2 Chr. 26: 18.

Verses 14-20. *Man of God* was said of Moses in view of his special work as leader of the people, and the lawgiver for God. He is named in the paragraph because he was of the tribe of Levi, as was Aaron his brother. Nothing outstanding can be said of his sons or their families, but they are given "honorable mention" because of the great importance of their father. The reader should not confuse the son of Moses, Gershom, with Gershon, son of Levi. Note the difference in the last letters.

Verses 21-23. Merari was the third son of Levi according to the list recorded here and elsewhere. The instance of Eleazar's daughters marrying their cousins, the sons of Kish, was according to Num. 36: 6.

Verse 24. *Chief of the fathers* shows that not every individual person who was born after Levi was named. The list of *polls* or heads included only those *that did the work*. The age limit finally was reduced to twenty years and over. See the comments at verse 3 on this subject.

Verses 25-27. This group of verses really should be considered in direct connection with the preceding one. By lowering the age limit of the Levites, (which was done by David near the end of his life), it increased the number of men who would be taken into the list. It would also reduce the average physical strength of the men by including those ten years younger than the ones at first numbered. But the Lord had given them rest from the enemy nations, relieving them of the hardships of the activities in the field. These men were to be in Jerusalem and be always ready to do the manual labor necessary for the duties of the priests. Another thing, the temple was about to be erected, and the headquarters of the nation would not be moved from place to place as was necessary while they depended on the tabernacle. Therefore, the service required for the assistance to the priests would be near home all the time, so that any man twenty years old or over could perform the service.

Verse 28. There is always some work required in connection with the religious service that is not strictly religious in its nature. This includes such as washing the animals, and the care of the building with its doors and various apartments. This work was performed by these men that were numbered from twenty years and upward.

Verse 29. This specifies some of the items of preparatory work in connection with the temple service. Somebody had to do the manual work of baking the loaves of unleavened bread that were placed on the table of shewbread each Sabbath. There were also many calls for cakes and bread to be offered on the altar of burnt sacrifices. (Lev. 2.) This created a demand for such articles and these men were employed in it.

Verse 30. Another service to be rendered in connection with the material sacrifices was the prayer and praise service. Some of these men referred to above performed the said services as members of the choir.

Verse 31. *Sabbath* is in the plural because every special or holy day was a sabbath. The term is used generally, and the writer then specifies some of the days that were considered sabbath or holy days besides the 7th day of the week. *New moons* always had to be observed as holy days. (1 Sam. 20: 5, 18, 24.) *Set feasts* means the ones with definite dates, such as the Passover which always came on the 14th day of the first month; Pentecost which always came 50 days after Passover; and Atonement which always came on the 10th day of the 7th month.

Verse 32. The tabernacle was at that time at Gibeon, with all the articles of the service except the ark. The service was necessarily incomplete due to the distance from the capital city, also because the ark was in a tent to itself. What service could be had, however, was to be performed by these Levites. It was intended also that they should have the similar work later on. This is evident by the reference to *the house of the Lord*.

1 CHRONICLES 24

Verses 1-3. This is an introduction to the subject matter of the chapter as a whole. *Divisions* means the groups of persons that descended from Aaron down to the time of this writing. Aaron had four sons, but two of them died leaving no children. The line of the priesthood therefore proceeded from the remaining two. By the time of David the eligible men descending from the two sons of Aaron came to number so many that he concluded to make some arrangement for some systematic method of administration.

Verse 4. The *chief men* were the ones among the descendants of Aaron's sons who were to head the lists that were to have charge of the priestly services thereafter. There were 16 such men in the group from Eleazar, and 8 in that from Ithamar.

Verse 5. The families of these 24 men were to furnish the lots for the service from then on. But in order to have proper procedure, and give some fair distribution of the work, the arrangement was decided by lot.

Verse 6. After the lot had been taken and the various households had been assigned to their position in the numerical order, the proper men made a record of the same, which became a part of the royal histories. That would avoid any dispute as to whose turn it was to serve at any given time. Smith's Bible Dictionary has the following to say about this course or turn method of administering the priesthood. "Courses. —The priesthood was divided into four and twenty 'courses' or orders. 1 Chr. 24: 1-19; 2 Chr. 23: 8; Luke 1: 5, each of which was to serve in rotation for one week, while the further assignment of special services during the week was determined by lot. Luke 1: 9. Each course appears to have commenced its work on the Sabbath, the outgoing priests taking the morning sacrifice, and leaving that of the evening to their successors. 2 Chr. 23: 8." This information is found also in Josephus; Antiquities, Book 7, Chapter 14, Section 7.

Verses 7-19. This passage gives the order of turns for the service of the priesthood as described in the preceding paragraph. The reader will be interested in the mention of *Abijah* in verse 10. In Luke 1: 5 is the account of the priest who belonged to that course, and who became the father of John the Baptist. The spelling is a little different in the N. T. but is the same man. *According to their manner* means according to the plan that David had established for them.

Verses 20-31. These verses are all grouped into one paragraph because no distinct interest is had in any one. It is a list of persons belonging to the blood of Levi, yet not of the "chief men" who formed the courses of the priesthood. There was much work required in the service of the Lord besides the actual service of the priesthood, and the men enumerated in this paragraph were used for that.

1 CHRONICLES 25

Verse 1. *Prophesy* is from NABA and Strong defines it, "to prophesy, i. e. speak (or sing) by inspiration (in prediction or simple discourse)." It has a very wide extent of meaning, but is used in the present instance to mean they sang with the accompaniment of these musical instruments.

Verses 2-4. A prominent fact connected with David was his love of music. He was an able player and we recall his work while a young man in the service of Saul. Now that he is in a position of authority, he devotes a great deal of attention to his choir. These men who are said to prophesy were some of the expert players and the king assigned to them some particular instrument to play in connection with the service.

Verse 5. A seer was a prophet in the ordinary sense of that word, whose duty was to speak the words of God concerning the future. But they were also among the musicians, and this man Heman was one of the prophets, and had a large family.

Verses 6, 7. The family of Heman, which included many sons and daughters, could play on various instruments, and the king used them in the service. The cymbals were used to beat time, while the psalteries and harps were stringed instruments that were used for service to God under the direction of David. Of course we will not forget that all of this arrangement for *the house of God* was preparatory, for no such house was yet built. David was not permitted to build it, but he was allowed to prepare for it. So he not only got much of the material ready for the building, but also arranged a vast system of talent among his subjects to engage in the public service to God when the time came for it. There were 288 of these talented persons ready for service.

Verse 8. With such a vast amount of talent available, it was necessary to make provision for an orderly execution of it; this was done by casting lots. *Ward* means duty, and the thought is that the lots were cast for the enlistment into the service of all the talents whether great or small. *Teacher . . . scholar.* Among the large number of musicians there were both the instructors and the ones still receiving instructions, and all of them were assigned to their proper place in the service by lot.

Verses 9-31. This entire paragraph has to do with the enumeration of the various musicians and their places in the service as determined by the casting of lots.

1 CHRONICLES 26

Verses 1-12. It was thought well to make a single paragraph of these verses because they all have to do with the subject of the porters. If any special attention is needed to some expression, it will be referred to its proper verse. There is so much space given to the porters of the temple service that some consideration will be given to the subject. A porter was a janitor or gatekeeper. The house of God that was built by Solomon was a complicated structure with many gates and doors, some of which were large and heavy. I shall quote the article in the Oxford Cyclopedic Concordance on this subject. "Porters were the doorkeepers and police of the temple (2 Chron. 31: 14). They were divided into companies, under the command of the 'Captain of the Temple,' and one division was always on duty, keeping guard day and night. Josephus says that it took twenty men to shut the great brazen gates (Acts 21: 30)." This information will explain the references to *mighty men of valor* (V. 6) and *strength* (V. 8) and *strong men* (V. 9) in the present paragraph. *Wards one against another* means they had their individual duties and were to take their turns after each other.

Verse 13. *Small . . . great.* These are from words that apply to age, meaning that no age limit was considered in the allotment of this service. The only thing considered when distributing the tasks was the particular family a man belonged to.

Verses 14-16. The four directions are named in the verses, and some particular man was placed at each of the gates with some part of the duty given him. *House of Asuppim* means a store-room that was located near the gates. It is very easy to see why such places would need special guards.

Verses 17-19. These Levites were assigned these posts as guards in addition to those named in the preceding paragraph. *Asuppim* is the same as the one mentioned before, and had these additional guards for the place. *Parbar* was a suburban annex to the main wall, and *causeway* had reference to some walkway connected thereto. The first mention of *Parbar* means the unit as a whole. Then in particular, there were four guards for the walkway and two for the wall of the annex.

Verses 20-27. The store-houses had not only guards for the places, but special charge was given for the things stored therein. Ahijah, a Levite, had some of this duty, and it included the gifts that had been made by the Israelites for the service of God. Also, the things that had been taken by David in his conflicts with the enemies were put in these store-houses, and the men named were to assist as guards.

Verse 28. Many of these spoils had been taken as far back as the days of Samuel and Saul. They had been kept in places of safety until the present time, and David valued them highly enough to make all these provisions for their continued safety. No one man can do everything, hence it was necessary to assign the responsibility to these men.

Verse 29. *Outward business* refers to the policing and governing of the country in general. For the purpose of external affairs these officers were appointed, and the force was managed by Chenaniah.

Verse 30. *Hebronites* and such like terms refers to locality classes and not to any particular family. Since *valour* means strength, and since these were officers to keep the peace, we can see the propriety in the selection of these men.

Verse 31. *Generations* means "family history." According to the family history of this man, Jerijah was a chief man. He and his fellows were "rounded up" for the service in the last year of David's life and reign.

Verse 32. The two and a half tribes were on the east of the Jordan. Being thus located at the distance from the nation's headquarters, they needed ample protection. David assigned 2,700 strong men to the policing of that territory. It was their duty to look after both the religious and temporal interests of the kingdom of David.

1 CHRONICLES 27

Verse 1. This is a sort of summing up of the men in the service of David. The orderly manner of their service is indicated in this verse. They served a month at a time and took their proper turns. The number of the forces that served in any particular month is suggested in the following verses.

Verse 2-15. There were 24,000 men serving each of the 12 months of the year.

Verses 16-22. In this paragraph the service is divided according to tribes. Out of each tribe the king selected *princes*, which means men of influence or prestige.

Verse 23. David's not taking the enumeration of those from twenty and under, and the reason stated, shows his motive for the numbering; it was his concern for the strength that lay in great numbers. Were they somewhat limited or uncertain, he would have enlisted every male who was physically able to do any kind of manual labor. The motive he had was what led him into the oversight concerning the ransom money. See Ex. 30: 12; 1 Chr. 21: 1-3.

Verse 24. At first thought this verse might seem to contradict Ch. 21: 5. But the sum there mentioned means only that when Joab saw the wrath of God coming, he ceased the numbering. He then gave over to David the report of the work done thus far.

Verse 25. No one man had exclusive charge of the interests connected with David's kingdom. Azmaveth was one among others who had some part of caring for the treasures. Jehona then must have been a rather important man, for his work attached him to the things stored in *fields, cities, villages* and *castles*.

Verse 26. Some preceding verses have told of men who had charge of the products of the fields and other sources. Ezri had oversight of the production itself, seeing that the ground was properly tilled.

Verse 27. This means Shimei was to care for the plants of the vineyards. Zabdi was to have charge of the product, to see that the wine was produced and stored in the cellars. These details may seem trivial to the reader, but we should get the lesson of the importance of having a system; doing things in an orderly method. Paul commended the church at Colosse for that. (Ch. 2: 5.)

Verse 28. This *sycamore* was a fruit tree somewhat like the fig tree. Baal-hanan was to care for these and the olive trees that grew in the low plains. The olive tree was cultivated for the oil of the fruit, and Joash was to look after its storage.

Verse 29. The *herds* of this passage means the larger animals, such as beeves. David was careful to see that full provision was made for the care of these animals by not assigning too much to any one man. The cattle feeding in *Sharon* and the *villages* had each a different man.

Verse 30. Camels were used for food and for transportation. They were among the most important beasts of service in old times; one man was charged with the care of these. The asses were used for plowing and transportation; Jehdeiah took care of these.

Verse 31. The many uses for sheep and goats are so familiar that it is unnecessary to comment. Jazib had the care of the flocks. He was a Hagerite, which was of one of the Arabian clans. *All these* applies to the men in the service of David who are mentioned in the several preceding verses.

Verse 32. A counsellor was one who gave advice and made suggestions. When some decision was made it was to be recorded, and Jonathan served in the capacity of advising and recording. His work was not as specific as was that of the king's official counsellor who will be presented in the next verse. Jehiel was engaged by David to act as tutor for his sons.

Verse 33. *Ahithophel* should be regarded as the king's special or official counsellor. He was the one whose advice was rejected in the case of Absalom, and who killed himself over it. (2 Sam. 17: 23.) *Hushai* is classed as a companion only, but finally became the more important as a counsellor. (2 Sam. 15: 32-37.)

Verse 34. Joab was the general of the army and the most important man of all.

1 CHRONICLES 28

Verse 1. This verse reports a call for a general assembly of all David's chief men. He knows he is near the end of his life, and plans to inform his people of what had been in his mind, also what he hopes to have done after he is gone.

Verse 2. The ark was a divine instrument for the service of God, ordained by the Lord himself. Yet its material was earthly and the forming of it was done by man. In view of such facts it was fitting to call the building David proposed to erect a resting place for the ark. But when he came to speak of it in connection with God personally, he claimed no higher honor for the temple than to call it a footstool.

Verse 3. See my comments at Ch. 22: 11 on the attitude of David regarding this matter of his being denied the privilege of building the temple.

Verse 4. Instead of feeling as if he were left out of all honor, David called attention to the particulars in which he had been favored. For one thing, his tribe was chosen to furnish the kings who were to reign in Jerusalem. Next, out of that tribe the Lord chose his father's family. Last but not least, of the eight sons his father had, he was the one chosen.

Verse 5. In continuing his specifications of favors David pointed out that of all the many sons he had, God had selected Solomon to be the next king. Not only was Solomon to be king, but was to be allowed the honor of building the house of God, something David had longed to do but was forbidden. It might be wondered why David had this feeling of preference for Solomon. There is no direct statement in the Bible on this subject. But we know that Solomon was a son of Bath-sheba, and the affair with that attractive woman, although connected with some bitter memories, must have left a feeling of favoritism in the mind of David.

Verse 6. David's reverence for God would naturally influence him to have profound respect for his activities. God had set Solomon on a pedestal of special favor by the endearing terms of *father* and *son*; David had been told all this. It necessarily impressed him with the outstanding importance of this son of the woman of tender memory.

Verse 7. *For ever* means "agelasting." Had Solomon been always true to God, the vast extent of his jurisdiction (see 1 Ki. 4: 21) would have continued to the end of that (Jewish) age. But the condition on which such favor was to be granted was that he continue in obedience to the Lord's commandments. *As at this day* means that the future king should serve God according to the law that was then in force.

Verse 8. This exhortation was addressed to the assembly of the great men mentioned in verse 1. It was in the sight of the congregation and in the hearing of God. It should always be remembered that God hears all that is said. That is important as to the things *we* say, and also as regards the instructions that are given us from any of God's authorized teachers. *Leave it for an inheritance.* This expression implies more than is generally realized. Many people act as if they were not responsible on behalf of the future generations. If they see fit to consume the land to which they have a title, they think it is no concern of others. This verse teaches that the men then in charge of the land were to conduct themselves in such a manner that the territory would be left for others after the present generations had passed away.

Verses 9, 10. This is a fine exhortation and came from an able and sincere mind. Had Solomon heeded it he would have been a happier man. The Lord must be sought if he is to be enjoyed. This is taught in Isa. 55: 6, 7 and Matt. 7: 7.

Verses 11, 12. God was very considerate of David even though he would not permit him to build the temple. He gave him the pattern *by the spirit*, which means he was inspired in delivering it to his son. More will be said on this subject at verse 19.

Verse 13. God directed David as to the courses or turns of the priests, and he handed the instructions over to Solomon.

Verse 14. All metal has weight, but the expression *by weight* means that David had it weighed and did not leave it for his workmen to guess at.

Verses 15. *According to the use* means the weight of the metal allotted to each piece was according to its needs, depending on the service to be had from it.

Verses 16-18. When Solomon built the temple he reproduced, in enlarged form, all the vessels and furniture that had been in the tabernacle service, except the ark. That had been housed in a special tent by David, and Solomon did not reproduce it.

Verse 19. *Hand* is from YAD and Strong defines it, "a primitive word; a hand (the open one [indicating power, means, direction, etc.] in distinction from a closed one)." So the verse means God gave David the power to write the description of the temple to be erected by Solomon. There should be no questioning of the work of Solomon in the vast architecture he used in the building. If the temple was not constructed as God wanted it, the reason was that the divine pattern was not followed. We cannot conclude that, for the Lord blessed the building at the prayer and dedication.

Verse 20. The task of erecting a building of such vast proportions was great. It was to require the work of thousands of men and call for the collecting of huge amounts of materials; hence the encouraging words of David were appropriate. Neither could such a great work be accomplished without the help of God, and David assured his son that divine help would be given him.

Verse 21. The *courses* or turns of the priests also would be assured for Solomon's service in things belonging to their line. In short, the talents of the entire nation would be at his command.

1 CHRONICLES 29

Verse 1. There was never more than one man chosen to be a king at the same time, nor to supervise a great work like the tabernacle or the temple. *Whom alone* means there was no other to compare with Solomon, or to stand any chance in the estimation of God. *Young and tender* means he was inexperienced in the matters soon to claim his attention. Were the building to be for man's use only, it would not have been so important; but it was for the Lord and must have the utmost attention.

Verse 2. Part of the definition of the original for *prepared* is, "appoint, render sure." That is the meaning it has in this place. David did not have any of the materials shaped up and ready to install in the building. He wanted to be sure of some to be waiting for Solomon's use, hence *prepared* or made sure that it would be there.

Verse 3. This is the passage cited when I was commenting on 1 Ki. 10: 13. There was a distinction between the possessions a king might have as a private citizen, and the ones he owned and controlled as king. It could be illustrated by the allotment of money the President is given for his expenses as Chief Executive, and the money he might have in a bank as his private checking account. *Mine own proper good* means his private goods, and *that I have prepared* means the valuables out of the royal treasury that he had "earmarked" for use in building the temple.

Verses 4, 5. *Gold of Ophir* is designated because the metal that came from that place was considered of special fineness. *Who then is willing,* etc. David informed his people that materials were ready for the temple, and then called for volunteers to work with them. Not that they were to begin the work at once, for David would not have been permitted to have that done. But he wanted to have workmen as well as the materials ready when the time came.

Verses 6-8. The people responded further than David requested. He had asked them to offer their *service* (from the same word as "hand" in Ch. 28: 19), but they offered also their valuables, and gave them willingly.

Verse 9. The literal value of the things offered was not the most important phase of the situation. That which caused David and the others to rejoice was the fact that they gave willingly. That is the same principle which pleases the Lord today. (2 Cor. 9: 7.)

Verses 10-13. These verses are self-explanatory, but I wish the reader to ponder them well, however, and note the strong expressions of gratitude and praise to the divine Giver of all good things. God is acknowledged to be the source of all good.

Verse 14. This verse brings to a specific view the thoughts expressed in the preceding paragraph. It is the same thought that Paul gives us in 1 Tim. 6: 7 and 1 Cor. 4: 7. It is true that the latter is speaking of spiritual gifts, but the idea is the same, that all we have came from God. Therefore, when we make a "gift" to God, we are merely handing back to him that which he has loaned to us.

Verse 15. *Stranger* means a temporary dweller, and the word could be used with reference to the places in the world and their relation to each other. But in this place David applies the word to those on the earth as a whole. That proves that David did not believe this earth to be the final abode of man.

Verse 16. This is the same as verse 14.

Verse 17. *Triest the heart* is said in direct connection with the fact that God had given his goods into the hands of man. It was to test his honesty and devotion.

Verse 18. *Keep this* refers to the state of mind the people then had. They were respectful toward God and willing to contribute of their means and labor for the advancement of God's interests. David prayed that such an attitude may be kept in the imagination (mind) of them ever after.

Verse 19. A special prayer was offered for his son that he might always have the right kind of heart toward God. *Commandments* referred to the requirements of God in general. *Testimonies* means these requirements had been attested and established. *Statutes* refers to the formal enactments of God. All of these terms may be used somewhat interchangeably, and the same law might possess all of the qualities at once.

Verse 20. *Bless God* means to adore him and to show it by the posture of the body; *worship* as used here means about the same. When one bows the head at the mention of a certain being, he is said to worship him. That is the sense in which the people worshiped the Lord and the king.

Verse 21. These sacrifices were voluntary offerings, prompted by the gratitude of the people for the favorable state of affairs, and the prospect of good things to come. A *drink offering* was an offering of wine, so called because it was the giving up of something that could have been used for a drink.

Verse 22. *Eat and drink before the Lord* signifies that it was one of the religious feasts that the Jews were permitted to have. (Deut. 12: 21; 1 Sam. 9: 12.) *Made David king the second time.* They had a second public formality or recognition of him as king. The principle involved would apply in general for persons of authority. The popular song "Coronation" has been criticized by some because it speaks of crowning Christ as king, whereas he has been already crowned. The objection ignores the figurative use of the term. Actually and literally, a man is made king but once, but every time a subject acknowledges the king, he may be said to have crowned him. That is the sense in which the people made David king in this instance.

Verses 23-25. We must remember that the books of Chronicles are brief and do not claim to give all the details. Because of the character of said documents we will not find them always chronological. This paragraph is out of line as to date, for David was yet king. It is in line as to the thought. One of the outstanding items of David's prayer and request was that the people would respect his son who was to reign after him. (Ch. 28: 1-8.) The inspired writer goes into the future far enough to tell us of the answer to the prayer for Solomon, then drops back to the proper date to finish the account of David. The direct history of Solomon will come in next book.

Verses 26, 27. This is a summing up of the reign of David. *All Israel* is said with reference to the partial reign ascribed to him at first. Judah was the only tribe that accepted him for 7 years, then finally all the tribes. (2 Sam. 2: 8-11; 5: 1-3.)

Verse 28. This is another general statement. *Good old age* does not refer to the actual length of his life, for many men lived longer than he. But he was not cut off by any misfortune of violence or disease; he died of natural causes.

Verses 29, 30. *Samuel, Nathan* and *Gad* were national prophets. They not only spoke the Word of God when occasion called for it, but each of them put many things into writing. *Book* is defined as "history," and the details of the happenings of their days were put into their histories, for the fuller information of the people then living. For the purposes of future generations the Lord had certain portions of their works put into the book that was to become a part of our Bible. See also my comments on the word "Chronicles" at 1 Ki. 14: 19.

2 CHRONICLES 1

Verse 1. This and several verses following corresponds with 1 Ki. 3: 1-15. *Was strengthened* denotes that Solomon was established on his throne. It sometimes happens that a man may take his place on the throne, but be in an uncertain condition because of some disturbance in the nation. It was not so with Solomon for all elements of the nation were favorable to him.

Verse 2. *Solomon spake.* The second word is one with several meanings. It is rendered in the A. V. the most frequently by "speak" and "answer." In a few instances it is translated "command." The present verse merely says that Solomon spake to the people. We must conclude, therefore, that what he said included what was necessary to inform the people of the king's desire of them.

Verse 3. See my comments at 1 Ki. 3: 2 on "high places." The temple had not yet been built, so it was necessary to go to the tabernacle that was at Gibeon.

Verse 4. The ark had been separated from the tabernacle at the battle with the Philistines. (1 Sam. 4.) It never was in its original place again, but was taken from place to place; first among the Philistines, then with the Israelites. It was at Kirjath-jearim for at least 20 years. (1 Sam. 7: 2.) David finally moved it to Jerusalem and put it in a tent that he had pitched for it in the district of the city called Mount Zion or City of David. (2 Sam. 6.)

Verse 5. The brazen altar was originally located before the tabernacle, just as it is described here. The statement indicates that a general disturbance had been made of the tabernacle and its furniture. This was caused by the Philistines, but we have no specific information of when it was done.

Verse 6. The altar represented the major part of the congregational worship of the Jews. Solomon respected it by going to Gibeon to offer sacrifices upon it. His reign was just beginning and he was in the state of sincere devotion to God that led him for several years. It was fitting that he begin the great career with a season of public devotions, hence the statement in V. 3 that *all the congregation* went up.

Verse 7. God did not tell Solomon he might have anything he wished as is so commonly taught; he merely asked him what he wished. Had Solomon asked for something that was displeasing to the Lord we have no indication that it would have been granted.

Verses 8, 9. The gratitude of Solomon first fixed his attention on the favor that God had shown David his father. His prayer accordingly was connected with the promise contained in that favor, and he wished the kingdom to be confirmed on him.

Verse 10. Solomon realized that the favor shown to his father would avail him very little if he must depend solely on his own strength. He asked for *wisdom* and *knowledge*. The first has special reference to the natural skillfulness of the mind, the second to the information that might be acquired by such a mind. *Go out and come in* refers to his dealings with the people. To *judge* the people means to guide them in the vast numbers of interests that would come up.

Verses 11, 12. God never gives to man that which would be wrong for him to have. Solomon was promised a number of things he did not ask for. The principle underlying the whole situation pertains to the chief motive that was controlling Solomon. Riches and the other things named were not wrong in themselves, else God would not have given them. But it would have been wrong for them to be the chief motive of Solomon's reign. As an illustration of the thought, Christians may find much pleasure in the association with acquaintances in the general assembly, but it would be wrong were that the primary motive that brought them together.

Verse 13. See my comments at 1 Ki. 3: 2 on *high places*, one of which is mentioned in connection with Solomon at Gibeon. The capital of his kingdom was Jerusalem, hence he had to leave the tabernacle to be in the proper city.

Verse 14. Smith's Bible Dictionary says a chariot was "a vehicle used either for warlike or peaceful purposes." Solomon did not have any wars, therefore he used the chariots for peaceful purposes. He wished to have some of them at hand and these he kept in Jerusalem. Others were kept in cities set apart for the purpose.

Verse 15. These statements are for comparison to indicate the wealth of Solomon. The sycamore was a species of fig tree and abounded in that country. The cedar was a valuable and highly prized tree, but Solomon was able to have them in as great number as the common sycamore tree.

Verse 16. Bringing these horses out of Egypt was contrary to Deut. 17: 16, but the Lord was very lenient and tolerated it for the present. The linen yarn was obtained *at a price*. One word used to translate the last one is "worth." The thought here is that the linen was paid for at its full value. Smith's Bible Dictionary says this: "Egyptian byssus, a flax that grew on the banks of the Nile, was exceedingly soft and dazzling in whiteness. This linen has been sold for twice its weight in gold."

Verse 17. Paying such a price for a chariot and a horse indicates the wealth of Solomon. In paying such a price for these things, the standard of value was set, and the kings of Syria and the other foreign nations had to pay the same if they wished to purchase them.

2 CHRONICLES 2

Verse 1. The *house* was the temple, and the *house for his kingdom* was the palace.

Verse 2. *To oversee them* means that the laborers worked under other men. All rules may be abused, but it is true that a man needs a "boss" over him to direct his activities as a laborer.

Verse 3. *Huram* is another spelling for "Hiram." The Mosaic system of government was secular or civil as well as religious. As king of a secular nation, therefore, it was proper for Solomon to have friendly dealings with Huram, another secular king. He did not forget that a friendship had existed between his father and the king of Tyre, and referred to it in his address to him.

Verse 4. All of the purposes for the proposed house mentioned in this verse were ordained by the law of Moses. The king of Tyre was given assurance, therefore, that Solomon was not planning on starting some new practice that might jeopardize the peace.

Verse 5. The house that Solomon proposed to make was to be great. But there should be a just call for such a structure, else the other nations might wonder about the intentions of the neighbor. Solomon sets that matter in its true light by the statement *for great is our God above all gods.*

Verse 6. While the God whom Solomon served is great, he does not want to imply that he, an unworthy man, could construct a house worthy of Him. So he justifies his intentions by the explanation that the house is to be used in which to burn sacrifices. In other words, if man is going to prepare a building that could be available for service to God, nothing would be too good for him.

Verse 7. David had engaged skilled workmen in Judah to be ready for the service under Solomon. Solomon now wants to supplement these by skilled men from Huram's country. The metals named were for the plating of the framework of the buildings. The *purple* and other colors named referred to fabrics of linen, to be used for the vails.

Verse 8. The trees were for the inner part of the framework, and the metals were to be used in overlaying it. The cedar and fir were species of evergreen trees, and were produced in the territory of Huram. The *algums* were imported from outside. Smith's Bible Dictionary says: "The almug (algum) was brought in great plenty from Ophir for Solomon's temple and house, and for the construction of musical instruments . . . The wood is very heavy, and of a beautiful garnet color."

Verses 9, 10. *Beaten wheat* means threshed wheat. The weights and measures of Biblical times present so much variation as to their value that it is often difficult to discover just what the amount is. I can do no better in this instance than quote the translation of Moffatt. "200,000 bushels of grain for food, 200,000 bushels of barley, 180,000 gallons of wine, and 180,000 gallons of oil."

Verses 11, 12. Tyre was a leading city of Phoenicia, a country lying between Palestine and the Mediterranean Sea. Being so near the country of the Israelites, its people had many opportunities of learning something of the God of Israel. The frequent demonstrations of divine power made them somewhat familiar with the Lord, hence this king speaks of him in much the same language as was used by the Jews. The conclusion that Huram formed was that love for his people would be the reason for placing over them such an unusual king as the son of David. This message of congratulations was put into writing and sent to Solomon.

Verse 13. In response to Solomon's request (V. 7) for a skilled workman, Huram sent a man who had been in the employ of his father, whose name also was Huram, and he was to supervise the mechanical work of the temple and its furniture.

Verse 14. This verse says the mother of Huram was of the tribe of Dan, but 1 Ki. 7: 14 says she was of the tribe of Naphtali. The explanation is that she was by blood of the tribe of Dan but lived in the territory of Naphtali. This man was to cooperate with the skilled workmen of Solomon's country.

Verse 15. Solomon had promised (V. 10) to furnish these provisions for Huram's workmen, of which he is here reminded. *His servants* means the workmen of the country of Tyre who were to labor in a service to Solomon.

Verse 16. *Lebanon* was a district of Phoenicia containing the famous trees of that name. The timber was to be put into the water and formed into rafts or floats. It could then be moved downward to Joppa which was a seaport of Palestine. From there it would be transported by vehicles drawn by beasts of burden to Jerusalem, for use in building the temple.

Verses 17, 18. The *strangers* were the foreigners who were scattered throughout the country of Israel. They had been enjoying the protection and other benefits of the country, now Solomon had them registered for service in his building project. He divided them into proper distribution for his service. There were three groups, those who worked the material, those who moved it, and those who supervised the work.

2 CHRONICLES 3

Verses 1, 2. *Mount Moriah* was a spot within the boundaries of Jerusalem, and first made famous by the offering of Isaac by Abraham. On a geographical and historical subject, the scholarship of the world should be the basis for our conclusions. I shall therefore make a few quotations as to the location and identity of this spot. "The Offering of Isaac. (Gen. 22.) From Beer-sheba Abraham took his son Isaac, at God's command, to offer him as a burnt offering in 'the land of Moriah.' Some authorities accept the Samaritan tradition, that this place was Mount Gerizim; but we see no sufficient reason to dissent from the general view, that it was Mount Moriah, at Jerusalem, ten centuries afterward the site of the Temple."— Rand-McNally Bible Atlas. The next is from Smith's Bible Dictionary. "Mount Moriah. — The elevation on which Solomon built the temple, where God appeared to David 'in the threshingfloor of Abraham the Jebusite.' It is the eastern eminence of Jerusalem, separated from Mount Zion by the Tyropoeon valley. The top was leveled by Solomon, and immense walls were built round it from the base to enlarge the level surface for the temple area. Tradition which first appears in a definite shape in Josephus, and is now almost universally accepted, asserts that the 'Mount Moriah' of Chronicles is identical with the 'mountain' in 'the land of Moriah' of Genesis, and that the spot on which Jehovah appeared to David, and on which the temple was built, was the very spot of the sacrifice of Isaac."

Verse 3. *Was instructed* means that Solomon gave instructions to his workmen to guide them in their laying the ground plan for the building. The 20 x 60 cubits applies to the main part of the temple not counting the many adjoining parts.

Verses 4-8. For information regarding this paragraph, the reader is requested to see my comments on 1 Ki. 6th chapter.

Verse 9. In using nails in the construction of a building, it would be necessary to use a hammer, and we know there would be some sound. This should be considered when commenting on 1 Ki. 6: 7, a passage often misunderstood.

Verses 10-13. This *most holy house* corresponds to the second room in the tabernacle, called the "most holy" place. The two cherubims also corresponds to the two in the tabernacle, but they were larger. They were made large enough to take up the entire space of 20 cubits that was the size of the room. *They stood on their feet* may seem to be an insignificant expression. It is a contrast with the posture of the cherubims that were in the tabernacle. Those creatures were on the mercyseat, and the position of their feet is not stated. The ones in the temple were not on any piece of furniture; that would mean they had to "stand on their own." Also, instead of facing each other as did the ones in the tabernacle, these both had their attention focussed on the building.

Verse 14. The vail constituted the partition between the holy and most holy rooms in the building. It served the same purpose as the vail in the tabernacle described in Ex. 26: 31-33.

Verse 15. These pillars were over 50 feet high. The *chapiter* was an ornamental cap or head, and it was seven and a half feet high.

Verse 16. The chains were for holding these ornamental pomegranates.

Verse 17. Proper names usually conveyed some special meaning. *Jachin* is defined in the margins of many Bibles as "establish," and the lexicon agrees. *Boaz* is of rather uncertain meaning, but the margin gives us "fleetness." The idea expressed by Solomon in these large pillars with such names, was an acknowledgement of the favor of God extended to him in his undertakings.

2 CHRONICLES 4

Verse 1. This *altar of brass* corresponds to the "brasen altar" of the tabernacle. We will not criticize the enlarged size of this one over the old. We have already learned that Solomon received divine instructions on the building of this house, therefore the work was right in the sight of God. We should keep in mind the fact that the nation was growing all the time, and the needs for service would grow with it.

Verse 2. In the place of the laver which Moses made, Solomon made a vessel that was so large that it was called a sea. It was 15 feet across and seven and a half high.

Verse 3. Under *it*, that is, under the brim of the sea, were two rows of work in the form of oxen. They were small for there were ten to every cubit. *Cast, when it was cast*, means the mould was formed with these ornamental oxen so that they were all cast together at the same time the sea was cast.

Verse 4. According to 1 Ki. 7: 45 these oxen were made of brass. They were large enough to serve as a base for the large sea or tank, and were arranged so that the faces of three of them could be seen from each of the four sides.

Verse 5. The walls of the sea were about three inches thick and the brim was ornamented with formations like lilies. All of this was cast with the sea in the same operation. *Held 3,000 baths* means its capacity was that—it could hold that much, but it did not need to be filled to capacity. It usually had in it only 2,000 baths. (1 Ki. 7: 26.) According to Moffatt the capacity of this tank was 24,000 gallons.

Verse 6. The law of Moses required that the beasts to be offered on the altar be washed. These ten lavers were for that use, leaving the sea or large tank for the use of the priests. They were required to wash their hands and feet every time they went into the house of the Lord. (Ex. 30: 19-21.)

Verses 7, 8. The only thing needful to mention about these is the fact that Solomon increased the number of the articles over what was in the tabernacle. It was all satisfactory to the Lord, for he blessed the whole institution when it was completed. The nation was growing in numbers and becoming more important in the eyes of the nation, and it was fitting that the institutions of its public service be enlarged.

Verse 9. A special court was made for the priests, and the *great court* was for the people in general, hence its increased size.

Verse 10. The sea or large tank was placed before the east end of the building. It was set over at the right-hand side of the space and facing southward.

Verses 11-16. This paragraph is a summing up of the foundry work that Huram did for Solomon. There is no information other than has been already given and considered.

Verse 17. The size and number of castings that Solomon had made prohibited their being done in an established foundry. Strong describes this *clay* as thick loam. That would explain its usefulness in forming moulds for the casting of the brass.

Verse 18. *Could not be found out* does not mean it was physically impossible to weigh the material, but it was so great that no attempt was made to do so. 1 Ki. 7: 47 expresses the thought very well.

Verses 19-22. This is another summing up of some of the work of Solomon. He reproduced or duplicated all of the vessels that had been in the tabernacle except the ark of the covenant.

2 CHRONICLES 5

Verse 1. Solomon respected his father's interest in the work of the Lord. 1 Ki. 29 gives an account of the things David had prepared and dedicated for the work.

Verse 2. The transfer of the ark was to be an event of much importance. The sacred vessel had been separated from its proper place since the early days of Saul. (1 Sam. 4). David had secured royal possession of it and housed it in a tent devoted to its exclusive use, located in Mount Zion in Jerusalem. Solomon called for this representative gathering of great men to witness the event.

Verse 3. *Feast . . . seventh month*. This was the feast of atonement. (Lev. 16: 29, 30.) It was the time when the high priest went into the Most Holy place in the tabernacle, where the ark had formerly been kept.

Verses 4, 5. All the elders of Israel, meaning the more experienced and influential men had a part in this great movement. There were some things, however, that none but Levites were allowed to do, hence they are mentioned in connection with the elders. *Brought up the ark and the tabernacle.*

This sounds as if the transaction was one and the same as to location. Such was not the case, though, for the ark was right there in Jerusalem, while the tabernacle and the other articles of service were at Gibeon. It was not destined ever to be used again in the service, but was brought to the capital city and stored out of due respect.

Verse 6. This great sacrifice was a sort of celebration or rededication of the ark, which was the most exclusive piece of furniture in the tabernacle or temple.

Verses 7, 8. The *priests* were the proper ones to have charge of the ark. *Oracle* and *most holy place* were names for corresponding rooms. The latter was what it was called in the tabernacle, and the other in the temple. They were alike in that no one but a priest had any right to go into them while they were in service. (Heb. 9: 7.)

Verse 9. This strange verse is explained in my comments on 1 Kings 8: 8.

Verse 10. *Nothing in the ark save*, etc. Heb. 9: 4 names the three things that had been put into the ark, and Ex. 16: 33, 34; Num. 17: 10, and Ex. 25: 16 gives the account of their being put there. I can find no information as to how or when two of them came to be missing when Solomon moved the ark into the temple.

Verse 11. In 1 Chr. 24 is an account of the arrangement for the priests to serve in their turn. On this special occasion the rule was suspended, and all of the men eligible for the office participated. Let us note, however, that before they did so they were sanctified for the occasion.

Verse 12. This verse refers to the choir that had been collected by David, and consecrated to sing and play on the musical instruments.

Verses 13, 14. Some effort has been made to draw a distinction between the place where these instruments were used, and that part of the building that was considered holy. The point attempted is to show that God did not favor instrumental music even in Old Testament times, and neither does he now. The point is erroneous and unnecessary; God favored many things then that he does not now. But a close study of this passage will show us these facts: God endorsed this instrumental music by shedding his glory on the service. Furthermore, the spot where it took place and that was *filled* with the glory of the Lord is called *the house of God*. This glory was so great that it was too much for the physical endurance of the priests.

2 CHRONICLES 6

Verse 1. *Then said Solomon*, etc. I have commented in much detail on this speech and prayer of Solomon in 1 Kings 8. The reader is requested to consult that comment to save space here. However, I shall group several verses and call attention to a few special expressions of interest.

Verses 2-10. *Loins* is from CHALATS and refers to the thick part of the body. The ancients believed that the reproductive germ of a man came from that part of his body. That is why we have so frequent a reference to a man's "loins" when speaking of his offspring. Gen. 35: 11 had predicted something along this line, and Solomon acknowledges the fulfillment.

Verse 11. Of the three things that were once in the ark, the most important was the tables of the covenant. They were still therein and Solomon mentions the subject in direct connection with the placing of the ark in the house of the Lord.

Verses 12-23. There are two expressions in this paragraph on which I will offer comments. In V. 14 the mercy of the Lord is promised to those "that walk before thee with all their hearts." The blessings of God have always been made conditional on the obedience of man. The other is in V. 21 concerning the prayer of Solomon for the sake of the people. He asks the Lord to forgive the sins of the people *when thou hearest*. The prayer of Solomon was accepted, which means that sins were actually forgiven in those times, not just "rolled forward."

Verses 24, 25. The same idea about forgiveness at the time of prayer is expressed in this paragraph. The specific condition on which the favor is to be granted is that the people *return and confess*.

Verses 26, 27. In the days of special providence, God occasionally punished his people by withholding rain; there is an account of it in 1 Ki. 17. The scourge was to be removed upon the penitence of the people. They were to express that penitence by praying *toward this place*, which means the temple. *Taught them the good way* refers to the teaching they received the "hard way," which means in the school of experience.

Verses 28-31. Nothing much that is new is offered in this paragraph. It is interesting, however, to note the numerous misfortunes that are enumerated in one verse. We should be impressed with the vast resources of the Lord for carrying out his will.

Verses 32, 33. We generally think of people on the "outside" as not having any right to the institution of the Lord. But we again must remember that the Mosaic system was a combination of religion and civil government. It is always in order for aliens to participate in the benefits of our country. On that basis it was proper for the strangers (aliens) to participate in the privileges of the Israelite country.

Verses 34, 35. *By the way that thou shalt send them.* This is said on the subject of war. It shows that God had something to do in the action of warfare at that time. If war is wrong morally then it always was wrong. That would mean that God sent people out on a mission that was wrong, for even the most ardent pacifists will admit that God endorsed war in the old times.

Verse 36. *No man which sinneth not.* This declaration is in agreement with the teaching of 1 John 1: 8, 10. There is no pleasure in the thought that all men sin, but there is much encouragement in the thought that God understands, and has made provisions of mercy for all who will become penitent for their sins.

Verses 37-39. Solomon made a conditional prediction that actually came to pass. The same prediction is made, in more specific and pathetic terms, in Psalms 137. Then we may see the fulfillment of this woeful state of mind in Ezk. 37: 11. It should be noted that Israel was in Babylonian captivity at the time the last passage was written, and that would make it actual history. The history of an event that had been predicted is what proves its fulfillment, so we have a noted instance before us of a conditional prophecy that became a fulfilled fact. The history of Israel shows that God heard the groaning of his people in Babylon, and brought them out after all the purposes of that punishment had been accomplished.

Verses 40-42. It is refreshing to observe the devotion of Solomon as it is connected with the temple. Only when the prayers of the people shall have been directed toward that holy institution did he expect God to hear them. That principle holds good today under the New Testament teaching. Only when our religious activities are offered through the spiritual temple, the church, will God accept them. (Eph. 3: 21.)

2 CHRONICLES 7

Verse 1. When the brazen altar of the tabernacle was first put into service, God started the fire on it miraculously. (Lev. 9: 24.) Now when the new service is offered to God, it is fitting that he indicate his acceptance of it by this demonstration.

Verse 2. The condition was the same as in Ch. 5: 14. The splendor of the Lord's glory was too much for the physical endurance of the priests.

Verse 3. The presence of God's glory was so bright that all the people saw it. The effect upon them was profound, and they performed the custom of the times under conditions of extreme respect. They became prostrate in the posture of their bodies, and thus worshiped the Lord. But it was not the actions of fanatics under excitement, for they gave a clear and highly appropriate reason for their conduct by saying, "The Lord, his mercy endureth for ever."

Verses 4, 5. This account is given also in 1 Ki. 8: 62-66. The gratitude felt for the goodness of God prompted the king and the people to make this vast offering.

Verse 6. The priests did the part exclusively belonging to them, and the other Levites used the *instruments of music of the Lord.* This is an inspired statement, so we must know that after David had made the musical instruments for religious service, the Lord accepted and blessed them.

Verse 7. The altar of burnt sacrifices originally would take care of all the animals required in the regular or set feasts; also for the occasions of offerings for sins of individuals. But the occasion of this dedication was very special, and an emergency was created. In view of that, Solomon was authorized to use the extra space of the court as a place for the great number of sacrifices.

Verse 8. *Hamath* and the *river of Egypt* were two opposite points on the boundaries of Palestine. This feast had to be celebrated in Jerusalem, but the verse means there were Israelites from all that territory present at the feast.

Verse 9. These activities were special and had some items not provided in the law of Moses. But again we will not forget that a new epoch in the history of the nation is starting, and many things are being done that will not be repeated after the regular establishments of the law are resumed. So in the present verse is seen the duplication of the seven-day period; one for the altar and the other the regular period for the feast that came yearly.

Verse 10. The day of atonement came on the 10th of the month. Add two periods of 7 days each and we have the 24th day of the month. But many of the people had come from a distance (V. 8) and Solomon released them the day before the expiration of the time so they could go to their homes.

Verse 11. *House of the Lord* means the temple, and *the king's house* means the palace. *Prosperously effected* means he succeeded in accomplishing his plans.

Verse 12. This verse is very informative. When God says he has *heard* a prayer, he means he has granted it. This idea has been mentioned several times when speaking of the forgiveness of sins in that day. It is important also that God accepted the temple as the place for sacrifice.

Verses 13-16. In this paragraph the Lord repeats some of the things for which Solomon had prayed and promises to grant them.

Verses 17, 18. God did not forget his promise to David, that he should have a son to sit on his throne. Neither did he forget the condition on which the promise was made, that the son was to keep the *statutes* and *judgments* of the Lord. The difference between the two words is rather technical. The first refers to the formal enactments of the Lord as set ordinances. The second has special reference to the decisions which God makes as occasions require. However, the distinction is so slight that for all practical purposes, whether called by statutes, ordinances, commandments, ordinances, law, or any other equivalent terms, the importance is the same. More than one is sometimes used in one sentence for the purposes of emphasis.

Verse 19. *Serve* and *worship* are two more words that are generally used interchangeably, yet have a slight distinction in meaning. The first denotes that the person performs obligations imposed by the gods, and the second refers primarily to the attitude of mind toward them.

Verses 20, 21. The things threatened here came to pass, and it is recorded in 2 Ki. 25: 9. The house was destroyed by the Babylonians and never rebuilt until about 75 years later, which was after the fall of Babylon.

Verse 22. The warnings given out to the people of Israel were so well known that when the calamity came the public understood why it was.

2 CHRONICLES 8

Verse 1. Solomon was 20 years building the two houses. *House of the Lord* means the temple, and *his own house* was the palace for the king.

Verse 2. Solomon offered some cities to Huram (Hiram) king of Tyre. They did not please him, and although he seemed to accept them at first, he would not keep them, so he returned them to Solomon. That is the meaning of *restored to Solomon* in this verse. These cities evidently were not very desirable, and that is the reason the king of Tyre objected to them. Solomon then improved them for occupancy by Israelites.

Verse 3. Solomon never engaged in warfare, yet this verse says he *prevailed* against the city of Hamathzobah. That means his authority was such that he overcame all opposition and took possession.

Verses 4, 5. When cities already in existence are said to be *built*, it means they are improved and fortified.

Verse 6. *Store cities* were those in which he kept his chariots and horses, and other valuable products that were brought in from Egypt and Ophir. They were kept in these cities that were rendered suitable for safety, and convenient for use when desired.

Verses 7, 8. *Pay tribute* means they were compelled to pay taxes in the sense of tariff, for the support of the government whose protection they were enjoying. They were compelled also to do bodily service for Solomon's kingdom.

Verses 9, 10. Solomon never made war against any nation. There are needs, however, other than military, for soldiers' services. One thing, "to be prepared" is one way of avoiding actual military actions, and doubtless the keeping of this "standing army" of

250 chief men with the great numbers under their command, was one of God's means of effecting the reign of peace predicted for Solomon.

Verse 11. Solomon had 700 wives and 300 concubines. (1 Ki. 11: 3.) But a man will normally love only one woman in the way a husband should love his wife. The one whom Solomon thus loved was the daughter of Pharaoh. She is the heroine of the Song of Solomon. While he was engaged in the work of the two great buildings, he kept his beloved wife in Mount Zion, the most highly esteemed spot in Jerusalem. This was to be temporary, however, until he had the place prepared where she was to have her permanent residence. (1 Ki. 3: 1; 7: 8.) That was in connection with one of the buildings that were built in the vicinity of Mount Moriah, in the eastern part of Jerusalem and thus different from Mount Zion which was in the south part of the city. On this subject see my comments on Ch. 3: 1, 2. Since Pharaoh's daughter was an alien, Solomon did not consider it proper for her to reside in the most sacred spot in the city, the spot that was connected so affectionately with the memory of his father, and also the special regard for the Lord. It is strange that he would be so concerned for the dignity of God's institutions when the residence of his wife was under consideration, and yet was led to accept her as his wife, contrary to the will of God. It is another instance that shows the predominance of the flesh over the spirit.

Verses 12, 13. *After a certain rate every day* has reference to the established requirements of the law. Solomon was attentive to observe the specific demands laid down by Moses, as well as the extra sacrifices he offered on special occasions. His example teaches us that a person cannot substitute his own voluntary services for the specific requirements of God. *Three times in the year* referred to the three yearly feasts when all males of the Israelites were required to go to Jerusalem. Those occasions are not always identified by the same names, due to the various activities connected with them. For clarification of the subject I shall follow each expression in italics with corresponding ones for the same periods. *Unleavened bread;* the passover. *Feast of weeks;* pentecost. *Feast of tabernacles;* the day of atonement.

Verse 14. After the various activities connected with the dedication had been ended, Solomon put the regular services in their proper order again. The *courses* or turns of the priests had been arranged by David (1 Chr. 24: 1-19), and Solomon observed the arrangement respectfully. The *porters* were janitors or gatekeepers, and they also served by *courses* or turns.

Verse 15. *Priests* and *Levites* are mentioned as separate groups. That is because all priests were of the tribe of Levi, while not all Levites could be priests; only the family of Aaron had that right.

Verse 16. *Was prepared* means the work was completed. The verse is a summing up of the work of Solomon, telling us that his great task was brought to completion.

Verses 17, 18. Solomon wished to import this gold from Ophir because it was reputed to be of unusual fineness. As the sea travel in those waters was somewhat uncertain, Huram (Hiram) sent some of his men to serve as guides in the adventure.

2 CHRONICLES 9

Verse 1. See my comments on 1 Ki. 10: 1 for this place.

Verse 2. *Told her all her questions* is a way of saying he gave her the answers to all her questions.

Verse 3. *Seen the wisdom* signifies that she had seen his wisdom proved.

Verse 4. *Sitting of his servants* refers to the orderly manner in which the servants of Solomon attended the meals. That systematic routine applied also to the services the various persons rendered to their master. The queen of Sheba observed also the grandeur of the whole array of architecture connected with the temple. *No more spirit in her* is figurative, meaning she was overcome with astonishment.

Verses 5, 6. The report of Solomon's splendor was great enough to bring this queen from a far country to see him. Notwithstanding it was that great, the report was not half as great as the facts would have justified. That is remarkable, for the common thing is for such reports to be exaggerated. It is a fine example of the faithfulness of God's promises. We may misunderstand and incorrectly describe the good things to be received from God, but it would be impossible to overdraw the *degree* of his favors; we could not represent them in too high a quality.

Verse 7. The queen's statement, ascribing happiness to the servants of Solomon, was based on the fact that they could hear the wisdom coming from him. What a wonderful conclusion it was she formed, placing wisdom above material advantages.

Verse 8. True love is often indicated by the kind of favor it leads one to bestow on the one loved. The queen of Sheba connected God's love for Israel with his giving them this wise man for a king.

Verse 9. See my comments on Gen. 32: 13 for the explanation of why the queen made these gifts to Solomon.

Verse 10. See Ch. 8: 17, 18 concerning this gold. The comments on the following verse will explain the algum trees.

Verse 11. The algum is called also the almug tree. According to Smith's Bible Dictionary, it was a wood with fine grain, and was of a beautiful garnet color. *Terraces* comes from a word that means a staircase. The timber of the algum tree would be well adapted for that use. Being hard and fine grained, it would be suitable also for the making of the musical instruments.

Verse 12. See the comments I have offered at 1 Ki. 10: 13 and 1 Chr. 29: 3 for explanation of this misunderstood passage.

Verses 13, 14. According to Moffatt's translation, the 666 talents of gold was nearly 29 tons. *Chapmen* were wandering or traveling tradesmen, and they brought much gold to Solomon in the form of tariff. The merchants in general, also, paid tariff for the traffic privileges. The gold and silver that was turned over to Solomon from the kings and governors was in the form of tribute. This was exacted because Solomon "reigned over all kingdoms" in the territory named. (1 Ki. 4: 21.)

Verses 15, 16. These articles were made for ornamental purposes and placed in this house for exhibition. *House of the forest of Lebanon* referred to the palace. This subject is explained in detail at 1 Ki. 7: 2.

Verses 17-19. Ivory is a pretty substance, yet it was covered and put out of sight with gold, another pretty material. But there was a physical reason for using ivory for the body of the throne. Its texture was such that it would be free from shrinkage, and it also would endure the test of bending by its flexibility. For more comments regarding these lions see 1 Ki. 7th chapter.

Verse 20. Silver was *not anything accounted* which means it was not thought much of in those days. Solomon's glory (Matt. 6: 29) consisted not only in the costliness of his wearing apparel, but also in the show and beauty of his articles of service.

Verse 21. According to Smith's Bible Dictionary, this *Tarshish* was a seaport that could be reached through the Red Sea. The ships of the two kings, Solomon and Huram, united every three years in a trading voyage to this city. They brought to the realm of Israel a supply of useful materials such as named. The peacocks were used for ornamental purposes only, not for breeding, since the males only were brought. The apes were doubtless used merely for whimsical purposes.

Verse 22. The reader is given such declarations as this verse to impress him with the fulfillment of God's promises. (1 Ki. 3: 13.)

Verse 23. The inspired writer is the one who says that God put the wisdom in the heart of Solomon. This should be considered by those who deny that Solomon was inspired. It is true that all good things come from God, and the wisdom a man has naturally could be said to have been put in his heart by the Lord. But Solomon already had that when God made the promise of 1 Ki. 3: 12, which shows that the wisdom he had was a direct gift from God, which is the same as inspiration.

Verse 24. These "presents" were official tokens of recognition of and subjection to Solomon, according to the practices of the times. See the comments at Gen. 32: 13.

Verse 25. This account does not agree, in figures, with 1 Ki. 4: 26. I have gone into detail at that place, and the reader is requested to consult it.

Verse 26. *The river* refers to the Euphrates River. This is not learned from the lexicon, because the original could mean any body of water that had some prominence. But other passages that deal with the same subject name the river. (Gen. 15: 18; Deut. 11: 24.) *Land of the Philistines* refers to the western boundary since that narrow tract lay along the Mediterranean Sea. The *border of Egypt* has the same significance as *river of Egypt* which was part of the southern boundary of the promised land. This whole territory had been promised to Abraham and his seed. (Gen. 15: 18.) Solomon was the first man fully to realize the enjoyment of that much territory, due to the disobedience of the national leaders.

Verse 27. Stones and sycamore trees were very common. Solomon's resources were so great that gold was as plentiful in Jerusalem as stones had been, and the elegant cedars were as numerous in Jerusalem as the sycamore trees were in the lowlands.

Verse 28. This was a violation of Deut. 17: 16, 17. God was lenient toward Solomon for the sake of David, and did not punish him directly for this error.

Verse 29. There were many books written in the days of the kings that were never made a part of the Bible. But they were good histories, and were referred to very often for the benefit of the readers who might wish more detailed information.

Verses 30, 31. *All Israel* could be understood as a contrast with the partial rule of David. He had the rule over one tribe only for seven years, then received it over the whole nation. *Slept with his fathers.* See 1 Ki. 2: 10.

2 CHRONICLES 10

Verse 1. Chronicles differs from the book of Kings in that the major part of it is the history of the kingdom of Judah, or the two tribes. Incidental references will be made to the ten tribes because of their connection with Judah, but the run of the history will concern Judah only. Jerusalem was the national capital, but the inauguration ceremonies for Solomon's successor took place at Shechem.

Verse 2. While Solomon lived he heard of some actions of Jeroboam who aspired to be king. Accordingly he threatened him so that Jeroboam fled to Egypt. Hearing of the death of Solomon, Jeroboam came out of his exile and back into the land of Israel. He remembered the favorable predictions that had been made for him (1 Ki. 11: 31) and came home with that motive in mind.

Verse 3. It would be expected that the people in general would learn about the prediction that had been made to Jeroboam. There had previously been a division of sentiment in the congregation as indicated by such expressions as *Israel* and *Judah*. (1 Sam. 11; 8; 2 Sam. 2: 10; 3: 10; 12: 8; 19: 43.) The formal division of the nation, therefore, was about to come, and needed only a spark to set off the blast. Jeroboam was invited to attend the ceremonies at Shechem, where he acted as spokesman for the dissatisfied elements among the congregation.

Verses 4, 5. The statement the people made as to the service given to Solomon was true. The two great buildings, the temple and the palace, required 20 years of time and many thousands of man hours of hard labor. All of that was necessary and no criticism was made against Solomon; it was mentioned only as a statement of fact. Now the work was done and there was no call for such service to continue. We might think the people were sincere in their address to Rehoboam, for their statements were true. There was no indication, however, that the new king intended to continue the rigorous services of his father. The whole situation shows the people were seeking a pretext for the break they had already determined upon. Rehoboam took the case "under advisement" for three days.

Verses 6, 7. The corresponding passage in 1 Ki. 12: 7 suggested that Rehoboam "serve" the people. That did not mean that the king was to "divide his authority" with the people, as some persons often teach, but that he would serve the best interests of his people by ruling wisely. The same thought is expressed with different words in the present passage. Rehoboam could have taken the advice of the older men without surrendering one mite of his rightful authority.

Verses 8, 9. The influence of association is indicated by the words *that were brought up with him*. Many times a boy's "pals" have more influence over him than do older people, or even his parents. How true are the words of Paul in 1 Cor. 15: 33.

Verses 10, 11. These young men had the erroneous idea that threatened severity could take the place of wise directions in regulating a people. They failed to realize that one of the surest ways of acquiring obedience from a subject is to assure him that his best interests will be considered in all government over him. The severe expressions suggested were figurative, of course, and used for comparison only.

Verses 12-14. *Advice* is from the same word as "counsel" in Psa. 1: 1, where it is related to the ungodly. The nature of the counsel, however, would not necessarily prove that the ones giving it were ungodly persons. We should be slow in forming that conclusion in this case, for the Lord had a hand in the affair as we shall see in the next verse. However, that would not justify any unwise motive of the acting parties.

Verse 15. God always takes care of his predictions, and in so doing often uses human means in carrying them out. If, in fulfilling God's plans unconsciously, the agents do unwise things, they are not excusable just because their deeds proved the predictions of God. The Assyrians were fulfilling God's plans when they subdued the ten tribes. But they were condemned because of their motives in the deal. (Isa. 10: 7.) God has predicted this misfortune for Rehoboam of which we are now learning, hence his every action was to be according to the prediction.

Verses 16, 17. *All Israel* means the ten tribes. They revolted from the inauguration of Rehoboam and went to their homes. The rest of this day's events is given in 1 Ki. 12, showing the formation of the kingdom of Israel. The two kingdoms are afterward referred to as the Kingdom of Judah and the Kingdom of Israel. They are sometimes designated simply as Judah and Israel. In secular history they frequently are known as the Northern and the Southern kingdom. *David . . . own house.* The 10 tribes recognized David as a prominent head of the kingdom of Judah. That was true in that he was of the tribe of Judah, as were all the kings who afterward reigned in Jerusalem, the city that contained the important Zion, or "City of David."

Verses 18, 19. Rehoboam was rash enough to think he could subdue the revolt. He took his financial officer with him and went among the 10 tribes, thinking to exact the usual taxes from them. But the people slew the taxgatherer, which caused Rehoboam to hasten back to his own capital city.

2 CHRONICLES 11

Verse 1. It seems that Rehoboam had not yet learned his lesson. The disastrous experience of his treasurer should have made him know that the 10 tribes were lost to him. He did not realize it though, and made preparations for war with a view of forcing the tribes back under his rule.

Verses 2-4. *Man of God* was one of the special names for a prophet. Instead of speaking directly to Rehoboam, God spoke to him by this prophet. (Heb. 1: 1.) The division of the nation into separate kingdoms was ordained by the Lord as a punishment for the sin of idolatry, according to the prediction of Ahijah. (1 Ki. 11: 30-35.)

Verses 5-10. *Built the cities* denotes the remodeling work that was done. Rehoboam improved and fortified these cities which had already existed. *Fenced cities* means walled cities, one of the items of fortification.

Verse 11. *Strong holds* is from METSURAH, and Strong defines it, "a hemming in, i. e. a mound or a rampart, fortification." These were places adapted for defense by their natural setting. Rehoboam made them stronger and stationed soldiers in them, who were supported by a store of provisions.

Verse 12. *Having Judah and Benjamin on his side.* By providing each city with strong weapons he made sure his standing with Judah and Benjamin.

Verses 13, 14. This is the first account we have of the side the Levites took in the division of the tribes. In the original record we have the two and the ten tribes only mentioned. This passage informs us that the Levites pulled off with the 10 tribes. Jeroboam rejected them and they went back to the kingdom of Judah. We cannot feel too favorably toward them for returning to the right place, for if Jeroboam had accepted their service, we have no evidence that they would have rejected his offer. However, we are pleased that they went back, for that gave the kingdom of Judah, the one with the capital at Jerusalem, the lawful priesthood.

Verse 15. The priests whom Jeroboam ordained were to act for him in three classes of service, named in this verse; *high places, the devils,* and *the calves.* The first is commented on at 1 Ki. 3: 2. The third refers to the idols described in 1 Ki. 12: 28. The second does not have the meaning usually conveyed by that word. It is from SAIR and Strong defines it, "shaggy; as noun, a he-goat; by analogy a faun." It has been translated in the King James version by devil 2 times, goat 23, he goat 1, kid 28, satyr 2. It thus has a somewhat indefinite significance as applied to the priests under Jeroboam. When these priests acted in the sacrificing of these goats, the dominant idea Jeroboam had was to adore the animals sacrificed instead of the true God for whose sake he was pretending to offer them.

Verse 16. *Them* is the pronoun for the Levites in V. 13. When they went back in a body to Jerusalem, it had an influence on many individuals in the other tribes, who refused to go to the calves at Bethel or Dan, but went instead to the place which God had ordained for the national worship, which was at Jerusalem.

Verse 17. The effect of this returning of the Levites and other individuals was a strengthening of Rehoboam. For three years he served God faithfully and was a powerful ruler and God was for him; but he relaxed in his devotion. This is recorded in 1 Ki. 14: 22-24, also in the chapter following the one we are now studying.

Verses 18-21. The account of these several wives which Rehoboam took is not given as a criticism. Plurality of wives was suffered at that time and Rehoboam was not any worse than the others. But his numerous offspring helped him to be strong in the execution of his office. *Loved Maachah above* is like the case of Solomon who really loved the daughter of Pharaoh. A man can love only one woman as a husband is expected to love his wife. But they took a plurality of women for the purposes of mere fleshly gratification, and for advantages in the social and political world.

Verse 22. The rule of succession was for the oldest son to be king after his father. But Rehoboam loved his wife Maachah and that caused him to feel partial toward her son Abijah. Accordingly, he prepared for the succession by making him his chief among the brethren, having a rule over them under his father.

Verse 23. This wise distribution of his children among the provinces of his kingdom is what was meant by my comments on Vs. 18-21. And because there was such an advantage in having many of his own flesh and blood offspring to be stationed in places of importance, he *desired many wives.*

2 CHRONICLES 12

Verse 1. The period of Rehoboam's strength as a righteous king was described in Ch. 11: 17. It is again referred to in this verse, and the indications are that his greatness was misused. Instead of showing gratitude to God for his good fortune, he became vain and forsook the Lord.

Verses 2-4. It was a usual practice of God to punish his people by bringing some foreign nations against them. In the case of Rehoboam, the king of Egypt was suffered to come against Jerusalem with a large force of charioteers and other people. He took over the walled cities scattered over the territory of Judah, then went up even to the capital at Jerusalem.

Verse 5. Again the Lord used a prophet to communicate to the people. Shemaiah came to Jerusalem to explain to Rehoboam and his leading men why they were suffering the humiliation of the Egyptian invasion. They were told plainly it was because they had forsaken God, therefore they were left in the hands of Shishak.

Verse 6. The message of the prophet was received with respect. The people became penitent and acknowledged the righteousness of God's dealings with them.

Verse 7. The penitence of man is never overlooked by the Lord. However, he will not go to the other extreme and release the disobedient entirely from just punishment. In this case he promised not to be as severe as he had intended.

Verse 8. Experience is a good teacher, and in many cases will rivet the lesson on the mind more closely than theory. By being in subjection to the king of Egypt for a while, the people of Judah were to learn the difference between serving God, and serving the foreign countries.

Verses 9-11. See my comments on 1 Ki. 14: 25-28 for explanation of this paragraph.

Verse 12. There were two facts that caused the Lord to become lenient at this time: one was humility of Rehoboam; the other was the existence of some good in Judah. *In Judah things went well* means that there was some good still left in Judah. So all in all, there was reason not to be too hard on the nation.

Verses 13, 14. This is a general summing up of the life of Rehoboam, covering the short period of his good rule, and the rest of the period when he forsook God.

Verse 15. There were books written by various persons that are not included in our Bible. They were not inspired in all cases, but were good histories. Those who wished more details than were given in the Biblical account could consult the said books. Rehoboam and Jeroboam started their reigns at the same time, and as long as both lived they were in a state of war with each other.

Verse 16. *Slept with his fathers* is explained at 1 Ki. 2: 10.

2 CHRONICLES 13

Verse 1. A brief reference to the reign of Jeroboam is made only to show the date of the reign of Abijah. The narrative will concern the kingdom of Judah primarily. But in giving us that history it will be necessary to report some things pertaining to the 10 tribes, since the two kingdoms never were on peaceful terms.

Verse 2. *His mother's name*, etc. Such an expression is found in the history of Israel very frequently. It is because the kings had a plurality of wives and the reader was to be informed as to which of a man's wives was the mother of the man considered.

Verse 3. *Set the battle in array* denotes that Abijah got his forces together, consisting of brave and strong men to the number of 400,000. Jeroboam did likewise with twice the number of select soldiers. The division of the 12 tribes into separate kingdoms was by the ordinance of God, and it was in vain that any attempt was made to prevent it. Yet the Lord always had a preference for the kingdom of Judah because it was the inheritance from David. In the wars which took place between the two kingdoms, God took a hand frequently and helped the side that was worthy. When the Lord was with a certain side, great numbers or other apparent advantages possessed by the other side would avail them nothing.

Verse 4. *Mount Zemaraim . . . in . . . Mount Ephraim.* It would be confusing to read of one mount being in another. But the last term had reference to a large territory which included the specific mount of the same name. The territory contained also the mount where Abijah stood to make this speech.

Verse 5. The covenant God gave to David was indeed intended to be perpetual, but it was based on the condition that all the subjects be obedient to the law of the Lord. *Covenant of salt* is figurative, and means that the covenant was to be perpetual, even as material would be that is preserved by salt. In Num. 18: 19 and Mark 9: 49 salt is used figuratively to indicate something perpetual.

Verse 6. *Servant of Solomon* and *son of David.* Note the contrast in the standing of the two persons. Jeroboam was but a *servant* of Solomon, while the latter was a *son* of David. And this son was to have his father's throne in peace, and transmit it to future generations in the same condidition.

Verse 7. Vain men means "empty" or "worthless" men. *Belial* in the Old Testament is not a proper noun, but is descriptive of any men who are low and wicked. The king charged that men such as he had described had brought the conspiracy against Rehoboam. *Young and tender* denotes one who is inexperienced because of his youth.

Verse 8. Abijah further charged that a multitude of evil men had a mind to withstand the kingdom of the Lord, and that, too, when it was in the hands of the sons of David. The *golden calves* are the idols that Jeroboam had set up at Bethel and Dan, to keep his people from Jerusalem, the place for the lawful sacrifices.

Verse 9. See my comments at Ch. 11: 13, 14. It was fortunate for the true worship that the Levites came back to the kingdom of Judah; however, the motive of the 10 tribes in casting them off was sinful. Their sin was especially great in that the priests they ordained to take the place of the lawful ones officiated in vain worship. *No gods* was said in reference to the golden calves mentioned above.

Verses 10. This verse is a picture of the lawful service. The Levites in general were for the service indirectly connected with the priesthood, and the sons of Aaron the particular ones of the Levites who were to officiate in the priesthood.

Verse 11. Not only did Judah have the lawful priests, but their service was in connection with the divinely ordained articles of furniture.

Verse 12. Abijah made a final appeal by the warning that God was with him and his people to be their captain in battle. *Trumpets to cry alarm* referred to the instructions of Moses in Num. 10:9. The significant statement is made that the battle of the 10 tribes would *not prosper* because it would be *against the Lord God of your fathers*. This great principle of truth is taught by Paul in Rom. 8:31.

Verse 13. The speech of Abijah was in vain. *An ambushment* is a body of troops lying in concealment. Jeroboam had his main forces with him in the front of the battle, while the ambushment was in the rear.

Verse 14. When the action began, the men of Judah realized their situation. They resorted both to divine and human means for help. That is, they *cried unto the Lord*, and the priests *sounded with the trumpets*.

Verses 15, 16. *Shout* is from RUWA and Strong defines it, "figuratively to split the ears." The shout alone could not have caused the victory. But it exhibited their faith in God who responded by smiting the forces of Jeroboam, and they fled before the men of Judah. They did not escape defeat, however, as we shall see in the next verse.

Verse 17. This was a remarkable battle, and, as far as I can recall, was without a parallel in all history in the point of the number of the slain. We should bear in mind the fact that no great destructive means existed at that time for warfare. The usual weapon was the sword or spear, and required hand-to-hand fighting. But the victorious army slew 100,000 more men of the enemy than it had in its own entire forces. The explanation lies in the great truth that the Lord was with them, and against him no force can prevail.

Verse 18. The success of the battle just ended is accounted for by the fact that Judah *relied upon the Lord God of their fathers*.

Verses 19, 20. *Cities* and *towns* differ mainly in size and corresponding importance. The towns were the same as villages, and were connected in some sort of dependency with the cities named with them. *Bethel* is the most important city in this group, because it had one of the golden calves that Jeroboam set up. The effect of this great battle was to render the king of Israel weak the rest of the reign of Abijah. He finally was stricken with some sort of sickness and died.

Verse 21. While Jeroboam grew weaker, Abijah grew stronger. His marrying the 14 wives gave him the large number of children attributed to him, and that contributed to his strength as a king.

Verse 22. Iddo was a writing prophet, although his works were not included in the Bible. Like many others already mentioned, his writings were good history, and persons could consult them who wished a more detailed account of the various subjects than were to be found in the regular compilation.

2 CHRONICLES 14

Verse 1. *Quiet ten years* means there were no war activities in that time. *City of David* was called Mount Zion also, and was the most prominent part of Jerusalem.

Verse 2. *Right in the eyes of the Lord* is a more significant expression than is realized many times. Almost anything would be right in the eyes of some men; the real question is, what does the Lord consider to be right.

Verse 3. *Strange* means "foreign or outside." Strange gods, then, would be gods outside of the authority of the true God. *Images* is defined in the margin of some Bibles as "statues." They had been erected at the *high places* (see my comments at 1 Ki. 3:2), for which the sacrifices were offered on the altars referred to in the same connection. See comments at 2 Ki. 17:16 for explanation of the *groves*.

Verses 4, 5. The reformation of Asa was scriptural and logical in its order. He first had the unlawful practices stopped, then commanded the people to resume that which was lawful. It would not have been of any use to profess the lawful service while continuing the evil kind. The same principle holds good today. If a man expects the Lord to receive his services, he must first cease his evil practices.

Verse 6. *Fenced cities* were those with walls, built around them for defense.

Verse 7. *Build these cities* does not mean to start them, but to improve and fortify them. *While the land is yet before us*, and *given us rest*, are significant expressions, and are related in one principle, "in time of peace prepare for war." This is an old saying that is wise, and shows the motive that Asa had at the time he proposed his work on the cities. They were then in his possession, and he was not occupied with war. It was an opportune time, therefore, to "strengthen the things that remained." But the inclination for war was so general that Asa was destined not to be at rest always as we shall soon see.

Verse 8. Asa not only prepared for the future by the works he did on his cities, but he formed and maintained a strong military force which is described in this verse. *Targets* were large shields for defense against the spears and darts of the enemy. The *spears* were long poles with points of metal at the end, used by casting against the foe. *Shields* were similar to the targets except that they were smaller. These instruments of aggression and defense were wielded by an army of several thousand men who were strong and brave.

Verse 9. *Chariots* were vehicles so constructed as to be useful in battle, although they could be used for purposes of transportation also. They consisted of a single pair of wheels on an axle, upon which was a car with high front and sides, but open at the back. Such an arrangement would serve as a defense against the enemy that was being faced. The opening at the rear would make it convenient when the occupants wished to leave the chariot, either for hasty retreat on foot if the chariot horses were killed, or when it was decided to make a hand-to-hand attack. There were 300 of such vehicles with their equipment, also a *host* or army of a million soldiers that confronted Asa for battle.

Verse 10. *Set the battle in array* means they drew up in battle formation.

Verse 11. *Nothing with thee to help* denotes that great numbers will not count for anything against the Lord. The Ethiopians had brought a large force against the people of God. Asa relied on the strength of his God, and in that faith he offered his prayer "just before the battle." The situation was the same in principle as that in the case of David and Goliath. That was one where physical strength was to be pitted against the large. The present situation with Asa was to put small numbers against the large.

Verse 12. To smite means to strike or hit another, either with the result of immediate destruction, or with lesser effect. In the case at hand the effect of the smiting was to cause the enemy to flee. *Before Asa* and *before Judah* are stated in this way because Asa was the king of Judah. The two terms, then, mean the same forces.

Verse 13. God could completely destroy an enemy on the ground. However, he desired man to have a part in the work, so the foe was first smitten sufficiently to make him flee, then the servants of the Lord were to pursue and make their attack *Before the Lord* and *before his host*. These phrases are in keeping with the thoughts just expressed. The Lord and his people were to be workers together. We may read of the same principle as taught by Paul. (1 Cor. 3: 9.) The *spoil* was the loot or valuable personal property taken from the enemy.

Verse 14. *Smote all the cities* means they smote the people in them. This smiting was severe enough to cause the inhabitants to be afraid of the Lord, and so much that they yielded up their spoil or personal valuables.

Verse 15. To smite the tents of cattle would mean the tents were attacked and the beasts captured. Thus ended successfully this battle of Asa against his enemies.

2 CHRONICLES 15

Verse 1. The prophets were not always under the inspiration of God; it was only when some communication was to be delivered. (Heb. 1: 1.) At the time we have reached in our study, God wished to give a message of encouragement and instruction to Asa, and sent his Spirit upon the prophet for that purpose.

Verse 2. Note the condition on which the Lord would be with his people, *while ye be with him*. That condition was always in force whether expressly stated or not.

Verse 3. God has always been, and his law was in existence at that time. Israel had been without God for the reason indicated in the preceding verse. They were without law simply because they had forsaken it. The priests were expected to be teachers of the law of God. (Lev. 10: 8-11; Deut. 17: 9; Mal. 2: 7.) They had become negligent of their duty and the prophet complained about it.

Verse 4. The constancy of God's compassion was indicated when the people returned and sought his favor, and they were not disappointed in their expectations.

Verses 5, 6. *Those times* refers to

the periods described in V. 3. As a punishment for the disobedience of his people, God suffered the foreign nations to come against them to vex and damage them.

Verse 7. The prophet was not implying that Asa was then guilty of neglect as described, for he had very recently waged a courageous battle against the heathen. The speech was for the purpose of encouraging him, and he was assured of being rewarded.

Verse 8. Oded was the father of Azariah, who was really the prophet. In a statement of respect his father was named as the prophet, although his son was the man who delivered the message. Upon the message of the prophet from God, Asa made a more thorough reformation still, by removing the idols from the territory of his own proper domain, and also from the extra cities that he had taken from the general territory outside, known as *Mount Ephraim*. After clearing out the institutions of false worship, he renewed the true service that belonged to the great altar before the temple.

Verse 9. This movement was recorded in Ch. 11: 16. It is gratifying to read the motive that prompted these *strangers* from the other tribes to come to the side of Asa; it was their seeing that God was with him. Too often we see men "line up" on a certain side merely because it seems to be the winning side, not because it is the right side. To associate with a man because God is with him is the supremely good motive.

Verse 10. *Third month* was the one in which the feast of weeks or pentecost came. That was one of the three occasions on which all the males were required to go to Jerusalem.

Verse 11. These offerings were voluntary contributions out of the things they had taken from the enemy. It does not mean, necessarily, that the beasts were slain. They were given over to the ones having charge of the service of God.

Verse 12. These strangers from the tribes of the northern kingdom had been tainted with a mixed worship and were very unsettled as to the true God. The evidence was convincing to them that a half-hearted service would not count for anything with God. They now *entered into a covenant*, which means they agreed with the Lord that they would give their whole heart to him.

Verse 13. The age of the Mosaic Dispensation was one with military phases in its execution. Violators of the law were liable to physical punishment. In order to be prepared against future departures into the ways of the heathen about them, these new arrivals at the temple of God threatened to inflict the penalty of death on all people who hesitated at seeking the true object of their devotions.

Verse 14. The threat of such severe punishment was emphasized by an oath. In order that none would escape the notice, the oath was accompanied with loud voices and with instruments made for producing heavy sounds.

Verse 15. This is more or less a general statement, going back to the previous chapter where the record may be found of the victory over the enemy. *Rest round about* refers to the freedom from war.

Verse 16. The title of queen was an honorary one only; the full form is "queenmother." Yet it is a considerable honor and not lightly to be considered. But the mother of the king had made herself unworthy of the title by her idolatry. Asa showed his faithfulness to God by not allowing his flesh and blood interests to interfere with his devotion to the Lord.

Verse 17. *But the high places . . . nevertheless.* These two expressions modify each other. There was something wrong about the high places, but not as bad as some other things since Asa was spoken of favorably in spite of such places. See the comments I have made on the subject at 1 Ki. 3: 2.

Verses 18, 19. When kings and other great men obtained valuables from their enemies, they generally appropriated a goodly portion of them to the Lord's service. Asa carried out such an action in his devotion to the God of Israel. He had a prosperous reign and was free from war many years.

2 CHRONICLES 16

Verse 1. Baasha was king of Israel which was the kingdom of the 10 tribes. With a few exceptions there was a state of war between the two kingdoms all the years of their existence. Baasha *built Ramah* which means he fortified it with the intent of blockading Jerusalem, since the two cities were not far apart.

Verses 2, 3. We will always remember that the Jewish nation was secular as well as religious. It had dealings with other nations as a temporal power, and such relations were not necessarily wrong. However, in the dealings with other temporal powers, the kings of the nation of God should never have left the Lord out of their calculations. Damascus was the capital of Syria, a country just north of Palestine, and hence a near neighbor of the 10 tribes. An alliance had previously been formed between the two kingdoms. Now that Judah is about to be attacked by the king of Israel, Asa thinks to divert his attention by turning his ally away from him. With this in view, Asa appropriated some of the treasurers in the house of the Lord. Since the object was in the interests of that house, as Asa saw it, we can see a favorable motive in his act. We should not consider the offer of the silver and gold as a bribe in the ordinary sense of that word. It costs money to carry on war, and if the king of Syria is to do so on behalf of Asa, he should be supported in the expense.

Verse 4. Ben-hadad king of Syria accepted the proposition of Asa and sent his soldiers against Israel. *Store cities* were the ones containing the magazines of supplies for military and other uses.

Verse 5. The plan of Asa had the desired effect of drawing away the attention of Baasha. He stopped the work of fortifying Ramah and left the materials behind him.

Verse 6. *Took all Judah* means that Asa called the people of Judah into his service for the special work. The materials that had been brought to Ramah to oppose Asa were used to help him instead. They were used to fortify two cities of Judah that were important to the welfare of the nation.

Verse 7. Good men are subject to mistakes. Asa did not give the Lord his due consideration in the plan to draw off the king of the 10 tribes (see remarks at Vs. 2, 3 above). A prophet was sent to chastise Asa for his mistake, and to punish him with a military loss in that the Syrians were allowed to escape completely.

Verse 8. The main point in this verse is the truth that great numbers do not count when opposed to the Lord, nor does the victory for the Lord depend on numbers.

Verse 9. God sees everything in all places, and understands the full strength as well as the weaknesses of all. He is ready to help those who put their trust in him. The punishment that was threatened against Asa was not directly upon his body; it was to affect his condition of peace in the kingdom. The period of peace that he had been enjoying was to end and wars would come instead.

Verse 10. Human nature manifests some strange traits at times. The *seer* or prophet of God was not responsible for the unpleasant message, yet Asa put him in prison for it. His rage did not stop at the prophet, but he *oppressed* or tortured some of the people at that time. Blind spite could have been the only motive for such conduct. We are not elated over the errors of this good man who was so nearly always righteous. The fact that God had the truth about it put into his Book for the information of man, is another proof that the Bible was not the production of human beings. They would have extolled the goodness of Asa, but suppressed his mistakes.

Verse 11. As an explanation of this verse, see the comments at 1 Ki. 14: 19.

Verse 12. Opponents of medical doctors may think they have a point here, but they do not. Those were days of special providence, and important servants of God had reason to appeal for divine help in times of distress. The failure to do so was one of the weak points in the life of Asa.

Verse 13. *Slept with his fathers* is explained at 1 Ki. 2: 10.

Verse 14. Abraham and other prominent men of Biblical times prepared their own burying places. Asa had made a sepulchre for his body and his friends laid him there. They added some things to the place by preparing a bed filled with various spices. *They made a very great burning for him.* Moffatt's translation gives us "bonfire" in the place of *burning*. Such a demonstration was done at times in the same spirit as were other acts of respect for the remains of loved ones. See Jer. 34: 5.

2 CHRONICLES 17

Verse 1. This verse is a continuation of the preceding chapter. Jehoshaphat was a son of Asa and is classed among the good kings. As there was a state of war between Judah and Israel practically all the time, Jehoshaphat girded himself for the conflict.

Verse 2. Jehoshaphat distributed his

soldiers, placing them in the *fenced* or walled cities. *Garrisons* were military posts that had soldiers always in them, and the posts were fortified against invasion. The king went outside his own territory and established garrisons in the cities which Asa had captured from the territory known as Mount Ephraim.

Verse 3. The life of David as a whole was good, but the purest part of it was at the beginning. This is why we have the comparison to the *first ways* David. He is called the father of Jehoshaphat by way of respect for his place in the royal line. David never did serve Baalim; the reference to that subject here is to make a favorable comment on the life of Jehoshaphat, in addition to his following the good ways of David.

Verse 4. *Not after the doings of Israel.* Without a single exception, the kings of Israel were idolaters. Jehoshaphat was one of the few of Judah who were not.

Verse 5. *All ... brought ... presents.* This signifies that Jehoshaphat had the support of his whole realm, for they were faithful in paying their dues for the maintenance of the kingdom, and for the royal splendor of the king.

Verse 6. *Lifted* is from an original that has a rather unfavorable meaning primarily. However, it is sometimes used in a good sense, meaning to be exalted in the right way. The connection shows that Jehoshaphat was influenced by the exalted principles manifested by the Lord's ways. His work against idolatry mentioned in the close of the verse justifies the remarks in the beginning of it.

Verse 7. *Sent to his princes ... to teach.* The idea is that he sent word to these princes to do the teaching. *Obadiah* and *Zechariah* are the same names as two of the minor prophets, but that is a coincidence only. These men were merely some princes or leading men in the service of Jehoshaphat.

Verse 8. The princes named in the preceding verse were outstanding men, but were without any official designation. In addition to them, the king selected some men from the tribe of Levi. A still more special selection was made of the Levites; some of whom were priests. This distinction is explained by the fact that all priests were Levites, but not all Levites could act as priests; only the family of Aaron could.

Verse 9. *They taught in Judah* means the priests taught. That was according to the system that God designed for the continued instruction of his people. (Lev. 10: 11; Deut. 17: 9; Mal. 2: 27.) This work had been neglected according to the charge made by Azariah in Ch. 15: 3, and Jehoshaphat was trying to correct the defect.

Verse 10. God had frequently told his people that he would bless them and bring the other nations in subjection to them. Now that the requirements of the law were being carried out under the directions of Jehoshaphat, the Lord caused the kingdoms around them to fear to the extent that they did not undertake any war against him.

Verse 11. The absence of war was not the only indication of the subjection of the kingdoms, for they brought *presents* and *tribute silver.* The first was a diplomatic courtesy (explained at Gen. 32: 13), and the second was a specific charge of financial support for the kingdom of Judah.

Verse 12. The *castles* were fortified places to defend the country against invasion of the enemies. The *cities of store* were the ones equipped for storage of provisions.

Verse 13. *Business* is from MELAKAH and Strong defines it, "properly deputyship, i. e. ministry." It means that Jehoshaphat had official and military representatives in the cities of his kingdom. He had brave and strong men with him also in Jerusalem.

Verses 14, 15. This paragraph is interesting mainly in giving a statement of the strength of Jehoshaphat's defense.

Verse 16. *Willingly offered himself* is equivalent to our system of "volunteer" service. This man was one of influence and had 200,000 strong and brave men under him, all for the defense of the king of Judah.

Verse 17. The weapons of warfare differed from each other. It would be good strategy to group the men using each class of weapons for the purpose of unified action. This Benjamite was given command over 200,000 men who used the *bow* and *shield.* The first was to use against the enemy, the second as a defense from the enemy's darts.

Verse 18. *Ready prepared for war* means they were trained and ready for military service upon call.

Verse 19. The forementioned men

were "in waiting" always at the immediate call of Jehoshaphat. Besides all these, the king had his men stationed in all the *fenced* or walled cities scattered over his territory.

2 CHRONICLES 18

Verse 1. *Joined affinity* signifies that he formed an alliance with him. We are not given any reason why Jehoshaphat made this move, and it was a strange one in view of the character of Ahab.

Verses 2, 3. See the comments on a like passage in 1 Ki. 22: 3, 4.

Verse 4. Jehoshaphat is classed among the good kings of Judah, although the project to which he agreed was ill-advised. However, he was unwilling to venture out on the important proposed action without some information, and the method of obtaining such in those days was through the prophets. (Heb. 1: 1.)

Verse 5. Prophets, like other teachers, sometimes give instructions they think will please their hearers regardless of whether they are correct.

Verse 6. Jehoshaphat knew of the disposition of men to be popular, and had some doubt with regard to these 400 prophets. He did not directly deny their being the prophets of the Lord. He merely asked if there were some other prophet *besides* them.

Verse 7. Ahab was naturally inclined to favor the 400 prophets because they favored him; by the same token he would not like the other prophet. When a man does not want to hear unpleasant truth, he dislikes the one who might give such to him. Ahab expressed himself along that line and was rebuked by Jehoshaphat.

Verses 8, 9. Ahab had no way of evading the unpleasant situation, so he sent a servant to bring the prophet Micaiah before the two kings. As it was to be a meeting of a military nature, and one conducted jointly by the rulers of two great kingdoms, it was proper to provide a special place for this hearing. Accordingly, they selected a *void* or open plot of ground near the gate of Samaria, Ahab's capital.

Verses 10, 11. While waiting for the prophet sent for to arrive, the 400 who were already present were not silent. One of them, Zedekiah by name, made a material gesture for emphasizing a prediction he wished to make. He had made some horns or pointed instruments of iron to use for effect in his speech. He made the prediction that Ahab would *push* or gore the Syrians until they would be consumed, which means completely defeated. All the others of the 400 joined in with the flattery and urged the attack.

Verse 12. As the conversations recorded in the foregoing paragraph were going on, the messenger had arrived in the presence of Micaiah. He tried to prejudice him by reference to the 400 prophets who had spoken their minds already. The natural desire to be "on the side of the majority" was appealed to by the messenger, when he told Micaiah the purpose of his visit. He suggested that his word would be like that of the other prophets who had spoken favorably to the king.

Verse 13. This speech of Micaiah was similar in principle to the one made by Balaam to the messengers of Balak. (Num. 22: 18.)

Verse 14. Much of the meaning of a speech is indicated by the voice and facial expression of the speaker. We cannot see nor hear Micaiah as he makes this speech, but we are sure that it is made in irony. That is language used for a meaning directly opposite of the way it sounds.

Verse 15. *The king* was Ahab since he was the one who had sent for Micaiah. (V. 8.) He detected the irony in the speech and chastised him for it. Ahab would welcome any favorable prediction, but he would want it to be given in seriousness. *Adjure* means to make an oath. He meant to charge Micaiah to tell the truth as if he were under oath.

Verse 16. Micaiah then spoke seriously and described a vision that the Lord had given him. In that he saw the defeat of the forces of Ahab.

Verse 17. In disgust and despair, the king of Israel broke into the scene with an "I-told-you-so" statement.

Verse 18. But Micaiah was not through with describing his vision. He had been permitted to witness a scene in the presence of the throne of God. The *host of heaven* would mean a numerous mass of celestial beings, ready to do the bidding of the Lord.

Verses 19-22. For explanation of this paragraph see my comments on 1 Ki. 22: 20-23.

Verse 23. Again I ask the reader to see the comments on 1 Ki. 22: 24.

Verse 24. This is explained at 1 Ki. 22: 25.

Verses 25, 26. *Bread* and *water of affliction* means the coarse fare often served to prisoners. This was a threat of humiliation to be imposed on Micaiah.

Verse 27. Micaiah staked his reputation as a true prophet on the outcome of the venture that Ahab was about to make. He called attention of the people to it, so that when the affair was ended they would remember what had been said.

Verses 28, 29. The two allies prepared to go up to battle. Let it be borne in mind that the king of Syria did not know he was to meet the king of Judah. Ahab was thinking of that, and planned to elude the Syrian weapons by not appearing in the attire of a king. Jehoshaphat would be the only one in such robes and hence would be the target for the foe. If this scheme could be carried out, Ahab hoped to frustrate the prediction of Micaiah and so be able to return in peace as he had boasted.

Verse 30. To take the king is about the same as taking the army. The Syrian king, thinking only of the king of Israel, gave the orders recorded here.

Verse 31. The charioteers were not personally acquainted with the Israelite kings. Seeing one man in royal robes, it was natural to conclude that he was the man wanted, and they were about to make their attack on Jehoshaphat who made an outcry. Ordinarily that would not have availed to ward off the attack. The verse says *the Lord helped* him which accounts for his escape as explained in the next verse.

Verse 32. This is the explanation of how the Lord helped Jehoshaphat; it was by revealing to the Syrians the fact that they were pursuing the wrong man.

Verse 33. This verse is the same account as given in 1 Ki. 22: 34. The reader is asked to see the comments at that place.

Verse 34. Ahab had requested his men to carry him out of the army. The request was not granted, but he was held up in his chariot by assistants through the day while the battle raged, and he died in the evening.

2 CHRONICLES 19

Verse 1. Ahab was a wicked man and deserved being defeated in the battle with the Syrians. Jehoshaphat was unwise to become an ally of such a sinful person, yet he was a good man and the Lord favored him. After the conflict with the Syrians he was permitted to return in peace to his own capital in Jerusalem.

Verse 2. *Wrath* is from a word otherwise translated anger or rage. There was no special action threatened against Jehoshaphat, neither will anything of the kind come to him. The prophet Jehu was sent to him to give him a "scolding" for his folly in associating with such a wicked man as Ahab, a man who hated the Lord. However, since the alliance had not actually injured the cause of God in Judah, this rebuke was the worst that was done to him.

Verse 3. The good traits of Jehoshaphat were acknowledged, and he was given credit for having a right kind of heart.

Verse 4. Jerusalem was the dwelling place of this righteous king. But he was not content to sit down idly and see the people drift away from God. He *brought them back* means he turned their interests and conduct toward the Lord. It was similar in principle to the work of John the Baptist as predicted in Mal. 4: 6.

Verse 5. *City by city* is another way of saying that Jehoshaphat located a judge in each of the *fenced* or walled cities throughout the territory previously named.

Verse 6. God was blessing the reign of Jehoshaphat. The institutions, therefore, that he put into force would receive the divine favor. That is why he told these men that they would be judging *for the Lord*.

Verse 7. The kind of *fear* the judges were to have was respect or regard for the Lord. He would not be partial nor selfish in his judgments, neither would he tolerate such work if performed by the men whom he had appointed (through Jehoshaphat) to handle the causes of the people.

Verse 8. *Set* is used in the sense of appoint, and these Levitical men were to advise the people. *Judgment of the Lord* pertained to the judgment they were to render regarding the Lord's matters. See Lev. 10: 11, Deut. 17: 9, Mal. 2: 7. *Controversies* would refer to subjects under the law where personal interests between men were in dispute. *When they returned to Jerusalem* is said with reference to the time following the experience with the Syrians. See the first verse of this chapter.

Verse 9. Many of the words in this verse are for emphasis mainly. The significant one is *fear*, which means the respect due unto the Lord.

Verse 10. Almost every word used regarding the institutions of God could be used interchangeably, because the difference in meaning is slight or technical. Yet there is a distinction to be observed or else they would not be grouped as they are. *Blood and blood* refers to the items where the shedding of blood was in dispute. That is, where the question of murder was under examination, or where capital punishment would be the penalty were the person being investigated found guilty of the sin charged against him. *Statutes* are the formal or set enactments of God, and *judgments* are the divine conclusions on emergencies that would come up in the dealings between man and man. *This do and ye shall not trespass* means that if these judges would do the things just required of them, they would not be guilty of trespass.

Verse 11. Amariah was *chief priest* which was the same as high priest. He was the most dignified official in the Mosaic system, hence it is said here that he was over the people in *matters of the Lord*. It might be asked whether all matters were not a concern of the Lord; they are, in a general sense. But the matters in which the high priest officiated were specifically such because they took him into the most holy place in the temple. Zebadiah was ruler, or had charge of the things in the palace of the king. That is, what the high priest was to the house of the Lord, Zebadiah was to the house of the king. *The Levites* refers to the work of that tribe as a whole, and they were to operate in connection with these other men. *Deal courageously* was an exhortation for them to be brave and firm in their service to the Lord, and they had the promise that they would be blessed for it.

2 CHRONICLES 20

Verse 1. *Moab* and *Ammon* were the sons of Lot. Their descendants formed two of the noted nations of Biblical history. Because of their near relation to Abraham, God would not permit the Israelites to attack them as they did the other people. This favor was abused by them at times, and we now read of a threat of war coming from them.

Verse 2. The Dead Sea is the place meant. The Moabites and Ammonites were east of that body of water. *This side Syria* is a very indefinite term as locating the people then threatening war on Judah. Syria was a term applying sometimes to a large territory northward of Palestine. *This side Syria* would thus mean that the invading people were from a territory east of the Dead Sea and south of Syria. At the time of this notice to Jehoshaphat, the invaders had reached Engedi, a town on the west shore.

Verse 3. *Jehoshaphat feared*, which means he realized the danger confronting him. In times of great peril the true servants of God will seek for his help. It is necessary to manifest the proper frame of mind before the Lord will be entreated. Fasting was not generally commanded, but it was approved when done voluntarily. In the great distress of their situation, Jehoshaphat called upon the whole nation to observe a season of fasting; but the service in the homes was not enough as we shall soon see.

Verse 4. There are certain acts of worship that can be done privately or in the home, and others that are done collectively. In the Christian Dispensation the latter can be done only at the place of the regular meetings of the church. Under the Jewish Dispensation they had to be done at Jerusalem. So we read of the Jews leaving their places of residence and coming *to seek the Lord*, which brought them to the place where he had recorded his name, and that was in the temple.

Verse 5. *Judah* and *Jerusalem*. This Judah, though an extended territory, had to be represented at Jerusalem in order to have a lawful assembly. The *new court* was a part of the temple where the public was allowed to be. It was called *new* with reference to its being more recently built than the one around the tabernacle built by Moses.

Verse 6. The question form of this language is a reverent way of making a positive expression, acknowledging these great things of God. *Rulest . . . kingdoms . . . heathen*. This great truth is not generally realized. Nebuchadnezzar had to learn of it by a humiliating experience. (Dan. 4.)

Verse 7. God does not have to be reminded of his promises to get him to perform them. The mentioning of them in a prayer is done by way of expressing one's faith in the Lord; also to show the logic of the faith as to its basis. God had driven out the heathen in order to fulfill the promise made to Abraham, so it would be reasonable to expect him to repel these heathen invaders now threatening the descendants of Abraham. *Friend* is from AHEB and Strong defines it, "to have affection for." Abraham loved God and showed his affection for him by doing what he was commanded without hesitation.

Verses 8, 9. The sentiments of this verse were uttered by Solomon in his prayer at the dedication of the temple. (1 Ki. 8.) The evil anticipated by the "wise monarch" was about to come on the nation and Jehoshaphat made his appeal according to that prayer. The principal basis for expecting the favor of God at this prayer is the fact that *thy name is in this house.*

Verse 10. The reference to *Mount Seir* means that some Edomites had joined in with these others to invade Judah. The three groups were near of kin to Abraham and were spared when the Israelites were on the march from Egypt.

Verse 11. *Behold how they reward us.* This is a brief way of saying these people were rewarding evil for good; not showing due appreciation.

Verses 12, 13. In a state of complete despair, the congregation waited for some promise of relief from God. They realized that no human might, however great, could meet the forces of all these intruders. It must have been a solemn and pitiable sight, the husbands and wives, and the children cringing near their parents, longing and begging for some kind of assurance from God.

Verse 14. Following the general practice, God called upon one of his servants to give a message to the people. The line of names mentioned was to show the connection between this man and the tribe of Levi. That tribe furnished the priests, and the priests were expected to give knowledge to the people according to Lev. 10: 11, Deut. 17: 9, Mal. 2: 7. Not that Jahaziel was a priest, but he came of the priestly tribe, and it would be fitting to use him for the special occasion of information.

Verses 15, 16. Not only did Jahaziel assure the people of relief, but that the battle would be a supernatural one; was really not to be their battle. All of this is understandable when we recall that God would not permit the Israelites before to attack the descendants of Abraham. Now that it is necessary to oppose them, the Lord will take a hand so that the procedure will be consistent with the former restrictions.

Verse 17. *Stand ye still and see,* etc., was used the most literally that the famous saying was ever used. About all the people will need to do on their part will be of a ceremonial or religious nature. It is true they were told that on the next day they would go out *against* the enemy. But it would not be to engage physically in the battle. They were to be there for the exercises just mentioned, and to *see* the great and unusual salvation the Lord will perform for them.

Verse 18. This verse gives us one clear meaning of "worship" as used in the Bible. The king and his people are said to have prostrated their bodies with faces toward the ground. In doing this they are said to be *worshiping.* The New Testament recognizes also a wide range of meaning for this word, from the complete subjection to all the requirements of the Lord, down to the mere act of respect toward another.

Verse 19. Levi had three sons of whom Kohath was one. Of the family of Kohath one son was Korah, and these Korhites came from him. They were an important branch of the singers in the temple service, hence are mentioned in this connection here. They sang with a *loud voice on high* because the nation was assembled in great numbers, and the singing was to be heard by the people.

Verse 20. In obedience to the instructions of V. 17, the people left the temple the next day to go toward the vicinity of the invading host. On the way the king made an encouraging speech to them; that they should have faith in the word of God that had been given to them by the prophet. *Believe his prophets, so shall ye prosper.* The popular doctrine of "faith only" is not justified here. They had been already told that the battle would be fought by the Lord, not them. Now then, all that was left for them to do as far as the actual fighting was concerned, was to believe.

Verse 21. *Consulted with the people* does not mean that Jehoshaphat "divided his authority" with them. Moffatt renders it, "after his counsel to the nation." This counsel included the instruction that the singers were to carry on their services while they were marching to the scene of their triumph.

Verse 22. An ambushment is a group of men lying in an unseen place, and ready to make an unexpected attack. We shall see in the next verse that this ambushment consisted of some men of the Ammonites and Moabites, detached from the main body of the soldiers, to strike from their lurking place against their own people.

Verse 23. These soldiers of Ammon and Moab first attacked the Edomites who were in the general army. When that unit was destroyed they turned on each other with their weapons until they had committed military suicide. This fulfilled the prediction of the prophet that was made in verses 15-17.

Verse 24. *Watch tower* comes from a single Hebrew word, MITSPEH, and Strong defines it, "an observatory, especially for military purposes." The people of Judah marching toward the enemy arrived at this watch tower, and from that post they saw the condition that had come about by the actions described in the preceding verse. They could then realize what the prophet meant in the prediction recorded in verses 15-17.

Verse 25. The people with Jehoshaphat saw that they had no soldiers to fight since they were all dead. It was customary under the rules of war to take possession of the valuables found on the bodies of the enemy army, and also the other personal property among them, such as the cattle and other things of value. The amount of all this spoil was so great that it took three days to collect what they were able to take with them, and even then they had to leave some of it.

Verse 26. Nearby was a valley that was suitable for an orderly assembly. To this place Jehoshaphat brought the people for a season of praise to God for the victory that had been given them. They *blessed the Lord*, which means they praised him as the source of the great blessings just bestowed upon them. This valley probably had no special name before this time, but the occasion which brought about the gathering suggested a name that would be appropriate. The word *Berachah* means "blessing," hence the valley received the name given it here.

Verse 27. After the services in the valley, Jehoshaphat led the people back to the capital city. *Judah and Jerusalem* are named in this way because the last word names the capital of the Kingdom of Judah. The meeting in the valley took place the day after they had completed the taking of the spoil. It was fitting to gather at the regularly established headquarters for a more official season of religious services.

Verse 28. A *psaltery* was a stringed instrument of music to accompany the voice. A *harp* was the national instrument of the Hebrews. According to Josephus it had ten strings, and was played upon with a plectrum, an attachment worn by the finger. A *trumpet* (called also a cornet) was a loud-sounding instrument, made of the horn of a ram. The first two were stringed instruments while the third was a kind to be played with the mouth. These were made by David according to Ch. 7:6. The joy of the people for their relief from the threatened war caused them to come to the headquarters to engage in a praise service, and these instruments were used with it.

Verses 29, 30. The providential victory of Judah over their enemies had its effect on other peoples. It caused them to fear God in the sense of being afraid to undertake any warlike action against the people of God.

Verses 31, 32. This is a general statement of the reign of Jehoshaphat, including the events that we have already learned about. Giving his mother's name was because most of the men in those days had a plurality of wives, and we are to be informed which of the wives was the mother of the man being considered.

Verse 33. Jehoshaphat was one of the good kings, but, adhering to the rule of the inspired writers, the weak points were not overlooked; one of those was the retaining of the *high places*. The reader may see the explanation of these places in the comments at 1 Ki. 3:2. They were not just what should have been used, yet not as bad as some other things. *Had not prepared their hearts*, etc., means they were not fully adapted to the service of the Lord, so a degree of leniency was shown.

Verse 34. Not all of the speakers

and writers in the olden days contributed writings that were placed in the Bible. That does not mean that there is any weakness in the Book which God handed down to us. Not all of the things that were done by Jesus were recorded in the writings of the New Testament. (John 20: 30, 31; 21: 25.) If any person in the days of the Israelites dominion wished further details on the subject, he was referred to these extra writings. And to show the reliable character of such writings, a reference was made to the favorable mention of them in the other places. Jehu has been named in a favorable manner in 1 Ki. 16: 1.

Verses 35-37. See the comments at V. 33. Among the weak points in the life of Jehoshaphat were the things mentioned in this paragraph. He was too friendly with these unworthy persons; however, the Lord did not charge him with the wicked things they did. He was made to suffer some disappointment in his plans, also to receive a reprimand from the prophet; such was the punishment he received for his errors.

2 CHRONICLES 21

Verse 1. *Slept with his fathers* is explained at 1 Ki. 2: 10. The *city of David* was a burg or department in Jerusalem of great importance. It was called Mount Zion also, and was the location of David's house.

Verse 2. All of these brethren of Jehoram were younger than he, hence not regularly entitled to the throne.

Verse 3. *Their father gave them;* refers to a time before the date of V. 1. The statement is made to show us that the younger brothers of Jehoram had not been encouraged by their father to expect the kingdom, although they were given much consideration otherwise. They received large bounties of precious metal, also the possession of fenced or walled cities. But the seniority of Jehoram entitled him to the throne, and his father had appointed him as his successor before he died.

Verse 4. Jehoram was a wicked man, and was unreasonably suspicious of his younger brothers. There was no indication that they expected to reign, for their father had settled the matter before he died. When a man makes a distribution of his possessions personally while living, it indicates he does not want some other arrangement made after his death. As far as we can learn, these brothers had accepted their father's settlement, content with the favors that had been bestowed upon them. Notwithstanding, and utterly regardless of all the considerations set forth in the preceding verse, Jehoram was evil-minded toward his brothers and determined to remove them from his presence. These innocent victims were murdered soon after the new king took the throne.

Verse 5. *Reigned in Jerusalem* is an expression used frequently. It is to keep us clear as to which city was the capital of Judah. This is important from the fact that other cities have, from time to time, been the headquarters of the people of God; but one only, Jerusalem, was the capital of the original kingdom.

Verse 6. *Walked . . . ways . . . kings of Israel.* Such a comparison was sufficient to classify any man, for every king of Israel (the 10 tribes) was an idolater and otherwise a wicked man. But while all of them were wicked, some were worse than others, and among the very worst ones was Ahab. *For he had the daughter of Ahab to wife;* the writer accounts for the wickedness of Jehoram by this fact. That is significant, and let us get a view of the great danger connected with the marriage between God's people and those who are not. Serious difficulties are always likely to result.

Verse 7. *House of Davd* means the family of David. The throne passed from father to son on down through the generations, unless an exception was made due to some serious fault of the heir. The Lord had promised David that his descendants should come upon the throne of Judah in their proper order, and thus the sins of Jehoram were overlooked and he was permitted to retain his seat.

Verse 8. The revolt of the Edomites fulfilled the prediction made by Isaac to Esau, recorded in Gen. 27: 40. After Jacob had stolen the blessing of his father from Esau, the latter begged for something in the form of a blessing. Isaac then made the prediction, "When thou shalt have the dominion, thou shalt break his yoke from off thy neck." The Edomites were descendants from Esau, and their revolt in the days of Jehoram fulfilled the prediction made by the aged patriarch, Isaac.

Verses 9, 10. It was natural that the king of Judah would try to overcome the rebellion of the Edomites, so he attacked their forces near him and slew many of them; the revolt, however, could not be put down. And the success of the Edomites encouraged the city of Libnah, a royal one of the Canaanites, to rebel against Jehoram. This revolt also was allowed to succeed, *because he had forsaken the Lord God of his fathers.*

Verse 11. We have seen already (1 Ki. 3: 2) that the *high places* were not always such bad things, yet were in an unfavored class. And when built by a man like Jehoram, were always used for evil purposes. In the literal sense, fornication means unlawful intimacy between the sexes. The evil is used to illustrate the unlawful religious intimacy between the people of the Lord and any other god. The people of Judah were encouraged by the wickedness of Jehoram to commit both fleshly and spiritual fornication. In fact, the two kinds seemed to go together, as in the case of the men of Benjamin (Num. 25) an outstanding instance. Rev. 2: 14 expressly connects fornication with the idolatry of this occasion. The reader is advised to see the remarks made on this subject at Num. 25, in the first volume of this Commentary.

Verses 12, 13. Elijah was a national prophet but not one of the writers of the Bible. The writing he did was on special occasions such as the present one to Jehoram. The ways of Jehoshaphat and Asa, kings of Judah, are contrasted with those of the kings of Israel (the 10 tribes). That was because the latter were, without exception, idolaters. *Go a whoring* means to go lusting, and is spoken here with reference to spiritual uncleanness. See the comments at V. 11. The closing statement verifies the comments made about the brethren of Jehoram at Vs. 3, 4.

Verses 14, 15. The throne continued in the line of David's house in spite of the wickedness of Jehoram. But God did not let him escape all personal punishment, for he was to be smitten miraculously as will be noticed later on; his own family also was to be plagued.

Verses 16, 17. Many misfortunes can come to a royal family without changing the occupation of the throne. Among the things brought against Jehoram was the enmity of such heathen nations as the Philistines and Arabians that were located in the same general territory as the Ethiopians. They could not overthrow the throne, but were suffered to confiscate the treasures that were then accumulated in the king's palace. Besides taking these valuables, they had kidnapped his wives and all of his sons except Jehoahaz (also spelled Ahaziah). He was the youngest son and not entitled to the throne according to the law of inheritance. However, he was to receive it because of the absence of the oldest brother as explained here.

Verses 18, 19. This affliction was predicted in V. 15, hence it was brought on by a miracle. It was a fatal disease but not swift in its progress, for he lingered on for two years. It was a decaying form of disease, so that in the last stages his bowels were expelled from his body in the process of regular discharges and resulted in his death. *Made no burning* refers to the burning of incense and sweet odors that was practiced often in connection with the burial of noted persons. (Ch. 16: 14; 1 Sam. 31: 12.)

Verse 20. This is a summing up of the life of Jehoram. *Without being desired* is translated by Moffatt, "with no one to regret him." Being a descendant of David, he was buried in the *city of David.* His personal corruptions were so great that he was not buried in the sepulchres allotted to the other kings.

2 CHRONICLES 22

Verse 1. The dividing of the Bible into chapters sometimes interrupts a thought. This verse is a continuation of the close of the preceding chapter. *His youngest son,* then, means the youngest of Jehoram. The explanation is given, also, of why the youngest son was *made king;* it was because the others had been slain. It should be further observed that had the oldest son been living to occupy the throne, the words *made king* would not have been used. The simple statement would have been given that he reigned, without the explanation preceding it as to why it was so.

Verse 2. The account here gives 42 years as the age of Ahaziah when he began to reign, whereas it is 22 according to 2 Ki. 8: 26. The scribes were not inspired men, and their work was to copy the manuscript of the inspired original. A worn or faded copy could easily be misread, especially in the matter of numbers which was expressed by letters. This does not affect the authenticity of their work, for

Jesus never called them in question on that point, even while making other serious charges. Had they been inaccurate in the important features of their work as transcribers, we are sure that the Lord would have mentioned it, for that would have been more serious than any of the other evils of which he accused them. Athaliah is called the *daughter* of Omri; that is from a word with a wide extent of meaning. Strictly speaking, she was the granddaughter of Omri, in the same sense in which Belshazzar is called the son of Nebuchadnezzar (Dan. 5: 22), when he was his grandson. Athaliah was the daughter of Ahab who was the son of Omri. The wickedness of Ahab was commonly known, and by jumping back a generation to the grandmother, who also was a wicked person, the character of Ahaziah's mother can be understood.

Verse 3. This verifies the remarks on the preceding verse. Since Ahaziah's mother was the daughter of Ahab, her counsel for the son was tinctured with the evil principles of that man, who also was influenced by his wicked wife Jezebel.

Verse 4. *House of Ahab* is the antecedent of *they*, and sets forth the source of Ahaziah's training. This bad influence resulted in his destruction.

Verse 5. There were two men named Jehoram, one a king of Israel and the other a king of Judah. And each of these names also was sometimes spelled "Joram." Another fact that might cause some confusion was their living and reigning at the same time in a part of their reigns. These thoughts should be kept in mind while reading the names; switching back and forth between Judah and Israel. The influence of evil counsel was shown in that Ahaziah formed an alliance with the king of Israel in warfare.

Verses 6. In the battle with the Syrians, Joram, king of Israel (the 10 tribes) was wounded and went to Jezreel for treatment. Ahaziah (here called Azariah) further showed his interest in him by visiting him in that city. The outcome will give an instance of the evil consequences of association with unworthy characters.

Verse 7. The destruction of Ahaziah had been determined by the Lord, and the occasion for bringing it about was this very circumstance of his coming to Jezreel to see Joram. While calling on him, the word came that Jehu was approaching. Now this man had been chosen by the Lord to overthrow the house of Ahab, of which Joram (or Jehoram) was a wicked member. To oppose Jehu, therefore, would be the same as opposing the plans of God, and that was what Ahaziah did when he joined in with the wounded man, and went out against Jehu.

Verse 8. Jehu was really engaged in executing the judgment of God on the house of Ahab, when he came across some chief men of Judah who had been serving Ahaziah. Upon meeting these men Jehu slew them, which was the beginning of Ahaziah's downfall.

Verse 9. When Ahaziah saw that defeat was about to come he tried to escape and had succeeded in reaching some hiding place in Samaria, capital of the 10 tribes. He was found and brought before Jehu where he was slain. He was given a respectful burial because he was the son (grandson) of Jehoshaphat, who was a very righteous man.

Verses 10-12. Athaliah was a wicked woman with wicked ambitions. The *seed royal* means the near relatives of the royal line, one of whom would ascend the throne in the absence of a direct heir. In order to acquire the throne for herself, she formed the awful plot of murdering all of these relatives. One was enabled to escape by the watchfulness of his aunt, who hid him in a private room for six years, during which time Athaliah reigned by usurpation.

2 CHRONICLES 23

Verse 1. When an heir to the throne was too young to act as king, the affairs were managed by the priest in those days. Joash was but an infant when he barely escaped death at the hands of Athaliah. The woman who saved him was the wife of Jehoiada the priest. When the boy was in his seventh year, this priest concluded it was time to do something on behalf of the rightful heir to the throne. He formed a group of army men who were captains over hundreds of soldiers.

Verse 2. As a starter for the action, they went throughout the various cities and gathered the Levites, together with the elderly men of Israel (Israelites in general), and came to Jerusalem, the capital of the Kingdom of Judah.

Verse 3. *Covenant with the king* means the covenant was on his behalf.

The procedure was being handled by the priest since the king was but a young lad. *He said* means the priest said, for he was leading the movements for the king.

Verses 4, 5. The arrangement described was to safeguard the important transaction about to be undertaken. Not only was the throne then being held unlawfully, but it was by an unscrupulous woman who was already guilty of multiple murder. Nothing must be left undone to prevent her escape from the fate due her. The priest classified his forces into three parts. The ones from the priestly tribe were to guard the entrances to the temple, giving special attention on the sabbath days. Another group was to stand guard at the king's palace, while another part was to stand guard further outward, protecting the foundation of the gate. The above assignments were for special groups of men and at special places. Then the people in general were to be on hand for any possible need. The courts of the temple were open to the public, and the bulk of the citizens received orders to be present in these courts.

Verse 6. The priests only were allowed to enter the temple proper, but their service was to be protected from possible violence by the people "standing by" in the courts. This grand setup appears to have been intended as a permanent arrangement, but no one knew just when the opportune time would come for the climax nor how long it would take; every precaution must be taken.

Verse 7. It was not customary for a new king to be crowned in the manner that was being planned for Joash. But the circumstances were very unusual, in that a woman had usurped the throne, wading to it through a torrent of blood. The king was to be escorted in and out of the temple, the Levites forming the bodyguard in close contact.

Verse 8. The orders of Jehoiada were obeyed to the letter. *Dismissed not the courses* refers to the courses or turns that David had instituted for the priests, after the eligible men became too numerous to be needed at the same time. (1 Chr. 24.) But the occasion now is exceptional, and called for the combined service of all eligible men.

Verse 9. As possible violence was feared, the priest gave the men the weapons that had belonged to David, the first king of the tribe of Judah.

Verse 10. The spot selected for the crowning act was in front of the temple, facing the altar. The armed men formed a guard that reached from side to side of the temple.

Verse 11. Within this impressive setting the king was given his position. There, with the guard all ready for any possible emergency, a crown was placed on his head. The august formality was concluded with the anointing of the king by the priest and his sons, and the acclamation, "God save the king."

Verse 12. While the foregoing actions were proceeding, Athaliah was in the palace which she was occupying unlawfully. The sound made by the people caught her ears, and she came to the temple to investigate.

Verse 13. When she arrived at the house of the Lord an imposing scene met her. The young king, whom she thought she had murdered, was at his post by the entrance, wearing the royal crown. Nearby was the retinue of chief men, ready to support him by force if necessary. At the same time, the mighty chorus of singers and trumpeters, accompanied by various instruments of music, all sounded in the ears of the wicked usurper like a death knell. She rent her clothes, which was a custom when people were under great tension from grief or anxiety. With a despairing wail, like a swan song, she impudently shouted, *Treason, Treason.* There is an old saying that a thief sometimes tries to divert attention from himself by crying, "Stop thief." Such an attitude was manifested by this wicked woman.

Verses 14, 15. *Ranges* means the rows of soldiers. *Forth of the ranges* means to bring her out through or between the rows of soldiers, to conduct her from where she was to some other place for execution. He had told them not to slay her in the house of God. She was such a wicked woman, and did not deserve even to have the honor of being slain in such a holy place. As they began their death march, the priest gave orders to kill any who would try to follow. Curiosity alone might be the motive for following, yet it might be for the purpose of interfering with the execution. But whatever the motive, such persons must be killed. The place selected for the execution was very appropriate for such an unworthy person. It was at the horse gate, "by the way by which the horses came into the king's house." (2 Ki. 11: 16.)

Verse 16. This verse is similar, in some respects, to the call that Moses made on the occasion of the golden calf. (Ex. 32: 26.) The wicked woman had suffered idolatry to creep into the practices of the people. The woman was out of the way, now it would be in line to clarify the stand of the people. The priest formed a covenant between the new king and his people, that they should be known as the people of the Lord, not of Baal. They agreed to the proposition as the next verse will show.

Verse 17. This verse is what verifies the statements on the preceding one. Actions speak for the heart, and by declaring themselves in favor of the true.

Verse 18. It would be expected that the worship of Baal would disrupt the lawful kind. Now that the evil had been destroyed, the way was opened to reinstate the true service. *Offices* means the duties; Jehoiada appointed the duties or offices or official tasks pertaining to the house of the Lord. These tasks could be performed only by the Levites, lawfully, and by those particular Levites who were priests; the descendants of Aaron. *Distributed in the house of the Lord* denotes that the priests were given their particular assignments so that the whole service would be orderly.

Verse 19. The porters were the same as janitors, but the specific item of such a job that was expected of these men was to watch the doors, and see that no one entered who was unclean. The law of Moses was very definite in requiring all who participated in the sacrifices to be clean.

Verse 20. The persons mentioned had been at the temple, engaged in the ceremonies of crowning the king. The proper place for the ruler was in the palace, hence Jehoiada had this great assembly to attend the king as he was escorted to the throne. *High gate* refers to one more important. It is described in 2 Ki. 11: 19 as "the gate of the guard." It was fitting to bring the king in through a gate that was guarded, for a revolution about the throne had taken place, and every precaution was in order.

Verse 21. The mere fact of a woman having been slain should not cause rejoicing. The motive of the rejoicing was the knowledge that a murderous usurper had been slain.

2 CHRONICLES 24

Verse 1. It was a common practice of historians to make a brief statement that covered the life of a prominent man, in general, then follow with the details. The entire life of Joash was only 47 years, because he met a violent death as we shall see.

Verses 2, 3. This paragraph also is a general statement, extending over the entire life of Joash. As long as he had the good influence of Jehoiada to guide him, he did what was right. He listened to the wise counsel of the priest even in the selection of wives, when he became old enough for marriage.

Verse 4. The antecedent of *this* is the birth of the children of Joash. The statement shows that the king, though being influenced by the good priest, yet was acting "on his own" since he was no longer a minor. All buildings are subject to decay, especially if neglected. The interest in idolatrous worship had detracted from the building where the true worship was practiced. Joash wished to undo the damage by repairing the house of the Lord.

Verse 5. The Levites in general, and the priests in particular, were told to go out at once and begin collecting money from the people. It was expected that much time would be required to complete the work, hence it is stated they were to attend to this collection *from year to year*. But they were told to be prompt in starting the collecting, an order that was not obeyed.

Verse 6. Jehoiada was doubtless feeling the weight of years. He was a good man and interested in the work of the Lord, but had become somewhat slow in promoting the work of collecting the money. The reference to the law of Moses does not mean that the repair of the house of God, such as was needed just now, was specifically meant by the law. At any time that money was needed for the Lord's service the people in general were to furnish it. The Levites were not required to make this contribution since they had no income resulting from production.

Verse 7. The usual degeneration of a building referred to above, was not the only thing that had damaged the house of the Lord. The sons of Athaliah had used violence against it, and had taken the treasures out of it and used them in the service of Baalim (plural for Baal).

Verses 8, 9. This chest was a slotted box to receive the money. Since it was a special collection, it was proper to provide a convenient place in which the people could deposit their gifts. The obligation laid upon them by Moses referred to the law of contributions in general; the special collection would come under that law. The proclamation was spread throughout the country, but the people were to bring their money to Jerusalem and put it in this chest.

Verse 10. *Rejoiced, and brought in.* This is suggestive of the same principle taught by Paul in 2 Cor. 9: 7. God will not bless a gift that is offered while the donor is in an unwilling frame of mind. It must have been a genuine pleasure to contribute to such a worthy cause that was before the people of Judah. Their holy temple had been violated through the influence of one of the wickedest of women, and its treasures turned over to a false god. That woman was out of the way and the true worship again was being restored. *Until they had made an end* means the contributions kept coming in until sufficient funds were collected to pay for the needed repairs.

Verse 11. The space in the chest would not hold the entire amount of money required for the work on hand. When it was necessary to empty it, two men took charge of the money.

Verse 12. This verse is a simple business statement of how the money was put out after having been collected from the people. The setup indicates that men with the proper trades were employed to repair the house.

Verse 13. *Work was perfected* means it was completed. To set the house *in his state* denotes that it was put back into its original condition and reinforced.

Verse 14. Since the holy vessels had been taken out of the temple, it was necessary to get some more. Hence a part of the money was used for that purpose as well as for repairing the house. The verse covers all of the days of Jehoiada regarding the service. After the building had been repaired and the holy vessels replaced, the true service of sacrifices was reinstated and continued.

Verses 15, 16. Jehoiada was a priest, but he was buried *among the kings* because of his good deeds in behalf of the Lord and his house. It will be remembered that he virtually was a king while Joash was young, and influenced him for good. It was fitting, therefore, to give him that kind of a burial.

Verse 17. This is a verse where we may "read between the lines." *Obeisance* is from a word with a wide range of meaning. Strong defines it, "a primitive root; to depress, i. e. prostrate (especially reflexively in homage to royalty or God.)" In the King James Version it has been translated by, bow down, humbly beseech, fall down, crouch, etc. Since "humbly beseech" is one of the meanings, the connection shows that the princes had "an ax to grind," and preceded their petition with a flattering attitude toward the king. It had the effect they desired, for it says the king hearkened.

Verse 18. *Idols* were always wrong, *groves* were usually so. But there was a certain amount of indefiniteness about the right and wrong of them. See my comments at 2 Ki. 17: 16 on the groves and trees. *Judah* and *Jerusalem* are mentioned together because the first was the name of the kingdom, and the second was its capital.

Verse 19. The prophets had a great work to perform in the time of the Old Testament. They uttered the predictions of God when directed to do so, and were the ones who stood on the "walls of Zion" to admonish the people concerning their duties, and the danger of departing from the living God. *Would not give ear* corresponds to Isa. 1: 3. The reason the people did not know any better in the days of that man of God was, they "did not consider." In the days of Jehoiada, or soon thereafter, the people "would not give ear." As one result, they overlooked their duties and brought upon themselves the wrath of God.

Verse 20. *Spirit of God came*, etc. The prophets, like the apostles of Christ, were inspired only while writing or speaking the messages of God. Zechariah was inspired to deliver an admonition to the people. *Stood* is from a word with both a literal and a figurative meaning. Doubtless it was used in both senses here. It was important that the hearers see the speaker as well as hear him. The same precaution has been taken in other cases, for we read that Ezra stood upon a pulpit of wood (Neh. 8: 4). It was true also that Zechariah was above or over the people in importance and knowledge. He explained that God had forsaken them because they had forsaken him. Zechariah was not a prophet in the ordinary sense of the word, but was specially inspired for the occasion so that he might give the people authoritative instruction.

Verse 21. This stoning is mentioned by Christ in Matt. 23: 35, but in that place Zacharias is called the son of Barachias, while our present passage shows him to have been the son of the priest Jehoiada. Smith's Bible Dictionary gives a reasonable explanation by saying that Barachias was his grandfather. There is nothing strained about the explanation, for we are sure of some other instances where a grandson was called a son. Belshazzar is called the son of Nebuchadnezzar in Dan. 5: 22, when we know he was his grandson, according to secular history, for Nabunidas, father of Belshazzar, married the daughter of Nebuchadnezzar, and Belshazzar was their son. Rawlinson, Ancient History, Page 49. *In the court* is equivalent to *between the temple and the altar* in the statement of Jesus.

Verse 22. The pronouns are somewhat confusing. The antecedent of *his* in both cases is Zechariah. *Him* refers to Joash, while *he* in both instances means Zechariah. Using the nouns for the pronouns, the verse would read thus: "Joash the king remembered not the kindness which Jehoiada, Zechariah's father had done to Joash, but slew Jehoiada's son. And when Zechariah died," etc. *Require it* means that the Lord would require the guilty person to suffer for it. The suffering will be shown in the events to be recorded in the next few verses.

Verse 23. Syria was the country just north of Palestine. The *host of Syria* means the army of that government. They came to Jerusalem, which was the capital of Judah. The *princes* were leading men among the people of Judah, and were destroyed by the Syrian army. When they got the men of Judah under control, they took their personal belongings from them and sent them back home to their king. He was at Damascus because that was the capital of Syria.

Verse 24. *Small company* is mentioned to emphasize the fact that the Lord was helping the Syrians. If they could overcome a *very great host* of the Israelites, it would have to be by the help of God. In helping the Syrians against Joash and the princes of Judah, the threat was carried out that was meant by the words *require it*.

Verse 25. The army of Syria was content at the havoc that had been wrought against the princes of Judah and the property that had been acquired; they did not care about Joash personally. Besides, he had fallen a victim of some disease and could do no harm to anybody, so the invaders left him to his fate, whatever that might be. But the king was not destined to escape personal judgment even though the Syrians departed from him. Being in bed, his own servants attacked him because of his wrongs against the sons of Jehoiada. There was nothing right in the actions of Joash in his treatment of the sons of the priest, but two wrongs do not make one right. These servants of the king did wrong also when they took advantage of him in his sickness, and assassinated him. They not only slew him, but further dishonored his body by refusing it burial in the sepulchres of the kings.

Verse 26. The most interesting fact of this conspiracy is that it was headed by some descendants of Lot, the Ammonites and Moabites.

Verse 27. A reference is made to some "outside" history. See my comments at 1 Ki. 14: 19 for explanation of such a subject.

2 CHRONICLES 25

Verse 1. The place where Amaziah reigned is given because the kingdom of the 10 tribes had other cities for its capitals. Jerusalem was the original headquarters of God's people, and Judah was favored in that it retained possession of that city. The mother's name was given because the kings had plurality of wives and the writer wished us to know which was the mother of the man being considered.

Verse 2. Due credit was given always to the actions of men, but their failings also were noted. The shortcomings of Amaziah will show up partly in the history.

Verses 3, 4. Amaziah would have reigned after his father, although he had been permitted to live out his natural lifetime. The fact of his receiving the throne much earlier than was to have been expected, did not blind him to the great guilt of his father's assassins. Therefore, as soon as his possession of the throne was made certain, he executed those conspirators.

Verse 5. Warfare was the "order of the day" in those years, and it was important that the king be prepared. *Judah and Benjamin* are both mentioned because both tribes were included in the kingdom, although Judah gave the name to it, being the larger tribe.

Verse 6. It was not an unusual thing for a king or other military leader to hire soldiers into his service. Such men are called mercenaries, and the arrangement is not considered necessarily objectionable. However, there was a special reason why it was an unfavorable movement in the case of Amaziah.

Verse 7. A *man of God* means some man sent from God for a special reason; to deliver to Amaziah a protest against his hiring men out of the kingdom of Israel (the 10 tribes). God was not favorably disposed toward that kingdom and would not prosper any work attempted in connection with it. *Ephraim* is a term that came to be used, both in history and the writings of the prophets, to refer to the 10 tribes. It is well worded in Smith's Bible Dictionary thus: "After the revolt of Jeroboam the history of Ephraim is the history of the kingdom of Israel, since not only did the tribe become a kingdom, but the kingdom embraced little besides the tribe."

Verse 8. Amaziah was further warned that if he insisted on using these hired men of Israel he would fail in the battle. An additional reason was given for not using the legions of mercenaries in the words, *God hath power to help, and to cast down.* If a battle is not favored, all the multitudes in the world would not give a man success. This is taught also by Paul in Rom. 8: 31.

Verse 9. Amaziah was convinced that he should not use the hired soldiers. But he was worried about the money he had paid them in advance and which he could not get back from them. The man of God assured him that the Lord would more than repay him for his financial loss.

Verse 10. Amaziah dismissed the men he had hired out of Ephraim (the 10 tribes), and told them to go home. We would take that as a special favor, to have all that money and yet not have to fight. The account says they were angry over it. The explanation is that it was a shock to their military pride. They felt that it was the same as if Amaziah had said to them, "I can get along in my battle just as well without your services as with them, so you may go home." They will show their resentment by their actions before the affair is over.

Verse 11. *Valley of salt* was a region not far from the Dead Sea, otherwise called the Salt Sea. *Children of Seir* means the Edomites because Mount Seir was a central point in the territory occupied by that people.

Verse 12. War is a terrible procedure, and includes various methods of destruction. The Edomites who could not be captured alive were slain in battle. There were 10,000 who were taken alive and were to be destroyed in a mass. It was accomplished by thrusting them down a rocky precipice.

Verse 13. This verse records the revenge that was intimated at verse 10. The men whom Amaziah hired and then dismissed, "took their spite out" on him by attacking some of his cities and killing many of the inhabitants.

Verse 14. The conduct of Amaziah in this case is difficult if not impossible to explain. It does not have the small token that Ahaz had on a similar occasion (Ch. 28: 23) which will be considered at the proper time. There is nothing present over other instances of idolatry. What we know is that mankind has always been inclined to worship a god that can be seen and touched.

Verse 15. God sent a prophet to speak to Amaziah. (Heb. 1: 1.) The reasoning of the prophet was very logical. If Amaziah was able to defeat the Edomites in spite of their gods, why would he worship them as if they were being stronger than he?

Verse 16. *Art thou made of the king's counsel* was another way of telling the prophet that he had not been asked for any of his advice. The king further threatened to use violence against the prophet. He did not offer any more advice, but made a prediction that God would overthrow him for rejecting the counsel of a prophet.

Verse 17. *Took advice.* The first word is not in the original as a separate term. The second is from YAATS and Strong defines it, "a primitive root; to advise; reflexively, to deliberate or resolve." Among the words by which it has been rendered in the A. V. are determine, devise, purpose. That makes the matter clear. Amaziah felt above taking any advice from another, but made up his own mind, urged on by the success of his encounter with the Edomites. With that fact to puff him up in pride, he resolved to make another try at battle to win more glory. *See one another in the face* when said by one military man to another was the same as challenging him to close contact in battle.

Verse 18. The king of Israel (the 10 tribes) understood what was prompting Amaziah's challenge, and tried to get him to drop the case, by telling him a fable. In order to appreciate the force of it we must understand that the cedars of Lebanon were always considered among the loftiest and most elegant of trees. A thistle would be about as much of a contrast as one could imagine. Next, transfer the thought to people whose social ranks were as different from each other as were the artistic qualities of the cedar and the thistle. To ask a cedar for his daughter in marriage to the son of the thistle would be the height of insult. Even the beasts of the field would be shocked at the impudence of such a proposal upon hearing it, and put an end to the affair by trampling down the thistle. This fable was a figurative hint to Amaziah of the fate that would come to him for his inappropriate challenge.

Verse 19. The king of Israel then spoke seriously and correctly. He explained to him that his success over the Edomites had puffed him up, and advised him to stay at home.

Verse 20. God never forces a good man to become a bad one, nor leads him against his will to do the wrong thing. But if he chooses to commit a grievious iniquity that deserves some appropriate and special punishment, then he often does direct him into the channel that will bring upon him the needed penalty. This is the explanation of the verse, in which we have the sin noted for which the punishment was brought, *because they sought after the gods of Edom.*

Verse 21. The expression used in verse 17 is repeated here, meaning that they came into close contact in battle. The spot of the encounter was Judah's territory.

Verse 22. *Put to the worse* denotes that the battle went against the army of Amaziah. The actual number of casualties is not stated, but the defeat was so severe that the men of Judah fled from the field of battle and sought shelter in their camp.

Verse 23. The king of Judah was permitted to live, but was captured and taken to his capital, Jerusalem, where he was released. But Joash had been admitted into the city with its king in custody, after he had destroyed part of the wall.

Verse 24. Joash took advantage of his presence inside the city of Jerusalem to plunder it and take its treasures as booty of war. While at it, he also plundered the palace of its valuables. *Hostages* is from two Hebrew words that mean, when combined, the holding of persons regarded with high esteem as an assurance against future disturbance. Amaziah had intruded into the rights of Joash, without provocation and against good advice, and he might do so again. Hence these persons were taken along with Joash as he returned to his capital at Samaria. Obed-edom was the man who had given refuge for the ark when it was being transported toward Jerusalem. (1 Chr. 13: 14.) That good man would be highly esteemed by the people of Judah, and they would be careful about his safety. Because of these facts he was taken in hand by Joash, along with other *hostages*, when he left for his own kingdom.

Verses 25, 26. These verses are not in chronological order, but are a general statement of the life of Amaziah. See the comments at 1 Ki. 14: 19 in connection with references to outside books as further reading matter.

Verse 27. Going back into the history of Amaziah, the writer picks up the circumstances of his violent death. Conspiracy is always regarded unfavorably, as being an unlawful way of accomplishing a result. However, it is the inspired writer who connects this conspiracy with the fact of Amaziah's having turned away from following the Lord. That would give the conspiracy a show of having a good motive at least. When the king recognized his danger he fled to Lachish, an important city not far from Jerusalem. The conspirators followed him to that city and slew him there. He was brought back to Jerusalem for burial. The *city of Judah* is a general term referring to Zion in Jerusalem, according to 2 Ki. 14: 20. He was brought *upon horses*, which indicates that the conspirators regarded their action as being justified under the rules of war. According to Smith's Bible Dictionary the horse was used exclusively for warlike purposes. We may be confused about why Solomon was said to have been so much interested in horses, when he was a man of "peace" and never had a war. But his connection with them was commercial. See 1 Ki. 10: 28, 29.

2 CHRONICLES 26

Verse 1. *The people ... made him king*. It means they went through the ceremonies of anointing him. The fact of his being the son of the last preceding king was what entitled him to the throne. The name *Uzziah* and *Azariah* are used interchangeably, so the reader should not be confused by the use of either. It is significant that "all the people of Judah" had a part in placing Uzziah on the throne. It shows the unity of the nation in the sentiment in favor of him.

Verse 2. *Eloth* was a city in the land of Edom, and it is sometimes spelled Elath. It seems to have been at one time taken over by the king of Judah, then allowed to fall into bad repair and slip out of the use of the nation. Uzziah *built* it, which means he repaired it so that its usefulness was again made available.

Verse 3. Uzziah (or Azariah) began to reign when but a youth, and had one of the long terms. His mother's name is given because his father had more than one wife.

Verses 4, 5. It is very necessary to consider the two verses together, for that will include the reference to the good priest Zechariah. In that dispensation the Lord depended upon the priests to be spokesmen to hold the people in the line of duty by their work of instruction and warning. See Lev. 10: 11; Deut. 17: 9; Mal. 2: 7. They were not left to their mere human knowledge, *but had understanding in the vision of God*. It is affirmed that God made the king to prosper while he relied on him.

Verse 6. The walls of cities were regarded as their main fortification. In breaking down the walls of these Philistine cities, Uzziah was weakening their defense. At the same time he was destroying their strength, he was erecting towns in the territory of the same people, which could be used for his own opposition against them.

Verse 7. In verse 5 it is said that God prospered Uzziah when he sought unto him. Hence we read that when he went about the work described, God helped him to the desired end. He also gave him success against the Arabians, a people descended from Ishmael, who were hostile against the children of Israel.

Verse 8. The Ammonites were descendants from Lot, and, although related by blood, were always at enmity with the people of God. But Uzziah brought them into subjection, for they *gave gifts*, which means they paid taxes for the support of the government. Uzziah was so successful in his government that he became known by the people as far away as the borderland of Egypt.

Verse 9. The walls of Jerusalem had a number of gates and each had a special name. Not all of them had any particular meaning, however, but were given as a mark of distinction for purposes of reference. The *towers* were a sort of lookouts for observation uses, and they were located at the various gates. The king also reinforced the *turning* or corners of the wall, which made them more firm against attack, when the enemy brought his battering-ram to bear.

Verse 10. An enemy would not always come against the walls of a city for battle, but would pitch his camp in the *desert* or open field, hence Uzziah built some towers in such places. He *digged many wells* to care for his cattle from time to time. These wells were made all over the territory, both in the low and high ground. These preparations were not all for military uses alone, *for he loved husbandry* or agriculture.

Verse 11. While interested in agriculture, Uzziah knew he should be prepared against invasion by the enemy, hence he provided himself with a *host* or large company of fighting men. They were not a big crowd of men with no systematic method of operation. They were organized for service under the command of special men in the cabinet of the king. *Jeiel* was ordinarily employed as a recorder and MAASEIAH was a ruler or leader among the people in peacetime activities. But these men took charge also of the troops when it was necessary to go out in the military line. *Hannaiah* was one of them, being one of his captains.

Verses 12, 13. The numerical strength of the king's army was 2,600 men at the head, and 307,500 men under them. This was a mighty array of forces and helped the king in his stand against the heathen nations about him.

Verse 14. No body of soldiers can be of service to their superior without weapons, so the king furnished all his men the necessary armaments. The *shields* were large plates of metal that could be held up against the missles of the enemy, and the *spears* were long poles with sharp heads to hurl by the hand against the foe. *Helmets* were caps with metal plates for the protection of the head. *Habergeons* were coats made of leaves of metal, so arranged that the wearer was protected, yet was free to move his body as necessity demanded. They might be compared to the feathers of a large bird, but made with strong metal.

Verse 15. These *engines* were instruments of a military nature only, and the name was never used in the Bible as we use it now. They could hurl large stones or other forms of ammunition, and do so with great force. Uzziah placed these engines on top of the towers mentioned in a previous verse. He placed them also on the *bulwarks* or fortified walls about the city. He used them to hurl two kinds of missiles, large stones and darts. All of this equipment helped the king so much that he became generally known as a strong man.

Verse 16. We have here a situation expressed the opposite of what Paul used in 2 Cor. 12: 10, where he says, "when I am weak, then am I strong." Uzziah was strong in worldly accomplishments and possessions. Instead of showing appreciation by making proper use of his advantages, he became vain or weak in mind, and overestimated his rights. He presumed to act in a service that had been specifically assigned to another class of men, the priests of God. The handling of sacrifices was generally done by the priests, yet it could be done lawfully by others and frequently was so done. But the burning of incense was the exclusive work of the priests, and they were from the family of Aaron, who was of the tribe of Levi. See Ex. 28: 1; 1; 29: 29, 30; Num. 18: 8.

Verse 17. *Azariah* the priest should not be confused with the same form that is sometimes used for the king Uzziah. This priest took 80 *valiant* or brave other priests with him and went into the temple after the king. Surely, the presence of this large group of men ought to impress the king with their dignity. It should induce him to give respectful attention. He knew that his proper place as king was in the palace, and that these other men were in their allotted place, the temple. But when a man presumes to go beyond his bounds, he is not likely to listen to reason.

Verse 18. All of these men *withstood* Uzziah, which means that they stood against him in his unlawful actions. They made a kindly but firm speech to the king, and gave him the reason for their opposition to his doings. It was not because he was not a good man morally, nor because he did not know how such work ought to be done, nor because it was not the right time and place for such service. It was because he was not the right official for it. The words *burn incense* give us the direct key to the work and rights that distinguish the priests from all other servants of God. Uzziah was informed of this, and was told further that he would be dishonored for his trespass.

Verses 19-21. If a man is shown to have committed a sin, and he is humble enough to acknowledge the sin, God is always gracious and willing to pardon. The sin of Uzziah at first was in presuming to perform an unauthorized service. But the sin for which he was punished was his attitude toward it when he was rebuked. An authorized man of God declared to him the error he was committing and admonished him to cease. Not only that, he was told it would result in his dishonor and destruction. If a legitimate physician advises a man of a dangerous disease present in his body and points out the remedy, the victim generally feels grateful for the information, even though it is bad news. But Uzziah was so unreasonable that he resented being shown his own danger, and gave way to anger. The words of Solomon (Prov. 15: 10) were verified by the conduct of this king: "Correction is grievous unto him that forsaketh the way: and he that hateth reproof shall die." Leprosy was not a disease that was suddenly fatal, but it was a loathsome one, and subjected the victims to great humility. The law of Moses required a leper to be in perpetual quarantine. (Lev. 13: 45, 46.) Realizing his condition, Uzziah was quick to get out of the temple and go into the perpetual isolation required by the law. While he lived he was technically the king, although not permitted to act as such. During the remainder of his days the affairs of the kingdom were administered by his son Jotham.

Verse 22. Isaiah was one of the writing prophets. He lived at the same time with Uzziah and naturally would have something to say about him. See Isa. 1: 1; 6: 1.

Verse 23. *Slept with his fathers* is commented upon at 1 Ki. 2: 10. The kings usually had special sepulchres set aside for their bodies. Uzziah was a king, but because *they said, he is a leper*, his body was honored only by being buried in the general field of the burying ground, not in the spot of the kings' sepulchres.

2 CHRONICLES 27

Verse 1. The 16 years of the reign will not include those of his service before the death of his father, but the period of his own right as king.

Verses 2. *In the sight of the Lord* is a significant expression. Many things are right or approved in the sight of men that are wrong before the Lord. In fact it is usually that way. (Luke 16: 15.) *Howbeit* is the same as "except." The language of the verse might seem as if his not entering into the temple was an exception to his following in the righteous footsteps of his father. We know that it was right for him not to enter the temple as his father did. The exception is not made to the statement pertaining to the righteous conduct of Uzziah. The writer made a general reference to the life of the former king and said that his son followed in his steps. Then, realizing that part of the life of Uzziah was not right and should not have been imitated, he added the exception noted. And while the life of Jotham generally was good, he was somewhat short of his duty in not curbing the corruptions of the people.

Verse 3. When historians are writing up the good deeds of kings or other prominent men, they generally point out the things that indicate their interest in the public good. Hence we are told that Jotham built (repaired) the *high gate* which means the upper or most important one. It was so considered because it was "the king's gate eastward." (1 Chr. 9: 18.) *Ophel* was a prominent elevation in the vicinity of Jerusalem and there was a *wall* or tower there; Jotham repaired that place.

Verse 4. Always it should be remembered that when a man is said to have "built" something, it does not necessarily mean that he constructed it for the first time; it often denotes that he *rebuilt* or repaired it. *Castles* and *towers* were institutions for defense and other military purposes. Jotham was concerned about the security of the nation, and took all these steps with that in view.

Verse 5. Jotham was so victorious in his wars with the Ammonites that he forced them to pay him tribute for three years.

Verse 6. The success of Jotham is explained by the fact of his regard for the Lord. *Prepared his ways* means he established his conduct in the light of what the Lord would consider right.

Verse 7. This verse refers to some "outside" writings covering the same subject matter that has been considered here. See the comments at 1 Ki. 14: 19.

Verse 8. This is a repetition of verse 1.

Verse 9. *Slept with his fathers* calls for the comments at 1 Ki. 2: 10. Jotham was buried in the *city of David*, otherwise called *Mount Zion*, a main spot in Jerusalem.

2 CHRONICLES 28

Verse 1. David is called the father of Ahaz by way of respect. There had been many generations since him, but he was the first king of the tribe of Judah.

Verse 2. Every king of Israel (the 10 tribes) was an idolater, hence this general reference to them which is done so many times. There were three methods of shaping the metallic idols; carving, hammering and casting or *molten*. *Baalim* is the plural form of Baal, and that form was used sometimes because there were so many places where an image was erected to that false god.

Verse 3. The valley of *Hinnom* is sometimes connected with the *son of Hinnom* with reference to the offspring of the founder of those rites. *Burnt incense* means he offered sacrifices in that valley in service to the heathen deity. On the offering of human sacrifies see the comments at 2 Ki. 16: 3.

Verse 4. Idolatrous sacrifices were wrong wherever practiced. The mention of all these places is to show the degree of iniquity to which Ahaz had gone. *High places* (see 1 Ki. 3: 2) were the elevations made by man, the hills were those made by nature, and the trees were those either planted for the purpose of idolatry, or were selected out of the groves and consecrated to the false worship.

Verse 5. God frequently punished his disobedient servants by delivering them into the hand of some other man. A man can be killed but once, yet Ahaz was smitten by two different men. That is because when a certain king *smote* him it means merely that he was attacked. The severity or extent of the damage is never determined by that word. Thus we read that the kings of both Syria and Israel (the 10 tribes) *smote* this king of Judah. Of course, many of his men were smitten to the extent that they were slain, and that would be regarded as being an attack upon him.

Verse 6. This is a specification of the statement in the preceding verse. *Pekah* was a king of Israel, and God suffered him to kill 120,000 men of Judah in one day, as a punishment for their departure from the true God.

Verse 7. *Man of Ephraim*. For the third word, see comments at Ch. 25: 7. The men whom Zichri slew were important, being closely connected with the king, either by blood or service.

Verse 8. *Children of Israel* is a term that applies usually to all the tribes, but in this verse applies to the 10 tribes only. However, being all Jews, they are called their *brethren*. *Women, sons, and daughters* would indicate a general capture, and not the soldiers only, as is so often done. The *spoil* means the personal property of the people. They brought them all to Samaria because that was their capital.

Verse 9. When God uses a man or nation to punish another man or nation, he never allows any boasting over it. This will be manifest many times when we come to the books of the prophets. The kingdom of the 10 tribes was used in the present instance as an instrument in God's hands to chastise the kingdom of Judah. They did what they were supposed to do and no fault will be charged against them on that score. But the spirit in which they did it, and the motive they had as to the future, was displeasing to the Lord, and he determined to rebuke them. Again we see the use that God made of the prophets. (Heb. 1: 1.) The prophet *Oded* was the one selected for this occasion. The point was made that God had the kingdom of Judah punished because he was *wroth with Judah*, and not because of any merit of the kingdom of Israel. If a parent punishes his child while in anger, the purpose of the discipline may be defeated. The people of Israel had attacked Judah *in rage*, and that was objectionable to the Lord.

Verse 10. This verse reveals one of the motives the people of Israel had, and that was to put those of Judah under a state of enforced servitude. In other words, they had the intention of reaping some special advantage out of their service to God. The reference to their *sins against the Lord* was a hint that a similar judgment might be meted out to them unless they corrected their ways.

Verse 11. The kingdom of Judah had been sufficiently punished by the loss of their goods, and the humiliation of their citizens. It was proper, therefore, that they not be made further to suffer. In a final word of exhortation, the prophet told them to release the captives.

Verses 12, 13. The men named in V. 12 were representative ones, and they accepted the admonition of the prophet Oded. They took their stand against the men who had been conducting the war operations. They objected to bringing the captives into the vicinity of Samaria, and denounced it as a sin against the Lord. They said that already there had been an offense committed against God, and that by bringing these captives away from Judah they would be adding to the trespass, and would bring upon them the divine wrath.

Verse 14. The foregoing speech was directed toward the men in the army, because they were the ones who had taken possession of the captives. Upon hearing the rebuke of the princes (leading men named in V. 12), they surrendered the captives and spoil.

Verse 15. When these princes (named in V. 12) got possession of all that had been taken by the soldiers, they used the articles of clothing for the benefit of the captives. Having been stripped of their personal property, they were in need of the things required for bodily comfort. These were provided out of the very things that had been taken from them. They gave them food and drink, and further administered to their comfort by anointing them. That was a practice of ancient times that had more than one meaning. It contributed to the sanitary and medical benefit of the person receiving it, and also indicated to him an attitude of respect. See Psa. 23: 5, Luke 7: 46. Having given the captives these tokens of compassion, they placed them on beasts of burden and took them back into their own land. The particular spot to where they took them was Jericho, a prominent city in the possession of the tribe of Benjamin, a part of the Kingdom of Judah. It was called the *city of palm trees* because of the prevalence of that tree, which was a very useful one. Smith's Bible Dictionary describes the palm tree thus: "The palm tree frequently attains a height of 80 feet, but more commonly 40 to 50. It begins to bear fruit after it has been planted 6 or 8 years, and continues to be productive for a century. Its trunk is straight, tall and unbroken, terminating in a crown of emerald-green plumes, like a diadem of gigantic ostrich-feathers, these leaves are frequently 20 feet in length, droop slightly at the ends, and whisper musically in the breeze. The palm is, in truth, a beautiful and most useful tree. Its fruit is the daily food of millions; its sap furnishes an agreeable wine; the fibres of the base of its leaves are woven into ropes and rigging; its tall stem supplies a valuable timber; its leaves are manufactured into brushes, mats, bags, couches and baskets. This one tree supplies almost all the wants of the Arab or Egyptian." After delivering the captives to their own country, the princes of Israel returned to their own capital, at Samaria.

Verse 16. Later on in the chapter we will learn that God saw fit again to humble Ahaz for his unrighteous life. Again the punishment will be administered through the agency of the heathen nations. Common reason should have told the king that if the Lord decided to punish him by bringing one foreign nation against him, it would be in vain for him to call upon another for help. But he evidently did not consider, for we are told that he called on the Assyrians for help.

Verses 17, 18. The invaders named in this paragraph had been causing Ahaz much trouble, and that was the reason he sent for the Assyrians referred to in verse 16. The Edomites were east, and the Philistines west of Judah. They sent bands of men who took part of the people captive and carried them out of their own land. Others of the invaders took possession of some of the towns and dwelt in them.

Verse 19. This verse explains why the Lord had brought the nations against his people. It was too bad that the nation had to be brought down on account of their king, but he was their representative and acted on their behalf. *Naked* is used figuratively and means that the people were exposed to the insults of a foreign power, who dispossessed them of their valuables and left them in want.

Verse 20. *Tilgath-pilneser* was a king of Assyria, the nation mentioned in V. 16. Ahaz called for him and he came; but instead of relieving him, he became his enemy.

Verse 21. Ahaz thought he could hire the king of Assyria. To obtain something with which to induce Tilgath-pilneser to help him, Ahaz even plundered the temple and the palace, also the houses of his leading men, and gave the loot to the Assyrian king. It was in vain, for the king refused to help him.

Verse 22. Distress is supposed to make a man sober minded and cause him to look to the Lord of Heaven for help. Ahaz was not so affected by his afflictions.

Verse 23. It is difficult to explain the density of some men's minds. The people of Damascus, capital of Syria, had defeated Ahaz, but he had much reason to understand that they could not have done so had not God used them for that purpose. Instead of ascribing their success against him to his own true God, he gave it to their false gods. He was so foolish as to offer sacrifice to them, thinking they might help him. Instead of being any advantage to him, they were his *ruin* or cause of his downfall.

Verse 24. Ahaz "went the limit" in his sins against the Lord. The *vessels* of the house of God were the various implements used in the different services. The word is from KELIY and Strong defines it, "Something prepared, i. e. any apparatus (as an implement, utensil, dress, vessel or weapon)." These articles were made of precious metal. They could be melted and recast into altars or other things for some use designed by the one having charge of it. Ahaz wanted to use this material for his corrupt service of idolatry, so he plundered the temple of its sacred instruments, closed the doors, and thus abandoned the lawful worship. He then used the metal for making altars for the service of idolatry, placing them in every *corner* or prominent angle in Jerusalem. We may find a parallel in principle in some of the practices of professed Christians. They will deny the lawful use of the Bible and the Church, then try to use them for their own plans. The holy creations were for the exclusive purpose of benefiting mankind morally and religiously. God made them to prepare man for usefulness in this life and for happiness in the next. But they are often plundered and made to serve the social and financial interests of professed worshipers of God. All such will be condemned by the Lord, even as Ahaz was condemned.

Verse 25. The wicked king of Judah was not content with corrupting the capital city with his idolatry. He made *high places* (see comments at 1 Ki. 3: 2) in the different cities of his realm, and used them as places for sacrifices to false gods. *Provoked* has no word in the original at this place, but it is used in the same sense in other places as applying to God. It is from NAATS and defined in the lexicon, "a primitive root; to scorn; or (Eccl. 12: 5) by interchanging for NUUTS, to bloom." In the A. V. it is sometimes used in the sense of "give occasion to." We should not think of God as being like men, and giving way to evil passions at the instigation of human creatures. Yet the misdeeds of man will cause the occasion for the Lord to express his anger in some form of punishment for the offender.

Verse 26. See 1 Ki. 14: 19 and comments, in connection with this paragraph.

Verse 27. *Slept with his fathers* is treated at 1 Ki. 2: 10. The people of ancient times were particular about their burying grounds, and classified them according to the merits of the ones buried. Ahaz was a king of Judah and was entitled to burial in the capital of his kingdom. But he had been a wicked man and was not placed in the sepulchres that were set apart exclusively for the kings.

2 CHRONICLES 29

Verse 1. We are beginning the study of one of the best kings of Judah. The expression is repeated that he reigned in Jerusalem. It meant much, especially up to the date at which we have arrived. There have been two distinct kingdoms, or divisions of the original kingdom. One of them was composed of the 10 tribes who revolted from the original and formed a kingdom that had more than one capital at various times. The other division was composed of two tribes, Judah and Benjamin (including Levi after the 10 tribes had rejected him), and its capital was at Jerusalem, the original headquarters. It was informative, therefore, when writing about the kings of Judah, to say that they reigned in Jerusalem. Hezekiah's mother was the daughter of Zechariah, a prominent name. There were at least 28 men with that name mentioned in the Old Testament. Some of them were of the tribe of Levi and some of other tribes. We should therefore not attach any special importance to the name in the present verse.

Verse 2. David is called the *father* of Hezekiah as a term of respect, and because David was the first king from the tribe of Judah. The original is defined by Strong, "a primitive word; father in a literal and immediate, or figurative and remote application." It is rendered in the Old Testament by father 670 times, chief 3, principal 1. Again let us note the proviso, *in the sight of the Lord*, when declaring that he did that which was right. "The Lord seeth not as man seeth." (1 Sam. 16: 7.)

Verse 3. Hezekiah did not delay going about the work before him. He started it the *first month* of the *first year*. He opened the doors because Ahaz had closed them (Ch. 28: 24). The temple had been let fall into disorder and Hezekiah repaired it.

Verse 4. *Priests* and *Levites* are mentioned as separate classes. That is because all priests were Levites, but not all Levites could act as priests. Yet there were services for the Levites besides that of priesthood. *Street* means an open area or space, not necessarily an avenue. The space east of the temple was where Hezekiah assembled these men, for the purpose of making a speech to them.

Verse 5. *Sanctify* means to consecrate one's self to the service of God. The worship of the Lord had been corrupted by the preceding king and the temple been closed to the true service. There is no indication of literal filthiness being present, but the very state of neglect, due to the idolatrous interests of the king, suggested a religious corruption whose stagnation reached to heaven. The Levites were charged to alter all these conditions, and thus to *carry forth the filthiness* out of the holy house of the Lord.

Verse 6. More than once our attention has been called to the idea that a thing should be right "in the eyes of the Lord." This verse gives us the same principle on the negative side, something that is evil in his eyes. A thing might look good as far as man could tell, but look sinful as the Lord would see it. We should accept the divine verdict and act accordingly. *Habitation of the Lord* refers to the temple, since that was the place where God recorded his name in that Dispensation. See Deut. 12: 12; 14: 23. When Ahaz closed the doors of the house of God and directed the attention of the people away from that place, that was when they *turned their backs* against the Lord.

Verse 7. The *porch* was a vestibule entering the main room of the building. By closing the doors to the porch, the entrance to the house was cut off. Such an action resulted in putting out the lamps and stopping the burning of incense.

Verse 8. Because of the evils described above, the Lord poured out his wrath on his people by subjecting them to the surrounding nations, who were suffered to trouble the kingdom with commotion. The *astonished* referred to the surrounding people looking on as well as to themselves. The *hissing* referred to the derision or ridicule that the nations cast at the people of Israel after they had been brought down in shame. *Judah* and *Jerusalem*. The first word is the name of the kingdom, the last its capital.

Verse 9, 10. *For this* means that the misfortunes that had befallen their families had been brought on them on account of the sins just mentioned. Hezekiah proposed that a new promise be made to the Lord, offering to be rededicated in service to him, hoping thereby to escape the further divine wrath.

Verse 11. *My sons* is a term of endearment, and used in view of the relative positions of the speaker and the hearer. *Negligent* is rendered "deceived" in the margin, and the lexicon agrees with it. However, the warning for a person not to be deceived is said rather with the idea of arousing the hearer to a sense of his duty. A person can sometimes be deceived by inattention to duty as surely as by some positive false teaching. The purpose of Hezekiah was to remind these Levites of their duty. And, in order that they might realize it all the more, he told them that they had been chosen for a special work, one of the items of which was to burn incense.

Verses 12-14. Among this list of names the reader should distinguish the three sons of Levi; Kohath, Merari and Gershon. These men personally had been dead for many years, but their individual lines of descendants had been registered and their proper assignments of work carefully observed.

Verse 15. These men responded favorably to the exhortation of the king. A general definition was offered at verse 5 for *sanctified*, but I shall give the information found in Strong's lexicon or dictionary. The word is from QADASH and defined, "a primitive root; to be (causatively make, pronounce or observe as) clean (ceremonially or morally)." From this the reader will see that the explanation given at verse 5 is about as specific as we should make it. When a person divested himself of anything that might disqualify him for a particular task, then went to work at that task, it could be said that he had sanctified himself for the work.

Verse 16. This verse indicates that there was some actual filth accumulated in the house besides the figurative uncleanness described at verse 5. There is nothing said as to what that filth was nor how it got there. It would be natural for any place to become unclean if neglected, if said place had been used for serving various kinds of food and burning literal incense. So these Levites "cleaned house" by taking this accumulation out to a brook for disposal.

Verse 17. The work of these Levites began on the first day of the year. Verse 3 says that was the day on which Hezekiah opened the doors of the house. The whole transaction, therefore, the work of the king, his speech to the Levites, and the beginning of their work of cleansing the house, all started at once, and that was right at the beginning of Hezekiah's reign.

Such punctuality in attending to the Lord's business is worthy of imitation by all of us. The task was no little one, for after they had worked 8 days they had got to the porch only, but that constituted the major portion of the work. Then in 8 days more the whole job was done.

Verse 18. The Levites did not merely make a general report, but specified the items of work they had done. Such a report indicated a sincere interest in the reform movement that Hezekiah was sponsoring. The altar of burnt offering was not in the temple proper, yet it was named in connection with the cleansing of the *house of the Lord*. That shows we cannot make too fine a distinction between the various parts of the divine structure. In some sense it was all the house of the Lord.

Verse 19. *Cast away* means the vessels were tossed to one side as of little use or value. It was natural that such articles would be damaged by such treatment, so the Levites *prepared* or repaired and cleansed them and made them suitable for use again.

Verse 20. *Rulers of the city* were the officials of the place, but were men who were interested in the affairs about the temple. Being citizens of Jerusalem and members of the Jewish nation, they would very properly offer some services to the Lord, hence were called together by the king.

Verse 21. Leviticus 4 gives the instructions for the sin offerings, and by that chapter it can be seen that these rulers of the city brought the proper beasts for the occasion. The offerings were for the *kingdom*, the *sanctuary* and for *Judah*. The first refers especially to the domain or landed estate, the second means the temple, and the third applies to the people who were in possession of the landed estate. The offerings were furnished by the people, but the ceremonies were handled by the priests.

Verse 22. The bodies of the beasts were to be burned on the altar, but the blood was sprinkled on it. There are two reasons why the blood was taken from the animal. Blood would not burn without a miracle while the flesh would. Besides, the blood being *the life* (Lev. 17, 11), it must be separated from the body of the beast, thereby signifying that the animal was dead. It is the same reason why we have two separate articles in the Lord's supper, the bread and the fruit of the vine, and they are kept separate. In that way we *show the Lord's death* when we have the two items.

Verse 23. *They* laid their hands means the ones furnishing the creatures that were to be offered in the sacrificial services.

Verse 24. The rule was that the persons offering a sacrifice were to do the killing. In this instance the priests did it. No reason is given for the exception, unless it is in the statement that the blood of cleansing was to extend its benefits to *all Israel*, and not merely to the ones bringing the animals to the latar.

Verse 25. *Cymbals* were made of plates of metal and struck together in rhythmic accord with the music. A *psaltery* was a stringed instrument to accompany the voice, and a *harp* was a larger stringed instrument and often used independent of the voice. The statement is made that these instruments were set in the *house of the Lord*, and the thoughts in v. 18 show that the term has a general meaning, including the whole structure with its outer parts. According to the wording of the King James version, this arrangement was by divine authority. *For so was the commandment of the Lord by his prophets.* The American Standard Version renders this as follows: "For the commandment was of Jehovah by his prophets." Moffatt's translation gives us, "(for the Eternal had transmitted the order by means of his prophets)." Ch. 5: 13, 14 shows us that when the musical instruments were used, the glory of the Lord *filled the house of God*. Thus no distinction can be made between the particular parts of the building. The truth is that whatever or wherever the place was that was being considered, that which was filled with the glory of the Lord was where the musical instruments were used, and was called "the house of God." It is a mistake, then, to say that God never endorsed instrumental music in worship offered to him in Old Testament times. But all of this is no authority for such music in the New Testament worship. If it is, then we have authority for animal sacrifices now, for we know they were used with divine command in that time. The reason David is mentioned so much in connection with the musical instruments is that he was an outstanding musician, and was the originator of many of the instruments. He was an inspired man in his teaching, and when he gave his instructions for the use of the instruments in the services to God, he was acting by divine authority. Had such an extensive practice been displeasing to the Lord, he surely would have been chastised for it, as he was in the cases of other mistakes, such as those about Bathsheba and the numbering of Israel.

Verse 26. *Instruments of David* means the ones he invented and put into use with the Lord's approval. The trumpets were sometimes made of the horns of animals and were played by blowing into them as a man plays a cornet. These instruments had been especially designed for the use of the priests. (Num. 10: 8.)

Verses 27, 28. In this paragraph we see the combination of the musical instruments with the animal sacrifices. The whole procedure was under the jurisdiction of Hezekiah the king, and the statements of the paragraph are those of the inspired author of the book. Among those expressions are, *song of the Lord, with the trumpets,* and *instruments ordained by David.* All of this agrees with the comments on verse 25, etc.

Verse 29. It would be considered, and properly so, that all of the activities of the preceding verses were acts of worship. Why, then, does this verse say that after they had made an end of the offering, the king and others *worshipped?* The answer is in the very general meaning of the word in the Bible. Any act of respect can truthfully be called an act of worship. In this instance the writer was thinking of that meaning of the word that pertains to the posture of the body; *they bowed themselves.*

Verse 30. *The words of David* evidently mean the Psalms, and it is so translated in Moffatt's version. It would be fitting to use his compositions in their worship, since they were using his musical instruments. They used also the compositions of another inspired man, Asaph the *seer* or prophet.

Verse 31. Hezekiah commended the people for their good conduct. *Thank offerings* would be the sacrifices they offered to express their thankful feelings for the good things of God. The ones who took part in the services are said to have been of a *free heart.* That agrees with the teaching of Paul in 2 Cor. 9: 7. Any gift offered to God that comes from a regretful heart will be fruitless as far as any reward from the Lord is concerned. Only a cheerful giver will be rewarded.

Verses 32, 33. God does not have any personal need of the gifts from man. Neither does the great number of such gifts signify anything just because the number is large. The point of interest is in what the large number indicates. Verse 31 had said that the ones making the sacrifices or gifts were the people with a free heart. The large number, therefore, tells us that there were great numbers of the people who had the right attitude toward God, a fact worthy of rejoicing.

Verse 34. The distinction is again made between the priests and the Levites. The former were those particular Levites who were descended from Aaron. They had not made themselves fit for the service in sufficient numbers to do the work. They were supposed to *flay* or skin the animals. While that was primarily a work expected of the priests, yet any Levite could lawfully do it. And as there was a shortage of qualified priests, the other Levites helped them. It is said that the Levites were more upright in qualifying themselves for the work than were the priests. It often occurs today that the people from whom we have the right to expect the most, are the least forward in doing it.

Verse 35. *Burnt offerings* and *peace offerings* are terms of the major sacrifices provided for in the law of Moses. Details of them may be read in Lev. 1 and 3. The *fat* was one of the parts of animals that must never be eaten (Lev. 7: 23,24), but must be burnt on the altar. The verse closes with a statement that includes all of the activities described in the chapter. In this summing up statement no distinction is made between the various parts of the building; it is all called *house of the Lord.*

Verse 36. Hezekiah rejoiced over the general conditions. The people were *prepared,* which means they were put in condition to render acceptable service, and the king gave God the honor for it. *Done suddenly* refers to the readiness of the people.

2 CHRONICLES 30

Verse 1. The 10 tribes had recently been taken off into captivity by the Assyrians; the details of that event are given in 2 Kings 17. But a number of individuals had escaped and got back into the home land, and were scattered through the different territories that had been the possession of the tribes. (V. 6.) This explains the reference to *Israel* and *Judah*. The letters of Hezekiah were addressed to them as a whole, with specification of the ones who had descended from Joseph, namely, *Ephraim* and *Manasseh*. The first of the national feasts required by the law was the passover, which normally was observed in the first month.

Verses 2, 3. Hezekiah was not a religious official exclusively, so it was appropriate that he hold a consultation with his leading citizens on so important a matter as the great feast. Their conclusion was that the conditions called for the provision made in the law for a substitute date. Num. 9: 6-11 stipulates that if the people are disqualified by uncleanness to partake of the feast in the first month, it should be done in the second. Ch. 29: 17, 34 tells of that condition which was in the way of observing it on the original date. Another thing, on account of the general state all over the country, the people had not come together at Jerusalem. Therefore, the decision was to notify the Jews in the scattered districts to come to that city.

Verse 4. The king and the whole congregation (those already in the city) were in agreement on the subject, which caused them to be pleased.

Verse 5. *Established a decree* means it was decided officially by the assembly to make the invitation apply to the whole country. Beer-sheba was at the southern, and Dan at the northern extremity of the original kingdom of Israel. A reference to these cities was a figurative way of referring to the whole country. The passover had been neglected for a long time and not observed as the written law required.

Verse 6. *Posts* were persons sent out in a hurry on any mission at hand. In the present instance it was to take the letters of proclamation that had just been decided upon by the consultation between the king and his princes. These letters were not invitations merely; they were the *commandment of the king*. The letters were addressed to the children of Israel as a whole, for a reference was made to the common ancestors of them all, Abraham, Isaac and Israel. (Jacob.) This is the place that tells us some of the captives had escaped from the Assyrians, and were back in their original home country in the several possessions.

Verse 7. God made a distinction between the leaders of the nation, and the individuals in the nation who could not prevent the public transgressions. When we come to the books of the prophets this will manifest itself many times. These letters recognize this distinction, and exhort the escaped captives to profit by the mistakes of their leaders and not fall into the condemnation of God.

Verse 8. *Stiffnecked* is a figurative word for being stubborn. The opposite of it is to be willing to *yield yourselves unto the Lord*. *For ever* means "through the age," and it denotes that the sanctuary or temple was to be regarded as holy through that age or dispensation. The wrath of God will be turned away from all his faithful ones.

Verse 9. The fate of their brethren still in captivity was somewhat dependent on the conduct of these escaped ones. If they will turn to the Lord, he will see that their fellow-citizens still in the land of captivity shall be given compassion, so that they too may return to their own country.

Verses 10, 11. Before the kingdom of the 10 tribes was taken into captivity, there were certain individuals who were true to God, and came to the place of lawful worship. (Ch. 11: 16; 15: 9.) Now that some have been so fortunate as to escape their captors and get back home, they were yet unappreciative of their freedom and refused to respect the call of the *posts* or runners. Others, however, *humbled* themselves, which was indicated by their obedience to the orders. It can truthfully be said that pride is the cause of all rebellion, and humility is what prompts obedience.

Verse 12. God does not force men by direct miraculous power to be righteous; he offers inducements to persuade him in the right direction. If man yields to the inducements and does the right thing, then it may correctly be said that the action was by the *hand of God*, as it is asserted here. The people of Judah were united in heart to do the thing that God required. This verse tells us that the king and his princes were issuing their orders *by the word of the Lord*. That made it divine law for the situation at hand, and placed a solemn duty before the people.

Verse 13. *Unleavened bread* refers

to the same occasion as the *passover* in verse 2. See the comments on this subject at Ch. 8: 13.

Verse 14. The *altars* were those that had been put there for idolatrous worship, whether for the burning of animals or incense. *Kidron* was a brook or depression near the city, and used as a dumping ground for these corruptions.

Verse 15. The *second month* was substituted in the place of the first month, which was the original date. But we should bear in mind that the Lord was the one who made the substitution. (Num. 9: 10, 11.) Man has no right to make any change in the divine ordinances, but when God makes a change, it is not only right but necessary to observe the change. *Were ashamed* refers to the humility of mind with which the priests made themselves fit to partake of the passover. Here it was, a whole month after they should have done it, but were unfit for the service on account of their uncleanness. Now that God had graciously allowed them "another chance" to perform the required service, it was fitting that they do so with deep humility.

Verse 16. This verse reports the regular procedure that was *according to the law of Moses.* Leviticus 1 shows that it was the duty of the priests to handle the blood of the animals, after the givers had done the killing. Thus far, then, the performances going on were as originally ordained by the law.

Verse 17. This verse reports a change in the original ordinance. The chapter in Leviticus referred to above shows that the man bringing the beast for sacrifice was the one to do the slaying, then turn it over to the priest. But an unclean person was not allowed to do this killing. There were some of the private individuals who were not clean, and others in their class or rank did the killing for them.

Verse 18. Strictly speaking, if a Jew did not find himself fit to kill the animal, neither should he have considered himself fit to eat of it. But human imperfection manifested itself in this instance, and many who were not qualified to slay their beast went ahead anyway and ate of it. The inspired writer says that in so doing they ate of it *otherwise than it was written.* God is merciful to his creatures and suffers many things that are short of duty. The whole situation as Hezekiah faced it was so out of order that much allowance was made. These people who ate of the passover while unclean did wrong, and the fact is not overlooked; but the king was a righteous man and prayed for them, thus acting in the role of a mediator.

Verse 19. The prayer of Hezekiah was on condition that the people bring their hearts into the proper attitude toward God, even though their bodies at that particular time were not ceremonially cleansed.

Verse 20. The prayer of Hezekiah was heard as an intercessor or mediator for the people, and they were *healed,* which means the Lord removed all of the disqualifications from them without requiring them to go through any further ceremonies.

Verse 21. Some of the musical instruments were larger than others, and would make a stronger sound. They were the ones used on this occasion. The Levites as a tribe, and that part of the tribe qualified to act as priests (the descendants of Aaron), were so glad because of the goodness of God, that they combined their more important instruments with their praise. *Day by day* means they performed this each day of the feast.

Verse 22. The entire period of the feast was one of joy and gladness and praise to God. *Spake comfortably* means he had a "heart to heart" talk with them. He spake to the Levites—not to the whole tribe in this case, but to the ones *that taught,* and Lev. 10: 11, Deut. 17: 9, and Mal. 2: 7 shows that it was the priests who were to do the teaching. The *peace offerings* that were offered in connection with their confessions are described in Lev. 3.

Verse 23. *Took counsel* signifies that a consultation was held. Such transactions are generally called for when some subject of importance has become present. After this consultation the group repeated the performance of the 7 days just past; that is, they had another feast of 7 days in direct connection with the first 7 days. It was not like the changing of the date as in the instance of the passover date. It was more in the nature of a continuation of the feast already in progress. It could not strictly have been said to be a repetition of the ordinance as a separate observation of it, and considered as done the second time, for the feast had not been closed entirely yet. The occasion for the extension will be shown in the following verses.

Verse 24. There were certain specific requirements in the law concerning the set feasts. Ex. 12: 15-17 and Lev. 23: 6-8 gives the law of the 7 days of unleavened bread. This was not to be changed nor substituted by anything else. But the children of Israel were given wide privileges in the performance of their animal sacrifices and religious feasts. There was no restriction as to the frequency or number of such exercises. In the present instance the king and his leading men had given large numbers of animals to the people, which they might offer to God in sacrifices. A fact that doubtless accounts for this gift was that the movement seemed to have gained headway and caused several of the priests to join the work of purification. The early part of the chapter showed a condition of neglect in the matter of cleansing. Many men who should have been engaged in the religious exercises were prevented on account of uncleanness, and they had not been sufficiently interested to change their condition. But the zeal of others evidently stirred them to action, and a great many more of the priests qualified themselves by putting away their uncleanness. That called for more animals and more time for their sacrificing, hence the statements of this verse.

Verse 25. The kingdom of Judah was composed mostly of that tribe, but the priesthood was in the tribe of Levi, and that part of the tribe that descended from Aaron. *Strangers* is from a word that means persons from the outside. Certain Israelites scattered through the territory of the 10 tribes had come to Jerusalem to the feast. Since they were from the "outside" of Judah, they were called "strangers." All of these are said to have taken part, not only in the sacrifices and feast, but in the rejoicing.

Verse 26. The set feasts of the law had doubtless been observed, but the extent of the exercises was exceptional, and that was what caused the great rejoicing.

Verse 27. The *priests* and the *Levites blessed* the people. Primarily that word means to kneel, but here it says they *arose* to bless the people. The meaning is that they pronounced a benediction on them as they were dismissed.

2 CHRONICLES 31

Verse 1. Public professions of loyalty to God are not enough. The Israelites conducted an earnest and prolonged season of devotions to the true God. They made many sacrifices and much blood was shed in service to the one Lord whom they declared to be the one and only Being entitled to their worship. But had no actions been taken to remove the means of the false worship, their professions of faith would have been empty. So they "showed their faith by their works" by attacking the things that had been used in idolatrous worship. These consisted in the *images* or statues; the groves or trees consecrated to false worship; the high places (see 1 Ki. 3: 2) devoted to false worship, and the altars used on which to burn the animals in sacrifice to Baal. These reform measures were taken all through the home territories, those cities of Judah and Benjamin. The work also was extended to the places that had been occupied by the 10 tribes. After completing the national cleansing, the people returned home.

Verse 2. At such a time as we have been considering, all of the items of the public service would naturally suffer some neglect. Thus the king found that the original setup of the priesthood had been somewhat disrupted. In 1 Chr. 23: 6 and 24: 1-19 is a record of these courses of the priests that David had arranged and he restored it. The particular work that was intended to be done by the several classes of citizens was again assigned to them. Some of that work pertained to the sacrifices, while other men were given parts to perform that pertained to the praise service.

Verse 3. The occasions for sacrifices named in this verse were the *set feasts*, or those regularly established by the law. They were not to vary as to date (except as God made the variation as he did in the passover for the 2nd month), purpose, and manner of observance. They were not considered as individual services, but were for the nation as a whole. That was the reason that the contributions for them on behalf of the kingdom were to be taken from the substance or products of the king; that is, they were to be taken from the royal stores. It should be observed that these *set feasts* were according to what was *written in the law of the Lord*. Now they are found only in the "ceremonial law" that was given through Moses, yet that law is here called the *law of the Lord*. This all condemns the doctrine of the sab-

2 Chronicles 31: 4-13

batarians who try to distinguish between the law of Moses and the law of God.

Verse 4. *Portions of the priests and the Levites* refers to the support that was to be given them for their services. They were not permitted to have a tribal possession as were the others, and therefore had no productive means of income. The other tribes were to give a tenth of all their income, and that was to go for the support of Levi. They were to receive also certain parts of the animals that were offered on the altar, which they could use as their food. See Num. 18: 8-24.

Verses 5, 6. This paragraph is a showing of the response the people made to Hezekiah's commandment in verse 4. We are impressed with the promptness with which they came up with their duties, for it says they did it *as soon as the commandment came abroad.* They brought in their *tithes* which means the tenth.

Verse 7. *Foundation* was the starting of the collection of the fruits of the land. They were added unto the third month until the seventh, when the collection was complete. It will be interesting to note that pentecost came in the third month, and that was when the Jews brought the "firstfruits" unto the Lord. (Lev. 23: 17.) The seventh month was the one in which the great day of atonement came, followed in a few days by the feast of tabernacles. Also, by that time the year's crops were all in, so that these *heaps* mentioned in this verse would be complete by then.

Verse 8. It is significant that Hezekiah and his princes, or leading men, blessed the Lord *and* his people. They could not have given the products had not the Lord caused them to grow. But after they were made to grow, the Lord expected the people to show their appreciation by the return of part of them to him.

Verses 9, 10. *Hezekiah questioned* means he made inquiry about the resources for all the piles of produce, and of the use that had been made of them. The information was furnished by the chief (high) priest. God wants his servants to put the divine interests ahead of all others; yet he does not require them to go undernourished in so doing. The children of Israel had been sufficiently fed and were still able to offer this great store for the Lord's service. We are reminded of Paul's teaching along this same line in 2 Cor. 9: 8-10. This is not the particular place to enter into any speculation about "special providence." I do not believe, however, that any faithful child of God ever suffered bodily harm by reason of his contributions to the work of the Lord. Hezekiah saw the bountiful supply of foodstuff, and seemed to wonder if the people had been deprived of their actual needs by making such gifts.

Verses 11, 12. The produce had been temporarily piled up while the amount was incomplete. Now that the collection was finished, it was necessary to make better provisions to care for it. The *chambers* were storehouses, suitable for housing the products of the field and herd, to be used later as the service demanded. Someone must be made responsible for the proper distribution of this store. One man, Cononiah, was made head of the entire department, with helpers under him. *Offerings and tithes* indicates that there must have been a difference. That is true, and it is as follows. Every Jew was required to give a tithe or tenth of his income to the Lord. If his flocks brought ten young animals into the world, one of them must be turned over to the Levites to be used in the service of the Lord. If the field prdouced a hundred bushels of wheat, ten of it were to be turned over. But in addition to all the tithes, a Jew was encouraged to make voluntary offerings. For instance, the man who brought the ten bushels out of his crop of 100 bushels, could offer an additional five bushels if he wished, and when such a contribution was made in connection with the tithes, it was called an offering. The two words were often used interchangeably, which suggests the following observation: All tithes were offerings, but not all offerings were tithes.

Verse 13. We can see that the work was well systematized into a food administration. Cononiah was chief, with a personal helper in the association of his brother Shimei (V. 12), and now the men named in this verse were to have the more direct charge of the work of distribution. They were called *overseers* which would be called foremen in the industrial language of our day. Hezekiah was the king and Azariah was the high priest, and they jointly commanded the whole procedure. That was very fitting, for the one was "chief executive" of the government, and the other was the supreme authority in regard to the religious activities. In a system such as the Mosaic, a combination of religious and secular principles, we would expect to see some men who were assigned to their proper places in the nation.

Verse 14. This has to do with the receiving and distribution of the things brought in by the Israelites in their service as citizens. The law of Moses made certain requirements of all persons regarding their income, and someone would be needed to see that the things were taken care of. Kore was in charge of the east gate, to receive the products coming from that direction and placing them where they belonged in the service of the temple. *Oblations* comes from several Hebrew words, but all have practically the same meaning, referring to that which is given for the altar or other service to God. It is thus the same as the *offerings*, but the distinction of *freewill* offerings is explained by a closer study of the law. Certain offerings were stipulated and required of the children of Israel, and they were not left to decide the matter. In addition to them, it was permitted to make voluntary gifts to the service, and such were called *freewill offerings*.

Verse 15. *Next him* means next in rank. The law did not assign any major possessions to the tribe of Levi. They had no use for it since their time was to be taken up in the service about the temple. But they needed homes, and they were provided by giving them certain cities scattered through the possessions of the other tribes. And when the turn or course of any particular group came, the ones needed at the temple would come up and serve. In the meantime they would reside in their own cities, but while there they would have to be supported. This verse is an explanation of that part of the great system.

Verse 16. The Israelites observed their birth records in different methods at different epochs. At this time they entered the names of their sons when they were three years of age. Then, as they came up into maturity and were called into the priestly services, their support from the offerings was furnished as the need demanded.

Verse 17. It should constantly be remembered that all priests were Levites, but not all Levites were priests. And while the record of births started when the boy was three years old, the attention of the overseers was centered on those 20 years old.

Verse 18. To the *genealogy* ("pedigree or family list") was a certain portion given. That was necessary because the fathers had been *sanctified* or set apart to the holy work of the priesthood. They had no opportunity to produce the necessities of life, therefore their wives and little ones had to be cared for out of the tithes.

Verse 19. A *suburb* in Bible language was not what the word denotes today. Instead of meaning the outlying parts of a city, it meant the open area surrounding it. The word is from MIGRASHAH, and Strong defines it, "a suburb (i. e. open country whither flocks are driven for pasture); hence the area around a building, or the margin of a sea." The question is sometimes raised, why would these priests need any ground if they did not engage in the production of crops. They were supported out of the gifts of the tribes. Included in those gifts were the animals turned over for the use of these men of the family of Aaron. Since the animals would be brought to these families as they were produced, and also since they would not be consumed at once, they needed an area in which to keep them. These suburbs or open fields of pasture were used for this purpose.

Verses 20, 21. This paragraph as a whole is a commendation of Hezekiah for his good life and work. It is not in the nature of flattery, but states a logical reason for the favorable treatment he received from God. *Every work* that he attempted for the house of God prospered, and the reason for it was the fact that he did it *with all his heart*. It has ever been the desire of the Lord for his people to be in earnest about their work and not be halfhearted in the doing of it.

2 CHRONICLES 32

Verse 1. *These things* means the doings described in the preceding chapter. *Established* refers to the completeness and righteousness of the things; that no just complaint could be made against the conduct of the realm of Judah. If any harm or inconvenience comes against the kingdom, it cannot be laid to any neglect of the man on the throne. This disposition was possessed by a heathen king, Sennacherib, king of Assyria. This nation had Nineveh as its capital, and the territory bordered on the Tigris River, situated east and north of Babylon. It was a great and powerful country, and not long before the time we have reached in our study, had carried off the kingdom of Israel (the 10 tribes) into captivity. This tragic event is recorded in 2 Ki. 17. Elated, doubtless, by the success of his predecessors against the Jews, the king of Assyria thought to subdue the remaining kingdom of Judah. He accordingly marched into the country and established camps against the fenced (walled) cities.

Verse 2. When an invader settles his camps around the important cities of a country, it may be expected that he will not stop until he has reached the capital if possible. Hezekiah saw the forces of Assyria and concluded that the king of that powerful country would eventually come to Jerusalem.

Verses 3, 4. Hezekiah held a counsel with his leading men concerning the situation created by the Assyrian invasion. It was decided to shut off the supplies of water about the city so that the invader would not have them to use in the siege. The chief men cooperated with the king and they carried out the plan to stop the water supply.

Verse 5. Further measures of defense were taken by building a set of walls around the city, planting towers or lookouts on the inner one. He also repaired Millo, a special fortification within the city, near the division called the City of David.

Verses 6, 7. Defensive preparations in the way of forts and walls are not enough when the safety of a nation is at stake. Active warfare may be necessary to repulse the enemy. Hezekiah realized this and went about getting ready for the conflict. Captains are required for the orderly conduct of warfare. The king assembled his forces in the street near the city and gave them an encouraging speech. He assured them that they had more forces than the enemy had. This, however, did not necessarily mean that the numerical count with them was actually greater than was possessed by the Assyrians. The idea that Hezekiah had will be revealed in the next verse.

Verse 8. The two forces that Hezekiah was comparing are expressed in the terms *arm of flesh* and *Lord our God*. With such consideration on which to base his statements, we understand why the king made the assertions that are given in the preceding paragraph. Such comparisons have been made in other places in the Bible, as far as the principle involved is concerned. The 10 spies shrank from their duty because they felt as helpless as grasshoppers by the side of the powerful characters inhabiting the land of Canaan. They did not consider that even an insect, if standing on the side with God, would be a "majority" as far as strength was concerned. Paul taught the same idea in Rom. 8: 31 where he asks: "If God be for us, who can be against us?" The words of Hezekiah cheered the people; they *rested* on them, which means they relied upon them. The history in 2 Kings 18 shows that the king of Assyria retired from the siege after being given articles of ransom by Hezekiah.

Verse 9. In a year or two after the events of the preceding paragraph, Sennacherib made another expedition into Hezekiah's territory; but he did not go in person. He was occupied with a siege against Lachish, an important city south of Jerusalem. From this place he sent his leading servants to act for him against Judah. According to the account in 2 Kings 18, the leader of those servants was named Rab-shakeh, but some secular authorities say that was a military title and would apply to whomsoever the chief of the nation put at the head of his army, or a detachment therefrom.

Verse 10. Whether the name mentioned in the preceding verse was a personal one, or an official title, the spokesman tried to persuade the people of Jerusalem to desert Hezekiah. He belittled the ability of their king and derided them for remaining in the city to suffer the results of the siege.

Verse 11. The Rab-shakeh warned the people in Jerusalem that they would die of hunger if they listened to Hezekiah. Some spies or other secret informants must have been busy, for the reference the spokesman made to Hezekiah's reliance on God was true.

Verse 12. The pronoun *his* refers to the same *Lord our God* named in the preceding verse, and thus constitutes a falsehood. It was not the altars of God, but those of Baal that Hezekiah had thrown down.

Verse 13. This vile heathen made no distinction in his respect for the gods of the different countries. He impudently referred to the countries whom his master (Sennacherib) had subdued in spite of their gods.

Verse 14. The irreverent comparison to heathen gods is repeated in this verse. *My fathers* means the ancestors who had gone against other rulers in spite of their gods.

Verse 15. Rab-shakeh stated what was untrue in principle. The God of Israel had delivered them from the Egyptians, and Syrians, and Edomites, and Ammonites, and others too numerous to mention. And soon this vile man will learn that God can deliver his people from so powerful a nation as the Assyrians.

Verse 16. *His servants* means the servants of Sennacherib. He was personally at Libnah, having departed from Lachish (2 Ki. 19: 8), but was being represented by his servants, chief of whom was this one referred to as Rab-shakeh.

Verse 17. *He wrote* means that Sennacherib wrote the letters from Libnah. He made the same impudent comparison between the two kinds of gods, the true God and those of the heathen nations that Rab-shakeh had made by mouth before the wall of Jerusalem.

Verse 18. It is the part of a coward to pretend confidence in himself, and to threaten the opponent in a way to frighten him. There were those in the Assyrian host who could speak the Jews' language. They did so here, in order to impress their hearers all the more.

Verse 19. *Against God . . . as against the gods*, etc. This means they put the God of Israel and the gods made by the hands of men in the same class. Such irreverence was bound to work its rebuke sooner or later.

Verse 20. This verse is a brief account of the exercises of these two great men on behalf of the Israelite nation when the Assyrians were threatening it. See 2 Ki. 19.

Verse 21. Sennacherib had a strong force of soldiers who were in camp under him. When the letter and prayer of Isaiah and Hezekiah were come up before God, he sent a destroying angel out through the camp and *cut off all the mighty men of valor*. 2 Ki. 19: 35 says the number was 185,000. This humbled the haughty king, and he left the position at Libnah for his home land. But the return home did not give him any honor, for some of his own offspring murdered him while he was performing service to his heathen god.

Verse 22. The same God whom the Assyrians had so wickedly blasphemed, overcame all opposition and brought deliverance to his people. In bringing this great victory to them over the Assyrians, other threatening nations were brought down also.

Verse 23. In this verse we have the words *gifts* and *presents* both used. This indicates some distinction although the words are generally used interchangeably. For the general meaning as used in the Bible, see my comments at Gen. 32: 13 and 1 Sam. 10: 27. According to the definitions in the lexicon, the *gifts* were things of practical use, such as could be put on the altar of sacrifices, or be appropriated to the financial support of the kingdom. The *presents* were things considered desirable because of being rare, such as precious gems. But the outstanding thought is the same in both articles, and means that the nations made public and official recognition of the kingdom of Judah.

Verse 24. *Sick to the death* means that his sickness was going to be fatal if something would not be done to cure it. But that was done, and a miracle was performed to cure the disease, and also a sign or other miracle was performed to assure him that he not only would recover from his present illness, but would live a stated number of years. For a fuller account of this matter see 2 Ki. 20: 1-11.

Verse 25. The best of men will make mistakes, and often it is when they have been favored the most. After Hezekiah had his health restored, and was given assurance of many more years of life, he became puffed up and failed to show appreciation for the favors. That is the meaning of *rendered not* in this verse. By his unwise conduct, the wrath of God came down on the nation and its capital. The details of that are set forth in 2 Ki. 20: 12-19.

Verse 26. It is not the man who never makes any mistakes (there are none such) whom the Lord will bless, but the one who, after he has done wrong is willing to humble himself and repent. That was what made David "a man after God's own heart." Hezekiah humbled himself before God and his repentance was recognized. Certain marks of the divine displeasure were bound to be brought upon the country, but Hezekiah was spared the pain of seeing them personally.

Verse 27. The *riches and honor* came from the nations that brought their tokens of recognition as stated in verse 23. The *treasuries* were depositories made safe and convenient for storing the precious metals and other articles of great value.

Verse 28. *Storehouses* for grain and *stalls* for animals were for the same purpose as the depositories for gems and metals. They were needed for the proper care of the things that God had given the king. We have the basis for the lesson in connection with the parable of the "certain rich man" in Luke 12: 16-20. The two instances are alike in that the surplus of crops made it necessary to build additional storage room. But Hezekiah was not condemned while the other man was. The explanation is that the man in the parable was not condemned for building greater barns to care for his crops. He would have been condemned had he not done something to care for them. His sin was in the wrong use of them that he proposed to his soul.

Verse 29. The cities did not produce the flocks, but they provided a means of caring for them. With such provisions at hand, the king was free to keep in possession some of the things that would otherwise have been disposed of. Since God had given him all this substance, Hezekiah felt that he should take proper care of it.

Verse 30. This *watercourse* was a spring and its waters had been running down through a valley named Gihon, and was thus being wasted. Hezekiah *stopped* this spring which means he curbed it or put it under control so it could be directed down near the city of David. In this way the spring was made to be of service. His works were made to prosper because they were good and helpful to the people.

Verse 31. This refers to an error in judgment that Hezekiah made. The fuller account is in 2 Ki. 20: 12-19.

Verse 32. The reference to the account in Isaiah's writings will be found in chapters 36-39 of the book in our Bible, bearing the prophet's name. As to the reference to the *book of the kings*, see comments at 1 Chr. 14: 19.

Verse 33. The highest honors that could be given a man by the manner of his burial were bestowed upon Hezekiah, and the whole nation manifested its respect for him at his death. *Slept with his fathers* is explained at 1 Ki. 2: 10.

2 CHRONICLES 33

Verse 1. The statement is again made that the king reigned *in Jerusalem*. The importance of it is in the fact that other cities had been capitals for the people of the Jews, but Jerusalem was the original and most authoritative one.

Verse 2. Manasseh was classed with the bad kings, but not as wicked as some of them. I wish the reader to note again the words *evil in the sight of the Lord*. The real test of whether a thing is right or wrong is if the Lord considers it so. *Whom the Lord cast out* is said to give us a view of the evil that was in the life of Manasseh. He was guilty of the same kind of sins that caused God to cast out the heathen.

Verse 3. *High places* might not have been so bad (see comments at 1 Ki. 3: 2) had they not been used for an evil purpose, but when used in connection with other things that denoted idolatry, they were wrong. Baalim was plural for Baal and expressed in that form because there were so many altars erected for sacrifices to that god. The *groves* were the sacred trees, whether planted for that purpose or appropriated to idolatry out of the forestry already growing. *Host of heaven* means the planets and other heavenly bodies.

Verse 4. This verse may be a little confusing unless the right words are emphasized. The house of the Lord was in Jerusalem, therefore no complaint could be made as to the place where the altars were built, had it been right to build them at all. But those altars represented the name of Baal, and that is the point of the criticism. The thought can be brought out by emphasizing the words *altars* and *my name*. It will then be seen that the sin committed was in building *altars* in that place, when the Lord had said that *his name* should be there. It was a question of whose name should be planted there.

Verse 5. The altars discussed in the previous verse were built in the main room of the house of the Lord for the worship of Baal. Manasseh then erected altars in the courts (adjoining rooms) of the house. These were for worship to the *host of heaven*, which means the sun and moon and other heavenly bodies.

Verse 6. *Pass through the fire* calls for the remarks at 2 Ki. 16: 3. The valley mentioned was a depression in the earth south of Jerusalem. That place was so named because of the use made of it by a wicked family named Hinnom. Among the various forms of worship for idolatry was the burning of human sacrifices. *Observed times* means he practiced witchcraft and consulted fortune tellers. All the rest of the verse pertains to the various forms and methods resorted to in seeking knowledge that human beings are not supposed to have. Not that men can actually learn the forbidden facts, but the desire and efforts to obtain them always will be displeasing to God. On the genuineness of the claim for this unlawful knowledge or information, let the reader see comments at 1 Sam. 28: 12.

Verse 7. There were three methods of forming the images; cast or molten, hammered, and chiseled or carved. Manasseh had one of the last kind made and put in the house of God. The language of the verse is the same in meaning as verse 4.

Verse 8. The promise never to remove his people from the land was based on the conditions stated in the verse. *So that they will take heed* is another way of saying, if they will take heed, etc. The *whole law* is general and includes everything that Moses had delivered for their government. The other words are almost the same in meaning. *Statutes* means the formal enactments, and the *ordinances* holds out the idea of things that had been ordained, calling attention to the fact that there was authority behind them. *By the hand of Moses* is very significant in view of the efforts of the sabbatarians to discount the authority of Moses. Since these laws were given to the people from God, it does not lessen their authority and binding effect to have been given through this human agency.

Verse 9. To do *worse* than the *heathen* is comparative. In view of the advantages that the people of God had enjoyed, in the way of enlightenment and evidence, they should have been far above such foolish practices as the ones they did. With that all being considered, their conduct was truly said to be worse than the heathen.

Verse 10. In addition to the information stated in the preceding verse, God spoke directly to the king and his people about their conduct. *Would not hearken* is the same in thought as the statement of Isaiah in Ch. 1: 3 of his book. It is there declared that the reason God's people did not have any better knowledge of his way was, "my people doth not consider." A specific instance of such stubbornness is seen in the present case.

Verse 11. This should not be confused with any of the national captivities. It was a special judgment upon Manasseh by which he was temporarily dethroned and taken off to Assyria. I shall quote from the history of Josephus on this event; Antiquities, book 10, chapter 3. "And when they perservered in the same course of life, God raised up war against them from the king of Babylon and Chaldea [that territory was then in control of the Assyrians], who sent an army against Judea, and laid waste the country; and caught king Manasseh by treachery, and ordered him to be brought to him, and had him under his power to inflict what punishment he pleased upon him."

Verses 12, 13. The punishment brought Manasseh to repentance and prayer. God is ever compassionate toward those who become truly penitent, and he heard the prayer of this humiliated monarch and caused him to be released. In the same place in Josephus the history is continued as follows: "But then it was that Manasseh perceived what a miserable condition he as in, and esteeming himself the cause of all, he besought God to render his enemy human and merciful to him. Accordingly, God heard his prayer, and granted him what he prayed for. So Manasseh was released by the king of Babylon, and escaped the danger he was in."

Verses 14-16. After his repentance Manasseh tried to "show his faith by his works." He improved the wall that was near the water supply which Hezekiah had arranged, which was on the west side of the city. He put military captains in all the fenced (walled) cities of Judah, and thus was concerned about the defense of the country. He not only improved the temporal features of the country, but was active for its religious interests also. He removed all the articles used in heathen worship in the temple, and cast them out of the city. The form of worship that had been going on in behalf of the heathen gods, naturally caused the true worship to be neglected and its altar to be let go down. Manasseh accordingly repaired it and proved his sincerity about it by offering sacrifices thereon. *Peace offerings* were one item of the major sacrifices prescribed by the law in Leviticus 3. *Thank offerings* were not necessarily any specified kind of offerings. The term has reference more to the motive or occasion for making the offering. After setting the example, he then commanded the people to serve the God of Israel, not those of the heathen about them. On this part of Manasseh's reformation, Josephus gives us his account which I will quote, and it is in the same section of his history already copied from above and is as follows: "And when he was come to Jerusalem, he endeavored, if it were possible, to cast out of his memory those his former sins against God, of which he now repented, and to apply himself to a very religious life. He sanctified the temple, and purged the city, and for the remainder of his days he was intent on nothing but to return his thanks to God for his deliverance, and to preserve him propitious to him all his life long. He also instructed the multitude to do the same, as having very nearly experienced what a calamity he was fallen into by a contrary conduct. He also rebuilt the altar, and offered the legal sacrifices, as Moses commanded; and when he had re-established what concerned the divine worship, as it ought to be, he took care of the security of Jerusalem." The reader has frequently been cited to "outside" reading matter, and shown inspired examples for it by what some of the writers of the Bible have done. The Bible does not have need of human defenses, yet it is helpful and encouraging to find that authentic secular authors corroborate the statements of the inspired Word. Another thing, the Bible does not claim to give all the details of the subjects treated, and if the secular histories gives some more of them, it is perfectly in order for the student to avail himself of them.

Verse 17. See the remarks on *high places* at 1 Ki. 3: 2. That will help to understand why the subject is mentioned in the way it is here.

Verses 18, 19. *Rest of the acts*, etc. This is another reference to what we have been considering as "outside" reading, and explained at 1 Ki. 14: 9. The *seers* were prophets, and called by that name sometimes because of the meaning of the word. A prophet is able to *see* into the future, and would thus be a *seer* on the same principle that one who does, is a doer. God used these seers to admonish and otherwise instruct the king (Heb. 1: 1). In the comments on *high places* referred to in V. 17, a distinction was made between those places in view of the different motives and uses that were made of them. In this paragraph the word is used in its bad sense, for it is associated with the religious groves and graven images, and they were always idolatrous.

Verse 20. *Slept with his fathers* is explained at 1 Ki. 2: 10. The kings had their private homes in addition to their use of the palace. These homes had some land about them that could be used for various purposes. If a king had met the full favor of the public sentiment, he was buried in the special location set aside for the royal sepulchres. If it was otherwise, he was laid in some other place. In the case of Manasseh the burial was in the private grounds about his house.

Verse 21. Amon received the throne by regular succession, being the son of the preceding king. He reigned *in Jerusalem*, an oft-repeated term. The force of it will be realized more, perhaps, if we were to word it, he reigned in Jerusalem; not Hebron or Shechem or Tirzah or Samaria. These places all had been used as headquarters for certain Jewish kings, but Jerusalem was the original and most authoritative capital.

Verse 22. What Amon did was approved by the people who were as evil as he, but *in the sight of the Lord* his doings were sinful. *Sacrificed* and *served* are used in a way to imply a distinction between them, which is true; but it is mainly in the sense of the degree in his devotion. To make sacrifice might merely mean to go through the formalities of the altar actions. *Serve* is from ABAD and Strong defines it, "a primitive root; to work (in any sense); by implication to serve, till, (causatively) enslave, etc." It therefore means to bend the energies of mind and body in a daily routine that practically enslaves one to the object of his admiration. Such a life would be commendable if lived in the service of the true God.

Verse 23. Amon did worse than his father in that he did not humbly repent of his sins. He *trespassed more and more*, which means, as expressed in the margin, that he multiplied his trespasses. Technically, this word means to encrouch upon the rights and property of another, but in this instance the original means something more serious. The first definition in the lexicon is "guiltiness, a fault." In the A. V. the word is rendered by "sin" 4 times. The expression about Amon means that he got worse and worse in his sinful life, including all of his idolatrous activities and daily conduct.

Verse 24. The life of Amon was so bad that he provoked his own personal servants to a rash action. Finding him in his own residence, they murdered him. This was an unlawful deed, for a man in authority should be removed by lawful means if done at all.

Verse 25. "Two wrongs do not make one right" is an old saying. It was evidently the principle on which the citizens of the nation acted in their treatment of the assassins. The sinful life of Amon did not justify the servants in murdering their king. The law of capital punishment would call for the execution of these servants. The people of the land, therefore, were acting lawfully when they slew the assassins of the king. His son would have become king through the established rule of succession, independent of the formalities of these citizens. But their ceremonies were to be a sort of public protest against the action of the murderers of the preceding king.

2 CHRONICLES 34

Verse 1. In stating the length of a reign, all of the years are counted from the time the king became the legal occupant of the throne until he quit it, either by death or otherwise. But in case he is too young to act in person, the high priest who is in service acts for him until such time that he can take upon himself the duties of a ruler. There was such a case in the reign of Joash or Jehoash. (2 Ki. 12: 2; 2 Chr. 24: 2.) That is what was done in the case of Josiah, for he was but 8 years old when he became king, and his entire reign continued 31 years.

Verse 2. These commendations of Josiah apply to his reign after he became ready to take active part in the affairs of the kingdom, and hence after he was old enough to be held accountable for his conduct; this will appear evident in the next verse.

Verse 3. The eighth year of his reign would be when he was 16 years of age, and when he would be considered responsible. It was at that time that he *began to seek after the God of David*. But he still was not very forward in the affairs of the kingdom. Like a judicious person, he spent 4 years in seeking after God, in which time he grew in years and knowledge. Such a preparation would qualify a king to act wisely. Accordingly, after 12 years of preparation, and in the 20th year of his life, he began to take action. He started a work that was destined to develop into one of the greatest reformations in the history of that nation. He began by purging out the high places that had been devoted to idolatrous sacrifices, and destroying the groves that had been used to shelter the images of the false gods. Not only did he destroy all of the actual trees and groves of trees that were so used, but he destroyed all of the images of those trees that had been made in imitation of such plants. He also destroyed the statues that had been erected to the heathen gods, whether they had been made by casting or chiseling.

Verse 4. *In his presence*. Josiah ordered his men to destroy the altars of Baalim while he looked on, making sure thereby that the work was done. The images or statues had been erected over the altars, as if the gods were present and beholding the service rendered to them; all of such were destroyed. *Made dust* is said of the *groves* in the same sense as it is said of the images, thereby implying that they were made of metal. It will be well to quote from Smith's Bible Dictionary on this subject. "Grove. A word used in the Authorized Version, with two exceptions, to translate the mysterious term ASHERAH, which is not a grove, but probably an idol or image of some kind. It is also probable that there was a connection between this symbol or image, whatever it was, and the sacred public tree, the representation of which occurs so frequently on the Assyrian sculptures." There was nothing strange about the making of such metal images for worship. If the heathen nations worshiped certain trees, it would be consistent to make images of them. As a result of that practice, we will read of instances where the groves were cut down and destroyed, when it means these metallic images of the trees. They were first burnt so as to have them in a corroded condition, then ground into dust and strewn on the graves of the ones who had been worshipers of them. That was done in contempt of such gods, to demonstrate their utter helplessness. Those gods not only were unable to save their followers from death, but could not defend themselves from being crushed and consigned to the last resting place of their deluded devotees.

Verse 5. This is a very brief account of the subject concerning the burning of these bones. Read the prophecy about it, with the fulfillment, in 1 Ki. 13: 1, 2, and 2 Ki. 23: 16, 17. This treatment of the bones of the priests would be for the same purpose as that done to the dust of the grove, recorded in the preceding verse.

Verse 6. The cities named were in the former possessions of the 10 tribes. Those tribes had been in Assyrian captivity for almost a century, but many of the traces of their great corruption were left in the land, and Josiah extended his purging reformation into that territory. It was fitting that he do so, for the nation of the 10 tribes was then toiling in slavery among the heathen, and it was in punishment for the worship of these false gods. How appropriate, then, for him to destroy the images.

Verse 7. Having completed his tour of reformation through the communities of the places named, Josiah returned to his own capital. *Land of Israel* sometimes applied to the whole of Palestine, but in this instance refers to the territory of the 10 tribes, of which Samaria was the capital.

Verse 8. All buildings without exception are subject to decay, and especially if neglected through interest in outside matters. Having completed his purge of the land, and taken the idolatrous images out of the temple, Josiah next turned his attention to repairing the temple. This was in the 18th year of his reign, which shows that he spent 6 years in the purging of the country. All of the men he called upon to see after the repair work were important ones. Shaphan was a scribe (2 Ki. 22: 3), Maaseiah was governor (about the same in rank as our mayors) of the city, and Joah was a recorder, a position about the same as a secretary.

Verse 9. The work that Josiah commanded to be done required money, so the men named in the preceding verse went to a lawful place for it. The Levites had been receiving money from various sources and out of various communities as they kept the entrances to the temple. Acting under orders from the king, these men went to the Levites and got the money, then went to the high priest, which was in order to make a proper accounting within their responsibility.

Verse 10. After they had made their proper report, and under the supervision of the high priest, the highest official over the temple, they put out the money to pay for the labor of the repair work. It was all done in a businesslike manner, contacting first those who were overseers or foremen, who in turn would expend it on the men who *wrought* or worked on the repairs.

Verse 11. An *artificer* was "a fabricator of any material" according to the definition in the lexicon. When used in connection with a building, it would refer to the man having general oversight of the formation of its structure. The *builders* were the men who actually did the bodily work according to the directions of the *artificers*. These two classes of men would know what kinds of material were needed for the repairs, so the money was supplied to them to go out and buy them. *Couplings* were braces or brackets, placed in the angles or corners of the building to support it. To *floor* is translated "to rafter" in the margin. The lexicon will admit the definition, but it also would retain the translation in the text. It is defined, "to impose timbers (for roof or floor)" So it means any heavy pieces of wood necessary to repair the building. *Houses* is in the plural because there were the temple and palace, and both had been neglected by the preceding kings and had fallen into disrepair.

Verse 12. This verse gets nearer to the working forces of the great project set in motion by Josiah. A former verse named the more superior men, this names the men actually doing the work. *Did the work faithfully* would include the fact that they obeyed their foremen as to how the work should be done, also that they worked and did not shirk. Not only was the building needing repairs, but the musical instruments that David had introduced had been somewhat tossed aside and had to be repaired or replaced. And since they were used in connection with the worship, and since that was always in the hands of the Levites, it was in order that the matter of those instruments be attended to by *other of the Levites*.

Verse 13. There were tasks in connection with the repair work that could properly be performed by persons from any of the tribes, but the major portion of them came from the tribe of Levi. That was especially true of such tasks as clerical services, and the responsibility for guarding the gates, which was done by the porters.

Verse 14. *Money that was brought* means the money that had previously been deposited in the treasury of the temple. It had to be taken out in order to follow the instructions of the king for the repairs of the temple. *Found a book.* This has been the occasion for many fanciful speeches, intended to enlarge on the neglect of the Bible of which so many are guilty. In order to put emphasis on the instance, they even add their imagination by saying that the book was found amidst the rubbish that had been allowed to accumulate in the house of God. There is nothing said about such a subject. All that can justly be said is that no attention had been given the book previously, but that the program the king had put into action caused a closer inspection of all the surroundings. It is significant that the book was found when they were visiting the place where the money was deposited. That money was taken from the incomes of the people, and was added unto almost constantly. That fact would discount the idea that the book was "hidden in the rubbish." It was found at the same time these men were thinking about the repair work ready to be started in the building, and thus when the attention of all was more alert to the conditions. Many professed children of God today might "find" the Bible in the same sense that is applied to the case under Josiah. A Bible might be lying on a table or in a library shelf and be unnoticed for years, until some person called attention to the importance of reading it. And if it should then be done, many half-hearted Christians would be as surprised as Josiah was, when they discovered how far they had drifted from their path of duty.

Verse 15. Hilkiah was high priest and second to none in authority over matters pertaining to the religious activities. The scribes, however, had the special work of copying the law, and it would seem consistent with their role to handle what copies that were already written. So the high priest turned over the book to the scribe.

Verse 16. The wording of this verse might be a little confusing, as it sounds as if Shaphan made two trips to see the king. The thought is that he had to make a report to the king anyway, so while he was at it he just took the book along. No doubt that fact figured somewhat in the act of the high priest in putting the newly found book into his hands. He knew that he soon was going to see the king, and hence would be the first to have occasion to tell him about the book. But before bringing up that subject, he made his report on the conduct of the king's servants, that all things were done according to the royal orders.

Verse 17. Shaphan did not stop with a general statement of the work of the servants. He gave the detail of gathering together the money that was available in the house of the Lord, and making proper distribution of it; it was placed in proper hands.

Verse 18. Having made his business report, the scribe then mentioned the subject of the book. He told the king who had found it and delivered it to him. The king did not take the book but had Shaphan to read it in his hearing.

Verse 19. Men as well as women wore certain loose clothing over their inner garments. There was a custom of tearing the skirt of the garment at times of great grief or anxiety. Where or when this practice started I do not know. When Josiah heard the reading of the book he rent his clothes. That was not in protest or disrespect for what the book said; he had great reverence for it; but he was shocked at the awful situation it indicated they were in, and determined to make further inquiry.

Verses 20, 21. Moses was the writer of the law of the Lord and he completed his work. If any new or specific information were needed, it had to be learned through the prophets or other inspired persons who would be given messages for the occasion. (Heb. 1: 1.) Josiah knew that the nation had departed from the law in many respects, but had not realized how far, until Shaphan had read it before him. Accordingly, he was concerned about getting direct instructions from the Lord, and commanded these persons to *enquire of the Lord*. His attention to **the material improvements of the temple was now diverted and centered** on a spiritual reformation, even more intense than what he had done in the beginning of his reign.

Verse 22. Strong, in his lexicon, says a prophetess is an inspired woman. In all of the dispensations, God has occasionally used inspired women in his work. Miriam was a prophetess (Ex. 15: 20), who was still under the Patriarchal Dispensation. Philip had four daughters who prophesied (Acts 21: 9), and that was in the Christian Dispensation. Now we have Huldah as an inspired prophetess. But we must not forget that all such were temporary arrangements of God, and that when he finally got his Revelation to man complete, all miraculous methods of information were discontinued, and mankind was left solely to depend on the written Word which is perfect. (1 Cor. 13: 10; James 1: 25.) The men appointed by the king went to this prophetess for information concerning the crisis that Josiah feared was at hand. The woman's husband had the care of the sacred garments that were worn by the priests while in active service. She would very logically be dwelling nearby, so the text says it was in the *college*. The marginal reading is "second part," which agrees with the lexicon. It is from MISHNEH and the definition is, "a repetition, i. e. a duplicate (copy of a document), or a double (in amount); by implication a second (in order, rank, age, quality or location."—Strong. Moffatt's translation gives it that she lived "in the second ward" of Jerusalem. It is thus clear: she was an inspired woman, yet occupied a secondary residence in the city where her husband had the important assignment of caring for the sacred garments.

Verses 23, 24. *Evil* is a word with wide extent of meaning, including adversity and affliction. In this verse it has special reference to the things that had been warned about in the writings of Moses. Many of these are written in Deut. 27 and 28. Huldah did not give any new information as to the curses that were to come, only that the ones already written about were soon to be brought upon them.

Verse 25. All forms of service to false gods were displeasing to the true God, but the burning of incense seemed to be the highest indication of devotion, and was especially offensive to God. That was the reason that it was the special thing that distinguished the rights of the priests from all others. (Ch. 26: 18.) *Shall not be quenched* is a final decision, from which nothing can move the Lord. All of the reformative work of Josiah could not save the nation from the impending doom. But even in the midst of the conditions, and just as God was affirming that nothing could change his mind, he still admonished sinners to repent and seek the favor of God. It is natural to wonder if there were not some contradictions in the actions of the Lord. There were not, but we need to consider that God's dealings with the nation as a whole was one thing, and those of individuals was another. For a more detailed discussion of this subject see my comments at 2 Ki. 22: 17.

Verse 26. This verse is for the personal benefit of the king. It will be an instance of the distinction referred to in the preceding verse. Let it be noted that Josiah was credited with seeking information *of the Lord*, even though he was applying to the prophetess. The thought is important; it signifies that the words of any of the persons who are inspired of God, are divine words, and he who disregards them is guilty of having disregarded the words of God and of disobeying them.

Verse 27. *Heart was tender* means it was penitent toward God. Had Josiah been resentful and inclined to justify himself and the nation, both he and the nation would have been punished. Instead, he performed the actions that were the accustomed signs of penitence in those days (the actions described in the body of this verse).

Verse 28. The doom of the nation was sealed, and all of the work of Josiah could not stop it. But on account of his personal righteousness, the Lord promised to delay the national calamity until after he was gone. *Gather thee to thy fathers* has the same meaning as "slept with his fathers," which is explained at 1 Ki. 2: 10. *Gathered . . . in peace* means that he will not die as a casualty of the great tribulation threatened upon the nation. It cannot mean that he would die "from natural causes," for Ch. 35: 20-24 shows that he died by violence. The *peace* promised him consisted in the fact that his eyes would not *see all the evil* that was to be brought upon his beloved country.

Verse 29. *Elders* is not an official term, but refers to the older men among the people, and who would be expected to be leaders in judgment.

Also, men who would be foremost in feeling the weight of responsibility for the actions of the nation. Josiah wished to have these leading citizens with him as he held a consultation with certain officers and the populace in general.

Verse 30. This was a solemn assembly. It was composed of *all the men of Judah* (that were present) and the local citizens of the city. The *priests* and *Levites*, which means that portion of the tribe that was of the priestly family, and the tribe as a whole. *Great and small* means old and young. There were many thousands of people in the land, so we know they could not all have gone up *into the house of the Lord*. The verse means, therefore, that all of the ranks or sections of the population that are named, were represented in the gathering. Josiah did not depend on his memory to present the case to the assemblage, but read the book in their ears.

Verse 31. *Stood in his place* means he stood in a spot that had been prepared for him, to be in the sight and hearing of the crowd. The king personally *made a covenant*, signifying that he, for one, promised to walk after the Lord. *Commandments* refer to the law in general; *testimonies* are the words that had been attested and found to be correct; the *statutes* mean the fixed and formal enactments of the law. *Heart* and *soul* are practically the same, but the two words used together add emphasis to the declaration. To *perform the words* denotes that they not only heard the words read, but would proceed to put them into practice. It suggests the statement in James 1: 22.

Verse 32. Josiah caused the audience to agree to the covenant he had made with God. They not only promised to do so, but the inspired writer states they did it.

Verse 33. This verse is a general statement of Josiah's activities, including the work then in the future as well as that already done. The work of reformation that this righteous king performed was still in its infancy when this verse was composed, but the inspired writer gave a complete coverage of the work while on the subject. Note it says that *all his days* the people followed the Lord. We shall see them soon forget it after Josiah is gone.

2 CHRONICLES 35

Verse 1. This passover was the feast instituted by Moses on the night the children of Israel prepared to leave Egypt. It was so named because the Lord made certain exceptions to a great destruction of life among the families. All the firstborn of the Egyptians, and any others who did not observe this feast, were to be visited with the death of the oldest member of the family. If a family of the Israelites carried out the requirements of this ordinance, which included the sprinkling of blood over the doors of the homes, the death angel would pass over that house. It was then established as one of the set feasts of the nation, to be observed on the 14th day of the 1st month of each year. (Ex. 12.)

Verse 2. *Set the priests in their charges* indicates that Josiah required some system to be observed. The priests were assigned their several duties, and were encouraged to carry on the divine service that had been given into their hands.

Verse 3. The Levites (of whom were the priests), were to teach the people. Read Lev. 10: 11; Deut. 17: 9; Mal. 2: 7. *Put the holy ark in the house* implies that it was then outside its own proper room. Ch. 5: 7 states that it was placed in there by Solomon, and there is no evidence that it had been taken out. Moffatt's translation of this passage shows a different construction of the language, which agrees with all the known facts and I shall quote it. "Since the sacred ark," said he, "was placed inside the temple built by Solomon the son of David, king of Israel, and you have no longer to carry it on your shoulders, see to the worship of the Eternal your God, and of his people Israel."

Verse 4. In the general disorder that had befallen the nation, the orders or courses that David had instituted for the priesthood had shared in the confusion. Josiah instructed them to adjust themselves to the proper places again.

Verse 5. This verse is practically a repetition of the preceding one. But the importance of proper order was so great that the king did not wish to take any chances on the men being short about their performances. *Stand* is from an original word that has a very wide extent of applications; all of them, however, are in just two major classes; either figurative or literal. The priests were to continue in the holy place that had been appointed for them in the law. One family was not to encroach upon the work or place of another, but was to observe the order given to their forefathers.

Verse 6. After the instructions of the several preceding verses, the people were told in direct terms to *kill the passover*. It reminds us of the introductory instructions that Moses gave the people on the night of the first passover. (Ex. 12.) *Sanctify*. In every passage of the Old Testament this is from the same Hebrew word, which is QADASH. Strong's definition is, "a primitive root; to be (causatively make, pronounce or observe as) clean (ceremonially or morally)". A man was not permitted to partake of the passover if he were unclean in any sense, hence the full definition would apply in the command that Josiah gave the people. One illustration of ceremonial uncleanness would be where a man had touched a dead person. Actual uncleanness requires no illustration to make it understood by the reader. *Prepare your brethren* was addressed to these Levites, who will be in charge of the feast. They were to transmit the order of the king to their brethren of the nation, and see that they removed any defect, either ceremonial or actual, that would hinder them from partaking of the feast. *Word of the Lord by the hand of Moses*. This is another instance that shows the writings of Moses to have been the Lord's word. It is a solemn rebuke for the sabbatarians who presume to distinguish between the two as to authority of the word.

Verse 7. The vast number of animals that Josiah gave to the people indicates the size of the group assembled for the feast. Under the circumstances, he knew that few of them would be provided with the beasts, so out of his own private property he made the donation. Mention is made of bullocks which might be a little confusing, since the sheep or goat only was used in the passover. But the feast of unleavened bread of 7 days followed the passover immediately, and in that period they observed an *offering made by fire*. (Lev. 23: 8.) This would call for the larger animals.

Verse 8. The princes were leading citizens of the country but not necessarily officers. Having been favored with an abundance of possessions, they willingly shared them with the people, also with the official and unofficial members of the tribe of Levi. Hilkiah and Zechariah and Jehiel had charge of the temple. The first was high priest, the one who found the book that caused this great movement of reformation. It would be particularly appropriate for him to show a practical interest in the work of reconstruction, by giving out of his possessions unto the common priests, so they could have wherewith to sacrifice to the Lord. *Small cattle* has no words in the original, but is followed by the conjunction *and*, which connects with the word *oxen* which we know are the larger cattle. The connection, therefore, justifies the words *small cattle*, meaning lambs of the sheep or goats, since all animals were called cattle.

Verse 9. The men named were *chief* of the Levites. The word is defined in the lexicon, "a head person of any rank or class." So they were not necessarily officers, but outstanding men of the tribe. Such men would likely have more property, and they graciously shared it with their fellow-Levites, so they could take part in the great feast. *Small cattle* takes the same explanation that is made in the preceding verse.

Verse 10. Everything was "all set" for the important observance. Each man took his place for duty, whether he were a priest and ready for the direct service at the altar, or of the other Levites, and ready for secondary work in connection with the ceremonies. And the whole procedure was according to the king's commandment.

Verse 11. The animal was killed by having his throat cut. That caused the blood to be available, and it was first used by the priests by sprinkling or dashing it by hand on the altar. Then the other Levites would flay (skin) the carcass and prepare it for burning on the altar.

Verse 12. Certain parts of some of the animals were to be burned on the altar. Certain other parts were to be given to the people for their individual service to the Lord. This is the explanation of the verse.

Verse 13. The passover was the set feast for this time of the year, and the law required that it be roasted, not boiled. (Ex. 12: 8, 9.) Other offerings that the people made along about the same time could be sodden, which means they were boiled. The cooking was done in whatever vessels were convenient. After being cooked, they were divided among the people for food.

Verse 14. *They* in the verses now being considered means the Levites in general. They had to do the bulk of the work, while the priests (the Levites who came from Aaron), had to do the official work about the altar. After the congregation had been waited on, these unofficial Levites were released to get ready for their own offerings. And while they were at it they prepared for the priests also because they had not had any time to do so for themselves. The *fat* is specially mentioned because it was the most important part of an animal that was offered on the altar. It referred to the richest portion, such as the suet and the material that clung to the kidneys and intestines. It had no reference to what is commonly called "fat meat."

Verse 15. The *sons of Asaph* were a school of poets and musical composers founded by Asaph, according to Smith's Bible Dictionary. The word "school" means group or class in about the same sense as we speak of a "school" of fishes. David had appointed this group to the song program in connection with the passover.

Verse 16. Promptness was manifested by the persons charged with the preparations, for they were all accomplished in one day. The immediate orders came from the king, Josiah, but originally they were ordained through Moses at Sinai.

Verse 17. All of the people, whether male or female, were permitted to be present at the feast of the passover, but the males only were required to be. That explains why the verse says that those *that were present* kept the feast. The entire feast required 8 days; and 7 of that period was the feast of unleavened bread, and it was preceded by the passover. The period as a whole is frequently referred to in the Old and New Testaments by either term, passover or feast of unleavened bread. If that is kept in mind it might save the student of the Bible some confusion.

Verse 18. This verse makes a comparison that goes back to *Samuel the prophet*. The corresponding passage in 2 Ki. 23: 22 goes back to *the days of the judges*. But there is no contradiction for Samuel was one of the judges as well as being a prophet. (1 Sam. 7: 6.) There was a specific formula for observing the feast of the passover, and that did not allow for any variation. It would be questioned, then, how there could be any such comparison made as is done here. The comparison is to the number of persons participating and the zeal manifested, not to the form of observance.

Verse 19. This wonderful passover observance was 13 years before Josiah closed his career. From that time on, however, we have very little information about him.

Verse 20. Preparing the temple had nothing to do with the movements of the king of Egypt. The writer merely mentions it in the way of dates; that the expedition of Necho was after the repair of the temple and the reformatory work that accompanied it. By such a statement, the reader will be informed that the sad affair about to be reported did not interfere with the life work of the good king. The king of Egypt made a tour against a city on the Euphrates. To do so he had to travel across some territory in which Josiah felt an interest, not far from Nazareth. But he was passing along peaceably and not making any disturbance against the land of Palestine. However, Josiah went out with the intention of intercepting him.

Verse 21. We do not know why God wished the people of Charchemish chastised. But it was not the only instance in which one heathen people was sent against another, by the ordinance of the Lord. (2 Ki. 5: 1.) It was done also after this in the days of Nebuchadnezzar (Ezk. 26: 7), and later in the days of Belshazzar (Dan. 5: 28). It was a meddling with the work of God, therefore, for Josiah to interfere with the march of Necho.

Verse 22. This verse shows that Necho was telling the truth when he said that God was with him. The inspired writer is the one who tells us that the words of Necho were *from the mouth of God*. Josiah committed the one great mistake of his life in this case. He disguised himself in an attempt to escape defeat. He should have remembered the like conduct of Ahab (1 Ki. 22: 30-37), and the failure that he suffered. But he persisted in his own way and thought to elude the danger that usually confronts a man when he goes out to battle; especially in a cause that is not his business.

Verse 23. The *archers* were those who used the bow and arrow, a common weapon of warfare in those times.

The simple statement is made that they *shot at* Josiah, but the rest of the verse shows they hit him. *Sore wounded* is worded "made sick" in the margin. The lexicon would agree with it, for part of the definition is, "to be weak, sick, afflicted." The idea is that he was not only critically hurt, but was still fully conscious and could feel the sickening effect of his wound.

Verse 24. A *second chariot* was one in reserve, not in direct line of combat. It was thus used as we would use an ambulance, and served to bring the wounded king to his capital at Jerusalem. The statement *and he died* is made after the one about his being brought to Jerusalem. That does not make it mean, however, that the death occurred after arrival. It is just a common form of expression in the Bible, where the several facts of a circumstance may be named with very little regard for their chronological order. The corresponding passage in 2 Ki. 23: 30 plainly says that the servants *carried him in his chariot dead.* Where two different, but not conflicting accounts of an event are given, one more specific than the other, the one that is clearer should be used to explain the other. Josiah was critically wounded, but death was not instantaneous, for he felt and announced his terrible condition. It was a considerable distance from the scene of the tragedy to Jerusalem, and the king did not live to see it. He was buried in one of the family tombs. Judah was his proper realm and Jerusalem was its capital. The whole nation mourned the passing of one of the best kings it had ever had.

Verse 25. Jeremiah was one of the writing prophets and wrote two of the books in our Bible. But, like many other writers of old, he wrote or expressed some things that have not been handed down to us. It was very natural that he, "the weeping prophet," should lament the death of so good a man as Josiah. The singing men and women expressed their sentiment in their composition. *To this day* means to the day this book was being written. It is similar to a common expression of writers in current publications, "as we go to press." *Made them an ordinance* denotes that they established it as a custom to mourn the sad fate of their good king. *Written in the lamentations* does not have any special reference to the book bearing that name. It is from a word that is defined, "a dirge (as accompanied by beating the breasts or on instruments)."—Strong.

Verses 26, 27. For comments on this thought see 1 Ki. 14: 19.

2 CHRONICLES 36

Verse 1. *Made him king* refers to the ceremonies of publicly acknowledging him as their king; he was actually made king by succession. It might be compared to the inauguration rites of a man who has been already elected to an office.

Verse 2. Jehoahaz was the ruler by natural rights and thus the regular heir to the throne, yet he held it for 3 months only. The circumstances that made his reign so short will be reported soon.

Verse 3. The inspired record does not explain why the Egyptian king was suffered to take such a prominent part in the affairs of Jerusalem. This is the same king who was opposed by Josiah, father of Jehoahaz. The Assyrians were in power at the time of Josiah's death, but were nearing the end of their rule. In fact, it occurred in the beginning of the reign of Jehoiakim, of whom we will read in the next verse. Jehoahaz was dethroned and the land *condemned,* which means it was put under a tribute of money.

Verse 4. We are not told why Necho changed the name of Eliakim to Jehoiakim, but the name was recognized afterward by the writers of the Bible. The simple statement is made that Jehoahaz was taken to Egypt. But Jeremiah the prophet said he was to die there, never having seen his native land again. (Jer. 22: 11, 12.)

Verse 5. This reign of 11 years included the years he was sitting on the throne, but subject to the king of Babylon. Soon after he was put on the throne by Necho, the Assyrian power was overthrown by the Chaldeans, otherwise known as Babylonians, of whom Nebuchadnezzar was ruler at the time. As soon as he came into power in Babylon, he went to Jerusalem and induced Jehoiakim to acknowledge his supremacy; but after 3 years he rebelled against that relationship. (2 Ki. 24: 1.) The king of Babylon then put him under greater subjection. Jehoiakim was permitted to occupy the throne in Jerusalem for 8 years longer, but subject to the king of Babylon. (2 Ki. 24: 2-4.)

Verse 6. The events of this verse came at the end of the entire reign of

Jehoiakim that was referred to in the preceding verse. The corruptions under the reign of this king were so many that God became weary with them and caused the Babylonian king to come up to Jerusalem and take him from his throne. More details of the affair are given in 2 Ki. 24: 2-4. The king was bound with fetters to be taken to Babylon.

Verse 7. Nebuchadnezzar also took the valuable vessels of the temple with him, and placed them in his own temple in Babylon, which was his capital. This great event may be said to have completed the first captivity, which was begun at the end of the third year of Jehoiakim. That was also the beginning of the famous 70 years captivity, of which we will hear much when we come to the study of the prophecies. That is, the beginning of the 4th year of Jehoiakim marks the date, not only of the beginning of the "seventy years captivity," but the date of the 1st of the "three captivities." I have gone so much into detail about these "three captivities" at their account in the book of Kings, that not much space will be taken for it here. I ask the reader to consult carefully all the comments on 2 Ki. 24 and 25.

Verse 8. There is very little said as to the details of Jehoiakim's reign, either here or in the corresponding passage in 2 Ki. 24. Hence we have a very clear reason in this case, why it was so often stated that the "rest of the acts" of rulers was written in those outside reading books. See the comments at 1 Ki. 14: 19.

Verse 9. Jehoiachin has two other forms for his name in other parts of the Bible, and it will be well for the student to bear them in mind in order to avoid confusion. They are, Jeconiah and Coniah. The common text says he was 8 ears old when he began to reign. The corresponding passage in 2 Ki. 24: 8 says he was 18. The one in Kings evidently is the correct one. But the critic of the Bible will have nothing to boast about, or to claim it to have been the work of man. The difference is too plain not to have been noticed by the men who composed the volume, had it been the work of uninspired man. Had the two accounts been so written originally as they now stand, the mistake would have been noticed by the writers on their first reading of it, and would have been corrected. But a blurred manuscript could easily have been misread by a copyist. Jehoiachin at the age of 18 years, was old enough to be "on his own" in the kingship. He was an evil ruler and the Lord suffered his political superior (Nebuchadnezzar) to take him away into the captivity.

Verse 10. Jehoiachin was permitted to reign but a few months when Nebuchadnezzar came up against him and his capital, and took him away to Babylon. At the same time he took the *goodly* vessels of the house of the Lord; that is, he took some of them. Verse 7 says he took *of* the vessels, which would still leave a part of them, and at the time we are now considering he took some more of them but left some. He made a change in the rulership also. Jehoiachin was only 18 years of age when he was taken from his throne. It is not likely that he had any children to inherit his place. But the entire regime was under the subjection of Babylon anyway, so that whatsoever changes that country would see fit to make could be expected. Men had more than one name in those days and they were used interchangeably. For instance, Mattaniah was one name and Zedekiah another of the same man, and he was a son of Josiah. Another thing to remember is that a relative of a man was sometimes spoken of as his own relative of the same rank; so a man's father's brother might be said to be his brother. It was that way in the case at hand. Zedekiah was really the brother of Jehoiakim, father of Jehoiachin, but here spoken of as his brother. We should consider 2 Ki. 24: 17 and 1 Chr. 3: 15 in connection with this verse, in order to get this relationship clear in our minds. The taking of Jehoiachin to Babylon constituted the 2nd of the three captivities already spoken of. Because he reigned such a small fraction of a year, any date based on the years after "Jehoiachin's captivity" or on the number of years of Zedekiah's reign would be the same date. The fuller account of Jehoiachin's captivity is given in 2 Ki. 24: 10-16. It can be seen at that place that it was the most important of the "three captivities" in the way of casualties. At that time the king of Babylon took away most of the vessels of the temple and stored them in the heathen building in his own capital city. He took also the best portions of the inhabitants, leaving only the poorest sort of the people. Among the great men whom he took away was the prophet Ezekiel. (Ezk. 1: 2; 40: 1.)

Verse 11. This verse is a general statement of the entire reign of Zedekiah. Some of the details of the reign will be given in the following verses. Other details are recorded in the writings of Ezekiel, scattered through several chapters of his book. From these different sources it can be seen that the 11 years of the reign of Zedekiah were filled with evil. He was rebellious and proud, and unmindful of his obligation to the king of Babylon.

Verse 12. The conduct of Zedekiah was evil *in the sight of the Lord*. That is what counts, whether man approves or not. Humility is placed opposite of evil, and it should be so placed. Pride is manifested in more than one way. If a man refuses to cease his evil ways, the Lord considers it to be an evidence of pride. That is especially true if he has been admonished and offered instruction. This wicked man had just such opportunities in the service of Jeremiah the prophet. In Jer. 21 is the record of the circumstance when Zedekiah sent to the prophet for information. It was given him, and he was admonished to submit to the rule of Nebuchadnezzar. He was further told that resistance would be in vain and that it would be better for him personally to cease his evil ways. But the admonition was spurned and he thought he could evade the doom that God had decreed against him and the nation for their disobedience.

Verse 13. In rebelling against Nebuchadnezzar, he not only was disobeying the word of God as spoken by the prophet, but broke his own word of oath with the Babylonian king. *Stiffened his neck* is a figure of speech found frequently in the Bible, meaning to become stubborn and unyielding to the law. The expression is used in this place with special reference to the obligation to Nebuchadnezzar, who was his superior at that time, having become so by the operations of war, and with the approval of God. *Hardened his heart* is another figure of speech, similar to the one just considered, and used with special application to his personal attitude to God. The thought is, that even though he might feel at liberty to oppose Nebuchadnezzar, he being a heathen king, yet he should have been considerate of his personal duty to the true God.

Verse 14. Although the Babylonians had put the king and his country under their rule, they had been lenient enough to leave the temple for their use. They could have continued in a partial observance of the services at least, in the holy building. But instead of doing so, this wicked king had even encouraged the priests and people in their heathen practices. They had carried their transgressions to the extent of polluting the temple that God had accepted and declared to be holy to him.

Verse 15. God is ever compassionate and desirous of sparing his people all the sorrow possible. The nation as a whole was bound to go into captivity to fulfill the divine decree, which was destined to rid it of its great national sin of idolatry. But that would not prevent giving personal favors to those who were righteous as individuals, or who would become so upon being admonished. This is another place where I will insist that the student read the comments at 2 Ki. 22: 17. In keeping with these principles, God continued to warn and admonish his people through his *messengers*. This is from the Hebrew word MALAK and Strong defines it, "from an unused root meaning to dispatch as a deputy; a messenger; specifically of God, i. e. an angel (also a prophet, priest or teacher)." So the word has a wide extent of meaning, but retains throughout the common idea of a special communication from one person to another. And this varied meaning of the word again reminds us of Heb. 1: 1. *Betimes* means to be prompt in whatever matter is on hands. It would apply not only to the promptness of God in recognizing the need for a message, and for making ready a messenger for the purpose, but also that the messenger would be prompt in attending to his duty.

Verse 16. They *mocked* the messengers, which means they derided or ridiculed them. They *despised* the words of God sent by the messengers, which denotes that they belittled them. This attitude was persisted in so long that the wrath of God was aroused against them, to the extent that the nation got beyond remedy. (2 Ki. 22: 17.)

Verse 17. The Chaldees were the same as the Babylonians as far as this history is concerned. Babylonians is the name derived from the country and its capital city. The Chaldeans were a distinct tribe of the people that had existed for a long time, and were in authority of the country at the time we are studying. God used them as his instrument for chastising his people. They were suffered to take over the temple, even using violence against the young men while they engaged in the service thereof.

Verse 18. Some of the holy vessels were taken at each of the previous raids, but at this time they were all taken, including the royal treasury, and the valuables of the princes.

Verse 19. The temple had been spared through the previous years that the Babylonians had possession of the country. But even such a favor did not keep the Jews from their evil practices; now the complete destruction will take place. The besiegers did not stop at the temple, but destroyed the city wall also. They likewise destroyed the *palaces* and their valuabe contents. We think of a palace primarily as the home of a king or other royal person. But there was only one of such in Jerusalem, while this word is plural. It is from an original that means any high and dignified structure. There were many of them in the city and they were all burnt. The beloved city of the nation of God; the capital of the mighty empire of David and Solomon was left in ruins by the relentless, destructive power of the Babylonians.

Verse 20. This verse is the climax of the 3rd captivity. (See comments at 2 Ki. 24: 1.) It came after a siege of about 2 years. (2 Ki. 25: 1, 2.) In that siege many perished from famine, and when the final assault was made, many died by the sword. Those who did not perish in the attack were carried off to Babylon to remain until the time of the Persian dominion. That event is mentioned because it coincides with the end of the "seventy years' captivity" that began with the 4th year of Jehoiakim. (2 Ki. 24: 1-4.) After coming to Babylon these Jews were made to serve the king as long as he lived, and then his successors until the end of the period described.

Verse 21. *To fulfill* refers to the preceding verse. That is, by remaining in captivity until the reign of Persia over Babylon, the prophecy will be fulfilled that was made by Jeremiah. That prophecy may be seen in his book, Ch. 25: 9, 11, 12; and Ch. 29: 10. The Babylonian captivity was to last 70 years, beginning with the 4th year of Jehoiakim in 606 B. C., and going to 536 B. C. In Lev. 25 is the law that required the land should rest every 7th year. It had been disobeyed until the land had been cheated out of 70 years. The captivity was to give it a chance to "catch up."

Verses 22, 23. This passage is the same as the first two verses of the next book, and the comments on it will be given there. The verses were attached to this book as a connecting link for the reader who might not have the Book of Ezra at hand. This was possible before the books of the Bible were collected into one volume.

EZRA 1

Verse 1. *First year of Cyrus.* This means his first year as ruler over Babylon. He had been king of the Persians for some 20 years up to the time of his taking this city. It will throw some light on this part of the subject to quote from Myers' Ancient History, pages 88, 89: "Cyrus the Great (558-529 B. C.) founds a Great World Empire.—The leadership of the Median chieftains was of short duration. A certain Cyrus, king of Anshan, in Elam, overthrew their power, and assumed the headship of both Medes and Persians. Through his energy and soldierly genius Cyrus soon built up an empire more extended than any over which the scepter had yet been swayed by Oriental monarch, or indeed, so far as we know, by any ruler before his time. After the conquest of Media and the acquisition of the provinces formerly ruled by the Median princes, Cyrus rounded out his empire by the conquest of Lydia and Babylonia." A more extended account of the taking of Babylon may be found in *Five Great Monarchies*, by George Rawlinson; Vol. 3, pages 69-72. Between the close of the preceding book, and the beginning of this, some 51 years have passed in history. That space of time was what remained of the 70 years' captivity after the taking of Zedekiah, last Jewish king to sit on the throne in Jerusalem. Many events that occurred in the course of the famous 70 years will be referred to and discussed when we come to the books of the prophets. It is enough now for us to know that the captivity came to an end with the same event that ended the Babylonian Empire, which was brought about by the victory of Cyrus over Babylon, which is mentioned above. Passing over the history of the 70 years for the present, the inspired writer takes up the line at the beginning of the reconstruction in Jerusalem under the orders of Cyrus. *By the mouth of Jeremiah.* The prophet had foretold the conquest of Cyrus over Babylon, which put him in position to release the Jews from captivity and to permit them to restore their city and country. See Ch. 33: 6-14 of the book of Jeremiah. *Stirred up the spirit of Cyrus king of Persia.* God has used various kings and other persons of the world, both good and bad, to accomplish his purpose. See Ex. 9: 16; Num. 22 to 24; 1 Ki. 19: 15; Isa. 10: 5, 6. Cyrus was one of the good (morally) heathen kings. On this point I shall again quote some history: "Almost universal testimony has ascribed to him (Cyrus) the purest and most beneficent character of any Eastern monarch." Myers' Ancient History, P. 90. Cyrus not only released the Jews from their bondage (yet retaining them as citizens under him), but authorized them to return to their former country. *Made a proclamation* was an official order put out to the public notice, but applying to the Jews. *Put it in writing* would be necessary for two reasons. The dominions of Cyrus now were so extensive that the proclamation would have to be circulated by postman. Another reason was to prevent any misunderstanding of the requirements.

Verse 2. *Lord God of heaven.* Cyrus was a heathen, but when God saw fit to use him he made himself known to him in the things he wished him to do. It had nothing to do with his moral character, before or after the service. He was used as an instrument of God for a certan purpose. But in order for him to be available for the work, it was needful for God to assure him that he was being directed by a Being whom he should not ignore. Moreover, he was given to understand that the conquests he had made over the nations and kingdoms were made possible by this very God. *Given me all the kingdoms of the earth.* This was no vain boast, but was in fulfillment of a prophecy of Daniel in his book, Ch. 2: 38-40. It pertained to the 4 great world empires of which we will hear much in later studies of the Bible. Those empires were, Babylonia, Medo-Persia, Greece or Macedonia, and Rome. Cyrus was king of the second of these world empires, hence it was necessary to give him all those kingdoms as he just claimed. He announced that he had been charged to build the Lord a house in Jerusalem. Not that he would personally supervise the work, but that he would see that the necessary provisions were made for the building. There was a political reason for this official procedure. Jerusalem had been destroyed while in a state of revolt, and the restoration of it might be interpreted as an act of renewed rebellion. In fact the attempt was made to bring such a charge as we shall see in the progress of operations. So without the sponsorship of Cyrus the work of rebuilding would fail.

Verse 3. Cyrus called for volunteers to take up the work which was *charged* upon him to have done. He gave his good wishes for the favor of his (the volunteer's) God upon him, and gave his royal authority for him to leave the borders of Persia and go to Jerusalem. But let it be noted that it was not merely a furlough to make a journey of pleasure. He was to go to Judah to *build the house of the Lord.* And since there are lords many and gods many, Cyrus specified what one he meant; the God of Israel. *He is the God* was not a primary acknowledgment of God as the supreme One. He meant to say that the God of Israel was the God to be recognized in Jerusalem.

Verse 4. The Jews are no longer captives, for that period was ended by the overthrow of Babylon by the Persians. But they are still the citizens of the country that is being ruled by the successors of the Babylonian Empire. That relationship makes them accountable to the Persians in all matters pertaining to a national government. Even their religious privileges are subject to the "powers that be," and their exercise will depend on the will of the same. Fortunately, the incoming government is friendly toward the people of God, just as the Lord had predicted by his prohpets that it would be. In taking possession of the Babylonian Empire, the Persians also gained control of the countries that had been under the control of that great power, which included Palestine and its adjacent territories. These facts should explain why Cyrus would have any business whatever in the affairs of the people sojourning *in any place.* Since that would include men who would be scattered throughout the various provinces in the Mesopotamian lands in general, as well as all Syria and Palestine, we should understand this verse in the light of the remarks at the beginning of this paragraph. Therefore, in all of the places indicated, there were individuals who might be interested in the restoration of the Jewish interests in Jerusalem.

The proclamation indicated in this verse was to make them feel free to show their friendliness toward that work, and be willing to assist it. It went further than permitting the men interested to lend a hand in the work. Such action would call for materials, and Cyrus ordered that the people of the communities among whom these others were *sojourning*, were to cooperate by furnishing them with materials for the building, and animals that they might use in their altar services.

Verse 5. *Then* is an adverb of time, referring to the proclamation of Cyrus, which was in the first year of his rule over Babylon and its possessions. Since the matter of dates has been brought up, I believe this is a good place to offer some explanatory remarks touching the chronological connection of this short, but comprehensive book. It covers two of the three important sections of the total reconstruction work that followed the "70" years. The three sections were, rebuilding of the temple (under Zerubbabel), the reformation of the worship (under Ezra), and the rebuilding of the walls of Jerusalem (under Nehemiah). The first is covered by chapters 1 to 6; the second by chapters 7 to 10, and the third is covered by the book of Nehemiah. The time consumed by the first was 21 years, reaching to the 6th year of Darius I of Persia. Nothing much was done further until the work of Ezra on the second section of the restoration. That began 58 years after the completion of the work of Zerubbabel. More will be said about that at the proper chapter; but now, let us come back to the immediate study of the present verse. The 10 tribes had been taken away by the Assyrians a century before the kingdom of Judah was overthrown by the Babylonians. The 10 tribes were in practically the same general territory as the others, but had become more or less interspersed with the people of the land, and their tribal distinction was not so evident. The 70 years just ended left the tribes forming the kingdom of Judah with their leading men still recognized as such, and they were the ones who took the lead in responding to the proclamation of Cyrus. We note that the priests and others of the tribe of Levi were among those who answered the call of the Persian king. The motive that prompted them to act favorably was the fact that God had *raised* or aroused their spirit. In other words, they were going to Jerusalem to work in the cause of the Lord because their heart was in the matter.

Verse 6. In verse 4 is the order of Cyrus for the people with whom the Jews were sojourning to furnish them with metals and animals. That order was obeyed, and in addition they gave them things that had not been specifically required. That is what is meant by the words *beside all that was willingly offered*.

Verse 7. The vessels mentioned here are the ones of 2 Ki. 24: 13; 25: 13-17, and 2 Chr. 36: 18. This conduct of Cyrus was consistent with the proclamation he had just made on behalf of the Jewish nation. These sacred vessels had been taken out of the land of Judah by the captors, and had even been disgracefully used by the heathen king Belshazzar. (Dan. 5: 1-4.) Hence all the rules of war as well as moral justice required that they be restored to their former and rightful owner. In saying that the vessels were restored, exception must be made, of course, to the ark. It was never accounted for after being taken from Jerusalem by the Babylonians. Smith's Bible Dictionary says: "It was probably taken captive or destroyed by Nebuchadnezzar, 2 Esdras 10: 22 [one of the apocryphal books], so that there was no ark in the second temple." Schaff-Herzog Encyclopaedia says of the ark: "It was probably burnt up in the destruction of Jerusalem by Nebuchadnezzar; and in the YOMA [a secular writing], it is said that there was a stone in the Holy of holies on the spot where the ark should have stood; and on this stone the postexilian (after the exile) high priests set the censer." The vessels that were still available will be numbered but not named in a following verse.

Verse 8. *Numbered* means he made a list or invoice of the articles with the knowledge of his own treasurer, and turned over to Sheshbazzar who was a leading man of the Jews. That action was for the protection of Cyrus' reputation as to honesty.

Verses 9-11. A *charger* is a basin to hold liquids and other loose matter. A *bason* is defined by Strong as "a covered goblet." *Second sort* is said of them because they were for a less important use. This is a clear instance of the thought in 2 Tim. 2: 20. These vessels were not in the tabernacle built by Moses. Solomon was permitted to enlarge over the work done at Mt. Sinai, which is why we read of so many things here that are not to be found in the tabernacle service. This assortment of vessels was placed in the hands of Sheshbazzar who was a prince; that is, a leading man of the land of Judah. He was made responsible for the transportation of the precious articles, as the group of Jews went out of the land of their captivity to their own country, whose capital was Jerusalem.

EZRA 2

Verse 1. *Province* is from MEDIYNAH, and Strong defines it, "properly a judgeship, i. e. jurisdiction; by implication a district (as ruled by a judge); generally a region." The land of Judah had been taken over by the Babylonians, and they in turn had lost it to the Persians, who had the "jurisdiction" over it at the time of which we are studying. That is why it is referred to as a "province." The statement means that the "children" or people who are about to be named, belonged to the province of Judah. A record was kept of births, making a notation of the city where the birth was registered. And when this exodus of former citizens took place out of the land of their captivity, each man returned *unto his city.*

Verse 2. *Came with Zerubbabel* is so worded because he was the chief man in that group, and the one who took the lead in rebuilding the temple. *Nehemiah* was not the one in the book of that name. It was common for more than one man to have the same name. Smith's Bible Dictionary says of this man: "One of the leaders of the first expedition from Babylon to Jerusalem under Zerubbabel." *Mordecai.* This is another name that might have referred to more than one man. Some authors make it mean the same as the one in the book of Esther, others say it was a different man. Either view could be correct since the events connected with the history of the two all happened within the possible span of a lifetime. The men named in this verse were leaders in the expedition. *The number of the men* who came with them will be given in several following verses. The ones named in the beginning of the several verses were family heads, and their descendants through several branches of the family "tree" are enumerated. It will not be necessary in every case to assign a paragraph to a verse.

Verses 3-35. This long group of verses is what was meant by the remarks at the close of the preceding paragraph. No information would be given were I to make separate comments on each verse. The ones that will be made will be more or less general. *Children.* The first impression this word makes on us is that it refers to a man's bodily offspring. It is proper that it should be so taken. However, let it not be forgotten that it may, and frequently does have a less definite meaning. I believe it will not be amiss to copy the definition of the original word that is in the lexicon. It is from the Hebrew word BEN, and Strong defines it thus: "a son (as a builder of the family name), in the widest sense (of literal and figurative relationship, including grandson, subject, nation, quality, or condition, etc." In the A. V. it has been translated by arrow, bough, branch, breed, calf, children, colt, foal, man, one born, people, son, them of, whelp, youth and others. The way it is used in these verses it means all of the members of the family tree whose head is the man named in the beginning of the verse. The Jews had a rule of being listed in the registers on file in their particular "home town." See Luke 2: 3, 4. Following that rule, these various family groups settled in their own proper city upon their return from their captivity.

Verses 36-39. Any man who was a lineal descendant of Aaron was eligible for the priesthood. It had been so many centuries since the time of starting said priesthood that many branches of the family had come into existence. The men named in this paragraph were some of those branches.

Verse 40. All priests were Levites, but not all Levites were priests. Hence the registers would be filed in separate classes. Some men who would not be permitted to act as priests, even though they were of the tribe of Levi, yet were authorized to perform certain special services; for that reason they were noted in the list.

Verse 41. Smith's Bible Dictionary says there was a school or group of musical composers that was founded by Asaph, and they are the ones meant in this verse. When the more elaborate services were formed in the days of David and Solomon, these professional singers were enlisted for the exercises.

Verse 42. The porters were janitors or gatekeepers. Their work was considered necessary and they were given a place on the recorded program.

Verses 43-54. The *Nethinims* were a class of servants given over for the rougher work about the temple. They had no official status, but waited on the men who were conducting the service of the house of God. There must have been a considerable number of them, for this paragraph lists the descendants of 35 men who were classed in that service. We do not have any definite statement of the tasks they performed. A fair example of the kind of service they did is the case of the Gibeonites in Josh. 9: 21-23. I do not mean these people were put in the same rank as the Nethinims. They were of a foreign blood while the Nethinims were Israelites. But the nature of service that was exacted of them will serve as an illustration of the kind of work done by this particular class of servants that happened to be called Nethinims.

Verses 55-57. The persons mentioned here were distant descendants of the individual servants of Solomon. The Nethinims were generally required to render service wherever and however needed about the temple. But Solomon had appropriated a number of them for his use as king, and the classification was continued to be recognized.

Verse 58. The special servants for the king were named above, but the number was reserved to be given in this verse.

Verses 59, 60. These towns were in the country of Babylon, and some of the Jews had been stationed there, but they were not able to prove their relation to Israelite blood. However, they were at least given the "benefit of the doubt" to the extent of being given what is popularly called "honorable mention" in our language.

Verses 61, 62. It had been established that no one should be allowed to have part in the priesthood but those in the blood line of Aaron. The Lord was very particular about this; so much so that he afflicted an otherwise good king with that most loathsome of diseases, leprosy, because he presumed to participate in the rights of the priesthood when he was not in that class. (2 Chr. 26: 18.) There were certain persons who the inspired writer says were *children of the priests*. Yet they could not show their "birth certificate" and consequently were excluded from the group that would be allowed to act in the priestly service. *As polluted* does not mean that they were considered as actually polluted. But the dignity of the priesthood was so great and the Lord was so particular about it, that people whose blood relation was doubtful were as objectionable for that office as if they were literally polluted.

Verse 63. *Tirshatha* is the original word, spelled out with English letters. The definition in Strong's lexicon is, "of foreign derivation; the title of a Persian deputy or governor." But that would not mean that this man was a Persian by blood. We recall that while the period of the captivity was over, all the people were still the subjects of the Persian Empire the same as other citizens of a country would be. That would account for the fact that the man authorized to take the lead in the movements would be called by the name used in the text. The evidence is, however, that he was of Jewish blood and understood the principles of the Mosaic law. The Urim and Thummim were the objects placed in the garments worn by the priest. See Ex. 28: 30. They were used in some supernatural manner in receiving communications from God (Heb. 1: 1), but were useless except when in the hands of the priest. (Num. 27: 21.) The persons mentioned in the preceding verse were excluded from the priesthood because of uncertain birth. Now the governor appointed by Cyrus to supervise the operations was not going to authorize any performance of the services until the lawful men showed up. They would be the men having the right to the priesthood; to handling the Urim and Thummim, which would be impotent in any other hands but those of a priest.

Verse 64. It must be understood that the number of the *whole congregation* means the leaders or heads, similar to the numbering in Num. 1: 46 and 26: 51. What I mean is, the comparison between these various numbers will give a fair estimate of the size of the congregation at the different times referred to. By such a comparison it is evident that the population was considerably reduced in course of the captivity. The ravages that were made into the personnel as well as the population in general accounts for this cutting down of the list. This was to be regretted, but at the same time the fact fulfilled several predictions on the subject. More than once the Lord had predicted that his people would be exposed to the hardships of captivity, which would destroy their sons and daughters, as well as their old men and women. But in connection with such warning and predictions, he also gave them the assurance that a remnant would be salvaged out of the wreck of the years. On this subject, which is a mixture of joy and sadness, see 2 Ki. 19: 30, 31; Isa. 1: 9; 10: 20, 21; Jer. 23: 3; Ezk. 6: 8; Micah 2: 12. This prediction is written in many other places which will be noted in the studies of the prophetic books, to be considered in a later volume of this Commentary.

Verses 65-67. The *whole congregation* mentioned in the preceding verse was independent of these secondary persons. But the large number of such, as well as the goodly number of animals, all shows the prosperous state of the Israelites in spite of their long exile in a heathen land. Another point is in evidence, and that is the kindness of the nation that had the jurisdiction over them. Instead of cutting them down to a mere token, and driving them out with a be-gone-and-the-sooner-the-better attitude. Cyrus sent them out with his blessing, and with financial aid.

Verse 68. Gratitude at least would have prompted these fathers to make this contribution for the Lord's work. They had been treated very kindly by the Persian government, and the materials furnished them were in order that the Lord's work in Jerusalem could be advanced

Verse 69. The amount of these offerings is stated which is great. However, that would not entitle them to any special credit were it not for the fact that it was *after their ability.* That is the basis upon which all of the offerings in the New Testament are to be made. See 1 Cor. 16: 2; 2 Cor. 8: 12.

Verse 70. After turning over the possessions in their hands to the work for which they had been given them, they retired to their homes. It is interesting to note that the several ranks and grades of the nation respected the assignments belonging to them as to residence, for it says they dwelt in *their* cities.

EZRA 3

Verse 1. *Seventh month* of the first year of Cyrus' rule over Babylon was the time meant. The people of various classes had taken up their residences in the cities that had been shown to be their proper location. Then, having been thus settled so that their families were cared for, the people next turned their attention to the city from which they had been taken 70 years before.

Verse 2. Since the altar service was the subject of immediate interest, it was fitting that the men of the priestly rank take the lead. Zerubbabel was the leader and main man to supervise the work of the first section of the restoration. When Nebuchadnezzar finally destroyed the temple, it would be expected that he had wrecked the furniture of it also. The *vessels* that he took were the smaller articles of the service, such as bowls and trays that were used for eating and drinking purposes. Now then, in order to reinstate the sacrificial worship, it was necessary to erect an altar. They had not offered any sacrifices to God while in captivity. This is a fact not known or realized by many Bible students. The nation was sent into captivity because of the sin of worshiping idols, and that consisted chiefly in offering sacrifices to them, either of animals or other material things. One of the things to be accomplished, by the exile in a heathen land, was their being completely cured of the sin of idolatry. In keeping with that object, they were not permitted to offer any sacrifices to God while in captivity. This subject, the various predictions pertaining to it, and the history that shows the fulfillment, will be treated at length in the volume of this Commentary that contains the study of the prophetic books. For the present, the reader is cited to the following passages. Deut. 28: 36; Isa. 1: 10-15; 2: 18-21; 43; 22-28; Jer. 33: 8; Ezk. 20: 38; Hos. 2: 17; Micah 5: 13; Zech. 7: 4-6. It will be seen, when all the history has been consulted, that the Jews were entirely weaned from idolatry when they came back from the captivity. And since they were not permitted to offer sacrifices during those 70 years, it is easy to understand their earnestness in renewing the lawful service when the way was opened up to them.

Verse 3. *Bases* is from a word that the lexicon defines as meaning a pedestal or a spot. Moffatt's translation gives us "spot," and the footnote in the American Revised Version says "spot." The idea is, the people were in fear because of the kind of men and women who were in that country. The

Jews had great faith in their God, and relied on his protection in times of danger. But they understood that the Lord required something in the way of service before bestowing his favor on his servants. The most evident form of faithful devotion was in the animal sacrifices on the altar. Therefore, they lost no time in getting the altar in its place to begin the service.

Verse 4. As fast as they could, they resumed the national ceremonies. The feast of tabernacles properly came in the 7th month, which was the month now reached. So they kept this feast *as it is written* (Lev. 23: 34). In observing this festival season they needed to follow the law to the number, and *according to the custom.* This custom is recorded in detail in Num. 29: 12-34.

Verse 5. The *continual burnt offering* was another name for the "daily sacrifice." (Ex. 29: 38-42.) *Both* does not apply to the offering just described. It is a Biblical way of saying that something was to be done in addition to what was just described. It is as if it read, "And afterward . . . offering, also of the new moons," etc. The thought is the fact that the people were so glad to be again in their own land where they could worship the true God, that they attended to all of the ordinances as completely as the circumstances would permit. In addition to the specified ordinances required, the people volunteered other sacrifices.

Verse 6. *From the first day* would be in accordance with the law of Moses. The new moon was a holy day, also the beginning of the month (1 Sam. 20: 24, 27), and that called for a sacrifice; hence the statement in this place. The work of building the temple would require much more time than it would take to arrange for these services, therefore they did the latter before starting on the major task before them. Such is the significance of the closing sentence of the verse.

Verse 7. Having got the altar worship under way, the people turned their attention to the great work of rebuilding the temple. They had been allowed to take money with them when they left Babylon, and they expended it on the workmen employed in the building project. Tyre and Zidon were cities in the country of Phoenicia, the territory that produced the famous cedar trees, celebrated in story and song. Solomon had procured this wood from the king of Tyre for the first temple, and now the Jews turned to that source for the same kind of timber. *Sea of Joppa* means the seacoast of Joppa, that city being an important shipping port on the Mediterranean Sea. From there the timber would be floated in rafts to some suitable port accessible to the territory of Judah. *According to the grant* refers to the permission that Cyrus gave the Jews to obtain materials for the building, and to pay for them with money obtained in the land of Persia proper, or other places under the same rule.

Verse 8. *Second year . . . to set forward the work of the house of the Lord.* This is a proper place to make some remarks as to dates and names, in order to keep the run of things clearly in mind. It should be borne in mind that all the civilized countries, practically, were under Persian rule at the time of which we are studying. What the Jews did was under the authority of various Persian kings, because the land of Israel had been taken over first, by the Babylonians, and they had given way to the Persians, making them the government over all lands, including Judah. Some of the Persian kings were favorable to the Jews and some were not. I will suggest that the reader draw a chart for reference while studying this and the following book. Make the chart as follows, with 6 perpendicular columns. At the top of the columns write the dates 536-529; 529-522; 522-521; 521-484; 484-464; 464-415. These numbers show the beginning and closing dates, B. C., of the reigns of the Persian kings named in the several columns. Next, put the following names in the 6 columns, from left to right: Cyrus, Cambyses, Smerdis, Darius I, Xerxes, Artaxerxes. Some of these men had other names in the Bible, and to keep the matter clear, put the following names in parentheses under the ones I shall denote. In the 2nd column write Ahasuerus, 3rd column write Artaxerxes, in the 6th column write Longimanus. This last name, however, is not in the Bible, but is a name given him by secular writers as a sort of nickname, meaning "longhanded." But it is well for us to use it to distinguish him from the Artaxerxes in the 3rd column. Now, having arranged your chart, have it near and put the information on it as I suggest while going on with the study. The first notation is in the first column as follows: "1st year, edict of Cyrus to rebuild the temple." Let it be understood that all references to 1st or 2nd or any other year, mean such a year of the period indicated by the dates at the top of the column. We have reached the *second year* of the 1st column in our study, but the notation to be made in addition to that just indicated, will be suggested a few verses down.

Verse 9. The men named are the ones of Ch. 2: 40. *Set forward the workmen* means they put them at their work, to get the house of God under construction.

Verse 10. Now make the following notation in the first column of the chart: "2nd year, the foundation of the temple is laid." The manual labor of the foundation was accompanied with the praise service of the priests. They were *in their apparel* which signifies they put on their priestly garments, and gave the service of blowing the trumpets, which were instruments similar to our cornets as to the manner of playing. Even a Levite would not have the right to wear the special garments unless he belonged to the priestly family. That is why the writer mentions the priests in connection with the apparel, then adds his reference to the Levites who used the cymbals, which were instruments of metal, and used to make a loud sound by beating upon them in rhythmic count with the trumpets that were being played by the priests. Not all or just any of the Levites were used this time, but those who had belonged to that group of musical composers known as the sons of Asaph. This musical program was *after the ordinance of David.* See 1 Chr. 6: 31; 16: 4, 7; 25: 1, 2.

Verse 11. They sang by *course* which means they sang in sections; not all of them sang at one time. That method prevented confusion, so that the people could respond intelligently to the service. They did so, for it says all the people *shouted with a great shout* after this praise service. The first word is from RUWA and defined "a primitive root; to mar (especially by breaking); figuratively to split the ears (with sound), i. e. shout (for alarm or joy.)"—Strong. The last word is from TEBUWAH, and Strong's definition is, "clamor, i. e. acclamation of joy or a battle cry." Taking the central thought of the words as a basis, the whole expression would properly be worded, "the people made the ears to vibrate with their acclamations of joy." The cause of all this demonstration was the fact that *the foundation of the house of the Lord was laid*, which gave a foresight of the restoration about to be accomplished.

Verse 12. This verse furnishes a practical illustration of an old saying namely: "Much depends on the viewpoint." All of the people were looking at the same object, yet some of them were made to weep, while others *shouted for joy.* The former were the older men who could remember the temple that had been destroyed by the Babylonians. While the present one was good, it was inferior to the first one, and that caused them to weep in regret at the contrast. The latter were the younger ones who were contrasting the brightness of the prospects in view of the foundation, with the dejected situation they had been in for so many years in captivity. That was what caused them to be joyous. This subject is treated in Hag. 2: 3.

Verse 13. This indicates that the crowd was almost equally divided, either as to the number in each group, or in the volume of their expression of feelings.

EZRA 4

Verse 1. The people designated as *the adversaries* were the classes who had been brought in to occupy the country after the Assyrians took the 10 tribes away into captivity. For information on this subject see 2 Kings 17. Doubtless they had grown to be a numerous band in the two centuries that had gone by since then. In that time the captivity of the kingdom of Judah also had taken place, and these folk probably thought that they would have continuous and undisturbed possession of the whole land.

Verse 2. Envy was certainly the motive for the proposition these *adversaries* made. If any glory should come from this building project, they wanted a share in it. There was some truth in their claim about sacrificing to the same God that the men of Judah worshiped. On this point let the reader again read, carefully, the account that is given in the 17th chapter of 2 Kings. It will be seen just to what extent these people sacrificed to the Lord.

Verse 3. Zerubbabel was the leader or superintendent of the construction work of the temple. The other men referred to were under him and had some prominent part in the work. The motive that prompted these *adversaries* to make the proposition they did would have made it wrong to let them into the work. But a still greater reason existed for refusing them. They were *adversaries* according to the inspired writer, and it would have been unsafe to permit them to have such an important connection with the sacred building. Another thing, Cyrus did not authorize any but the Jews to do this reconstruction, and that would have made them intruders to employ them as they suggested. Zerubbabel and his co-workers were true both to God and to Cyrus. They informed these people that it was the *house of our God*, which would make it inappropriate for the Lord's *adversaries* to take part in it. They also stated that their operations were according to the commandment of the king of Persia, and thus the whole project was not only a work of God, but was in harmony with the highest temporal authority over them.

Verse 4. This short verse is a general statement of the activities of the local citizens who were the *adversaries* of God's people. It merely says they *weakened* their hands, which means they "slackened" their hands in the work. It does not state how it was done, and that will be learned in the following verses. But before going on with the reading, make another notation in the first column of the chart as follows: "The work was hindered all the rest of the reign."

Verse 5. *Hired counsellors* would be about what we would mean were we to "employ an attorney." They wanted these counsellors to help devise some way of hindering the work of the temple. *Frustrate* means to "break up." One translation of the word in the A. V. is, "cause to cease". This verse makes a general statement of the length of time the hindrance lasted, but some following verses will give more details of the wicked actions.

Verse 6. This *Ahasuerus* is at the head of the 2nd column of your chart. In this reign these *adversaries* continued their opposition to the work of erecting the temple. No further detail is given of what they did except to write a letter to the Persian king in power at that time, whose name was referred to above. The notation to be made in this column is, "Work on the temple is still hindered."

Verse 7. *Artaxerxes* is at the head of the 3rd column of your chart. His reign was short, but much was done in that 1 year. The letter written by the counsellors to the preceding Persian ruler had its desired effect by causing the work to be hindered. Those who did the writing in the preceding reign were the hired counsellors and referred to by the pronoun "they." Whether the persons named in this and some following verses were the same men, we do not know. But we do know that they used their influence in behalf of the *adversaries* of the Jews. They wrote a letter to Artaxerxes the Persion king, who, we should bear in mind, was then in Babylon. The letter was written in the *Syrian* tongue, which was another form of Aramean. These two words are used somewhat interchangeably in the Bible, and yet there is a distinction that should be recognized at times, or confusion will result. I will quote from history a few paragraphs for the information of the reader, and he is requested to refer to this verse and its comments when there is occasion for the information. "*Aramaic languages* are so called from *Aram*, a geographical term which in old Semitic usage designates nearly the same districts as the Greek word, Syria. Aram, however, does not include Palestine while it comprehends Mesopotamia. (Heb. Aram of two rivers), a region which the Greeks frequently distinguish from *Syria proper*. Thus the Aramic languages may be geographically defined as the Semitic dialects originally current in Mesopotamia and the regions extending S. W. from the Euphrates to Palestine." *Britannica*, Vol. 2, p. 307.

"Etymologically, 'Syria' is merely an abbreviation of 'Assyria,' a name which covered the subject lands of the Assyrian empire, the subject-people being also called 'Syrians.' Afterwards, in the Graeco-Roman period, the shorter word came to be restricted to the territory west of the Euphrates, the designation 'Syrians,' however, being given to the great mass of the Semitic population dwelling between the Tigris and the Mediterranean, who are more accurately called Arameans." *Britannica*, 22-821.

"Aram, which occurs in Scripture with the same frequency as Asshur, is, like Asshur, a name concerning the application of which there is no doubt. Our translators almost always render the word, as did the Septuagint interpreters, by 'Syria' and the term though etymologically quite distinct, is beyond a doubt, in its use by the Hebrews, a near equivalent for the 'Syria' of the Greeks and Romans. It designates a people distinct from, yet closely allied with, the Assyrians, which, in the remotest times whereto history reaches, was established in the valley of the middle Euphrates, and in the tract between the Euphrates and the Mediterranean. This people, known to itself as Aramean, continued the predominant race in the country to the time of the Mohammedan conquest." *Rawlinson*, Origin of Nations, p. 234.

"Between the outer limits of the Syro-Arabian desert and the foot of the great mountain range of Kurdistan and Luristan intervenes a territory long famous in the world's history, and the chief site of three out of five empires of whose history, geography, and antiquities it is proposed to treat in the present volumes. Known to the Jews as Aram-Naharaim, or 'Syria of the two rivers'; to the Greeks and Romans as Mesopotamia, or 'the between-river country.'" Rawlinson, Five Great Monarchies, Vol. 1, P. 2. See also, in same volume, pp. 43, 179, 236, 262.

These men were subjects of the Persian power, but were of Syrian origin, hence they wrote their letter in that tongue. But since their king was a Persian, they realized they would have to send along also a Persian translation of the letter. That is what is meant by the words *interpreted in the Syrian tongue*.

Verses 8, 9. I do not know just how many different persons had a direct part in writing the letter, but evidently all of these who are named had something to do in forming the epistle A *chancellor* was an important official in the employ of a king. A *scribe* corresponded to our secretary. The difficult names in verse 9 are some of the groups that had been brought into that country after the 10 tribes were taken into captivity. The account of this transferring of the foreign clans is recorded in 2 Ki. 17.

Verse 10. In the account given by the writer of 2 Kings, Esarhaddon, an important king of the Assyrians, is said to have brought these people over to Samaria, while here it says Asnapper was the man who did it. But there is no difficulty on that subject. A king or other leading man is said to have done a deed, when he has it done by one of his officers. Smith's Bible Dictionary has this to say on this matter: "Asnapper (swift), mentioned in Ezra 4: 10 as the person who settled the Cuthaeans in the cities of Samaria. He was probably a general of Esarhaddon." After giving all those names, representing the various groups of persons cooperating in sending this letter, the writer sums up by the words *and at such times*, which corresponds to our "etc."

Verse 11. This verse is the introduction to the letter, with a general salutation that includes without naming, the various groups of people joining in the epistle that is addressed to the king of Persia. Their introduction concludes with the same words that mean "etc."

Verse 12. Jerusalem had rebelled against the king of Babylon (2 Ki. 24: 1), and had paid the penalty for it by being destroyed and its people taken into captivity. But that was over 80 years prior to this date. In that time the captivity had been ended and the captives had been given authority to do the very thing they were doing at the time this letter was planned. We should not become confused over mention of the *walls* as being set up. We know that it was in Nehemiah's time (75 years later) that the walls of Jerusalem were rebuilt. The walls mentioned here refer to the walls forming the foundation of the temple. It is true the adversaries feared that the entire city with its walls would be restored. But their immediate concern was for the walls of the foundation of the house. The language in Ch. 5: 3, 9, 16 and 6: 14 shows they used the word *wall* in connection with the house of the Lord.

Verse 13. These *adversaries* complained that if the work of the Jews was allowed to go on to completion, then the city would become independent and break off all diplomatic relations with the king. It is remarkable how forgetful an envious mind can be. At the start of this work, these very adversaries proposed helping with it. Now they claimed that such work was in rebellion against the king. Before, they pretended they wished to join in the work because it was on behalf of the God whom they all served. Next they opposed having the work done at all because of their loyalty to the king of Persia. When a man so glaringly contradicts himself, it is evident that he does not have an honest basis for his activities.

Verse 14. If either of the two motives these men stated was the true one, it was the first. Their support might be cut off if the king should lose some of his revenue. Selfishness was the true sentiment that prompted their activities, but they pretended to be concerned about the king's honor.

Verse 15. The paragraph contained in this verse states some truth and some error. What truth it has is used in a way to make a false impression. It was true that the nation of which Jerusalem was the capital had opposed other provinces, but it was because of their evil ways. It is also true that the city was destroyed when it rebelled against the Babylonians. But in referring to those facts, the writers connected events that were many years apart, and which occurred by far different causes. When the city was destroyed, it was done by the nation that God caused to come against it. And that was done in punishment for their taking up the corrupt practices of the very kind of people who were writing this letter to the Persian king. In asking the king to search the official records, they went far enough back to omit the later accounts, that showed the authority for the present work that the Jews were doing. That record, however, will be brought to light before the case is ended.

Verse 16. The previous warning was repeated and summed up in the words *have no portion this side of the river* (of Euphrates). They meant that if the government in Jerusalem was allowed to be reestablished, it would again take possession of all the territory west of the noted river.

Verse 17. The warning and suggestion of the letter had the effect intended by its authors. The king of Persia was intimidated into having the official records examined. All kings and other rulers keep an account of the transactions within their realms, and of other countries in any way connected with them. But king Artaxerxes did not cause a complete search to be made; he looked only for the item that was suggested to him by the letter. Having done so, he sent an answer, and this verse is the formal salutation to the persons whose letter is being answered, the ones named in verses 8, 9. *Peace, and at such a time* is a friendly expression as a part of the salutation. Moffatt's translation condenses the whole phrase into "Greetings, etc."

Verse 18. *Plainly read* means the letter was interpreted to the king so that he could understand it in his (the Persian) language, it having been written in the Syrian tongue (v. 7). The whole performance as to the composition of this letter and the accompanying explanation, might well be described as the act of handing a student in a foreign language a sentence to translate, and with it handing him a vocabulary. The difference in this case is, the servants made the application of the vocabulary for the benefit of the king.

Verse 19. This verse repeats practically what the letter declared (in v. 15).

Verse 20. This verse makes the report even stronger than did the letter. It admits that *mighty kings* had ruled in Jerusalem. A very important item in the Persian record is the declaration that the government at Jerusalem had ruled over all the countries *beyond the* (Euphrates) *river*. That was promised to Abraham (Gen. 15: 18), and actually realized by Solomon (1 Ki. 4: 21). So it is interesting to find the Persian records corroborating those in our Bible.

Verse 21. The command directed to be given would be a royal decree and effective at once. However, an intimation was made that the king was taking the subject under advisement for further investigation. He left open the prospects of another order that might change the one just given. We shall find that it did take place, but not in the reign of this king.

Verse 22. The urge for strict obedience of the edict was based on the welfare of the kings, meaning the kings of the Persian Empire. The question of what was right or wrong was not considered; only the advantages of these heathen rulers were given consideration in transmitting the royal decree.

Verse 23. Here is another place to make a marking on the chart. In the 3rd column write as follows: "Work on the temple is stopped by order of the king." The promptness of the men when they received the order is significant; *they went up in haste*. Another thing that should be noted is, they made the work to be stopped by *force* and *power*. The first word is from EDRA and the definition of Strong is, "An orthographical variation for DERA; an arm, i. e. (figuratively) power." The second is from CHAYIL and Strong defines it, "An army, or strength." The thought is, they were compelled to stop by physical force that was backed by the military units of Persia. The Jews would not cease to work upon the mere order of these counsellors. They had already had a test of that kind, when they had the proposal to help in the building project. (Vs. 2, 3.) There is no indication that the official letter was read or even shown to the Jews. They were told to cease a work that they knew had been ordered by a former king of Persia, hence were doing what they knew to be lawful. But when physical force was brought against them, the only thing that could be done was to stop.

Verse 24. This verse gives the authority for the notation just made in the 3rd column of the chart. By comparing the dates at the head of the chart, it will be seen that the work lay idle for two years.

EZRA 5

Verse 1. *Then* applies to the date stated in the closing verse of the previous chapter; the 2nd year of Darius. He is the man whose name you have at the head of the 4th column of the chart. You have him designated as Darius I, which is correct. He is known also in secular history as Darius Hystaspes. He was thus associated with the name of his father to distinguish him from a number of other Persian rulers named Darius. He was a good man, morally, and showed the same attitude toward the Jews as did Cyrus. He had a long reign, and it was in his 2nd year that the work on the temple was resumed. The verse says that Haggai and Zechariah *prophesied.* Strong's definition of the word is, "a primitive root; to prophesy, i. e. speak (or sing) by inspiration (in prediction or simple discourse)." This definition will help us understand the verse as a whole, especially when we have read the passages that will be cited soon. The verse gives the mere fact of these two prophets' speaking as the reason the Jews resumed the work. Now, I urge that before reading further in the present book, the student read Haggai 1, and Zechariah 1: 1-17. Be sure to read these passages carefully and more than once, then you will be prepared to understand the chapter we are studying. Although Cyrus had given the Jews the right to rebuild the temple to their God, they had let the threatening of the adversaries interfere with their work. The edict of Cyrus had not been repealed, for the Persians never canceled one of their laws, except by enacting a new one that would counteract the old. But there was no evidence that what the *adversaries* said to them was a law enacted by the king. Therefore, they should have paid no attention to it. It is true that force was brought to bear on them which they could not resist at once. They should have called for an investigation (as was done under Darius as we shall soon see), and then gone ahead with the work. But they were like many professed Christians. If some "unavoidable" circumstance causes an interference in their devotions to the Lord, they will often become indifferent toward their duty, and begin to show more interest in their personal affairs, just as these Jews did, as shown in the passages cited in the prophetic books. Then it becomes necessary for some man of God to get after them and rouse them to action. That is what these prophets did, and it produced the desired effect on the leaders. Now the reader should be prepared to understand the verses to follow the one of this paragraph. But before going further, put this notation in the 4th column of the chart: "2nd year, work resumed on the temple by order of the king." The basis for that notation will appear soon.

Verse 2. *Then rose up* means they became active after the two prophets delivered their messages. The messages contained exhortation and warning, and brought the Jewish leaders to realize how negligent they had been, and how nearly they had come to bringing the wrath of God upon them. Zerubbabel was a leading man of the tribe of Judah, and as general supervisor of the building. Jeshua, otherwise spelled Joshua, was a high priest, and hence a member of the tribe of Levi. These two men represented the material and religious interests of the nation at the time of its restoration. *Began to build* signifies they resumed the work of the house of God, that was stopped at the foundation 15 years before. The prophets helped them with their exhortations and encouraging speeches, addressed to the helpers of the work.

Verse 3. *This side the river* means west of the Euphrates. The Persian Empire had spread out over the civilized world which included the territory from the great *river* to the land of Palestine. Such a vast country could not be personally supervised by the king or any other one man, but had to be "sublet" to other rulers. All of them would be subject to the chief. Tatnai was one of those rulers, and

Shetharboznai was an officer under him. These men had some companions as helpers, and they were all concerned with the interests of their king in the territory placed under them. Their attention was called to the work going on in Jerusalem, and felt called upon to investigate. The circumstances show that it was a better motive that prompted these men in their activities than that of the ones in chapter 4. Those persons were envious, and did not make a sincere effort to get the right thing done. These last were true servants of their king, and were honest in their performances. They approached the group engaged in the work of the temple and asked for their authority in the building project.

Verse 4. The wording of this verse in the A. V. might be a little confusing. It sounds as if *we* were asking for the names of the workmen, but certainly that would not be true. Whoever the "we" represents personally, it means the ones connected with the work, and they had no reason for asking such a question. Instead, they were asked the names of the workmen, and the verse means to say what they told Tatnai in their answer. The American Standard translation words it, "then we told them," etc. The thought is, Tatnai not only wanted to know the authority for the work going on, but also the personnel of the men in charge of the work.

Verse 5. Tatnai and his fellows did not presume to interfere further with the work until they had communicated with their king. *The eye of God was upon the elders.* This accounts for the conduct of the Persian officers as stated in the beginning of this paragraph. So the work was to continue, pending word from the king.

Verses 6, 7. This paragraph introduces the reader to the letter that was sent to the King of Persia. The parties sending the letter were the ones who had made the investigation of the work going on in Jerusalem.

Verse 8. The expressions in this verse indicate that some progress had been made with the building. Mention is made of *timber,* which would not be put into the foundation. *Great stones* is rendered "stones of rolling" in the margin, and Strong's lexicon defines the word for *great,* "from a root corresponding to GALAL; weight or size (as if rolled)." It is an interesting subject, based on one of the methods used in ancient times for raising huge stones to their places in the buildings, in the absence of cranes or derricks, such as are used today. A ramp or sloping roadway was built of earth, the highest point of which reached the surface of the preceding course in the wall of the building. The stone was then rolled over and over on this ramp, with the aid of strong levers, until it reached the top where it was skidded into its place in the wall. The ramp was then lengthened and raised to correspond with the height of the previous stone, and another was rolled up the ramp to its place. This procedure was continued until the desired height of the wall was reached. *The great God* was not said in derision. We will recall that after the captivity of the 10 tribes (2 Ki. 17) some people from an outside territory were brought in to occupy the country. They adopted a mixed religion that included a nominal recognition of the true God. The term used did not indicate all that we would mean by its use, but to them it was a proper way of designating the God of the place where the reported work was going on. *Work goeth fast on* was said to impress the king with the urgency of the case.

Verse 9, 10. These verses correspond with 3 and 4, and need no further comment.

Verse 11. This part of the answer from Zerubbabel is not given in the first account of the conversation, but is made a part of the letter to the king. The Jews said they were the servants of the *God of heaven and earth,* while the expression originating with Tatnai was merely *the great God.* The difference will be recognized if you will reread the remarks in the preceding paragraph, expianatory of the expression of the Persian governor. He did not know about the God of heaven as we recognize him, but did think of him as the God of the temple. The *great king* that was mentioned by Zerubbabel and here repeated in the letter to Darius, was Solomon.

Verse 12. This is more of the answer of Zerubbabel to the inquiry of Tatnai. It is not likely that many persons who made this answer to him were living at the time of the captivity. But all such matters were put into the records and could be read by interested ones. This was a truthful though brief statement of the sad downfall of the kingdom of Judah at the hand of the king of *Babylon,* the *Chaldean.* These two terms are again used in the same connection. Babylon was the name of the territory, and Chaldean was the name of a prominent people who were in possession of Babylon at the time of which we are studying.

Verse 13. The letter omitted the 70 years of the captivity, and came directly from the beginning of the period's start to its ending. *First year of Cyrus* means the first year after he had taken Babylon; he had been a ruler over the Persians about a score of years before. The dates at the top of the chart show only his rule over Babylon. The letter states that Cyrus made a decree the first year he came into Babylon, that the house should be built to the Lord in Jerusalem.

Verse 14. We desire to keep our "bearings" and understand who is who, and why the various names and places are used in such close connection. For this purpose I shall make a brief statement on the subject. At the time the kingdom of Judah was captured, the territory around Babylon was in control of the Babylonians, otherwise called Chaldeans. At the time when the people of God had "served out their sentence" of 70 years, the territory had changed rulers and was under the Persians. When Cyrus the Persian came into power in Babylon, he found the Jews there, as a man would find a bird in a cage that he had captured from another man. And, just as a compassionate man would open the cage and let the bird go free, so Cyrus permitted the imprisoned Jews to have their freedom. To use the illustration further, as the compassionate man might take the interest to provide a suitable nest for the bird, so did Cyrus use his advantage as king to help the Jews find a desirable home and headquarters. If there were articles of service found in the cage that the bird could use in his new home, the good man would transfer them thereto. Accordingly, Cyrus found some vessels in the cage (Babylon) that really belonged to the prisoners, and that had been taken from their native home. These were restored to the rightful owners, but to insure their safe transportation, they were put into the hands of his own officer, which the text calls a governor. The margin renders it "deputy," which is evidently correct, since Tatnai was govenor over the territory west of the Euphrates River.

Verse 15. Don't forget that we are still reading the letter that was sent to Darius, in which the edict of Cyrus made 15 years before is being recounted.

Verse 16. The letter goes on to state that the edict of Cyrus had been respected; that the foundation was laid and the work on the building started. *Since that time . . . been in building . . . not finished.* These words mean that work had been held up through the years, but was again being put forward.

Verse 17. Thus far the letter was giving a true report of what Tatnai learned when he investigated what was going on in Jerusalem. Also, what was told him upon his inquiry for their authority for what they were doing. Having made the report, the authors of the letter wrote a closing paragraph, in which they requested that the royal records be consulted to see if the Jews were correct in their claims. It was also requested that the king return word as to what he wished to have done about the matter.

EZRA 6

Verse 1. Acting on the request of Tatnai, Darius ordered a search to be made for the account of the decree of Cyrus. It is significant that the royal records were kept in the same house where the treasury was, which indicates they were valuable.

Verse 2. Not all of the records were kept in one city. After looking through the ones in Babylon, they went to Achmetha, otherwise called Ecbatana, where they found a record. Strong says that this city was a summer capital of Persia. The verse says, however, that it was in the province of the Medes. The mention of this will call for some explanation, and it will require some secular history to get the subject clarified. The full title for the government we are now considering is the Medo-Persian, or, as it is more familiarly spoken, the Medes and the Persians. It will now be useful to quote some history. "Kinship of the Medes and Persians.—It was in very remote times that some Aryan tribes, separating themselves from the other members of the Aryan family, sought new abodes on the plateau of Iran. The tribes that settled in the south became known as the Persians; while those that took possession of the northwest were called Medes. The names of the two peoples were always closely associated, as in the familiar legend, 'The law of the

Medes and Persians, which altereth not.'" Myers' Ancient History, p. 88. See also, Herodotus, 1-130. "The leadership of the Median chieftains was of short duration. A certain Cyrus, king of Anshan, in Elam, overthrew their power, and assumed the headship of both Medes and Persians." Myers' Ancient History, p. 88. In the light of these historical facts, we should understand why some of the royal papers of the Persian Empire would be found in a city of the Medes.

Verse 3. Sure enough, they found the report of the Jews to be true. The record said that Cyrus had issued a decree in his first year in Babylon, favoring the rebuilding of the house of God in Jerusalem. The decree even specified the size of the building that was authorized to be built, with some other details.

Verse 4. This verse stipulates some of the materials to be used, and authorizes the king's treasurer to furnish money for the house, out of the royal resources.

Verse 5. This decree agrees with Ch. 1: 7-11, which is a statement of what Cyrus did regarding the vessels belonging to the house of God. The present verse shows that the king had good foresight in providing against future misunderstandings. He was not satisfied just to have the work done while he lived and could personally enforce his orders, but had the decree made a part of the official record for the protection of future generations. We can see the wisdom of his acts now that Darius is called upon to settle the dispute. Had the *adversaries* who first opposed the work been as fair as Tatnai and his aides, the work would have been completed long ago.

Verse 6. Up to this point in the return letter, the king has been relating what he found in the official records; that it was in harmony with the claim of the Jews. From this on the letter will contain his own decree in the matter. It is directed to the officials who sent the letter of inquiry. In order that no hindrance be had in executing the decree, the officers are mentioned by name. *Beyond the river* means the same river as *this side of the river*. The difference is in the point from where the expression is made. The former is now made from the east side of the Euphrates, while the latter was from the west side. *Be ye far from thence* is a nice way of telling them to get out of the way of the work.

Verse 7. They not only must get away from the work as far as being objectors, but must not hinder it in any indirect manner; they must *let the work of this house of God alone.* They were not even to insist on participating in the work as did the *adversaries* in Ch. 4: 2, but *let the Jews do it.*

Verse 8. While his officers were not to dabble in the work, they were ordered to furnish support in the way of materials. Not out of their personal property, but to draw on the treasury of that part *of* the realm *beyond the river* for expense money, and give it to the leaders of the work among the Jews.

Verses 9, 10. Great empires always keep accurate accounts of the things going on in their realms. We have seen that a record was kept of the Jews and the treatment done to them. That would necessarily include the account of their captivity and the occasion for it. And after being brought into the land now being ruled by the Persians, those people had been prevented from practicing their religious services of sacrifices and offerings. But God had opened the hearts of the heathen kings and caused them to see the righteousness of restoring the temple to the unfortunate Jews. It was appropriate, therefore, that the services belonging thereto be restored also. For the purposes of their temple service, the decree of Darius was extended to the order for animals for the altar, and other things needed in their congregational activities. Darius did not dictate what animals were to be selected, but left it to the priests at Jerusalem. It is noteworthy that the king requested prayer to be offered for him. That was a lawful request. In Jer. 29: 7 the Jews were instructed to pray in behalf of the city of their captivity, and in 1 Tim. 2: 2 is the command for Christians to pray for temporal rulers. This is all in keeping with other teaching regarding God's interest in secular governments. Dan. 2: 21; 4: 17 says that God takes a hand in governments of the world. It is proper, therefore, that the people of God should pray for those rulers.

Verse 11. It is an established principle that a law without a penalty is, in reality, no law at all. On that basis it was consistent for the king of Persia to attach a penalty for the violation of his decree. And it was in a very impressive form in which the offender was to be punished. He not only was to be executed by hanging, but was to furnish the material for his own gallows. *House be made a dunghill* means that the place where his house had stood was to be used as a place for refuse.

Verse 12. *Caused his name to dwell there.* The last word refers to the temple that was to be rebuilt by order of the king. He thus is offering an indirect prayer to God, asking him to support the Persian decree by punishing all persons who try to violate it. The whole document was made binding by the signature of Darius.

Verse 13. Upon receipt of the letter from the king, Tatnai, who was governor of the territory west of the Euphrates, and his aides, proceeded to obey the decree. It is worthy of note that they did so *speedily.*

Verse 14. This verse is a grand summary of the progress made in the rebuilding of the temple. In one paragraph all the factors are grouped that contributed to the final completion of the work. That took in the exhortations of the prophets, the commandments of God, and the various decrees of the Persian rulers who were friendly toward the Jews. The Artaxerxes mentioned is the one at the head of the 6th column of the chart. Thus far in our story he has not figured in the case, and will not for 58 years. But since the verse is a general statement of the fortunes of the Jews, the inspired writer could include the part this Persian will play in their affairs, for he will prove to be an important person in the matter.

Verse 15. This verse is short but very informative. The house was completed in the 6th year of this king Darius. The work on it was resumed in his 2nd year (Ch. 4: 24; 5: 1, 2). Hence the work on the body of the house was done during 4 years of the reign of Darius I. Here is the place to make another notation on the chart. In the 4th column write, "6th year, the temple was completed." While at the business of marking the chart, make the following notation in the 5th column: "The Ahasuerus of the book of Esther according to most authors." Some comments will be offered on this subject when we get to the book of Nehemiah or Esther.

Verse 16. Four classes of persons are named as taking part in this *dedication* or setting apart of the temple. The first is a general class; children of Israel. The priests, meaning the part of the tribe of Levi that descended from Aaron, in the second class. The third is the tribe of Levi as a whole, and fourth, any individuals left out in the ones mentioned above, but designated as being among the captivity literally. Some Jews were permitted to remain in Palestine during the 70 years. These people, of course, were enslaved under the Babylonians, but not actually taken into the land possessed by their captors.

Verse 17. The offering of *sin offerings* was not especially an acknowledgement of sin, although they had enough sins charged up against them to call for such sacrifices; but certain offerings were thus designated, regardless of the purpose for which they were given. Special attention is called to the word *twelve* in connection with the tribes of Israel. There is a doctrine in the world to the effect that the 10 tribes were lost in the captivity, and as yet have never been found. Well, the services that went on at this dedication, were under the supervision of the priests. They certainly would have known it, had these tribes been lost. And if so, they would have had no occasion for counting them when providing the sacrifices *according to the number of the tribes.*

Verse 18. There is no practical difference between *divisions* and *courses* as used here. There was some work that the priests only could do, being of the family of Aaron. The other Levites had a more general line of duty, yet could perform some things that no other tribe could lawfully do. Also, the number of eligible men in both kinds had grown so numerous, that it became necessary to have them serve in turns and sections. A part of the arrangement for the courses or turns of the priests had been fixed by David (1 Chr. 24: 1-19), which was far this side of Moses, yet with the approval of God. Therefore, *as it is written in the book of Moses* refers only to the *service,* not to the turns or courses. The outstanding thought we should get out of this paragraph is that of good order or system. That is taught in the New Testament. (Col. 2: 5.)

Verse 19. *Children of the captivity* means the children of Israel that had just come back from the land of the captivity, having been released by Cyrus.

Verse 20. *Purified together* refers to

the law of Moses that required all persons to be clean, both actually and ceremonially, before they were permitted to partake of the feasts. See Num. 9: 6-11 and 19: 11-22. These passages give the general requirements as to uncleanness, all conditions coming under the rule must comply with the law for ceremonial cleansing. These members of the tribe of Levi had attended to the demands of the law, thereby qualifying them to prepare the passover for the others as well as for partaking of it themselves.

Verse 21. The children of Israel who had come up from Babylon had to be purified according to the law. There were others who had been living in the land of Palestine and thus in connection with the *heathen of the land*. These last named persons had *separated themselves unto them*. This means the ones who had been living in Palestine in the midst of the idolaters of the country, complied with the law of purification, then joined themselves to the ones lately come in from Babylon. All of them together took part in the great feast, mutually rejoicing in the favorable situation.

Verse 22. The feast of unleavened bread was kept immediately following the passover. (Ex. 12: 18-20; 13: 7-9; Deut. 16: 3.) Politically speaking, the "land of the captivity" was a Persian territory and ruled by Persian kings. But from a geographical standpoint it was the old country of Assyria. That is why we have the expression *king of Assyria*, really meaning the Persian king. He had *strengthened their hands* as we have seen in this chapter, by furnishing them materials, and it was a time of great rejoicing among the people of God. Not only because their term of exile had been terminated, but the former oppressors were in power no more.

EZRA 7

Verses 1-5. *After these things* refers to the events of the preceding chapter. The small blank space on the paper between that and the present chapter represents more time in history than would seem possible, for it is an interval of 58 years. The dates at the top of your chart will show that to be the correct figure, but on such an important matter some quotations from authentic sources will be proper. I shall cite the following from Smith's Bible Dictionary: "Ezra, Book of, is a continuation of the books of Chronicles. The period covered by the book is 80 years, from the first of Cyrus, B. C. 536, to the beginning of the 8th of Artaxerxes, B. C. 456. It consists of the contemporary historical journals kept from time to time, containing, Chs. 1-10, an account of the return of the captives under Zerubbabel ,and the rebuilding of the temple in the reign of Cyrus and Cambyses. Most of the book is written in Hebrew, but from Chs. 4: 8 to 6: 19 it is written in Chaldee. The last 4 chapters, beginning with Ch. 7, continue the history after a gap of 58 years—from the 6th of Darius to the 7th of Artaxerxes—narrating his visit to Jerusalem, and giving an account of the reforms there accomplished, referred to under *Ezra*. Much of the book was written by Ezra himself, though the first chapter was probably written by Daniel; and other hands are evident." Quotations pertaining especially to our present line of study will also be found in Schaff-Herzog Encyclopaedia, volume 1, as follows: "*Ezra*, book of (a chronicle of events occurring between 536 and 456 B. C.), consists of parts, the first of which extends through Ch. 6. Between these two sections lies an interval of 58 years. . . . The second section (Chs. 7 to 10) has Ezra for its chief actor." On account of the importance of Ezra as a person, his family line is given back to Aaron, who was the first high priest under the Jewish Dispensation.

Verse 6. Ezra was not only a high priest but was also a scribe. The business of such men was to make duplicate copies of the law, which was done by hand, there being no printing presses or other mechanical means for such work. It can readily be seen that much was at stake for the correct preservation of the text. There were some rigid rules imposed on the profession to guarantee the genuineness of the copies. I shall quote here an extract from a standard author: "The copies of the law must be transcribed from ancient manuscripts of approved character only, with pure ink, on parchment prepared from the hide of a clean animal, for this express purpose by a Jew, and fastened together by the strings of clean animals; every skin must contain a certain number of columns of prescribed length and breadth, each column comprising a given number of lines and words; no word must be written by heart or with points, or without being first pronounced orally by the copyist; the name of God is not to be written but with the utmost devotion and attention, and previously to writing it, he must wash his pen. The want of a single letter, or the redundance [unnecessary repetition] of a single letter, the writing of prose as verse, or verse as prose, respectively vitiates [spoils] a manuscript; and when a copy has been completed, it must be examined and corrected within thirty days after the writing has been finished, in order to determine whether it is to be approved or rejected. These rules, it is said, are observed to the present day by the persons who transcribe the sacred writings for the use of the Synagogue." *Horne*, Introduction, Vol. 1, p. 217. Such requirements surrounding the copying of the sacred writings explain the silence of Jesus and other speakers and writers of the Bible as to the faithfulness of the scribes. Those men were condemned by our Lord for their loose living and hypocrisy regarding their own obedience to the law, but not once were they ever even as much as complained of, much less condemned, for any unfaithfulness in their work as scribes. And yet, had they been guilty along that line it would have been the most serious of faults, and Jesus would certainly have exposed them for it. His silence on that matter, therefore, is an assurance to us that we have the copies of the original writings of the inspired men preserved correctly. An occasional error of a copyist due to a worn place in a letter or numeral sign is too insignificant to deserve any attention. Ezra is said to have been a *ready* scribe, which means he was skilful or expert, thus making his work the more useful and dependable. Let it be noted that after mentioning the *law of Moses*, the inspired writer says of it that it was that *which the Lord God of Israel had given*. This is another instance which exposes those who would belittle the authority of Moses, or try to make a distinction between his authority and that of God. Of course we understand that the motive for this insult to Moses is in order to evade the guilt of inconsistency in their practice. They pretend to keep the law as still binding, yet dodge the requirements concerning animal sacrifices. In order to make a show of defense for their actions, they try to distinguish between the law of God and the law of Moses, a distinction the scriptures do not allow. Ezra had requested the privilege of going to Jerusalem to bring about some reforms in the service about the temple.

The king of Persia was influenced by *the hand of the Lord God*. That means that God had a hand in all the affair and brought it to the necessary conclusion.

Verse 7. Make the following notation in the 6th column of the chart: "7th year, Ezra and many other prominent Jews are permitted to go to Jerusalem to restore the worship." The classes named were outstanding men of the Jewish nation, and took active interest in the great mission for the reforms so much needed at the capital of their home country. *Children of Israel* is a general reference to the several sections of the workers in the services of God. The *priests* were the particular members of the tribe of Levi who came down from Aaron; the *Levites* was a term referring to the tribe in general. The singers were the ones forming a special group that had been looked to for that item of the worship, and it was a service that had received its first support from David. The *porters* were doorkeepers or janitors. The Nethinims were a special group of servants, considered as attendants for the other men in the public services. The last phrase of the verse is the authority for the notation just written in the 6th column of the chart.

Verses 8, 9. Incidentally, we may get some information in this paragraph on the meaning of certain expressions in the Bible. In the 8th verse it says Ezra *came* to Jerusalem. But in the 9th verse it says he *began* to go to Jerusalem on the first day of the first month, and on the first day of the fifth month he *came*. All of this shows that a writer may speak of the time at which a person starts to a certain place, and word it as if he were speaking of the time he arrived at the place. This should be considered when studying the subject of arrival of the women at the tomb of Jesus (Matt. 28: 1; Mark 16: 2; Luke 24: 1). In the case of Ezra, he came or started toward Jerusalem on the 1st day of the 1st month, but was 4 months making the journey. That would not be strange, considering the distance traveled, and the obstacles to be encountered in the journey. He could not have made the trip in that time, had it not been for the help of God whose *good hand* was upon him, which means that God took a hand in the expedition and caused it to be a success.

Verse 10. *Prepared his heart* signifies that he took his stand on behalf of the Lord. To carry out that determination, he would need to search the divine law in order to learn what he should do. He not only resolved to do the commandments as they pertained to his own conduct, but would teach the same to the children of Israel. This verse, short though it is, contains some fundamental principles pertaining to the conduct of man. Had Ezra been concerned in the liberty given him, only because of his personal enjoyment of the freedom, he might not have received the same assistance from God. But his motives were founded in the dignity of God's law, and the desire to instruct his Israelite brethren therein.

Verse 11. Ezra was a good man and was doubtless known as such to many of the nation. But the movement he was about to make was so great that he might have been questioned on his right to make it. I wish again to make some statements regarding the status of the Jews with reference to the government of the country. The 70 years of captivity had been ended three quarters of a century before. Yet the Jews were still subjects of the "powers that be" just the same as Christians in this country are subjects of the U. S. government. And if a Christian in continental America wished to go to some possession of the U. S. in another territory, it might be necessary to obtain some kind of paper or passport before he could lawfully make the journey. Likewise, the Jews were subjects of the Persian Empire at the same time they were servants of God. And to go out of the main land (Babylonia) into one of the provinces (Palestine), it was necessary to obtain a safe conduct through some formal document. For that purpose king Artaxerxes handed to Ezra this letter. The dual position of Ezra, scribe and priest, is kept before us, which should continually impress us with his importance. Besides, we have already seen from secular history, that he was the writer of this book. The same fact is indicated in V. 28 of this chapter, which will be commented on more at length when we reach that verse. Any man who did secretarial work, such as writing, would be called a scribe. Thus the inspired writer informs us that Ezra was a scribe of the words of the Lord, thereby designating his special work.

Verse 12. Artaxerxes styles himself *king of kings* which is to be understood as a statement for purposes of emphasis. The usual impression made by the word "king" is that it designates a person in the highest authority. The word itself cannot mean that, else there could not be a king of kings. And the term was not a vain display of pomp as a false claim of a heathen ruler. In Dan. 2: 37 the prophet told Nebuchadnezzar that he was a king of kings. An inspired man would not give to any ruler a title that is impossible of fulfillment. That the term under consideration denotes a rank of unusual authority is shown by the further speech of Daniel in the verse cited. After telling Nebuchadnezzar that he was a king of kings, he immediately told him why; that it was because he had been given power, strength and glory. The same was true of Artaxerxes, so that he was entitled to the claim he made of himself. There was a logical reason for using the title in connection with the decree about to be announced. If he was *king of kings*, there could not be any other king who might try to counteract this decree by another of his own. And by addressing the decree to Ezra, there would not be left any opening for some one else to lay claim to the privilege granted in the royal document. There might be other men having the same name, so the designation was made that it was the Ezra who was both a priest and scribe. *Perfect peace, and at such a time* means, "Greetings, etc."

Verse 13. A *decree* is about the same as a judicial sentence, in that it has the authority of the power in force at the time all back of it. This document was put into the hand of Ezra, but its benefits were to be extended to the people of his race. That no misunderstanding might be had as to who could benefit by it, the various classes were named; *people of Israel, priests and Levites*. The decree does not dictate that any should act against his will. Only those who were *minded of their own freewill* were to be affected. Hence it would have been unlawful for Ezra to try to compel any of the Jews to go with him, if he were to base his order on the authority of the king.

Verse 14. *Seven counselors* was an advisory board in the service of the Persian king. They joined with him in authorizing Ezra to make this journey to Jerusalem. It was understood that he was to make an investigation into conditions in the former capital of Israel. Said investigation was to be made in the light of the law supposed to govern the practice of that city. A copy of that law was then given to Ezra.

Verse 15. A heathen like Artaxerxes would not understand the full omnipresence of God as we do. His conception of him was that he was a God with a certain dwelling place. Hence we have him describing God as having his habitation in Jerusalem.

Verse 16. The silver and gold that Ezra could "find" would be that which he, as an authorized collector of revenue, would be able to lay hold of. In addition to such treasury, the people could bring forth out of their private stores of wealth, very much silver and gold. Ezra was hereby empowered to take all this wealth with him to Jerusalem, to be used in the temple service.

Verse 17. The money collected could not be used directly in the service of the house of God. But it could be used to buy animals and other articles for such use.

Verse 18. After obtaining all the animals that could be used in the temple, there might be a surplus of the money. The brethren of Ezra were authorized to join with him in deciding what to do with this surplus.

Verse 19. Some of the citizens would donate vessels of various kinds, who did not have money to give. All such were to be appropriated to the service. *God of Jerusalem* means the same as was explained in verse 15.

Verse 20. Even all of the sources mentioned for obtaining materials for the service of the God of Jerusalem might be insufficient to supply the demand. In that case Ezra was authorized to draw on the royal treasury for the needed funds.

Verse 21. The second grade officers of Artaxerxes were given the direct order so they would not have to rely solely on the word of Ezra. It would not be a small matter to open up the treasuries of the great king of Persia for the benefit of a former captive. The decree, therefore, was very opportune.

Verse 22. Even the details were taken care of. Some of the treasurers might be willing to give over to Ezra a part of the money, but not enough for the work. The order means, then, that whatever Ezra called for was to be given him, up to the amount stipulated. And no limit was placed on the amount of salt to be given. It might be wondered why salt would even be mentioned in connection with the services about the temple. Let the reader see Lev. 2: 13 and he will learn that salt was a part of the offerings made from grain, and grain has been mentioned in this verse.

Verse 23. Personal safety or advantage might seem to have been the motive of Artaxerxes in all of his treatment of the Jews. Specific reference is made to the *wrath* that might be put on the king and his sons were they to disregard the *God of heaven*. It is true that the fear of punishment was in his motive. That is not necessarily to be disapproved, for Christians are exhorted to a life of faithfulness partly on the basis of such fear. (2 Cor. 5: 11.) If Artaxerxes was familiar with the history of his nation and its predecessor, he knew something of the power of this God of heaven in overthrowing human kings. He knew also that two of his own predecessors on the throne of Persia, Cyrus and Darius, had been told by this same God to do certain favors for the Jews in the realm, and that the country had been favored by the same God because of its assistance to the unfortunate people. Thus a great motive was urging the king in his friendliness for the people of God.

Verse 24. To *certify* means to make known. Artaxerxes was making known to his deputies, through Ezra, what was his will on the subject mentioned. The particular item of his decree that was meant concerned the matter of taxes. All of the officers or special classes among the Jews that were engaged in the services about the temple were to be exempt from all financial obligation to the Persian government. This ruling was consistent with the general situation. The Jewish nation had been deservedly punished for its sins by being deprived of the use of the land. That sentence had been served out and the present generation was innocent of the great iniquity. It was right for the people to be restored to the enjoyment of their own country, and be given a chance to "catch up" on their wealth and resources as a nation, free from the burden of taxes imposed by the government.

Verse 25. The instructions given to Ezra were similar to the advice that Jethro gave to Moses on the subject of governing the people. (Ex. 18: 13-26.) *Beyond the river* means west of the Euphrates, since this was written in the land of the Persian capital which was east of the great river.

Verse 26. Two laws or authorities are considered in this verse; God's law and that of the Persian king. Artaxerxes had learned sufficient of the law of God and the conduct of the people regulated by it, to have respect for it. He was therefore willing to combine it with his own laws to the extent set out in the present conclusion. Four kinds of punishment were provided for as the penalty for disobeying either God's law or that of the king. As to which or how many of these penalties were to be imposed, it would be decided by the judges authorized in the preceding verse. Artaxerxes understood the fundamental principle involved in the operation of law—that a law without a penalty is void—and completed his great decree with naming the penalties.

Verses 27, 28. The preceding verse was the end of the decree and letter of king Artaxerxes. This paragraph is the language of the writer of the book we are studying. The pronoun in the first person is used four times, and in direct connection with the work that Ezra only was commissioned to do. We therefore know that he was the writer of this book. He blessed God for having put it in the king's heart to have the house of God adorned. This gives us an inspired explanation of why the Persian king acted as he did. Furthermore, I like to note the words *put . . . in the king's heart*. God can operate even on inanimate objects and cause them to move at his will. And he could force a king, like a piece of mechanism, to write and say just the things desired. But the great God of heaven wished the important work about to be accomplished through this heathen king to be entered into wholeheartedly. To do this he brought his influence to bear on his heart. The whole procedure was pleasing to Ezra. He was assured that in taking advantage of the commission given him by the king, he was also carrying out the will of his God, and he therefore felt no hesitancy in the proceeding. The true servant of God will do his duty in spite of the temporal powers over him, if he can. Yet how much happier he will feel if he can follow out his line of duty to the Lord, and at the same time be in harmony with the laws of the land in which he is living. With all these inducements to cheer him, Ezra proceeded to go into action by first calling together the persons he expected to cooperate with him in the reform work about to be launched in Jerusalem. We should keep in mind the time of present activities, that it is the 7th year of the reign of Artaxerxes.

EZRA 8

Verse 1. These *chief of their fathers* are the men referred to in the last verse of the preceding chapter. It was not expected that every Jew would make the journey to Jerusalem at this time, but the leading men among them, in order to accomplish the work at hand. The word *fathers* has special reference back to the beginning of the nation after they came out of Egypt. *Genealogy* means the family list. That is, when certain men are named, a jump may be made back to their forefathers to find the fountainhead of the person or persons, if two or more had a common ancestor.

Verse 2, 3. Some of these names are familiar, being among the early ancestors of the congregation of the Jews. Again, some cases are mere coincidents and should not be allowed to confuse us. The leading men of whatever unit is being considered will be named, then a sum of the number that went with them will be stated. Thus the number that was with the unit of this paragraph was 150 males. All of them were admitted to the expedition, having been represented in the *genealogy* or family list.

Verse 4. *Sons of Pahathmoab* is a general statement of the group the writer wished to consider in this unit. And out of that group he named Elihonenai, whose immediate father was Zerahiah. This man was associated with 200 males.

Verse 5. The next group was composed of the sons or descendants of Shechaniah. But not all of them could be represented in the movement, so a particular one was named to furnish the list. Jahaziel was the one chosen and the name of his son is not given, only that a son of his was given 300 males.

Verse 6. Adin stands for a group of seed of Israel, and both father and son who were selected are named. This son was given 50 males to journey with him.

Verses 7-14. Having considered several verses in detail, I believe the reader now understands the order or method followed, which applies to each of the verses in this paragraph. It was thought unnecessary, therefore, to take space for all of them separately. The thought that will be added, and that applies to each of the verses from the 3rd on down, is the fact that only males are mentioned. That is in keeping with the general plan of the Mosaic system, which required the males only to take upon them the activities of the national services. That was in consideration for the females as being the weaker vessels (physically), and hence not qualified for the journeys and other strenuous items of the system. The sum of all the males listed in verses 3-14 is 1496, which is quite an army of workers and travelers, planning to journey to the native country of their forefathers.

Verse 15. *Ahava* was the name of some small stream, or a town on a stream, located on the border of the Persian dominions proper, at which Ezra collected the men for his expedition to Palestine. The reader may remember that Ch. 7: 8, 9 recorded the arrival of Ezra at Jerusalem, yet here we are, encamped on the banks of a stream only a short distance from the starting point. But many places in the Bible are not strictly chronological. The passage just referred to is a brief statement of the entire event of Ezra's expedition from the Persian dominions to Jerusalem. The writer then goes back with his story to the events preparatory to the journey. They included the formation of the letter containing the decree of Artaxerxes, authorizing Ezra to make the journey. Having given us a copy of that document, the writer goes on with his story and has the expedition formed and assembled at the place named in the beginning of this paragraph. Before launching out upon the main part of the journey, Ezra took an inventory of his crowd. He discovered, after three days of search, that among the priestly group, there were none of the Levites other than the priests. The idea is that while there were some who were from the family of Aaron in the crowd, and hence composed a group of priests, yet the tribe of Levi in general was not represented. They would be needed for the more rugged service about the temple activities.

Verses 16, 17. *Then sent I* means Ezra summoned these men into his presence from the crowd that was there at Ahava. The first 9 men named were called chief or leading men. That would apply especially to their personal influence or prestige. The next 2 men were distinguished for their mental ability. These 11 men were sent with a commission to contact Iddo, another leading man at Casiphia, which was a district nearer the headquarters of the realm. The message to Iddo was that he should send along some *ministers* for the house of God, at which they were expecting to arrive. This word *minister* is what was indicated by the mention of Levites in verse 15. Please reread the comments in that place. The Nethinims were another group of servants that had been distinguished in the days of Solomon.

Verses 18, 19. *By the good hand* means God took a hand in the affair for their good. Such assistance guaranteed them the proper selection of a man, and consequently the man chosen had a pure lineage back to Levi, the head of the special tribe.

Verse 20. Lest we forget the information regarding the Nethinims, I shall here repeat it as far as can be learned from the sources. Smith's Bible Dictionary says this: "Nethinims (given, dedicated). As applied specifically to a distinct body of men connected with the services of the temple, this name first meets us in the later books of the Old Testament — in 1 Chronicles, Ezra and Nehemiah. The word and the ideas embodied in it may, however, be traced to a much earlier period. As derived from the verb *nathan*, i. e. give, set apart, dedicate, it was applied to those who were specially appointed to the liturgical [religious ceremonies] offices of the tabernacle." Young says they were "a class of persons employed as servants or assistants to the Levites; probably the Gibeonites and others reduced to servitude." Schaff-Herzog Encyclopaedia gives us the following: "Different from the Levites were the *Nethinims*, who performed the menial [less dignified but honorable] work for the Levites: hence they are mentioned along with the Levites (1 Chr. 9: 2; Ezra 7: 24). The original stock of the Nethinims were probably the Gibeonites, whom Joshua made 'hewers of wood, and drawers of water' (Josh. 19: 27). The Nethinims of 1 Chr. 9: 2, Ez. 2: 43, were probably sprung from captives taken by David in the later wars, who were assigned to the service of the tabernacle, replacing possibly the Gibeonites, who had been slain by Saul (2 Sam. 21: 1). Undoubtedly these Nethinims were obliged to keep the Mosiac law. From Neh. 10: 29 we know that such was the case in the post-exilian [after the exile] period." From this information we can see that the term is not a racial or religious one, but one of social state. Such a group of servants might have come out of any order of persons who were brought into a state of servitude as described. In the case now before us, there were 220 of them and they were listed according to their individual names. Ezra had sent back for some of the Levites to join the expedition, and these Nethinims very properly accompanied them.

Verse 21. The law of Moses did not generally require the practice of fasting. It endorsed it and even encouraged it by offering certain rewards for its observance. The time was at hand, in the judgment of Ezra, for a season of fasting and devotional service. They were about to start on the main lap of the journey, that was to take them through a wild and perilous country. Hostile persons would likely be encountered, as well as other dangers connected with such a territory. *Afflict* ourselves means to become humble and devote a season of time to serious prayer to God for safety.

Verse 22. It is evident from this verse that the Persian king had offered to furnish Ezra a military escort for the journey. The offer had been declined on the basis that he would rely on his God for protection. He had informed the king, though, that such help would come to those only who *seek him*. In accordance with that declaration, the appointment was made for the fast and other devotional activities of which we are now hearing. After refusing the offer of Artaxerxes, Ezra was ashamed to return to him to ask protection when he realized more fully the dangers confronting them.

Verse 23. The voluntary fasts consisted of more than the mere abstaining from food. Prayer and expressions of humility accompanied the period. *Intreated* means to "listen to prayer." The phrase signifies that God listened to or heard (favorably) the prayers of the people and of Ezra.

Verse 24. *Separated* is used in the sense of being appointed. The two men named and 10 others were specially called upon for the service soon to be described.

Verses 25, 26. In stating the amount Ezra *weighed unto these men*, it does not mean that he took just that much out of the supply on hand. It is another way of telling us that was the amount of the materials that had been given them by the king and his counsellors. Weighing it to the 12 men was for the purpose of checking afterward. As an illustration, a man might be handing a sum of money to another in settlement of an obligation. He may insist that the money be counted before they separate so that no misunderstanding could come up afterward. The same principle is taught in the New Testament (Rom. 12: 17; 2 Cor. 8: 20, 21; 1 Thess. 4: 11, 12). An honest man will not object to being "checked"; in fact, he will insist upon it. I have known treasurers of churches who never gave any statement to the congregation; if they were asked for it they would resent it. Something is wrong with a man when he does that way.

Verse 27. *Fine* copper is rendered "shining" in the margin. That fact signifies that it was the best grade since it would take a high polish. *Precious* as gold is likewise given another translation in the margin and is rendered "desirable." The lexicon agrees with it, because a material might be as desirable as gold, even though not as valuable in the market as a precious metal.

Verse 28. The word *holy* is used in the sense of being consecrated to God. The vessels and the metals, also the men having been charged with them, were appointed to the service of God in the temple, hence all was holy.

Verse 29. Ezra charged these men to weigh the valuables *before* the chief persons, which means to do it in their presence. That was for the same purpose that caused him to weigh them as they left his hands. See my comments at verses 25, 26. They were to be weighed in the presence of responsible persons. Special mention is made of the priests and Levites. The former were those members of the Levitical tribe who came down from the family of Aaron, the latter meant the tribe in general.

Verse 30. The priests and Levites not only took over the materials, but they took the *weight* of them. That was virtually a receipt for them, thus assuming responsibility for their proper disposition for the great work then about to begin.

Verse 31. According to Ch. 7: 9 it had been 12 days since Ezra started from Babylon. Most of that time had been spent at Ahava, completing the preparation for the main portion of the journey. On the 12th day of the 1st month they started, and the trip was successful through the good hand of God. That fulfilled the assurance indicated in V. 23 when the prayer of Ezra was heard.

Verse 32. *Came to Jerusalem* are 3 words that cover 5 months of time according to Ch. 7: 7. *Abode there three days* means there was nothing done for that length of time. A journey that had taken 4 months, and extended several hundred miles, would call for a brief period of relaxation.

Verse 33. After a 3-day rest, the silver and gold was turned over to the proper men and in the proper place. It was not only handed over, but was *weighed* in the presence of responsible officers and men who would be witnesses if they were needed.

Verse 34. The metal was weighed and the pieces counted or numbered, making it doubly sure that no misrepresentation, either intentional or unintentional, could be done. And furthermore, that no misunderstanding due to faulty memory might occur, the list was written down at the same time.

Verse 35. It had been over 100 years since the captivity took place, and many children had been born in the land of the exile. They are the ones meant in the beginning of this verse. They did not know, from personal experience, of the humiliation attached to a siege and capture. But they did know that they had been in a land where no worship had been practiced publicly except that for idolatrous gods. They could therefore feel grateful for the freedom now given them of serving the true God in his own appointed way. They expressed that gratitude by large numbers of sacrifices.

Verse 36. The king's *commissions* means his edict, contained in the letter shown in the preceding chapter. It was proper to deliver it to the officers of Artaxerxes in charge of his affairs *this side* (west side) of the river Euphrates. Upon receiving the decree they proceeded to obey it, and the result was the furthering of the work about the house of God in the hands of the Jews.

EZRA 9

Verse 1. One of the most outstanding predictions that appear in the writings of the prophets is that the Jews would be cured of idolatry by the captivity. That subject will be given complete discussion when writing on the prophetic books. This verse might seem to contradict that prediction by its charge that they were doing according to the evil ways of the heathen nations. The group named were the ones of old whose idolatrous practices had led the people of God into the condition that resulted in their downfall. But take note that the verse does not specify what the abominations were, except that some unlawful connection had been formed.

Verse 2. This is the place that tells us what was meant in the first verse of the chapter. The marriage between God's people and those of other nations had been forbidden by the law of Moses (Ex. 34: 16; Deut. 7: 3). That law had been violated by the Jews who had been living in Palestine. The reader will remember that a great many of the children of Israel had gone up there from Babylon in the days of Zerubbabel, 75 years before this period of which we are studying, and in that time these unlawful intermarriages had taken place. *Holy seed means* the children of Israel because they alone composed the nation that had been recognized as the people of God.

Verse 3. *Garment* means the main body of his clothing and the *mantle* was an outer piece, covering the upper part of the body. Many customs of old times seem odd to us, and we do not know their origin. But the actions of Ezra in this instance were part of the practices used in times of great anxiety or grief. *Astonied* is another form which means to be astonished or amazed.

Verse 4. To tremble at the words of God means to be respectful toward them, and to feel a great anxiety for those who have disobeyed. Such persons had brought the shocking report to Ezra, and now they gathered about him as he sat in his state of amazement. This sitting continued until the *evening sacrifice* which was at the middle of the afternoon. See Num. 28: 4, and the marginal reading in connection with it.

Verse 5. At that hour it would be necessary for Ezra to be concerned with the religious activities, including an address to God as well as the regular sacrifice.

Verse 6. *Increased over our heads* signified that their iniquities were not confined to their personal surroundings; that they had reached up to the notice of high heaven. Ezra was not personally guilty of any of the evils present, but his concern for the nation was so great that he was overwhelmed with humiliation.

Verse 7. This verse is a general view of the history of the people, going back to the first generations. As a whole, the record of the nation was one of shameful disobedience, and it had brought them into contact with the heathen lands, whose people had been suffered to afflict them with the sword and other means of torture.

Verse 8. This verse comes down to the more favorable conditions at present surrounding the better part of the congregation. *Little space* is a comparative term, referring to the period that followed the 70 years of captivity. The *remnant* was noted in Ch. 2: 64, which see. When *nail* is used figuratively it means a fixed place. It here applied to the assurance that, while the nation had been subjected to great humiliation, yet through the preservation of the *remnant*, the people of God would still have a secure abode in the *holy place*, which was the temple in Jerusalem. *Reviving* refers to the renewed hope that had been brought to the remnant by the favorable turn of affairs through the king of Persia.

Verse 9. *Were bondmen* refers to the 70 years of captivity, during which time God kept a jealous eye over his people. And when their term of bondage was served out, the people who had been God's instruments for the chastisement due them, were themselves overthrown. The Persians came into power and would have been the overlords to continue the bondage of the people of God. But that was not the divine will, and the new rulers were influenced to be merciful to the captives they found in the country they took over. *Reviving* is defined in Strong's lexicon as "preservation of life." That was not restricted to the physical life of the individual, but applied to them as a nation. By granting the Jews a release from bondage, and by authorizing the restoration of their temple, their national existence also was preserved. *A wall in Judah* means that a defense was assured them, since a wall about a city was one of its fortifications. While the word is used figuratively in this place, yet it had a literal application in its effect, for Ch. 7: 26 decreed that force should be used if necessary to protect the Jews in the privileges granted them by the Persian government.

Verses 10, 11. This paragraph starts with what is a question in form, but rather is an admission that something worthwhile should be done. The reasons for the admissions are then stated. The people had forsaken the commandments of God concerning the land into which they had been led by divine grace. They had been told beforehand that the people of the land were filthy and abominable. For that and other reasons they had been forbidden to permit marriages between their own young people and those of the nations. This law had been disregarded, and now Ezra made an admission in question form, that something should be done about it. This paragraph was addressed to God. It will be interrupted temporarily to give attention to the people.

Verse 12. In keeping with the agreement implied in his address to God in the preceding paragraph, Ezra then addressed himself to the people. It was on the subject that directly concerned the prevailing conditions, which pertained to their marriage relations. He forbade their marriages with the nations around them. They were not even to *seek their peace*, which means they were not to make any compromise with them in order to be at peace with them. As an inducement for such conduct, they were promised the best of the land for their enjoyment, and to be able to leave it for their children when they were gone.

Verse 13. Ezra then addressed himself to God again, and the whole speech was in the spirit of confession, and acknowledgement for the many favors they had received from the Lord. It also acknowledged that the punishment inflicted on them was less than they deserved. How different that spirit from what is so often manifested by the professed servants of God. We complain and speak of our lot as if it were unjust, when we should realize that if we were treated according to the just desert of our deeds, "we would long since have been lifting our piteous cries where hope and mercy can never reach." Let us read carefully and ponder Psa. 103: 10.

Verse 14. Ezra continued his prayer

and lamentation to God. While it was in question form, it was a declaration of the unreasonableness of their thought of disobeying God, after he has done so much for them. Should they do so, it should be expected that God would be angry with them and bring them to final destruction.

Verse 15. After exclaiming that God is righteous, Ezra gave a logical reason for his statement. It was the fact that they had *yet escaped*, notwithstanding the great sins of the nation. *Before thee in our trespass* means that their trespasses were exposed before God. *We cannot stand* signifies they had no justification to face the Lord in their awful sinful condition.

EZRA 10

Verse 1. Ezra *confessed* which justifies my remarks in the preceding chapter, that his questions were really the same as admissions. His prayer and other demonstrations affected many of the people. A large number of them gathered around him and joined in the general lamentation. Their confidence in Ezra must have been great. They were sure that such a good man would not have given way to expressions of grief and anxiety as he had without a just cause.

Verse 2. The audience about Ezra found a spokesman by the name of Shechaniah. He did not try to deny nor even excuse the evils of which Ezra had charged them; instead, he acknowledged all that had been brought against them. *Strange* wives means wives "outside" the nation of Israel, that being the meaning of "strange." In spite of the confessed sins, however, he did not despair of some relief. He evidently had faith in the mercy of God, for he expressed a hope concerning Israel. But we shall see that he did not think they could realize that hope without doing something to discharge their own obligations regarding the matter.

Verse 3. True to his acknowledgement of their wrongs, Shechaniah exhorted the people to correct the evil by putting away their unlawful wives. There was nothing morally wrong in the marriage with the foreign women. The sin was in disobeying the express demand of the law, that they confine their marriages to the people of their own nation. God wanted to keep a "strain" of blood pure from Abraham down to Christ, hence frowned upon taking in the people from another class. Besides, at that period of the world's history, idolatry was very prevalent, and the marriages among the heathen worshipers was sure to lead in the wrong direction. *Make a covenant* means to make a solemn promise to God. *My Lord* refers to Ezra, and *our God*, of course, means the God of heaven. Since Ezra was working in harmony with God, it was necessary to obey each at the same time. To *tremble* at the commandment of God means to have such respect for it that one would be afraid to disregard it.

Verse 4. In this verse Shechaniah addressed himself directly to Ezra. He advised him that he had the matter in his own hands of taking the lead in the work of adjustment. That was true since he was the *lord* over them and had the authority to act. He encouraged him with assurance that he would have the cooperation of the people.

Verse 5. The first act of Ezra was to call upon the whole assembly to take an oath to comply with the covenant that Shechaniah suggested. In his address to the audience he recognized 3 classes; *chief priests*, the *Levites* and *all Israel*. The first were the leading men who were the descendants of Aaron; the second was the tribe in general, and the third a listing of the congregation as a whole. The groups thus addressed by Ezra responded favorably and agreed to take the oath.

Verse 6. After securing the promise of the groups to correct the iniquity among them, Ezra "took time out" for a season of rest. He entered the room of one of the leading men, named Johanan. But it was not for the purpose of entertainment, for he was still mourning over the condition of the congregation. He even refused to partake of the necessities of life, he was so humiliated over the situation.

Verses 7. The first reaction to Ezra's demonstration of grief (V. 1) was the gathering to him of a great congregation *out of* Israel. After the decision to enter the covenant between God and all the people concerned, it was thought necessary to have a more complete representation of the nation. For that purpose a proclamation was made that *all the children of the captivity* should come to Jerusalem.

Verse 8. This is another instance showing that a law must have a penalty in order to be effective. It would require some time for the people to reach the city if they lived in the outer regions of Palestine; because of that, a period of 3 days was allowed. The penalty for defaulting was the loss of property, and being expelled from the congregation of those who had been victims of the captivity.

Verse 9. Two tribes only are mentioned by name, but that is not because that none of the other tribes were among them. We have abundant evidence (too much to cite now), to the effect that all of the tribes survived the captivity and returned to their home country. But Judah and Benjamin had been last in charge of Jerusalem, and it was natural that they would be especially in evidence at a time like this. It was in the 9th month, which made it 4 months since Ezra and his company arrived in Jerusalem (Ch. 7: 9). It was a time of rain, yet the great assemblage from all over Israel sat down in the street before the temple. They were in a state of uneasiness over the awful proclamation that had been given them by the couriers sent out by Ezra.

Verse 10. *Ezra the priest.* The reader has doubtless noticed that Ezra has been generally referred to in the third person. That might raise the question whether he could be the author of this book. That would not affect the question in the least. Moses is almost always referred to in the first five books of the Bible in the third person, even in the place where he is said to have been meeker than all other men in the earth (Num. 12: 3), yet we know he was the author of that writing. An inspired author would be writing of himself in the same sense that he would use if writing about another. We can therefore be sure that Ezra was the author of the book that bears his name. When he was ready to speak to the greater group that had come in answer to the proclamation, he informed them of the evil of which they were guilty. In marrying strange (outside) wives, they had increased the trespass of Israel. That showed that their marriage irregularities were not the only evils they had done.

Verse 11. Ezra demanded a confession of wrong from the people. But confession of sins only will not be sufficient. All wrongs that one commits must be corrected as far as possible, in order to obtain the forgiveness of God. Accordingly, Ezra called upon the guilty to separate themselves from the foreign people of the land.

Verse 12. A positive and unanimous response was made to Ezra's demand; all agreed to do as he had asked.

Verse 13. The request for more time is often an indication of indifference, or a means of evading an unpleasant task. I am sure the opposite was the case with these people. The magnitude of the work necessary to be done, and its importance in the light of the law violated, justified the request for plenty of time. Another thing, the inclemency of the weather was mentioned. That was not just because of the unpleasantness of the situation, for they had shown already that such would not keep them from doing what they believed to be their duty. They had come from the far borders of the country and sat in the street while the rain was coming down upon them, showing something of their courage. But the activities connected with sorting out the foreign wives, making sure that no lawful ones were imposed upon, yet being careful to get all of the others—all this would require time and would be hindered by the weather.

Verse 14. It showed wisdom to suggest some systematic method for handling the great work. And it is noteworthy that they did not expect the officers to "run down" the offenders to force them to comply with their duty. They proposed to have the chief officers of the congregation remain in the capital while the people came to them for the transaction. Since there were so many people concerned, it was suggested that *appointed times* be understood for the several cities. When each one's time came he was to appear before these rulers, accompanied by the proper officials of his city, and then perform whatever ceremonies would be required by those having charge. By having the elders and judges present they would be sure of attending to the matter in a lawful manner; also would have witnesses for it. The motive for this revolutionary movement was to turn away the fierce wrath of God.

Verse 15. Two priests, Jonathan and Jahaziah, were appointed to have charge of the work. Two other men of the tribe of Levi were given to them as helpers; they were Meshullam and Shabbethai.

Verse 16. *Children of the captivity* were the ones who had been exiles, but had come back to Palestine in the days of Cyrus. They were the ones who had taken the unlawful wives after coming from Babylon. They had agreed to correct the situation by putting away the strange wives. The priests mentioned in verse 15 took active charge of the ceremonies, but the transaction needed to be "checked" by other and superior men. For this work Ezra took some chief fathers and sat down to the task of reviewing the work that had been done. They began their work the 1st day of the 10th month. It had been started about the 20th of the 9th month (V. 9), which means that Jonathan and his helpers got a 10-day start ahead of Ezra's review work.

Verse 17. *First day of the first month* means, of the next year following the arrival in Jerusalem; so that we see the work of Ezra in examining the work of Jonathan required two months. All of this shows that care was taken in this serious business, so that the national personnel would again be pure.

Verse 18. As a rule, what is wrong for one man is wrong for another. A thing may be a greater wrong in one man, though, than in another, from the standpoint of his influence. For instance, a priest was more prominent in his position with the congregation, hence a wrong committed by him would be more outstanding. This is the reason this verse names certain men in the priestly group who had taken strange wives. The priests were expected to teach the people the law (Lev. 10: 11; Deut. 17: 9; Mal. 2: 7), therefore their sin was the less excusable.

Verse 19. The priests *gave their hands* which is a phrase that means they made a solemn promise to correct their wrongs. That was done first by putting away their strange wives; but that did not clear them before God. The law of Moses made provision that certain sacrifices should be offered to atone for sins called trespass. (Lev. 6: 6.) This service was performed by these men because they were *guilty*.

Verses 20-22. This paragraph is a continuation of the thoughts in verse 19. The same remarks would apply to these priests that were made at the preceding verse. But after having named a few of the priests and describing their actions regarding the strange wives, the inspired writer considered that to be a precedent for other like cases, hence the list making up this paragraph with nothing specified but their names.

Verse 23. All priests were Levites, but not all Levites were priests. The preceding paragraphs listed the names of some Levites who were priests. The men named in this were Levites but not priests. It would be taken for granted they would follow the example of other Levites in the disposal of their wives, and in other duties.

Verse 24. David had formulated a group of Israelites whose special part of the services was the singing. In 1 Chr. 6: 31 a reference is made to certain men whom he had set over the service of song in the house of the Lord. Their exercises were accompanied with instrumental music generally. Among the units connected with this service were *the sons of Asaph* (1 Chr. 25: 1), and the classification of singers finally became very distinct. The fact accounts for their being specifically mentioned in the list of men we are now considering. *The porters* composed another special group of servants about the buildings of the Lord. Their work was equivalent to gatekeepers or janitors. They were somewhat prominent and thus became entitled to special mention in the account of the irregular marriages.

Verses 25-43. This long list of names has been grouped into one paragraph because nothing peculiar to any one of them is said. The list starts with the words *of Israel*. That means that after the mention of the special classes included in the preceding verses, all the rest to be named as being guilty were Israelites in general.

Verse 44. One statement was made that was common to all of this long list; they had taken strange wives. The specification for some of them was that they had children by these wives. That, in fact, was one of the main objections to these unlawful marriages. God had promised to Abraham that he should have a numerous race of descendants, through whom a seed would be given to the world for a universal blessing. Also, these descendants were to compose a nation that was to possess the land to which he was being led. In order to accomplish the two promises to the patriarch, it was necessary to keep the blood line pure, unmixed with that of outside races. That is the special reason it was forbidden to beget children by wives of an alien nation.

NEHEMIAH 1

Verse 1. Make the following notation in the 6th column of the chart: "20th year, Nehemiah is permitted to go and rebuild the walls of Jerusalem." Since the events of the preceding book, 13 years have rolled away. (Ch. 2: 1.) We are told in direct language that Nehemiah is the author of this book. We will not be confused, therefore, by the use of the pronoun in the 3rd person. *Shushan* was another form of Susa, which became the capital of the Persian Empire from the days of Darius Hystaspes. At the time our subject opens, Nehemiah was in this city a personal attendant of the king Artaxerxes.

Verse 2. Nehemiah asked about the Jews who had *escaped*. We ordinarily think of that word as meaning one who had to elude his captor and get away without leave. It does not mean that in this place. The word is from an original that is defined "deliverance" in the lexicon. It is said with reference to the Jews who had been in captivity, but had been given their freedom by the ones who had them in their control. Many of these were in Palestine and living in the vicinity of Jerusalem; concerning them Nehemiah made his inquiry of some individuals who had returned to Persia.

Verse 3. The report given to Nehemiah was very disheartening. Mention was made of the condition of the walls. In the time of Zerubbabel (Ezr. 4: 12) we read that the walls were set up, having been thrown down prior to that, and the present account sounds as if the condition had just been made known. But we should remember that the time of Zerubbabel was almost a century before this experience of Nehemiah, and in that period they had again been let fall into decay. In those times of almost constant difficulties with neighboring governments, a wall about a city was of utmost importance. That is why there is such frequent mention of fenced (walled) cities. We may well understand, then, why Nehemiah was so affected by the report.

Verse 4. *Mourned certain days* merely means he mourned for some time. Fasting was not generally commanded in the law, but was endorsed when done voluntarily. It was common for men to go on a fast when under great concern or anxiety. Of course we would expect a righteous man like Nehemiah to pray also at such times.

Verse 5. To *beseech* means to pray very earnestly. *Terrible God* means he is a God to be respected and reverenced. God's mercy is offered on condition of obedience.

Verse 6. No human is absolutely perfect, and a man like Nehemiah would be the last to make such a claim. He therefore expressed his penitence in this prayer. His confession did not mean necessarily that his personal life had been corrupt in the things that brought about the downfall of his nation. It had been about 100 years since the captivity, and he could not have been directly active in the national wrongs. He was speaking rather for the nation as a whole. The New Testament teaches us that the eyes and ears of the Lord are favorable toward the righteous (1 Pe. 3: 12). In accordance with that truth, Nehemiah made his prayer to God.

Verse 7. *We have dealt* shows the prayer and confession referred to the nation as a whole, and not to Nehemiah personally. The *commandments* of the Lord mean his law as a whole. The *statutes* were the formal edicts or decrees enacted independent of the conditions, and the *judgments* were the decisions of the Lord rendered upon occasions that came up. However a decision was made on any special occasion, it became a fixed law for all other like cases.

Verse 8. *Commandest thy servant Moses* means he commanded Moses to give it to the people. This is another place that shows the error of those who try to distinguish between the "law of God" and the "law of Moses." They are the same as far as authority is concerned, so that all that Moses wrote is as much in force today as any certain part of it is. The word under present consideration plainly declared that if the people transgressed the law of God, they would be scattered among the nations. Nehemiah was mindful of the justice dealt out to his people, that it was in accordance with the word of God. But it had a redeeming feature which the prayer included, and it will be shown in the next verse.

Verse 9. On condition of repentance, God has always been willing to forgive his wayward people. Looking to that provision in the divine plan, Nehemiah pled for mercy and help for his afflicted people in Jerusalem. God had promised to recover his people even though scattered afar, when they would have returned to him in their hearts.

Verse 10. The Lord does not need any human information. He knows

Nehemiah 1: 11—2: 8

who are his people and who are not. The language of Nehemiah, therefore, was a part of an earnest prayer for divine guidance. He expressed his belief in the great power of God.

Verse 11. Most of this verse is the same as the preceding ones in its sentiments. Nehemiah had been praying for the help of God and in general terms. He now came to particulars and asked that God cause mercy to be shown him by *this man*. The antecedent of the pronoun is the king of Persia as the closing sentence shows. A *cupbearer* is described in Smith's Bible Dictionary as follows: "An officer of high rank with Egyptian, Persian, and Assyrian as well as Jewish monarchs. 1 Kings 10: 5. It was his duty to fill the king's cup and present it to him personally."

NEHEMIAH 2

Verse 1. It will be well to consult the chart again, noting that we are in the 20th year of the reign of Artaxerxes. *Wine was before him* means he was having an indulgence of his favorite refreshment. At such times Nehemiah performed his personal duty, to fill a cup and hand it to the king. Such a service was not a difficult one, and to render it to a king with the temperament this king seemed to possess would be a pleasant task. For these reasons Nehemiah had never shown such a state of sadness as he did at this time, which attracted the attention of the king.

Verse 2. Having noticed the expression on the face of Nehemiah, that it was unusual, the king made some remarks about it. He knew that his servant was not sick physically, therefore concluded the condition to be one of the heart. That was what he meant by the expression *sorrow of heart*, that it was a condition of great worry. Sore afraid means he was greatly concerned. He had not realized how much the worry of the report had affected his general attitude and facial expression.

Verse 3. With all due respect for his king, Nehemiah told him the cause for his sorrow. The place of burial was always considered as something sacred even by the heathen. It was an important explanation, therefore, for Nehemiah to make this report.

Verse 4. The king asked him what he wanted to do, and the indications are that he encouraged him to expect great privileges. Upon such a weighty matter Nehemiah did not feel ready to decide without divine guidance. That is why he *prayed to God*.

Verse 5. After his prayer to God, Nehemiah asked the privilege of going to Jerusalem to have it repaired in the walls.

Verse 6. The request of Nehemiah was granted. The hearing must have been very impressive. Artaxerxes had called for his wife to sit by him while the conversation was had. An esteemed personal attendant upon the king of Persia was about to be given leave of absence for a time, the length of which was to be determined by the servant. Ch. 5: 14 shows the time *set* was 12 years.

Verse 7. A man who has been in the employ of a great king should not be seen out from his territory without good cause. The secondary officers of Artaxerxes who were in the immediate vicinity of the capital might easily be made to understand why such a servant was at large. It would be different with the ones *beyond the river*, which means west of the Euphrates River. To avoid any difficulty, therefore, Nehemiah asked for letters showing his right to travel even as far as to Judah. Not only that the officers would not try to stop him, but would furnish him a conveyance.

Verse 8. The king granted to Nehemiah the letter he requested, which included the order for material from the keeper of the *forest*. Since this forest was a place of timber, and also since the original word is related to our English word "paradise," the reader might appreciate it if I take some space to quote from the authorities on the origin and meaning of the word, as follows: "PARADEISOS. '(Thought by some to be of Armenian, but by most, to be of Persian origin); 1. Among the Persians, a grand enclosure or preserve, hunting ground, park, shady and well-watered, in which wild animals were kept for the hunt; it was enclosed by walls and furnished with towers for the hunters.'—Xenophon, Cyropedia, 1-3-14; Anab. 1-2-7-9. '2. Universally, a garden, pleasureground; grove, park: Josephus, Antiquities, Book 7, Chapter 14, Section 4. Sus. 4-7-15; Sir. 24: 30; and so it passed into the Hebrew language, Neh. 2: 8; Eccl. 2: 5; Song of Solomon, 4: 13; besides in the Septuagint [Greek translation of the Old Testament] mostly for . . .; thus for that delightful region, the garden of Eden, in which our first parents dwelt before the fall: Gen. 2: 8. 3. That part of Hades which was thought by the later Jews to be the abode of the souls of the pious until the resurrection: Lk. 23: 43. But some (e. g. Dillman) understand that passage of the heavenly paaradise. 4. An upper region in the heavens: 2 Cor. 12: 4 (where some maintain, others deny, that the term is equivalent to HO TRITOS OURANOS in V. 2): with the addition of TOU THEOU, genitive of the possessor, the abode of God and heavenly beings, to which true Christians will be taken after death. Rev. 2: 7.'—Thayer. 'Paradise, a region of beauty; Armenian PARDES, a garden or park around the house, planted with grass, herbs, trees, for use and ornament. In the Hebrew form . . . , and Greek PARADEISOS, it is applied to the pleasure gardens and parks with wild animals around the country residences of the Persian monarchs and princes, Neh. 2: 8; Eccl. 2: 5; Song of Solomon 4: 13; Xenophon Cycropaedia 1-3-14. In like manner of the Jewish kings, Josephus, Antiquities, Book 7, Chapter 14, Section 4. Book 8, Chapter 7, Section 3. Hence in the Septuagint [Greek translation of the Old Testament], of the garden of Eden, PARADEISOS for Beb. . . . in Gen. 2: 8; Josephus, Antiquities, Book 1, Chapter 1, Section 3 . . . Hence in the later Jewish usage and in the New Testament, paradise is put for the abode of the blessed after death, viz. 1. The inferior paradise, or the region of the blessed in Hades, Luke 23: 43. Josephus, Antiquities, Book 18; Chapter 1, Section 3. 2. Specifically, HO PARADEISOS TOU THEOU, the paradise of God, the celestial paradise, where the spirits of the just dwell with God, 2 Cor. 12: 4, equal to HO TRITOS OURANOS in verse 3; see Rev. 2: 7 where the imagery is drawn from Gen. 2: 8.'—Robinson. '(Pers., in Heb. . . .), a park, a forest where wild beasts were kept for hunting; a pleasure park, a garden of trees of various kinds; a delightful grove, Eccl. 2: 5; Song of Solomon, 4: 13; used in the LXX [Septuagint] for the garden of Eden, or of delight, Gen. 2: 8; in the New Testament, the celestial paradise, that part of Hades in which the souls of believers enjoy happiness, and where God dwells. Lk. 23: 43; 2 Cor. 12: 4; Rev. 2: 7.'"—Greenfield. Note: from above it can be seen that PARDES in the Old Testament is similar if not equivalent to PARADEISOS in the New Testament. We know that the parks of the Persians have been discarded or will be, yet no one argues from that fact that the Paradise of God, whose name has been taken from those parks, will ever be discarded. A similar line of reasoning should be had with reference to the origin of the Greek word for Gehenna, which will be introduced in the New Testament Commentary. A word may originate from some thing or practice that finally ceases to exist, and yet still be applied to something that is permanent or endless in its existence.

Verse 9. Artaxerxes was very considerate of Nehemiah. He not only gave him letters of introduction to the governors west of the Euphrates, but furnished him a military escort. The preceding verse explains this all to have been the hand of God.

Verse 10. Sanballat was a Persian ruler under the authority of Artaxerxes, stationed in Samaria. Tobiah was a Samaritan by race, and a slave of Sanballat. The two were united in their opposition to the work of Nehemiah. They were unfriendly toward the Jews, and hence felt grieved to see anyone doing something in their behalf.

Verse 11. The situation was somewhat tense, so Nehemiah was not hasty in starting operations; he waited 3 days after arriving in Jerusalem.

Verse 12. Nehemiah knew that he would likely be opposed in his work. He did not want to expose himself to the enemy any more nor any sooner than necessary. His first investigation, therefore, was in the night. He went about it very quietly. He took a few men with him, evidently for protection only. He did not tell them what he had in mind, and did not let them have horses to ride. They had to go on foot while he alone had the use of a horse.

Verse 13. Of course we would not expect Nehemiah to make a minute inspection of all the parts of the wall, especially at night; he made a general survey. The cities with walls had gates at certain places where special interests would draw crowds. And the gates would be named after these special interests, or perhaps be located by some natural significance. The *dragon well* was a fountain having that name, for what reason we are not told. Since this fountain would be visited frequently, a gate was made in the wall at that place. One gate was called *gate of the valley* because it opened out near one of the depressions near the city. *Dung port*. The second word means "gate." The first is from SHEPHOTH and Strong defines it, "a heap of rubbish or filth." Smith's Bible Dictionary says the following about the subject: "The uses of dung were twofold—as manure and as fuel. The manure consisted either of straw steeped in liquid manure, Isa. 25: 10, or the sweepings, Isa. 5: 25, of the streets and roads, which were carefully removed from the houses, and collected in heaps outside the walls of the towns and fixed spots—hence the dung-gate at Jerusalem—and thence removed in due course to the fields." All of this information explains why there would be a port [al] or gate at this spot and be so named. Nehemiah made inspection at these places and found the walls and gates in a dilapidated condition.

Verse 14. Such places as fountains and pools would be visited frequently, which would call for the convenience of a gate. Nehemiah tried to inspect some of these spots but they were not passable for his horse.

Verse 15. He came up from another angle; by the brook. From here he examined the condition of the wall, then retraced his journey. He re-entered the city at the gate of the valley, the place where he had begun his tour of inspection (V. 13).

Verse 16. The persons named were outstanding citizens of the country. The priests were a religious class and the others were assorted according to either social or industrial classification. Nehemiah kept his preliminary investigation unknown to all of them, until he had returned.

Verse 17. After returning within the limits of the city he made known the conditions. We understand that the ruins of the wall were visible, so that the writer could refer to the various gates and other parts of the wall or structure. But the ruin was so great that it would be necessary to rebuild it as if it never had existed.

Verse 18. Nehemiah told his fellow Jews of the encouragement he had, both from God and the king of Persia. The effect of his report on the conditions, together with the encouraging assurances, was immediately favorable. They proposed going right to the work of building. *Strengthened their hands* means they took courage and resolved to take hold of the work with a willing mind.

Verse 19. The population of the country was a mixture of the various peoples since the days of the captivity. Sanballat had been placed in a position of authority under the Persians, Tobiah was a slave of his. The Arabians came from Ishmael, son of Abraham, but had become a race to themselves. They were known as foreigners to the pure stock of Israel. The whole group here named became concerned over the activities of Nehemiah. When Zerubbabel started his work about a century before, the "outsiders" offered to help but were rejected. Doubtless that had been recorded and Sanballat knew he would not be permitted to have anything to do with it. These enemies, therefore, took an attitude of "sour grapes" toward the work. *Laughed us to scorn* means they derided or made fun of them. *Despised us* means they belittled them, and in a flippant spirit accused them of rebelling against the king.

Verse 20. The attitude of the enemies did not discourage Nehemiah. He did not honor them even by denying their foolish accusation. Instead, he affirmed that God would help them so that the building would be done. Moreover, he gave them to understand that they would not be allowed to have any part in the matter.

NEHEMIAH 3

Verse 1. In this great work of rebuilding the walls of Jerusalem, all classes and ranks of men took part. The chapter recounts the order in which the different workmen were located on their jobs at the particular places on the wall. It was necessary to describe the separate parts one at a time, and in the order in which they were placed. But we should understand that all of the parts were built up at the same time (Ch. 4: 6). The description of the work started with the *sheep gate*. See my comments at Ch. 2: 13 on the importance of gates. Since this gate was where the description of the work began and ended, it must have been of special interest. I shall quote what Smith's Bible Dictionary says about it: "Sheep-gate, The, one of the gates of Jerusalem as rebuilt by Nehemiah. Neh. 3: 1, 32; 12: 39. It stood between the tower of Meah and the chamber of the corner, Ch. 3: 1, 32, or the gate of the guard-house, Ch. 12: 39; Authorized Version, 'prison-gate.' The latter seems to have been at the angle formed by the junction of the wall of the city of David with that of the city of Jerusalem proper, having the sheep-gate on the north of it. The position of the sheep-gate may therefore have been on or near that of the Bal el Kattanin." It is easy to understand why the sheep gate would be important. There were thousands of sheep driven into the city each year to be offered in sacrifice. It would be natural, then, that a place would be sanctified or devoted to such a sacred purpose. *Tower of Meah . . . Hananeel.* Towers were fortified structures elevated on the walls of cities and other places requiring defense. They served also as lookouts against any approaching enemy. There were no less than 6 of these towers on the wall of Jerusalem, two of which are named in this verse. These towers were given individual names, but the origin of such names is not told us.

Verse 2. Citizens from various cities came in a body to the work. The men of Jericho were given the place next to that of the high priest.

Verse 3. Smith's Bible Dictionary says that among the purposes of the gates of eastern cities was that of public markets. We understand, therefore, that the fish gate was the place where fish were bought and sold. That part of the wall was built by the sons of Hassenaah. Since the work was extensive and many workmen were needed, the mention of the men in given cases may be all we can know of them. The part mentioned indicates that a gate of such walls that surrounded the great cities had a very complete formation. They had to be made strong against the battering rams of an invading force attempting to overthrow the structure.

Verse 4. The simple information in this verse is the fact that *Meremoth, Meshullam* and *Zadok* each were placed in order upon the repair work of the wall.

Verse 5. Certain groups came in a body to the city to join in the work. These groups would be assigned to their proper places on the job, and it would then be up to the group to make their own distribution of the workers as to turns. The unit as a whole would get the credit for assistance in the project, although certain individuals in the unit might be shirkers. So in this place, there was the work of the Tekoites, people of Tekoa. The common people among them worked on the job, but the nobles or the ones who thought they were more important, felt above the work.

Verse 6. We have no information especially applicable to the *old gate.* It was doubtless so called because it was among the first to be built, and made on the general requirement for gates. Two men, *Jehoiada* and *Meshullam* were assigned this old gate.

Verse 7. A throne does not always signify the place of a monarch. The original word here is also translated by seat and stool. It means the headquarters of the man who was the governor of the province. It was near the wall and the persons named worked on that span of it that extended between this seat and the old gate.

Verse 8. The wall was evidently heavier or broader in some places than in others. Such parts would need no special fortification, but would be a fortification in itself. The tradesmen mentioned in this verse added certain fortifications to their repair of the wall, until it reached to the *broad wall* as stated above.

Verse 9. A *ruler* of the kind mentioned here does not mean specifically an official in the ordinary sense of the word. It is from SAR and Strong defines it, "a head person (of any rank of class)." It has been rendered by captain, chief, general, governor, keeper, lord, master, prince and steward. The meaning is, this man had a high prestige over one half of the city. It would be significant, therefore, that such a man contributed to the humble work of rebuilding the wall, consisting of manual labor.

Verse 10. *Jedaiah* lived either within the limits of Jerusalem, or near it on the outside. He was assigned that part of the wall near his house.

Verse 11. Malchijah repaired the *other piece.* That means the second section of the part that was repaired by Hattush in the preceding verse. One of the towers described previously in this chapter was near the furnaces or ovens. That would be an important point because of its connection with the provisions for the tables. It was necessary, therefore, that one of these fortifications be near these ovens.

Verse 12. Verse 9 told of one man with certain influences over half of the city. This verse tells of the other half of the city under a like oversight, represented by Shallum and his daughter.

Verse 13. *Valley gate* was so named because it opened out upon one of the

Nehemiah 3: 14-27

depressions near the city. The work of these people reached from this gate to the *dung gate*. See Ch. 2: 13 for comments on this place. Hanun's work stopped at this last gate.

Verse 14. The *dung gate* itself was repaired by Malchiah. He had a position similar to these other *rulers* already described. His home community was at Beth-haccerem which was near Bethlehem.

Verse 15. This fountain is referred to in Ch. 2: 14.' It was a place of much water for Nehemiah's horse could not pass over the spot. A gate was to be built there and the work was in charge of Shallum. This man was another *ruler* of the vicinity of Mizpah. Siloa is another form of "Siloam," and we recall that a pool was at that place (John 9: 7). The king also had a garden near the spot, and in connection with all these interesting things were some steps constructed leading from the district of Jerusalem called Zion or the city of David. The part of the wall enclosing all these objects was in charge of this same man, Shallum.

Verse 16. The name *Nehemiah* is a coincidence with the author of this book. He was another one of the kind of *rulers* that means men of influence. His territory was half of the town of Beth-zur. His work on the wall reached from that of Shallum to the part of the city where the burial ground of David was. His span of the work also passed the pool (2 Ki. 20: 20), and the *house of the mighty*, which was an arsenal.

Verse 17. The two Levites were Rehum and Hashabiah. The last named was another ruler, or man of personal influence, and his part of the territory for such prestige was half of the town of Keilah.

Verse 18. Bavai was the *ruler* having the other half of Keilah. He and several others named in the chapter were Levites.

Verse 19. Another *piece* means another section of the wall. *Armoury* is from NESHEQ and Strong defines it, "military equipment, i. e. (collectively) arms (offensive or defensive), or (concretely) an arsenal." *Turning of the wall* means the corner of it. This man repaired that part of the wall that went near the arsenal and on to the corner of the enclosure of the city.

Verse 20. Baruch had a section of the wall beginning at the corner that we have just turned, and reaching as far as the opening made for the house of the high priest.

Verse 21. The house of the high priest would certainly not be of excessive length. Yet Meremoth was assigned only that much of the wall as reached from the door of this house to the end of it.

Verse 22. *The priests* who worked on this job were the ones of the descendants of Aaron who were eligible for the office. There were a great many of them by this time. Not all who were thus qualified were in active priestly service, but all of them would be called *priests* as regards the work on the wall. However, the unit of these priests who worked on this section of the wall were the ones from a distinct locality called *the plain*. The singular pronoun is used when we know that a number of men worked. That is because each group would be under the foremanship of one man.

Verse 23. The three men named in this verse lived near the wall and they were assigned the section nearest their homes. That was not only a gracious provision, but it enabled them to lose less time getting to their work. It was necessary for them to go to their houses occasionally (Ch. 4: 23).

Verse 24. Certain men had homes near the wall, and their houses were used as the marking place of beginning of some section of the wall. Binnui had the section extending from the spot near the home of Azariah to the next corner of the structure.

Verse 25. This section was repaired by two men, and the part of their assignment began just at the corner that was left by Bennui, and extended past one of the towers described previously. This tower was especially important, because it overlooked the house of the king that was near the prison.

Verse 26. The Nethinims were a class of servants that originated in the days of Solomon. The objects that located the section assigned to them were, one of the gates and one of the towers referred to above. This particular tower was for the defense of this water gate, and it was on the east side of the city.

Verse 27. *Ophel* was a ridge of ground inside Jerusalem, and it was the site of certain dwellings. *Wall of Ophel* just means that part of the wall reaching that far. The Tekoites were inhabitants of Tekoa.

Verse 28. Some more of the priests (descendants of Aaron), lived near the wall connected with the horse gate. This was a gate used for the entrance of these animals when they were to be brought in for any purpose. These priests were permitted to have this portion of the wall. It would give them the same advantages mentioned in V. 23.

Verse 29. Zadok was another man who lived near the wall, and he had his work there, which joined up with the work of the priests. The man who worked near him was the janitor of the east gate. Such men were sometimes called porters.

Verse 30. The section of the wall considered in this verse was repaired by three men. The last one named lived near the wall. See comments at V. 23.

Verse 31. The section of the wall considered in this verse reached from the spot near the chamber or house of Meshullam to the corner of the wall. This span went near one group of the Nethinims; a location of merchants; and one of the gates of the city. This particular gate was named Miphkad for some reason not given in the history.

Verse 32. This section reached from the corner to the sheep gate, the place of the beginning. The last phrase means the beginning of the chapter and thus the beginning of the description of the project. The work was all in operation at the same time (Ch. 4: 6). We are not given any information as to the comparative extent or difficulty of the various sections of the wall referred to in this chapter. Neither do we know the exact number of men who worked on any given part. But since the whole work went up together, we must conclude that proper consideration was given to the subject. Just the right men and number of them, and with the proper qualifications, would be assigned to the several divisions of the great wall, so that no confusion or misfits would occur. The project went forward as one grand piece of work until it reached a harmonious and complete whole.

NEHEMIAH 4

Verse 1. Sanballat was the man who expressed his displeasure at first hearing of the coming of Nehemiah. He had no good feeling for the Jews and was grieved at the mere thought that anyone would do a favor for them. Now he was still more worked up over the fact that the wall was being built. He knew of the letters of authority that Nehemiah had from the king, and knew he would have no right to interfere. But he mocked or made fun of the work.

Verse 2. Sanballat feared lest his people become interested in the project of the Jews and perhaps lend them moral support at least. To prevent this, he tried to belittle the work, or to make it appear that they were undertaking that which was impossible. *Make an end in a day* is figurative, and implied that Nehemiah expected to accomplish the work in a very short time. He intimated that it would be an almost endless task to clear away the rubbish and get such a great wall built again. He failed to consider that the Jews had a God who was above all others, and that he would be a source of strength to his people in times of need or adversity.

Verse 3. It is almost amusing to observe how the enemy tried to encourage each the other. They were really feeling sorry for one another, but pretended to think the work of the Jews was a useless fabrication. Tobiah was near Sanballat when he was making his belittling speech. So he added his mite of condolence with the extravagant statement that a fox could overthrow the work. When a man will make such a ridiculous statement as that, it is evident that he is really concerned about the very thing he is belittling and pretending to regard as of no importance.

Verse 4. *We are despised* means they were being treated with contempt. Nehemiah heard of the reproachful sayings, and prayed to God that their reproach be turned back upon themselves. That is, be made to feel the sting of their own spiteful words.

Verse 5. The Bible teaches that God will always forgive when the guilty ones become penitent and comply with the terms of pardon. These enemies of the Jews were not God's people and would not be inclined to make the proper approach to him for the securing of forgiveness. If God did *cover* or *blot* out their iniquity and sin, it would be by sheer favor. Such forgiveness was what Nehemiah prayed God not to grant them.

Verse 6. *All the wall was joined together unto the half thereof.* Moffatt's translation words this, "So we built the wall to half its height all round."

The versions are both correct, but having the two, the thought is more clarified. The meaning is that all the parts of the wall were joined together as the work progressed. At the time referred to, the wall had been built up to half its proper height. The explanation for the success was the fact that the people *had a mind to work.* And it does not mean simply that they were active in the sense of being work-frenzied, but they were in tune with each other and cooperated in the whole proposition. Had that not been the case, the wall would have been built up at places, and lagging at others. As it was, every man worked in fellowship with his neighbor, and hence the wall was *all joined together.* This is a wonderful lesson to us on the advantage of cooperation in the work of the Lord. See Rom. 12: 16; 1 Cor. 1: 10; 3: 9; 2 Cor. 13: 11.

Verse 7. The persons named were a mixture of various clans and tribes of idolatrous people inhabiting Palestine at the time Nehemiah came to repair the walls. They had been living in unmolested enjoyment of the country for many years, and it grieved them to see the prospect of having their reign of iniquity disturbed. *Were made up* does not mean the walls were completed. The marginal translation combines the three words into one word, "ascended," and the lexicon agrees with it. Also, it agrees with the language in the preceding verse. Seeing the successful progress of the wall, these men were filled with wrath.

Verse 8. To *conspire* means to join together for some unlawful purposes. In this case it was with intent of fighting against the work at Jerusalem.

Verse 9. This verse combines the same items as a command of Christ to his disciples in Matt. 26: 41. One duty cannot take the place of another, and in spiritual matters the same person can watch and pray at the same time. But there was a special reason for different forces to be assigned to the separate items in the case of Nehemiah. The work was of a material nature, although being done for the sake of the Lord's cause. The watching, therefore, was also literal, because they had to be on the alert for a possible physical attack from the enemy.

Verse 10. Even some of the Jews became discouraged. They imagined that the work of removing the rubbish was too strenuous for those who were supposed to carry it away.

Verse 11. Nehemiah had to hear the boasts of the enemy as well as the complaints of the men of Judah. They said that before the Jews realized it, they would be among them to kill the workmen and thus put a stop to the work.

Verse 12. There were some Jews living by the enemies referred to in the preceding verse. They caught the discouraging spirit of the enemy and came to Nehemiah with their tale of woe. *Ten times* is figurative, meaning they repeated their disconsolate speech over and over again. I like Moffatt's rendering of the latter part of this verse, which is as follows: "they kept telling us, 'They are gathering against us from all quarters.'"

Verse 13. Nehemiah was not entirely indifferent to the threats of the enemies. He began to strengthen his defenses by placing some families in the low and high places, and armed them with swords and other means of combat.

Verse 14. Nehemiah spoke to the heads of the people in behalf of their families. Having them there in their sight, they should be impressed with the necessity of defending them. He bade them trust in the Lord who is great. Under him they could fight for their wives and children, with assurance that victory would be theirs.

Verse 15. The "war scare" was over as soon as the enemy learned that the Jews were preparing for the worst. They ceased their threatening for the time being, and the men resumed their work on the wall.

Verse 16. While Nehemiah was not frightened by the threats of the enemy, he decided not to take any chances. From that time he used a special plan for the work. It was especially arranged for the men of Judah to strengthen their morale, as they were the ones who had been foremost in the complaints. As a greater precaution, half of the servants of Nehemiah were released from active duty on the wall so that they could be on constant guard. They were prepared for this defense with various weapons, and also were covered with a habergeon. That was a sort of metallic coat that was worn over the other clothing for protection from the darts of the enemy.

Verse 17. There were the masons and others who worked on the wall. They had to be furnished with materials that were borne on the shoulders of men called "burden bearers," and some others were needed to lay the materials on the shoulders of the bearers. These three classes of workmen are meant in the forepart of this verse. Even all of these men were directed to carry a weapon in one hand. That would explain why they needed some to lay the load on the shoulders of the carriers.

Verse 18. We thus see that all the classes of workers, whether engaged directly on the wall or in attending on them, were armed and prepared to fight if need be, as well as to work. The same principle is taught in the New Testament. Christians are commanded to work (Phil. 2: 12), and to fight (1 Tim. 6: 12). The use of the trumpeter standing by Nehemiah will be shown in the following paragraph.

Verses 19, 20. The wall was very great and the workers were necessarily scattered so that not many would be in any one section. Should the enemy observe that fact, he might select some one of the more scattered groups and direct his attack there. The trumpeter was therefore expected to sound an alarm and all the others were to rush to the place attacked and help in the defense. This is another principle taught in the New Testament. See Rom. 12: 15; 1 Cor. 12: 26; 1 Th. 5: 14. Nehemiah taught his people the idea of being coworkers with God; that man's efforts were required, but they alone would not win. Hence they were told that "our God shall fight for us."

Verse 21. The spears were already mentioned in V. 16. The added detail is given here as to the hours put in at the work. They were from daylight to full darkness. There was no such thing as "overtime" on that project.

Verse 22. When active duties had subsided on account of the nightfall, there was still the necessity for the presence of the servants to act as guards. There never was a time when they could be said to be free from danger of the enemy. That is the same lesson that is taught in 1 Peter 5: 8.

Verse 23. The emergency created by the necessity of washing their clothes is what was referred to at Ch. 3: 23. See the comments at that place.

NEHEMIAH 5

Verses 1, 2. *We take up* means they needed corn for their children. They complained that the need was urgent because there were many of them. For this great need they were crying to Nehemiah.

Verse 3. Some of the people claimed they had to mortgage their properties because of the shortage, to get food for their families.

Verse 4. Still others complained that they could not pay the tax required by the king, until they borrowed money. And the loan had to be secured by their land and vineyards, the very sources of their living.

Verse 5. The poorer Jews were being thus oppressed by their more fortunate brethren. They protested having their children, which they called their own flesh, to be placed at the mercy of their brethren. They insisted, and with truth, that the flesh or bodies of them and their children was just the same as that of their more fortunate brethren, as far as value was concerned. They declared that their plight was not to be helped, on account of the hold the lenders had on them.

Verse 6. Nehemiah was righteously indignant at the heartless treatment of his poor brethren. He felt that no reason existed for their actions.

Verse 7. *Consulted with myself* means that he thought over the subject, to determine what to do and say. He then rebuked the guilty ones and accused them of *exacting usury* of their brethren. The law forbade taking usury from the brethren (Ex. 22: 25), and these nobles were violating that law. Nehemiah then assembled a numerous throng to oppose this cruel disregard for the divine ordinance that had been given from Sinai.

Verse 8. *Redeemed our brethren.* When Nehemiah came back to Palestine he found that some of their brethren had been sold to the heathen. He had managed to buy a great many of them back. Now the Jews were putting their own people into the same kind of reproach through their financial dealings. By taking advantage of their straitened circumstances, they were making slaves of them just as certainly as the heathen had done. When Nehemiah caused them to see their transactions in the true light, they were made speechless, doubtless, from a feeling of shame.

Verse 9. It is always right to do right regardless of any other consideration. But an added reason exists in the fact that one's conduct is observed by the public. The heathen who were in Palestine had known about the close dealings of heartless characters. Now if they behold these Jews mistreating their own brethren, it will cause them to think of their profession of religion with contempt. This idea is taught in the New Testament. See Rom. 12: 17; 14: 16; 2 Cor. 6: 3; 1 Th. 4: 12.

Verse 10. Had it been right to exact payments of food from the people, Nehemiah and his servants would have had much the better claim for such a privilege. He was not doing so, and exhorted them not to do so any more. That is, not to take usury of their brethren for the loans they were making.

Verse 11. When a man goes into the commercial or industrial world to make a financial investment, it may be perfectly just. But that does not prove that it is right to make a profit off of those whose bodily needs call for assistance. Nehemiah knew that the whole situation was brought by the sore need of the poor brethren, and not as a legitimate business investment. He therefore bade the creditors restore all the money and properties that had been exacted as security.

Verse 12. We cannot but admire the spirit of these creditors. They evidently had not realized the real principle involved in their dealings, for they promptly agreed to do as Nehemiah requested. And to make the matter binding, he called for the priests who had the authority to administer an oath. Under oath the men were caused to promise to carry out the requirements of Nehemiah.

Verse 13. Shaking his lap was a physical illustration to signify the complete undoing that was to come to all who would break their oath. After the demonstration and comments thereon, the whole congregation voiced approval. We have the gratifying information that the promise was carried out.

Verse 14. This verse gives the information on the *time* that Nehemiah set under the king in Ch. 2: 6. He had been made governor over the land of Judah, to act under authority from Artaxerxes. Special provisions were made for whosoever was the acting governor of the country, and Nehemiah could have eaten of them lawfully. But he and his brethren supported themselves through the entire period of 12 years. He considered the straitened circumstances of the people and did not have the heart to take advantage of his rights under the legal setup.

Verse 15. Judea (Judah) was a province of the Persian Empire after the fall of Babylon. Such distant units of that vast monarchy had to be under the supervision of local governors, and such officers drew their support from the money raised by taxation. The men who held that position before took advantage of that, and could do so lawfully as far as that was concerned. Nehemiah would have been lawfully entitled to the same privileges, but was so compassionate that he drew on his own private funds in order to relieve the poor people of the burden of taxation. The former governors not only made use of the tax money, but became oppressive in the exercise of their authority, and suffered their own servants to domineer over the people. The fear of God caused Nehemiah to have regard for his fellowman.

Verse 16. *Neither bought we any land.* This means that Nehemiah did not take advantage of the financial straitness of the people. They might have been compelled to sell their land to get their tax money, and Nehemiah could have obtained it under the terms of forced "tax sale," and thus to have enriched himself at the expense of the unfortunate. That would have put him in the class of the heartless characters spoken of by Christ (Matt. 23: 14) who would "devour widows' houses."

Verse 17. Nehemiah supported a large number of his own nation, and was so hospitable that many of the foreigners were invited to eat at his table.

Verse 18. *Prepared for me.* The last 2 words are not in the original. This vast amount of food was prepared for Nehemiah and his guests. A question may be in the mind of the student about where he obtained such a great supply of goods if he did not draw on the taxes of the land. We should remember that the Jews had been a free people for about a century. Their service to the king or other ruler was that of "hired servants." Nehemiah had a very high position of employment, in that he was a personal attendant of the king, with the honorable duty of serving him his wine. All the circumstances show that he stood high in the estimation of his royal employer, and it is reasonable to conclude that he received a liberal salary.

Verse 19. The prayer of Nehemiah for God's favor was based upon the good he was doing. That is the way it always has been with man's relation to the Lord. God is no respecter of persons, but does regard those who do good.

NEHEMIAH 6

Verse 1. In Ch. 4: 6 we learned that the wall was built up all around at the same time. That is what is meant in this verse by the words *no breach*. While the gates were not yet hung, the body of the wall was complete as far as it went.

Verse 2. The enemies had tried various means to hinder the work. They tried laughing at them (Ch. 4: 3), threatened to fight them (Ch. 4: 8), and next they tried to divert their attention by inviting them to a friendly meeting in one of the plains. Regardless of their purpose for such a meeting, had Nehemiah heeded their invitation it would have meant the loss of some time in the work of the Lord. Whatever time or effort is given to the cause of an enemy of the Lord, it is bound to be at the expense of the works of righteousness and to the advantage of evildoers.

Verse 3. The brief reply of Nehemiah is centered in the words *I am doing a great work*. There is no work possible as great as that of the Lord, and to switch from it to anything else whatsoever would be a downward move. That is why Nehemiah refused to *come down* to the enemies. Moreover, he said that he would not *leave it* and come down to them. That means that if a person devotes any of his time and effort to a work that is not the Lord's, he must necessarily desert that of the Lord; he cannot work at both at once. Christ taught the same thing in what he said about it being impossible for a man to serve two masters (Matt. 6: 24).

Verse 4. Persistence is a strong force and often will accomplish success when a single effort will fail. Sanballat knew this and tried it in his attempt to hinder the work on the wall. He made his proposition 4 times and was refused each time, so that his own persistence was matched by that of Nehemiah.

Verses 5, 6. The next move was to make a charge against Nehemiah and his brethren, that they were plotting a rebellion. They thought to strengthen the accusation by quoting a man named Gashmu. He was an Arabian and was supposed to add weight to the report. But it did not, for he was only a famous gossiper. The foolish statement was made that Nehemiah was building the wall with a view of becoming a king.

Verse 7. Everyone would know it to be a serious thing to make a prediction such as charged against Nehemiah. There was no truth in the accusation, but perhaps he might suspect that some of his over-zealous friends were doing such preaching unknown to him. If such should be going on it would reach the ears of Artaxerxes, and that would mean serious trouble. Now if Sanballat could influence Nehemiah to think such reports were going the rounds, he would become concerned and want to talk it over. So it was proposed that they *take counsel together*.

Verse 8. But Nehemiah understood the scheme and hurled back the accusation that Sanballat was making the report himself. He did not merely accuse him of helping to scatter a rumor that someone had started, but that he was the one who started it out of his own heart. That would mean that he was a wicked falsifier.

Verse 9. *They all made us afraid* is to be understood as meaning they thought to frighten them. They did not succeed as they hoped, for Nehemiah had faith in God. However, he was not blind to the wickedness of his foes, and felt the need of divine help. He therefore prayed to God for strength.

Verse 10. The agitation seemed to have some effect on one of the prophets. Shemaiah had *shut up* himself in his house, which means he was keeping himself close because of fear, real or pretended. Nehemiah had learned about it, and entered his house to have a talk with him. When he got on the inside, Shemaiah suggested that they seek a safer place for protection and named the temple. He pretended that it would be a better place at night because it was not a private residence.

Verse 11. Nehemiah had two reasons for not doing as Shemaiah requested. He was not frightened; and besides that, if he were he would not enter the holy building for personal protection from bodily harm.

Verse 12. By this time Nehemiah realized that this professed prophet had accepted money from Sanballat to pay him for making the false report.

Verse 13. The object was to get Nehemiah to take refuge in the sacred house, which would have given room for reproach against him. The temple was not built to be used as a fortress. Its purpose was religious only, and for Nehemiah to have fled therein for fear of these heathen would have been to desecrate it. Such an event would have been a sweet morsel for the enemies of the Lord to boast about.

Verse 14. This verse shows that it was some of the professed people of God who were being used by Sanballat as tools for his opposition against the work of Nehemiah. But he made his appeal to God, asking him to take notice of the conduct of these false servants. Even the prophetess Noadiah sold herself to the service of God's enemies, and tried to intimidate Nehemiah.

Verse 15. As this verse is so practical and literal, there is little that needs to be said by way of comment. However, the fact that such a vast project could be brought to completion in less than two months is a wonderful tribute to the unity of operations. What adds to the merit of the work is the fact that it was performed in spite of the constant opposition and attempts at discouragement. Perhaps the key to the success was in the expressions: "The people had a mind to work," and "We made our prayer unto our God." (Ch. 4: 6, 9.) It reminds us of Paul's language in Rom. 8: 31, "If God be for us, who can be against us?"

Verse 16. It would have been a wonderful feat to build such a wall in that length of time, had there been no opposition, and had everyone helped what he could. But it was a still more marvelous thing to accomplish it in spite of their activities in trying to make the whole project a failure. That was why the heathen hung their heads in shame and disappointment. They were forced to admit (to themselves) that these Jews had accomplished the work by the help of their God.

Verses 17-19. This paragraph is a reflective picture of what had been going on while the wall was in building. The writer had just recorded the successful completion of the work, notwithstanding the interference of the enemies, and he then wished to have a renewed picture of the opposition in direct connection with the final report. In that manner the immensity of the accomplishment could be the better realized. These nobles of Judah were influenced through some intermarriages with the heathen. In the heat of turmoil over Nehemiah's work there was much gossiping back and forth, and some attempts at tattling to him. The object of it all was to put him *in fear*, but their expectation failed as we have seen.

NEHEMIAH 7

Verse 1. The doors could not be hung until the wall was completed to its full height. Thus the order of the services would be as it is stated in this verse. The porters were the janitors or gatekeepers, and they could not be appointed to their several places until the gates or doors were ready for service. The singers were expected to do part of the religious exercises. That was according to an institution of David (1 Chr. 25: 1; 2 Chr. 35: 15). The Levites were the original ones to have the supervision of the sacrificial part of the services. All of these appointments were made by Nehemiah when the building work was completed.

Verse 2. Two men are named yet a singular pronoun is used. The idea is that Hanani was the principal one considered, and Hananiah was associated with him as a helper. The second man had been in charge of the palace. The reason given for the appointment of Nehemiah's brother is significant; it was because he feared God. What a wonderful motive for selecting a man to have an important work. No personal preference or feeling of relationship entered into the consideration. If a man fears God more than others fear Him, that shows a qualification that outweighs all others.

Verse 3. The gates were not to be opened until it was far into the day. While waiting for that hour to come they must be guarded. That is the meaning of *while they stand by*. Since it would be daylight the public would be stirring, and hence the gates should be secured. The porters were therefore ordered to see that they were shut and barred. In addition to the men on duty right at the gates, the inhabitants on the inside of the city were to be called upon for guard duty. Each man was to be assigned that part of the wall nearest his own home.

Verse 4. This verse explains the precautions required in the preceding ones. The area enclosed by the wall was large and not many residences had yet been built. For that reason it was necessary to make wise distribution of the forces available. After all the attempts at preventing the work while it was in progress, Nehemiah did not wish to take any chances for violence now that the work had been completed.

Verse 5. *My God put it into my heart* means that God spoke to Nehemiah and directed him to do the thing described. The importance of keeping the line of the generations as pure as possible was the purpose of all such transactions. Had the Jews never been taken from their own country, the danger of blood mixture would not have been so great. But the 70 years of captivity, and the period of almost a century that followed, had brought them into contact with the heathen. The precaution that Nehemiah was told to take had been followed out by Zerubbabel 90 years before, and now it was deemed well to repeat the investigation. For this purpose Nehemiah summoned a gathering of the people including the leaders among them. All of these people were to be "checked" according to the official register. At this time Nehemiah found the list that had been made *at the first*, and the examination was to be made according to that.

Verses 6-73. These verses are an exact reproduction of those at Ezra 2: 1-70. As I have commented at some length on the verses at that place, the student is asked to turn to it for his information on this paragraph.

NEHEMIAH 8

Verse 1. The people responded to the call of Nehemiah when he wished to investigate their "registration number." Now they have assembled again and are seeking information. They met in the street that was near a very important gate. It was the one opening out near the water supply of the city. That was why it was called the *water gate*. The information sought this time was different from that wanted when Nehemiah called them together. They wanted to hear from the book of the law. What a wonderful motive for coming together! Also, we are told that all of the people were in this gathering, and that they had met *as one man*. Ezra was the man called for and it was for a good reason. All of the copies of the law were made by hand, and the men who did that were called scribes, in which occupation Ezra was engaged. He was also a priest (Ezra 7: 11), but his position as a scribe also was what caused him to be called this time. As his work was to reproduce the law, he certainly would have a copy of it, and also would know how to read it. The reader should note that the *law of Moses* was what *the Lord had commanded to Israel*. This is another rebuke for those who try to make a difference between the authority of Moses and that of the Lord.

Verse 2. While Ezra as a scribe would be expected to have a copy of law at hand, there was a reason also for calling on him as a priest. Lev. 10: 11; Deut. 17: 9 and Mal. 2: 7 shows that they were counted on to be ready to teach the people the knowledge of God's Word. *Hear with understanding* is rendered "listen intelligently" by Moffatt's translation. The word for *hear* is from SHAMA, and Strong's definition is, "a primitive root; to hear intelligently (often with implication of attention, obedience, etc.; causatively to tell, etc.)." *Understanding* is from BIYN and Strong's definition is, "a primitive root; to separate mentally (or distinguish), i. e., (generally) understand." This information will show us that it was no supernatural gift that was meant in the description of the ones expected to receive the law. The Word of God is a plain book, and was intended to be grasped by any person with intelligence enough to be responsible. But even such minds will be expected to give earnest attention and exert some effort in order to comprehend the meaning. In other words, they are supposed to "consider," which Isa. 1: 3 says certain ones did not.

Verse 3. The reading of the law lasted from daylight until noon. That was a sufficient length of time for one session, for it was then necessary to look after the needs for physical food. But after stating to begin with how long the reading lasted, the writer described the manner of the forenoon's procedure in the course.

Verse 4. *Pulpit of wood* was the same as a platform or rostrum. It was necessary to stand in such a place, because the audience was great and it is always better for the hearers to be in view of the speaker and vice versa. No reason is given why the men named stood on the right and left hands of Ezra while he read the law. Some of them were priests, and their presence in that attitude would show great respect.

Verse 5. The writer connects the fact of the book's being opened in the *sight of all the people* with the other fact that Ezra *was above all the people*. That agrees with the remarks about a *pulpit* in the preceding verse. We should be impressed with the action of the people at the opening of the book; they all stood up. There could not have been seats for that vast throng, hence they were sitting on the ground. But their reverence for the divine document brought them to their feet. They continued in that posture from daylight until noon. It is remarkable what people will endure if their interest in the subject is great enough.

Verse 6. To *bless the Lord* means to acknowledge him as the source of all blessings or benefits. The people endorsed the words of Nehemiah by saying *amen, amen*. In the Hebrew lexicon the word is defined "truly." The lifting up hands while bowing the heads would form a position of great respect. *Worshipped* is from SHACHAH and Strong defines it, "a primitive root; to depress, i. e. prostrate (especially reflexively in homage to royalty or to God)." The word is used in this place with regard to the posture of the body, that it was one with the face *to the ground*. That could not mean that the face was in contact with the ground, for the people were standing. It means their faces were toward the ground in a pose of respect.

Verse 7. The men named were Levites, therefore the words following, *and the Levites*, means "who were Levites." Being of that tribe it is clear that they would be the ones to *cause the people to understand the law*. The explanation of the law intensified the attention of the people so that they *stood in their place*.

Verse 8. The preceding verse states generally that the Levites caused the people to understand the law; this gives the details. *Distinctly* is from PARASH and is defined, "a primitive root; to separate, literally (to depress) or figuratively to specify)."—Strong. *Sense* is from an original that means "knowledge or understanding." We know that more than one man would not be speaking at one time. Ezra was holding the book and doing the first reading. These other Levites would then "separate" the words one from another, and give what we would call a lexical definition of them. There is an interesting paragraph in a work of secular writing which I shall quote: "During the 70 years captivity, though it does not appear that the Hebrews *entirely* lost their native tongue, yet it underwent so considerable change from their adoption of the vernacular languages of the countries where they had resided, that afterwards, on their return from exile, they spoke a dialect of Chaldee mixed with Hebrew words. On this account it was that, when the Hebrew scriptures were read, it was found necessary to interpret them to the people in the Chaldean language; as, when Ezra the scribe brought the book of the law of Moses before the congregation, the Levites were said to have caused the people to understand the law, because they *read in the book, in the law of God distinctly, and gave the sense*, and caused them to understand the reading." *Horne*, Introduction, Vol. 1, p. 190.

Verse 9. *Tirshatha* is another word for governor. Nehemiah had been put into that office over Judah (Judea) by the king of Persia. In one sentence the dual position of Ezra, priest and scribe, is stated. It would be well for those marking their Bibles to make note of this subject. The effect of hearing the law was to cause the people to weep. There is little difference between *mourn* and *weep*. There is a slight distinction, however, when used in one sentence. The first has special reference to the state of the mind, the second to the facial and voice expressions. Nehemiah and Ezra meant that so much had occurred for which to be thankful that they should neither mourn or weep, but be joyful instead.

Verse 10. Instead of giving way to mourning, the people were bidden to take enjoyment in the blessings of God. The Jews were forbidden to eat fat, yet they were here told to eat it. The word is from an entirely different Hebrew original, with an entirely different meaning, from the one in the case of the restriction. It is from MASHMAN, and Strong defines it, "fatness; but usually (figuratively and concretely) a rich dish, a fertile field, a robust man." It can thus be seen not to have any relation to the fat of animals that the Jews were forbidden to eat. The people were encouraged to enjoy these good products of the land. They were told also to send *portions* (rations) to the poor people of the country. It is significant that the exhortation to send rations to others was based on the fact that the *day was holy unto our Lord.* We here have an approved example of celebrating a day as holy unto the Lord, by making gifts of things for the enjoyment of the body.

Verses 11, 12. The people carried out the instructions of Nehemiah and Ezra. They recognized the day as holy by making gifts of the good things of life. The reason for their response to the words that had been spoken to them was the fact that they *understood them,* an important consideration.

Verse 13. Having been informed about part of the law, the people came together the next day to get more details.

Verse 14. The next thing they learned was about the feast of tabernacles instituted in the law of Moses. That is found in Lev. 23: 40-43, where the purpose of the feast is given. It was to commemorate the fact that Israel had to dwell in tents while going through the wilderness, due to their irregular times for traveling.

Verse 15. The period was observed by cutting branches from several kinds of trees and setting them up into *booths.* The original for this word is defined in the lexicon of Strong, "a hut or lair." The branches were stood up in something like the form of an Indian tepee, thus making a sort of rude and temporary shelter. It was their dwelling for 7 days of the feast, the entire length of that institution. This practice would make them appreciate the permanent homes they had in Palestine, through contrast with the tents they had had to depend on exclusively for 40 years.

Verse 16. There was a general movement of the people to celebrate the great occasion. The different places mentioned were those of convenience for the putting up of such shelters. The houses had flat roofs which would make suitable places for them. The courts were the spaces surrounding them, similar to the "yards" or lawns of modern homes. Some selected the streets near the various gates of the city. After getting these booths or brushy tepees set up, the devout Jews lived in them 7 days.

Verse 17. The writer goes back to the days of Joshua for his comparison. Since his time the Jews had not done as complete a job of keeping the feast as they did this time under the influence of Nehemiah and Ezra. The experiences of the long captivity had taught them many lessons, and among them was that of appreciation for the blessing of being at liberty in their own land. That appreciation put them in the frame of mind to be "hungry and thirsty for righteousness," and to dig further into the divine law to see what duties were there required that they had been missing.

Verse 18. The feast lasted 7 days according to the law. During that time they had the law read to them. The day following the feast was a special one. *Solemn assembly* means a holy or sabbath day. Keeping it *according to the manner* means according to the ordinances in Lev. 23: 36. It will be well for the student to read carefully the entire 23rd chapter of Leviticus and see the connection with regard to what constituted a holy or sabbath day. In that chapter it can be clearly seen that holy days and sabbath days are the same.

NEHEMIAH 9

Verse 1. *This month* means the 7th (Ch. 8: 14). That was a very important month with the Jews, for in it came the great day of atonement (10th day, Lev. 16: 29), and the feast of tabernacles that we have been considering. Now it was given added prominence by the public reading of the law. On the 24th day of the month the people came together into a voluntary season of fasting and other customary items connected with times of great concern.

Verse 2. The law had restricted them from intimate association with *strangers,* which meant those on the outside of their own nation. They attended to that matter and made the required separation on this day. When the people of God commit a trespass against him, there are two things required to get back into the divine favor. One is to adjust the wrong, the other is to make confession of the same. The children of Israel did both with regard to their unlawful alliances.

Verse 3. Two fourths of a day would reach to midday which would be an occasion for partaking of the necessities of life. Such an observance was had at the first reading of the law (Ch. 8: 3, 9-12). This circumstance teaches us that even our religious activities are not expected to interfere with the actual needs of the body.

Verses 4, 5. In view of the preceding verses, I would conclude that from here on to the end of the chapter the writer is giving us some detailed information regarding the subject matter of those verses. The present paragraph very fittingly states the names of the men who led in the exercises, that they were Levites. That was appropriate in view of Lev. 10: 11; Deut. 17: 9; Mal. 2: 7. I shall make comment on the following verses because of the interesting subject matter. It will be found to be a resume of the dealings of God with his people, beginning with the creation and coming down to the exile in the land of the captivity.

Verse 6. This verse is comprehensive. All of the material things mentioned had been worshiped by the heathen, and the Israelites had been guilty of joining in with the iniquity. They were making confession of that sin, and, as a specific expression to show that their acknowledgement was not only sincere, but that it was logical, they said the things they had been worshiping had been the creation of the one true God, whom they now promised to serve.

Verse 7. *The Lord the God* was not merely a salute of honor, it had a significance based on the practice of the times. Lord means ruler and God means a being to be worshiped. These people had been ruled over by foreigners, and they had been worshiping false gods. This expression, then, was to distinguish between unlawful rulers and false gods on the one hand, and the true One on the other. The mere changing of a man's name might not mean much, but in this place it did. *Abraham* means "father of a multitude," while *Abram* means merely "high father." It was therefore a promotion to have the change made for Abram.

Verse 8. The promise made to Abraham that his descendants were to possess the land was made to him because God found him to be a man of faith. He proved his faith by his works, in that whenever he was told to do a certain thing he always did it. The nations mentioned were heathen people who usurped the possession of land already given to Abraham and his seed. Righteousness was ascribed to God on the basis that he kept his promises to his servants.

Verse 9. The afflictions in Egypt are described in Ex. 1, and the cry by the Red Sea is found recorded in Ex. 14: 10, soon after leaving the land of Goshen.

Verse 10. This goes back to the time prior to the event mentioned in the preceding verse. It refers to the 10 plagues, recorded in Ex. 7 to 12.

Verse 11. This event is recorded in Ex. 14. It has been questioned whether the word *dry* is to be taken literally. The lexicon defines the original word "dry ground," so there should be no difficulty over it. But even that term would not necessarily mean it was 100 per cent free from moisture. We do not always use it in our everyday practice in that way. We could speak of a man's wading out of a stream onto the dry ground even though the ground might be muddy. It was used in the present case with that general meaning. The *persecutors* were the Egyptians whose dead bodies were seen by the children of Israel on the seashore (Ex. 14: 30).

Verse 12. This unusual cloud was not a rain cloud. It was bright on one side and dark on the other (Ex. 14: 19, 20), and kept the Egyptians from approaching near the Israelites all the night as they were marching.

Verse 13. The history is now moved forward to Ex. 19 and several chapters following. From Mt. Sinai God gave his law to the people. Some of these terms are more specific than others. *Judgments* especially refer to divine decisions that were necessary in cases of emergency, *Statutes* mean the formal enactments which God made independent of any certain cases. *Commandments* are more general, including both the other kind. *True laws* is a term whose significance is that the laws of God are in truth.

Verse 14. *Madest known . . . holy sabbath.* This declaration opposes the teaching of sabbatarians, that the sabbath day had been observed from the beginning. Had that been the case there would have been no occasion for God to make it known as late as the gathering at Sinai. Another thing in this verse to notice, is the commandments of God were given by the hand of Moses. That rebukes those who would distinguish between the authority in the law of God and that of Moses.

Verse 15. The *bread* was the manna, and the water was furnished the children of Israel by having a rock at Sinai smitten.

Verse 16. This is an admission of

wrongdoing on the part of the *fathers*, which means their forefathers or early ancestors. Dealt proudly refers to their stubbornness and refusal to yield to the commandments of God. All disobedience may be charged to pride, and Paul teaches that in 1 Tim. 6: 3, 4. *Hardened their necks* is just another phrase for their stubbornness, and a stiff neck is used as a figure of it.

Verse 17. Ingratitude is a common weakness of man, and is one of the most deplorable kind. Being unmindful of the deeds performed by the Lord for his people, the Israelites became restless while Moses was in the mount. *Appointed a captain to return to their bondage.* This was done at the time the spies returned from their 40 days of research. The same is referred to by Stephen in his noted speech to the Jews (Acts 7: 40). He had a different instance in mind from that in Numbers, but it is on the same line of conduct. These people in their wonderful speech acknowledged the mercy of God that was manifested, and that he did not forsake his people.

Verse 18. The history of the molten (cast) calf is in Ex. 32. It would have been foolishly false to make a metallic image to worship only, but it was blasphemous to attribute their miraculous deliverance from Egypt to such a helpless thing. In doing that the children of Israel gave God cause for great provocation, so that it would have been just to cut them off from him entirely.

Verse 19. But God's great mercy tempered his justice, and caused him to continue his divine guidance by use of the supernatural cloud.

Verse 20. The spirit of God directed the sayings of Moses, and he then gave them to the people. In this way the Lord gave his spirit to his people throughout the period of their relations to him in the wilderness. Also, in special instances he gave inspiration to others. See Ex. 31: 1-3; Num. 11: 24, 25. Another reference is made to the miraculous supply of bread and water. The bread was rained down from the skies in the form of manna, and the water was brought out of a dry rock.

Verse 21. The naming of the 40 years as a period of miraculous support does not mean that God did not care for them at other times. But special interest is centered round that subject because the children of Israel were "on the go" during that time, and did not have time nor opportunity for producing the necessities of life; for that reason God provided them as needed. One method he used in supplying their needs was to prolong the wearing qualities of their clothes. Also their feet did not *swell*. This is from an original that Strong defines to "blister." Having no opportunity for replacing their shoes or sandals, and having to travel on foot, they surely would have become footsore had they not been miraculously cared for.

Verse 22. *Divide them into corners* is rendered by Moffatt's translation as follows: "allotting them every corner of the land," and the lexicon agrees. It means that God gave unto his people the land being held by the heathen. The ones that are named in this verse were east of the Jordan River.

Verse 23. When they entered Egypt they numbered only 70 (Gen. 46: 27), and they increased to over half a million men of war besides women and children by the time they left Egypt (Num. 1: 46).

Verse 24. The promise to give all the heathen nations into the hands of the Israelites was made conditional. They were to make no covenant with those nations, but they did not fully observe the conditions. As far as they did so the Lord drove out the foreigners, and this verse should be understood in that light.

Verse 25. This verse should be understood in the same light or with the same restrictions as the preceding one. *Fat* land means a land that was productive of the good things of life. Moses had promised that they were to go into a land already provided with these desirable things (Deut. 6: 10: 11).

Verse 26. This verse is acknowledging the ingratitude of the nation of Israel. To *cast the law behind the back* means to go headlong in their own selfish way, regardless of the way the law would have them go. *Slew the prophets.* This doubtless took place on numerous occasions, but a noted instance was that by Jezebel in 1 Ki. 18: 4.

Verses 27, 28. This paragraph has special reference to the period covered by the book of Judges. The *enemies* into whose hand God sold his people were the nations in Palestine who were there when they crossed over into that land. They had been warned not to have any covenants with them, but to drive them out. They did not do so and God then suffered them to oppress his people to punish them. After a while his compassion would assert itself and he would raise up a man to deliver them from their oppressors and rule them for a time. Such men were called judges in that book but are called *saviours* in this paragraph. This in-and-out or up-and-down experience of the nation of Israel continued for 450 years (Acts 13, 20).

Verse 29. *Testifiedst against them* was in order that they could not forget "what it was all about." That made their conduct to constitute a course of conscious disobedience. It placed them in the class of wilful rebels, entitled to the judgments of God. *Withdrew the shoulder* is figurative. Burdens were carried on the shoulders, and to withdraw the shoulder would mean to refuse to perform one's duty or to help others bear the burdens of life.

Verse 30. *By thy spirit in thy prophets*. This teaches that the prophets spoke to the people for God, and in order to do so needed to be inspired. See Heb. 1: 1.

Verse 31. The nation was not utterly destroyed, but it was not because it did not deserve to be. The reason was that God was merciful and not willing to see it given up to complete ruin. That is still the reason that man is suffered to live on in his unworthiness. See 2 Pe. 3: 9.

Verse 32. This plea does not deny any of the sins of the nation for which it had been punished. It is a plea for mercy and relief from the trouble. *Terrible God* means he is a God to be feared or respected, because he is a terror against evil. *Keepest covenant and mercy*. God never breaks his covenant with his people, but they often do so with him. In that case it would be just to reject them, but mercy intercedes in their behalf and gives them another chance to serve the Lord.

Verse 33. The speakers confessed that God was *just* in what he had brought upon them in the way of punishment. That does not mean, however, that they had received all that justice would have demanded. The reason they had not was the mercy of God.

Verse 34. No class of the nation, whether official or private person, had kept the law. This fact will be noticed in many places when we come to the prophetic books. But while all were guilty, the leaders were held chiefly responsible because of their position of authority which gave them some advantages over the people.

Verse 35. The advantages mentioned in a general way in the preceding verse are specified in this. *Their kingdom* and *large and fat land* made them especially responsible because of special opportunities for doing the service of God. The same principle was taught by Christ in Luke 12: 48.

Verses 36, 37. *We are servants;* but they were not bondservants. The end of the 70 years of captivity brought an end to their service of that class. But the land was still in the possession of the foreign powers, and the Jews were enjoying it by the favor of those powers. The land was productive after the period of the 70 years of rest. In fact that was the purpose God had for requiring the rest of every 7th year, that the land might become more productive of the necessities of life (Lev. 25: 6). The captivity gave the land this rest so that at the time this great speech was being made the land *yielded much increase*. But the Jews were enjoying it at that time as a favor from the heathen only. That made them virtual servants, whereas they should have been using it as if the land belonged to them. Such a privilege was the purpose of God upon the return from captivity and readjustment of all affairs. That readjustment was to come upon condition of a complete reformation of the nation. Such a work was in the intentions of the nation, and they made their long and penitent prayer and confession preparatory to a solemn covenant (or promise) to comply with the requirements of the law.

Verse 38. The prayer and speech concluded with an expressed determination to make the promise official and binding by *seal* or signatures. That could be done either by literally writing their names to the document, or by publicly authorizing Nehemiah and Ezra to put their names down.

NEHEMIAH 10

Verses 1-8. These men sealed or endorsed the covenant referred to in the preceding chapter. They were all of priestly families except Nehemiah the tirshatha or governor. It would seem very appropriate for him to give his name at the head of the list, being the governor appointed over the province and on behalf of the Jews. There are 3 names in the list that are familiar to Bible students, Jeremiah, Obadiah and Daniel. The similarity is only a coincidence and should not confuse the reader. It was not uncommon in those times for more than one man to have the same name.

Verses 9-27. *And the Levites* is the beginning of this list. All priests were Levites, but not all Levites were priests; none but the descendants of Aaron. So there was nothing farfetched in making two separate rolls of the names standing good for the covenant.

Verse 28. We should not conclude that all of the priests and general Levites were named in the first two lists. They were evidently some outstanding men who could be considered responsible persons. Others of the assembly then manifested their approval of the act. The reason they were favorable to it can be seen in the fact that already they had made great reforms in their lives. They had put from them their foreign wives and the children that were born of them. Such conduct was the main idea in the covenant proposed, so that would account for their willingness to cooperate with the endorsers of that great document.

Verse 29. *Curse* and *oath* are named as separate acts although there is not much difference. When used in one sentence the first means an offer to receive some severe penalty if a certain agreement is not carried out. The second means that the curse was supported by the oath; it was agreed to under oath. *God's law . . . given by Moses* are the terms that catch our eye again. They show that no difference can be made between what Moses wrote and what God spoke with his mouth.

Verse 30. One of the most, if not the most important of the restrictions of the law pertained to the marriage institutions. That was not especially from the legal standpoint, but because of a desire to keep a blood line pure from Abraham to the promised seed. For that reason the marriage with foreigners was forbidden.

Verse 31. It was agreed to observe the sabbath day according to the law of Moses, which included the stoppage of all commercial transactions. *Sabbath or . . . holy day.* There was no difference between the primary meaning of the two words, only that the first usually referred to the 7th day of the week. The phrase might well be worded, "sabbath or other holy days." *Leave the seventh year* means to let the land rest in that year. It was the violation of that law which brought upon the nation the 70 years of captivity. *Execution of every debt.* In Ch. 5 is an account of the oppressive treatment of the poor. The more fortunate were taking advantage of the others in the matter of lending money. They did so on condition of heavy usury, and to secure the loans they had taken from them their land. All such dealings were to be discontinued under the terms of the covenant.

Verse 32. The contribution stipulated here was voluntary, and in addition to the specific requirements of the law as to their income.

Verse 33. The preceding verse mentioned the service in general, this gives the specific services. The *shewbread* was the unleavened bread that must be placed on the table. It was in 12 loaves and was renewed every weekly sabbath. *Continual* means "regular," and applied to the meat (meal) offerings that were made in connection with other sacrifices. *Continual burnt offering* is a phrase referring to what is commonly called the "daily sacrifice." See Ex. 29: 38-42. *Of the sabbaths* was referring to the doubling of the daily sacrifice on the sabbath days (Num. 28: 9). The new moon was the first of the month (1 Sam. 20: 24, 27), and was always a holy day. The *set feasts* referred to the three annual feasts described in Lev. 23. This voluntary contribution was for the support of any or all of the divine services.

Verse 34. The Levites were not required to produce any materials, because they were not given an allotted portion of the land as were the others of the tribes. But this verse included the people, which accounts for the mention of the wood to be furnished After it was furnished by *the people,* the priests and Levites took charge of it and made the proper use in the service of the house of the Lord. Not all of the eligible men would be needed at one time, hence they *cast the lots* to decide the turns of service. The lot was one of the means used in Biblical times to decide questions. See Prov. 16: 33 and Heb. 1: 1.

Verse 35. The law had required that the first of everything be devoted to the Lord. It would include the first of the fruit of trees and of the ground.

Verse 36. *Firstborn of our sons.* The Lord never did require human sacrifices, but he did claim all the firstborn of their sons as his special possession (Ex. 13: 2). He later exchanged them for the entire tribe of Levi (Num. 3: 12). After that the Lord required a certain offering to be made upon the birth of the first child (Num. 18: 14-16). That is what these people meant to do when they agreed to devote the *firstborn of our sons*. Also, they owed a certain consideration to the Lord upon the increase of their beasts. All of these things were to be placed at the disposal of *the priests that minister in the house of our God*.

Verse 37. Grain that had been made ready for dough was not to be exempt from the contribution. In addition to the *first* of everything, the *tithe* or tenth of all crops of the ground must be devoted. It was turned over to the Levites because they had no ground of their own for farming.

Verse 38. *Tithes of the tithes*. The Levites had no means of productive income, so they lived on the tithes of the other tribes. They in turn were required to contribute a tithe or tenth of what had been given them by the other tribes.

Verse 39. All of these products were to be brought to the house of the Lord; not expect the priests to come after them. *Priests that minister*. Not all eligible men were acting at one time. Those who were needed for the service at any given time were the ones meant by these words.

NEHEMIAH 11

Verse 1. There were too many of the people for all to reside in Jerusalem, and besides this, they had their individual homes and it was natural for them to want to live there. It was thought necessary, however, for some to remain in the city. So the *rulers* agreed to dwell in the city. That word is from SAR and Strong defines it, "a head person of any rank or class." It could thus include men of the various offices if they happened to be outstanding through personal influence and efficiency. But it would be fair for them to have some help in the holy service, and the people agreed to furnish one out of every 10 to join their *rulers* in it. The selection was made by casting lots. See Prov. 16: 33 and Heb. 1: 1.

Verse 2. It was quite a sacrifice to to give up their home residences and dwell in the city. That was appreciated by the others who blessed them (extended best wishes) for the good deed. It was a service that benefited the whole congregation.

Verse 3. This and several verses following will give a list of persons, of the ones to reside in the city of Jerusalem, and the ones to dwell in other places.

Verse 4. The tribes of Judah and Benjamin had possessed the territory that included Jerusalem and that surrounding it, and those tribes naturally felt disposed to furnish a representation for the service. The group of names is given generation by generation to show the lineal connection with an important ancestor. He is here called *Perez*, which is another spelling for Pharez in Gen. 38: 29, in which chapter he is seen to have been a son of Judah.

Verses 5, 6. More of the descendants of Parez are named, then a summing up is stated of the number altogether which is 468. This will give us some idea of the importance of that son of Judah, conceived and born under such unusual circumstances. See Gen. 38 for the history of the case.

Verses 7-9. The little tribe of Benjamin had become sufficiently numerous to furnish 928 men for the service in the city. This particular group had its own supervisor whose name was Joel. The Judah named as second ruler is only another man with the same name as the one heading the tribe and it is a coincidence of names.

Verses 10, 11. There would always be a need for priestly services in Jerusalem. *Hilkiah, Zadok and Ahitub* are among the names with whom we are somewhat familiar.

Verse 12. Since the brethren of the priestly men numbered 822, it is easy to understand why all would not be named. Then another outstanding man is named, *Adiah*, and a few of his lineal ancestors.

Verse 13. The brethren of *Adaiah* numbered 242. Next another man is named. *Adaiah*, and a few of his ancestors, engaging in the work about the Lord's house.

Verse 14. The brethren of *Amashai* numbered 128. They are said to have been men of *valour*. This word in the Old Testament always comes from CHAYIL and Strong defines it as follows: "probably a force, whether of men, means or other resources, an army, wealth, virtue, valor, strength."

Its outstanding meaning is force or strength.

Verses 15, 16. These additional names of the Levites are given because of special reasons. *Shabbethai* and *Jozabad* were among some chief Levites, and they had the oversight of the *outward* business of the house of God. That is from CHIYTSOWN which Strong defines, "properly the (outer) wall side; hence exterior; figuratively secular (as opposed to sacred)." A system as extensive as the Mosaic would have much need for services on the outside of the capital city and on the outside of the temple that would be considered necessary though not strictly religious. The thought might be compared with the work of a janitor of a church house, keeping up the fires or mowing the lawn. Such work is necessary and yet is considered secular.

Verse 17. *Mattaniah* was a descendant of the sons of Asaph, already known to us as a unit of musical performers in the days of David. This man was appointed as leader of the song and prayer service. He had others associated with him in the exercise.

Verse 18. The *holy city* was Jerusalem, and of the great tribe of Levi 284 were therein. They were there because some services could be lawfully performed only by them; a special consideration occasioned by the event in Ex. 32: 26.

Verse 19. The gates of the city had to be opened and closed at proper times. They were also to be guarded against the entrance of questionable persons. The men with this job were called porters and there were 172 of them appointed.

Verse 20. Most of this chapter has dealt with the groups who were stationed inside Jerusalem. This short verse is given us to keep in mind the fact that the people of Judah not so employed were in order, each residing in his own inheritance.

Verse 21. The writer comes back into the city again to designate the location of some of the classes. *Ophel* is defined by Strong as "a ridge in Jerusalem." Smith's Bible Dictionary says it was evidently the residence of the priests. The Nethinims were a special class of servants so designated in the days of Solomon. There were some of them residing in this part of Jerusalem, and Ziba and Gispa supervised them.

Verse 22. *Uzzi* was a sort of over-seer-at-large in Jerusalem, to direct the services of the Levites. The singers, men following the practice instituted by the sons of Asaph in the days of David, had charge of that service in the house of God.

Verse 23. The singers were to serve in turns and the change was to be made daily. That made it necessary for a goodly number of them to be in the city all the time. *King's commandment.* We do not suppose that Artaxerxes was personally concerned with the religious activities of the Jews. But he had become favorably disposed toward them, and had given orders (Ezr. 8 and 9) that their wishes should be carried out.

Verse 24. *At the king's hand* means about the same as the remarks in the preceding verse. Moffatt's translation expresses the thought in this verse by saying the work was "in the hands of the king's representatives."

Verses 25-35. The subject matter of all these verses is practically the same, hence I have grouped them into one paragraph. It has to do with the more open parts of the country. The fields attached to the towns or villages were for the production of crops and cattle. These members of the tribes of Judah and Benjamin had the use of the land by right of inheritance. They were dispersed over the territory at points of advantage. Some of the places mentioned are familiar to us; among them are Kirjath-arba, Beer-sheba, Ziklag, Adullam, Lachish, Michmash, Bethel, Anathoth and Nob.

Verse 36. The Levites were not given landed estates under the law, but were to dwell in cities within the possessions of the other tribes. This verse means that sections of the tribe of Levi were located throughout the possessions of Judah and Benjamin.

NEHEMIAH 12

Verses 1-21. It will help to understand the apparent repetition of all these names to quote, in part, from Smith's Bible Dictionary. "The book of Nehemiah, like the preceding one of Ezra, is clearly and certainly not all by the same hand. By far the most important portion, indeed, is the work of Nehemiah; but other portions are either extracts from various chronicles and registers or supplementary narratives and reflections, some apparently by Ezra." Much of the discussion of this chapter, therefore, should be regarded as information on the state of affairs at different times. I shall make comments on the merits of the several verses, not always trying to settle upon any specific date for the incidents that may be under consideration.

Verse 22. *Chief of the fathers* is not an official title for these Levites. They had no extra classification under the law except that of having the execution of the law. But in the eyes of the nation in which they were living they were considered in the light of this phrase. That estimate was had of them down to the time of *Darius the Persian*. If the reader will consult the chart (see suggestions for chart at Ezra 3: 8) he will see that this king was reigning from 521 to 484 B. C. This will give us a good view of the light in which the Levites were held by the secular governments.

Verse 23. See comments at 1 Ki. 14: 19 for explanation of *chronicles*.

Verse 24. This special song and praise service was instituted by David, and the account of it is in 1 Chr. 25. *Ward over against ward* means they took their turns.

Verse 25. The porters were stationed at the gates, whence the name of their occupation. But the special task of the porters named in this verse was to guard the treasures coming in through the gate. *Thresholds* is from a word meaning "a collection of offerings," according to Strong's lexicon.

Verse 26. This verse is a statement showing that the various kinds of works described in the preceding verses were performed for several years prior to the time of the writing. The reader is requested to consult again my comments in the latter part of the first paragraph in this chapter. The activities covered the days of Nehemiah and Ezra, the most outstanding men in this part of the narrative.

Verse 27. During the building of the wall most of the congregation were living in their own homes, including the Levites. When the dedication of the wall took place it was especially appropriate to have them present, in view of their official position in the nation. They were counted on to join in the services with the music and singing.

Verse 28. The special group of singers responded to the call from the surrounding territory. *Netophatai* was a district in Palestine and it had a number of villages. The singers in those burgs came to the dedication.

Verse 29. *House of Gilgal* means the families in the neighborhood of Gilgal. That vicinity furnished some singers for the service, as did the families from the fields (country) around Geba and Asmaveth. The persons living in the territories named wished to be in readiness for the call to service. For that purpose they had built themselves villages (small dwellings) around Jerusalem.

Verse 30. The priests were the Levites who descended from Aaron. There were too many of them to be needed in active service at any one time. When the turn of any of the eligible men came, they had to observe the ceremonies of the law as to uncleanness that might have come upon them during the time they had not been serving. While in the exercises of ceremonial cleansing they extended it to include the wall.

Verses 31-37. One group was to climb up to the top of the wall and turn to the right. They were to be distributed along on the wall in the order named, and there they were to engage in praise service.

Verses 38, 39. This group turned to the left and were spread along the wall as far as the *prison gate*, or guard gate.

Verses 40-43. Nehemiah was in the last named group, and both groups halted and all joined in song and praise to God for the great mercies he had given the people.

Verse 44. The service mentioned in this verse has been referred to in previous passages, so nothing new is noted. It is well, however, to observe that some order and system had been arranged. *That waited* means the Levites who "stood by" to be in readiness when called upon to serve.

Verses 45, 46. *Ward* means duty or obligation; the singers and porters (janitors) both did theirs, which was according to the order that had been given by David.

Verse 47. *All Israel* means the congregation in general. They were required to support the service of God with their contributions. That is what is meant by *gave the portions*. The period that was being especially considered by the writer was that in the days of Zerubbabel and Nehemiah. A glance at the chart will show that to have comprised almost 100 years.

NEHEMIAH 13

Verse 1. *That day* means the day they had the reading of the law (Ch. 8). The Moabites and Ammonites were descendants from Lot. They had some of the same blood as did those descended from Abraham, but were always counted as enemies of God's people. They were to be permanently rejected from any relation with the congregation. The place where we read this is Deut. 23: 3-5.

Verse 2. The special complaint against these people was their alliance with Balaam, and they also had refused the Israelites the common necessities of life. It was at the time they arrived in the plains of Moab east of Jordan (Num. 22).

Verse 3. The obedience of the people was prompt; it was *when they heard the law.*

Verses 4, 5. There is a break in the narrative here. Sometime after the events leading up to the end of the preceding verse, Nehemiah's term of 12 years expired and he had returned to his duty with Artaxerxes. After he had left Jerusalem, the circumstances of these verses took place which I shall now notice. Eliashib was the priest and should have guarded the house of God with care. But he was influenced by Tobiah, who was a favorite slave of Sanballat, to allow him the special privilege of an apartment in the holy building. He occupied the space that had been devoted to the storing of the articles intended for the sacrifices. This was an awful desecration of the sacred house of God.

Verse 6. The information in this verse is what authorized the remarks at the beginning of the preceding paragraph. After Nehemiah had returned and resumed his service for the king of Persia, he heard of the corruptions that had crept into the service in Jerusalem. The king again favored him with a grant of leave of absence.

Verses 7, 8. Nehemiah again arrived in Jerusalem and found the reports to have been true. He was sorely grieved over the evil conduct of the priest, and cast out all of this heathen's household stuff.

Verse 9. The casting out of the secular materials would rid the place of the actual uncleanness. The law of Moses, however, would not be satisfied until the ceremonial cleansing was done. That was performed at the commandment of Nehemiah.

Verse 10. As a natural result of such an unlawful use of the space given over to Tobiah, the proper support of the Levites and singers had been neglected. Not only so, but the situation had frightened them so that they fled to their private dwellings.

Verse 11. Nehemiah rebuked the men who were guilty of the abuses described above. *Gathered them together* means the Levites and singers who had been crowded out of their rightful place, were all returned and encouraged to expect their support again.

Verse 12. In obedience to the commandment of Nehemiah, the people of the tribe of Judah brought the tithes of the products of the *treasuries* (storehouses) to be used according to the law that was given by Moses.

Verse 13. Nehemiah did not take any risk in the handling of the products. He appointed certain men to supervise them, and the selection was made from those who were *counted faithful.* Since their office (work) was to distribute these necessities of life to the proper persons, it was very advisable to put it in the hands of such men.

Verse 14. Nehemiah was a man of prayer and we read frequently of his turning to God. His prayer that God would not *wipe out* (forget) his deeds for the house of the Lord did not imply that he would be short in his rewarding of merit. The disciples were taught to ask God not to lead them into temptation (Matt. 6: 13). That did not mean that he would so lead them; it was to be their expression of confidence in the good leadership of the Lord. In the same sense, Nehemiah's prayer was his expression of his faith in the divine mercies and reward for righteousness.

Verse 15. The law against manual labor and secular business on the sabbath day was still in force. But Nehemiah found this was being violated and he rebuked the guilty ones while they were in the act.

Verse 16. The violation of the sabbath was not permitted even in the case of the heathen. The evil was made worse by the practice of the Jews, in that they patronized these unlawful transactions.

Verses 17, 18. Nehemiah did not merely rebuke the ones responsible for the corruption, but called their attention to some history. He reminded them of the punishment that God had brought upon their fathers for just this kind of sin. He accused them of *profaning the sabbath*, which was done by using the sacred day for worldly purposes.

Verse 19. *Gates . . . began to be dark* means that darkness began to fall on the gates. As soon as Nehemiah saw that condition in the evening before the sabbath, he ordered the gates closed to remain so until after the sabbath. As a precaution against any attempt to override the rule and bring in the produce, some guards were placed.

Verses 20, 21. It was well that the watchmen were set at the gates. Some commercial men lingered near them a time or two, hoping doubtless to catch an opportunity for trading contrary to the regulations that had been established. Nehemiah warned them that they would be given rough treatment if they did not leave. They heeded the warning and came no more on the sabbath days.

Verse 22. The Levites were all eligible for the service about the holy city, but ceremonial fitness under the law required them to be entirely separated from any common objects or practices. Hence they were commanded to make the necessary adjustments in their condition, that they could serve as guards at the gates on the sabbath.

Verses 23, 24. A reformation of the marriage situation had been carried out before this (Ezr. 9 and 10), but here were some who either were overlooked at that time, or had relapsed into the unlawful relationship again. And, as usual, when the good associates with the bad, the latter has the greater influence. The children of these unlawful marriages took up the language of the heathen.

Verse 25. *Cursed them* means he described their sinful state to their face. He even used physical punishment on some of them. Since the Mosaic system of government was civil as well as religious, it was fitting that special offenders be so punished.

Verses 26, 27. Nehemiah strengthened his criticism of their conduct by citing the case of Solomon. Even as great a man as he was affected by evil surroundings through his unlawful marriages. *Outlandish* is from NOKRI and Strong's definition is, "strange, in a variety of degrees and applications (foreign, non-relative, adulterous, different)." In 1 Ki. 11: 1 Solomon is said to have loved many strange (NOKRI) women. As far as the information goes, all of Solomon's wives were from a land outside of his own proper country. The force of the word may be seen by writing it "out-landish."

Verse 28. There was one special case of unlawful marriages noted by Nehemiah. A grandson of the high priest had gone so far as to marry a daughter of Sanballat, the man who was the enemy of the work from the first. *Chased* is from BARACH which is defined as follows: "a primitive root; to bolt, i. e. figuratively to flee suddenly."—Strong. The expression, then, means that Nehemiah used some kind of force that caused this man to run away as in fear.

Verse 29. Nehemiah was especially grieved because the sacred office of the Levitical priesthood had been defiled.

Verse 30. The holy office was rectified by expelling all strangers, people of foreign blood, and placing the *wards* or charges with the proper persons.

Verse 31. Nehemiah completed the reformative work so that the service could again be pure. He asked to be remembered only in proportion to the good he had done.

ESTHER 1

General remarks: The reader is requested to make the following notation in the sixth column of the chart: "Josephus places the history of Esther in this reign." It is true that most secular authors place the story in the preceding reign. I have accepted the word of Josephus in preference to the others because of the fact that he was an educated Jew, and certainly had better opportunity for understanding such a subject than the others. And especially is that consideration worth much in view of the fact that he lived many centuries ago, when the materials for historic writing were more plentiful than at a later date.

This book, like that of Ruth, contains a very interesting story of love and intrigue, that outshines any mere human composition. However, that was not the main purpose in giving us the book. Like the other book mentioned, it was composed to show the fulfillment of a very important prophecy, all of which will be revealed in course of the story. We should bear in mind that it is an inset historically into the main history of the Persian Empire. But the motive in giving it to us is to show the fulfillment of a prediction that God made many centuries before. The circumstances of the times brought about the opportunity for that noted completion of God's decree.

Verse 1. We have already seen in many instances that more than one man in olden times had the same name. This Ahasuerus is not the one in Ezra 4: 6, but one who lived many years afterward. As shown in the chart, he was the man who was called Artaxerxes (Longimanus) in secular history. He was the one on the Persian throne at the time that Ezra and Nehemiah performed their wonderful works. This verse shows him to have been a powerful monarch, and held sway over a large territory.

Verse 2. *Shushan* is sometimes spelled Susa. It was the capital of the Persian Empire at the time covered by this book.

Verse 3. *Power* is from a word that means strength and influence. The phrase means that the *princes and his servants* represented the most powerful men in his kingdom, *Persia and Media*. The government that was in world power at the time of our story is known in history as the Medo-Persian Empire. A quotation from Smith's Bible Dictionary will explain how the empire with its hyphenated title originated: "Of all the ancient Oriental monarchies the Median was the shortest in duration. It was overthrown by the Persians under Cyrus, B. C. 558, who captured its king, Astyages. The treatment of the Medes by the victorious Persians was not that of an ordinary conquered nation. Medes were appointed to stations of high honor under Cyrus and his successors. The two nations seem blended into one, and we often find reference to this kingdom as that of the 'Medes and Persians.' Dan. 5: 28; 6: 8, 12, 15." From this account we will understand why the two parts are in the name of the empire. The supremacy of the Persians over the Medes also can be understood, and will account for the fact that the monarchy is generally referred to simply as the Persian Empire. When the two names are used together, it is because that in point of date, the Medes were first, and hence the order in which the two parts are used. But the superiority as to power and extent was ascribed to the Persians. Not long after this powerful king came to the throne he made the banquet reported.

Verse 4. The festivities continued 180 days, during which the proud king exhibited his riches and other marks of glory. It was a season of pride and vanity, for the Persians generally were puffed up over the dignity of their authority.

Verse 5. The long feast recorded in the preceding verse was for the large gathering of notables out of the vast provinces of the king's domain. Afterward he made another feast for the members of his immediate household, or close attendants of the palace. In this feast no distinction was made between the classes of attaches of the court. The feast was held in the garden (fenced court) of the palace and lasted 7 days.

Verse 6. The whole scene was one of splendor, and the appointments suggested a week of the most abandoned dissipation. The king had pillars of marble erected, on which were suspended luxurious drapes of brilliant hues. These hangings were tied with linen cords that were passed through rings of silver. As this banquet was to last a week, provision was made for sleeping by furnishing beds made of gold and silver. These beds rested on a pavement of black marble, inlaid with materials of red, blue and white, forming a beautiful mosaic surface.

Verse 7. For many years it was thought proper style to have the pieces in sets for the table in similar patterns. Later people thought it was an advancement to have a variety, but the Persians thought of that long before us. The wine was served to the guests at the banquet in vessels, no two of which were alike. *Royal wine in abundance* means there was no shortage of the servings because they were taken from the king's own supply. His state of fortune was so great that the wine was unlimited.

Verse 8. *None did compel.* The law of the king was that each guest should be permitted to "take it or leave it" when the wine was offered. In that respect that heathen king manifested more decency than modern society leaders. At the present time it is regarded highly improper and offensive when a guest objects to drinking. It will be insisted that the guest "have a drink with me."

Verse 9. The dignity of the feast made by the queen differed from that of the king in that no authority was represented. But Vashti had the use of the royal apartments belonging to her husband. As the guests of Ahasuerus were men of his household, so the queen appropriately served her banquet to the women of honored rank.

Verses 10, 11. After 7 days of drinking the king became *merry with wine*. The first is from an original word with a variety of meanings. The connection here shows it means the king was "feeling good" as the saying often goes when speaking of one who has been "imbibing freely." It is characteristic of intoxication that it will intensify the coarser sentiments of the one indulging. Under the influence of the wine the king stooped to make a most disgraceful attempt upon his wife. He ordered her to come into the presence of his royal male guests to show her beauty. She is described in the text as being *fair to look on*. The key to the phrase is the third word. It is from an original that Strong defines, "a view (the act of seeing); also an appearance (the thing seen), whether (real) a shape (especially if handsome comeliness; often plural the looks) or (mental) a vision." It is easy to see in this definition that Vashti had a figure that was attractive, and one that would especially make an appeal to the opposite sex. There is a footnote in Josephus, taken from the writings of a Chaldean. This note states that Ahasuerus intended to show his wife to his male guests unclothed. This note is evidently correct, for the inspired writer tells us that she was fair to look on. That means she had a body that would attract the eye of a man. And it is said in direct connection with the other statement, that Ahasuerus wanted to show her beauty, *for* she was fair to look on.

Verse 12. Vashti refused to come at the king's commandment. Considering the purpose of the king, we can only honor her for her refusal to submit to the indignity. It was not an entirely unusual thing for a Persian ruler to call for his wife (Ch. 4: 10, 11), so Vashti had no reason to refuse to come at the mere fact that the king had called for her. Her refusal must therefore have been because she knew the purpose of the king in making the call. Every law of decency and self-respect would justify her action, and condemn the brutal and criminal attempt of the inhuman king. We would expect such a specimen of human flesh to become angry at the action of Vashti. He had been "stung" by his wife, the person whom he doubtless considered his personal property. Besides, it had been done to the knowledge of his royal guests, who evidently had been led to expect being gratified in their fiendish desire for immoral entertainment at the expense of this beautiful woman's honor and modesty.

Verses 13-15. Something must be done, the king thought, to cover the shame that had been heaped upon him by the disobedience of his wife. It was his practice to consult his *men which knew the times*. That means men among the sages who were supposed to give good counsel on the affairs of state. They were to advise what the law would authorize to be done to a queen who refused to obey her king.

Verses 16-18. Memucan was spokesman for the 7 wise men. He told the king that the action of Vashti had wronged him. But it would not stop there, for the report would reach the ears of the women of Persia and Media, and all over the country. When they would hear of the action of Vashti, and if she were allowed to "get by" with it, they would be encouraged to *despise* (belittle) their own husbands. If a queen can act thus against the king, then surely no other woman need obey her husband.

Verse 19. The whole proposition may be considered as a "face-saving" gesture. There would really be no need for a royal commandment that the queen come no more before the king. Under the rules already in force (Ch. 4: 10, 11), all that would have been necessary would be not to call for her. The action therefore was to create an appearance of authority over the queen. *Give her royal estate unto another* meant to demote her so that she would feel the humiliation as a penalty. Moreover, the decree was to be incorporated into the regular laws of the Persians and Medes. The object of that was to be sure that neither the king nor anyone else could revoke it. There was a foolish notion among those people that man could make a law that was so completely right that it could not be improved. If this decree of the king became a part of the regular statutes, the fate of Vashti's honor would be fixed. That is the significance of the words *that it be not altered*.

Verse 20. The preceding verse revealed the motive of the proposed decree as it would affect the king and queen directly. This one shows the other motive to have been concerned over the dignity of the men in general throughout the empire. When the decree became a part of the unchangeable law, it was then to be published to all the citizens. Such a serious action would certainly have a profound effect on all the wives with regard to their own husbands. Fearing a similar treatment for themselves, they would be induced to yield obedience to their lords.

Verses 21, 22. The king was pleased with the suggestion of Memucan. He doubtless was still smarting under the injury to his pride, and was in a mind to do anything that would seem to be in the nature of revenge. He later would have recalled the vicious edict had he the power to do so. But he sent letters into all the provinces of his mighty empire. They included so much territory that not all the people spoke the same language. The decree was therefore translated into the speech of each province. We have no information on the effect it had on the various people, when they received the hasty action of the haughty monarch. But the publishing of it was evidently a solace to the wounded pride of the king, and also must have given some satisfaction to the princes who had become uneasy over their own authority.

ESTHER 2

Verse 1. *He remembered Vashti.* This could not refer merely to an act of the memory, for the king would not forget his wife in that sense. *And what she had done* should be connected in thought with the other italicized words. Moffatt's translation which helps to clarify this place is as follows: "He recalled what Vashti had done and the edict against her." I will also quote Josephus on this incident: "But the king having been fond of her, he did not well bear a separation, and yet by the law he could not admit of a reconciliation, so he was under trouble, as not having it in his power to do what he desired to do." The thing that distressed the king most was the thought that his fleshly desires had been cut off from gratification by his rash edict. This conclusion is supported by what follows in the text immediately after the statement about his remembering her. The servants made their suggestion about the virgins in direct connection with, and as a solution for, the distress of the king. This proves the statement that his worry was over his disappointment at not being able to expect the gratification of his desires of the flesh.

Verse 2. We all would know that a purely sentimental love for his wife would not be satisfied by merely finding the virgins. But the servants knew the character of the king, and concluded that he would be appeased by the prospect of lustful indulgence. The virgins of the realm were to be sacrificed to his desires.

Verse 3. *All the fair young virgins* were to be gathered, not just some one to take the place of Vashti. The purpose of getting so many will appear soon. The word *fair* is from an original that means "a shapely and beautiful form of body." These girls were to be collected, as so many cattle, by officers appointed and authorized to take possession of them and take them from their homes. They were then to be turned over to *Hege*, spelled also *Hegai*. He is called a chamberlain in the text, but the word means a eunuch, supposed to be just the right kind of person to be entrusted with a group of young virgins being kept for the use of the king. They were to be taken to the capital city where the palace was located and placed in the *house of the women*, which was about the same as a harem. *Things for purification* will be noticed in V. 12.

Verse 4. *Pleaseth the king.* The first word is formed from two Hebrew originals, the first of which means "beautiful," and the second means "eye." So the phrase means that the girl having a body that looked beautiful to the eye of the king was to be put in the place of Vashti. The proposition was favorable to Artaxerxes (secular name for *Ahasuerus*), and he ordered it to be carried out. It will not be forgotten that God had a hand in this transaction as a whole, whose purpose will be seen near the close of this book. When the Lord has something special to be accomplished that requires the services of a not too virtuous man, he always finds the man already having the qualifications and therefore does not induce any man to become something he had not been before. But all these considerations do not justify the motives such a man discloses. I believe it will be well to make further reference to Josephus, and get his picture of this lustful king, and his shameful treatment of the girls: "And when the eunuch thought the virgins had been sufficiently purified, in the forementioned manner, and were now fit to go to the king's bed, he sent one to be with the king every day. So when he had accompanied with her [had intimate relations], he sent her back to the eunuch." The quotations in this and the first paragraph of this chapter are from Josephus, Antiquities, Book II, Chapter 6, Section 2.

Verse 5. Tribal relations were regarded very highly in ancient times, hence the pains taken in this and many other instances to trace them out.

Verse 6. The reader has previously learned that the Babylonian captivity was accomplished in 3 divisions or sections. That was while studying 2 Ki. 24 and 25. The 2nd one was in the days of Jeconiah, otherwise spelled Jehoiachin. At that time Mordecai was taken to Babylon, together with "all the princes, and all the mighty men of valor" (2 Ki. 25: 14). Ezekiel was another one of these mighty men.

Verse 7. *Brought up* means he nourished or reared the girl who was his cousin, her parents having died when she was young. Of course she would be in the same situation with Mordecai as to the captivity, hence we find her in Persia with him. *Fair and beautiful.* The first is from two originals, the one meaning "beautiful" and the other meaning, "outline, i. e. figure or appearance."—Strong. The last of the italicized words is practically the same in meaning as the first, and was used by the writer evidently for emphasis. The phrase means to describe a girl with a beautiful form, one to please the eye of a man like the king. We are not to suppose that Esther had no other qualities than those of her body. The story will show her to have been a modest, sweet, truthful, respectful girl, and genuinely unselfish. But those were not the traits that caused her to be chosen by the officer, for he did not know about them, neither did the king upon his first relations with her.

Verse 8. To the "outside world" it would seem as a matter-of-course event that Esther would be included in this group, since she possessed all of the general characteristics of body that had been stipulated. God's purpose in all this story was to get her into the intimacy of the king, and it was done by the drag-net method employed. Had that plan not been used, then some special one would have been necessary. But that would have roused the suspicions of the king and all the others concerned, and the intentions of the Lord would have been hindered if not prevented.

Verse 9. *Maiden pleased him* means she pleased Hegai (Hege). Of course it means she pleased him from the standpoint of the kind of girl that would likely please the king. *Gave her things for purification.* The officers sent out through the empire were to make a collection of all the eligible girls. That was a general and extensive work. Had they brought in some one who did not "pass inspection" under the eye of Hege, she would have been deferred at least for further examination. *Obtained kindness* means she was favored by him, by being given the necessary things for the season of purification (V. 12). *Such things as belonged to her* is merely a fuller statement than the one just before it. In other words, the eunuch was so well satisfied that Esther would rank high in the eyes of the king that he showed her great favor. He *preferred her* by giving her a special apartment in the house of the women. Maidens associated with women of distinction was a common practice in Biblical times. (Gen. 16: 1; 29: 24, 29; Ex. 2: 5; 2 Ki. 5: 2; Prov. 31: 15.)

Verse 10. Esther did not know any reason for not telling her relatives about her situation. She was merely doing what her cousin, who was older than she and who was her guardian, had told her to do. Neither do we know what Mordecai had in mind, unless he was being influenced by a Higher Power. The whole plan needed to be carried out wisely or it might fail.

Verse 11. Mordecai had a parent-like interest in Esther, having cared for her from her young childhood. There could have been nothing but the most affectionate nearness between them. He knew of the edict of the king, followed by the proposition of the servants. He also was aware that his precious cousin, who was also his ward, had been taken into the house of women, as a possible though involuntary candidate for the king's bed. If she were sent out of this house on that mission, what might be her lot after he is through with her. No wonder, then, that *Mordecai walked every day before the court of the women.*

Verse 12. There was nothing supernatural in this purification process. It was much in line with modern practices with perfumes and various kinds of "make-up" and application of cosmetics. The main difference was in the greater length of time used and the attention to formality observed. These girls were being prepared to spend a night with the king of Persia. It was possible for any given one of them to be chosen to succeed the deposed Vashti who had been exiled from the throne and bed of the king. Since the choice was to be made on the basis of bodily attraction, it was thought necessary to make every effort to please. By a liberal use of perfumes and other cosmetics the aroma of the body would gratify the olfactory sense of the king, the form of her body would please his eye, and both qualities would intensify the pleasure of another sense, that of touch or feeling. Every girl was required to spend one year in this preparation of her body before being called upon to go to the king.

Verse 13. The girls were to await their turns for going in to the king's private apartment. There is no definite information as to the things a girl desired to be given her to take into the bedroom of the king. Doubtless it referred to some of the little niceties that any girl might think would add to her personal charm.

Verse 14. Each girl spent a night with the king. In the morning she did not return to the *house of the women* from where she came, for her relation to the king had been changed. Having had intimate relations with him she was no longer a virgin and hence could not properly rejoin the other girls. But she was sent into the custody of a different eunuch, the one who kept the *concubines*. That word did not mean what it does today. The only practical difference between that and a wife was in regard to property rights. In those ancient times when plurality of wives was tolerated even among the Jews, there was no moral objection against a concubine. A significant thought here is that the girl was classed among the concubines after having intimate relations with the king. That was the only basis of marriage given by the Lord in the beginning. See Gen. 2: 24; Matt. 19: 5. After this one night's experience the girl was classed as a concubine only, and did not again come into the king's presence unless he called for her. That would mean that her night's association with him would not entitle her to any of the legal rights of property or royal dignity.

Verse 15. Esther left it to the judgment of the eunuch as to what things to take with her to the king's apartment. She fared as well as the ones who may have made special requests along that line, in the eyes of the observers. In fact, a womanly spirit and modest behaviour are the best ornaments a woman can have. (1 Pe. 3: 4.)

Verse 16. Esther was in Persia, but the writer used the Jewish calendar. She was taken into the king's house in the 10th month, named Tebeth. Ahasuerus had been reigning 7 years, and hence the selection of a woman to take the place of the deposed Vashti was in the same year that Ezra began his work (Ezra 7: 17).

Verse 17. *Loved* is from AHAB and Strong defines it, "a primitive root; to have affection for (sexually or otherwise)." All of the connecting circumstances show that the king's love for Esther included both parts of the definition of the word. Her form of body and other phyiscal qualities would respond to his sexual demands, and her sweetness of spirit would certainly arouse in him the deepest of affection. And so a girl of exquisite attractions in body and temperament was the agency used by the Lord to bring about the fulfillment of a great prediction. The following parts of the story will show that the king was completely charmed by his love for this maiden. He at once placed her in the honored position of queen of the realm and the sole object of his love. Such a situation was perfectly adapted to the great scheme in the mind of God, and proves the supreme wisdom in all of his performances.

Verse 18. The king was so happy over the finding of a companion for him in his life's relations that he made a great feast in her honor and named it for her. *Release* means rest, and the king granted a general holiday throughout the provinces in respect for this new wife. It was a custom to make gifts to friends on occasions of joy and gratitude. (Neh. 8: 10.) *According to the state* means the gifts were proportionate to the state ("means") of the king.

Verses 19, 20. *The second time* refers to another collection of girls. Josephus says the number of damsels brought together finally amounted to

400. Mordecai evidently did not know just what was going on "inside," and all the while, he was sitting at the gate. He had charged Esther not to tell any of her people what was going on. The record states that she respected his requests as she always had from her childhood. What a wonderful character she must have been. And these circumstances did not put her in the light of disobedience to her husband, for the thing that Mordecai asked her to do had nothing to do with the king's business.

Verses 21, 22. In the plot of a great story there will be items dropped in the course of the narrative that may seem not to have any bearing on the main subject. Then later, as the writer begins to take up these "loose ends" it can be seen that they were even some vital parts of the story. Such will be found to be so with regard to this paragraph, so note it well. The apparently casual presence at this gate gave Mordecai an opportunity to overhear a conversation between two of the gatekeepers. They were plotting to do violence to the king. He wished to have it made known to the royal husband of his cousin. No one would believe him but Esther, so he told her and she told the king. Acting on the information, the king ordered inquiry to be made. The conspiracy was discovered and the men were hanged. As this was an important event it was recorded in the official chronicles of the realm. The matter was given no attention further at the time, but it will come up again.

ESTHER 3

Verse 1. *After these things* means after the events at the close of the preceding chapter. We have no information as to why Haman was given the promotion mentioned. However, since it was a part of the plan being used for the fulfillment of a great prediction, we may justly conclude that the Lord had a hand in it. The fact that is the most significant is that he was an *Agagite*. This is from AGAGIY which Strong defines, "an Agagite or descendant (subject) of Agag." Next, "Agag" is defined by Strong, "flame, a title of Amalekitish kings." Now read 1 Sam. 15: 1-9, then Ex. 17:8-16 and you will begin to see "daylight" in connection with one of the most interesting and important dramas in history. The hand of God will be seen throughout.

Verse 2. *Bowed* and *reverenced* are practically the same. The first refers specifically to the act of bending the knees, the second is a comment on the first, meaning that in bending the knees they meant to reverence him. The king had commanded the servants to show this attitude toward Haman in recognition of his recent promotion. Mordecai refused to pay the required homage. It was not from the motive of disobedience to the king, for he had already shown much regard for him. Neither could we think of it as being from jealousy, for all of his conduct before and after this event showed him to have been a very humble man. The explanation will appear in the following verses.

Verse 3, 4. The servants naturally observed the actions of Mordecai. The only point that impressed them was the fact that the king had been disobeyed. They asked him why he had disobeyed the commandment of the king, and his answer was what aroused their curiosity as to the outcome. The last phrase begins with *for* and ends with *Jew*. Now we know why he refused to bow to Haman; it was because he (Mordecai) was a Jew. In connection with that we must remember that Haman was a descendant of the Amalekites who were confirmed enemies of the Jews. There was even a standing declaration of war between the Jews and the Amalekites since Ex. 17: 14-16, and Mordecai evidently knew about it. To bow to Haman would be like a citizen of one country paying homage to one of another country that was in a state of hostility.

Verse 5. Disappointed pride is one of the most active motives for evil. It goaded Haman into plotting two terrible schemes for revenge.

Verse 6. When Haman's attention was called to the attitude of Mordecai, he inquired about him and learned of his nationality. He then recognized him as one of some people scattered all through the provinces of the empire. His feeling of importance was so great that he thought he should have an extraordinary revenge to satisfy his wounded dignity. But it would not amount to much if only this one lone man were put down. He therefore conceived the horrible plot to have all the Jews slain.

Verse 7. Having concluded on the fiendish plan for wholesale destruction of the Jews, he resorted to a superstition in settling on the day to select for the mass murder. *Pur* means "lot," and he began in the first month to cast lots. This was done daily until the decision was indicated in some way by the sign that was connected with the superstitious practice. The lot fell on the 13th day of the twelfth month. That would give him plenty of time to prepare for the terrible event. Such preparation would include the edict of the king and its general proclamation throughout the provinces. Perhaps it would not have required all of that time for the plot of Haman, but the activities on the other side to counteract his wicked design would take some time also. This fact indicates that God took a hand in the lot when Haman resorted to it, and caused it to fall on that distant date in order to give his people opportunity for carrying out their role in this great drama. We know that God did use his enemies even to accomplish his will. He used Pharaoh (Ex. 9: 16), Balaam (Num. 24: 1) and the woman of Endor (1 Sam. 28). We are told also that he sometimes used the lot for disposing of questions. (Prov. 16: 33.)

Verse 8. *There is a certain people.* This was as definite as Haman would make his accusation. He might have known the nationality of the queen, and if so, he would not dare risk the results of indirect threat to her life. At any rate, he felt that he would secure the king's authority for his scheme were he kept in the dark about the whole truth. He contented himself with general but unfavorable reports about the conduct of this *certain people*. A part of his statement of their history was true, but did not show any disadvantage to the business of Ahasuerus. But one of his accusations was without foundation, for the history of the case shows the Jews to have been obedient to the laws of the realm.

Verse 9. Haman then asked for a decree from the king, authorizing the destruction of this *certain people*. Such a task would require the service of many men and they would need financial support for their time and labor. Haman agreed to furnish this out of his private funds. *To bring it into the king's treasuries* meant he would at once place this amount in the royal treasury, to be used in paying the servants for their time and activities in executing the decree.

Verse 10. The ring was used as a symbol of authority. Smith's Bible Dictionary says this about it: "The ring was regarded as an indispensable article of a Hebrew's attire, inasmuch as it contained his signet. It was hence a symbol of authority." The king expressed his approval of Haman's proposal by giving him his royal ring.

Verse 11. *The silver is given to thee* was the king's way of telling Haman to keep his money, but that he was authorized to carry out his patriotic purpose of destroying the enemies of the kingdom. Certainly, such a laudable service should be paid for out of the funds of the nation that would be benefited thereby.

Verse 12. Having consented to the request of Haman, preparations were made to publish the edict. The work was to be done in a formal manner, and for that purpose the king's scribes or secretaries were called to "take dictation." The work was done on the 13th day of the first month, and was to be executed or completed the same day of the twelfth month. *Lieutenants; governors; rulers.* These were the various men that represented the king's authority in the provinces throughout the vast empire. They differed slightly in rank according as the importance of their individual charges differed. *According to the writing thereof* means that the edict was written in the languages of the different people of the several provinces. The genuineness of the letters was made sure by being *sealed with the king's ring.* I will quote a little more about the ring from Smith's Bible Dictionary: "We may conclude from Ex. 28: 11 that the rings contained a stone engraven with a device or with the owner's name. The ring was used as a stamp to impress the name of Ahasuerus on the documents.

Verse 13. A *post* is defined in the lexicon as a runner; today he is called a postman. The terrible edict was so worded that the complete destruction of the Jewish race was to be accomplished, as far as it existed in the realm of Persia.

Verse 14. The official document was sent out 11 months before the time of execution. The reason for the general scattering of the edict was *that they should be ready* by the time the day came for the carrying out of the slaying and pillage.

Verse 15. The *posts* or runners were urged to publish the information as swiftly as possible. After they had been sent on their mission the king and Haman sat down to drink. We may be sure these two men had different motives for engaging in a round of imbibing. The king thought he was celebrating a fortunate escape from some national disaster at the hands of a gang of evil men. Haman thought he was regaling himself over a fiendish revenge for his wounded pride. There must have been something unusual in the whole proceeding, for the people of the capital city were perplexed. They could not have been aware of any visible reason for the harsh decree. In all of the years that the Jews had been interspersed throughout the empire, there had been no indication of trouble from them. Now to know of such a sudden and drastic decree was very confusing. Of course, the reader will not forget that the king was wholly unaware of the identity of the people against whom he had signed the edict.

ESTHER 4

Verse 1. The decree was known to Mordecai since it was made so public. It caused him to go into a period of mourning. *Sackcloth and ashes* were put on and about the body on about the same principle on which people once wore dark crepe after the death of a near relative. Rending the garment was done also as a sign of grief and anxiety. Mordecai displayed his forms of mourning through the central portions of the city, accompanying the material demonstrations with bitter outcries.

Verse 2. There were restrictions against going inside the king's gate while wearing mourning. Mordecai went as far as he could; he came before the gate.

Verse 3. The mourning became general because the Jews were scattered throughout the empire. Some went to the extent of lying prostrate with their bodies covered with sackcloth and ashes scattered over them.

Verse 4. Esther had the service both of maids and eunuchs or chamberlains. They saw the condition of Mordecai and told her about it. She did not know the reason for his strange behaviour, and sought to have his mourning attire removed and replaced with raiment. He refused the raiment and we are aware of his reason for it.

Verses 5, 6. Upon the refusal of Mordecai to accept the raiment sent to him by Esther, she realized that something very extraordinary was going on. The king had placed at her service one of his own eunuchs. She commanded him to inquire as to the reason for Mordecai's actions.

Verse 7. The refusal of Mordecai to use the clothing that Esther offered him was not from a spirit of ingratitude or sullenness. When her special servant asked for an explanation, Mordecai gave the information without evasion. He had learned even of the detail about the money that Haman promised to furnish to be applied on the expenses of having the Jews destroyed.

Verses 8, 9. There seems not to have been any attempt to conceal the plan for the destruction of the Jews, for Mordecai was able to furnish the servant of Esther a copy of the royal decree. Upon the strength of the order, Mordecai sent a request to her to *go in unto the king to make supplication for her people*. This was the first information that Esther had of the terrible decree of the king. While she knew it was a royal document, she knew also that Haman was the instigator of it. However unjust it might be, she felt sure that the king was in the dark as to the undercurrent flowing from the wickedness of this man. She also knew of the law of the court, that no one of any rank dared come into the court uninvited by the king. She accordingly sent the information to Mordecai stated in the next paragraph.

Verses 10-12. The harsh rule was to the effect that the inner court of the king was to be avoided by all men and women. No one dared venture therein uninvited, and if one disregarded the rule he was liable to suffer death. The only chance for escape lay in the graciousness of the king. Should he be pleased to suspend the rule in any given instance, he indicated it by extending toward that person his golden scepter. That was a rod or baton held in the hand of a monarch that denoted his authority. Esther stated this law in her reply to Mordecai, then told him that she had not been invited to come to the king for 30 days. We do not have any information as to why the king had not called for his beloved wife for so long a time. However, the fact that such a long period had passed thus might have been an indication that some unusual condition existed in which perhaps the king would not wish to be disturbed. If that were the case then it would be especially dangerous to intrude; this information was given to Mordecai by Esther.

Verse 13. Mordecai may have misjudged Esther. No one could know what she expected to experience through her relationship to the king. But Mordecai thought her refusal to grant his request was because of her confidence in that relationship, and the security she thought it would give her. He warned her not to depend on that feeling of security; that being in the king's house would not make her any safer than the other Jews when the edict of the king was ready to be put into effect.

Verse 14. *Enlargement* means literally room or space, which would mean that provision was made for escape from the destruction intended by the decree. Mordecai meant to express his faith in the providence of God, and the refusal of Esther to cooperate in the effort to avoid the destruction would not prevent the deliverance coming from some other source. *Who knoweth whether thou art come to the kingdom for such a time as this?* This means the same as if Mordecai had said: "Who knows but that thou wert brought to the kingdom at this time for the very purpose of bringing about the deliverance of thy people?" We are sure that his question was timely, and that God had indeed caused the procedure of selecting Esther as the queen.

Verses 15, 16. Fasting was not generally commanded by the law of Moses, but it was encouraged and blessed by the Lord. It was resorted to in times of great distress or anxiety. See 1 Sam. 31: 13; 2 Sam. 12: 21; Ezra 8: 21; Judg. 20: 26; 1 Chr. 10: 12. Esther had great confidence in the mercy of God. She also had much respect for Mordecai, and doubtless believed his plans were just. All of these considerations outweighed, in her mind, the law of her husband. *Not according to the law* was uttered to indicate that she had full realization of the seriousness of the thing she was about to perform. But it would be at the request of her beloved cousin, and after humble devotions to God. If, after such considerations, she took the risk of breaking the law, and "worst came to worst," all that could possibly come to her would be that she perish. In other words, if the request of Mordecai should have the effect he expected, the risk she would run would be more than justified. On the other hand, if the plan of Mordecai did not work, it could not make matters any worse than they would have been anyway, for she could only perish. With this spirit of loving resignation to whatever might be in store for her, she sent word to Mordecai of her decision.

Verse 17. Mordecai was cooperative also, and did as Esther bade him do in preparation for the great venture into the king's presence.

ESTHER 5

Verse 1. *Third day* means the last day of the period of fasting that Esther had ordered. Laying aside whatever clothing she might have been wearing appropriate for the fast, she put on her royal garments. That was in due respect for the king into whose presence she was about to venture uninvited. The king was seated on his throne in the *royal house*. This is distinguished from the *king's house*. That is because the palaces in ancient times were not always referred to in the same sense. Sometimes a king would maintain a house as his personal residence separate from the building he occupied as a king. Ahasuerus did this, and had his throne in the royal house which was near his personal residence.

Verse 2. The king saw Esther standing in the court. She had not been invited on that day, nor had she been called for 30 days. Her presence was a clear case of intrusion into the exclusive vicinity of the monarch of the great Persian Empire. By that act she exposed herself to the possibility of a sentence of death. Even though she was the queen, there was no provision made in the law for any personal exceptions. The only thing that could save her was the mercy of the king. Esther could justly have been thinking of the close attachment that existed between the king and herself, for a man with the emotional sentiments of Ahasuerus would doubtless have made them known to her in their previous intimate relations as husband and wife. But would even all that save her as she stood in the august presence of the great king whose established law she had violated? What a momentous crisis that was, both for Esther personally and for the Jewish people! It is significant to read that *when the king saw Esther the queen . . . she obtained favor in his sight.* As a cold, logical fact, we would know that it would be only after seeing her that he would have any occasion to act upon the situation. But the writer made the statement as emphasis on the power of her very appearance in his sight. The established signal of favor was displayed by extending toward Esther the golden scepter. With our mind's eye we can see her as she modestly and respectfully approached toward the throne, coming just near enough to touch the top of the scepter, a gesture in recognition of his supreme authority.

Verse 3. The king was completely charmed by the influence of Esther's presence. She had been his choice among the group of maidens of the realm who had been placed at his command. She was accepted because of his love for her, and that attachment was so strong that it overcame the fact that she had violated a fixed rule of the court. It went so far as to induce the king to commit himself to her wishes before he had the slightest idea of her purposes. He not only recognized her as the queen, but added the affectionate expression of her personal name, *Queen Esther*. When he told her she could have anything she wished, even to the half of the kingdom, he gave evidence of her complete influence over him. And this gives us further proof that God understood just what kind of person to bring into the plan predicted and set on foot at the battle of Rephidim. (Ex. 17: 8-16.)

Verse 4. The king offered half of his kingdom to Esther if she desired it. Instead of that, she merely wished that he and Haman accept an invitation to a banquet that she had prepared. It is true that it would be a great honor to have a king of the Persian Empire, accompanied by his recently-promoted prince, attend a banquet in the home of the queen. However, that was apparently such a small favor compared with the one she could have received, that we are bound to be filled with surprise. That is, we would be entirely perplexed over it were we not already aware that a great drama was "now showing," in which the fate of God's people and the fulfillment of a divine prediction were at stake. We may be assured that God was taking a hand in the affair and directing Esther, the wisdom of which will become evident later on.

Verse 5. The request of Esther needed to be authorized by the king regarding Haman. He was therefore called to prepare to attend the banquet, which he did with readiness, it being an unusual honor thus bestowed upon him. A banquet was a feast in which wine was used in large quantities. The word is used in connection with this feast in the next verse. An ordinary meal where the wine was not drunk might not have brought about the condition of mind on the part of her special guests that was desired. Hence Esther provided a feast where "imbibing" would be indulged in, and the king and Haman attended it.

Verse 6. When Esther appeared, uninvited, within the inner court, it was evident that she had some request to make. So there was a logical reason for the statement of the king at that time. There was nothing, though, in the mere fact of a gathering at a banquet that suggested any such motive on her part. But the king was under so great a "spell" in his devotion to this charming woman that he almost unconsciously invited her to make a further request.

Verses 7, 8. The request that Esther made the second time was exactly like the one made in the first instance except as to date. The next banquet was to be on the morrow. It would have been natural not to repeat such an extensive occasion as a royal banquet the same day, for physical reasons at least. But there was a far more important reason than that for letting a night come and go between this feast and the next one. Certain things must take place, both on the part of the king and others, that would require some time, and especially the nighttime, for bringing them about. Esther therefore asked her royal guests to attend her banquet on the morrow. *Will do tomorrow as the king hath said.* This means the same as if she had said: "Tomorrow, at the banquet, I will do whatever the king asks me to do." She expected the proceeding to come to some form of climax at the second feast, and that the king would give some kind of directions to persons in his charge. The statement in italics means she would be ready for whatever came. We note that nothing is recorded as to the king's accepting the invitation this time as was done at the first. That fact was to be taken for granted since the king had already fulfilled his promises.

Verse 9. "Every joy hath its sorrow," is an old saying, and it was certainly true with Haman. He departed from the feast full of pride over the distinguished honors placed upon him by the invitations from the queen. But that pride received a wound as he passed out at the gate. He probably had momentarily forgotten his feeling against Mordecai in the excitement of the banquet and its joyful social atmosphere. Now that the hated Jew was thrust upon his vision again, and that in an attitude of contempt, his rage almost knew no bounds.

Verses 10-12. Nevertheless, he restrained himself and rested on the hope of obtaining some consolation later in the midst of his home and friends. He went thither to report on his experiences of the day. *Called for his friends, and Zeresh.* We need not suppose that Haman's wife lived apart from him, that he would need to call for her to come. The statement means that after he called for his friends to come, he spoke to them in the hearing of his wife. Much of the speech was for the information of friends since it pertained to his family circumstances, of which his wife would be aware already. But aside from those items, the conversation had to do with the honors just bestowed on him, all of which was news to the friends and his wife.

Verse 13. The very sight of the Jew at the king's gate so irritated Haman that his enjoyment of the honors bestowed on him was lost. Mordecai was only one Jew, and the edict had already been started out to destroy the whole number of them throughout the realm. But that was not to take place until the 12th month, and this personal humiliation at the contemptuous attitude of Mordecai was constantly with him. Immediate relief from the distress against his pride was what he desired.

Verse 14. The suggestion to build a gallows for the hanging of Mordecai may have been from a personal impulse of Zeresh as far as her motive was concerned. But we should keep in mind the fact that God was in all this transaction, and was turning even the selfish motives of the enemies into usefulness for effecting the divine plans. This gallows will be needed in God's service, and it was well that the personal motives of Haman and his wife be made use of.

ESTHER 6

Verse 1. Any person is likely to have wakeful nights occasionally. Darius passed such a night (Dan. 6: 18). But we can understand the cause in his case, for he had just signed a decree that he felt was unjust. In the case of Ahasuerus it was different. It is true he also had authorized a decree that was unjust, but he had not learned of that as yet. There was no apparent reason for his sleeplessness, yet we are sure it was just another item in the wonderful drama being carried on by the Lord. When a person is unable to sleep, and no reason for it is known, he naturally seeks something to "pass the time." In the case of a king the most natural subject of interest would be the records of his kingdom, so this king called upon his servants to read them to him.

Verse 2. The servant "happened" to read the account of an attempt upon the life of the king. Now I will request my readers to turn to Ch. 2: 21-23 and note the comments on those verses. In the present paragraph we see the "loose ends" of the story being gathered up. The account showed the plot of the conspirators and their exposure. It told also of the patriotic service of Mordecai in getting the information to the king that saved his life. But no further action was taken as far as the record went. It has always been the custom at least to give a "reward of merit" of some kind to one who has performed an unusual service to another, and especially to as important a person as a king. But the one doing the reading said nothing along that line while pronouncing this chronicle from the official document.

Verse 3. The king evidently thought the full account had not been read. His question, then, as to what had been done in appreciation of Mordecai's action, was in the nature of request for the complete story. But he was told that he had heard all of the story, that nothing had been done for Mordecai.

Verses 4, 5. The king was determined on supplying what had been neglected in the case, and prepared to show his appreciation by bestowing some honor on Mordecai. Naturally he wanted to use the proper method and would employ some trusted servant for the purpose. So the king asked to learn who was available and who was in the outer court. Anyone would be permitted to come that far uninvited. Haman "happened" to be there at the very time the king made his inquiry. He had come, however, to seek the lawful entrance to the inner court, to ask for the slaying of Mordecai. When informed that Haman was there, the

Esther 6: 6-14

king gave order to have him brought in. Doubtless this invitation came before Haman had asked for it, and it must have been a joyful surprise. Under such an impression he came into the immediate presence of the king with great expectations.

Verse 6. We should keep in mind that up to the present point, the king knows nothing of the connection Mordecai has with the decree that Haman had caused to be sent out. He knows only that it was against "a certain people," but does not know that Mordecai and Esther would be involved. Therefore, when he makes his proposal to Haman, the king will be perfectly "innocent" of its relation to the divine plan. As far as the king was concerned, this affair which he was about to carry out would be only an incident to complete the routine of honorable reward of merit, so that the royal chronicles would show a regular form. And since Haman was one of his more important servants, he would be an appropriate person to suggest the procedure and also to put it into effect. In the light of all this he asked Haman for his suggestions. We would expect Haman to take just such a view of the case as he did. Had the king not recently promoted him? Had not the royal decree been signed at his request? Had he not been the only guest invited to the queen's banquet with the king? And now, had he not just been invited to come into the inner court even before he had asked for it? No wonder, then, that he said to himself, *To whom would the king delight to do honor more than to myself?* Everything indicated that he was the very one to receive the honor.

Verses 7-9. With the impression just described as his motive, Haman would naturally make the scene as dignified as possible. The procedure he suggested would place a man about second to the king in the point of show and pomp. There are no less than six items in the formula that he prescribed for the man to be honored. I shall briefly note the items from the text: *Royal apparel, crown royal, arrayed by the most noble prince, on horseback through the city, proclaim before him, horse the king rideth,* etc. What a display of glory that Haman thought he was arranging for himself!

Verse 10. With our knowledge of the whole background in mind, it would appear that Ahasuerus had the idea of punishing Haman by the order he gave him. That it was done as if he was saying to himself: "I will teach Haman a lesson that will humble him." Such was not the case, for he was still wholly ignorant of the true state of affairs. He did not know the connection that Haman and Esther and Mordecai had with the edict sent out. Instead of being a rebuke to Haman (which we can see that it was), the king would rather consider it something of an honor to him, to be entrusted with this important service for the king of such a great realm as Persia. But this very motive of Ahasuerus would make the order given to Haman all the more a sharp rebuke.

Verse 11. Of course Haman could not do otherwise than obey the order of the king. Even to have protested would have forced an issue into the limelight that he was not ready to meet. So he faithfully carried out the procedure suggested by himself and directed to be applied to the very man he hated most. It gives us an instance of the lesson taught by Jesus in Luke 18: 14.

Verse 12. When the march through the city was over, the procession ended where it began which was at the king's gate, since that was where Mordecai had been keeping himself most of the time. What feelings of mingled hate and shame Haman must have been having as he deposited the despised Jew in his accustomed place after this triumphant march through the city; a march of triumph for the Jew who had consistently spurned the haughty Haman. But it was a triumph of honor that he had not sought. And it was no wonder that Haman hastened to his home, with his head covered with sackcloth or some other article that indicated his utter dejection.

Verse 13. Haman received no comfort from his wife, as he did the first time he appealed to her. She evidently knew about the general history of the Jews, and that in all of their troubles they were successful in the end. But she must have been unaware of the full relationship between Mordecai and them, even though he was called a Jew. She finally suspected the truth about it and concluded that Haman was doomed to be the loser in any conflict with Mordecai. She stated this thought to him, and the same was agreed to by the wise men attending on him.

Verse 14. The affair of giving Mordecai an honorable conduct through the streets of the city took place between the two banquets given by Esther. Haman likely forgot about the second invitation because of his terrible shock at the exaltation of Mordecai. So he had to be reminded of his "social engagement," and urged to fulfill it.

ESTHER 7

Verse 1. *To banquet.* The second word is a verb and is defined in the lexicon, "to imbibe." That is the main item of the occasion, although it would imply also a feasting as an additional indulgence.

Verse 2. The king was still under the "spell" of his love for Esther. Ordinarily a man tries to express his love for a woman by making her a present of some valuable article. He may spare no expense within his possibilities, sometimes even bringing himself almost into bankruptcy. Ahasuerus could think of no gift that was good enough for this woman who had him overwhelmed by his devotion to her. So he told her to name the gift most desirable, the limit being nothing less than half of his kingdom.

Verse 3. Esther made her request general at first, merely asking that she and her people be spared their lives. This must have been one of the greatest surprises the king ever received. Being entirely uninformed of the identity of the people against whom he had signed the decree of destruction, he had no inkling of any danger to the Jews. He was also unaware of the nationality or race of his wife, and consequently had no idea of the peril overhanging her.

Verse 4. In continuing her answer to the king, Esther was actually recounting the terms of the decree that he had unconsciously signed against her and her people. However, she did not as yet reveal their race, nor the connection between them and the decree that had authorized Haman to start a movement of destruction. She explained that she would not have made any complaint had the edict required only that they be sold into slavery. It would have been a loss to the kingdom had the Jews been sold into bondage, for the price of their sale would not have been as great as the loss from the services of so good a people as hers. And neither would Haman have been able to make up for the loss, although he had pretended to have great wealth when asking for the decree. These last remarks are based on the concluding words of the verse, which may appear a little vague to the readers. I shall offer a few words of explanation. The *enemy* is Haman. *Countervail* means "make up for," and *damage* means loss. With these definitions in mind I will reword the last sentence thus: "I had held my tongue, although Haman could not make up for the king's loss." In other words, the sale of the Jews would have been a loss to the king, which Haman with all his boasted wealth could not have made up for the king. While Esther might have regretted seeing such loss to the king, yet she would have suffered it to go through, rather than cause any appearance of opposition to the royal decree.

Verse 5. The reply and questions of the king showed that he was entirely in the dark about what was going on. His words *where is he* especially indicated that he was wholly unsuspecting as to the guilty party.

Verse 6. This verse is brief but very weighty. It is the climax to all of the things that Esther and Mordecai had been doing, beginning with the 4th chapter. She wanted to be sure of her ground before springing the surprise upon the king. In order to that end she drew him on with her social program, and in the progress of that she could observe the complete willingness manifested to grant her any request she might make. Thus, after he had thrice offered her anything up to half of the kingdom, she concluded "the iron was hot" and ready to be struck. So there, at that second banquet, with the king still lost in his rapturous admiration for his lovely queen, and in the immediate presence of Haman, she told the king the answer. She used three words to describe Haman; *adversary, enemy* and *wicked. Haman* was *afraid* which means he trembled in the presence of the king and queen. The memory of the march through the streets of the city would come surging into his mind. Now that the queen had dared to accuse him at the inquiry of the king, and with an accusation that he knew to be true, the full extent of possibilities threw him into a panic of fear.

Verse 7. Esther displayed much wisdom by not stating the full details of her case in Vs. 3, 4. She told enough to give the king a shock, and start his mind working toward the desired conclusion. With that much of the situation arrayed before him, his nerves would be in a tension of concern for the welfare of his beloved wife. To think that anyone would dare wish to harm the idol of his heart was almost more than he could stand. The person who could be so unreasonably rash must undoubtedly be skulking somewhere like a cowardly spy. Imagine, then, his state of mind when the awful truth was stated to add its weight to his already outraged temper. No wonder that he arose unceremoniously from the banquet and left the room, as if shrinking from the vile presence of the man on whom so much honor had been heaped, but undeservedly. Haman was able to see the grave danger confronting him. The king had gone out, so his only means of contact to make a plea for mercy was through the queen.

Verse 8. Having brought the situation to this dramatic climax, Esther was overcome with emotion and lay down upon her bed. Haman was then desperate with fear and threw aside all discretion. In casting himself upon the bed by the side of the queen, we are sure he had no intention but to beg earnestly for his life. Nevertheless, the position was interpreted by the enraged king in the light that such a compromise would logically be taken. With an accusing question he spoke in the hearing of the ones present, calling attention to the threefold offense namely, *force the queen, before me, in the house.* The witnesses took the view of the case that was expressed by the king and resolved not to let the wicked Haman add one word more in his plea. They shut him off by covering his face, thereby smothering him as with a gag.

Verse 9. When Harbonah called attention to the gallows that Haman had erected he may not have thought especially of the use the king would make of it. The purpose was to cite another item of evidence, proving how wicked a man Haman was; that he had constructed an instrument for the destruction of the very man who had saved the king's life. But the suggestion was enough for Ahasuerus. He promptly gave orders that Haman should be hanged thereon.

Verse 10. The orders were carried out. The inspired writer added emphasis to the occasion by stating that the hanging of Haman took place on the gallows that he had prepared for Mordecai. This pacified the king's wrath because it struck out the man who was the author of the terrible conspiracy just discovered.

ESTHER 8

Verse 1. The word *house* is from an original with a various meaning. Its leading idea is household or family members. The verse means that Esther was given authority over the members of Haman's family, both immediate and distant relatives. In the meantime she had acquainted the king with her relation to Mordecai. This brought him into the royal favor so that he was escorted into the king's presence.

Verse 2. The king had taken the ring from Haman, previously given him as a badge of honor, and now gave it unto Mordecai. That action was a signal of authority, and Esther availed herself of it by placing Mordecai in charge of the house of Haman.

Verse 3. Esther had been favored so much by the king that she was encouraged to press for more. The immediate disposal of Haman and his family had been arranged for through the authority vested in Mordecai. But there remained the edict that had been signed by the king at Haman's request. It was still in force and only waiting for the date on which it was to be executed. Something must be done to counteract that, else the people of Esther will be destroyed. That was what she meant by the request to *put away the mischief of Haman.* Falling down at the feet of the king, she tearfully begged him for further consideration.

Verse 4. By holding out the golden scepter toward Esther, she was made to understand that she might make her wishes known and that they would be granted. There is every indication that no request of hers, within the possibilities of the king, would be denied her, so completely was he enthralled by his love for her.

Verse 5. Esther knew the rule of the Persian law, that no edict could be directly repealed; yet it might be possible to do something that could have the effect of an alteration or repeal. That was what she requested, but she made it on condition that the king felt entirely favorable towards it.

Verse 6. Esther was a Jewess and knew that the edict of destruction would include her by its terms unless some exception could be made due to her relation to the king. But regardless of any assurance she may have felt for her personal safety, her great spirit of humanity was moved for her people. She felt that she could never stand it to see them come to such harm. On account of this concern she made the request stated in the preceding verse.

Verse 7. We notice the king addressed both Esther and Mordecai because of their common relation to the issues at stake. The execution of Haman was placed in charge of Esther, and the reason for it was stated; that it was his attack upon the Jews.

Verse 8. The execution of Haman and his household was not enough. Some action must be taken to counteract his wicked designs against the people of Esther and Mordecai. This had to be done through some other edict, not by directly repealing the first decree. The king therefore gave authority to have the other edict drawn up and made binding in the established manner. Such a result was accomplished by putting the king's name on the document. But that might be done without his knowledge or consent, so an additional evidence must be used to close up the gap of uncertainty. This was done by using the seal that was on the king's ring, a sort of "notary" signal. The outstanding point of that act was the established rule that "no man may reverse it."

Verse 9. The official secretaries were called in again to "take dictation" on the important work of the new edict. It was done near the end of the 3rd month, and was to take effect on the 13th day of the 12th month. That would give a period of about 9 months in which it could be given full publicity. The document was to give authority to, and call upon, all the various subordinates in the realm of Persia to see that the edict on behalf of the Jews was carried out. It also authorized the Jews to take full advantage of the decree and be prepared to carry out its provisions.

Verse 10. *He wrote* means Mordecai wrote; not by his own hand for that was what the scribes or secretaries were called in for. But he dictated it and had it put down in writing and then attested in the forementioned manner. Copies of it were then sent by postmen on various beasts of burden, to all the sections of the realm where the Jews were scattered.

Verse 11. The terms of the edict were very sweeping. They gave the Jews the unrestricted authority for assemblage and for self-defense. This might be done to the extent even of killing their enemies who would attack them. They could also take possession of the property that had belonged to their foes.

Verse 12. The decree was to take effect on the very day that had been set for the enforcement of the former decree. The reason for such a date is obvious. It would not do to have it dated even one day earlier, for the Jews were to act in self-defense only, and no attack upon them would come before the prescribed date. And of course it would not do any good to date it later, for that would be after they would have been the victims of the other edict.

Verse 13. The decree was officially copied and sent to all the sections of the realm. It urged the Jews to be ready to avenge themselves when the day came on which the decree of destruction was to be put into force.

Verse 14. The *posts* were the same as postmen. They were urged on in their mission by the commandment of the king. It is evident that Ahasuerus was as eager as was Esther or Mordecai to have the vicious instrument of Haman intercepted.

Verse 15. Mordecai had manifested a spirit of humility from the beginning. There is no indication that he ever sought any honor. So the exaltation of which we read was placed upon him by the king unsolicited. It is significant that the city of Shushan (the Persian capital) rejoiced. Most of the citizens of the city were Persians, and the edict just sent out was on behalf of the Jews. But the injustice of Haman's activities was doubtless understood by the people. They were happy, therefore, to know that a harmless group of their subjects was to be spared the awful destruction intended by the wicked Haman.

Verse 16. *Light* is from OWRAH and Strong defines it, "luminousness, i. e. (figuratively) prosperity." Of course the idea is that the Jews were glad because of the prosperous situation they had the right to expect.

Verse 17. In the various sections of the realm of Persia, the Jews celebrated their joy by holding a feast. *Many of the people became Jews.* This means they became proselytes to the Jewish system. There were certain privileges that were allowed by the law that entitled a foreigner to be classed with the Jews. That had several restrictions, yet left the relationship in such a state that it gave to the proselyte much advantage. The circumstance shows one of the common traits of mankind. When special favor seems to be in store for certain classes, then others wish to "get in" on the favor. It is always well to see persons show an interest in things that are right. It would be more highly appreciated, though, were they to do so under circumstances that betrayed less selfishness.

ESTHER 9

Verses 1, 2. Since the preceding chapter came to a close, 9 months have passed. The date for the two famous edicts has arrived and the Jews have girded themselves for the conflict. They assembled in the cities, and were so successful in their own defense that the public mind was stirred up in their favor.

Verse 3. *The fear of Mordecai* means they respected him for his righteousness of life. Because of this the officers of the city helped the Jews in their defense.

Verse 4. Mordecai was in high standing in the household of the king as well as in the estimation of the people in general. He had not done anything that would be called great in the estimation of the world, but God was with him and was causing the tables to be turned in his favor.

Verse 5. The mention of *sword*, and *slaughter*, and *destruction*, is for emphasis. The general idea is that complete victory over the enemy was achieved by them.

Verse 6. If there would be any place where the citizens of a realm would have advantage it ought to be in their own capital city. But even that did not avail them anything in their aggression against the people of God.

Verses 7-10. This paragraph merely states the names of Haman's 10 sons as being among the slain. The importance of that fact will appear later. The additional news item is the fact that the Jews did not take possession of the spoil. The edict of the king would have permitted them to do so, but they spurned it with contempt.

Verse 11. All events of importance were made a part of the royal record. Because of that, the king was given an account of the number of casualties of the day. There would be a special reason for his interest in the subject, for he had given his official consent to the decree on the occasion, and had commanded its prompt execution when the time of maturity came.

Verse 12. All through the story we are studying, the king's regard for Esther has been much in evidence. He favored her with a piece of information connected with her previous requests. In this report he made separate items of the destruction of the citizens of Shushan in general, and of the 10 sons of Haman in particular. The second item was in reference to her chief concern, which was the fate of Haman's family. What have they done *in the rest of the king's provinces?* Moffatt renders this as follows: "What, then, must they have done in the other provinces of the king?" The thought is, if that much destruction of the enemies has taken place in just one city, there is no telling how much has been done in other parts of the vast empire. But even with that much accomplished in her favor, she was given the privilege of making further requests. She was assured that any request would be granted to her.

Verse 13. The next request of Esther was to the effect that the day's accomplishments be repeated on the morrow; that is, as far as possible. There could actually be more of the citizens slain, but the sons of Haman could not be slain again. But they could be subjected to the shame of the gallows. Their father had sought to have her cousin hanged but was slain thereon instead. Now she wished to render the merited disgrace more complete by having their dead bodies held up to public scorn.

Verse 14. True to his promise and also true to form of his previous favorable attitude toward Esther, he caused the 10 sons of Haman to be hanged.

Verse 15. Matters were going "their way" for the Jews, so that the slaughter of the enemy was continued even into the 14th day of the month. And again they did not deign to take advantage of the right to property. This movement was done in the capital city as Esther had requested.

Verse 16. While the attack was being repeated in the city, the Jews out through the provinces were also continuing their destruction of the enemy, to the number of 75,000. They again refrained from taking any of the prey of the enemy.

Verse 17. The 13th and 14th day had been periods of success against the enemy. The Jews observed the fact on the 14th day by having a feasting and period of gladness.

Verse 18. The Jews that were in the capital city extended the season of gladness; they included the 15th day in their festivities.

Verse 19. The same spirit of gladness that prevailed in Shushan and other large cities was manifested in the small towns. One item in the observances was the sending of portions (gifts) one to another. That was a custom that prevailed in ancient times. It indicates the righteousness and propriety of making gifts as expressive of joy and appreciation. In Neh. 8: 10 is an instance of this subject. In that case the Lord had been good to the people. They were then advised to observe a day in honor of the Lord, and a part of the exercises was that of making gifts.

Verses 20, 21. It has long been the practice of human beings to keep, in memory of great occurrences, some kind of formality. The Jews had a feast in memory of their deliverance from Egyptian bondage (Ex. 12: 14). Now they were directed by Mordecai to keep a feast in commemoration of the triumph over the conspirators acting with Haman. This observance was to be in honor of the 14th and 15th days of the 12th month.

Verse 22. The noteworthy feature of the great season was the idea of sorrow being replaced with joy. The time was celebrated by feasting among themselves, and by sending gifts to the poor. When there comes a time of general good feeling among the people of the land, it is wholly proper to celebrate it by making presents. They may do this first among themselves, then by sending gifts to those less fortunate.

Verse 23. *Do as they had begun* means the Jews determined to keep up the memorial feasts from year to year, in the same manner that was observed at the start.

Verse 24. The inspired writer goes back toward the early parts of the history and takes up the plot of Haman to destroy the Jews. *Had cast Pur* refers to the casting of lots that is described in Ch. 3: 7. Haman was an Agagite, and 1 Sam. 15: 8 shows that he was descended from the Amalekites. These were the people who opposed the children of Israel in Ex. 17. At that time God declared that he would put out the remembrance of Amalek from under heaven. It was gradually being fulfilled in this book.

Verse 25. This verse also is a brief recounting of the earlier transactions of the great drama now being shown through the inspired channel.

Verses 26, 27. *Pur* and *Purim* are forms of the same word which means "lot." It was used as a name of the annual feast that the Jews kept at the time now being considered. It was adopted in view of the method that Haman had used in determining the day for the destruction of the Jews. They wished to keep alive their appreciation of the escape from Haman's plot, and for this purpose they named the days, feast of Purim.

Verse 28. *Throughout every generation.* As a secular evidence of the truth of this account, I shall offer to my readers an extract from a metropolitan newspaper. The item is from the Chicago Herald and Examiner in the issue of Feb. 22, 1939, and is as follows: "*At Masque Purim Ball*—Celebrating the 2,500th anniversary of Purim, these pretty young ladies [pictured] appeared in costume yesterday at a rehearsal for the masque ball to be held at Temple Sholom." It is interesting to know that a statement in our Bible is verified by this authentic news item in a standard secular publication, many hundreds of years later.

Verse 29. *Wrote with all authority* means they had full consent of the king to write this letter. It was called the *second letter* in reference to the one in Ch. 8: 10. It was called *Purim* because of its being occasioned by the casting of lots (meaning of Purim), by which Haman had decided on the date for his destruction of the Jews.

Verse 30. The *provinces* were divisions of the realm of Persia. The word is from MEDIYUAH and Strong defines it, "properly a judgeship, i. e. jurisdiction; by implication a district (as ruled by a judge); generally a region." The Persian Empire was so vast that its territory had to be subdivided into these 127 districts, with secondary rulers over them. This letter was sent to the Jews in all these regions, and it contained words of *peace and truth.* That is, the peace offered to the Jews was backed up by words that had been attested and found to be true.

Verses 31, 32. The purpose of the letter was to confirm or establish the annual feast of Purim. After the decree had been published throughout the 127 provinces of the empire, the fact was *written in the book.* That means it became a part of the official records, such as were kept by all great empires.

ESTHER 10

Verse 1. *The land* means the main body of the empire. The authority of Ahasuerus was so extensive that he put the islands under this tribute or tax also.

Verse 2. For comments on *chronicles* see 1 Ki. 14: 19. Such important transactions as those about the Jews would certainly be made a part of the royal records. The reason for making this statement by the inspired writer, is the fact that we are interested in the history of Mordecai and his connection with the people of Persia.

Verse 3. *Mordecai the Jew was next unto king Ahasuerus.* The book of Esther furnishes us with at least two important facts and lessons. It shows the complete destruction of the descendants of the Amalekites (Ch. 3: 1; 7: 10; 9: 12), which fulfilled the prediction made in Ex. 17: 14. It gives also a clear example of the truth spoken by Jesus, that, "whosoever exalteth himself shall be abased; and he that humbleth himself shall be exalted." (Luke 14: 11.)

JOB 1

General remarks: I shall not attempt to discuss all the questions raised as to the exact date when Job lived. The "authorities" do not agree on the subject, but that is not of so much importance to us. The main thing to remember is that he was an actual person and not an imaginary one. In Ezk. 14: 14, 20 he is named in connection with Noah and Daniel, and in the same sense. No one who accepts the Bible at all ever denies the actual personality of two of the men mentioned, and hence that of Job should be regarded in the same light. Strong's lexicon gives us the direct and simple definition, "the patriarch famous for his patience." James refers to him (Ch. 5: 11) as a real man, and we have no reason to consider him otherwise.

As to his race or nationality I shall quote from Smith's Bible Dictionary as follows: "Job, the patriarch, from whom one of the books of the Old Testament is named. His residence in the land of Uz marks him as belonging to a branch of the Aramean race, which had settled in the lower part of Mesopotamia (probably to the south or southeast of Palestine, in Idumean [Edomite] Arabia), adjacent to the Sabeans and Chaldeans." According to this, Job's blood was a mixture of that from Abraham and the other branches of people under the Patriarchal Dispensation. Other points of interest as to Job's place in the great Book of God, and the central line of thought running through the book, will be noted as we pursue our study.

Verse 1. The character of Job is the outstanding fact of this verse. *Perfect* means he was completely righteous before God, and feared or reverenced him. To *eschew* evil means not only to refrain from doing it but to shun or avoid it.

Verse 2. The story will come back to this verse in the outcome. Let the reader take note of the number and sex of Job's children at this place.

Verse 3. The narrative will come back also to this verse, so it will be well to mark it. *Substance* is from a word that Strong says means "live stock." *Household* is from ABUDDAH and Strong defines it, "something wrought, i. e. (concretely) service." It is the word for "store of servants" in Gen. 26: 14. So Job was blessed with a family of sons and daughters, a possession much prized in Biblical times; an abundance of various animals, and many servants to wait upon him in the enjoyment of his property.

Verse 4. The sons would hold feasts in their houses, each taking his turn to act as host to the others. To these feasts the sisters were invited. All of this indicates a united and thus a happy family. That was a condition to be considered as a great blessing, for not all families are thus congenial. While a parent would regret to lose a child, however unworthy or unpleasant in disposition, yet the loss of so agreeable a group of children would be felt the more keenly.

Verse 5. It would be no surprise if the sons should commit some trespass in the course of the festivities, for—

getting themselves in the enjoyment of the occasion. On the mere possibility of their doing so, Job would go through with a service of sacrifices in their behalf at the conclusion of each feast. The question naturally arising is, what good would it do for one man to offer sacrifice for another? The answer is in the fact that Job was a father in the Patriarchal Dispensation, in which the head of a house or family group was priest for the group. His acts, therefore, would be a benefit for the members of the group. We are told that "Noah found grace in the eyes of the Lord" (Gen. 6: 8). Nothing is said about the lives of the sons, because they were all in the Patriarchal Dispensation. Hence the action of Job would benefit his sons. But we should note the devotional spirit of Job in that he did not wait until he was directly called upon to atone for the sins of his sons. *It may be* was all the motive he needed for making the sacrifice. And nothing would be lost even if no irregular conduct of his sons had been committed. Sacrifices were always in order, whether definitely needed or not, and if no act of the sons had called for the service, the exercise would be accepted as a freewill offering.

Verse 6. *Sons of God* are the same beings meant in Ch. 38: 7. They were not sons of God as that term is used in the New Testament, or even in the Old Testament as pertaining to God's earthly servants. The next verse will show that the gathering referred to was not on earth, hence these were not human beings. Moffatt's version gives us "angels." We do not know what was the purpose of the meeting, other than to give the angels opportunity to present themselves in humble adoration before their Lord and Creator. It would appear that God at various times permitted special gatherings in the celestial region. See an instance in 1 Ki. 22: 19-24. Neither do we know why Satan was suffered to be present at that gathering, except that it was a link in the chain of events which the Lord was forging for another of his great dramas. We should not be disturbed over the idea of the presence of Satan in the region of the eternal life. Bear in mind that the judgment day has not come yet, and that certain conditions and actions may be tolerated that will not be after the final day. Such an experience as that recorded in 2 Cor. 12 will never take place after the eternal settlement of things has occurred. And so for wise reasons the Lord suffered Satan to be present in the solemn gathering.

Verse 7. *Whence comest thou?* means "from where have you come?" That indicates Satan had been in some place other than the one where this great assembly was being held. The answer stated that Satan had come *from . . . the earth,* etc. This is what proves that the gathering was not on earth and that the *sons* of God were angels.

Verse 8. We may "read between the lines" without speculating. We read (1 Pe. 5: 8) that the devil walks about as a roaring lion. So between the lines of this verse we can read that Satan had been going up and down in the earth, spying on the servants of God and hoping to get in one of his darts of temptation. In such a tour he would logically meet up with Job, but fail to make any progress against him. The Lord threw this fact as a challenge to Satan.

Verses 9-11. Satan did not deny the Lord's claim about the righteousness of Job. But, like many human beings, tried to "explain it away" by giving it a questionable motive. To make it brief, he charged that Job's service to God was on the basis of a bribe; that he was serving the Lord purely from a selfish purpose, and that if his earthly possessions and interests were taken from him he would curse God.

Verse 12. The Lord gave Satan the privilege of stripping Job of everything he had outside of his body. Even had this special commission not been given to Satan, we know that he has at times manifested great power. In the universe there are three shades or degrees of power; human, superhuman and infinite. Man has the first, God has the third. Between these extremes we have seen various limited degrees of power, sometimes manifested by men, sometimes by animals and sometimes by the devil. We should always bear in mind, however, that all power comes from God, and that every creature in the universe will possess just the amount of power that God sees fit to let him have. When the magicians in Egypt failed at the plague of lice, they explained that it was because it was "the finger of God" that had brought that plague. That was an admission that the superhuman acts which they had performed were by the power of Satan. And so we see Satan given the power to damage Job miraculously, with restrictions.

Verse 13. There was nothing unusual in this gathering at the home of Job's oldest son. Verse 4 states that it was a practice for them to gather in turns for that purpose. For some reason not revealed to us, the devil chose such an occasion for carrying out the program of destruction against the family and property of Job.

Verses 14, 15. The destruction was accomplished in parts and through various agencies. The first calamity was the theft of the beasts of service and the death of the servants who had been working them, all except the one who escaped to bear the news to Job. The *Sabeans* were a people related to the Arabians. They were a wild-like clan and given to making raids into the territory of others. This great misfortune was reported to Job by the messenger who had escaped.

Verse 16. *The fire of God* meant only that it was a supernatural fire. The messenger would not understand the situation and attributed it to God. The sheep and the servants caring for them were destroyed by fire, all except the one who was let escape to carry the news to Job.

Verse 17. *Made out three bands* means they divided them into three groups among their forces. That was good strategy and was done by others in times of urgency or distress. (Gen. 32: 6-8; 2 Sam. 10: 9-11.) The Chaldeans were a strong race of people residing in the Mesopotamian lands. They stole the camels of Job and slew the men caring for them, all except one allowed to escape to be the bearer of the news.

Verses 18, 19. The story of Job's misfortunes starts with the feast at his oldest son's house. It is remarkable that all of the events about the animals and servants occurred while that feast was going on. They must have taken place in rapid succession, for according to V. 4 the feasts were of one day's duration. The whole setup is interesting and shows a plan so arranged as to grow with tension as it neared the climax. By selecting a time when the sons and daughters were feasting, their attention would not be drawn to the destruction of the property so as to rush to the defense. Furthermore, by starting on the animals and their caretakers, the less valuable of Job's property would be lost first. Of course, the loss of even such assets would ordinarily be calculated to arouse the owner's anxiety. Then, just after the tension had been drawn almost to the breaking point, here came the final blow, the destruction of his children. He certainly cannot stand such a heavy stroke. Surely, Satan will be the winner in such a contest.

Verse 20. But Satan was doomed to disappointment on this occasion. Job arose and rent his mantle. That was an established custom in olden times when one was in great distress or anxiety. It thus did not indicate any spirit of resentment. Instead, if Job does the right thing even after having torn his garment, it will prove his self-control more certainly than if he had made no demonstration. In other words, a calm and respectful behaviour after such a customary demonstration would mean more than if he had not first put on the demonstration. We are therefore eager to see how he conducts himself afterwards. The record states that he *fell down upon the ground and worshipped*. What a masterful exhibition of self-control mingled with profound respect for God!

Verse 21. Even Nicodemus knew that a man could not return to his mother's womb (John 3: 4), and Job did not mean it that way. The thought really is in the word *naked*, and means that, as "we brought nothing into this world, it is certain we can carry nothing out" (1 Tim. 6: 7). This truth agrees with the fact that what we have was given us by the Lord. And if the Lord gave us all that we have, it would certainly be all right for him to take it back whenever he saw fit. Job was completely resigned to that consideration and praised the Lord that he had permitted him to have these blessings for even a part of his life.

Verse 22. Job would have had no way to prevent the loss of his posessions had he been so minded, and thus the sin of which he could have been guilty was that with his lips. Had he accused God of acting foolishly it would have been a sin. The same principle holds true today. We are warned not to criticize the wisdom of God. (Rom. 9: 20.)

JOB 2

Verses 1, 2. This meeting and conversation were like that in Ch. 1: 6, 7. The student is requested to read the comments at that place for explanation of this.

Verse 3. The Lord again called attention to the character of Job. We should observe carefully the description of this righteous man, for it was said of very few other men, if it was said of any other. The outstanding characteristics were that he was *perfect, upright, feareth God* and *escheweth* (avoideth) *evil.* Strong defines the original for *integrity,* as "innocence." *Without cause* is an expression that comes from one Hebrew word, which is CHINNAM. Strong defines it, "gratis, i. e. devoid of cost, reason or advantage." The word has been translated in the Authorized Version, as nought 6 times, as nothing 1, in vain 2, without wages 1, and others. The idea is that no reason had existed for afflicting Job before, neither would God reap any personal profit from it were he to afflict him now.

Verse 4. The answer of Satan was practically the same in thought as the first one. *Skin for skin* is a figure of speech, using the word "skin" in two senses. That is, it is used in the first instance to represent his skin in the natural sense, and in the second to represent his life or existence. When we would say that a man would give his very hide (skin) for a certain thing, we mean he would give the last item he possessed for that thing. And so Satan meant that a man would give up his last bit of belonging if he could only retain his life. That Job would be willing to lose all of those possessions outside of his body, if by so doing he could retain his hold on the favor of God and still live.

Verse 5. On the basis of the above reasoning, Satan challenged God to threaten the life or health of Job, and then Job would curse God to his face.

Verse 6. In the first instance God gave Satan full power over the interests of Job outside of his body. This time he extended his power to the region of his body, but with the restriction that he must not cause his death.

Verse 7. It is the inspired writer who says that *Satan smote Job.* This proves that Satan can wield supernatural power when the Lord is willing for him to do so. The restriction placed upon him was that he do nothing that would cause Job's death. We may be sure he would design to give him an affliction that would cause the most possible suffering short of death. For that purpose he smote him with *sore boils.* The second word is from SHECIYN and is defined, "from an unused root probably meaning to burn; inflammation, i. e. an ulcer."—Strong. So we are to think of Job as being afflicted with burning ulcers or running sores. Just one such spot on a man's body is often enough to render him frantic with distress. But not one spot on Job's body was exempt, for the sores started at the sole of his foot and covered him to the top of his head. Reason would tell us that the filthy discharge from the ulcers would impose themselves upon his eyes and nearby tissues, and even encroach upon his lips and mouth.

Verse 8. No friendly nurse was near to ease the misery with ministrations of soothing bath or other alleviating services. And there is no indication that he could have the services of a physician. In fact, since it was a diseased condition that was miraculously brought on (although the nature of the disease itself was not miraculous), it would not have availed him anything could he have been treated by a physician. The most that such a professional man could have done would be to use one of the crude surgical instruments of those times called "scrapers." In the absence of such services Job had only the use of a *potsherd.* That was a "broken piece of earthenware" according to Smith's Bible Dictionary. With this sort of an instrument Job sat down in the ashes for shame and distress, and scraped off the accumulation of the discharge from the sores. Thus we see him; his property and children all gone, and that by violence, and his own body attacked by a loathsome disease. The entire surface is viciously irritated by burning ulcers, and the repulsive matter is trickling down and over him constantly.

Verse 9. God intended that a man's wife should be his greatest earthly helper. (Gen. 2: 18-20.) When the storms of life threaten his feeble bark, and the trials and afflictions seem more than he can bear, he is often saved from complete dejection by the sympathy and love and encouraging words of her who is the sharer of his burdens and the keeper of his honor. How indescribably opposite of all this is the case if she fails even to cooperate with him. And how much worse, still, is the case, if she becomes outspoken in her opposition to his good purpose. Job's wife treated with contempt his determination to retain his *integrity* or innocence. *Curse God and die* means to take a final fling at the Lord as being the cause of his misfortunes, then be sullenly resigned to his fate which would doubtless be a miserable death, after such a disgraceful apostasy from the true God.

Verse 10. When Job lost his children and property he did not speak evil against God. When his health and comfort of body deserted him, he still maintained his respect for the Lord. Now when the greatest of all blows came, the desertion on the part of his wife, he still repelled all attempts to draw him away from his devotion to God. He told her that she spoke as one of the *foolish* women spoke. The original word has a more serious meaning according to the lexicon of Strong. Its definition is, "foolishness, i. e. (morally) wickedness; concretely a crime; by extension, punishment." Moffatt gives us, "You are talking like an impious fool." From these critical sources of information we can see how Job regarded his wife. He meant that her attitude was criminal and deserving of punishment. It implied also that she was a slacker in her obligations to God in that she was not willing to take her share of the unpleasant parts of life along with the pleasant. Then the writer adds the conclusion stated before that Job did not *sin with his lips*. See comments on Ch. 1: 22 about sinning with the lips.

Verse 11. *Friends* is from REYA and Strong defines it, "an associate (more or less close)." The word does not necessarily mean one who is as near as the term is generally used. These men were former companions of Job and friends in a general sense. No doubt they were genuinely interested in the welfare of their associate, and would wish to see him regain his health and enjoyment of life. It is the inspired writer who says they came *to mourn with him and to comfort him,* so we are sure that was their real purpose. If they manifest error in their course of reasoning, it will not be through lack of sincerity, but from lack of knowledge. The three friends were from different localities but in communication with each other, for they came by *appointment* to meet with Job. *Eliphaz* was a descendant of Esau through Teman. (Gen. 36: 11). *Bildad* descended from Abraham through Shuah. (Gen. 25: 2.) *Zophar* was one of the people of a district in Judah called Naamah. (Josh. 15: 41.)

Verse 12. *Knew him not.* We are certain this was not meant literally, for they knew it was Job and not someone else. I shall quote the entire definition for NAKAR, the Hebrew word for *knew:* "a primitive root; properly to scrutinize, i. e. look intently at; hence (with recognition implied) to acknowledge, be acquainted with, care for, respect, revere, or (with suspicion implied), to disregard, reject, resign, dissimulate (as if ignorant or disowning)."—Strong. I hope the reader will take note of all the elements of this definition. Considering the different shades of meaning as seen in the definition, and the circumstances connected with the case, I would render the phrase, "saw no resemblance of Job as they had known him." Yet they knew that it was their very friend Job, but O, what an awful condition he was in! They were forced to weep aloud for grief. They also rent their mantles and used dust in the manner of the times when profound sorrow was felt. *Toward heaven* means they put the dust on the tops of their heads, indicating that they were completely under the burden of woe.

Verse 13. *Grief* is from a word that is translated also by pain and sorrow. No doubt that all of the elements of the word were present. We know that Job was in constant pain from his condition, and we are sure also that such a state surrounding him would produce profound grief. This terrible condition was so visible that it overcame the speech of the three friends. Even at a distance his condition had appeared so depressing to them that they were brought to audible weeping and the other indications of compassion described in the preceding verse. Now when they came into his immediate presence, and could realize the whole situation of Job, they were rendered speechless. The scene was so overwhelmingly sad that I have not the words to describe it fully. All parties were seated on the ground, in seeing and speaking distance of each other, but for one whole week not a word was spoken. Through the long period of 7 days and nights, abject silence was their mute acknowledgement of the unspeakably low estate of their friend.

JOB 3

Verse 1. *Cursed his day.* The first word is not the severe term that is usually seen in its use. It has the sense as if Job had said, "My day was a very unprofitable one." The connection shows he had reference to the day of his birth.

Verse 2. This is a proper place to make some remarks on the several statements of Job about his condition.

It has been charged that Job was really not very patient since he had so much to say about his afflictions. Such a criticism overlooks two vital truths. God wished us to have an inspired account of the experiences of Job, and that made it necessary for him to give us all the details. Another thing, the meaning of patience is misunderstood. It does not mean the false pretense of having nothing to complain of when all the indications were to the effect that the complaints were many and just. The fundamental meaning of the word is perseverance. Job complained much of his afflictions, yet he never permitted them to move him in a single instance from the path of righteousness. That is what constitutes true patience. And so, as he was writing by inspiration, the greater the detail used in describing his condition, the more significance we will see in such statements as in James 5: 11.

Verse 3. *Day perish* means that said day would better not have come. *Day* is used as a date in general, and night refers to the period in that date when childbirth usually takes place.

Verse 4. From a figurative viewpoint, Job regards his birthday as so useless that God might well rule it out of all the record of facts.

Verse 5. Job pictured the elements of creation as challenging his birthday, questioning its right to be recognized, because of the great emptiness it brought him.

Verse 6. So unprofitable has the night of his birth proved to be, that it should be stricken from the calendar.

Verse 7. *Solitary* is from a word that means fruitless. Since the night that ushered him into the world had proved to be so fruitless, there was nothing over which any voice could be joyful.

Verse 8. *Mourning* is from LIVYATHAN and Strong defines it, "a wreathed animal, i. e. a serpent (especially the crocodile or some other large sea-monster)." The curse due the night of his birth was so heavy that it could well require the strength of one who could raise up a sea-monster.

Verse 9. As complete darkness would compare with a state of worthlessness, so Job pictured the day of his birth thereby; he even specified the divisions of the period. In the beginning of night the stars are wont to furnish some light; as the night draws to an end the dawning from the sun again brings some light. But on the occasion of that fateful event of his birth it was all inappropriate.

Verse 10. The pronoun *it* refers to the day of Job's birth. Now then, because it brought him forth he pronounced the curse upon it described in the several preceding verses. And in the present verse he makes the complaint that the day did not obstruct his mother's womb so that he could not have been born. This desolate picture of Job must not be criticized, for there is another similar expression in the New Testament. In Matt. 26: 24, Jesus told of a man who would have been better off had he never been born. That was not because his fate was anything to be compared with that of Job; the likeness is in the idea of escaping from an unfavorable experience by not being born.

Verse 11. If the first described escape could not have taken place, then he wished that he might have been born dead, or at least to have died immediately at birth.

Verse 12. One meaning of *prevent* is to assist. The knees assisted the life of Job while he was held thereon. This assistance was especially accomplished as he was in that position and nursed his mother's breasts.

Verse 13. Had the foregoing wishes of Job been allowed to occur, then he would have been saved all his present distress, and instead of all this sorrow he would have been at rest. This, by the way, is against the teaching that death ends all there is of man. Job believed that if he had died in his mother's arms he would have been at rest. An unconscious person has no appreciation of rest, therefore Job believed that the death of his infant body would have brought him consciousness and rest.

Verse 14. *For desolate places* Moffatt gives us pyramids, and the lexicon supports the rendering. The pyramids were built as burial places for the kings. Job gives us to understand that death places all mankind on a level whether king or infant, and the rest that an early death would have brought him would have afforded him something far better than the pomp of royalty with all its outward show of pleasure.

Verse 15. The thought in this verse is practically the same as the one in the verse just considered, and the reader will please consult that passage again.

Verse 16. This is similar in thought

to Vs. 10, 11. Job expressed a wish that he had had a premature birth so that his existence would have been *hidden*.

Verse 17. *There* is an adverb of place and refers to the state of those who had the lot described by the foregoing verses. That lot may briefly be summed up by reference to a death that occurred before one had to enter the trials of life. It was the idea of Job that an early death could bring him only a state of rest. *There*, in such a state, the wicked would indeed cease from troubling.

Verses 18, 19. The desirable experiences described in these verses would be the lot of the one pictured in the verses we have been considering. The whole passage of the last several verses describes the condition of one who passed out of this life while pure, thereby escaping the sorrows of the world of sin and sinners.

Verse 20. *Wherefore* means "why is it?" *Light* is used in reference to the mature existence of a man when he is compelled to undergo the misery of misfortune; Job could not see the reason for such an experience.

Verses 21, 22. The unfortunate person described above would rather die than live, and he would gladly obtain it by greater exertion than that used by the searcher for gold. Of course it must be understood that Job would not commit any violence against himself in order to obtain death. His comparison was only for the purpose of expressing his natural yearning for rest in death.

Verse 23. This verse starts the same as V. 20, then makes mention of a man whose *way is hid*. The phrase in italics means that the man is "at the end of his row" and does not know where to go next. *Hedged in* means about the same as the preceding phrase commented upon. It might be illustrated by a man who had found himself at the "dead end" of a street since it says that God had hedged him in.

Verse 24. *Sighing* and *roaring* are used to refer to the same thing in this place. The comparison to *waters* is made for two reasons; waters have long been considered as a figure of troubles, and the full flowing of waters illustrates the volume of Job's ills.

Verses 25, 26. We do not have any information about how or when Job had the thoughts expressed in this paragraph. There is a certain amount of uneasiness that is natural to any man, but this seems to have been something special in the experience of Job. The word *yet* is not in the original and should not be in the translation, for it makes a false impression. The word sometimes has the force of "nevertheless" and is more commonly so used. That would not be correct in this case because there is no contrast between the thoughts on each side of the word. If it is retained in the text at all it should be used in the sense of "and furthermore," which is one of its meanings. That would make the paragraph teach that Job first had fear and dread of some kind of misfortune, then it came upon him in reality.

JOB 4

Verse 1. It should be remembered all the way through the book that these friends of Job were not inspired men. They will speak much truth and also much error. The report of their speeches is inspired, but the speeches themselves will not be so. I shall comment as far as seems necessary on their language, but wish the reader to keep constantly in mind the fact that they spoke on their own authority and that their main theory was false. All through the conversations between them and Job their position was to the effect that God never afflicts a righteous man; that Job was afflicted; therefore, Job was not a righteous man at the time of their consideration. Such was the formula if stated logically and the argument throughout will be on that basis. Job denied the theory and offered as proof the known fact that good men as well as bad were seen to be afflicted sometimes. That being the case, it follows that afflictions are not proof that the victim was unrighteous, and therefore his afflictions must be attributed to some other cause. This statement of the respective positions of the three friends on one side and Job on the other will be referred to frequently and the reader is requested to take full notice of it for his information as the story proceeds.

Verse 2. Eliphaz made a sort of apology for speaking to Job but declared that he just had to speak.

Verses 3, 4. This paragraph was to remind Job of the teaching he had given to others. The purpose was to present a basis for accusations against him; that he had no excuse for the sins that had brought his present distress upon him.

Verses 5, 6. The idea thrown at Job is that he did not have the courage to "take his own medicine." *Is not this thy fear, etc.*, was a taunt for Job meaning that such was all that his professions of confidence amounted to.

Verses 7, 8. This paragraph exactly states the position of the three friends. Please read my comments on V. 1 for explanation of this passage.

Verses 9-11. *The blast of God* means the force of God's acts against the wickedness of men. A lion is strong and hard to overcome, yet it can be done when a greater force comes against him. Job had been a strong force but the blast of God was overcoming him. *Lion perisheth for lack of prey* is a figure of speech. Just as a strong beast will fail when the prey is gone, so the great professions of Job are coming to nought for lack of God's favor to keep them in a good showing.

Verses 12-16. We do not know whether Eliphaz really thought he had this vision or was drawing on his imagination. At any rate, he professed to have some "inside" information that he wanted to pass on to Job. Of course we would expect it to be along the line of his theory as to the reason for the afflictions of his friend.

Verse 17. This implies a false accusation against Job. He never claimed to be even as just as God, much less to be more so than he. He only denied that his afflictions were a punishment for any injustice of his.

Verse 18. Eliphaz spoke the truth about the angels (2 Pe. 2: 4; Jude 6), but that had no bearing on Job's case. It had not been shown that he was guilty of folly.

Verses 19-21. If God will not tolerate sin and folly in his angels, he certainly will not suffer creatures of the earth to escape. That is true but did not figure in the case of Job because he had not been convicted of any wrong conduct.

JOB 5

Verse 1. Eliphaz challenged Job to appeal to some righteous person to see if he could obtain any help. The argument was that if he had not done something wrong, the saint would come to his rescue upon his appeal to him.

Verse 2. It is true that wrath will kill a foolish man, but it likewise will kill a righteous one who happens to be a victim. See the comments at Ch. 4: 1.

Verse 3. *Taking root* is a figure of speech referring to the former good estate of Job. *Cursed* means he thought little of it because of its reversed condition; even so, Job's good situation was made low through the effects of his own folly according to the argument of the speaker.

Verse 4. The gates of cities were the places where the citizens came and went, and if all was prosperous the happiness of the children was assured. However, if a man became unworthy his children would have to suffer for it when they attempted to return through the usual channel at the entrance to the city.

Verse 5. The children of the wicked will even be deprived of the necessities of life at the hands of evil persons. There will be no relief for them because their father has gone wrong and thrown himself outside of the help of God.

Verse 6. The gist of this verse is the same as if he had said: "Affliction and trouble do not come from just nowhere or without a cause."

Verse 7. The argument of Eliphaz is as follows: "All natural effects come from natural causes, so Job's afflictions are the logical effect of something." The argument is correct but misapplied; just because there can be no effect without a cause is no reason for referring to Job's case. There could be numerous causes for the effects that were present, therefore it cannot be claimed that the particular cause designated by Eliphaz was the true one.

Verse 8. This verse gave some advice to Job. The speaker assumed that Job had turned from God and that it would be well for him to return. The claim had not been proved and therefore the advice was out of place.

Verses 9-12. Everything asserted in the paragraph was true, but still there was the missing link in the argument of Eliphaz. Job would have agreed to all the claims made for the greatness of God, but that would have had nothing to do with his afflictions. The greatness of God would not necessarily require that any man whosoever should be afflicted unless some cause existed for such punishment to be administered.

Verse 13. While the statement of this verse has nothing to do with Job, it is a true one and has been quoted for many generations. It is even quoted by Paul in 1 Cor. 3: 19. However, that does not prove that it was inspired when Eliphaz uttered it. Paul even quoted from the literature of the heathen (Acts 17: 28), but that only shows that the apostle accepted the statement as being true and he gave it his endorsement. The meaning of the present statement is that just when a man of worldly wisdom thinks he has a scheme arranged for his own advantage, the Lord will use that as a trap to capture the "wise" man.

Verses 14-16. Eliphaz said so many things that were true but they had nothing to do with Job. Had he been guilty of some special sin he would have needed the exhortations spoken to him, but he was as sure of all these truths as was the one speaking to him.

Verse 17. See my remarks on verse 13 regarding quotations from uninspired sources; this idea will need to be kept in mind or confusion will result. The mere reference to a statement does not prove it to have been written by inspiration since the Bible makes frequent mention of heathen writers with approval of the statements quoted. However, if an inspired man quotes an utterance with his approval, then it becomes inspired. The present verse should be considered in the light of these remarks.

Verses 18-22. This paragraph says some very good things about the doings of God, but Job did not need the instruction, for he was already aware of them.

Verse 23. These are figures of speech since a stone could not form nor break a league. A beast would know nothing about being *at peace* with a man, and so the whole passage means that a man would prosper if he trusted in God.

Verses 24-27. The paragraph as a whole pictures the success of a man who is true to God. Job did not need the information and we shall see that he does not notice any of these remarks when it comes his turn to speak.

JOB 6

Verses 1, 2. Job made no direct reply to the speech of Eliphaz, for he believed that his own problem was underestimated. *Grief were thoroughly weighed* means that his grief deserved a fairer consideration.

Verse 3. If the grief of Job could be literally weighed it would be found to outweigh the sand of the seashore. *Words swallowed up* means he did not have words to express his grief fully.

Verse 4. *Arrows* is used figuratively and refers to the afflictions that Job was suffering. *Within me* has reference to the manner of wounding with an arrow. If a man could find an opening in the armor of another, he could get his arrow through that opening and *within* the victim or into his body.

Verse 5. A beast will not complain when he has what he needs. Job reasoned that his complaints were just because he lacked the comforts of life.

Verse 6. The complaints of Job were just and as reasonable as it would be to object to food that had been improperly seasoned, or not seasoned at all.

Verse 7. This verse gives us a terrible picture of the unfortunate condition of Job. Because all of his property had been destroyed and his family and friends were no more, there was no one to provide him with food. Such a condition compelled him to eat things that he formerly would not even have touched with his hands.

Verses 8, 9. The substance of this verse is a wish of Job that he might be allowed to die. He would prefer death to life under such fearful conditions as were then overwhelming him. But it would be a sin for a man to destroy himself, therefore Job's wish was that *God would destroy him* by some kind of miraculous means.

Verse 10. Job believed that man was conscious and could be happy after death. See the comments on Ch. 3: 13-17 for this phase of the subject. But the present verse does not reach that far with the subject. Job means that whatever method God would see fit to use in bringing about his physical destruction, it would be pleasant compared with what he was then suffering. The reason for such a conclusion was the provocation that Eliphaz was adding to the situation by his false reasoning. *I have not concealed*, etc., means he had never evaded any of the words of God, therefore there were no hidden truths that would make Job dread anything from God.

Verses 11, 12. In these verses Job says practically the same things he has already said. He does not think he has much to live for, therefore it would be just as well for God to take him out of this world.

Verse 13. This verse is in the form of a question, but it really means to express an assertion. It is about the same as if Job would say: "Help and wisdom have forsaken me, and there is none of it with me."

Verse 14. Job accused Eliphaz of overlooking the respect he should have for the Almighty. Because of having done that, he has not pitied Job as he should.

Verse 15. In this passage Job recognized his three friends as his brethren. I wish the student to see my comments on Ch. 2: 11.

Verses 16-18. The sum of this paragraph is a comparison to the unsteady, temporary, off-and-on nature of many streams. They are uncertain as to their continuance, and just as one might think of refreshing himself by them they are gone. This would be particularly true of the streams that are fed by snow. When the sun's rays would become warm they would soon disappear. That illustrated the fickleness of the friendship of Job's brethren as he considered it.

Verses 19-21. *Troop of Tema* means the caravans of the people of Tema who were descendants of Ishmael. They were wanderers and in their traveling would desire to obtain water for themselves and for their beasts. When these tourists thought of getting such refreshments from these streams they would be doomed to disappointment by their sudden disappearance. Likewise, just when Job would look to his friends for comfort they disappointed him.

Verses 22, 23. Job had not asked these friends to give him any of their property to replace what he had lost. He was willing to endure such a loss as that if they had only not made his lot more bitter by their false reasoning.

Verse 24. Up to the present point in the conversation Eliphaz had not spoken anything to Job that he did not already know. That is why he said *teach me and I will hold my tongue.*

Verse 25. *Reprove* is another form of "prove." Job meant that the argument of Eliphaz did not prove anything on the subject under consideration.

Verse 26. Another meaning of *reprove* is "dispute." Job asked Eliphaz if his purpose was merely to dispute or contend against the words he was hearing. A man in as *desperate* condition as that of Job would likely give forth words like a whirlwind. But it would not be fair for a man to wage such a contest when he was in possession of all his good things and the other man was as downcast as Job.

Verse 27. Job did not accuse Eliphaz of literally injuring the helpless as it is worded here. But such an act was an illustration of his unjust attacks on Job.

Verses 28-30. This paragraph amounts to a challenge for Eliphaz to "get down to business" and come to the real issue. If Job was lying or making false claims it ought to be *evident*, and his *friend* was called upon to expose it.

JOB 7

Verse 1. There is one very pitiable feature of this case that I have not mentioned and it will be done now. In all of Job's afflictions he had not been told why it had come about. He did not believe the position of the friends, but he did not profess to understand the background. Because of not knowing why the afflictions were allowed to come he likewise did not know that they were supposed ever to end as long as he remained in the land of the living. Had he known that it was for the special purpose of a test and that as soon as the test had been carried through he would be restored, it then would have been easier for him to endure it. But the only consideration there was to keep him true through all the afflictions was his faith in God. He just supposed that "his fate was the common fate of all; that into each life some rain must fall," and that he would just have to bide his time.

Verses 2, 3. The *shadow* is the closing of the day when the slave would get to cease working; he would naturally wish for that time to come, and the hireling would look forward to the moment when he would receive his wages. The strain of mind in these servants is used to illustrate the state of Job's mind as he looked to the time when his day of sorrow would be over.

Verse 4. A state of continual unrest was what Job was describing in this verse. He would wish for the night because it was supposed to bring him rest. Then when it came and he lay down, his spirit of unrest made him wish it would be day.

Verse 5. The running ulcers that covered Job's body would naturally cause an open condition all over the surface. That exposed him to all kinds of filth that would be connected with the situation. Sitting among the ashes he would be helpless against the accumulation of the dust that would be caught by the sores that were open. This matter then formed *clods* which Strong defines in the original as "a mass of earth." Such a condition would attract the blowflies and they deposited their germs. That brought the *worms* as the text says and which Strong defines as maggots. Thus we see Job with our mind's eye, sitting there in the ashes, and the filthy pus oozing out and over his body. The flying dust has been caught by the open sores and it has formed into clods inside the sores. To add to all this, the maggots have hatched out of the germs deposited by the flies, and their creepy, wriggly, constant motion helps to keep Job's sickening agitation constantly with him.

Verse 6. Ordinarily we think that "time goes so slowly" when conditions are such as those being suffered by Job; the illustration is used in a different sense. A weaver's shuttle darts back and forth in the work as if it were nervously looking for a place to stop and rest. Yet it does not get to rest but must go on and on endlessly from one stroke to another. Likewise the days of Job were being constantly passed away from one alternation to another with no prospect of relief.

Verse 7. Job compared his life to *wind* in about the same sense that James called it a vapor (Jas. 4: 14).

Verse 8. This verse has been a favorite saying for many years when people were referring to the fleeting existence of human life. The force of the statement, however, has been overlooked. A man might refer to some date years ahead and say that when that time came no eye would see him. But that would still leave it possible for the speaker to live a long time. But this verse says that the eye that *hath seen* him would see him no more, which indicated that the end was near.

Verses 9, 10. The unbeliever in a future life would use the first of these verses to prove his theory. It is not fair to do that, but all of the connection should be observed. I will suggest that the reader underscore the last 5 words of verse 9, then underscore words 6, 7, 8 in the next verse. He will then have the expression *shall come up no more to his house.* That will be the truth, for we all know that the dead are never to come back to the earth to live.

Verse 11. Job gave Eliphaz to understand that his grief was too great to allow another the right to silence him.

Verse 12. This is another verse in the form of a question but is meant for an assertion. Job meant to tell Eliphaz that his attempt to regulate or influence a man with such a volume of emotion as that now possessed by him (Job), would be like trying to curb the sea or its monsters.

Verses 13, 14. The speeches of Job were a mixture of replies to the false reasoning of his friends interspersed with descriptions of his troubles. In this paragraph he reported an experience similar to what he described in V. 4.

Verses 15, 16. Job would rather die than live on with the weight of sorrows then bearing down on him. The same thought was expressed in Vs. 8-10; but he will not do anything by violence in order to get release from this life.

Verses 17, 18. Job was again ignoring the presence of Eliphaz and speaking as if to God only. He admits to the Lord that his life was not worth much in view of the present troubles and the satisfaction of a life in another world.

Verse 19. Job was protesting being constantly aggravated by Eliphaz. By the phrase *till I swallow down my spittle* is meant about the same as if he had said: "Can't you leave me alone for even a second?"

Verses 20, 21. *I have sinned.* This does not admit that the position of the three friends was correct. Job never denied being human and subject to human weaknesses, he only denied that his present afflictions were a specific penalty for some sin. But he was confused about the whole situation and asked, *why hast thou set me as a mark against thee?*

JOB 8

Verses 1, 2. The three friends took turns speaking to Job, while he had to do all the talking for his side. In all of the speeches of the three we will see the same thread of thought, accusing Job of having done some great sin and receiving the afflictions as a punishment. In this paragraph Bildad charged Job with being what the modern language calls "a windy speaker."

Verse 3. This affirms that God is never unjust in any of his dealings, which was something that Job never denied.

Verses 4, 5. Bildad even intimated that the afflictions were because of the sin of Job's children. But that theory will not hold good, for even if they had done wrong they were not living then. Neither would the afflictions of Job be in punishment for sins of his children committed before their death. In Ch. 1: 5 we read that Job was faith-

Verse 6. This is the same old doctrine of the three friends. *Awake for thee* means that God would be merciful to Job if he would purify himself by proper actions.

Verse 7. Bildad unconsciously predicted the very thing that did occur (Ch. 42: 12), but it did not come on account of the reasons that Bildad was assigning to it.

Verses 8-10. Bildad presumed to exhort Job to take a lesson from the forefathers. That was good advice but was not needed, for Job had already been credited by the Lord with being better than any other man in the world. (Ch. 1: 8.)

Verses 11, 12. This is the same old argument; no effect without a cause. Job admitted all that but that did not even touch the question of what was the real cause in the case under consideration.

Verses 13, 14. The very point in dispute is what these friends always assumed. The hypocrite's hope will perish but it had not been proved that Job was a hypocrite.

Verse 15. Bildad intimated that Job was leaning on his house (his claim of being innocent) and that it would not sustain him. Even at the very moment it was beginning to topple as evidenced by the afflictions being suffered.

Verses 16, 17. For a while man may prosper as Job did, and be compared to a green and lively plant.

Verse 18. But if the false support is taken from the plant it will go down, and the surrounding territory will deny that it ever knew the plant. The argument is that when Job is finally cut down he will be forgotten as was the plant that had been cut off from moisture.

Verse 19. The man who rests upon false security as Job has been doing will fall and others more worthy will take his place.

Verse 20. If God will not cast away a perfect man and yet has cast off Job, it follows that Job is not a perfect man. This again is the same argument but it leaves out a link. It has not yet been proved that Job is even cast away, much less proved that it was because of his imperfections.

Verses 21, 22. The argument is that if Job will become perfect by atoning for his sin, it will cause all his enemies to be *clothed with shame*.

JOB 9

Verses 1, 2. Job admitted the statements that had just been made by Bildad as far as the facts were concerned. There really has not been any difference between them on that phase of the subject; the point of dispute has been the application to be made of those facts. Job was a very afflicted man and he also was a human and made mistakes in life the same as other men. But the friends claimed the afflictions were sent to punish him for his sins while he denied it. In the present paragraph the argument of Job is that if all sin is to be punished by some special lot then all men would be going through some form of punishment. This agrument is couched in his words *how should man be just with God?*

Verse 3. Using nouns instead of pronouns this would read *if God would contend with man*, etc. Job did not believe that God would consent to argue with him; but if He did then he would not win one argument in a thousand.

Verse 4. No man can harden himself against God and succeed. Job meant to admit that he could not contend with God, but that did not mean that his afflictions had been sent for a punishment.

Verse 5. When it comes to describing the greatness of God, Job will show that his friends cannot outdo him. This and several following verses will deal with the subject of God's greatness.

Verse 6. We know the earth does not rest on literal pillars so the term is used figuratively. The thought is that God is able to handle the earth according to his will. That was demonstrated when he caused the shadow to go backward in the time of Hezekiah. (2 Ki. 20: 11.) That was done by reversing the motion of the earth.

Verse 7. This took place in the time of Joshua when he commanded the sun to stand still. (Joh. 10: 12, 13.) The word *riseth* in the text here is from ZARACH, and the part of Strong's definition that applies is as follows: "a primitive root; properly to irradiate (or shoot forth beams)." That is what occurred in the case of Joshua; the sun did not shine during the period which was the same in effect as if it did not rise.

Verse 8. *Which* is not in the original here and in a number of other verses nearby. It has been supplied from V. 5, second phrase. There it is from ASHAR which Strong defines, "a primitive relative pronoun (of every gender and number); who, which, what, that." Since the name of God was introduced in V. 2 we should use this word as a masculine pronoun and make the verse read, "He alone spreadeth out the heavens." It means that God is master of the earth and sky.

Verse 9. These are names of heavenly bodies and the passage means that they were made by the Lord.

Verse 10. The wonderful works of God are beyond the knowledge of man; therefore the present state of Job should not be allowed to cause confusion.

Verses 11, 12. This whole passage simply means that God's power and wisdom are beyond the comprehension of man.

Verses 13, 14. *Proud* is from an original that means to bluster or urge with active strength. It means a person who is generally hard to subdue. Job's thought is that God's anger will cause even such determined characters to shrink away. If that is the case then a modest man like Job would have nothing to say in answer to Him.

Verse 15. The thought in this verse is about the great difference between God and the best of men. The most righteous man living should not feel qualified to contend with Him, seeing he would not have any answer that would be just.

Verse 16. All apparent contradictions are clear when the real thought is observed. If God should respond to man's prayer it would not be on the ground of the merit possessed by the man; it would be purely the goodness of the Lord.

Verse 17. *Without cause.* God has a good reason for all that he does. Job meant that he had not given the Lord any cause for afflicting him. We know that was true, and that it was all brought about by the challenge of Satan (Ch. 2: 4-6). The pitiable part of this matter is the truth that Job did not know what occasioned his trials.

Verse 18. We must not forget that one object to be accomplished by this book was to show how a man of God may be patient under trial. To do that it was necessary to give the readers an inspired account of those afflictions. This verse is one of many in the book that are given along this line.

Verses 19, 20. Job described his afflictions in many passages but did not know "what it was all about."

However, he never once thought of complaining to God of any injustice having been done him. If he even thought that he had grounds for complaint, he did not feel able to contend with the Lord.

Verse 21. Notwithstanding all that might justly be claimed for his character, Job still regarded himself as an unworthy worm of the dust.

Verses 22, 23. Job has contended all along that afflictions do not necessarily indicate the wrath of God. His basis for such a position is the fact that both good and bad men have to suffer them at times, a fact of which all of us are aware.

Verse 24. God is said to give certain things when the literal fact is that he merely suffers men to have their own way that they might learn a lesson by their own experience. That is the meaning of Ezk. 20: 25, 39; Psa. 81: 12; Acts 7: 42; Rom. 1: 24 and 2 Thess. 2: 11. Such is the meaning of the paragraph now being considered.

Verses 25, 26. This paragraph will take the same comments as Ch. 7: 6.

Verses 27, 28. Job means that it would be useless to try to forget about his troubles. It would be false cheer were he to try making himself think that nothing much was the matter with him, for he might just as well make up his mind that he was "in" for more afflictions. The word *innocent* is not one with a meaning concerning guilt. Moffatt renders the last words of the verse, "I know thou wilt not let me off."

Verse 29. Job never has admitted that his afflictions were a special "judgment" sent on him. Yet he has been free to acknowledge that he partook of the same weaknesses common to man and the same tests of faith were necessary. This verse should be explained on that basis; that since he was like all other men and subject to vanity, it would be useless to expect any exceptions in his favor.

Verses 30, 31. Job's teaching in this passage is that at best a man would not be worthy of God's favor if measured on the basis of strict justice.

Verse 32. God and man are not in the same class of individuals, therefore Job would not estimate the Lord on a human basis.

Verse 33. *Daysman* is rendered "umpire" in the margin of some Bibles and the lexicon will sustain the translation. Job means that even if he had an umpire to decide without any partiality he would decide in favor of the Lord.

Verses 34, 35. If God should remove all indications of human weakness then Job might feel free to justify himself. But he had no reason to form such a conclusion if his own worthiness constituted his chief basis of thought.

JOB 10

Verses 1, 2. The awful state of affliction being endured by Job must be kept before the mind of the reader because of the main purpose of the book. (Ch. 3: 2, 3.) That will account for the many places throughout that devote so much attention to the subject. As a man, no doubt Job felt the sting of his sufferings; but as an inspired writer he was giving us a true description of his condition.

Verse 3. Apparently God was giving rough treatment to a part of his own creation. In doing that he was giving the enemy something to boast about.

Verses 4, 5. It appeared to Job that God was treating him in the same manner that a man would treat him if he had it "in for him."

Verse 6. Job had no knowledge of any particular sin for which he should be so grievously tormented. Yet it appeared that God was making a search "by scourging" as it were, to see if some secret sin existed in Job's life.

Verse 7. Job had a clear conscience before God, therefore he was assured that no one could snatch him from the Lord's hand.

Verse 8. *Destroy* refers to the destruction of Job's family and property and the loss of his health. God had allowed such a condition to come upon Job although he was the Creator of all those things.

Verse 9. Job knew that he was made out of the earth and was destined to return to it; he feared that such a change was about to occur.

Verse 10. When milk is poured out it is lost and Job used the illustration in view of what he had lost. One meaning of the original for *curdled* is to shrink or become diminished, and Job had certainly been diminished by the Lord.

Verses 11-13. This passage is an acknowledgement of the favors of God that had been bestowed on Job notwithstanding all his afflictions.

Verse 14. Job had denied all along, in his conversations with his friends, that his afflictions were a special judgment, yet he admitted that if he did commit sin he would deserve the judgment of God.

Verse 15. Job would expect the severe judgment or chastisement of God were he to commit wickedness knowingly. Yet, even though he was not aware of any specific sin, he would not feel inclined to boast of it. On the humble basis of his admission of unworthiness Job asked for the mercy of God.

Verse 16. God had suffered afflictions to come on Job as if a fierce lion were pursuing him. In spite of that, however, the divine favor had been great.

Verse 17. *War* is used figuratively and refers to the attacks being made on Job by his many afflictions as if by an invading army.

Verses 18, 19. The uselessness of his birth is the subject of this paragraph. See my comments at Ch. 3: 10, 11 for explanation of the passage.

Verse 20. This verse is a pitiable plea for just a few days of comfort before Job was to pass from the earth.

Verses 21, 22. This doleful description of the state of man after death applies only to the fleshly part. What Job said in Ch. 3: 13-17 showed he did not believe that death ended it all for the spiritual part of human beings.

JOB 11

Verses 1, 2. The third one of the "friends" was the next speaker. It should be observed that no attempt was made to meet the arguments of Job; all that Zophar could do was to accuse him of talking too much.

Verse 3. Accusations of falsehood were all the remarks that could be thought of.

Verse 4. This verse is a false acccusation, for Job never claimed to be "clean" in the sense that Zophar used it. *Thine* refers to God and Job knew that he was not perfect in the sight of the Lord. He only claimed that his afflictions were not sent from God as a special punishment.

Verse 5. The time will come when God will speak, but Zophar will be one against whom he will direct his divine remarks.

Verse 6. *That which is* means that the wisdom which is known to man is much less than the wisdom of God. The last half of the verse is the same theory that has been claimed from the beginning.

Verse 7. Job never made any such claim as was implied by this question. Not knowing all about God would not prevent him from knowing more than did his friends.

Verse 8. *Hell* is from a word that has a figurative meaning in this place intended to represent the opposite of heaven. The idea is that God is higher and deeper than all other beings or things.

Verse 9. This verse was said for the same purpose as the preceding one. But Job already believed what it said and thus the remarks of Zophar were unnecessary.

Verse 10. The ability of God to control things is the subject of the forepart of the verse. In view of his great might it would be foolish to attempt any hindrance to the Lord, a truth known to Job as well as to Zophar.

Verse 11. God knows all about vain or empty men and can see through all their wickedness in whatever form it may exist.

Verse 12. Some men are as vain or empty as a wild ass's colt, yet they will pretend to be wise. This was said as a reproach upon Job but was false.

Verses 13-15. This paragraph is a concise and direct statement of the position of the friends of Job. He was being afflicted for his sins, and if he would repent and make proper amends he would restore himself in the sight of God.

Verse 16. After Job would have restored himself to God's favor by proper acknowledgment, he would feel so good that all his past misery would be forgotten.

Verses 17, 18. Zophar unconsciously uttered a prophetic statement of the final state of Job. (Ch. 42: 12.) But that state did not come to him as a result of doing what the three friends were demanding of him.

Verse 19. *Many shall make suit unto thee.* This was another unconscious prophecy and the fulfillment may be seen in Ch. 42: 8.

Verse 20. This was a true statement but had no bearing on Job's case. The friends of Job made so many remarks that were unrelated to the controversy under consideration, and the real issue was thereby thrown into confusion.

JOB 12

Verses 1, 2. This is a form of language known as irony. That means language used in a sense just opposite of the outward and apparent meaning, and the purpose of such language is ridicule. The idea was that if the three friends were as wise as they pretended to be, when they died there would be no wisdom left.

Verse 3. Having spoken with irony in the preceding paragraph, Job next spoke directly and in a serious mood. *Who knoweth not*, etc., is the point that I have been emphasizing in many of the paragraphs of this book. The three men stated many truths, but Job knew them already and they did not have any bearing on the case.

Verse 4. Job was really a just and upright man, but the friends talked to him as if he were one beneath the notice of God.

Verse 5. A man who is not in trouble himself will think lightly of one who is. He will disregard such an unfortunate person the same as he would a lamp of which he did not feel the need.

Verse 6. This verse states facts that prove Job's position in the argument to be correct. If all afflictions are in punishment for sin, then how does it come that men who are known to be sinners are prosperous?

Verses 7-10. This paragraph refers to the providence of God in his creation. The beasts are blessed through the same divine creation as is man, and through that great impartial Providence the good and bad share alike in the temporal blessings of God. This great fact disproves the main position of the friends of Job.

Verse 11. The Creator has adapted all of the creatures of his work to the things that were created for their use and enjoyment. Thus the ear was made in such a manner that it could appreciate language, and the mouth was so made that it could receive and make use of food.

Verses 12, 13. The value of experience is the substance of this paragraph. These friends were not young (Ch. 32: 4, 6, 9), and hence their age should have brought them the wisdom of experience; however, they did not show much indication of it.

Verse 14. God is the one who is spoken of in this verse. It declares that when a man would oppose the works of God he will meet with defeat.

Verse 15. God's control of the elements that he has created is the leading thought in this verse.

Verses 16, 17. God knows all about man and can overrule the wisest of them.

Verses 18, 19. This is along the same line of thought as that in Dan. 4:17.

Verses 20, 21. God's wisdom and power are far above that of all earthly characters. The cases where this was proved are too numerous to mention, but Pharaoh is a noted example of His superiority over all others.

Verse 22. Light and darkness are the terms in this verse that express the leading thought. God's might is frequently illustrated by contrasting terms, such as heaven and earth, earth and sky, dry land and water, etc. In the present verse it is light as contrasted with darkness.

Verse 23. Just one example will be cited in confirmation of this statement. God caused his own people to increase to over half a million of men (Num. 1:46), then destroyed or reduced them to a mere remnant of 42,000 (Ezra 2:64).

Verses 24, 25. God caused his own people to wander through the wilderness 40 years, after they had given way to a spirit of despondency. (Num. 14:1-4.)

JOB 13

Verses 1, 2. Job stated what has been observed from the beginning of this story, that the friends said many things that were true but he already knew them; also, they had no bearing on the case in controversy. The few assertions that might have been a basis for an argument were not true.

Verse 3. Job would prefer to make his appeal to God, for he would be given due consideration in the hearing, and not be misrepresented as the friends were doing.

Verse 4. Using the physician as the illustration Job likened his friends to one who entered a case without the remedy necessary to it.

Verse 5. They would show more wisdom by keeping silent than by their talking, since what they said was false in most particulars; this thought is also in Prov. 17:28.

Verses 6, 7. God does not need the assistance of any man, much less one who would use deceit in his speech.

Verses 8, 9. The friends professed to be in harmony with God. Job's proposition was that they come to "close quarters" with him and see if their contentions would stand the test of the divine scrutiny.

Verse 10. If they insist on attacking Job at close range while remaining at a safe distance from God, it is likely they would justify a wicked man if they could do so secretly and also at a safe distance from God.

Verses 11, 12. This paragraph is a rebuke to these men for their lack of respect for the Lord. They were forgetful of the many evidences of God's greatness. He compared their fickle memories to ashes and clay.

Verse 13. Job insisted on "having his say" in the controversy and after that he would be willing to take the consequences.

Verse 14. *Wherefore* means "why," and Job asked why he was willing to take his life in his own hands in the manner just intimated.

Verse 15. This verse answers the question raised in the preceding one. It means that no amount of affliction, even though it would be severe enough to threaten his life, would shake his confidence in God. But even though such a severe state of affairs as that should come, Job would deny that it was for the purpose assigned to him by the theory of his three friends.

Verse 16. Job would disclaim being a hypocrite for such a character would not have any chance of being saved; yet he felt sure of his own chance for salvation.

Verses 17, 18. This paragraph describes the confidence Job had in the justice of his position. Since his argument did not rest on the ground of any claim to great righteousness, he was ready to face the test if called upon to do so.

Verse 19. Job was so confident that he was innocent of the things they were charging against him, that if anyone should prove the contrary it would kill him.

Verses 20-22. The *two things* Job requested God to do for him were, *withdraw thine hand* and *call thou*. Those two favors would encourage Job to speak.

Verses 23, 24. This plea of Job was that which might be made by any devoted man of God. He was not conscious of any particular wrong, as his friends had been arguing, but made his confession on the general basis that man is frail and in need of the mercy of God at all times in his life on earth.

Verse 25. The weakness of Job was compared to a beaten leaf and withered stubble.

Verse 26. Like most human beings, Job realized that he had made mistakes in the days of his youth, and his present experiences caused him to realize it more.

Verses 27, 28. This paragraph is another description of the unfortunate conditions of Job. It was necessary that he give us a description of his experience. The purpose and manner of such a report received a more extended explanation at Ch. 3: 2, 3, and the reader is requested to consult those comments again.

JOB 14

Verse 1. It would be natural for us to think, "All men are born of women, hence the statement is meaningless." We will appreciate the statement more after a little closer examination of the originals. That for *woman* has a wide range of meaning the outstanding one of which is "mortal." *Man* is from a word that has the idea of "human species." The phrase therefore might well be worded: "The species of creatures that is born of a mortal," etc. The additional words of Job are based on the truth in the first of the verse. The history of mankind also verifies the statement, and that fact further disproves the oft-repeated claim of the three friends, that trouble or affliction comes to man as a penalty for some special sin.

Verse 2. The only point in this verse is the shortness of human life; the same thought is given in Jas. 4: 14. There is no comparison between man and flowers except as to the uncertainty of the length of existence on earth.

Verse 3. The verse means to ask the friends if they think it is fair to require such a person to contend with another like him. Since mankind in general is subject to the frailties described above, it is unbecoming for one of such to set himself up as judge of another in the same class and involved in the same conditions.

Verse 4. In view of the argument of the three friends, and of the facts established at V. 1, the *clean* man would be such a person as Job (and yet all men are in the same class as he). Therefore, it would be impossible for anyone to produce a clean man, because to do so it would be necessary to bring a *clean* thing out of that which is *unclean* and that could not be done.

Verse 5. Job was addressing himself to God in whose hand is the life and existence of everyone. *Determined* and *number* should not be allowed to confuse us. It does not mean that God arbitrarily limits the exact length of man's life. The key to the passage is in the words *are with thee*. God alone knows just how long any man is going to live, but that time will be brought about by the various conditions that may prove to be his lot in this earthly existence. *Appointed his bounds* was done when man was cut off from the tree of life and made subject to "vanity." (Rom. 8: 20.)

Verse 6. Much of the language of Job was spoken as if addressed directly to God. However, it was also intended to suggest to the friends what they should do. The present verse is one of such and means for the friend to let Job alone and allow him to live out his days unmolested by others.

Verses 7-9. Besides the two thoughts expressed in the preceding paragraph, very much of Job's teaching was intended for the benefit of all mankind. This paragraph showed his belief in another life; it was expressed by a comparision to the renewal of the life of a tree through its roots even after the body had been cut down.

Verse 10. A materialist is one who says there is no part of man that exists or is conscious after death, and that when one dies all there ever was of him goes into the grave. Such a theory is one form of infidelity and puts human beings in the same class with dumb beasts. The present verse is claimed to prove the theory because it says that man *wasteth away*. According to 1 Thess. 5: 23 man has three parts and the body is one of those parts; it is the part that wastes away. The question *where is he* shows there is something about man besides the body, for we all know *where* it is after death. Job did not answer the question in this place but we will have seen beyond all doubt that he believed in another life after death, before we are done with the various declarations made by him reported in this book.

Verses 11, 12. That part of man called the body will lie down in death and *rise not; till the heavens be no more.* The last phrase in italics clearly teaches there will be a resurrection when the time comes for the heavens to *be no more*. Certainly there will be no resurrection before that time comes.

Verse 13. Job would have preferred death to life in misery if it had pleased God to release him from this life.

Verse 14. All punctuation marks in the Bible have been added by man. Most of them are correct but we should be careful not to be misled by them. The question mark in the verse is not correct, for Job had no doubt of another life. The statement has the force of a positive declaration as if he had said, "Though a man die, he shall live again." Because of that belief Job was ready to wait for the *appointed time* to come when his vile, decaying, diseased body would be changed into one of deathless vigor and of immortal structure.

Verse 15. *Thou shalt call* agrees with the exact words of Jesus in John 5: 28, 29.

Verse 16. *Numberest my steps* means the steps on earth are limited by the restrictions that God has placed on all mankind. See Gen. 2: 17; Rom. 8:20; Heb. 9: 27.

Verse 17. *Sealed up in a bag* means that God knows all about the conduct of man even though it is unknown to others.

Verses 18, 19. The point in this paragraph is the power of God over all things in the universe, including man who was made in his own image.

Verse 20. *Countenance* is from a word that also means "face." This is an impressive statement to my mind. And it is contrary to the teaching of the materialists who say that all there is of man goes to the grave at death. If that were so, then who or what is sent away as the text declares?

Verse 21. Some part of man does not go away or his sons would not *come* to honor him. If it meant that they honored his memory, they could do that in their own homes without coming to any other place. *He knoweth it not* because his sons came to honor his dead body at the funeral and of course *he* (his body) would know nothing about it.

Verse 22. I like the way Moffatt renders this verse which is as follows: "But his kinsfolk grieve for him, and for him his servants mourn."

JOB 15

Verses 1, 2. The "friend" who first spoke to Job took his turn again. Let not the reader expect much new material in this speech. When a man holds to a false theory he can think of very little to say that even looks as if it belonged to the subject. In this paragraph Eliphaz merely accused Job of being a windy declaimer.

Verses 3, 4. In addition to accusing Job of using vain talk, he charged him with being unwilling to pray which we all know to have been a false accusation.

Verses 5, 6. About the only comment that should be made on this paragraph is that it is a bundle of false accusations.

Verses 7, 8. This verse intimates that Job had claimed to possess all knowledge, and that he ranked far above all other men. Even a glance at the speeches of Job that we have heard so far will deny the charge.

Verses 9, 10. Job had not said that the friends were without knowledge. They had stated much truth and he did not deny it. All that he did claim was that the things they knew and stated had nothing to do with the case. That is what he meant in Ch. 6: 25 when he asked, "what doth your arguing reprove" [prove].

Verse 11. No, the consolations of God were not small with Job. In fact, they were the only ones he counted on for these friends were offering him none.

Verses 12, 13. *Heart carry thee away* was his way of saying that Job was beside himself and saying things that he did not realize.

Verse 14. This was an implied false accusation. Job never claimed to be innocent, but that his afflictions were not a special punishment.

Verse 15. This might be said to be true for 2 Pe. 2: 4 says that angels do sin.

Verse 16. Men as well as angels will be treated according to their conduct. Job has been teaching the same thing all through the controversy.

Verses 17-19. Eliphaz pretended that he was about to impart some great and new truths to Job; we shall see what they were if he had any to tell.

Verse 20. But they turned out to be untrue, for wicked men are as free from pain as any other class of human individuals.

Verses 21-23. This again was not true to the facts. The wicked man has frequently been among the most prosperous of the creatures of the earth.

Verse 24. Instead of the unrighteous one being afraid, he is boastful and feels prepared to do as he pleases in spite of all opposition, human or divine.

Verse 25. The wicked person stretches out his hand against God, it is true, but he has clothed himself with a feeling of security that will finally prove vain.

Verse 26. *He* (the wicked man) *runneth upon him* (God). It represents a wicked human being making a charge upon God as if he were a warrior's steed decorated with flashy ornaments and indications of strength and accomplishments.

Verse 27. This is an exaggerated description of a prosperous person who is puffed up by his own sense of importance.

Verse 28. This wicked man is so powerful that he can overcome the disadvantages of cities that had fallen to decay and ready to be heaped in ruins.

Verses 29, 30. Eliphaz wanted to impress Job concerning his own threatened downfall by describing the failure of this wicked one.

Verse 31. This was good advice but entirely off of the subject being discussed.

Verse 32. *Before his time* means the defeat of the wicked will come prematurely.

Verse 33. *Shake off unripe grape* has the same meaning of prematurity as the italicized words in the preceding verse.

Verses 34, 35. This paragraph and most of the ones preceding in this chapter stated much truth. However, it was truth already known to Job and was taught by him. But it was all outside of the subject that was supposed to be under consideration.

JOB 16

Verses 1, 2. *Miserable* is rendered "troublesome" in the margin and it is supported by the lexicon. It means that the speeches which they made on pretense of consoling him were only a bother to him. They did not tell him anything but what he knew, and it had no bearing on his situation.

Verse 3. *Vain* words were those that were empty or useless, and their words were such because they did not touch the subject, much less solve the problem.

Verse 4. This verse shows the well-known idea expressed in the statement, "Put yourself in my place and see how it will appear to you." If that were done, Job would have as much reason to reproach the "friends" as they professed to have against him.

Verse 5. But if Job could actually exchange places with them, he would speak real words of comfort to them instead of debasing them as they were doing him.

Verse 6. As the case stood, all of the remarks of Job were ignored although he had the facts on his side of the conversations.

Verse 7. *He* and *thou* both refer to God because he had suffered the conditions to come upon Job. That applies even to the provocation caused by the *desolate* company that had come into his presence. This is the same thought as expressed by *miserable comforters* mentioned in V. 2.

Verse 8. Job was so ill or undernourished that it was reflected by the emaciated appearance of his face.

Verses 9, 10. *He* and *they* in this paragraph are the "friends" who have been tantalizing Job with their false reasoning. *Smitten me upon the check* was said figuratively. They had not made any physical attack on Job, but their scornful reference to the wasted condition of his cheek was as bad as if they had struck him there.

Verse 11. Job did not believe nor did he mean that God put him into the hands of the ungodly as a means of punishment. Yet he considered this opportunity for persecuting him as coming from God for some purpose not yet known to him.

Verses 12, 13. This paragraph is a figurative description of the misfortunes that God had suffered to come upon Job. *Taken by the neck* was said in reference to a familiar practice in war. By getting hold of one's neck it made it possible to use the sword more effectively in slaying the foe. *Gall* is bitter and when used figuratively refers to the bitterness of afflictions.

Verses 14, 15. This is some more description of Job's misfortunes. When *horn* is used figuratively it refers to power or prosperity. The language means that Job's fortunes had been reversed upon him.

Verse 16. Through daily and constant weeping, Job's face was stained with the mixture of briny tears and the pus from his sores. And he had spent so much time in this sorrowful crying that his eyelids were inflamed and swollen and had the appearance of one near death. I shall frequently ask the reader to turn back to the comments at Ch. 3: 2, 3 and consider them in connection with the places where Job seemed to take so much pains to describe the depth of his misfortunes and suffering.

Verse 17. Again Job disclaimed any guilt that had called for this suffering.

Verse 18. The thought in this verse is that his blood should not be silenced. If it were covered then its cry would *have no place*. Instead of that, he wants his blood to be allowed to cry out for justice as did Abel's in Gen. 4: 10.

Verse 19. Earthly "friends" had turned against Job and falsely accused him. But there was One on high who understood and would some day bear witness to his innocency.

Verse 20. While Job's friends scorned him and poured contempt on his tears, he would turn his face toward God who can "wipe away all tears." (Rev. 21: 4.)

Verse 21. Job's friends had been pleading with him to confess to a guilt which he did not have. He prayed for some one to plead with God in behalf of the unfortunate.

Verse 22. Job believed in another life after this, but he did not believe that mankind would again live on the earth. (Ch. 7: 9, 10.)

JOB 17

Verses 1, 2. Job was not only ready for the grave apparently, but his days were being made more bitter by the provocation of mockers. Because of such a sorrowful condition he turned his attention to God.

Verse 3. *Strike hands* means to join hands in support of another. Job pleads with God to give him someone to help him in his burdens instead of making them heavier.

Verse 4. *Thou hast hid* is a negative term. It means that God had not given these friends a heart of understanding that they might use better reasoning.

Verse 5. Job did not want the friends to flatter him, for even the children of flatterers are in danger. What he wanted was for them to speak the plain truth.

Verse 6. The original for *tabret* is from another Hebrew word that means a drum; something to beat upon. When used figuratively it means something to be held in contempt and be cuffed about as a football. The people had been using Job in that way.

Verse 7. The condition of Job's eyes was described at Ch. 16: 16. *Members* means his limbs. They had become so lean from his afflictions and undernourishment that they looked like skeletons. Doubtless his observers said he was but a shadow of himself.

Verse 8. Job knew that he would receive little comfort from his "friends," but he believed that upright men would be *astonied* (astonished) at their hyprocrisy.

Verse 9. Job had confidence in the conduct of the righteous and believed all such would become stronger and stronger.

Verse 10. This verse was addressed to the three friends. *Come thou* is an obsolete way of saying, "see here and listen to me." He then told them there was not a wise man among them.

Verse 11. The misfortunes of Job had changed all of his plans.

Verse 12. Ordinarily we think of night more unfavorably than of day. The verse is merely a picture of the upside-down experiences that had been forced on Job.

Verse 13. If Job should think to find solace by looking into the future, all he could see was the grave. His lack of accommodations was like a man who had no light to see how to make his bed.

Verse 14. In this verse the terms *father, mother* and *sister* are used figuratively because they signify nearness to one. Job had been closely connected with corruption and the worms that had been ever creeping over him.

Verses 15, 16. Job asked what hope he had of being relieved of the worms that infested his body. He then answered the question by a reference to the *pit* which here means the grave. He expected to have no relief from all these pests until his body went with them to the grave, at which time they would *rest together in the dust*.

JOB 18

Verses 1, 2. It was Bildad's turn next to speak. This paragraph means that he wants Job to keep still so the rest of them could speak.

Verse 3. This was a false accusation. Job had even admitted many of the things they had said, but denied only that they pertained to the case.

Verse 4. How absurd was the statement in the light of what we have read. Job has been meeting all the claims of the friends with sound reasoning. But such extravagant remarks as these of Bildad give evidence that he is at his limit of his words.

Verses 5-10. I have grouped these verses into one paragraph because they all are to the same effect. They give a good description of a foolish and boastful man, but the information was unnecessary, for it did not apply to this afflicted man.

Verse 11. This implied what was untrue for Job had manifested unusual courage amid all of his terrible afflictions.

Verses 12, 13. This paragraph implied that Job was stricken with hunger and other destitute conditions as a result of his sins. That has been exposed many times.

Verse 14. When *king* is used figuratively it has the significance of something gigantic. The verse means that a character like the one just described will be confronted with huge troubles that will terrify him.

Verse 15. This king of terrors will take possession of the evil man's tabernacle and treat him as if it were not his own by rightful possession, but that it belonged to this "king." *Brimstone* was used to indicate the burning shame that would envelop the habitation of the wicked person, all of which is not to be denied.

Verses 16-18. This paragraph will take the same comments as Vs. 5-10.

Verse 19. It was true that Job lost all of his family, but it was not true that it was because of any fault of his.

Verse 20. Yes, no doubt that the people who lived after Job's day were astonied (astonished). However, it was because of the remarkable recovery that he made.

Verse 21. All of this verse was true but had no application to Job. Therefore the speech was wasted as far as the real issue was concerned.

JOB 19

Verses 1, 2. The suffering that Job was undergoing was severe enough without being tormented with the misapplied words of these friends.

Verse 3. *Ten times* is just a figure of speech referring to the many times Job had been reproached by the false speeches forced upon his ears.

Verse 4. If Job had been as sinful as they charged against him, no one was injured by it and therefore they should keep still. That is the meaning of his words *error remaineth with myself.*

Verses 5, 6. If their charges were admitted they should even then be willing to keep still. What more could they ask Job to do in the way of amends since *God had overthrown* him with afflictions.

Verse 7. *Wrong* is rendered by "violence" in the margin and refers to Job's afflictions. He complained that his hearers did not pay any attention to his cries of pain and anguish. Instead, they added to it by their false accusations.

Verses 8-10. *He* refers to God whom Job understood to be the one who allowed the misfortunes to come on him. He has never disputed the claim of the "friends" that God had brought on the condition. The disagreement has been as to why it was brought. The friends have maintained that it was for some specific punishment for Job's sin, while he has denied that in view of the fact that all classes of men are afflicted.

Verse 11. This verse is more along the same line of thought expressed above.

Verse 12. The great number of Job's afflictions is compared to a division of soldiers making an attack upon a helpless position.

Verse 13. *Brethren* must refer to Job's fellow citizens and more distant relatives. His immediate family had been entirely destroyed by the disasters of Ch. 1.

Verse 14. *Kinsfolk* could refer to Job's immediate family since they had all been taken from him. *Friends* is not in the original and the sentence means that the folk who had formerly observed him now overlooked him. *Forgotten* is from an original word that means to be "inattentive." It therefore does not mean they actually had a lapse of memory about him, but that they felt above noticing him due to his lowly condition.

Verse 15. We recall that Job's flesh-and-blood relatives had been taken from him by violence, but he still had a sort of home with professed servants. But all of these, too, had come to be "above" him and treated him as a stranger.

Verse 16. A servant in the olden times usually responded very promptly to the call of his master. Job's servant not only failed to do his bidding but did not so much as answer him. And all this notwithstanding the fact that his afflicted master begged for service. The most ordinary sense of sympathy should have moved even a superior to give Job some assistance, much more a servant whose duty was to do so.

Verse 17. We recall the attitude that Job's wife had shown toward him in the beginning of his afflictions (Ch. 2: 9); we here see some more of that attitude. She treated him as if he were a stranger on account of his objectionable appearance. *Children's sake* would have to be in the sense of the sake of their memory, for they had all been destroyed.

Verse 18. *Young children.* The first italicized word is not in the original. The second is from a word with a wide range of meaning, and the expression means that the offspring of the citizens treated Job with disrespect.

Verse 19. This verse means that the most intimate associates whom Job had had turned against him and spurned his love.

Verse 20. There is a familiar expression used in reference to a person who has become very lean which is that such a one "is nothing but skin and bones." That is what Job meant by the first part of this verse. *Skin of my teeth* is a highly figurative statement, that Job had barely escaped total destruction.

Verses 21, 22. Job has denied all through the discussions that God was afflicting him for the purpose of punishment. However, he did believe that God was doing it for some purpose not revealed, and he begged his friends to pity him instead of making his sufferings worse by falsely accusing him.

Verse 23, 24. Job has made many declarations of his faith in God, also of his belief in the prospect of another life. He was so positive about it that he had no fears that future developments would prove him to have been mistaken. And because of this assurance he wished that many assertions on the subject were even inscribed in a rock for its permanence, so that the future would be able to confirm his professions of faith. After making this wish, he made another and one of his most glorious declarations of faith in another life which will be considered soon.

Verse 25. There are several words in this verse that should receive a critical examination in order the better to understand and appreciate the noted passage. *Redeemer* is from GAWAL and is defined as follows: "A primitive root, to redeem (according to the Oriental law of kinship), i. e. to be the next of kin (and as such to buy back a relative's property, marry his widow, etc.)"—Strong. *Liveth* is from CHAY and the definition of Strong that pertains to our use is, "Alive . . . strong . . . life (or living thing)." *Stand* is from QUWM and Strong's definition is, "A primitive root; to rise (in various applications, literally, figuratively, intensively and causatively.)" Young defines it, "To rise up; be established; stand firm." It has no reference to the posture or condition of the body. The verse then means that Job's bondage to affliction will be lifted from him and all of the hopes of final deliverance from this world of decay and suffering will be realized. The "nearest of kin" is the divine One who has power to redeem and he will show that he has such power over the things of earthly decay by bringing them out of their "bondage of corruption" [Rom. 8: 21] at the resurrection of the "latter day."

Verse 26. *Worms* and *body* are not in the original as separate words. *Skin* is from a Hebrew word that is itself from another Hebrew word that means, "to be bare," the idea being that about all of his fleshly being will have been destroyed after death. *In my flesh* is rendered "without my flesh" in the R. V. I have examined Moffatt's translation and others in the light of the lexicon and believe it to be correct. I request the reader to consult the same for the fuller information.

Verse 27. Job expected some day to see the Lord face to face and not have to depend on what others could tell him. And this hope he held for himself as against the consuming desire he had to see God.

Verses 28, 29. This paragraph is a little difficult in its form of expression. Its meaning is to warn the friends of the judgment of God against them when the divine truth will be finally made known.

JOB 20

Verses 1, 2. Zophar's second turn to speak came next. It will be well to state again the position of the friends in the discussion. They claimed that God never afflicted a man except as a punishment for some sin. Since Job was afflicted it meant that he had sinned and should make full amends for it in order to be restored to health. Job did not claim to be absolutely perfect, but he did deny that his affliction was a special punishment from God since all classes of men were known to have afflictions. In this discussion the friends stated some truths but they had no bearing on the issue being considered. In this paragraph Zophar stated his reasons for speaking again, that his thoughts drove him to it.

Verse 3. *Check of my reproach* means that Job had reproached Zophar by checking his thoughts; for that reason he just had to speak again.

Verses 4, 5. Job would readily have agreed to the statement about the wicked man's triumphs. Therefore, there was no point made on the discussion at hand.

Verses 6, 7. The shameful humiliation of the man who was proud of his apparent successes is the subject of this paragraph.

Verses 8, 9. These figures of speech describe the final downfall of the man who attains greatness in an unrighteous manner. He will become practically invisible because even the place he once occupied will be vacant.

Verse 10. According to the translation in the margin of the Bible this verse means the children will become victims of other people. That is correct, for it was to be a condition unfavorable to this evil man.

Verse 11. In this place Zophar even intimated that Job was being punished for sins committed in the days of his youth.

Verses 12-15. This paragraph claims that the sins of Job may have brought him pleasure while committing them, but that afterward they would turn against him. Such was the argument Zophar was making regarding the experiences of Job.

Verse 16. A man might suck the poison of asps and not realize that anything objectionable would result. Afterwards the effects of the poison would show up in some form, just as the effects of Job's sins were manifesting themselves in his afflictions.

Verse 17. The desirable things the wicked man looked for will be denied him; he will not get to see them to enjoy them.

Verse 18. *Shall he restore* means he shall not get to keep the fruits of his labor. Instead of retaining the things for his own use, others will possess them.

Verses 19, 20. A glance at the statements of God as to the righteousness of Job (Ch. 1: 8) will show this paragraph to be a false accusation.

Verses 21, 22. Just at the time when Job was the most prosperous it was all taken from him. All of this was a true statement but it was not for the reason that Zophar was contending it to have been.

Verses 23, 24. This passage shows a false claim. Job did not "flee" from the condition in the sense of resenting it. Instead, his attitude was indicated by the wonderful expression found in Ch. 13: 15.

Verse 25. This verse was supposed to describe Job as being like a man who ran from a weapon but who was overtaken by it. That was another false claim although the affliction had been great enough to be compared to the worst of weapons.

Verse 26. *Fire not blown* means a weak fire, one not fanned into a strong blaze. Even such a weak fire would consume Job because he was unworthy to survive. The last of the verse means that any who might wish to remain with Job would be brought down.

Verses 27-29. There is nothing new in this paragraph. It repeats the same line so often let out before and describes the lot of any man who would disobey God.

JOB 21

Verses 1-3. The friends seemed to get much satisfaction out of their talking. Job wanted to have some of the same kind of satisfaction or consolation. He requested them to listen to him for a while after which they might *mock on* if they wished.

Verse 4. Job was not looking to man for justice, therefore man had no reason to interfere with his complaining.

Verse 5. In view of the thought in the preceding verse, Job asked them to take notice of his condition and then keep still until he made his speech.

Verse 6. At every notice that Job took of his condition he was filled with fear.

Verse 7. There are several verses on the position that Job has maintained all through the discussions. He said that unworthy men were known to be favored by the good things of life, therefore the misfortunes of one man did not prove him to be sinful. This and some following verses are on that line of thought.

Verse 8. The children of wicked men are often seen to be successful thus giving them much to be happy over. On the other hand, Job had lost his children by violence.

Verse 9. The homes of wicked men are often known to be secure, while those of Job's children had been destroyed by a storm of wind.

Verse 10. This verse means that the live stock would reproduce. *Casteth not her calf* means the calf would not be born prematurely.

Verses 11, 12. The children of the wicked are often numerous and happy, and are able to engage in exercises of pleasure.

Verse 13. *In a moment* indicates they will die in peace; not suffer from a lingering disease before death.

Verses 14, 15. The success of their plans for pleasure causes them to feel independent of God. On that account they will say, "Depart from us." Being thus successful they cannot think of any reason for serving God.

Verse 16. The pronouns in this verse are used a little vaguely. The thought is that the persons being considered are acting independently of God.

Verse 17. The wicked are not always successful; Job has not claimed they were. He maintained only that they were as likely to be so as were the righteous. But they also are liable to feel the wrath of God as against evil doers.

Verse 18. When *stubble* and *chaff* are used for purposes of comparison it is to indicate lightness. The characters are likened thus because they are so unimportant that they will soon vanish away as the chaff disappears before the wind.

Verse 19. *Iniquity* is from AVON and is sometimes translated, "punishment of iniquity." It is true that God will punish the best of his children. (Heb. 12: 6.) In view of that it would be no reflection on Job if his present afflictions were a chastisement from the Lord. That still would not prove the theory of the three friends.

Verses 20-22. Knowing that these unpleasant experiences may come to the man who displeases God, surely a man would not stubbornly disobey him as the friends had been intimating against Job's conduct.

Verses 23-25. I have made one paragraph out of these verses so the reader will see and appreciate the argument of Job. The first and last of the verses should be considered especially. The experiences of the two men in them are just opposite to each other, yet one of them is as likely to be sinful as the other. The words of the middle verse are figurative, meaning the man is healthy and prosperous.

Verse 26. The frailty of all human beings and their common lot in the grave is the subject of the verse. It brings to mind some words of an old song, "Six feet of earth makes us all of one size."

Verses 27, 28. The arrogant questions of the friends implied that Job was wicked though he was prosperous. But now *where are the dwelling places* he once had?

Verse 29. Job would have his accusers take information from almost anyone. They would be able to speak from observation and form a better conclusion than the "friends."

Verse 30. The New Testament teaches this same truth in 2 Pe. 2: 9. Since all are to get their just dues at last, the wicked will not be punished in this life.

Verses 31, 32. The pronouns refer to the wicked man. He is not to be punished in this life, therefore no one can confront him face to face with his doom. No, he will go to his grave the same as other men and remain there until the day of accounts.

Verse 33. *Clods of the valley* is a poetic reference to the grave. It is the same valley referred to by David in Psa. 23: 4 except that he meant the ordeal of death itself, while Job meant the narrow vale of the grave where the body will rest after death. In comparison with the afflictions of the body while in this life, the cold earth will be a place of sweet rest.

Verse 34. In view of Job's belief in the final plans of the Lord, he considered the so-called comfort offered to him by his friends as a false one.

JOB 22

Verses 1, 2. Eliphaz was the first speaker of the three "friends." He is now about to make his third and last speech to Job. The position will not be changed, but he will repeat many of the assertions that have already been made. He asked if a man could be as profitable to God as to himself. Any one would answer it with a negative but that would not touch the question at hand.

Verse 3. It is of no advantage to God to have a man live a righteous life. This is the teaching of Eliphaz and all people will agree with him, Job not excepted. That is, the Lord would not be personally benefited by the righteousness of man and it is not for that purpose; it is for the benefit of man's soul.

Verses 4, 5. God will not argue with man in order to get him to do right, yet Job ought to repent of his wickedness.

Verses 6-10. Since Job denied being guilty of any specific sin, Eliphaz named a number of them as suggestions in hope that he would admit them.

Verses 11-14. Eliphaz implied that Job was making his claim of innocence because he did not really know how great and wise the Lord is.

Verses 15-17. Job was asked to recall the experiences of wicked men who had lived before him and profit thereby.

Verses 18-21. Again Job was bidden to take a lesson from the experiences of the generations who lived before him.

Verses 22, 23. Eliphaz came directly to his old theory and exhorted Job to repent.

Verses 24-30. This whole paragraph is on the same line. If Job would acknowledge his sins and make amends then the Lord would abundantly bless him.

JOB 23

Verses 1, 2. *Stroke . . . heavier . . . groaning.* Job had been accused of complaining unjustly. He affirms that he had underestimated his afflictions.

Verses 3-5. The friends have charged that Job would not face God with his problems. He maintained an opposite attitude and wished that he might be permitted to come into nearness with Him to plead his cause.

Verse 6. Job believed that God would be more considerate of him than his friends.

Verse 7. *There* means the *seat of* the Lord referred to in V. 3. Job believed he would stand some chance in the presence of God.

Verses 8, 9. God was invisible to the human eye and hence was not taking the part of Job in any outward manifestation.

Verse 10. It is pathetic to know that Job was in the dark as to why he was being afflicted, except he believed it to be some kind of a test for him. He was not bitter over it but looked forward to the time or place when the test would be over and he would come out of it in the favor of God.

Verse 11. Job's confidence in the future was due to his faithfulness in treading the pathway of righteousness.

Verse 12. Job regarded the words of the Lord above all other necessary things.

Verses 13, 14. The subject of this paragraph is the wisdom of God. It is to be esteemed as perfect although we cannot always understand its workings.

Verses 15-17. Job was filled with awe at the presence of God. *Maketh my heart soft* means he felt humbled under the divine influence. He would have preferred death before the present afflictions came had that been the will of God.

JOB 24

Verse 1. *Times are not hidden* means that God knows all about man and his conduct. That being so, why are wicked men suffered to be prosperous?

Verses 2-10. This entire paragraph is a description of the ways of wicked men. The argument of Job is that if such wicked men can be thus happy and prosperous, the misfortunes of another do not prove him to be wicked as the friends have been arguing.

Verse 11. The wicked are able to quench their thirst by the wine of their own production, thus enjoying the fruit of their own labors.

Verses 12. These wicked men may impose on others until they groan, yet God does not stop them with any punishment in the way of afflictions.

Verses 13, 14. This paragraph should take the comments on Vs. 2-10.

Verses 15-17. The New Testament has this teaching on the attitude of unrighteous men toward light (Jn. 3: 19-21). The burglar observes the conditions while he has the light to assist him, then uses the cover of darkness to help in his wicked action.

Verses 18-25. In grouping so many verses into one paragraph I am not depriving the reader of any comments that otherwise would have been offered. Job has argued from the start that men who have been successful have been as free from afflictions as the unsuccessful ones. From that fact he based his denial that his afflictions were sent on him as a punishment for sin. That position made it logical for him to give much detail to his description of men who were prosperous though wicked. He closed this paragraph with a demand that his friends disprove his words.

JOB 25

Verses 1, 2. Bildad's turn came next; his was the second in order of the speeches. It is significant that his speech was very brief and contained nothing new. The strength of Job's position has been shown by the fact that the friends were unable to answer a single one of his arguments. Instead, their speeches became weaker and weaker, and Bildad finally was able only to make this weak speech of 6 verses. The next in line would have been Zophar, but he will not be heard any more at all. This paragraph describes the greatness of God, all of which is admitted but is not to the point.

Verse 3. The power of God is likened to a king with many soldiers at his command.

Verse 4. No man can be just in the sight of God and Job was foremost in teaching that truth. As to the last sentence, Job had already affirmed its answer in the noted passage of Ch. 14: 1-4.

Verse 5. God's power to stop the shining of the moon does not prove any objection to the light of that body. The stars are material things and not subject to the laws of righteousness.

Verse 6. Of course one man would be a worm if his father were one. The word is from two different originals that have practically the same meaning. The idea is that man is of such lowly origin that he will perish like a worm. In view of that no man should think to compare himself with God. To all of this Job would have given his approval but it was not on the subject.

JOB 26

Verses 1, 2. This is the beginning of Job's speech of 6 chapters. The three friends have been given turns to argue against him. Here we have the wonderful spectacle of three healthy men, in possession of all their faculties and blessings, taking turns attacking one man. This one man was unaided and was compelled to talk against the 3 men while he was overwhelmed with disease and stinging from the loss of family and property. But he was strong in the righteousness of his cause. In this long speech Job will give us many truths, not only such as will directly concern the issue between him and the three friends, but will be instructive for all of us. Much of the speech will be on the goodness and greatness of God.

Verses 3, 4. The language is in question form but is intended to be positive as declaring the greatness of God.

Verse 5. *Dead* is from a word that means "ghost," and is used here in the sense of something unseen to man. The myriad of creatures in the sea unknown and unseen by man have been the work of God.

Verse 6. *Hell* in the O. T. is always from SHEOL and Strong defines it, "hades or the world of the dead (as if a subterranean retreat), including its accessories and inmates)." It has been translated in the A. V. by grave, hell and pit. This verse means that God knows all about the unseen world, and things that would wish to cause destruction are subject to His power.

Verse 7. The earth is not resting on any material known to man that could support such a ponderous weight. Therefore it is like hanging it on nothing.

Verse 8. We can see the clouds floating through the air over us and holding the moisture in suspense. When it rains the *clouds* have changed to water according to the law of the Creator, and thus it is not the clouds that are coming down. The familiar term "cloudburst" is a misleading one for there is no such thing in reality. As long as the vapor is uncondensed the cloud will remain intact.

Verse 9. *Holdeth back*. The second word is not in the original and adds no important thought to the text. The first is from ACHAZ and Strong defines it, "a primitive root; to seize (often with the accessory idea of holding in possession)." The verse means that God has complete possession of his throne and can hide it from the universe at his will.

Verse 10. The *compass* (archway) of the sky corresponds with the circle of the earth. That circular globe, revolving, causes the alternations of light and darkness.

Verse 11. The heavenly bodies obey the commands of God. (Josh. 10: 12, 13; 2 Ki. 20: 11.)

Verse 12. *Divideth* is from a word that means to quell or manage with his power. Jesus gave a demonstration of that power in Mark 4: 37-41.

Verse 13. Many of the verses treat of subjects that are widely different except that all show the power of God. To *garnish* means to cause to shine; the sky glistens by the power of God. Even the *crooked* (fleeing) *serpent* was made by divine power.

Verse 14. God's great works are not fully appreciated by man. These are only a portion of the many wonders of creation.

JOB 27

Verse 1. *Parable* is from MASHAL and Strong uses "discourse" as one meaning.

Verse 2. *Judgment* means a verdict or decision. Job was not the one who decided on this condition of his. It had been made by the Lord without even notifying him.

Verses 3, 4. Although he did not know why God had suffered him to be smitten, Job had determined not to say the wrong thing about it.

Verses 5, 6. Let us remember that Job believed God to have been the one who suffered all the afflictions to come on him. However, he held out to the last that the friends were wrong in their explanation of it.

Verse 7. This was a mild wish that proper punishment would come upon all men who were so wicked as to be the enemies of Job.

Verse 8. Job could not afford to maintain his present attitude if it were knowingly wrong. Such would be hypocrisy and that kind of character will lose his soul.

Verses 9, 10. It would do no good for the hypocrite to cry unto God in time of trouble. This would be a sufficient reason for Job to behave himself sincerely now.

Verse 11. Job believed he was *by* (in) *the hand of God*. That would put him in possession of knowledge about God's ways so that he could impart it to others.

Verse 12. The three friends had seen many indications of Job's faithfulness to God. For this reason they were inexcusable in talking against the unfortunate man.

Verse 13. *This* refers to statements yet to be made concerning the lot of wicked men who are successful for a time.

Verse 14. The wicked man may be blessed with many children, but they will be liable to die by the sword. Another thing that often comes to the children of wicked men is hunger, in spite of the previous prosperity of their fathers.

Verse 15. *Widows shall not weep*. That is, some unexpected and sudden calamity will cause the death of the men and the widows will not be on hand at the time to weep personally or in direct connection with the calamity.

Verse 16, 17. We wish to avoid confusion as to the fate of the wicked. Job had claimed only that such characters often were prosperous and happy; he never did claim they would always be so. Therefore, they are liable for the lot here described.

Verse 18. The house of a wicked man will be as uncertain of continuance as the life of a moth, and as temporary as a booth made for some brief use.

Verse 19. *He is not* means the rich man will open his eyes soon to find that he is not a rich man any more.

Verse 20. *Waters* used figuratively means floods of trouble. The wicked rich man is destined to be overthrown by the terrors of disappointment.

Verse 21. The *east wind* is connected with *a storm*. Smith's Bible Dictionary says this about the east wind: "The east wind crosses the sandy wastes of Arabia Deserta before reaching Palestine, and was hence termed 'the wind of the wilderness.' Job. 1: 19; Jer. 13: 24. It blows with violence, and is hence supposed to be used generally for any violent wind. Job 27: 21; 38; 24; Ps. 48: 7; Isa. 27: 8; Ezk. 27: 26." But if something can be destroyed by even such a wind it is very uncertain.

Verses 22, 23. When the wicked rich man comes to his deserved lot he will be spurned by good men who fear God.

JOB 28

Verses 1, 2. A *vein* means a mine and to *fine it* means to refine it. Iron and other metals are taken from the earth and separated by fire. Likewise are the fires of affliction used to try the faith of men.

Verse 3. These valuable materials have been deposited in the earth by some power other than man. This is proved by the fact that he has to *search out* through the *darkness* of the earth's depths in order to find them.

Verse 4. Just when the ground under foot had become dry, causing man to forget about the water, floods came rolling over him. It all shows the helplessness of man and the workings of God independent of man.

Verse 5. Bread is produced by the earth, but the efforts of man are necessary to bring out that which is concealed below the surface.

Verse 6. Gems and precious metals are stored within the coarser parts of the earth. These were not put there by man, for since he has to labor hard to get them he would not have placed them so nearly out of his own reach.

Verse 7. In studying the several verses along in this part of the chapter we should not lose sight of Job's main purpose. He wished to extol the wisdom of God above all other considerations. One of his methods of thought to that end was to refer to the countless items of value hidden in the earth. They are not visible to the eye, not even to that of man. The explanation of his ability to dig and find them is in the reasoning faculties by which he was led to search for them, and this ability was given to him by the Lord. This should help us understand the present verse. The path leading to these great items of value is the path of wisdom just described, not that which can be seen with a mere physical eye such as that of a bird or beast. No, this path is unknown to the fowl or vulture because their eye cannot see it. Only the eye of wisdom given to man by the Lord can see that path.

Verse 8. This verse is explained by the comments on the preceding one.

Verse 9. *He* refers to man and his accomplishments in the field of mechanics. God has given man a mind by which he can reason on the laws of nature and thereby accomplish all of the deeds mentioned in the several verses of this chapter.

Verse 10. This verse refers to the canals and ditches that man has been able to make by his knowledge of nature's laws.

Verse 11. This is seen in the dikes and levees that man has made.

Verses 12, 13. Job said this wisdom was not in man; that is true of man if he is not connected with God. But God has honored man with the power of reasoning that enables him to go after the useful things of earth that his fleshly eye, such as the birds and beasts have, could not have seen.

Verses 14, 15. The wisdom of God which has been graciously portioned out to man cannot be valued by the materials in the sea or the sources of precious metals.

Verses 16, 17. Not even the gold of Ophir with its famed fineness, nor the most precious gems can purchase this wisdom.

Verses 18, 19. *Coral* and *pearls* both are products of the deep sea and prized very highly for their ornamental purposes. Yet they are to be found beyond the eye of all living creatures and were finally discovered by man due to the intelligence which his Creator gave him. The wonderful beauties of nature existing far beyond the eye of all beings, speak volumes of praise for a God who operated independent of all other powers. I cannot refrain from quoting a stanza of the memorable Elegy by Gray that is directly on this point. "Full many a gem of purest ray serene, the deep, unfathomed caves of ocean bear. Full many a flower is born to blush unseen, and waste its sweetness on the desert air." I will round out this line with a reference to the words of Jesus in Matt. 6: 28-30, which I request the reader to see.

Verses 20-23. If such wisdom is beyond the natural faculty of man, and if it cannot be bought with all the most valued treasures of earth, from where does it come? Job asked this question and then answered it when he said *God understandeth the way thereof.* Yes, God is the source of all wisdom and power. He made the earth with its countless hidden treasures and then directed man to *subdue it* (Gen. 1: 28). In order that man might be able to carry out that instruction God gave him his reasoning factulties by which he has been able to accomplish the works that have been described in this chapter. The moral of the lesson is that, after man has been able to uncover these hitherto hidden things, he should be overwhelmed with the desire to praise such a glorious Creator, and feel grateful for the honored privilege of serving him while on the earth.

Verses 24-28. These verses are a continuation of the thoughts in the preceding ones. The grand conclusion is in the last verse; *to depart from evil is understanding.*

JOB 29

Verse 1. The Word *parable* means speech or discourse.

Verses 2, 3. I think it well again to call the reader back to the comments at Ch. 3: 2, 3. With those thoughts in mind we will expect to have Job go into many details in describing his affliction of body and mind. One of the most pathetic sources of grief is a reminiscent view of past scenes that were pleasant; pleasant but now gone, perhaps never again to be enjoyed.

Verses 4, 5. I believe this is the most pathetic passage in all of Job's utterances. His mind went back to the time when the *secret* (intimacy) *of God* hovered over his home. The presence of the Almighty was in evidence all the time and made holy the joys he had in the family ties that kept his children about him. The smiles of their faces reflected the light of the good Lord who had given them to him. Even the expressions of pain that sometimes shadowed their countenances reminded him that they were his own flesh-and-blood offspring, and that he had another occasion of tendering to them his loving care to drive away those lines of anguish and make them give place to the beams of gratitude. Now they were all gone, never to come back as far as he knew.

Verse 6. This is a figurative description of the better days gone by, when Job was abundantly blessed with the good things of life.

Verses 7, 8. The gates of ancient cities were the places where diplomatic conversations took place. Job had once been among those who took part in such gatherings. When he did so the young men *hid themselves*. That means they kept at a respectful distance because of their regard for him. And even the old men rose to their feet when he took his seat in their councils.

Verse 9. *Princes* were not officials but men of outstanding influence. At the presence of Job they kept silence so great was their regard for him.

Verses 10, 11. This paragraph gives further account of the attention given Job.

Verse 12. This and some following verses will explain that the respect given to Job was not in the spirit of flattery. It was because he was a friend to the poor.

Verse 13. Job helped the man ready to perish by supplying him with the needful things. This caused that man to pronounce his blessing on the benefactor. The Pharisees would "devour widows' houses" (Matt. 23: 14), but Job rejoiced the heart of the widow by supplying her with the necessities of life.

Verse 14. Paul instructed the disciples to put on the Lord Jesus Christ (Rom. 13: 14), and Job wore the garment of righteousness.

Verse 15. This means Job assisted those who could not see their way, or who were unable to travel in their needful walks of life.

Verse 16. All known cases of destitution Job relieved. A call might come to him that was somewhat uncertain as to its worthiness. He did not dismiss it on the pretext that it was doubtful but made inquiry to learn if it was a worthy call.

Verse 17. When it was necessary Job would use force to defend the helpless against the wicked who would rob them of their goods.

Verse 18. Job believed that by following such a righteous course he would be permitted to end his days in his own home.

Verse 19. Using a plant for illustration that sends its roots into the waters and lives, Job thought of his own past prosperity.

Verse 20. The bow was one means of defense in ancient times. Job's successful defense was compared to one who always had his bow ready for action.

Verses 21-25. This entire paragraph pertains to Job's position of influence among the people. Please read my comments at Vs. 6-9. His advice was sought and followed without contention. But all of this was while he was prosperous, strong in body and able to serve others.

JOB 30

Verse 1. The preceding chapter closed with statements showing the honorable standing Job had with leading citizens. That was when he was prosperous and in good health. All of that changed when he became poor and otherwise unfortunate. The picture of his fallen standing is graphically drawn here. He had owned some dogs to protect his sheep. Some men were not considered good enough to associate with these dogs, and now their sons were snubbing Job.

Verses 2-8. This paragraph describes the people to whom reference was made in the first verse. *Old age was perished* means their fathers were dead and they had been driven to desperate resources for their support. They had to dig up *mallows*, a kind of herb used for pottage, and use them for food.

Verse 9. Men who had come to the shameful state of dependency as the preceding paragraph describes were considering themselves as too good to respect Job. He was their *song* and *byword* which means he was the subject of their jokes.

Verse 10. To spit in one's face was an act of the greatest contempt. It was considered so much in that light that God told Moses such an act would render a person unclean for 7 days. (Num. 12:14.) Now these vile creatures dared to use that act to express their contempt for Job.

Verse 11. *He* means God had cut himself loose from Job. *They* means Job's enemies and *bridle* means a curb or restraint. These enemies had given themselves to unrestrained persecution of the unfortunate man.

Verses 12, 13. These young enemies would force the feet of Job from his chosen path. *Have no helper* means these enemies found Job with no helper to resist them.

Verses 14, 15. Like a mighty flood that knows no bounds, these enemies came against Job with their persecutions.

Verse 16. The *soul* or life of Job was practically all relaxed from being overwhelmed by his afflictions.

Verse 17. The ulcerous sores that infested the surface of his body had finally gone in and attacked the bones.

Verse 18. This verse describes what must have been a very uncomfortable condition. *Garment* is a general name for Job's clothing and *coat* is rendered "a shirt" in the lexicon. Naturally the collar of a shirt fits closer to the body than the more outward articles of apparel, and would be a more approprite illustration of what he was describing. The discharges from the ulcers had been penetrating all of his clothing until they had become dry and stiff and tightened about his body like the close fitting of a shirt collar.

Verse 19. *He* means that God had suffered Job to have this terrible affliction.

Verses 20, 21. *Thou* refers to God and the paragraph is describing the afflictions that he had caused to come upon Job. *I cry* should not be thought of as applying to the prayers of Job in his religious devotions. The *cry* was the physical longing for relief from his sufferings. *Didst not hear* was because God's plan of teaching Job required that he go on with the afflictions until the desired result was accomplished.

Verse 22. *Wind* means the blast from God had reduced Job to want.

Verse 23. Job had never had it explained to him as to why he was made to suffer. He expected it to continue until death. *House* is a figurative name for the grave.

Verse 24. This does not deny the resurrection, for Job has given abundant proof that he believed in such a coming event. He means God would not perform a miracle to prevent anyone from going to the grave.

Verse 25. Other unfortunate men had received the sympathetic help of Job.

Verse 26. *Good* and *evil* are not moral terms here; they refer to temporal blessings and misfortunes.

Verse 27. When used figuratively *bowels* refers to the emotions and yearnings. The condition was *prevented* or preceded by Job's afflictions.

Verse 28. As a person without the sun would be in darkness, so Job's afflictions spread over him the cloud of mourning.

Verse 29. Under the same figure of speech used in the preceding verse, Job was put in the same class with these creatures of the night.

Verse 30. The condition of Job's skin and bones was literally caused by the ulcers.

Verse 31. Musical instruments are used generally in times of joy. Dispensing with them figuratively means that sadness had taken the place of joy.

JOB 31

Verse 1. Job did not confine his remarks to general statements of denial. The three friends had made many accusations against him that were false. He denied all of them and besides that, he specified a number of prevalent evils in conduct and protested his innocence. *Covenant* with his eyes is figurative, of course, and means he promised himself not to look with longing upon a virgin.

Verses 2, 3. *What portion* means that he would not receive any consideration from God were he to be guilty of the wrongs referred to in the preceding verse.

Verse 4. God knew all about Job's ways and would chastise him if he were even to long after that which is sinful.

Verses 5, 6. *Weighed in an even balance* signifies Job was willing to be tested. If his conduct proved to be evil he would submit to the discipline of the Lord.

Verse 7. The eye might behold something that is alluring and sinful. One would not be guilty if he merely saw the sinful thing, but he would be if he walked after the thing his eyes had beheld. In that case the evil thing would cling to him which is the meaning of the words *blot, cleaved* and hands.

Verses 8. *Let me sow*, etc., is a clear instance of what is meant by "cursing" another. To wish some misfortune to come to one is the meaning of the word when it is used concerning the action of a man who is uninspired.

Verses 9, 10. This is another curse that Job was wishing on himself if he could be found guilty of the sins he had been describing. *Grind* is from TACHAN which Strong defines, "A primitive root; to grind meal; hence to be a concubine (that being their employment)." This might seem to some as a severe wish, but Ch. 2: 9 shows this woman not to be worthy of a better consideration.

Verse 11, 12. Job justified his severe wishes by the greatness of the crimes he had been describing, if he had been guilty of them.

Verses 13, 14. If Job were unjust with his servant he would expect to receive the judgment of God.

Verse 15. The meaning of this verse is that Job and his servant had the same origin, therefore he had no right to abuse his servant.

Verses 16, 17. *If I have*, etc., implies his denial of the wrongs described.

Verse 18. The meaning of the verse is that all his life Job had administered to the needs of others instead of imposing upon them.

Verse 19. This is another assertion that Job had supplied the naked with clothing.

Verse 20. The *loins* are a major portion of the body, and to protect them with warm clothing would be a righteous deed.

Verse 21. The gate was the place where decisions were rendered. Job means he did not oppress the unfortunate with a suit just because he was sure of success. This is the significance of the words *saw my help*.

Verse 22. This was another of the curses I have been writing about. It was a severe expression but was intended to show how confident Job was that the friends could not convict him of sin.

Verse 23. One reason Job would not have committed the wrongs described was in the knowledge he had of God's *terror* against evil doers. He felt that he never could have withstood the awful wrath of the Lord.

Verses 24, 25. Job had once been rich, but that was no sin provided it did not make him vain; the record we have shows that it did not.

Verses 26, 27. If a man were to kiss his hand in salutation to the sun, that would be an idolatrous act. Job was denying that he had done any such thing.

Verse 28. Had Job done homage to the sun he could have justly been punished by the rulers. It would have been a denial of God, and the same was taught in Matt. 6: 24.

Verse 29. Job teaches that it would be wrong to take pleasure in the misfortune of others, even if they be personal enemies.

Verse 30. If it would be wrong to rejoice at another's calamities, it would likewise be wrong to wish for such a thing to come upon him.

Verse 31. The members of Job's household never had reason to complain of not having that which was necessary to satisfy their requirements.

Verse 32. Job was given to hospitality which is one of the qualifications of elders in the New Testament (1 Tim. 3: 2).

Verse 33. The word *Adam* is from an original that could apply to mankind in general. It is true that man in general is disposed to hide his sins and the marginal rendering gives it that way. But the Hebrew word used here has its first application to the first man. The trial of evasion from guilt was made manifest in Gen. 3: 10. Job denied having resorted to such conduct.

Verse 34. If Job were ever challenged to meet any accusation he was not afraid to do so. No multitude could have frightened him into hiding behind his own door.

Verse 35. A righteous man is not afraid to face his accusers. Job wished that his adversary had committed himself in writing.

Verses 36, 37. Had the adversary done as wished in the preceding verse, Job would have faced the issue squarely, for he would have had no fear of the results.

Verse 38. David wrote "The earth is the Lord's and the fulness thereof (Psa. 24:1). A man may claim the land as his own but that is true only in a limited sense. God intended it to be for the support of humanity while the earth remains. Because of that no farmer has the right to misuse his ground. He must take care of it for the next generation and leave it to them in as good condition as he received it. Job claimed that he had never misused his land so that it could have cried against him.

Verse 39. The preceding verse shows the wrong of misusing the land because of the rights of the land itself. This verse considers the wrong of taking the fruit of land belonging to another without paying him for it. Such teaching shows the right to rent land to another for hire.

Verse 40. This verse is a summing-up curse or wish for an evil to come. It means that if Job had been guilty of the things described in the several preceding verses, then may these misfortunes come to him. *Cockle* is defined by Strong as any noxious or useless plant. *Words of Job are ended* means that Job ended his long speech to the three friends who had been opposing him in his position.

JOB 32

Verse 1. The second clause might be misunderstood unless it is given proper consideration. It makes Job appear in an unfavorable light; making him seem somewhat self-righteous. That is not correct as the whole history of the case has shown. The statement represents the accusation of the three friends and it was false. Job often mentioned his own weaknesses and also admitted that his afflictions were from God. But he denied them as being a special chastisement for his sins. The friends were unable to meet the facts and arguments of Job and therefore ceased talking with him.

Verses 2, 3. Elihu is referred to in some reference works as one of the friends of Job; the Bible does not so classify him. In fact, it puts him in a class alone for in V. 3 it is stated that he was angry *against his* (Job's) *three friends*, which indicates he did not represent either side of the controversy as against the other. He had the same erroneous idea of Job the three friends had namely, that he *justified himself rather than God*. We have already seen that such was not the case. But he was correct in his criticism of the three in that they could not answer Job's arguments and yet condemned him. The speech of Elihu, like that of the friends, was not inspired in itself but was recorded by inspiration. It also was like theirs in that it took the wrong position as to the reason for Job's afflictions. I shall comment on the speech of Elihu, but before reading further here I will request the student to read my comments at Ch. 2:11 and 4:1. With the foregoing explanations as a background let us study the speech of Elihu.

Verse 4. Both Job and the three friends were older than Elihu. Since he will profess to disagree with all of them it was fitting that he wait until Job as well as the three friends had finished talking before he presumed to speak.

Verse 5. In the preceding verse I said that Elihu would profess to disagree with the three friends. However, we shall see that on the real issue between Job and them, Elihu took the same position as the three friends.

Verses 6, 7. Through respect for age, Elihu waited until Job and his three friends were done speaking. He thought that days (age) should produce the wisdom of experience, and so he waited to see what these older men would say.

Verse 8. *Inspiration* is from a Hebrew word, and a part of Strong's definition is "intellect." The expression of Elihu means only that he intended on speaking with the mind or intellect that God has given to man.

Verses 9, 10. There are exceptions to about all rules. On that basis Elihu felt justified to speak since these men who were older than he had not shown the wisdom expected of old age.

Verse 11. Elihu claimed that he had been an attentive listener to the speeches of the three friends who professed to be answering Job's speeches.

Verse 12. Regardless of whether Job's position was correct, Elihu observed that the friends had not answered his arguments.

Verse 13. The friends may try to explain their failure to answer Job by saying God helped him form his speeches; that they were not his own thoughts.

Verse 14. The idea of this verse is that Elihu proposed to speak on his own; not get his arguments from anyone.

Verse 15. *They* refers to the three friends and their utter failure to answer Job.

Verses 16, 17. After Job concluded his long speech, Elihu waited for a while to see if either of the three friends would reply. Silence reigned instead of speech and that prompted Elihu to enter the argument.

Verse 18. *Matter* is from an original that means "words." Elihu meant his spirit or intellect was urging him to speak.

Verses 19, 20. *Belly* is from BETEN and the part of Strong's definition that applies here is, "the bosom or body of anything." Wine was put in pouches (called bottles) made of skins of animals. As the wine began to ferment the skins would have to stretch and would burst if too old a skin were used. (Matt. 9:17.) Elihu used the wine bottle or skin to compare his own being as filled with words and threatening to burst unless he could obtain relief by speaking.

Verses 21, 22. Elihu was evidently warning Job not to expect favorable words on account of any personal influence. The three friends had spoken unfavorably to Job and Elihu had rebuked them for it in Job's hearing. Now it might be that Job would expect to hear an opposite kind of words; hence the remarks of this paragraph.

JOB 33

Verse 1. Having prepared the mind of Job to hear his candid speech, Elihu addressed his remarks to him, begging him to hear him as he spoke.

Verses 2, 3. *Mouth* in the first instance means an opening or mouth in general. In the second place it refers especially to the inside of the mouth. The idea is that Elihu's tongue had been trying to speak even in the palate of his mouth, therefore he opened it so the tongue could talk freely.

Verses 4, 5. Elihu was again claiming to be prompted by the Lord to do his speaking. He made the same claim when talking first to the friends in Ch. 32:8.

Verse 6. Elihu stated that he was formed of the same kind of material as Job. For that reason he should be ready to listen to him because he was speaking to him instead of God; that he was a spokesman for God.

Verse 7. Elihu was trying to calm Job in advance by assuring him that he would not be hard on him. This was all unnecessary, for Job had already shown that he could withstand strong attacks from a critic.

Verse 8, 9. Elihu started out with the same false accusation that the friends had repeated so often. Job had never claimed to be *clean* in the sense of their charge. He frequently admitted he was weak and erring, but denied he was being punished for it.

Verses 10, 11. This paragraph is a continuation of the claims that Elihu charged Job with making, but the charge was unfounded. Job never claimed that *he (God)* counted him as an enemy although he did freely admit that the Lord was bringing the afflictions on him for some purpose unknown to him.

Verse 12. Had this conversation been a part of some "open forum" meeting, Job would have voiced a hearty "amen" to it. I mean the last clause, for he has admitted from the start that God is greater than all other beings.

Verse 13. Job was not striving against God, but was objecting to the erroneous charges being made by Elihu against the unfortunate man.

Verses 14-16. Elihu's theory was that God's voice is not always recognized. Finally, however, the human mind awakes to the fact that the Lord has spoken.

Verses 17, 18. When the voice of God is understood it will be known why he has spoken. The purpose was to save man from the evil effects of his ways.

Verse 19. *Chastened also with pain* is the expression that is directly on the point at issue. Elihu meant that Job's afflictions were a chastisement from God. That was the identical position of the three friends which Job denied.

Verse 20. A man's illness may be so cruel upon him that it will take from him his appetite. That is why he *abhorreth bread.*

Verse 21. This verse fairly described the condition of Job at that time. It was no additional information, for practically the same thing was stated by

Job in Ch. 30:17, which the reader is requested to read again.

Verses 22-24. The unfortunate man will be brought near to death as a punishment for sin. Yet if he will listen to the messenger at hand and accept the advice offered he will have mercy shown to him.

Verses 25, 26. The restoration described in this verse is somewhat overdrawn. But Job really did have his former good condition restored in the end. However, it was not accomplished through the means suggested by Elihu.

Verses 27, 28. This paragraph teaches the same thing couched in the position of the three friends. Briefly stated it would be that Job should confess his sins. If he would do that he would be lifted out of his present state of affliction.

Verses 29, 30. Elihu explained to Job that God often worked along the line described in the preceding verses.

Verses 31-33. Elihu intimated that Job was permitted to speak if he had anything to say in reply to him. He professed to be in sympathy with Job and would gladly agree with him if possible. But Job evidently saw no reason to speak as nothing new had been presented. Elihu was therefore suffered to continue his speech.

JOB 34

Verses 1, 2. *Men* is not in the original; the paragraph was meant for general use.

Verse 3. The adaptation of the ear to language is as natural as food to taste.

Verse 4. This was a suggestion to use the faculty of hearing to determine what is good. It implied that if that were done the words of Elihu would be accepted.

Verses 5, 6. It will help to clarify this paragraph if we enclose all of it in quotation marks after the word *said*. It misrepresents Job, for he never contended that he had no transgression. He maintained all the while that the afflictions were not connected with any sin that he may have committed.

Verse 7. Job paid such little attention to the scorning or derision that was thrown at him that Elihu used the illustration of a man drinking water freely.

Verses 8, 9. This was a direct false accusation. The intimation that Job was a sinner was far enough from the real issue; but this wild statement was false almost to the extent of being vicious. Job never dignified it even with a denial.

Verse 10. This verse is addressed to men in general as was the 2nd verse. The implication is that if God were to let Job "get by" with his wickedness he would himself be guilty of wickedness.

Verse 11. This verse states a truth, that God will give every man what his deeds deserve. Job believed that doctrine as firmly as anyone.

Verse 12. This verse has the same meaning as verse 10.

Verse 13. No man gave God his control over the earth, but rather God has disposed or arranged the universe himself.

Verses 14, 15. If God should withdraw his support from man he would utterly perish and return to dust.

Verses 16, 17. Elihu asked Job to give him close attention as if he were going to make some important statement. It turned out to be the same false accusation that has been made against Job by the three friends and now by Elihu.

Verses 18, 19. It would be highly improper to charge even a human being with wicked conduct. It would be much more so to charge such against God.

Verse 20. If any man should be so rash as to charge God with wickedness, he will utterly perish.

Verses 21, 22. God sees all the actions of man. There is no darkness dense enough to hide man from the divine Being.

Verse 23. *He* means God and the thought is that he will not impose on man; therefore man will have no reason for contending with God.

Verses 24-26. I trust the reader will not lose sight of the real issue. Job was being terribly afflicted and Elihu claimed it was a special punishment for his sins. In order to show it to be just, a great many sentences were spoken to describe the greatness of God and his mighty treatment of sinners. Job admitted the greatness of God as freely as did his accusers, so there was no difference of opinion there.

Verse 27. *Turned back* means they backslid and did sinfully.

Verse 28. The backslider misused the poor people and caused them to cry unto God; when they did so their cry was heard.

Verse 29. It is in vain to oppose the works of God. This is true whether attempted by a nation or an individual.

Verse 30. God will not suffer a hypocrite to reign lest the people be misled. It is true that God takes some notices of the kind of men who rule. (Dan. 4:17.)

Verse 31. This verse was a direct challenge to Job to confess his sins and promise to do them no more. It was the real issue of all the controversy.

Verse 32. Elihu intimated that Job should seek enlightenment so that he would know to do iniquity no more.

Verses 33, 34. This means that God would not operate according to the opinion of Job. Regardless of whether he was favorable or not the Lord's plans will go through.

Verses 35, 36. Job has been accused of sin, now he was charged with ignorance in his speeches. Elihu then prayed that Job would be given a complete test for his likeness to wicked men. The whole attitude was erroneous and cruel against Job.

Verse 37. This means that Job had sinned against God at the beginning. When he was punished for it he stubbornly refused to repent.

JOB 35

Verses 1, 2. Elihu represented Job as saying he was more righteous than God. Not that Job actually made the claim in so many words, but that his refusal to acknowledge his sins in the face of his afflictions meant that.

Verse 3. Here was another false statement. Elihu made as if Job asked what advantage there would be in his being righteous instead of sinful.

Verse 4. Although the whole thing was false, Elihu pretended that Job had asked the question and then he proposed to answer it for the benefit of him and his friends.

Verses 5-7. Job was told to observe the wonders of creation above him. These things are not affected by the conduct of man, whether good or bad.

Verse 8. No, the conduct of man will not have any effect on creation; but it will have effect on the sinner and upon his fellow man.

Verse 9. A specific instance was cited to show the evil effect of sin. The oppressed are made to cry out in their oppression.

Verses 10, 11. Elihu intimated that Job was ignoring God, who is the source of true knowledge. This was such a groundless charge that no further attention was given it; it did not deserve the dignity of a reply.

Verse 12. *There* refers to the creatures which God made. They are not the source from which to expect knowledge. If one cries to them instead of to God then will be brought to pass the thought expressed in the words *none giveth answer*.

Verses 13, 14. This was another false insinuation. Job never denied having to meet God, but rather rejoiced at the thought of seeing him. (Ch. 19: 25-27.)

Verses 15, 16. Because the judgment of God was not realized by Job, he had given himself over to words contrary to knowledge.

JOB 36

Verses 1-3. Elihu made bolder claims for his knowledge than did the three friends. He boasted of speaking for God, yet in the end we shall see that God will entirely ignore him in his dealing with the controversy.

Verse 4. Elihu could not justly claim to possess the charity spoken of by Paul which "vaunteth not itself." (1 Cor. 13:4.) The statement is as if Elihu had said to Job, "A man with perfect knowledge is here before you."

Verses 5, 6. God is mighty but will condescend to bless the afflicted when he humbles himself and acknowleges his sins.

Verse 7. This verse states a truth already referred to in the 35th chapter and agrees with Dan. 4:17.

Verses 8, 9. *Sheweth them their work* means that God will chastise kings when they do wrong. This he will do by letting them be bound in fetters.

Verse 10. *Openeth their ear*, etc., means he will cause them to listen to Him.

Verses 11, 12. This paragraph states an important truth that is taught in many places in the Bible. However, the information was known to Job as well as to Elihu.

Verse 13. The hypocrites do not appear to be concerned about the wrath of God but pretend to be at ease. In so doing they are storing up wrath for the future. This thought is taught in Rom. 2:5.

Verse 14. The hypocrites will come to shame in early life and suffer the lot belonging to unclean persons.

Verses 15, 16. God delivers the poor out of affliction when they are worthy. Job might just as well have been enjoying such favor from God. The reason (according to Elihu) will be shown in the next verse.

Verse 17. Job had failed to receive the favor of God because he was wicked. We know that Elihu made a false accusation here.

Verses 18, 19. If Job does not repent and confess his sins he will be destroyed by the wrath of God. When such a lot comes to him he will be unable to escape even with a ransom of gold.

Verse 20. Night figuratively means error and Job has been accused, falsely, of desiring it.

Verse 21. Job did not choose affliction directly. His choice was iniquity, according to Elihu, and affliction was the result.

Verses 22, 23. God is so great that no man is able to teach him. Neither should any man criticise the works of God.

Verse 24. Job was told to magnify the work of God. He had already magnified the Lord and Elihu had opportunity of hearing it. See Ch. 9: 2, 3; 19: 25, 26; 24: 1; 26: 7, 8, and the entire 28th chapter.

Verse 25. This verse is the same in thought as Psa. 19: 1.

Verses 26-33. If the student will carefully read chapter 28, he will think that Elihu got his ideas for this paragraph from that.

JOB 37

Verse 1. *This* refers to the great things ascribed to God in the closing verses of the preceding chapter. Elihu meant that his heart was all in a flutter over it.

Verse 2. The personal pronouns in this and several following verses refer to God. (Ch. 36: 26.) Elihu was exhorting Job to give attention to the voice of God.

Verse 3. *It* refers to the *sound* of the previous verse and denotes the thunder that God sends throughout the heavens. This thunder was preceded by *his lightning* which was the cause of the sound.

Verse 4. This verse is a follow-up of the preceding one. *After it* means after the lightning of the other verse. The *voice* which follows this *lightning* is then plainly called thunder. We know that a downpour of rain often follows a loud peal of thunder, which is the meaning of the last sentence.

Verses 5, 6. This paragraph is a repetition of the preceding ones. We have the specific information that Elihu was talking about God since his name was used.

Verse 7. *Sealeth* means "to stop," and the thought is that the great storm just produced put a stop to the activities of man for the moment.

Verse 8. The storm drives the beasts into their shelters.

Verse 9. The usual weather conditions were described in this verse and were considered as the work of God.

Verse 10. This verse describes the effects of cold. It brings frost and by freezing the waters they are *straitened* or held in check.

Verse 11. *Weareth* means to overburden. By reducing the vapor to water the cloud disappears and the rain comes down.

Verse 12. God has full control of the weather.

Verse 13. Sometimes a storm comes *for correction*, such as in Ch. 1: 19. Elihu implied that God sent the storm upon Job's children as a punishment for sins.

Verses 14-17. How unnecessary were all these assertions about God's works! Job knew about them and had never denied it.

Verse 18. *Glass* as we understand the word was unknown in olden times. The word means "mirror" and the object was produced by polishing the surface of fine grained metal. It was here used to compare the brightness of the sky.

Verse 19. Elihu called upon Job to suggest something to say about God; that it was difficult on account of human *darkness* or ignorance.

Verses 20-22. This paragraph merely stated some facts about God's control of the elements.

Verse 23. The power of the *Almighty* is beyond the comprehension of man. *He will not afflict* did not express the complete thought of Elihu. He meant that God would not send affliction unless there existed a cause for it. In the case at hand the affliction was caused by the sins of Job.

Verse 24. God will not favor the man who is *wise of heart*. This was a true statement but had no bearing on the subject that Elihu pretended to be discussing.

JOB 38

Verse 1. When the Lord got ready to enter the controversy he completely ignored Elihu. We are not told why he did so but we are sure that nothing had been said, in addition to that of the three friends, that deserved any attention. God spoke to Job with the accompaniment of a *whirlwind*. That would secure and hold the attention of those whom he wished to address.

Verse 2. *Words without knowledge* means that the speakers had been talking about things that they did not understand.

Verse 3. *Loins* in the O. T. is from different originals but the general meaning is the vigor or strength of man. To *gird the loins* meant for Job to summon all the human strength he had for the task about to be placed before him. And since he was to be called upon to answer certain questions, we know that *loins* was used figuratively, meaning that Job was to use his greatest strength of mind in answering. We should note very carefully that Job was to answer the questions *like a man*. That means he was to answer them from the standpoint of human knowledge. The answers would be clearly correct if they were done by using the one and greatest of all names which is God. The questions in this and the following chapters present a challenge to the unbeliever that he cannot meet. If he answers them by saying "God did it," he then gives up his position as an unbeliever. But if he refuses to let God into his speech he will not be able to answer the questions. In the study of this tremendous speech of God let us keep in mind always that Job was to answer the questions *like a man*, which means from a human standpoint, not regarding the existence of God.

Verse 4. If there is no higher power than man, he was present at the foundation-laying of the earth; but was he?

Verse 5. What power decided on the dimensions of the earth?

Verse 6. If man is the highest power in the universe (as the unbelievers claim), then he should account for the foundation of the earth.

Verse 7. *When* has the meaning of "at which time," going back to the time when the foundation of the earth was laid. Since that was before the creation of man, the *sons of God* were of necessity the angels. Moffatt so translates it and it agrees with the thought on Ch. 1: 6; please read my comments at that place. Psa. 89: 6 also gives light on the subject for these "sons of the mighty" are connected with the persons "in the heaven."

Verses 8-11. The clouds cover the sea and it is completely shrouded in darkness, all without the actions of man. *Hitherto* refers to the bounds of the sea. Man can build partial bounds in the form of dikes or levees, but even they are often demolished by the relentless power of the waves. Who, then, has held the sea in its bounds as we know them through all the years; it was not man.

Verse 12. Man can time the recurrence of daylight but he is powerless to lengthen or shorten the day.

Verse 13. *It* stands for the *dayspring* or dawn mentioned in the preceding verse. It *takes hold* or reaches to the ends of the earth. *Wicked might be shaken* means that the darkness is chased away by the daylight and that deprives the wicked of their chance to operate. (Ch. 24: 16, 17.)

Verse 14. *It* undoubtedly stands for the *earth* in the preceding verse. The pronoun is used in that verse after the mention of the *earth* and again in this one. The verse means that the earth turns just as we know it to do. The statement was made to explain God's method of alternating the day and night. *They* refers to the limits surrounding the earth, such as the sky that *stands* round the earth as a garment.

Verse 15. This has the same thought as V. 13 and Ch. 24: 16, 17.

Verse 16. Someone might answer that man has walked on the bottom of the sea. Yes, but it had not been done in the time of Job, yet the things that are found now were there when man first reached the depths.

Verse 17. Man knows that he must die yet has no explanation for it. If there is no higher power than man he should know as much about death as he does of life.

Verses 18-20. This takes the same comments as Vs. 12, 13.

Verse 21. If man is the highest order of life, then he was present when the light was ordained; but was he?

Verses 22, 23. This paragraph asked a question that was prophetical of an interesting scientific discovery made in the course of World War I, in which some ammunition was prematurely exploded. I shall quote the explanation that was given me by a student in chemistry: "The rain, falling through the atmosphere, which was partially saturated with carbon dioxide (CO_2) absorbed some of the gas and formed a weak acid. This was carbonic acid. H_2CO_3, which is found in soft drinks and in baking powder, etc., after it acts. The water containing some H_2CO_3 was used in the making of explosives, but was unsafe because the H_2CO_3 decomposed, forming new compounds and causing detonation. It was discovered that water obtained from snow or hail on high peaks could be used successfully. This discovery led to the more important discovery that CO_2 was causing the trouble. Water, freezing high above the comparatively heavy CO_2, fell on the mountains, and contained none of this gas. Of course there are easier ways of obtaining the gas-free water, but that was the way it was done in that particular incident."—Stafford Zerr, chemical student in Ball State Teachers' College, Muncie, Indiana. Thus we have a modern scientific discovery that verifies a statement of the Bible made several hundred years ago, before man knew anything about it. This all goes to prove there is a higher power than man.

Verses 24, 25. This is commented on at Vs. 11, 12.

Verses 26-28. Since it rains in places where no man has been some power higher than man must cause it.

Verses 29, 30. This is explained at Ch. 37: 10.

Verse 31. The Pleiades are called the "seven sisters" in popular folklore. Smith's Bible Dictionary says this: "The Pleiades are a group of stars situated on the shoulder of the constellation Taurus. The rendering 'sweet influences' of the A. V., Job 38: 31, is a relic of the lingering belief in the power which stars exerted over human destiny." Regardless of its being a fanciful belief, it challenges man's power over the cluster of stars.

Verse 32. *Mazzaroth* is called the zodiac today, and *Arcturus* is the name of another constellation that figures in our almanacs. We are not especially concerned with all the notions that may be had of these heavenly bodies. The point is that unbelieving man will look to them for results and influences over which he knows he has no power. Until man can show some control over these bodies he must admit they were made by a power higher than man.

Verses 33-38. This whole paragraph is practically on the same line of thought as much of the preceding verses. It challenges man to show his control over nature.

Verses 39-41. These dumb creatures could not care for themselves purely through their own intelligence; yet they exist independent of man, proving existence of some higher power.

JOB 39

Verses 1-8. Much of the argument of God's speech to Job is based on the perfection of creation over which man knows he has no power. This paragraph cites a number of items along the above line.

Verses 9-12. This *unicorn* was a wild ox of great strength and ferocity. Man has been able to bring him under subjection by using his superior intelligence, but he was not able to create him with the disposition to serve man.

Verses 13-18. Since the ostrich can *scorn the horse and his rider* she is not the product of man. No, man did not give to the bird her wings, but instead, he has taken the suggestion of flying from the bird. This proves that birds fly by a power higher than man.

Verses 19-25. These verses have been grouped into one paragraph because they are on the one subject of the horse. That noble beast was not the product of man, for he has a strength that is greater than that of man. It is true that man can manage him, but it is accomplished through his superior intelligence over the beast. Had man created him he would have made him so that both physical and mental power would have been naturally under that of his maker.

Verses 26-30. See the remarks in the preceding paragraph concerning the flying of the birds. Man is an imitator of the bird in devising mechanical means for traveling through the air. This proves that the actions of birds are the result of some power other than man.

JOB 40

Verses 1, 2. God interrupted his line of speech to challenge Job. Let us again note that the whole address was made for the purpose of showing the weakness of man when contending (as a mere man) with his Maker.

Verses 3-5. Job acknowledged the challenge and spoke as a representative of human beings, which was to show the dependence of such upon God.

Verse 6, 7. This takes the same comments as Ch. 38: 1-3.

Verse 8. Uninspired man often puts his own judgment ahead of God's judgment.

Verses 9-13. If there is no higher power than man, then he should be able to manifest the abilities described in this paragraph.

Verse 14. This means that if mere man can do the things described in the foregoing paragraph, then it would be proved that man is what he is by his own power and that he is the highest force in the universe.

Verses 15-24. Since this entire group of verses pertains to the same creature, I have made one paragraph of them. In the margin of some Bibles the *behemoth* is defined as an elephant, but every characteristic ascribed to him is true of the hippopotamus. Moffatt so defines it from the original and Strong defines it, "a water-ox, i. e. the hippopotamus or Nilehorse." The argument is that this creature defies the strength of man. He lives and thrives in regions where man does not and gives every indication of having been created by some power other than man.

JOB 41

Verses 1-9. *Leviathian* is from a Hebrew word that Strong defines, "a wreathed animal, i. e. a serpent (especially the crocodile or some other large sea-monster)." Moffatt's version and Smith's Bible Dictionary also render it crocodile. The word is also rendered, "great water animal" by Young, and "whale, dragon, serpent, sea-monster" by Robinson. The works of reference seem to intimate some indefiniteness as to the actual creature meant. The description as given in this chapter also seems to have both the crocodile and a large fish in mind. Part of the statements would apply to one and part to another. But the point under consideration is that man is frail when compared with the great brutes, and it is true of either of the ones named. I therefore shall refer to either as the language of the text suggests.

Like the argument made about other creatures in the universe, the might of the one now being considered is cited to show the helplessness of man. It is true that man today can master this beast or brute by his late knowl edge of scientific mechanics. But had man been the maker of all such creatures he would have known from the start how to manage them, and would not have needed to learn it by "the hard way" of experimentation and discovery.

Verse 10. If man is not able to master this monster of the sea, who then could contend with the power that created it?

Verse 11. *Prevented* is from QADAM and Strong defines it, "a primitive root; to project oneself, i. e. precede; hence to anticipate, hasten, meet (usually for help)." The word as used here means to help God and the question means to ask who has helped God in any of the works of nature.

Verse 12. *I* stands for God who declares that he will *not conceal*, that is, he will not refrain from mentioning all the parts of leviathan.

Verses 13, 14. This is a further challenge, expressed in figurative language, for man to match his strength against the creature being considered.

Verses 15-17. *Scales* is from MEGINNAH and Strong defines it, "a shield (i. e. the small one or buckler); figuratively a protector; also the scaly hide of the crocodile." These scales resemble somewhat those of a large fish. Man did not form them for the crocodile or fish, but rather has he learned from them to make metallic armor for himself.

Verse 18. *Neesings* is another word for sneezing. In the field of figurative language we should be careful to avoid speculation, and always remain within the bounds justified by the known facts. For instance, we know the inspired writer was describing a literal, fleshly creature. Whatever figures he used must be understood to be only some comparison to the thing named. Let us be careful not to formulate some far-fetched applications. When the hippopotamus sneezes, the vapor he forces from his nostrils would appear like a ray of light, and it would be reflected at the same time from his eyes.

Verses 19-21. The breath of this large beast would be charged with the temperature of his body which is likened to the heat of a lamp.

Verse 22. This creature is so mighty that what might have been meant as pain to him will fail, and he will be able to rejoice over the feeble attempt.

Verses 23-25. This is a description

of the powerful physical body of the beast.

Verse 26. The things named are articles of attack and defense used by man. The meaning is that all of them will be of no avail in an encounter with this monster.

Verses 27-29. By comparison only this beast is said to be able to masticate iron as easily as straw. Other parts of the paragraph take comments at V. 26.

Verse 30. His hair is so coarse that it is compared to stony points; he buries them in the mire on the floor of the sea.

Verses 31, 32. This paragraph evidently has special reference to the whale. (See my remarks at verses 1-9.) The statements are almost literally true. Standing on the rear deck of a large boat one can trace with his eye the path the boat has just traveled by the foamy light streak on the surface of the water.

Verses 33, 34. This sums up the might of the monster that has been described. The helplessness of man in contact with the creature is the point of the writer.

JOB 42

Verses 1-6. We should not lose sight of the thoughts expressed at Ch. 38: 3 and 40: 7. This book as a whole is inspired of God and Job was the human instrument through whom the document was given to man. However, in conducting the great drama, it was necessary for Job to take the role of an uninspired man and do his best to meet the inquiries put to him *like a man*, or from a human standpoint. This whole paragraph must be considered in the light of these comments. Full acknowledgment was made of the great power and wisdom of God. Uninspired man had exposed his ignorance by pretending to contend with the Lord. *Hear, I beseech thee*, etc., was a confession that man ought to let God speak while man hears and accepts the teaching. *Eye seeth thee* could not be literal in view of Ex. 33: 20, but refers to the arguments that had been made from the works of God in creation. By having the eyes turned to those things they would actually *see* the evidence of God's existence. In view of such a forceful situation, the arrogance of man would call for a practical reformation. Job acted as a representative of such a man by making the humble acknowledgment and by prostrating himself in dust and ashes.

Verse 7. The comments in the preceding paragraph are verified by this verse. God expressly said that Job had spoken the right words while the three friends had not, but instead they had kindled the wrath of God against themselves.

Verses 8, 9. These people were all living under the Patriarchal Dispensation in which the animal sacrifies composed God's religious headquarters. The three friends had sinned by their speeches while Job had not. Therefore, not only did they need to offer a sacrifice and Job did not, but they had to do so in the presence of Job, who acted as a priest.

Verse 10. *Captivity* is from SHEBIYTH and Strong defines it, "figuratively, a former state of prosperity." It means that after Job had officiated in the offerings for his friends, and when he had prayed for them the Lord accepted the service. God next remembered Job and reversed his condition by restoring his "former state of prosperity." He did not stop at merely restoring what he had in the way of health and happiness, but doubled the riches that he once possessed.

Verse 11. This verse exhibits one of the commonest weaknesses of many people. When a person is in sore need of help his so-called friends often desert him. Then if he becomes more fortunate they will pretend to be in full sympathy with him and offer great congratulations for his better estate. Job did not show any bitterness over the situation but entertained his guests in his own home. The gifts mentioned were according to the custom of the times. See comments at Gen. 32: 13; 1 Sam. 10: 27.

Verse 12. See my comments at verse 10.

Verses 13-17. Job was comparatively a young man when he had his siege of affliction. After that he was able to beget 10 children and then live 140 years. Of course we should understand that while much of this experience could have been possible through the ordinary course of nature, yet the special providence of God was certainly in evidence also. The statement that he saw his descendants to the fourth generation proves that the main portion of his long life came after the second family had been given to him.

www.ingramcontent.com/pod-product-compliance
Lightning Source LLC
Chambersburg PA
CBHW070835160426
43192CB00012B/2193